# Our Times, Our Lives

To Rose with my
very best wishes.

Love, E. Otto

Dec. 2008

# Our Times, Our Lives

*by Jozef and Eve Otto*

iUniverse, Inc.
New York  Lincoln  Shanghai

# Our Times, Our Lives

iUniverse, Inc.

For information address:
iUniverse, Inc.
2021 Pine Lake Road, Suite 100
Lincoln, NE 68512
www.iuniverse.com

ISBN: 0-595-33563-2

Printed in the United States of America

For Joe, Lia, Ed, and Sandy

Freedom is a hard-bought thing—
A gift no man can give,
For some, a way of dying,
For most, a way to live.

Freedom is a hard-bought thing,
A massacre, a bloody rout,
The candles lit at nightfall,
And the night shut out.

Freedom is a way of living,
A song, a mighty cry.
Freedom is the bread we eat;
Let it be the way we die!

# Contents

# ACKNOWLEDGMENTS

The idea for this book sprang from a conversation with my neighbor and friend, Carol Limoges, a retired high school teacher. For many years Carol and I have occasionally come together for coffee and a chat at her house or mine. As I recall, it was in the year 1983 when, after Jozef had a conversation with Carol about his experiences during World War II, Carol said to me, "Eve, you should write a book! It would be great to set Jozef's memoirs on paper for your children to read. I will help you with editing." I answered her that I had no idea how to write a book. I never had written anything more than letters and sometimes a composition at school in Holland. I also didn't know enough of the English language to write. Believe it or not, this conversation went on intermittently for about two years until I gave in and, with the encouragement of my husband Jozef, began writing this book.

I started when Jozef and I were in Florida for two months visiting our oldest son and his family. When the weather was cool and rainy, we stayed inside at our rental place, which was located close to the beach. It was there that I began to write the book in earnest. The first years I wrote everything by hand. Later with the popularity of the computer, I taught myself how to type and entered my book on the computer. The most difficult part was to write about the traumatic experiences of Jozef's life. Besides doing a lot of research I also read many library books concerning war to get some idea of what it must have been like to be on the battlefield.

Of course Jozef and I don't remember everything, but certainly we recall what was most important. Sometimes we had conflicting recollections or disagreed about what actually took place. Throughout all those long years of writing, my husband has always been very patient with me. I am grateful for all the help Carol has given me through all those years. Without her, this book never would have been written. I am also thankful to my son Ed, who always was there when I was in trouble with my computer. And I would like to thank my grandson Eric, my granddaughter Ashley and her mother Marlene for helping me with some of the early typing. It has taken about eighteen years from the very first word I wrote until the last sentence. I know this book is not a masterpiece by any means, but it is the story of our lives.

# PART I

## GOING HOME
### (Jozef's Story)

# PREFACE TO PART ONE

My father was born in 1887 in Czestopowo, east Prussia, which is now west Poland. Poland has known more war than peace. I think this is because it is totally locked in and isolated—a victim of its own geography, as it has been throughout its history. It lies between two powerful countries: Russia to the east and Germany to the west. To the north is the Baltic Sea and to the south are Czechoslovakia, Romania, and Hungary. For a hundred years Poland did not exist as a nation. This happened after a war at the beginning of the eighteenth century when the country of Poland was divided between Germany, Austria, and Russia. The western part of Poland became Germany, even though it was called Polish territory. We were under German rule, but they left us alone with our Polish traditions. Then in 1920, a few years after World War I, Poland once again became a nation with new borders. But those borders were greatly altered once again after the Second World War of 1940-1945.

Besides his parents, my father's family consisted of five brothers and one sister. After his grade school in East Prussia my father had gone as a teenager to Wanne, Germany, for further education. He stayed in that town with his oldest brother who had gone there earlier and lived there.

In that same town of Wanne my mother, Marina Kazmierzak, was born in 1894 of Polish parents. My grandmother (the mother of my mother) was born and lived in the small town of Lubin, East Prussia, before she married my grandfather who lived in Wanne, Germany. It was there in Wanne that my mother grew up. Her mother died when she was only 12 years old. She had no sisters or brothers. Some years later, my father and mother came to know each other in Wanne and were married there in 1913.

As World War I was raging across Europe bringing death and destruction to that part of the world, my father was somewhere deep in Russia fighting with the German Army. Since Poland at that time did not exist as a nation but was under German rule, my father had to serve in their military force.

At that time my mother lived in Wanne, West Germany. This was not far from the Dutch border and close to her grandmother (the mother of her father) who owned an apartment building in that town. On September 3, 1917, my mother gave birth to me, her first son. Her firstborn child was my sister Irene.

Mother had not heard from my father for some time and feared the worst. She presumed he had been killed in that terrible war, so when I was born, she gave me the name of Jozef, my father's name.

After the First World War was over, my father came back home to his thankful young wife and family only to find that Germany was filled with chaos. After living in Wanne for a few years he decided to take his young family to Czestopowo, West Poland, where his parents' family and my mother's family lived nearby in Lubin. Besides my parents, our family then consisted of three children. My sister Irene was three years older than I, and my sister Victoria was two years younger. My three brothers Stanley, Marian, and Kazek were born later in Poland.

When he moved back to Poland, my father went into training at the Police Academy. While he was in training there, my mother and her children lived for a time in my grandparents' home in Czestopowo. Later when my father had become a member of the Polish Federal Police and was stationed in many different towns at the beginning of his career, we moved around a great deal. Finally, when I was about eleven years old, my father settled in the small town of Miedzychud on the river Warta, in west Poland.

Jozef Otto, Poland, 1937.

Jozef and Marina Otto (Jozef's parents) with their first child, Irene. This photo was taken in 1914 in Germany.

The Otto family in 1935, Poland: Irene, Jozef, Mother, Father, Victoria, Stanley, a playmate, Kazek, and Marian.

# 1

# *GOING TO SOUTHEAST POLAND*

*Miedzychud, West Poland, January 1938.* The whistle blew, and slowly the train moved forward out of the small station of Miedzychud. Leaning out of the train's open window, I waved goodbye to my family who were standing on the almost empty platform. Early that morning my parents, two sisters, and three brothers had brought me to the train to see me off on my trip to east Poland where I planned to work and live.

As the train gained speed, I looked one last time at my family who were still waving but slowly disappearing in the haze of the cold winter morning. There was my father in his police uniform. Earlier he had firmly shook my hand and said, "Go with God, my son." He was a firm but good man who had gone through difficult times and worked hard for his family. He loved my mother and his six children very much. My mother stood beside him. In my memory I still see her standing there holding my father's arm. She was a pretty woman and had kept her slim figure even after having borne six children. My decision to live far away from home had not been easy for her to accept—she wanted me to stay close to the family. I then looked at my three younger brothers who were yelling goodbye to me while waving their arms in the air. The youngest, Kazek, was only ten years old. Fine boys, I thought, the two oldest maybe a little wild sometimes, but they were good boys. They would keep my parents on their toes. Standing behind them was my sister Irene. She was the oldest of the children and always was a great help to my mother. She was the serious one in the family, always helping out and keeping her four brothers in line, or other times she was reading and studying for school. Irene was much different than my younger sister Victoria, who was high-spirited. I knew I would miss Victoria the most of my siblings. Since she was closest to my age, she and I always played together when we were children. Later in our teens we went dancing many Saturday nights with friends in a restaurant which was located on the beach of a large lake. We always had a lot of fun there, especially when she or her girlfriends tried to teach me how to dance. Victoria was a very bright girl, always earning top grades in school. I never could beat her in math, no matter how hard I tried.

As the train went around a bend I took one last look in the direction where my family stood, but they had become a hazy blur and were out of sight. The train moved faster and the small town of Miedzychud where I grew up fell behind us. I had no idea that I would never see my father again and not see my mother, sisters, and brothers for thirty-two years.

As soon as I closed the train's window and sat down on the hard wooden bench, we crossed the railroad bridge of the broad river Warta. This great river is very busy with ships coming and going from Poland to Germany. As the train continued on its journey, my thoughts soon drifted back to my younger days. How well I remembered the warm summer vacation days in Miedzychud when I went swimming with my friends in this mighty river. We always went to a small inlet of the river which was a short walk from where I lived. As soon as we came to the inlet and reached the bushes which grew close to the water's edge, we peeled off our clothes and soon were roughnecking, mud fighting, and jumping from the slippery boulders which lined the riverbank. What fun we had! Of course our parents didn't know this. They would not have approved of our adventures there.

The town of Miedzychud was surrounded by forests and lakes large and small. As child I went fishing alone many times or at other times with friends. First I had to get some bait which I did by finding snails or bloodsuckers on the edge of the water or just by unearthing worms. I then got a pin and a string from my mother's sewing basket and my wooden pole. Most of the time I caught some small fish from which my mother later made fish soup. Because we kids didn't have watches, we guessed the time we should be heading for home—which was always "just in time." As I remember, most mothers in those years were very strict about having their children home on time, especially for supper. If we arrived too late for supper, we simply did not eat that night. Taking other foods from the pantry would have been out of the question. This way, we learned in early childhood to be at the dinner table on schedule.

It was about an hour later when the train slowed down as we almost had reached Poznan, the largest city in west Poland. I had to wait there for more than a hour to transfer to another train that would bring me into eastern Poland the next day. Slowly the train rolled into the terminal and came huffing and puffing to a stop. I took my suitcase, walked down the pull-out stairs, and looked around for a place to sit in this large terminal where trains stopped, arriving from Germany, France, or Italy. As soon as I had left the train car, I noticed a very cold wind blowing and decided to find the station's restaurant and wait there. It was interesting to see all the differently dressed people in the busy terminal. Many of them were wearing the native costumes of the region or country where they lived.

As I was sitting in the restaurant drinking a cup of coffee and eating one of the sandwiches my mother had made for me, I thought about the first time I had been to this large train station, when I had gone to work for a bakery in Poznan more than a half a year before. The idea of working at a bakery started when I completed grade school and my father and I decided that I should go to trade school. One of my father's acquaintances owned a bakery, and we both thought that it would be a good idea for me to go into that trade. At that time in Poland when a boy was accepted into a trade school, the government paid for his tuition. In return, he was required to belong to the National Guard. So for the following three years I was a very busy boy. From 3 a.m. until noon, I worked in the bakery of my father's acquaintance, and from 4:00 to 8:00 in the evening I went to trade school. I had to go to the National Guard one evening. We learned about weapons, and one Sunday per month we spent the whole day on field exercises. The other free Sundays I played my favorite sport—soccer. Sometimes, though, my schedule was a little too much for a young, busy man, and I remember that many times I felt as if I was sleepwalking to the bakery so early in the morning.

Two years later, I graduated from trade school at the age of 18. To get my certificate to be a licensed baker, I had to work for three years in a bakery. Since I had already worked two years in a bakery, I worked another year in the same bakery where I had started in Miedzychud. Then one day, after I had received my baker's diploma, I decided I wanted to go and live in Poznan and work in a bakery there to get more experience. Since the city of Poznan was not far from where we lived, I went on the train one day and found work in a bakery located close to the downtown area. The bakery was much larger than the one in Miedzychud, and I enjoyed making many different pastries and cakes. Late on Saturday afternoons I went home on the train and returned late on Sundays back in Poznan.

I probably would have stayed there in that bakery in Poznan if the letter not had come from east Poland. I had worked about five months when I got a letter from the brother-in-law of the baker I worked for. He asked me if I would be interested in coming to work for him in Gwodzec, east Poland, which is not far from the Carpathian Mountains. Later, if everything went well, I could become his partner. I knew the man because he had also owned a bakery in Poznan that had failed. He had gone to southeast Poland (which is now Ukraine) close to the Russian-Romanian border.

This man's name was Jan Wagner. He had gone to Gwodzec a year before with his wife, son, and daughter. With the help of the government, he had opened a bakery there. The government was interested in helping Polish businessmen go to southeast Poland and start businesses in Gwodzec and other towns. Few Polish people lived in that whole area of southeast Poland. The vast majority of the people who did live there were Ukrainians, White Russians, and Jews. Most of the businesses were Jewish-owned. Before 1920 that land belonged to Russia, but since the coming of new borders, it belonged to the new nation of Poland. The Polish government thought it was a good idea to bring more Polish people into that area, especially businessmen.

For awhile I had thought about the offer. I also had some lengthy discussions with my parents about whether it would be wise for me to go to Gwodzec, an area of Poland where the people were poor and life was a struggle. I knew it would be a big decision for me, but I could always go back home if things didn't work out. I also knew that my parents were not happy with the idea that I would be going to live so far away from home in case I wanted to stay there for always. The only transportation at that time was by trains which were fueled by coal and, at top speed, traveled 45 to 50 miles an hour. It would take a long time to travel if I wanted to go home for a visit. The distance from my parent's home in Miedzychud to Gwodzec in east Poland was about 600 miles. A great distance in that time was 50 miles away. Finally, one day I made my decision. I wanted to go to east Poland, to Gwodzec, and work there with Jan Wagner in his bakery. Maybe it was adventure I wanted.

Looking at the pocket watch my father had given to me before I left on my journey, I noticed that it was almost time for my connecting train to arrive. Carrying my suitcase and the bag of sandwiches, I walked to the platform from which my train was going to depart. While waiting there I noticed the many people who were going on the same train as I was and told myself that I should enter a car quickly after the train stopped and passengers got off. This I did, and I was lucky again to find a window seat. Even though there were no passengers standing, the train car was full of men, women, and children—people like me going someplace, somewhere.

After a short wait the train began to move and with the customary clanging sounds of wheels, we soon left the terminal and Poznan behind. As the train built up speed, it traveled over the beautiful winter landscape of Poland. We stopped at busy towns to let passengers off or on, and went through small villages where the people waved at the travelers in the speeding train. We passed snow-covered hills and ancient castles that appeared like magic out of nowhere, and we rode along-side forests that stretched as far as the eye could see. Yellow lights from the winter sky fell in streams through the dry branches of the trees. While I looked out of the window, I dreamed of an exciting life for me in an unknown area of the far southeast part of Poland. I was young and free and full of dreams and hope.

The other passengers in my train car included two older men, a young couple, and a mother with her two young sons. At first the boys laughed and teased each other and enjoyed looking out of the window at the landscape and towns. Later in the afternoon when the winter sun was setting over the land, it became dark outside, and there was not much more for the two boys to see. As soon as the lights came on in the train, the young mother settled her sons down with a book and told them to read. As I looked at the oldest boy who was about twelve years old, I thought about the time when I was his age and had a goat that I named Magda. I got her from a family who lived farther up on our road. They were moving to France and didn't know what to do with their goat. Since they knew that I loved animals, they asked me if I would take care of her. At first Mother didn't want anything to do with the animal, but later she gave in and said I could keep it. And so the three-year-old black and white goat came into our family.

As a child I had always loved animals and I kept quite a collection of them, including rabbits, chickens, and pigeons. Around our large house in Miedzychud we had much property, which was great for keeping animals. The chickens could run free, and I did not have far to go to gather food for my rabbits. Sometimes in the summer my pigeons would fly in through the open kitchen window and my mother would tell me to keep my pigeons out of her kitchen—*or else!* I also had a dog named Bello. He was a mutt, but to me he was the best dog that a boy could have and he was always near my side. Since school was not my favorite place to be, I could hardly wait until school was out. I would run all the way home to the animals who awaited my return. As soon as I was close to our home, Bello would run to me—happy to see me again. After greeting my mother, putting my books on the table in my room and changing into my play clothes, I went outside to gather food for my rabbits. While my pigeons flew from the roof of a small build-ing and acted happy to see me, the chickens came out from wherever they were at that moment.

I not only enjoyed very much the animals that I kept at home but also the ani-mals in the forest. I liked to go off by myself into the lush wonder of the forest and look for rabbit holes. The forest was a large area of tall broad-leaved trees and was located close to our house. After finding a hole, I would just sit there and hope rabbits would come out. In spring there were always a lot of baby deer, and I would sit on toppled-over tree trunks and watch them for the longest time as they leaped and played around their mothers. I enjoyed watching ducks and geese when they came down with the first warm spring breeze, sliding over the water and later building their nests on the lakeshore between the tall grass and reeds. In the winter when the snow was deep and the sunshine was glistening through the bare tree trunks, I followed footprints of deer, rabbits, and mice and sat on the side of the lake. As my fingertips and toes became ice cold, it amazed me that so many creatures could live through the cold winter under the thick ice. While the train was traveling at high speed, I still could feel the careless freedom of that time. I had been young then, and life was simple and clear and full of possibilities.

It must have been about midnight when the train slowed down and stopped at a small town. As soon as we stopped, the two older men and the woman with her two sleepy children got off the train and soon disappeared in the cold winter night. Since no new passengers entered our car, I found myself with plenty of room to lie down on the wooden bench. I tried to sleep, but it was difficult. Later I must have dozed off because when I woke up, the first morning light was streaming across the countryside. As I looked out the window, I knew that we had arrived in east Poland, and I wondered how we were from the large city of Lvov where I had to transfer to another train. The landscape that I saw was cultivated and here and there was forest. It reminded me of west Poland, and it brought back memories to me about a trip I took with my father when I must have been about twelve years old. My father had asked me if I wanted to go with him on vacation. He told me that he had one week of vacation time coming and wanted to go to Czestopowo where his family lived. Of course I wanted to share this exciting adventure, especially since we were going by train. It would take us about three hours riding.

When I was a child the trains looked like big black monsters to me, especially when they rolled into the station. The people always carefully stepped back a little on the platform before the train came to a stop. The train ride with my father was exciting, and I wished that all my friends could see me—me sitting in a train! We passed towns and villages and woods and rivers, and with my nose close to the window I saw the world pass by. It was also a great experience to see my grandparents again, whom I had not seen since we had moved from Germany and had stayed with them when we came to Poland. Nor had I seen my uncles, aunts, and cousins who lived there.

My father also wanted to visit the village where he was born. It was about four miles from where we were staying with his parents. Because we had no transportation, Father and I started walking. After we had walked about three miles my father suddenly stood still and, pointing his finger to the far horizon, said to me, "Look, son, all the land surrounding us, as far as the eye can see, once belonged to your mother's family. Your mother came from Polish aristocracy. Her grandfather was a Polish knight. Far back into history they were great landowners who owned not only large areas of land, but also whole villages where the people lived who worked for them. Not far from here," my father continued, "is a very old preserved church which is not used anymore. Your mother's grandfather had that church built. In its churchyard are the graves of your forefathers. The Church Preservation League still cares for it. The family name is Kazmiercsak," my father said. "But your mother's grandfather was a playboy and mismanaged his responsibilities. In time he lost everything. When his estate was sold, half of the money, by law, went to his wife and son, who was your mother's father, who was then about five or six years old. His wife, my mother's grandmother, bought apartment buildings in Wanne, Germany, with the money."

As Father and I walked farther we came to the village where my father was born and where some of his family still lived. It was interesting to meet more of the uncles, aunts, and cousins. Wherever we came to their homes, we had to sit down in the large kitchen where the family would gather around the big wooden table. We ate warm homemade bread together with chunks of smoked ham from their own smokehouse and drank fresh buttermilk. Everything we ate was homemade and tasted delicious. The houses in the villages were different from what I was used to. They were well built, but old, with bare wooden floors, heavy beams on the low ceilings and small windows and doors. It had been an interesting visit for me. Not only had I met my grandparents and cousins again but also many of my family members whom I never had met before. I also learned about the family history and the small villages that entire families would occupy for generations. When Father and I returned home a few days later, I had many stories to tell my mother and sisters.

I was still dreaming about that trip with my father when I noticed that the train had slowed down and we had come to the city of Lvov in southeast Poland. Lvov is a big city with a large train station where it seemed that all the passengers got off. As soon as I left the huffing train, I noticed that I had come to an area of

Poland which was different from my home. Even though the city was large and the people who lived there were more modern than in the other small towns and villages of east Poland, I noticed immediately a difference in their clothing and language which was more the East Slavic language of the Ukrainians. Even though it was early in the morning, there was the usual hustle and bustle of many people as in all large train stations. Soon I began looking for my connecting train to the town of Kolomayia and found out that I would have to wait more than a hour before it arrived. I went to the station's restaurant and sat down with a sandwich Mother had made and a cup of hot coffee.

While eating my breakfast, I noticed a young boy of about thirteen who was carrying a suitcase that he put on a pull-wagon. It reminded me of the time when I was about the same age and would carry suitcases in my pull-wagon from the train station of Miedzychud. The suitcases belonged to people who went to our local health resort in the forest, which was a 20-minute walk from the station. Our town had only two taxis, and they were not always around when people arrived by train. Of course, the travelers were happy to see someone willing to help them with their suitcases and gave me generous tips after I delivered them and their luggage to the resort. I always managed to make money one way or another. Sometimes I collected old iron scraps and sold them to a buyer. Other times I collected old clothing and sold it to the same man, but I needed many garments to make any money. In spring and summer, I picked herbs in the fields and forest for a local pharmacy. Even though I never made much money doing all of this, I always gave most of my earnings to my mother, keeping only a little for myself.

As I woke up from my daydreaming, I noticed it was almost time for my train to arrive. The early morning train from Lvov to Kolomayia was crowded with people who probably were going to work in the small towns surrounding that big city. Luckily there was a place for me to sit and, using my folded-up winter coat as a pillow, I soon dozed off. After a few hours I woke up and noticed the train pulling into the station of Kolomayia where I had to take the train to Gwodzec, my final destination. I now had traveled about 24 hours and was glad I was almost there.

The morning was chilly with the sun shining through a thin fog as I walked and waited at the platform for my train to arrive. I looked around at the low buildings and houses that surrounded the station and thought that it looked like one of the typical towns that I had seen in pictures of the far southeast regions of

Poland. How little I knew then that I would be back in this town of Kolomayia two years later under completely different circumstances.

◆     ◆     ◆

About one hour later the train stopped at the small town of Gwodzec where I had to get off. I had reached the end of my trip. As the door opened, I gathered my suitcase and stepped down on the platform. Since the station was small and only a few people were around, it would not be difficult for Jan Wagner and me to find each other. As I walked toward the exit, I saw Jan standing there. He had been waiting for me. He looked the same as I remembered him—tall and good-looking. The moment we saw each other, Jan walked forward and embraced me with a big smile. I think that he had not been sure that I would come, and he wondered if I had changed my mind. After a heartfelt greeting we left the station and walked to Jan's home.

My first impression of the town of Gwodzec, about 8,000 people, was that it was not an especially great place to begin a new life. I noticed that the houses were small and were made of some sort of stucco, with only the more important buildings made of stone. The self-made small houses of the peasants were constructed from clay and straw and were built further up around the center of the town. There were no paved streets, only wide sidewalks that were made of cement. "This is fine in the dry season," Jan told me as we walked to his house, "but when the rains come, it is impossible to walk from one side of the street to the other."

Jan's house was near the center of town with its small shops and the open market place. As soon as I walked into his house, I was welcomed by his wife Lidia, a slim and pretty women with dark curley hair and dark brown eyes, and their teenage son and daughter. All four were pleasant people who liked to laugh and tease each other a lot. They gave me a bedroom to use as my own and, even though the room was small, I could see from my window the snowcapped mountains of the Carpathians. It was not long until I felt like a member of their family. I would stay in their home until I had to leave which was almost two years later.

The people of Gwodzec spoke mainly Ukrainian, which is closely related to the Russian language and which was difficult for me to understand. They looked so different in their colorful clothing and boots with their faces brown from the wind and sun. It was a completely different world from the one I had left in west Poland. As I think about this town which was built close to the foot of the Carpathian Mountains, it brings back images and emotions I thought forgotten. I remember thinking that this town where I was living now was one of those small places where one was born and raised, married, had children, and died. Where one spoke their own language and nothing that occurred outside their town could possibly be of any concern to them. But I loved it there. The weather was great, and the people were very friendly. The surroundings were beautiful and hilly, with grapes growing on the hills and tobacco growing in the valley in the late summertime. In the background stood the spectacular Carpathian Mountains. It all looked so peaceful. Although the people were poor, new blood came into the area, and new businesses opened up. Everywhere there were high hopes for a better future.

Jan Wagner's bakery business was satisfactory and was the only Polish bakery in Gwodzec. The other bakery in town was Jewish-owned. Jan's bakery was built adjacent to his home. It was a good-sized place with massive workbenches and a large oven. Since we had no electric mixers and had to make everything by hand, it was hard working there. We baked wheat, rye, pumpernickel, and graham bread. After we rolled out the dough, we baked the breads in a double deck oven heated by wood or coal. The breads were great—crusty on the outside and moist and soft on the inside. We cooled the breads on large racks and then brought them to our store via horse and wagon. The store was located a few minutes from the bakery. The loaves were sold in the store without wrappings because the breads had to stay crusty—wrappings make the crust soft.

Two days per week were designated Market Days. For those days we baked special bread that was twisted and soft and as good as a sweet roll. We always sold much of this bread to the farmers, peasants, and other people from surrounding villages who came to the open market. We also baked sweet rolls and coffee cakes without fruit fillings. Usually they were made with poppy seed, cinnamon, or almond paste. The unfrosted cupcakes were baked on Saturdays, as were the eclairs. We had sugar, butter, and anise cookies every day.

I soon made friends in Gwodzec. They were primarily boys and girls from the Polish people who lived there. The Ukrainian and Jewish boys and girls usually had their own places to gather. When not working, as on Sundays, we would come together. after church services in the town's community building for some fun. We would hang around, play volleyball or listen to accordion music, and sing and dance. Or, when the weather was hot, we all decided to go swimming for the whole day in a bend of a small fast running river. There were no movies or other theaters in town; however, we did not miss them. We made our own good times. Sometimes I had a date with one or another pretty girl, but I was never interested in long relationships.

I lived in that small town of Gwodzec with Jan Wagner and his family for almost two years and I wished that things had gone on as they were. I am sure that I would have stayed there. I know it was not a town for everyone and, though sometimes I was lonesome for my family, I liked it there. Jan and I probably would have been successful in the bakery business if the war had not come. Soon everything would change, and our world would turn upside down.

# 2

# *THE RUSSIAN PRISON CAMP*

For some time now Jan and I were uneasy about the rumors of war. I never quite believed that it would happen. I suppose I hadn't wanted to believe in war. Early one morning while baking I said to Jan, "Why war? Why would the Germans start a war again! They haven't recovered yet from World War I!" While Jan took the loaves of bread out of the oven he said, "Jozef, the Germans have sixty divisions along the Polish border waiting for Hitler to find an excuse to attack without a declaration of war, and I am sure he will find one. No one knows what kind of war it will be or when it will begin, but there is little doubt that we'll have one." When I asked Jan if he thought that this war could have be prevented, he said. "I don't think so, Jozef. Those things build up until they seem to have lives of their own. Then nobody can stop them anymore." I answered Jan that I thought something should have been done years ago, when everyone knew Hitler was building a huge modern military force.

We all knew that life in the 1930s had been hard and difficult for everyone in the world with its deep economic depressions. Adolf Hitler, who came into power in 1933 and was named Chancellor of Germany, became a dictator. He and his fanatic Nazi Party had promised the people of Germany more land and a better life. The ones who did not trust Hitler and his Nazi Party, and who disagreed with all his promises, were put in prison or were killed. We also knew that the Nazis hated many people including the Polish, but above all they hated the Jews who they blamed for all the ills in the world.

◆　　　◆　　　◆

In the early morning hours of September 1, 1939, Jan and I listened to the radio when we heard the radio announcer interrupt the music and said with a trembling voice that Germany had invaded our country Poland. The assault began with heavy air and artillery attacks. The German Army, as we later came to know, was the most efficient and terrifying force the world had ever seen on the ground and in the air. While the German mobile armor units provided for fast deadly troop movements, the mighty Luftwaffe (German Air Force) controlled the skies.

It is difficult to describe how I felt. I was worried about my family in west Poland. They lived not far from the German border so they would be the first ones to be occupied when the German Army invaded Poland. I hoped there would not be much fighting where they lived. There was nothing of importance for the Germans to fight for, I believed. I tried not to think too much about it, but of course I did. Poor Poland, which had been free from oppression for only 19 years, was again thrown into another war. The topic of everyone's conversation was the war, and we all kept on hoping and praying that this would be a short war, and that it would soon be over. We all said to each other it cannot last long. We really didn't believe it would.

September 3rd came. It was my twenty-second birthday. All of us went about the day the way we always had as if nothing could happen to change anything. We baked bread and cookies and cake as usual. People have to eat, we thought. Jan had turned on the radio in the bakery so we could stay informed about the latest news of the war. Then later that day we heard the news—England and France had declared war on Germany. World War II had started on my twenty-second birthday.

On September 5, 1939, I was called to the Polish Army in the city of Kolomyia and had 24 hours to report for duty. From that moment on my life changed drastically. That same evening I wrote in a letter to my parents that I was drafted into the Army and would write another letter again as soon as I could. Since everything is chaotic during a war, I hoped that they somehow would receive my letter. I then said goodbye to the friends I had made in Gwodzec who stayed behind. I barely slept that night. Early the next morning I said goodbye to Jan's children and his wife Lidia who had taken such good care of me during the time I was living at their home. I then left with Jan to the train station. We both hoped that this war would not last long and then we would go on as before. Arriving at the station Jan and I embraced and wished each other good luck. It seemed as yesterday that I had arrived there in Gwodzec and Jan waited for me. A little later the train rolled out the station and headed northward to Kolomyia, the town I came through on my way to Gwodzec almost two years before.

As soon as I arrived at the military camp, they took care of the necessary paper work. I then went to get my head shaved and was given a soldier's uniform, a cap with the Polish silver eagle and high-top shoes. I then received a rifle, a blanket, and whatever a soldier would need in time of war. It was crowded in the camp and everywhere soldiers were waiting, sitting or stood stacked on stairs. The air was full of shouts. Men called each other. They shouted numbers. Because of the steady murmur of hundreds of voices, sleep was impossible that night.

I was placed into a division which was formed chiefly of reserve soldiers. The following day the divisions were sent further into southeast Poland, close to the Russian border. It was expected by the Polish Generals that Russia would invade Poland. First Germany would invade Poland from the West and then Russia would invade Poland from the East. Some time before, Russia and Germany had made a pact to divide Poland in half—the West for Germany, the East for Russia. How little did Russia know that Germany would conspire against it. Later in June 1941 Germany would invade Russia.

Our infantry division settled near the Russian border, took position, dug trenches and foxholes in the hard, cracked soil which begged for moisture, and we waited. The assault came in the early morning hours of September 17, 1939. Russia began the invasion with troops of overwhelming force. Soon the air filled with the roar of massive artillery fire. The sound of screaming artillery grenades seemed to come from all around us and exploded everywhere. One landed and exploded near me. It almost covered me with dirt while I was sitting in my foxhole with my rifle ready to shoot any Russian soldier that happened to show up. Everything seemed unreal to me. We waited the whole day, but no Russian infantry attacked our soldiers. Only the murderous fire of the heavy artillery went on. The shells came and exploded, plowing up the earth around me, filling the air with smoke and dust, killing and wounding our soldiers. It was like a nightmare. How unprepared and scared I was. What I had learned in the Reserve all those years had not prepared me for this. I thought about my father and the stories he had told me about when he had fought against the Russian Army far into Russia twenty-two years before. I remembered when he had said to me a few years earlier, "Even if you are scared to death, never run out of your foxhole during an attack because you will become a clear target for the enemy." I don't recall how many times that I would see what he was talking about some years later. It was a deadly mistake made by soldiers who panicked and started to run.

Later in the evening of the first day, the artillery slowed down to a splattering of shelling. Our infantry scrambled out of the foxholes and trenches, and in small groups we headed for the army kitchen on wheels. After we ate our rations and talked, we went back to our places in the ground. While some of us took up guard, others tried to rest. We attempted to sit as comfortably as we could in our holes during the night with our rifles between our legs. Many times that night while sitting in the foxhole I asked myself what the purpose was of all that suffering.

It was some time after predawn when the Russians attacked along the whole perimeter so that no sector could come to the assistance of another. First the shells came again, high and low. They screamed over the heads of our men, came down, and exploded—killing and wounding many of our soldiers. It was not much later that morning when the Russian infantry attacked us. We tried to hold them back, but it became a bloody battle. I think that it was there on that battlefield I lost my innocence. At one time I crawled out from my hole to assist a wounded soldier who was in front of me. Shrapnel had blinded him, blood was running down his face, and with his arm outstretched, he walked as in a daze. I put him down beside me and told him to lay low.

The enemy started to come in overwhelming force. Men ran and shouted. There were yells and screams. Dust and smoke filled my lungs. Then suddenly I heard the rattle of rifle shots and Russian shouts close by. I aimed my rifle and started shooting towards the sounds. As I pulled back toward some bushes with the blinded soldier at my side, one of our men ran past me. He held his arm high in the air, Russian gunfire had torn his hand off at the wrist.

I don't know how long the battle had been going on. War wipes out the normal subdivisions of time. It must have been late in the afternoon of that same day when an order came from our general. We had to fall back and form a new line for the morning. The third day came with more fighting. These were days of insanity, and when I saw our soldiers being killed and wounded, I knew then that war was a total waste of human life. Many a time I thought, "Time may be slowed down with all this fighting, but we cannot stop the Russians."Our soldiers were not a match against the Russian troops and after three days of bloody fighting we got the order from our Army General to surrender. East Poland was now under Russian control. The German Army had more difficulty in conquering west Poland. Poland's best troops had been sent earlier to the West front to fight the Germans. It took four long weeks before the Polish troops, which were desperately defending their capital Warsaw, surrendered to the Nazis.

During that time when so much was happening all at once, my thoughts went many times to my family in Miedzychud and what happened to them. I would know nothing of their lives during the rest of the war. All communication between the Nazi occupied countries and the free world was broken for five long years.

◆    ◆    ◆

The Russians took us as prisoners of war. First they seized our weapons and then they separated the officers from the soldiers. In later years we came to know that the Russians had shot our officers in the back of the head. A few years after the Russian assault, the Germans discovered mass graves of about 10,000 Polish officers, victims of the "Katyn Massacre." Katyn was then in Russia; today it belongs to the Ukrainians.

After a few hours of marching while Russian soldiers pushed us on, we came to a large, open field that was surrounded with rolls of heavy barbed wire. Coming there we soon found out that there were no tents or any kind of roof above our heads—no bathrooms—nothing. The first thing we did in our enclosure was dig trenches that we used for bathrooms. Soon the prisoners were sitting on the hard ground or standing in bunches, depending on where they came from in Poland, I guess. The married ones were the most worried; they worried about their wives and children. Others worried about their businesses. But we all worried about the fact that we were prisoners of war and about what the Russians were planning to do with us. We were lucky that the weather was dry and sunny. That first night when darkness settled over the huge camp, I rolled myself in my blanket and tried to rest. I didn't know where I was on the Polish-Russian border, but it really didn't matter. The war was lost. It was all over. Later I thought that the war couldn't be over.

Most of the men soon collapsed in sleep, but sometimes during that first night in prision camp some of the Polish soldiers would start to curse and shout and no one restrained them. Later I heard the Russian Army rolling into Poland. First I didn't know what all that noise was that I heard further away. I wondered where it came from. Sometimes it sounded like the hooves of horses and the sounds of rolling wagons. Other times I thought I heard the humming of motors or other heavy equipment. The whole night there was a continuation of sounds of moving objects. I finally must have fallen asleep, because when I awoke, I wondered if I had only dreamed it.

Then in the first morning light, I saw where all that noise had come from. It was the Russian Army moving west in long columns. As I watched, I saw through the dust that the Russian Army consisted not only of Russian soldiers, but also of soldiers from Mongolia and Ukraine. I saw also Tartars, Chinese, Turkomans and Lithuanians soldiers. There was a great mass of pointed Asiatic hats sitting in army trucks, on wagons pulled by horses and in armored vehicles. Many were marching on foot into East Poland. It went on all throughout the day and throughout the second night. I also saw hundreds of empty horse-drawn flat wagons and couldn't figure out what they were for. A week later we would see them going back to Russia stacked high with coal, hay, machines, and boxes upon boxes of other items. They stole it all out of our country. They were plundering Poland.

The Russian soldiers who were guarding our "camp" were a bunch of tough looking, poorly dressed guys. They were from an Asian race; they appeared to us as if they were Tartars. With their uniforms dirty and unbuttoned and cigarettes dangling from the corners of their mouths, they looked as though they could have killed us any minute. That second day we again received no food and hunger began to gnaw. The night was chilly and we slept in small bunches sharing the blankets and coats that we had to keep us warm.

On the third day of our imprisonment, we got our first food. It was a bowl of watery soup with a piece of hard bread. I think the soup was made of some war-killed horse, but we were so hungry that anything would have been good. After that first meal we were given one bowl of thin soup a day with some bread.

In the prison camp I got acquainted with two men who were in their early twenties like I was. They were cousins, but I have forgotten their names. They came from the Carpathian Mountains where their parents owned farms and raised sheep. These cousins had served in the regular Army for two years and had been stationed in the town of Kolomyia. They knew the whole area very well because they had known the villages that were close by and the roads between them. At night, as the cold wind blew, we three huddled together to stay warm. We put our coats on the ground and piled our blankets on top of us. The weather was still dry; no rain had fallen yet, and the soil was parched. Sometimes we filled the days talking to each other about our lives, the war, and what the future would hold for us. Other days we would just sleep. Because of the little food we got, we became very hungry. I was thankful I stayed healthy, since many of the prisoners became ill or got diarrhea.

It was not long until all kinds of rumors went around the camp. One of them was that the Russians were sending trains to transport us to Siberia where we would work in the mines. We all knew that when prisoners were sent to Siberia, it was seldom that they came back from there alive. Siberia was a forsaken place in Northern Russia. Siberia was where political prisoners, criminals, and other people who the Russian Bolsheviks did not want were sent to work in mines.

We must have been in the prison camp for eight or nine days when one evening we saw heavy clouds forming on the far horizon, and it looked like the dry weather would soon come to an end. The last thing that we needed now was rain! But luckily it didn't rain that night. The following morning the cousins were talking to each other for the longest time. With their voices down they were speaking in their native mountain language, and I couldn't understand what they were saying. Then the cousins approached me with a daring plan. They wanted to escape. They asked me if I wanted to go with them. It would be risky because guards were stationed every hundred meters and always walked their beat. We would be shot on the spot if they saw us on the other side of the wire. We heard rifle shots almost every night and were sure that they were firing at Polish soldiers who tried to escape from the prison camp. The cousins told me to think about it carefully first and to give them my answer the next morning. I did think about the danger, but it did not take me long to make my decision to try to escape with them when the time came. There was not much of a choice; I sure did not want to go to Siberia.

For the next few days we carefully planned the escape. Though the huge sky was heavy with clouds, the weather was still dry. Since the cousins knew the terrain well, I left most of the planning to them. One night it started raining and I thought it would be a good night to escape. I cannot remember why we decided to delay our plan and not go that night; it must not have been the right time.

The following day seemed endless. I knew that if it would rain again our chance to escape would come that night. The whole day I had to fight my fear and tried to sleep as much as I could. It had stopped raining that morning, but when the day ended, black clouds formed once again. It started to thunder, and the rain fell relentlessly—harder than the night before. We had no roof above our heads, so we were sitting as pigs in the mud in pouring rain. There were puddles everywhere, and as I walked, the mud sucked at my shoes and held them. Soon we were soaking wet and small streams of water were falling from my cap over my face, but I felt nothing but excitement and fear.

When we planned our escape a few days before, we had moved closer toward the wiring so we could carefully study the guards and the rolls of barbed-wire fencing. When we first came in the camp, the Russians had told us to stay away from the barbed wire and not to come closer than twenty meters from it. There were so many guards that we had to have our escape timed perfectly. As we watched intently, thunder rolled overhead and the night became black. Suddenly the oldest of the cousins, keeping his voice down, said, "Let's get the hell out of here." We rolled up our wet, muddy blankets, waited until one of the guards passed by and, lying as low as possible, crawled through the slimy mud twenty meters to the rolls of sharp wire. We had to be fast if we wanted to succeed. One of the cousins and I lifted the thick and heavy wire up with our rolled blankets. We used the rolls of blankets so our hands would not be injured on the hundreds of sharp barbs. Then one of the cousins rolled under the wire to the other side. He and I held up the wire, and the other cousin slid under it. Both of them held the wire up, and I slipped under it to escape. These were terrifying moments which seemed to last an eternity. We started to run as fast as we could. The mud in the fields clung to our shoes and seemed to hold on to them and delay our escape. Moments later we disappeared into the dark rainy night and left the prison camp behind us.

It seemed as if hours had passed before we stopped running to catch our breath and adjust ourselves. We listened intently for sounds of following Russian soldiers but it was quiet. The rain and the distant thunder were the only sounds we heard. We knew then that our escape from the camp was a success. The three of us breathed a little easier.

It was difficult going. Not only the mud slowed us, but the rain washed away our strength. Suddenly I noticed that my teeth were chattering from cold and wetness. Nothing made sense. It was all insane; the rain, the mud, and the wild night. Our soaking wet wool coats were heavy and stiffened our walk. We came to an unpaved farm road and stopped. The two cousins oriented themselves and said that they wanted to go in a southwest direction. I still cannot figure out how they knew in that dark rainy night which direction to go. I think they had grown up in nature, in the mountains back home, and the instincts that such nurturing brings forth benefits the senses. The rain no longer fell heavily and, utterly exhausted, we trudged on for a few more hours. I followed in the cousin's footsteps because they seemed to know where they were going. We talked little that night as we found our way further and further away from the prison camp.

While there had been danger, there was no fatigue; but now with the danger gone, I never felt so tired, so hungry, or so cold. The cousins felt as bad as I did, and the younger of the two was shaking uncontrollably. The poor food from the last few weeks had weakened us and made our physical condition not very good. There had to be a place somewhere where we could sleep or at least rest for awhile, I thought. We stopped often for a drink, which we took from one of the ditches.

The rain was still coming down as we reached the outskirts of a small village. It was very early in the morning just before daybreak and it seemed to us that we were in a village that belonged to a great landowner. There were many barns and other buildings. Cautiously, we went to one of the large barns and, as we opened one half of the barn door, we found it was stacked with hay. Since the cold and fatique were getting to us we decided we would rest there. Slowly we found our way into the dark barn and moved as far back as possible into the hay. We then cleared an area large enough for the three of us to hide in. Anyone who would come into the barn for hay would not be able to see us. We took off our wet clothing and spread it out to dry a little. More than I wanted food, I wanted to sleep. I couldn't control my trembling body and buried myself in the hay; it felt good—dry, warm, and soft. The straw smelled of the woods and fields in the sun back home and I felt the overwhelming peace of it. Finally I stopped shaking and dozed off to sleep while outside a light rain pattered down on the roof.

I must have been sleeping for some hours because, when I woke up the sun was filtering through the openings of the barn walls. It took me a few moments to sort out in my head what I was doing there in the hay. Then it suddenly occurred to me that I was a fugitive, not knowing where to go. Beside me, half buried in the straw, the cousins were whispering to each other in their native language and I wondered what plans they had next. When they noticed that I was awake one of the cousins told me that they had an uncle living at a farm only a one night's walk from where we were. Maybe he could help us. The cousins plan was to go to their home in the mountains and from there maybe we could escape to Hungary. After we put on our cold, damp uniforms, we made ourselves as comfortable as possible and waited. We had decided to wait until later that day after dark before we would attempt to go farther. Three soldiers in Polish uniforms would be a give-away as to where we came from.

The hours passed slowly. Hunger began to gnaw at us, and our stomachs grumbled in protest. Luckily during the night in our flight from the prison camp, we had consumed enough water from the ditches and were not thirsty. One of the cousins wanted to see if there was a vegetable garden close to the barn so that he could gather something for us to eat. His cousin and I were against this. "Too risky," we said. "Better hungry than captured." During that day we heard voices of peasants outside the barn or heard them walking around. We would look at each other and keep very quiet. That day no one came inside the barn for hay.

As soon as it was turning dusk, we left our hiding place and, after first cautiously looking around for peasants or Russian soldiers, we quickly left the barn and the small village behind us. We avoided the roads and walked through the fields. Although it had not rained any more that day, the walking was still difficult since the fields were muddy. We walked as much as possible on the grass that lined the side of ditches as we traveled in a westerly direction, all the time looking for something to eat. Luck was with us. We crossed a large potato field. In the light of the moon we saw some potatoes that some peasants probably had left from the harvest. We washed them in water from a ditch and ate them—peel and all. It was the first time I had eaten a raw potato in my life. The cousins told me they had eaten them before. The little bit of sand between my teeth was good for my stomach—or so they said. After I had eaten a few raw potatoes, my hunger pains left me. We walked on for the rest of the night, talked little and hid behind bushes when we heard any sound.

Early in the morning we reached the outskirts of another small village. It was still almost dark when we came to a farmhouse with some outbuildings. The cousins told me that it was their uncle's farm. When we approached the house we saw a light burning through a window. The uncle was probably awake, we thought, so the youngest cousin knocked on the door and waited. A few minutes later the door slowly opened and the farmer almost fainted when he saw three men in Polish uniforms—ashen, dirty and unshaven—on his doorsteps. He then recognized that two of them were his own nephews and let us in. Soon I noticed that the man was frightened and I wondered why.

After we sat down around the wooden table in his kitchen, the cousins asked their uncle if he could help us and if we could stay for a while before going to the city of Kolomyia. It was there where one of the cousins had a sister living and where we maybe could stay until we safely could go further to the cousin's home in the mountains. We told him about the last few weeks—when the war had started and how we fought against the Russians. We talked about being taken prisoners and about our escape from the prison camp. But the uncle seemed upset and afraid and said that many of his neighbors were Ukrainians and that some of them helped the Russians. He said that many of them were not to be trusted. Some were spies and 'soldier catchers' for the Russians. He went on to say that many of those Ukrainians had murdered whole Polish families in the last weeks since the Russians had come. I knew that the Ukrainians always wanted their own country and now probably hoped that Russia would give the land to them when they were free of Poland. While the uncle was looking at us he said, "There is not much I can do for you. What would you like me to do?" We understood then that there was no way we could safely stay at the farmer's house without putting him and his wife in danger.

We talked to him for a long time while his wife put black bread, sweet-smelling goat cheese, blood sausage, and a jug of sour milk on the table. We were extremely hungry after two days without food (except for the potatoes) and from the weeks in the camp when we got only a little food to eat once a day. The farmer's wife suggested that we would be much safer if we were wearing Ukrainian clothing instead of the uniforms that we had on. Mainly the farmers and peasants of the villages in eastern Poland wore Ukrainian clothing. But how were we to get such garments, we said while looking at each other. The woman interrupted us and said, "Well, let me think about it for awhile and find out what I can do."

It was decided that the next day the uncle would go to Kolomyia to see the cousin's sister. Perhaps she could give us more help. In the meanwhile, the uncle said we could stay in his barn. Following a few hours of talking about the war and the family, and after eating some more food, we went to the barn, which was set away from the farmhouse. The day was gray, and the sky was heavy with clouds but it was not raining. Cautiously looking around us at first, we went inside the barn and hid in the warm dry hay. My only thoughts were of sleep.

The farmer's wife ran a surprising errand for us the following day. We could hardly believe it when she came back with a Ukrainian outfit for each of us. The cousins looked great in theirs; they were taller than I was. My loose linen top was no problem, but my white linen pants were much too long. As I tried them on, one of the cousins started to laugh, and then we all laughed so hard that I thought we would never stop. I think we needed to laugh more than anything else. The farmwoman grasped her scissors, made a few snips, and there I was a Ukrainian farm boy. Our uniforms, damp blankets and overcoats we left behind. The farmer said he was going to burn them after they were dry.

Two days later, after sunset, we said goodbye and thanked the uncle and his wife for everything they had done for us. We walked the whole night through, and stayed off the roads. Early in the morning when the city was still sleeping, we carefully made our way to the home of the cousin's sister in Kolomyia.

The cousin's sister was a woman whose husband had been a professional man in the Polish Army. She had neither seen nor heard from him since the beginning of the Russian invasion. She was a dark haired small built woman about in her early thirties with no children. Her name was Irene Sobien. She lived alone in her house and said she was happy to help us. She told us that we could stay in her basement as long as we needed. We talked for the longest time that night about all that had happened to us and our country Poland. The next day Irene said that she was getting civilian clothing for us, the Ukrainian farmers pants and tops were not a good idea to wear in Kolomyia. It was sure a good feeling to finally take a bath and put on clean, dry civilian clothing after all those weeks.

The basement we were hiding in was made of stone blocks and had a cool damp cellar smell. There was a small window in the middle of a wall, which we covered with a cloth so it would not look suspicious when we had the kerosene lamp burning. Concealing the dim flame became almost a ritual, as it was our only means of light. We were lucky each of us had a straw mattress on the floor. The blankets we had were old but warm. In the corner stood a table and some chairs. Our days were filled with playing cards, reading, talking, and waiting.

We got the news about the war and the situation in Poland from Irene's radio. All radio stations in east Poland were now under Russian control. The news was uncertain and unreliable, with communications wrecked throughout the country. Before long we listened every day to a radio station that came out of Slovakia. It told about the many killings that occurred in east Poland. We heard about how Jews and Ukrainians arrested many Polish soldiers and shot them to death. They murdered many Polish people; sometimes whole families were killed for no apparent reason—just because they were Polish. It made us angry, and we said to each other that our time for reckoning would come.

# 3

# *THE CARPATHIAN MOUNTAINS*

The city of Kolomyia, which always had been a military town, was now crowded with Russian soldiers. The house we were staying in was on a main street. It was a wide street with houses and shops built one against the other. As we heard from Irene, the Russians and Ukrainians would pick up every young man they saw on the street. They thought any man could be a Polish soldier; therefore, they interrogated everyone. Our plan was to wait until the Russians settled into their functions of running the city of Kolomyia. When the Russians settled, most of their soldiers would be leaving, and we felt it would be safer at that time to take a train to the town of Warogta. This pretty town is a ski resort at the foot of the Carpathian Mountains. From there we planned to walk to the village in the mountains where the cousins came from. If everything went as we hoped it would, we would attempt to escape over the Carpathian Mountains to Hungary and to freedom.

After weeks of hiding in the basement, it became difficult to tell whether it was day or night. It seemed to me one endless period. I would lie on the mattress as I listened to familiar sounds from the outside—birds, the rattle of wagon wheels on the street and cars driving. I heard the clicking of high-heeled shoes and the giggling of girls as they passed. All those familiar sounds would take me back home, and I longed for my family.

One week followed the other and the two cousins and I began to get on each other's nerves. I thought I would be driven crazy if I sat in that basement any longer. I felt that I had to get out of there. I told the cousins that I was going to Gwodzec, the town that I came from before I went into the army and the town where Jan Wagner lived. I wanted to have my papers and some other things that were important to me. I wanted to get some of my clothing, especially my winter coat before I would try to go over the mountains to Hungary. Before I left for the army I had Jan store everything away for me. Gwodzec was about a seven-hour walk from where we were staying in Kolomyia. I felt that I could make it there in one night of walking. At first everyone was against the idea that I would leave our hiding place and attempt that long walk by myself. They thought it was too risky to attempt this. But after some discussion, Irene said to me, "Jozef, you could follow the railroad track at night and that will bring you into Gwodzec." After we talked it over for a few days, the younger of the cousins said he would go with me.

One evening when the weather was right, the cousin and I left the basement. We stepped outside and breathed in the cold night air. It felt good after breathing stale air and being confined for weeks. But we also felt weak and out of condition. My legs bent beneath my weight like rubber, as did my partner's. It was like if we were sleepwalking We had no problem finding the railroad track and started walking beside the railroad ties . The moonlight was yellow and lit up our surroundings. Close by we heard the traffic sounds, which disappeared after we walked for only a short time. It was a long distance to walk, and I was thankful that the younger cousin had decided to go with me. He probably also had been tired of hiding in the basement, and needed to get out of the house. I felt the cold against my face, and it felt good. Walking became easier; we rested once in awhile. Nobody crossed our path that night.

Very early in the morning we reached our destination. Jan Wagner's house was easy to find since the railroad track was not far from his home. When we arrived at his house I knocked on his door Jan opened it. Happily and surprised he and his wife asked us to come in. They had been wondering what had happened to me since I had left their home. For most of that morning we talked about all that had happened in the last months. Jan had closed the bakery because not only very few supplies were coming in, but also he and his wife were planning to go back to Poznan in west Poland with their children. They did not feel safe living between the Ukrainians anymore now that the Russians had come. All of their family was living in Poznan, and they would feel better and safer if they lived in the old familiar city with their family during this difficult and unsure time.

It was the next morning when Jan unexpectedly said to me, "Jozef, I am going with you to Hungary. My wife and children will be fine in Poznan, and I will wait out the war in Hungary." He said further, "Jozef, the war is not expected to last long. Then there will be better times. You and I both know it." I never knew nor did I ask Jan why he decided to go with us to Hungary. He must have felt it was the right decision for him at that time. In war, sometimes decisions have to be made quickly, and they are not always the right decisions.

That same day Jan went to a Jew and sold all of his family's furniture. The following morning when the man came with his wagon to take away most of their possessions, Lidia cried and I felt sad for her. Early that same evening Jan brought his wife and children to the train station for their trip back to Poznan. I never saw Jan's family again.

The three of us walked back over the railroad tracks that night. When we left Gwodzec, I looked back along the way we had come. I thought about that small town where I had been happy for almost two years and had wanted to stay. But now with Jan's family and the bakery gone, I knew that I would probably never return to Gwodzec again.

Early in the morning when we entered Irene's house through the back door, we saw a man about thirty-five years old sitting in the living room talking to her. He told us his name was Michael Jablanski and he was a Polish Air Force pilot in hiding. He had heard about our plan to go to Hungary from Irene, who was a friend of his sister. So here we were with two more men, making it five people in the small stuffy smelly basement.

It must have been about twelve days later when we decided to make our move out of the basement to the Carpathian Mountains. Many of the Russian soldiers had left Kolomyia and everything started to settle down in the city. We still had to be very careful. With Russian support, the Ukrainians with red bands around their arms were like dogs, sniffing out anyone they thought could be an enemy of the Russian Bolsheviks. Of course, I have to say, most Ukrainians were good and peace loving people, but too many of them were not and were feared by the Polish people who lived in southeast Poland at that time.

The townspeople went about the days again as they always had, seemingly peaceful in a time that was neither calm nor peaceful. We began our plan for our journey to flee to Hungary. In the last few weeks Irene and her friends, who had helped her with buying food for us, had tried to learn everything we would need to know about the comings and goings of the Russians and the whereabouts of the Ukrainians.

First of all we needed train tickets. We all had a little money, some more than others, but we got enough cash together for the five of us to go by train to the ski resort town of Warogta, as we had planned. One morning Irene went to the train station with her girlfriend and bought our tickets for the following late afternoon. The next day came; we all felt excited to finally leave our shelter and start our jump to freedom. We said goodbye to Irene who had taken such good care of us.

We hoped her husband would come back to her safely. We thanked her for all that she had done for us. She cried as we disappeared one by one into the dark. It was the end of November 1939.

◆      ◆      ◆

We planned to walk separately to Kolomyia's train station, at about one-minute intervals. We thought it would be safer than walking together. We also would keep an eye open for each other, but aside from that, we each were on our own. The day was dark and cold as I walked through the streets of Kolomyia. It felt so good to be outside again away from the cramped, damp basement. The five men, including me, had been on edge in the last weeks and sometimes our tempers had gotten the best of us.

Since I didn't know where the train station was, I had to concentrate on Jan who walked ahead of me. He in turn was following one of the cousins who knew the way around Kolomyia. Because of patrols we avoided the main streets as much as possible. It was about a 15-minute walk to the station where I saw, to my relief, many civilians. Quickly I went through a gate, the same as Jan had done before me, showed my ticket and found my way to the platform where I blended in with the crowd. While I kept an eye on Jan and the oldest cousin, I walked past people who were waiting for the train to arrive from Lvov. From Irene we knew that the Russians had opened an office at the train station and that there were many Russian soldiers and police walking around. I stayed out of their way as much as I could. Luckily, we did not have long to wait until the train from Lvov to Warochta arrived.

When I entered a train car, I saw there was standing room only. It was full of people sitting, standing or sleeping, while others were talking or just staring out of the train's window. As the train moved out of the terminal and gathered speed, I saw that the other four of our group were in the same car. We did not look at one another nor speak together. At the first stop a few passengers got out, and I found a seat beside an older woman. She started to talk and talk, which was fine with me because it gave me a cover. At the next stop other people boarded the train, and it stayed very crowded. I think that most people rode this train at the end of the day to go home from their work. So far everything was going as we had planned and hoped for.

After about a one-and-a-half-hour train ride with many stops, we arrived in Warochta. It was a town where well-to-do people from the larger cities in east Poland always came to ski in wintertime. The plan was to leave the train separately and meet behind Warochta's train station. The day before when we had left Kolomyia, the cousins had drawn a picture of the station so we all would know where to go. The moment I stepped out of the train car, I kept an eye on the oldest cousin and followed him at a short distance. After a short walk beside some small dark buildings I came to the back of the station where it was very quiet and dark. I noticed that the train station was somewhat on the outskirts of Warochta with almost no people around. As soon as we five men were together, the oldest cousin gave us instructions to follow each other again, but not too closely. A few moments later we walked silently down the street that was in front of the station. As I remember, it was a pretty street with many small stores and eating places for tourists and skiers. They were all closed—probably waiting for better times. We watched carefully for Russian military but we didn't see any soldiers. At times we passed townspeople who looked at us briefly. A little later the street turned into a dirt road that connected the small mountain villages. It was there that we came together again and started our walk to the cousins' houses that were somewhere in the foothills of the mountains.

As soon as we left the town lights, it became so dark that we could hardly see the road in front of us. The cousins, who were familiar with the dirt road, had no problem, as they had walked the narrow path many times before. Sometimes they turned around and said to us, "Are you okay?" Luckily it was not long before our eyes got used to the dark. We noticed that the small winding road was climbing on the side of a mountain. One after the other we silently followed the cousins.

It was around midnight when we reached a small farmhouse with a dim light showing through the rear window. As we walked to the house, a dog started to bark and another light went on. The oldest cousin knocked on the door while we waited. Slowly the door opened. All I remember is that I heard crying and laughing and screams of happiness from the family for the next 15 minutes, especially from the mothers. The youngest cousin's family lived in a farmhouse next door to the one we had entered. They all ran over—half dressed—with big grins on their faces. The families had worried about what had happened to their sons; they had heard nothing from them since the war had started. Now here they were, both of them, alive and well. So much bad news had gone around the villages in the last months about the murders of civilians by the Ukrainians, the terrible massacre in Warsaw by the Nazis, and the takeover of the East and West by Russian and German armies.

After things had settled down and everyone was introduced, the women cooked food for the hungry, unexpected crowd. When the brother of the youngest cousin, his name was Frank, heard of our plans and we all talked some more about it, he said, "I will take you over the mountains. It is too dangerous in the wintertime if you don't know your way." He continued, "I grew up here in the mountains, and I know them as well as you know your own backyard." He then said he would lead us through the mountains for two days. Then, after reaching a certain area, he would give us careful directions and point us further on the way to Hungary. Looking at us he said, "After we reach that area, I will go back and return to my village alone."

Later that night the youngest cousin told Jan and me that his brother Frank knew that area of the mountains so well because he was a smuggler. Sometimes he was gone for a long time alone by himself in the mountains between Hungary and Poland. It made me feel a little better to know that someone knew the way through the mountains. The plan had been for us to leave the next morning at daybreak. All five of us were very tired and soon went to sleep—wondering what the next day would bring.

Early the next morning one of the cousins woke us up; it was time to go. I took my belongings and, after a simple breakfast that the mothers had prepared for us, I stepped out of the house into the cold, early morning. It was still dark, but graying in the east, when the six of us gathered together for our journey to Hungary. As I looked the group of guys over, I realized how poorly we were prepared for this trip. However, I did feel that our clothing was sufficient. Jan, Michael, and I had long winter coats which we wore over woolen sport jackets, and Frank and the cousins were in their sheepskin coats. Irene and her girlfriend had given us wool hats, scarves, and gloves; but we had no equipment—only five blankets between the six of us to keep warm at night. Despite our warm clothes, our short soldier boots were not made for mountaineering, especially not if we came into snow. Jan interrupted my pessimistic thoughts and said that it was time to get moving.

With Frank as our guide, we started our journey. Frank was a man of small stature in his early thirties, agile, keen, and fast. He turned out to be a good leader, driving us, but always concerned about our safety. Many times he would stop when he noticed one of us get too tired. He was married, but I don't remember much more about him. Next in line came Michael. He was a handsome, well-built man, about in his mid to upper thirties. He was a professional in the military and a captain in the Polish Air Force. He had been stationed in southeast Poland when the war broke out. He spoke very little to us and only then with a few words. I think he came along with us only to escape from the Russians and Germans and wanted to be left alone. I don't know if he had any family, he never said.

Then came Jan, my friend and partner. He was the oldest of our group—in his early forties. He was very handsome and tall and always polite under any circumstance. He was worried about his wife and children and hoped that they had reached their family in west Poland. Like everyone else, he thought that the war was not going to last long, allowing him to return home as soon as possible.

Next came the two cousins. Born and raised in the mountains, they were of a different breed. Back at the prison camp when they had asked me to escape with them, I had not fully trusted them. I knew that they had needed a third man for their escape, and I had taken my chance. Many a time they could have gotten rid of me if they had wanted to. But when we were in Kolomyia in the basement for so long, I got to know them better. I knew then that I could fully trust them. They were rough on the outside but were good natured and honest, caring men. Neither of them was married but they both had girlfriends in Warogta.

And then there was me. I was 22 years old, the youngest of the group, standing 5 feet 8 inches with blond, curly hair. I always had been interested in sports and was very young when I started playing soccer or any kind of ball game. When I was a teenager, I was a runner in the 3 and 5 km run. I had developed good strength and endurance because of my athletic activities. My interest in girls was not high at that time. "Too time consuming," I had said. "Too much bother." Sure, I liked to look at pretty girls, but I felt I had no time for them. This war in my country bothered me a great deal, and I thought, "Didn't we fight a war to end all wars some years back?" But I was sure that the British and the French, and who knows, maybe the Americans too, would destroy the German Army in no time. The Russians would pull back, and the war would be finished in perhaps a year—maybe sooner. Then I was going home.

Walking the first few miles in the foothills of the mountains went easily enough, even though the altitude was already much higher. We saw sheep and cows roaming around free. They belonged to one of the other farmers who lived there. The weather was clear and crisp, and soon the first sun rays peeked over the treetops. It was the first time I had ever been in the mountains, and what mountains lay ahead of me! They were enormous and covered with snow. Behind the mountains were other mountains, and others were behind them. They seemed to go on and on endlessly. It was overwhelming for me at first and somewhat frightening to think that we had to go through them before we could reach Hungary.

The Carpathian Mountains is a range about 1400 km long. It is Europe's second largest mountain range, second only to the Alps. It stretches from the boundaries between Russia and Hungary and continues through Romania.

The first day we hiked steadily on with the oldest cousin leading us. We had left the small mountain farms behind us and soon the terrain became more rugged with no roads or trails to follow. Sometimes we climbed steep hills and over the largest boulders I had ever seen. Then we dropped back down again through bramble bushes until we came to a plateau. At midday we came to a forest of tall pine trees on the side of a mountain where our leader decided to stop. We would rest and eat a few bites of the pumpernickel bread and dried sausage the cousin's mothers had packed for our journey. We quenched our thirst from one of the many mountain streams where the water was running clear but very cold. Since we had decided that we would rest for a while I looked for a large boulder to sit on. After finding one and climbing it, I admired the mountain peaks covered with snow, brilliant in the sunshine. What a great place to camp and hike here during a summer vacation, I thought, but then in a more peaceful time. I looked out over the forest, dotted by yellow clearings and patches of brown. Frank interrupted my dreaming by telling us about the mountains and what to expect the next day when we would be heading into unexplored territory. He also said that we would encounter snow. After this rest, we continued on.

At the end of a long day of walking and climbing, I was very tired and longed for a good night of sleep. Now that the sun had gone down, it became very cold. Frank had told us about a hut he knew of, not far from where we were. We would stay there our first night. It sounded good to us—shelter and rest. We soon reached the little house, which was made of timber. I noticed that a chimney was built on the side and knew there was a fireplace. With all the trees growing around, I though we could build a good fire. I could hardly wait to feel the warmth of the flames and lay myself down to sleep. I thought we might even be able to make something hot to drink—just hot water would be fine with me. We went inside the small dark room and looked around. It smelled of straw. I saw the fireplace, two small single beds, a table, and two benches to sit on. Frank and the cousins decided that the first thing to do was to make a fire in the fireplace so we could warm ourselves. We went outside and gathered dry branches and some large pieces of wood.

Although everything was damp, it was not long until the fire started. Jan and I put some more branches on the fire and were ready to stretch our hands out to get warm, when thick smoke billowed out of the fireplace and began to fill the room. The smoke became so bad that everyone began to cough and almost choked and had to run outside. I think the chimney was completely blocked. Who knows how long it may have been since that fireplace was used. Or perhaps birds or squirrels had built nests in there. Frank propped the door wide open as far as it could go, but the smoke left the room very slowly. I think there was no wind that night, and it was very damp in the forest. Whatever it was, there we were sitting outside in the penetrating, damp cold, cussing and complaining and waiting for the smoke to leave the cabin. It took at least an hour before we could go inside again. By that time we were more tired and colder than we had been before. Even though the room was still filled with smoke, we didn't want to stay outside any longer. Jan and Frank each took a bed, and the rest of us found a place on the floor and tried to sleep. We coughed and coughed, and I think none of us slept very well that first night in the Carpathians.

It was the second day. The sun was not yet over the eastern mountains when Frank said it was time to eat something, gather our stuff and move out. We needed an early start, for we had a long day of walking and climbing ahead of us. Of course, after a night of fitful sleep none of us were rested but, later as we went outside, the crisp cold of the mountain air made us shape up fast. After a few hours of steady climbing we came into higher altitude which gave some of us problems breathing. Frank said that we could expect this, and that the journey would become increasingly more difficult. He also said we could rest when we needed to. The terrain was very rugged, and we saw the first snowfall on the shrubs and branches of the fir trees. The weather was clear but a drastic change in the conditions could come at any time. We were not prepared for bad weather, and I realized for the first time that this trip was going to be an awesome challenge.

Hour after hour we climbed. As I struggled on, working my way over fallen trees, I grew exhausted and the cold and fatique got to me. Everything I carried seemed to weigh more at each step. Even the smallest objects tugged heavily on my shoulders. One by one we started to throw away bags of belongings, leaving behind only our personal things which we had carried on us. I kept only my two pair of socks, papers, billfold, and comb. Even those things in my coat pockets began to hurt my skin through the layers of my clothing. After a few more hours of climbing, we came into a thick blanket of snow. We rested again and ate more of the bread and sausage, taking handfuls of snow to quench our thirst. The water in the small streams became too cold to drink. Frank, with his usual odd sense of calm, urged us on and said we must keep moving again.

By now we were high on the side of a mountain. For miles I could see nothing but rocks and cliffs. I stared unbelieving. The trees had become smaller and thinner and were slowly disappearing. The snow was almost knee high, and the going was moderate. Frank had told us earlier to be careful of how we stepped because snow is like quicksand. He also said not to look upwards too much but rather to watch for fallen rocks. It was bitterly cold and with each breath I could feel the hairs in my nostrils freeze. We moved in a single file, one behind the other—Frank, then the two cousins, then Michael, then me. Jan Wagner walked last. I had noticed that it had become more and more difficult for Jan to keep up with us. This concerned me. Jan was not the athletic type, and he was older than we were. As I looked over my shoulder at him, he gave me a sign that I should not worry about him. I now realized how treacherous and hostile this country was. The air was thin and painfully cold. It took so much effort to push my legs through the deep snow. My whole body had started to ache, and my muscles protested the abuse.

Silently we climbed our way further up along the edge of a steep cliff. The strong wind was out of the north, and there was a sharp gust of wind. Suddenly there was a scream from behind me. In an instant I turned around and, to my horror I saw Jan slide down in a sudden blur into the steep ravine, and then he was gone. It was a terrifying sight. Within seconds he had disappeared in a cloud of snow. There was a deadly silence. What had happened was too fast for comprehension. I screamed. I thought my heart stood still, and the world around me started to disappear. It is difficult to describe the next moments. Frantically, we began to scream his name. We hoped somehow that he had not fallen too far down, maybe he was on a small ridge and he would hear us and would scream back to us. But the only sound we heard was from the ice cold north wind. As the minutes passed, our certainty grew that there was no hope for Jan. While looking down into the ravine, I shouted to Frank, "Let's get down there; can't we try!" Frank put his arm around my shoulder and said, "I am sorry, Jozef. He doesn't have a chance. It is impossible for us to go down and search for him. We can do nothing." Even though there was no sign of life from Jan, I could not—or would not—accept that he was gone.

I don't know how long we stood there, somehow still hoping for a sound from Jan from deep below. I was devastated and felt the start of nausea deep inside my stomach. Nothing made sense. I felt extremely cold and tired. After what seemed an eternity, Frank urged us to go on. "We have no choice," he said calmly. Slowly and silently we fell in line again—one behind the other. As I took one last look down into the deep snowy ravine, I thought about the fact that nobody was ever going to find him there in the thousands of square miles of mountains and wild animals around. I staggered on with great effort, thinking about Jan and about his family who would never see him again.

It was now late in the afternoon, and the going was very difficult. I think we all were exhausted, physically, mentally, and emotionally. When we reached a small flat area, Frank decided that we should make camp there. He told us to push the snow to the side and make a circular wall about three feet high. Within the cleared circle all of us could lay together. When we were finished with our circle, Frank told us to take our shoes off our wet feet and put our dry socks on. The risk of our feet freezing would be smaller if we put them in our sweater sleeves so our legs would stay warm, he said. We put some of our outer coats on the ground and laid the blankets on top of us. We then huddled close together in an effort to keep each other warm.

The night was windless and very cold. It was so very quiet there high in the mountains. As I lay there staring into the darkness, I looked up at the infinitude of clear bright stars. I had never seen them so bright before, and they have never seemed so bright since. Perhaps one more star was given to the evening sky, I thought. A flood of sorrow came over me for the loss of Jan. I felt emptiness and a sense of panic, and I wept. I pondered how life could turn around so suddenly. Just a few months ago, we were happy. Jan, his wife and children—we all dreamed about a good life in east Poland. Now life was shattered for all of us. I cursed the war as I closed my eyes and tried to sleep.

It was now the third day. The sky was still dark when we woke up that morning; yet, the brightness of the white snow gave us enough light to eat a little. Then, when the peaks of the mountains caught the first rays of the sun, we started on. That day there was more uphill climbing on the side of the mountain before we would level off. We rested every ten minutes because the air was very thin and the cold was excruciating. I started to ache badly. The wind was at our backs, but sometimes it would turn around swiftly and push down from the mountain. We were in some of the most inhospitable terrain that I had ever seen in my life and never have seen since. I couldn't help but think that a heavy snowstorm would leave me and my partners lost and at the mercy of the elements. I didn't want to think about Jan, but I could think of nothing else. Why did it have to happen to him.

Later in the morning, Frank got us together and told us that he was returning to his village. He pointed toward peaks of low mountains, a short distance away, and said, "Just follow a straight line toward that area. When you get around to the other side of those mountains, you will be in Hungary. You will see the guardhouse in a distance." We hated to see him leave us. We gave him all the food we had left, for he had to travel back over the same route we had taken. It would take him a few days to get back to his home, while we had to travel only one more day. There was plenty of snow around us to get water. And we felt that we could do without food for the rest of our journey. After saying goodbye, Frank, our guide, disappeared from our sight.

We looked at each other and had a feeling of loneliness and even helplessness. Frank was deeply missed; however, we thought that we could make it by ourselves for just one more day. With Frank returning home and Jan tragically lost, there were four of us—the two cousins, Michael the pilot, and me. Silently we started on and struggled several more hours through the deep snow in the direction that Frank had pointed us. Suddenly a thick mist formed over our heads and descended all around us. We had to stop; visibility became zero and soon we could hardly see each other. There was an eerie silence around us. It was so strange, so white, that I thought I was on a different planet.

It was unbelievably cold now. Although it was only about 3:00 in the afternoon, we had to stay where we were. It was too dangerous to go any farther. Clearing a small area once again, we pushed the snow into high walls around us just as we had done the night before. We took our shoes off again and put our feet into our sweater sleeves. The mist created a ghostly atmosphere around us where nothing had definition or solidity. Bundled up together under blankets we started to talk about the war, wondering what was going on in Poland. In the last week we had heard nothing about the war, and we questioned what had happened since. As the long night wore on, I curled more tightly into a ball, fighting a battle with the cold. My muscles contracted, causing me to shiver and shake. I didn't understand why I couldn't control them. I was uncertain that I would make it through the night, but perhaps, I thought, it would be easier to give up—to surrender to the cold. Then thinking about my family, I knew that I would never give up until the battle was over. Finally, I fell into a fitful sleep. Huddled together, the four of us amazingly survived that incredibly frigid night.

The fourth day dawned. As it grew light that morning, my every muscle ached not only from climbing the mountains through the heavy snow but also from uncontrollably shivering throughout the night. We had no food, but somehow I was not hungry. I think my survival instincts had taken over. We were still in heavy clouds and could see nothing. We huddled together, and waited about an hour or more until it became lighter. Finally there was enough light to see what we were doing and leave our "nest." We were ready to face whatever was coming. We walked further in the terrible cold and utter desolation hoping that sometime that day we would see the guardhouse.

The going was slow and difficult. I cursed the deep snow and could not understand why I was sweating inside my clothing while frost formed on my eyebrows. Even my brain seemed frozen. Suddenly the clouds lifted, the sun shone through and soon there was an immense deep blue sky above us. Sunlight poured over the endless snow mass, and boulders glistened in the sunlight. The view was limitless. Below us, dark patches of pine trees were standing tall. Even though my mind was not clear, I remember thinking what a breathless view it was.

After we had dragged ourselves a few more hours, the snow seemed to become more compact. Suddenly we felt as if we were beginning to descend. We realized that we had passed the highest point of our journey. We had climbed over the Carpathian Mountains. The struggle to put one foot in front of the other to climb upward was over. But by going down, having my muscles in reverse, it hurt even more. Every inch of my body was one large ache now. Over and over I told myself, "Just ignore the pain! Just don't think about it!" During the next hours nobody talked. There was only silence. We just struggled on, each with our own mental and physical torture. Then suddenly we saw it in the distance—the guardhouse! What a fantastic sight it was to see that lonely building in the white wilderness. Standing there in the deep snow and under a brilliant sunshine we hugged each other and tears welled up in our eyes. We were thankful that finally our misery was almost over. If only Jan could have been here with us, I thought as we went on with great effort. At last we were in Hungary—we had reached freedom!

The guardhouse had looked so close, but to reach it seemed to take an eternity. For four more hours we painfully staggered forward. I was near the end of my endurance when we finally reached the large block house. I don't remember much after I got there, only that guards gave me warm milk to drink and bread with bacon to eat. They examined me to see if I had frozen my legs or any other body parts as many other people had. Soon I was asleep on the straw-covered floor of a large room along with other people. Years later I learned that about 11,000 people had died as they attempted to scale the Carpathian Mountains in order to escape the Russian and German armies.

# 4

# *GOING FROM HUNGARY TO YUGOSLAVIA*

When I awoke that morning in the guardhouse in Hungary, I was disoriented. I had slept so soundly that it took a good few minutes for me to get my bearings. I looked around the large room. There must have been about thirty men lying in the straw—some still sleeping and some just waking up as I was. I saw a large fireplace in the corner where wooden logs were burning high in red flames. It felt wonderful—warm and dry. I looked for the two cousins and the pilot, but did not see them. I thought that they must be in another room. I tried to get up, and I barely succeeded, for it seemed that every muscle in my body was stiff and refused to work anymore. Slowly I found my way to the other room where I saw guards bending over a man who lay on the floor. Both his legs were almost black; it looked as though they were frozen from his knees down.

Against a wall was a table where men were sitting to eat. Other men were standing or sitting on the floor, eating and talking to each other. A guard told me to take some of the food and drink from the table. There was bread, bacon, and warm milk just as the day before. I asked the guard about my friends who had come in with me. He said that since they didn't ask questions of anyone who came over the Carpatihan Mountains, he had no idea who or where my friends were. Many men had arrived the day before, coming from over the mountains. He told me that I had to go to the village for registration. Perhaps there I could find out about my friends.

Before I knew it, I found myself with three other men sitting in a large horse-pulled sled going down a narrow, winding road. It was misty, and I didn't see much of where we were going. I remember only that it was a long ride to the village. The sled stopped beside a small government building where we had to register and obtain a train ticket. I was to go to the city of Estergom where I would be given 'further care' as they told me. The train was to leave from the station in about three hours. When I asked about my friends, they told me they could not give out any names of people who had registered for security reasons.

I went outside and looked around. The village was small, but there were people everywhere. I saw a few women but most of the people were men who had come mainly from Poland to escape the war. On my painfully stiff legs I started walking through the small pine-lined streets hoping to see the cousins and the pilot, but there was no sign of them anywhere. I felt weak and exhausted as a result of the last few days and had to rest someplace. I went back to the government building and sat down on some stairs outside while looking around hoping to see a familiar face. I had been there awhile, when someone said to me, "Are you looking for someone?" I looked up and saw a man who was perhaps a little older than I. He wore a Polish police uniform. I told him that my friends with whom I had come from Poland had somehow disappeared. He said the same thing had happened to him. He and his friend had also gotten separated the day before when they arrived at the guardhouse in a state of exhaustion. The man's name was Adam Krasowski, and he came from Warogta, Poland. Somewhat later as we walked together to the small train station, we discovered that Adam had a train ticket to the same city as I did. The Hungarian government did not send too many people to the same city or town, but instead spread them out over the whole of Hungary. I found out later that many men were sent to refugee camps in that country.

As the train arrived, I looked around the station once more in the hope that I would see the cousins. But I would never see them again. I think, they probably stayed in or around that mountain village. They had told me earlier that they had relatives living there, and they probably waited out the war while staying with them. Perhaps the pilot had frozen body parts, as so many other people had, and was sent directly to a hospital. Or, since he was an officer, maybe he was sent to another place.

As the train left the station, I took one last look at the Carpathian Mountains. I thought about Jan, whose body was buried there deep in the snowy ravine and probably would never be found. I tried not to understand why things happened—they just did. I only knew that I missed Jan.

The ordeal so high in the mountains is a distant memory, but the loss of Jan, the stress, the savage cold, and the painful exhaustion I would never forget.

Only Adam, two other men and I went by that train to the town of Estergom about a two-hour train ride west of the village. Adam turned out to be a very pleasant and easygoing guy. He was a slender man, two years older and a little taller than I was. He was not married and talked much about his brother who was in the Polish army in west Poland. He wondered what had happened to him after the Nazi attack on Poland. When we arrived later at the train station in Estergom, we were brought to a large house that was next to the station. Originally it must have been a home where a family had lived before, as it had rooms upstairs, a kitchen, and other rooms downstairs. There was no furniture; probably all of it had been moved out before the stream of refugees arrived from Poland.

After our small group had registered, we were assigned rooms. Adam and I were in the same downstairs room, while the two other men went upstairs. Adam and I shared the room with four other men. On one side of me was a professor; a nice man about in his upper forties. Because of the German invasion, he was called to his reserve unit where he was a major. Later after the fall of east Poland, he had escaped to Hungary. On the other side of me was an artist. I didn't like him and left him alone. The two other men were not in the room when we arrived.

When we were settled in our rooms, we were told that we could eat anytime and as much as we wanted in the train station's cafeteria. Of course, that was the first thing we did. We were very hungry, and the food tasted great to us. To this day I still remember what we were eating. It was chicken soup with large pieces of chicken as well as lots of paprika. Later I would find out that the Hungarians put paprika into and on top of everything they cook. We also had cheese sandwiches. When we had eaten until our stomachs were full, we went back to our rooms feeling much better. By now it was evening. We met the two other men who were staying with us and talked about our lives and our families back in Poland until late at night. So far no one had heard much news from Poland and the war. For the following three weeks eating, talking and waiting would be the routine of our lives. After a few days my strength had come back after the ordeal in the mountains, as did Adam's. In the afternoons Adam and I would sometimes take a walk into the city of Estergom—an old city that lies on the Isza River. It has a large Cathedral that we visited. But it was winter and we had no money, so there was not much for us to do.

One day Adam and I heard about a camp outside of Estergom where there was a Polish cavalry regiment. The whole regiment, including horses, had escaped from Poland in September over some mountain road and into Hungary. We were told the camp was located on the other side of the city. One early morning Adam and I decided to walk to the camp for a visit. As soon as we got there, we heard that most of the soldiers and officers had already been sent to France by the Polish government in exile. The rest would soon follow them to join the French army. As Adam and I walked back to the house, we started to talk about the soldiers and how maybe we could join the French army also. After the war was over, which we thought would not be long, we would go back to Poland. As we got back to our room, we told the professor what we had learned and about our plan. He said to me, "Jozef, go. If I were younger and not married, I would go with you, but I must stay here and wait out the war."

Now the problem was how to get money to buy a train ticket to Budapest for Adam and me. We needed to get to the Polish Embassy which was located in the Budapest, the capital of Hungary. Then the professor said, "In the cavalry camp is a soldier who comes here about once a week. He pays for whatever you have to sell."Maybe you have something he could buy. Adam, who still had his police uniform on, had nothing that was worth selling. I looked over my long winter coat. It was the only thing I had which was worth money. A few days later that soldier from the camp came to see if there was anything for him to buy. He probably resold it to someone else for a good profit. When I told him about my coat, he said, "I will give you four pengos for it." A pengo was about one dollar at that time. I told him it was worth at least forty pengos because it was a really good woolen coat. Well, the end was I got only six pengos for it.

The following day, late in the afternoon, we said goodbye to the professor and the other men in the room and just left. I don't know if the Hungarian agents kept an eye on us or not in that time. As soon as we arrived at the train station, we learned the price of tickets to Budapest and discovered that we did not have enough money for both tickets. After some discussion, we decided to buy tickets to a town that was located before Budapest. We were hoping the conductor would come for our tickets before we reached that town. Then we would stay on the train, and maybe he would not come back before we reached Budapest. I paid four pengos for the tickets. The two pengos that were left I put in my pocket.

It was very busy at the station with people everywhere, coming and going. After we had waited a short time, the train to Budapest arrived and people hurried to the train cars to find a place to sit. We soon noticed that all the seats were full by the time we got there. We began looking into other cars and finally found one which was not even half full. We couldn't believe our good luck! When we opened the door, we noticed that there were only women sitting in the car. As soon as we were inside, a heavy built woman started to yell at us, her arms waving in the air. Soon the other women joined her in yelling at us. We could not understand what they were saying, and we just looked at them. The heavy woman then opened the train door and called the conductor who came in a hurry. He took us both by the arm and almost threw us off the train. He scolded us while he pointed to a sign that we could not read. We later found out that it said "Women Only." In a hurry we found standing room in another car. Later Adam and I would laugh about it many times.

Soon the train left the station but stopped many times on its way to Budapest. We began to get worried when we reached the town that we had bought tickets for because the conductor had not yet come around. In the meanwhile, we had found two good seats together and planned to act as if we were sleeping as he came by to collect our tickets. As soon as the train had left the last village, we saw the conductor coming. We slid ourselves down in the seats into a sleeping position and closed our eyes, acting as if we were sound asleep. The conductor came by for our tickets, but he overlooked us. He probably knew that we were refugees from Poland since it was not difficult to miss that—Adam in his Polish police uniform and me without a coat in midwinter. As he passed by us we looked at each other and breathed a little easier. We had bypassed another problem. It was late in the evening when we arrived in the city of Budapest, the capital of Hungary.

◆    ◆    ◆

Here we were in a city of about a million people. Night had arrived, and we had no idea how to get to the Polish Embassy or even where it was located. We decided to wait until the morning when it would be light. The Budapest train terminal was large with many platforms upstairs and downstairs connected by large halls. Because it was late in the evening with no trains coming in anymore, it was almost deserted. We decided to stay the night at the train station and lay on a bench hoping to get some sleep. We chose benches that were away from the other benches on the platform. After we settled ourselves and were half-asleep, a railroad night watchman came by and woke us. He spoke to us in Hungarian, and we could not understand what he was saying. We thought he meant for us to get off the bench and go out of the station. So we got up and instead of going out of the train terminal, we looked for another bench. After we found one, we laid ourselves down and fell asleep again. It couldn't have been more than an hour when there was the watchman again pulling on our sleeves motioning for us to get up. We walked farther down the platform and found another bench, only to be woke up again. This occurred at least five times and I thought there would never be an end to that night. It seemed to last forever before we saw the first morning light.

By now we were very hungry and cold and I missed my warm winter coat. I still had the two pengos in my pocket and hoped we could buy something to eat for that money. It was very early in the morning as we walked out of the large train station. Once outside we looked around. Which way to go now to the Polish Embassy? Wide streets ran to the left, to the right, and in front of us. Large hotels and other buildings lined the beautiful streets. We decided to take the street directly in front of us, but first we wanted to look for a place to buy something to eat. After we walked for awhile, some of the large beautiful stores opened up displaying their Christmas merchandise. Because of all we had gone through, we had forgotten that it was close to Christmas.

We came to a small quaint bakery where in its window were displayed the most delicious looking pastries and breads. Adam and I looked at each other. We knew that was what we wanted! We went inside the small, but very nice store where it was warm and where the smell of breads and pastries was overwhelming. It was hard to decide what to buy for the two pengos. Finally we decided to buy a loaf of bread and with the leftover money buy some sausage in a meat store. This would fill us more than a piece of pastry, we thought, even though we licked our lips just looking at all the sweets. So with the warm bread under our arm, we looked around for a place where they would sell sausage. We did not have to look far because a little farther along the wide street we saw a meat store. We went inside and with the leftover money we pointed to the bacon—it must have been the cheapest. So there we were, bread and bacon, but now we had to find a place where we could sit down. We did not see a park anywhere. Walking futher we arrived at some large buildings which looked like apartments. We saw wide stairs going up and decided to climb them, maybe we could find a warm place inside to sit down. After climbing the stairs there were large heavy glass doors which we opened and saw other large steps going up. Since it felt nice and warm there inside, we decided to eat our "meal" sitting on the steps. We settled ourselves down, broke our bread and divided our bacon. When the food was more or less halved, we began to eat. We licked our fingers and ate everything we had. It was a great meal! Then we had to find that Embassy.

As we walked farther on the same street, we came to a shop which seemed like a second-hand store. While passing we both glanced in the window and saw a man standing who looked like he might be the owner. We went inside and, since he appeared to be a Jew, we asked him if he could understand Polish or German and could help us. I think the way we were dressed the man must have thought that he could sell us some clothing. He said that he could speak German and yes, he was more than happy to help. He then said that we were close to the Embassy and pointed us the way. After thanking him we walked a few blocks further, and there it was—the Polish Embassy. Our national flag was blowing in the morning wind and never looked so great to Adam and me.

We entered the marbled lobby of the Embassy and went to the first desk we saw. After we told the clerk who we were and that we wanted help to go to France, the clerk sent us to another room. There officials wanted to know much more about our plan and interrogated Adam and me for a long time. Finally they said that they would help us and gave us each four pengos. A husky man of about forty came into the room and took Adam and me to a guesthouse (some sort of hotel). It was about four stories high and consisted mainly of small bedrooms, a bathroom, a sitting room, and a dining room. We noticed that some of the rooms were occupied by other men. While we looked around, the man told us to rest a while and that he would be back in a short while. About a hour later the same man returned and took us back to the Embassy where he led us to a storeroom filled with clothing. We each got a full set of new clothing, as well as a pair of shoes and a winter coat. We got the same style and color coat; only the size was different. Later we came to know that this whole organization of helping Polish men was financed by the English and French governments.

We went back to our "house," took a bath, and put on our new clothes and shoes. It felt wonderful, especially for Adam who was still wearing his Polish police uniform. We left our old clothing and shoes behind. We felt ourselves rich. We had a good warm bed, three meals a day, a bath anytime we wanted one, and four pengos in our pockets. I would stay there in Budapest for eight days.

Budapest is made up of two cities; one is Buda, and the other is Pest, separated by the historic Danube River. Buda started its long history in Roman times. Before World War II, Pest was one of the most enchanting and gay places of Europe. With its many museums and theaters, it is still a great city to visit today. Every day we went somewhere in Budapest. It was the first time in my life that I had seen such a big city. We saw the great bridges of the Danube, which connect Buda with Pest. The bridges are hundreds of years old and are built of stone and marble with many statues of people who were famous long ago. We visited the great ancient churches and two of the many museums. Yes, Budapest is a great city, and we enjoyed every minute of it. Too bad that we had no money to go to the famous night spots where the gypsy dancers whirled in their colorful costumes.

Then one morning the same husky man from the Embassy came to our room. He told me to gather my belongings and to come with him to the Embassy. Two men from another room also had to go with him. Even though Adam was not told to come with us, he came along as we wanted to stay together. When we arrived at the Embassy, the two men and I were given tickets for the train to the city of Baja. The train would be leaving immediately they told us. Since Adam didn't receive tickets for the train, we went to the agent and asked if we could stay together, but he said, "No! I have my orders and only you and the other two men are going—not Adam." Of course, we were very disappointed that we were to be separated. Adam and I had become good friends. This was the second time I had to be separated from people with whom I had experienced difficult times. First Jan and the two cousins and now Adam. These were friendships made during special circumstances. We did not want to separate, but there was nothing we could do about it. We were in a strange country and were dependent on the system. Adam and I said goodbye and hoped that somehow we would meet each other again someday.

The train ride to Baja took a few hours. The city of Baja lay south of Budapest, close to the Yugoslavia border. An agent was waiting for us at the train station when we arrived. He explained in broken Polish that he would take us to a house where a family lived, and there we would stay for a few days before being placed with another family in that city. The following day the same agent came and took us to the health office where we got shots to prevent typhoid and diphtheria. The shots did not bother me at first, but the next day when I went for a walk, I slipped on some ice and hit my arm against a mailbox. Even today I still can feel the pain from that incident. My arm swelled up like a balloon.

The next day the agent came again and told me to go with him. The other two men had to stay behind with the family until further orders. After some walking we came to the outskirts of Baja where I saw some nice looking houses with large gardens. We entered one of them and, when the door of the house was opened, I looked into the broad smiling face of a woman; her arms lovingly embracing me. Behind her was her welcoming husband. They took me inside their home, which was richly decorated. Beautiful heavy carpets were on the floors and suddenly I felt as if I had come home. As it turned out, besides their native Hungarian language, the man and woman could speak German also. Since I could understand and speak some German, I was happy to be able to communicate with them because the Hungarian language was a puzzle to me.

While the lady of the house was making coffee and cutting large pieces of homemade poppy-seed coffee cake, she talked to me. She said she had a married son and two granddaughters who lived close by. Her husband told me that he was retired from his flour mill and that his son had taken over the business. After we had eaten cake and coffee, they took me to my bedroom; it was a room made for a prince. There was carpet on the floor and beautiful paintings on the walls. And what a bed—a thick, heavy bed with warm down quilts and a big soft pillow. I felt as though I had landed in heaven. That same evening, the son and his family came over to meet me.

In the days that followed I became almost like a member of the family. The woman was like a grandmother to me, always taking care of me and forever baking and cooking for her family. The grandfather was a quiet man and did not speak much. After I was there a few days, he took me to the flour mill and showed me around and explained the operation there. Many people worked in that mill which operated day and night. One evening a few days after I had arrived, the oldest granddaughter, who was about nineteen, came over to the house. She wanted to teach me the Hungarian language, but I had to teach her the Polish language in return. I think by the time that I left there, she could speak Polish better than I could speak Hungarian. Maybe that was because I saw no use for it, as I knew I would soon be leaving Hungary.

One day the son and father asked me if perhaps I would want to work in the mill for a few hours each day. I didn't have to think about it for long. Sure I wanted to work there. It would keep me busy, I thought, and I would earn some money in doing so. I knew that the grandfather received money from the Embassy for keeping me in their home, but I needed my own money. I started working for about four hours each day. There was all kinds of work for me to do, and it made me feel good to work again. I received fifteen pengos a week for doing my work, as well as coffee and pastries after work every day. On Saturday nights the granddaughter would take me to a movie, or we would go dancing with her friends and her boyfriend. On Sunday the whole family, me included, went to church, and afterwards had dinner at the son's house. Yes, I had a normal and good life there. The whole family was very nice. One day the grandmother complained to me and to her family that I made my own bed. She didn't like that very much as she wanted to do that for me. They treated me like one of their family.

After four weeks, the grandmother asked if I would be interested in having them adopt me. At first I thought she was joking, but after awhile both she and the grandfather talked about it to me again. Then the son expressed his approval. He told his parents that he would be glad to help. They knew that the Polish refugees, who had been sent to Baja, were on their way to France and there they would join the French Army. The family thought it was a shame that such a nice young man as I was would have to go to a far-away war. If I would be adopted, I could stay legally in Hungary, of course, and would not be sent to a refugee camp. One of the grandfather's best friends was a retired judge. He could complete the paperwork so I would legally be their son and could stay in Baja. I could work full time in the flour mill and live with the family and later, if I wished, I could get an apartment of my own. I did not expect this at all. It was a complete surprise to me. I asked them to give me some time to think about it. I didn't want to hurt their feelings by telling them that I had no intentions of staying in Hungary.

Many times I wondered if or when the agent would ever come for me. On the radio there was no news about Hitler and the war. The British troops were in France and further, it was a quiet situation in Europe. Then, after I had been with this family in Baja for about seven weeks, the agent came to the house one morning. He told me to be ready to leave the evening of the next day and to which house I should go. I would be able to continue on to France. Years later I found out that many Polish soldiers, who had fled from Poland during that time, had stayed in Hungary the rest of the war years. Even more had stayed in Romania, for it was to Romania where the Polish government had fled before going to England.

Soon the whole family was over at the house. They all were sad and again asked me to stay. But I had made my choice and told them that I felt I had to go to France. Later in France, there were many times when I would regret that decision. The following day, late in the afternoon, I said goodbye to that wonderful family, especially to the older couple, who had cared for me so well all those weeks.

I walked to the house where the agent and five other Polish ex-soldiers were waiting for me. The agent told us that we would be going to Sombor, which is a town in Yugoslavia over the Hungarian border. Even though Yugoslavia was a neutral country and did help the Polish men, this could not be done legally. Since we had no Yugoslavian passport, we had to cross the border illegally. The point of entering into this country was going to be a night's walk, mainly along railroad tracks, from Baja. The agent would bring us to a certain point, and from there on, we would find our own way to the train station of Sombor. There another agent, this time from Yugoslavia, would meet us.

◆     ◆     ◆

It was now the third week in February 1940. "Here I go walking again," I thought as we left the town of Baja behind and turned toward open fields. There were no hills or forests—just open grassland with here and there a tree or some shrubs. It was cold and on the ground was a sprinkle of snow. After we walked about one-and-a-half hours, going in a southern direction, the agent said he had to leave us, and that we must go further in a straight line. We would come to a railroad track and should follow it in a southeastern direction. He told us some points to look for—like a little old deserted guardhouse—so that we would know that we were on the right track. Then he turned around, wished us good luck and, saying we should have no problems, disappeared into the darkness.

The other five men, strangers to me, and I had walked a kilometer or so further when we saw what looked like puddles of frozen water. Since it was dark, we thought it maybe was a frozen swamp area, I don't know. They were everywhere—some small, some covered much larger areas. We could walk around some of them, but others were so large that we had to walk across them. As I walked over an area of frozen water, I suddenly plunged through the ice with my right foot and leg. The water was freezing cold. I pulled my leg out of the hole in the ice and found my shoe was gone—stuck in the mud below. While angry at myself I tried and tried to locate the shoe but had no luck. Then the other men tried, but nobody could find it. It was buried somewhere in the muddy bottom. "What now?" I cursed. I would need both shoes on during the night as I was going to walk for so many hours over the railroad tracks. The only thing left for me to do was to put my two extra pairs of socks on the right foot and continue on. The extra pair of socks which we always carried with us on long trips were made of thick wool yarn, and I hoped that they would last for a long while.

We continued farther on, one following the other. Walking was comfortable at first. But it was not so fine anymore after we had walked about four hours. We walked on the side of the track because walking on the railroad ties was too tiring. They were unevenly spaced and too far apart for comfortable steps. Little stones started to tear my socks, and I felt the skin on my feet breaking up. We rested awhile, and the other guys started giving me their extra socks when they saw my bloody feet. We had now walked about eight hours. Luckily the moonlit night was windless and dry, only it was very cold.

Finally we saw the little empty guardhouse on the side of the railroad track which the agent had told us to look for. By now we had become tired, thirsty and exhausted. So far we had not seen a stream of water to quench our thirst. No one had taken anything to drink with them when we had left Sombor thinking it would be not so far to walk, and we had to travel light. While painfully going further I thought it must not be too long until we would arrive in Sombor. After some resting we walked a few more hours and still no Sombor. My foot was bleeding and hurt badly. I was angry over the situation I had gotten myself into and decided that I simply had to concentrate on getting to Sombor whatever it would take.

We now had walked, with some rest in between, for thirteen hours and still there was no Sombar. The going was rough, and the walking got slow. For the last few hours we had walked in silence each struggling on over the railroad tracks. In all this time only one train had come and gone over the track. We had not seen one person in all those hours. Finally, daylight came. We noticed that the flat, featureless landscape had changed into farmland with here and there a small farm house with outbuildings. Every step I took now was a painful throb; my foot was swollen and raw. When I finally thought I could not take it any longer, there in a short distance I saw a small church tower rising above trees and I knew we were in Sombor. How thankful we were to have finally reached our destination. We had walked for 15 hours without food and with only very little water to drink. Water that we drank from a small stream which we passed just before we reached the sleeping town of Sombor.

As we entered the almost empty train station of Sombor, a tall man with mustache came to us. He seemed to appear out of nowhere. He was the agent. Immediately he took us to a house where they gave us food and water. The agent and another man, probably another agent who was in that house, saw that I could barely walk and took care of my injured foot which by now was almost double in size. The skin was hanging, and I was in great pain—especially when they poured iodine over the open wounds. Then they told us we could sleep for a few hours before we had to board the early evening train to Belgrade. Belgrade is the capital of Yugoslavia and is the location of the Polish Embassy. It was there where we had to go and where they would help us further to France. When the agents woke us up later that afternoon, my foot was still badly swollen and would not fit into a shoe. Also I was in too much pain to walk on it. After some discussion between the agent and the other man, it was decided that I had to stay behind while the others went ahead by train to Belgrade. I stayed in my bed and slept most of the time, not caring much about the fact that I had to stay behind. I sure was not feeling well.

When I woke up the next day, the swelling in my foot had gone down some-what. They measured my foot, and later the agent came back with three different sizes of shoes. One shoe fit. It was about three sizes too large and two sizes too wide, but with my bandage on, it felt good enough. After I had my breakfast and felt much better, the agent came back into the room with two men and told me that they would be my traveling companions to France.

As it turned out, we later would be together for four years in the same battal-ion in England. One man was Richard Craff and the other was Josef Lizsowski. Richard, a 6 feet slender man, was an architect from Dansig and Josef was a law-yer from Krakow. He was short and skinny and with his black hair I thought that he was a Jew, but he wasn't. Both men were around 30 years old. They both turned out to be very pleasant companions. By 5:00 that afternoon we got our train tickets to Belgrade. The agent took us to the train and told us that another agent would be waiting for us at the train station in Belgrade. It seemed that everything was well organized. The agents who worked on orders from their Embassys and with approval of the country were taking good care of us.

After a three-hour ride in a train which stopped at every small town along the way, and while learning more about my companions, we arrived in Belgrade where an agent took us by tram to an old hotel close to the Polish Embassy. Before leaving he told us to be at the Embassy the next morning. The three of us slept in the same room, and after a good night's sleep my foot felt much better again. The next day at the Embassy, officials wanted to know everything about us. We were fingerprinted, and our pictures were taken for passports. They gave each of us five dinars (about five dollars). They also exchanged about 50 pengos for me. This was the money I had left from my earnings at the flour mill in Hun-gary. The Embassy told us where we could eat and that we would be staying at the same hotel that we had stayed in the night before. It was about the same setup there in Belgrade as the one we had in Budapest. We had to wait for further orders, they said.

When we left the Embassy, we three went on a short (since my walking was not too good yet) sightseeing trip into the city of Belgrade. First we went to a cof-feehouse and had coffee with a big piece of pastry. It was something we three probably were hungry for. Every day we went somewhere together. We saw the palace of the King; we went to movies; and we visited large stores. We noticed soon that Belgrade was not as nice and well kept and pleasand city as Budapest was. One day we saw a movie theater that looked nice on the outside. The three of us bought tickets and went inside. There we came in a room with a low hanging screen and with only benches to sit on. We noticed the public was somewhat tough looking. About half and hour into the movie, loud fighting noises came from a few benches to the front of us. The light in the theater went on, and there in the front were about six men fighting each other with long knives. We took one look and got out of that theater as fast as we could. We had no plans to stay there in Belgrade in a hospital with knife wounds.

About a week later we were called to the Polish Embassy. They gave us our passport pictures and told us that we had to go to the French Embassy. When we came there the French officials gave us our French passports. Later we would have a good laugh because of what our passports said. They indicated that all three of us were citizens of France. I was a music student; Josef became an engineer; and Richard stayed an architect. We were given train tickets to France, and we were to leave the next morning. They explained that we would go by International Express Train to Venice, Italy. There we would wait one and one-half hours before boarding another express train to Milan. We would reach the city of Lyon, France, at 10:00 at night. Early the next day the agent took us by tramway to the train terminal. He wished us good luck as the train began to leave. As the express picked up speed, I looked out the window. Finally, I thought, here I am on my way to France, and this time I don't have to walk.

I never before had gone by express train, and I was amazed at the high speed it traveled through the landscape. It was much different from the old trains I had traveled on before, which had stopped at every town and village. The roomy train cars were very comfortable, as were the soft cushioned seats. After Jozef, Richard, and I had seated ourselves, we started to talk about the experiences we had gone through since we left our homes in Poland. Later my mind wandered back over the last five months when I joined the Army to fight the Russians and my escape from the prison camp and the endless waiting in the basement in Kolomyia. I thought about the terrible flight through the mountains. I still could feel the cold and the pain in my body. I thought about Jan whose body was laying somewhere in a ravine. I could never get him out of my mind. I thought about those wonderful people in Baja, Hungary, and about my walk without my shoe over the railroad track and how glad I was that my feet had healed so fast.

The train traveled at high speed toward the large city of Zagred, Yugoslavia. It would make its first stop there. From Zagred we went further on to the large harbor city of Triest, Italy, on the Adriatic Sea where the train paused to let passengers off and on again. As we continued, the train traveled on a railroad track that was built on a dike. On both sides of the dike was the blue water of the northern part of the Adriatic Sea. It was the first time in my life that I had seen so much water. I had never been near a sea. In Poland we had always lived far from the ocean. I enjoyed watching the large ships which were coming and going. Until now, I had seen those large ships only in my schoolbooks when I was a boy. Too soon our train stopped at Venice, Italy, where we had to transfer to another express train going to Milan and then to Lyon, France. As the agent in Belgrade had told us, we had one-and-a-half hours to wait in Venice before boarding. We decided to take a short sightseeing walk. Although we did not see much of that famous city in the short time we had, it was enough to make me wish to go back there in the future.

When we returned to the station, my traveling companions and I made ourselves comfortable by sitting on a bench while waiting for our train to arrive. A group of about twelve people—men, women and children—came and were standing just a little distance from us. It looked as if they were waiting for their train to come. They started to talk loudly to each other using their hands for more expressions. It did not take long until they were almost screaming at each other, waving their arms and hands. We looked at each other, wondering why those people were in such a big argument here at the station. As the "situation" started to become worse, their train arrived. Suddenly, to our amazement, the group now started to embrace and kiss each other as passionately as they had "argued." It was the first time we had encountered native Italians.

After a few hours of speeding through the Italian landscape, past plains and forest and groomed little towns, we arrived at Milan's very old and massive train station. It was our last stop in Italy before arriving at our destination of Lyon, France. After the short stop at Milan, the train soon rolled through the peaceful French Alps, which connect Italy to France. Here nothing suggested war or even a thought of war; it was as if this soaring mountainous land had never known destruction and never would experience it. Tragically, four years later many soldiers and their officers, especially Americans, would be killed or wounded there in the battles of France. So many of the places I had come through since I left war-torn Poland had been peaceful and lovely. Nowhere had war torn up the soil and spread fire, death, and destruction yet. It was still a beautiful and peaceful place there in the France Alps. I saw the wooded mountain slopes and small roads, white and winding in the sunshine, going to small mountain villages surrounded by evergreen trees and rushing mountain streams. Soon the sun was setting, not gone yet, but almost gone, in an orange glow behind the mountains.

# 5

## *FRANCE*

It was late in the evening when we arrived at the city of Lyon, which is in southeast France. In Belgrade the French officials had told us that when we arrived in Lyon, we should look first for the Military Office that was conveniently located under the train station. It did not take long for us to find it because signs were posted telling the many French men, who were called for military duty, where to go. As soon as we walked into the office, I saw a black person for the first time in my life. He was a soldier sitting behind a desk and doing office work. In Poland some years before, I had seen a "black" person. He had been a man with black-painted face and hands and had been standing in a horse-pulled wagon that was decorated with commercial signs advertising shoe polish. But now, here was a real black man. As I was curiously looking at him another black soldier walked in and went behind another desk. I think they came from Algeria or another French colony out of Africa.

After a short wait a French soldier came in and took the three of us to a large hall where we were assigned beds. Before he left he told us to be ready at 7:00 the next morning. The large basement hall must have been set up temporarily for all the French soldiers who came in late at night as we had, and needed a place to sleep before going further on to different military camps in France. By a dim light I saw long rows of bunk beds, most of which were occupied by sleeping men. I noticed that in many beds a black man was sleeping, and it gave me a strange uneasy feeling. The hall was dirty, and it smelled musty. The blankets they gave us were totally filthy, but we were tired so it didn't matter much to us and soon we were asleep. It was my first night in France.

The next morning after Josef, Richard and I had eaten our breakfast at the railroad cafeteria, we were sent by train to Bressuere with many other soldiers—most of them French. After we arrived at that city, we walked about three miles to a large camp where the French Army Headquarters was located. There at one of the offices they interviewed us and took all the information they needed.

After they seemed satisfied with our papers and other records, we received 5 francs (about 5 dollars) and a French soldiers uniform. Richard, Josef, and I looked at each other. Here we were—French soldiers! My thoughts went back to the time, just a few months ago, when I wore my Polish soldiers uniform. Later in southeast Poland I walked in peasant clothing, and I looked like a peasant farm boy.

A French soldier took us to our sleeping quarters, which happened to be in a prison. It was a very large building and looked as if it was at least 200 years old. It seemed like it had not been used for a long time. They must have opened it up again because of the long stream of Frenchmen who had been called for war duty and needed a place to stay. The prison cells were very small with only a tiny cracked window that let in some dim light. The floor looked as if it was made from clay. It was very bumpy—perhaps from the pacing of many prisoners who were confined in that cell long ago. I had a "room" with Richard while Josef went to another "cell." During the day we were outside where we filled the hours by talking to a few other Polish soldiers who also had fled from Poland.

After we had been in Bressuere for three days, we left one morning with a group of about 100 men. We traveled by train to Versailles, a trip of about 2 ½ hours. Later when we got off the train, we walked from the Versailles train station to the camp. This camp was huge and held thousands of soldiers. Long rows of big tents, which held about 40 men each, were set up on large fields. Besides the large dining tents, there were many permanent buildings. First we went to an administration building to register. Here they checked us in and assigned us to our sleeping quarters in one of the large tents. We were lucky as Richard, Josef, and I had our assigned cots close together. Besides the soldiers, there was a sergeant and two or three corporals in every tent. The sergeant would be our instructor, and the corporals were his helpers.

The first week we had to learn the basics of artillery. Most of the French soldiers I tried to talk to were older than I was and had served in the army before. It was a refresher course for them. Since we three didn't want to be placed in the infantry, Richard and Josef, who had never served in an army before and had faked (as I had) being in the Reserve Artillery of Poland, worked hard to understand the basics. For them it was easier because they both could speak and understand French which they had learned at their University of Poland.

When we had been in that camp for about four days, I thought to myself, "What an Army, what an Army." There was little or no discipline and poor communication. If one came to training or not, nobody cared. If one came to training and just sat there in the grass and did nothing, nobody cared. We trained with weapons from the War of 1914-1918, and nobody cared. But the food must have been good, because I don't remember much about it. Since there was little to do in the camp in the evening, we usually walked to Versailles, a suburb of Paris. Versailles is a beautiful city. If the weather was good, we liked to sit in one of the many sidewalk cafés, drink a glass of wine and watch the pretty French girls walk by. We had received five francs when we came to the camp, but we sure couldn't do very much with five francs. A bar of soap and a glass or two of wine, and that was it. The French Army also gave us cigarettes, but they were very strong. Since I was a non-smoker, I gave my cigarettes away.

Our instructor, Stanley Stock, liked to spend his time talking to us. He could speak good Polish and told us that he was born in France from Polish parents. During our conversations, we discovered that his parents came from the same area where my family lived in Poland. Stock, as I would call him, loved to hear about Poland. He tried to teach me to speak French so it would be easier for me to get around. Stock had been in the French Foreign Legion for 19 years and had fought in Africa, in Algeria and in Morocco. While he was fighting in Siam, which is now Vietnam, he had lost half of his right hand. Many times he said, "I was young then and stupid to ever enlist in the French Foreign Legion." He had retired from the Foreign Legion after his injury until France had declared war on Germany the year before in 1939. At that time the French Army called up every available man. With half his hand gone, Stock was still healthy enough to be an instructor for the Army. After a week there in camp, he came to me and said, "I would like to show you Paris, and I will pay for everything."

Of course, I wanted to see this great city! Since next the day was Saturday, we left early in the morning by bus to Paris which was only a 15-minute drive from our camp. Paris! What a city! Even though France had declared war on Germany, there was as yet no fighting in France. Paris was the City of Light and was unsurpassed by any other metropolis in the world. The first place Stock took me was to the "House of Joy." Since I had never been in a place like that, I had no plans to go inside. Finally Stock said to me, "Come on, Jozef, just come in and wait there in the waiting room for me. If you change your mind, I will pay for the girl's service." As soon as we entered the "house," Stock was gone. I was left alone sitting at a table in a beautiful pink-and-blue decorated room. There was expensive furniture all around. About fifteen young women, ages 16 and older, were sitting in chairs around small tables, walking, or just standing nearby. They must have come from all around the world since they were not only white, but also black, brown, yellow, and whatever other colors. They all were beautiful and very sensually dressed. I could not understand why such pretty girls could live as they did. How green I was! After twenty minutes, Stock returned to my table where I was sitting very uncomfortably. He asked me once more if I would like to use the service provided by one of the other young girls, but I just could not do this.

We went further into Paris and saw the great gray medieval Cathedral of Notre Dame and stood on one of the fine bridges that spans the busy Seine River. We went to the Eiffel Tower and to the Arc de Triomphe. It was dark when we arrived back at our camp that night. It had been a most impressive day for me. Paris, Capital of France has more than two thousand years of history. It has fantastic buildings, boulevards, sidewalk cafés and a great love for gaiety. I would see Paris three more times with Richard and Josef who also had never before seen this beautiful city. Stock was again the guide on these trips and always paid for our lunches at one or another sidewalk café.

The second week that I was in that camp, I was assigned to the communication platoon. I had to learn everything from installing telephone lines, to Morse Code, to operating telephone switchboards, and everything that had to do with communication in wartime. We did not have radios in the French Army, so radio communications were non-existent in that time. While I had gone to the communication platoon, Richard and Josef stayed in the artillery, but in the evening we would walk to Versailles. For the second time we got five francs, but it just was not enough to do anything special with. The third week I learned more about communications, and on the last Saturday we went to Paris again. This time we walked to the Pantheon of Paris, an original temple which, in ancient times, was dedicated to the Gods. It is one of the best-preserved buildings of ancient times. Many tombs, which are located inside the Pantheon, hold the remains of illustrious Frenchmen.

The next day, Sunday, after we attended field church, Sergeant Stock told us we must prepare to leave this camp. On Monday morning we would be going to another camp by the name of Kitky Dann. It was somewhere near the city of Le Mans—a two-hour train ride southwest of Paris.

Kitky Dann was the largest military camp I ever saw. It was mainly an infantry camp. There they formed the infantry divisions from the many battalions that had come together. The second day after I arrived at Kitkie Dann and went to supper, who should I see sitting there on a bench eating his evening ration, but Adam. I could hardly believe my eyes! What a pleasant surprise! As soon as he saw me he got up and with hands outstretched he came laughing to me. We embraced and, of course, we had to tell each other many stories. Adam said to me, "When you went by train to Baja in Hungary, I was sent with four other men through Yugoslavia to the Adriatic Sea. From there I went by ship via the Mediterranean Sea to the south of France close to Marseille. I have been in France for two months." Adam and I soon found out that we had been assigned to the same battalion, which was going to Le Forse.

After I had been in Kitky Dann for about four days, I woke up in the middle of the night. I had to go to the bathroom, but since the bathrooms were quite a walk from where my tent was located, I decided to go behind a large tree that was growing nearby. It was dark outside, and the lighting at the camp was turned down to a dim light. As there were bushes growing all around, I looked at the ground as I walked so I would not trip over anything. When I reached the tree, something hit my head. I glanced up to see what it was and saw that it was a pair of military boots. As I looked more closely, I noticed that the boots belonged to a soldier who was hanging on a rope from a branch of the tree. It was an eerie sight to see someone hanging from a tree in the dark of night. When I had finished what I had come there for in the first place, I went straight to my tent and to the sergeant who was fast asleep in his bed. When I woke him up and told him what I had seen, he looked at me with an irritated look on his face and said, "Don't bother me. Go to sleep. We'll see about it tomorrow." I returned to my bed and went back to sleep thinking about the poor guy who was hanging there. When I got up the next morning and looked outside, the hanging man was gone. This was not the first time that a soldier had committed suicide and hanged or killed himself in one or another way. It was usually done by a gunshot, the easiest way. Nobody paid much attention to it.

It took a week to organize the divisions and for the first time we were issued weapons. They were old and probably were from World War I. The French Army then sent my battalion further south to an area called Le Force.

◆        ◆        ◆

It was now 6 April 1940. Le Force was an area of flat land with hundreds of acres of young evergreen trees—maybe 10 years old. It looked as if the French were growing a new forest there, maybe for a recreational purpose, I don't know. The French Army had formed a long defense line made up of many divisions to hold back the German troops in the event of an attack. Our division of about 20,000 soldiers took positions on the second defense line.

My company sleeping quarters were large empty cow barns. Four long rows of men could sleep in each of the barns. The floors were covered with hay for us to sleep on. Richard, Josef, Adam, and I found a place close together again. After we put our blankets and belongings down on our places, we went outside to look the area over. In front of the barns was a nice sized lake with trees all around it. In another time, it would have been called pretty there. Close by was a small village and further away, here and there, were farms scattered around. On one side of the cow barns there was a road that must have been connected with other small towns. It looked to us as if the place had been a dairy farm that the army had cleaned up for its own use. Not too far behind the barns were a few small houses, probably where the people who took care of the place used to live. We later found out that the owner of the dairy farm lived further away with his wife and seven daughters.

Our food was served from large kettles outside in a field. One day it would be rice, and the next day it would be macaroni. It was always prepared in the same way with pieces of meat and very fat gravy. With our evening meal we got two pieces of bread and one piece of cheese. We were to save the hunks of bread and cheese for breakfast the next morning. There was coffee to drink, and in the barn was a large barrel of apple cider from which we could drink any time.

The first night, after we went to the barn to go to sleep, we did not know where to put the bread and cheese for our next day breakfast. I rolled everything in my jacket, and placed it under my head as a pillow. It was not long after everyone in the barn had taken care of putting his breakfast away, that we were asleep. It must have been in the middle of the night when I was awakened by something that was scratching under my head and making peeping noises. I put my hand under my head and felt a tail of something slipping through my fingers. I knew immediately it was a rat that was after my breakfast. The next morning almost everyone's bread and cheese was gone. As we soon found out, the rats came from the lake. The problem now was what to do about the rats so that we would not lose our breakfasts to them anymore. We decided to hang a rope from one of the beams above our heads and somehow connect our breakfast on one end of it. I think it took us the rest of the day to get enough rope from the farmers who lived around the village.

Then that evening after we received our evening meal and our breakfast, Richard, Josef, Adam, and I and two other men placed our bread and cheese together in two of our food containers. They had no lid on it and were about two inches high. During the day it also served as our drink container. We made a sort of sack from a shirt, twisted the rope around it and hung the whole thing from a beam above us. As night came, we waited. It did not take long, and here the rats came. We heard them running along the beams above us. The creatures must have been trying to slide down the ropes or perhaps jump on the 'sacks' because one of them fell down close to my head and ran away. We made some adjustments with the ropes and had no more trouble with the rats. But every night we would always hear them scurrying around the barn looking for food. Somehow we got used to them. What I did not get used to were the lice. Ever since I was in France, I had terrible trouble with those nasty little suckers. The longer we were in France, the worse it became. Many times in the following weeks I would wash my clothing in the lake. I did not always use soap to do my laundry, but I just wanted to drown those lice. However, it became a losing battle, and I just had to learn to live with them. But I never did get used to the itching and scratching.

On April 9, 1940, the German Army invaded Denmark and Norway. Because of the poor radio communication system in the French Army, we knew nothing of this important event until much later when we were in England.

My days in Le Forse were filled with everyday practice—laying lines to the observation post at the infantry and serving a small telephone switchboard. Most of the time I was doing nothing—but just watching the artillery practice their stuff. While some of the guys and I played soccer or another ball game in the afternoons, others went to the village to look around for girls. In the evening some of the French soldiers went to the bar and came back with bottles of wine. Many of the soldiers in our barn were retired from the French Foreign Legion. They all seemed to know each other from other wars or from far away deserts. While they were playing cards and drinking wine, they told of their lives. They told the most gruesome stories about raping nuns in churches in Spain or about the murders they had committed in the deserts, including all the brutal details. Many of those men were homosexuals, and for me their stories were just too much. I was one of the youngest soldiers there in that barn and had never heard of the things they were talking about. In those months in Le Forse I grew up quickly living with those ex-Legionnaires.

After our breakfast and reveille on Sunday mornings, we went marching with the lieutenant to the church in the village. Since it was a small church, our battalion was divided into two groups and attended the church service at different times. Of course, not everybody went to church. There were the soldiers who had guard duty and the ones who simply did not go to church. France was mostly a Catholic country, but they did not force us to go to church; however, the Army sure made a point of it that we attended mass. Many times, as we marched into the front door of the church, some of the soldiers marched right through the church and out the back door.

Our priest was a chaplain from the French Army. The first Sunday we went to church, we noticed there was no altar boy to help the priest. At the end of that first service, the priest asked if there was any man who had ever been an altar boy. He asked if someone would please help him with the service the next week. Well, as it finally worked out after some talk back and forth, Adam and I volunteered. For the rest of the Sunday services we attended in the little church in Le Forse, Adam and I became altar boys. We gave the priest the wine chalice and rang the bell. I had forgotten the Latin words I was supposed to say while assisting the chaplain, but he understood and said them himself. Every week after mass he would say, "Jozef, you and Adam are the best altar boys I have ever had!"

On a farm close by lived a family who had a daughter about 21 years old. The girl was somewhat retarded. Soon the story went around the camp that if you wore a religious medallion, she wanted you to be her boyfriend. Almost every night as soon as it was dark and the family at the farm had gone to sleep, the girl's suitors got the ladder from the barn and placed it under the window of the her room. Then out of the first "boyfriend's" pocket came the medallion, and she allowed him to come inside her room. After a half hour when he came down the ladder again, he gave the medallion to the next suitor who then crawled up the ladder and through the small window of the girl's room. This went on every night for about a month. Usually it was some of the Legionnaires who were her "boyfriends." Then one night it so happened that a heavy-set suitor climbed up the ladder and tried to get through her window. Halfway through he got stuck. As I heard later, he made such a racket trying to squeeze himself either in or out of that small opening that the girl's father woke up. He came out of his house with a shotgun and started firing at the guy hanging halfway outside of his daughter's window. Two other men who had been waiting for their turn had hidden around the corner of the house. As soon as they heard the shooting, they came out of hiding and overpowered the farmer. The heavy-set "suitor" had somehow worked himself loose from the window as soon as the farmer shot him in his behind.

I was in the barn when his friends brought him in and laid him down in the straw. Some fellow soldiers had a bottle of cognac which they poured half of it over his behind to disinfect the wounds and gave the other half to "the patient" to drink. With a knife, they started to remove at least a dozen pellets from his bottom. It was like an operation party with drinking and laughing and everybody assisting the "doctors." The party lasted late into the night. When the "operation" finally was over, his rump was covered with gauze, which they had taken from first aid kits. The heavy suitor did not want to go to a doctor because the injury would have been reported to the Military Police and everyone would have been in trouble. But it was the end of the nightly procession to the "fun house."

Our regiment Commander Colonel went for a walk every evening with his mistress. It happened one night when the couple went for their stroll, three soldiers hid themselves in the woods close to the road. As soon as the couple passed their hiding place, they jumped out of the bushes, grabbed the colonel and beat him up so bad that we would not see him for two weeks. After the soldiers had beaten the colonel, they raped his mistress. The next morning the Military Police came, and everyone in the camp was interrogated. They asked every soldier if he had seen or heard anything concerning this matter. The interrogation went on for three whole days and of course, nobody had seen or heard anything. Later I heard that the three soldiers who had beaten the colonel and raped his mistress had done this just for the fun and had a good laugh about it. These kinds of actions were nothing new to this group. First of all, there was such poor discipline in our unit and then, with the ex-Legionnaires, one could always expect anything anytime.

At night I sometimes would lay awake and wonder why and for what reason I had come to France. The French Army was nothing like I thought it would be. We had no idea what the Germans were up to or even where they were. Even our officers did not seem to know anything. We had absolutely no idea that on May 10 the Germans had invaded Holland, Belgium, and Luxembourg. I thought, "How can you fight an enemy without knowing their whereabouts or anything about them?" The days came and went with the same everyday routine. At night I was lying on straw in a rat-infested barn, scratching my skin raw because of the ever-biting lice. Many times my thoughts would go back to Baja in Hungary, and I would wonder why I left those wonderful people there and abandoned a good life. But I had made my choice and had to live with it.

# 6

# *ESCAPE FROM FRANCE*

It was about June 10, 1940. The weather had become quite hot and dry there in France. It was Sunday morning, and we had just come back from church service. Richard, Josef, Adam, and I, along with some other Polish soldiers, was sitting in the grass close to the road by our barns. We were talking while we waited for our lunch to arrive which was always served early on Sundays. Suddenly we heard the sounds of trucks coming. When we looked up we saw heavy English trucks loaded with English soldiers going in southern direction. One truck after another passed our barns, yet we did not think much about it. As we watched the long line of trucks, we didn't know that these troops were evacuating from France and were leaving for England. As they passed, the English soldiers would point their thumbs upward, pointing towards the sky. After awhile, one of the soldiers who was sitting with us asked, "Why do you think they are pointing their thumbs up to the sky?" Richard looked at him and said, "Don't you know? They are telling us that pretty soon we will all meet in Heaven!" We had a good laugh about it.

The mess truck with our lunch arrived, and we left our place by the road. Soon we did not think about the English trucks anymore. What none of us knew was that the French, Canadian, and English troops had been fighting hard in Southern Belgium and Northern France. Germany had invaded France on May 16. England had sent twelve divisions of men into France to help the French stop the German troops who advanced rapidly further into France. But as I later came to know, the Allied troops were no match for the German power of superior weapons, disciplined assault troops, and large concentrations of tanks. On June 5, Germany had sent one hundred and forty divisions into France to open an attack toward the south. They split the French Army into many separate units. Much later I found out that the German troops took Paris on June 14, 1940.

*June 16, 1940.* It was about 5:00 in the morning when a screaming alarm awakened me. "What now?" I thought as I jumped from my sleeping place in the barn. I put my pants on while going outside with the rest of our soldiers. All of us were wondering what was going on. The captain told us that toward the horizon the guards had seen parachutists jumping out of German airplanes. It was unclear where they were and how many of them had come down. As I later learned, Germany's tactic was to cut off the enemy defense lines by landing their paratroopers behind the enemy lines.

After we had a lineup, we got the orders to take our rifles and enter the forest. We were ordered to support our infantry, which was a few kilometers in front of us. If the German paratroopers landed between the infantry and our location, we would fight and disarm them before they had a chance to organize themselves on the ground and attack us. An few hours later, after I had moved with my company into the young and dense forest looking for the German paratroopers, I heard noises coming from in front of us. We thought it was the German paratroops and went down on the ground, ready to overpower or shoot the enemy. Then suddenly we saw our infantry coming toward us shouting, "The war is finished!" Not understanding the meaning of any of this, we turned around and with the soldiers of our infantry went back in the direction of the barns. Soon we came back on the road where we had walked earlier before we had entered the forest. To our amazement we saw on that narrow road a stream of English, Canadian, and French soldiers sitting in Army trucks or walking, all going south. Amongst them were desperately fleeing civilians. We couldn't understand what was happening.

As soon as we arrived at our barns, the guards told us that while we had been searching for German parachutists in the forest, all our officers had fled in cars and had gone south. The guards, who were also ready to leave, shouted, "Everybody is running!" I could not understand any of this. I saw the same questions in the eyes of my army buddies. This is not what I thought it would be, I said to myself. It is all wrong! Why is everyone running, and why hadn't our officers dismissed us? Not one of them had stayed behind to tell us, "Men, you are all on your own from now on. Save yourselves."

What we did not know was that the German troops advanced rapidly and with great force toward Southern France. The British War Department who had evaluated the fighting in France had realized that the situation was hopeless and had given the order to withdraw from France. As soon as that order from England came, the Canadian, English, and Polish troops were leaving France on any kind of ship that was available from any port. From Dunkerque, Bouglogne, Le Havre or St. Nazaire—from any harbor where a ship could take them to

England. The French communication network was so poor that nobody knew the situation in France, and especially not us, the reserve units.

It was not long until there was an avalanche of soldiers and civilians on many roads of France trying to escape the German Armies. The French soldiers from our unit took their belongings from the barns and, with their rifles, disappeared among the crowd on the road. Here we were—Richard, Josef, Adam, and I and some other Polish soldiers. At first we did not know what to do. We had no relatives or friends in France where we could go and stay with—we had nowhere to go. We had no money because we had not been paid for the last week. Earlier when we were paid, we were given very little money. Here we were in a strange country. We had just the uniforms on our backs and old rifles in our hands. The only thing we did know was that we definitely did not want to fall into German hands. So we decided to follow the French soldiers. We thought they would know where to go and how to get there. And then on that hot miserable day, I started the most terrible trip of my life.

My friends and I and some of the other Polish soldiers started to walk together, going south as everyone else was doing. We soon discovered that there were many hundreds of other people on the same road. Conditions became worse by the hour. A silent, hurrying mass of people was flowing in a southern direction. Besides the France troops there where soldiers from different countries, many of them sitting in Army trucks. There were civilians with horse pulled wagons laden with odds and ends. I saw small cars that were crammed with people inside and people pushing their pushcarts. They all were fleeing the German troops that only a day behind us. It became chaos. Nothing seemed real. The roads were dusty and narrow, the earth was dry and cracked, and on the roadside the ditches were covered with hard dry grasses. The sun was high and hot and beat down on the people on the road.

It must have been in mid-afternoon on that first day of our flight when we saw in the distance German fighter planes coming out of the sky. They were Messerschmitts that flew fast and low. First they circled overhead, probably to locate a target. They must have seen the many soldiers on the road because suddenly one after the other, they swooped over the crowded road and started their deadly fire with devastating effects, ripping the road and soil apart. It was terrible! People panicked and ran every which way. Some dove into a ditch as I did. Others ran into the fields or fled back over the road in the direction they had just come from. We all tried to hide somewhere, but there was no place to hide. I saw the fighters turn around and come back again, swooping over the people and spitting their violent fire. I heard children screaming in terror and the anguished cries for help from the wounded. I heard the screams of horses whose legs snapped when, still harnessed to their wagons, they fell into the ditches. These were terrifying moments. It seemed like an eternity until finally the fighters flew away and left us.

When the world came back into focus, I slowly got to my feet, climbed out of the ditch and looked around. The scene was like a battlefield. Bodies of dead soldiers, civilians, and horses were everywhere, lying in the rubble and the dust. Men cursed, shouted and wept. But I think the worst of all were the wounded, since there was no medical help. Many of them died there on that road as they bled to death. Their bodies were left behind in ditches by sobbing friends or loved ones.

As the smoke drifted away, I looked for my friends. When the fighters had started the attacks, I had seen that they also dove into the ditch. Miraculously I found them. None off us had been wounded, but we were all shaking and in a state of shock. We went further again on the shell pitted road, passing people with bewildered eyes who were sitting on the ground attending their wounded friends or family members. Dead horses, still harnessed to their wagons, became a real obstacle on the narrow road. Walking was difficult. I wondered if the fighter planes would come back again. The human stream struggled along the open road in the hot sun and became disoriented in this total confusion.

As the day wore on, conditions did not become any better. We became very thirsty, and our feet started to burn. Those stiff hard leather army shoes were not made for walking long distances. Whenever we saw a lake or a stream, we stopped. With my face in the stream, I drank the cool water. I then sat down on the ground and took off my shoes and put my feet in the water to ease the burning. While I was sitting by one of the streams, I wondered why there were so many flies.

Sometimes while walking on the road, we got water from a farmer who lived close to the road. But most farmers closed their doors to the fleeing people and wanted to be left alone. Later we became separated from the Polish soldiers we had started this journey with. Maybe somewhere at a crossing they had gone a different way, or maybe they got hurt or lagged behind us. We did not see them again.

Later in the afternoon we heard the German fighter planes coming again. They swooped over the road and started their violent attacks. Terrified soldiers and civilians were desperately running for their lives. Once again I jumped into a ditch and prayed that I would not be hit. Finally the planes left and disappeared in the distance. I felt as though I was in a daze when I crawled out of the ditch and looked at the death and the destruction that surrounded me. Yells and screams from the wounded and shocked people filled the air. I looked at the people whose faces were streaked with blood, and I felt a need to help them. But there was so little I could do for them. I continued to wander, all the while scanning the faces of soldiers. I was looking for my friends. One by one we found each other again. None of us were hurt. We continued our long march under the hot sun. In the distance we heard the sounds of cannons.

We had no food with us as many other soldiers and civilians had. We also had no money to buy food as most of the French people did. They would buy something in one of the stores in a village we passed. Many times they would offer us something to eat or drink while they sat on the side of the road where we also would sit to rest.

As we walked along the road, we heard many of the French soldiers talking about where they were planning to go. Even though I couldn't always understand what they were saying, Richard and Josef could understand that some soldiers said they would go home or to the home of a family member or to a friend's house somewhere in France. Others said they would go further into southern France or to Spain. Some of them were talking about that they would go in a southwest direction and hope to reach the coast. Perhaps they could go by ship to England. Since none of us had family or friends in France, we thought this last plan would be the best for us. We talked more about it and decided we also would go southwest and ultimately arrive on the coast of France. We had no idea where we were or how many miles we were from the coast. We just followed some of the French soldiers who wanted to escape the Germans that way.

We continued walking until dark. During the last hours of daylight, we did not talk to each other anymore. We were exhausted, but despite the pain in our feet, our extreme fatigue, and the hunger that gnawed at us along with the thirst, we had traveled rapidly enough the last hours. But now we needed to rest. The dusty ditches with hard dry grass were full of people who had walked through the terrifying day and were resting or trying to sleep. We each found a place between other soldiers and civilians.

As I was lying there in the ditch, I looked up at the full moon that was illuminating the landscape with its cold light. My thoughts went back to that incredibly cold night high in the snow-covered mountains. That night I had looked up at the moon also and had prayed to God to grant me yet another day. Now some months later I was lying in a ditch somewhere in France and doing not much better. Memories of Jan washed over me. Somewhere a dog was howling, and a child was crying. I told myself to try to sleep and get my strength back. Maybe tomorrow my comrades and I could get some food. I tried to shut off the stream of thoughts which had come to me.

Night had passed and a new day came. I woke up when it was still dark and I noticed some people had already left, others were ready to leave, and others were still sound asleep. I looked for my buddies and found they were ready to go. We started our second day, wondering how and where we would be by evening. We had nothing to eat and were very hungry. We drank water from a nearby stream and started off.

After a few hours of walking, we noticed that fewer people were on the road than the day before. I guess that on the many crossing points, soldiers and civilians went different ways depending on what their plan was and where they wanted to go. I also think that many of the civilians left the roads as soon as possible. It was just too risky for them to walk amongst the soldiers because of the air attacks that were aimed at them. By midmorning we decided to rest a little while.

A French soldier who had bought a long loaf of French bread in one of the villages we had passed also sat down on the side of the road. He probably noticed how hungry we were, because he gave each of us a piece of his bread. Soon other people started to share their food. We were very grateful to them that they were willing to share the little food they had with some gray-faced strange soldiers. It was soon after we had eaten and rested that the German airplanes came over once more. "Here we go again," I thought as I dove into a ditch and listened to the bullets clatter on the road and people scream. As I was lying in the ditch, I thought that if I would be killed nobody there in France would care and that I would be buried in a strange country. My parents would never know what had happened to me.

After they strafed the road a few times, the airplanes left. We heard the sounds of cannon fire in the distance. Adam and I wondered how far behind us the Germans were. It could not be too far, we thought. While walking further along the shell pitted road with Adam, we noticed Richard and Josef straggled farther and farther behind us. We thought they would catch up with us later when we rested. Finally, we threw our rifles away into a ditch. They had become too much of a burden for us to carry any longer. Many other soldiers had thrown their weapons away the day before.

This day also turned hot, and soon our feet started to burn again. I got blisters on my feet, and they became sore. We rested at a small stream in the shade of some trees. The cool water felt so good on our burning feet that now had open sores. While we were sitting there hoping the fighter planes would not come back, I said to Adam, "When this war is over, I'll go home and sleep for a week and eat for 10 days straight." While washing our socks in the water, we thought about all the food we would eat. After we drank some more and washed the sweat and dust from our faces, we got up to continue on. I put my socks on my shoulder to dry. At first I tried to walk on my bare feet, but that was not possible because of the debris which lay all over the road. We noticed that Richard and Josef had disappeared somehow as if swallowed by the people on the dusty road.

A few hours later the German fighter planes came again, and there it started all over. Close over the road they came, opening their deadly fire, and it became hell once more. Into a ditch I went not seeing the bramble bushes which lined the ditch and scraped me badly. After I thought the planes were gone, I scrambled out of the ditch. A few seconds later they were back or maybe there were more, I don't know—I don't remember. Back I went into the ditch again. Over and over they came—back and forth—strafing the road. When the planes finally left, I again climbed out of the ditch. The first thing I did was look for Adam. I looked everywhere but I did not see him. I started to think the worst, but then I thought that if Adam had been killed or wounded, I would find him. He would be lying here somewhere. I don't know how long I looked for him. He was nowhere to be found. Finally I found myself left with a few French soldiers.

The heat was now profound. It seemed as thought the earth would catch fire and explode. The air quivered. Now I seemed to be walking outside of myself, wondering what the devil I was doing on that road. But it was too much trouble to stop my feet from moving, and so I didn't try. Somehow I did not care anymore, and while struggling on in exhaustion, I said to myself, "Each man for himself. You've got to make it. It is your only hope." Soon I began to lose my sense of time.

Somehow the day passed, and it became dark. I stumbled into a ditch. There were only a few soldiers sleeping a little farther on. When I laid myself down, I suddenly felt very lonely, and a sense of panic came over me. Here I was in a strange country, not knowing where I was or where I should go. I was hungry and had no money for food. The Germans were close at my heels, and worst of all I had lost my friends. But I think most of all, I feared the unknown. I was in a desperate situation and felt utterly miserable, and I dozed off thinking about Adam. I thought that maybe he had taken the wrong road; nobody was thinking clearly anymore, and there were other roads when the fighters came. Finally, I fell into a sweaty, restless nightmare that brought no rest.

When I woke up the next morning, a chaplain was lying beside me. I wondered where he came from because I had not seen him the night before when I had laid down to rest. At that time only a few soldiers were lying in the ditch further away. This man was alone and was a chaplain in the French Army. He introduced himself to me in French but soon found out I could not speak that language very well. After I told him, as good as my French allowed me, that I came from Poland and was now in the French Army, he looked at me and laughed. He then started to speak Polish and told me that he had come from Poland some years before. The Catholic Council had sent him to France because there was a shortage of priests there.

His name was Kaminski, and he was in his middle thirties. He was raised in Krakow, a city in South Poland. He had been stationed with the French Army not far from where I had been. He and some of the soldiers from his company had also fled when the German Army came closer, but somehow he got separated from them and now was alone. As soon as we started to walk together on the road, the chaplain said to me, "I am going to the Port of St. Nazaire to see if I can find a ship which will take me to England." He then continued, "St. Nazaire is a large harbor and not too far from here. I know the way." I looked at him and could hardly believe what I heard. How could I be so lucky that this chaplain had come just at the right time?

We had walked for about an hour, when we came to a village. While the chaplain went to a store which was located just off the road, he said "Jozef, here we will eat and rest." As he was inside, I looked for a place for us to rest and found one in the shade of a large old tree just beside the store on a small area of grass. It did not take long before Chaplain Kaminski came out of the store carrying milk, a large loaf of French bread, and a big piece of cheese. I couldn't believe my eyes. Food! How fortunate I was to have met someone with money to buy food! When I had started out that morning, I knew I needed food badly. I felt immensely tired and had not much strength left anymore to walk again so far. I must have eaten my meal like a hungry dog, because Chaplain Kaminski looked at me as if he could not believe where I had put it so fast. While I licked my fingers, I said to the chaplain, "Did you ever eat anything that good?"

After we rested awhile, I felt somewhat better and got some of my energy back. As we continued on walking along the dusty road, the chaplain told me about his life in the priesthood in France; how very poor life was in the small town where he now lived. When he came from Poland, he was sent to school in France to learn the language and about the French people. Since the beginning of the war, he had been a chaplain in the French Army with the rank of Captain. He had never had so much money in his pocket since he left Poland. He said the French people are difficult to understand. They are very nationalistic, and it is difficult for an outsider to be accepted into their lives.

The weather was hot and dry again. The sky was clear, there were no clouds; the sun shone down without pity. It had become quiet now, and we saw no more civilians on the road. The horses and wagons were gone also as were the cars and military trucks. There were only small groups of soldiers left. I thought they were going to St. Nazaire as we were, in the hope of finding a ship on which they could flee to England and escape internment in a German prisoner of war camp.

As we trudged along the road, I wondered what happened to my friends and where they were, and if I would ever see them again. My feet bothered me a lot; they were painfully swollen. Only the knowledge that I was close to St. Nazaire kept me going. Chaplain Kaminski's feet were not much better than mine were. We rested often under roadside trees and along ditches because walking became difficult for him. That day there were no German Messerschmitts coming over to attack us. I don't know if I could have survived another day of air attacks.

It was somewhat later in the afternoon when we saw about twenty German bombers flying in the sky with incredible slowness, no more than a two hundred meters above the fields. Then from afar, we watched the planes drop their bombs on the City of St. Nazaire. We heard the rolling explosions and saw the fires erupt. We watched as the smoke rose high in the cloudless sky. Earlier I had hoped to reach the city in the afternoon so we could find out where the harbor was and perhaps find a ship, any kind of ship, that was to go to England and could take us.

It was at this time that I had the hardest time with the chaplain. Not only did his feet ache unbearably, but he was also completely exhausted. He would say to me, "Jozef, you go on without me. I cannot make it anymore." But I felt that I could not leave him. He had come to me at a time when I was desperate and hungry, and now I felt it was I who had to help him. Had fate brought us together? Perhaps. So, slowly, with many stops to rest and to urge him to continue on, we finally reached the area close to St. Nazaire late in the evening under a red sky.

When we walked on the road to St. Nazaire, the chaplain and I had wondered many times why we did not see any civilians anywhere, anyplace. There was no traffic of any kind. Later I came to know that the Germans had already bombed St. Nazaire a few times before, and most of the citizens had left their city. As we approached St Nazaire, it seemed to us that the entire city was engulfed in flames. The fires were everywhere and smoke filled the air. It was a terrible sight. We heard huge explosions coming not only from the city itself, but also eruptions that seemed to come from what was probably the harbor side. But all we could do now was watch from a distance as the city burned. The chaplain and I decided to spend the night close to the city. Maybe tomorrow, we said, we could take a better look at the situation. We knew also that we had very little time; any time now we could expect to see the Germany Army or perhaps paratroopers falling out of the sky.

Not too far back, we had noticed a field with stacks of hay and had seen some French soldiers going into the field. We retraced our steps along the road we had come on. It did not take long until we found the field again where we observed soldiers in and around the haystacks. We looked around us and found a haystack that was not too far from the road. It looked good to us, so the chaplain and I took the shoes off of our painful feet, and soon we burrowed into the soft hay. I was wet with sweat.

The day had been hot, and the night was barely beginning. I felt ill with exhaustion. While I was lying in the haystack, I looked to the west where the sea was. To the northwest was England, to the northeast were the Germans, to the south was Spain and I was in the middle. I wondered how I had gotten myself into this mess. I prayed. The sky was red over the burning city of St. Nazaire.

When I awoke in the early morning hour, the fourth day of my terrifying journey, it was still almost dark. While I oriented myself as to where I was, I suddenly heard a woman's voice yelling in French through a megaphone at the top of her lungs. She was shouting that there was an English ship anchored in the harbor. And as I could understand, she said it was there to rescue soldiers. The chaplain and I jumped up and saw a French military truck parked on the road not far from us. I grabbed my shoes and started to run toward the truck. My legs trembled under me, and I almost fell as I looked down at my swollen feet. "This is it!" I yelled, "This is it!" I could not believe it. An English ship was waiting in the port, ready to rescue us. It was the answer to my prayers. A feeling of new hope came over me. Suddenly I felt an unbelievable relief. The chaplain was running beside me when suddenly he stopped and said, "My shoes, I forgot my shoes." He ran back on wobbly legs to the haystack and found them. As I waited for him, I saw other soldiers coming out from other haystacks in the field—all running to the waiting truck. After we were all in the truck—there were about fifteen of us—the woman yelled once more through the megaphone. No more soldiers came out of the fields. As the truck sped off, she looked around once more, but all that we saw was the smoke that was lying as a veil over the fields of St. Nazaire, blurring the ruins of the city.

The truck sped down the road for about ten minutes and then we came to a stop. We jumped out and saw an English destroyer lying at the end of a pier. I saw English sailors standing close to a ladder which was leaning up against the ship. Another English destroyer was lying further out from the harbor. I thought it was a mirage—an illusion, a part of the insanity and chaos of the last days.

When all the soldiers who had been in the truck approached the ship, the sailors dressed in dark blue uniforms asked us in English if we were French or English soldiers. When we said that we were French soldiers, the sailors shouted, "Hurry, Hurry!" They had us climb the ladder and go up on the deck. No civilians were allowed to go on board. Also on the pier were men in civilian clothing beckoning to the sailors to let them on board ship. The men argued that they were soldiers, had bought civilian clothing and had thrown their uniforms away. But the sailors told them they had orders not to allow civilians to board. Later we learned the driver and the woman of the military truck took those men somewhere else where another ship (a coal ship) was waiting to take civilians with them to England. Thousands of men were rescued this way on all kinds of ships and boats and taken to England in that summer of 1940.

As soon as we were on deck, the ladder was pulled up. The ship left the harbor hurriedly. As it moved away, I took one last look at the smoking city of St. Nazaire, a city I had never heard of before in my life, but which now I would never forget. I looked at the countryside of France where I had been for four long difficult months, and I wondered where Adam, Richard, and Josef were. Were they hurt, or worse, had the strafing German fighter planes killed them? I thought about my family in Poland and wondered what happened to them under German occupation. I wished they could see me now and know that I was on an English warship going to England. I looked a long time at the land under the smoke. It was behind me now. I had left it under the red sun.

This was the first time in my life that I was on an ocean and a ship. I never even had seen a picture of a warship. I looked around me. I saw that the English sailors were standing beside their anti-aircraft guns, ready to shoot down any German planes that happened to show up. I noticed that the ship was made of dark gray iron—nothing else. It had a large amount of cannons and machine guns of all sizes and sort on board. I came to know that destroyers protect the convoys of ships on the seas from enemy airplanes and submarines.

We were not allowed to go below and had to stay in a designated area on the deck of the destroyer. I think they were careful so we would not bring in any kind of germs of who knew what kind. We were dirty, unshaven, with gray sweaty faces and hollow eyes, and I think they also wanted no part of the lice we carried with us. Soon the English sailors came around with tea and biscuits which all of us greatly appreciated. We all were exhausted and looked around the deck for a place to rest. I found a good spot and sat down; the chaplain was beside me. The first thing we did was to take our shoes off. As I looked at my swollen feet, I said to them, "We made it! Dear Lord, we made it!"

I must have dozed off for awhile when suddenly I woke up and saw big waves all around me. One moment I was on top of the waves; the next moment the ship was going down into what looked to me like the bottom of a large bowl. Then the ship went up again, riding high on the top of a wave. It seemed as though any moment the high waves would crash over the ship as we went down again. I was scared stiff! But as I looked at the sailors and saw them talking to each other and laughing, I said to myself, "If they are not afraid, why should I be?" I tried to sleep some more, but I could not. Some of the French soldiers were hanging over the rail of the ship, disposing their tea and biscuits into the sea. The trip from St. Nazaire to England over the turbulent Atlantic ocean and English Channel would take twenty-four hours.

Later in England, I came to know that June 19, the day I left France early in the morning, thankfully rescued by an English destroyer, was the day that the last English ship left the port of St. Nazaire. That same day in the afternoon, German tanks rolled into the destroyed city. The fall of France was on June 22, 1940.

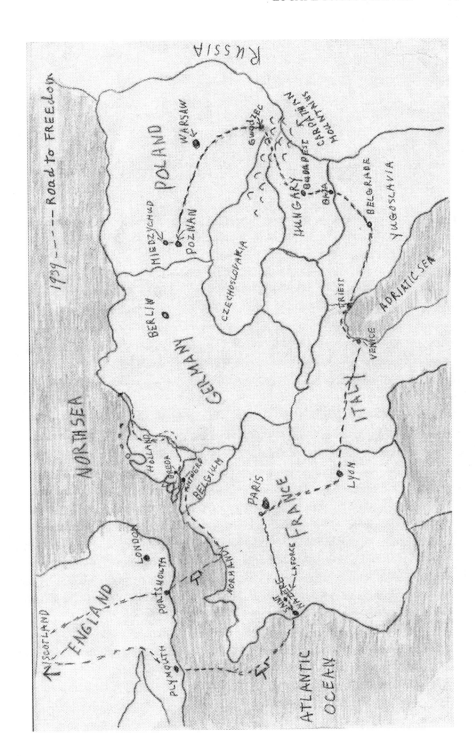

# 7

# *SCOTLAND*

The night seemed endless, but a new day finally came. During the night, between naps on the slippery gray iron deck of the destroyer, the Chaplain and I had talked with the other soldiers. Some of them were seasick and others were, as we, very tired but could not sleep. I was, and always have been, an easy sleeper under any circumstances, but on the deck of that ship going up and down on the turbulent water, it was just not possible. While looking over the endless expanse of the sea and watching the sun climb up, my hopes rose with it. Those moments on the open sea looked so peaceful in a world that knew no peace. Here I was going to England, something that had been the farthest from my mind. It was God's will or destiny, whatever you want to call it, that I was not going home, not yet anyway.

Soon I saw in the distance the white beaches of England gleaming in the early morning sun. We had reached England. The Chaplain and I did not know much about that country and wondered what kind of situation we would find there. We didn't know quite what to expect. It could not be any worse than in France, we said. As I looked to my left, I saw further up a convoy of many supply ships. They were guarded by four destroyers, probably for protection from German submarines or planes which, as I learned, were always hunting the convoys. I think the convoy came from America or Canada on the way to an English harbor. The English channel was filled with minefields. We saw little orange flags about every quarter of a mile where mines were floating just below the surface of the water. Our destroyer was steering right between those buoys. It was like a highway between rows of corn.

After the rough sailing over the Atlantic Ocean from St. Nazaire, the water had become calm as we reached the southwest coast of England and the large harbor city of Plymouth. There on the English Channel we had to wait in a line with many other ships before it was our turn to enter the harbor. It took more than three hours until finally our destroyer moved slowly into the harbor which teemed with ships of all sizes. It was a very busy place with many warships of the British Royal Navy coming and going. Also there were many supply ships being unloaded by tall cranes. This large harbor with all its ships was very impressive to see.

As soon as our destroyer had anchored, we went off the ship and were taken by military truck to a camp just outside the city of Plymouth. While I was sitting in the truck going through the city, I noticed the clean streets which were lined with trees, the beautiful Victorian houses, and the many fine churches and stores. The whole city looked so pleasant. People waved and smiled at us from the sidewalks. It looked like such a different world here than the one I had left in France.

We did not know then that the beautiful city of Plymouth would be heavily damaged by German bombers just a few weeks after we arrived in England. The Nazis bombed that city five nights in a row and left it with half the homes, shops and churches destroyed and many of its citizens dead. For the rest of the war, Plymouth would be bombed over and over again—especially the harbor. All of the children of Plymouth and most of the citizens who could leave, found refuge in inland towns and villages in England and Scotland.

The camp where we went was especially set up for the many soldiers who came to England after the British had decided to pull out of France. For the last few weeks the British destroyers and all kinds of other ships had rescued the trapped Allied soldiers from the beaches of Dunkerque and the harbors of France. When the truck stopped, we got off and entered a long tent. There we were interrogated by English, French or Polish officers. We had to show our papers, and then they asked us a thousand questions. I think they had to be sure there were no German spies among us. Finally when the officers were finished with their interrogations, they took us outside to a place where breakfast was served on long tables. We got large slices of white bread, butter, cheese and marmalade, coffee, and of course, English tea, which was England's favorite drink. It was my first breakfast under English sky. The English soldiers who took care of us were a bunch of pleasant and helpful guys. Grinning, we looked at each other. What a difference this was from France! Little did I know that I would remain in England and Scotland for four long years before returning to the mainland of Europe.

When we had finished eating our great breakfast, they took us to another tent where each of us was given a small container. We were asked to empty our pockets of all personal belongings and place them in the container. Then we had to undress completely and throw all our clothing on a large pile. I think they burned all the clothing. It was the only way to get rid of the lice which were embedded in every article of clothing. They handed us a piece of black soap (I think it was a disinfectant soap), and we stepped under one of the showers. As soon as I scrubbed myself, my skin started burning like crazy. Probably I had scratched my skin open here and there and now that soap was biting me. "I can't win," I thought, but I was thankful for finally being able to shower and wash away all the dust, grime and lice from France. Since the day I had been stationed in Le Force, all of us soldiers had used the lake to bathe in as there were no showers available. None of us had taken a freshwater bath or shower in three months. From a long table I took one of the many towels which were piled high.

After shaving our beards, we went on to another place where doctors examined us and asked questions about any shots we had previously received. After the visit to the doctors, we went into another tent. There we were issued our new underwear, socks and our British soldier's uniform. While I was putting on my uniform I thought, "This is the third different uniform I've worn in ten months—first Polish, then French, and now British." Soldiers who had swollen feet or had open sores on their feet were given gym shoes in addition to the hard stiff English military shoes. We were to wear the gym shoes until our feet were in good shape again. Along with clothing, we also were given English cigarettes.

Finally, we were directed to one of the large tents which were set up on the field. The Polish men were together in one tent; the French in another, and the Canadians in a third. "At last, a bed again," I thought as I walked into the tent and laid down on one of the military cots. A little later a Polish officer came in and said, "You can do whatever you want. If you would like to sleep the whole day, that is fine. But remember, lunch is served at 1:00." After he left I think I fell asleep immediately as did most of the other men who had been sleeping in ditches and open fields in the last days.

I remained at that camp for about a week. I cannot remember much about it, only that we had to be checked by a doctor every day. Many of the soldiers had become sick because of their ordeal in France. I and the majority of the men from our tent spent the week mostly sleeping and eating. A depression had come over me, and I felt as though I didn't care about anything. Then one day we were loaded on trucks and driven to a large military camp near Liverpool. We stayed there for two weeks before they took us to Glasgow in Scotland.

In the meantime, while I had arrived in England, the war in Europe had been extended. Aldolf Hitler's Ally, Italy, fought hard in North Africa and on the Mediterranean Sea. The British considered this a vital point for their ships in establishing control over the Mediterranean Sea and especially for control of the Suez canal which was the road to the Middle East and the oil fields. Italy, which had air bases in its North Africa colonies, needed the oil fields in the middle East very badly as did Germany and the British.

◆     ◆     ◆

*July 1940.* The camp, which was located close to the city of Glasgow in Scotland, was an all-Polish camp of about 1000 soldiers. Many of the men had already been there a few weeks before I arrived. The small tents in that temporary camp, which we ourselves had to set up, held only six men. We soon found out that the weather in Scotland was not the greatest. It was cool, cloudy and gray most of the time with many days a misty rain coming down. Since we were lying on straw mattresses on the ground, our bedding and clothing soon became damp. We sure were glad it was summer. The days there were filled with different kind of sports. Of course I mostly played soccer, but I also liked to play volleyball. Besides an occasional trip to the movie theater, we did nothing.

At the end of August of that year, while I was still at that same camp, they sent me to a new established driver and mechanic school for six weeks. At the school I learned everything about driving trucks, cars and motorcycles. We learned how to take care of them, replace parts and do general repair work. I liked this course; it gave me something to do and had a purpose to it. The course was taught every day except Sundays. On Saturday evenings I would go with a few other guys to a bar for a Scots beer, or we would wind up at a dance hall. I couldn't speak English very well yet but was learning fast, especially when we would sit down with some of the Scottish girls and, of course, the conversation was in English. I had bought myself a Polish-English dictionary and every day I taught myself a few word of English. After the six-week course at the school I received my Driver's Diploma and was qualified to drive any kind of motor vehicle.

Meanwhile the German Luftwaffe (Air Force) increased its channel warfare against convoys and England's coastal defenses. Sometimes many Allied ships were lost because their fighter plane protection did not arrive soon enough. There were not enough airplanes and trained R A F (Royal Air Force) pilots to replace the ones shot down.

The English people were afraid of an invasion by Germany, and they were not ready for this. They knew that only that stretch of water called the English Channel, interrupted the Nazi's conquest of the world. The English also knew that the German Armies were not a match for the English Army which had left most of their weapons behind in France. The English men and women now started to work 24 hours a day in the factories to build up their R.A.F. aircraft and Armed Force's guns and weapons.

Germany had thought it would be easy to invade England from France across the English Channel, which I think, would have been successful for Germany since the British Army and Air force were not strong enough to defend themselves against the overpowering forces of Germany. But Adolf Hitler made a serious mistake. He thought that, instead of an invasion, the English people would ask him for peace and surrender when his Luftwaffe would send enough bombers over England. Hitler's generals were amazed over Hitler's decision. Most of them wanted to invade England immediately before the British would have time to recover and prepare for a German attack.

Then in the beginning of September 1940 Hitler ordered day and night bombing raids on London and other major cities. Huge flights of German bombers swarmed over the cities. They dropped their loads of death and destruction. The damage in the crowded city of London was terrible. By the end of the war thousands of houses, office buildings, stores and churches were destroyed or set on fire. Thousands of civilians died. On the night of September 15, 1940 alone, 1000 bombers attacked the large cities in England. In November of that same year the English town of Coventry was completely destroyed with most of the citizens killed when German bombers attacked it. These attacks, mostly at night, continued throughout the rest of 1940 and further into 1941.

It must have been about the middle of October when all Polish soldiers were sent to St. Andrew and vicinity in East Scotland. It was there that commanders organized and formed the First Polish Artillery Regiment and the Polish Infantry Battalions. The artillery remained in St. Andrews; the infantry was stationed in towns around St. Andrew. Our company of about 120 men lived at Westerly Castle. This castle was not large, but it was very nice with a gray stone tower poking above enormous trees in the driveway. It was a few hundred years old and probably built when most of America was still a wilderness. Later I learned that it was owned by an elderly Scottish lady who was a widow. She had lent her castle to the army for the duration of the war. All the furniture in the castle had been removed, and straw mattresses were placed on the floors. All of us soldiers were assigned a room. About ten in each room. A very large open fireplace, fed by wood logs, gave warmth in each of the high large rooms. I stayed with nine other men; three judges, a former border guard from Poland, and a smuggler. The other Polish men in the room had come from France where they had lived and from where they had escaped to England. They were a nice bunch of men and we got along well with each other. I would stay there at that Castle for nine months.

The day after I had arrived at Westerly Castle, I walked that morning with my breakfast chow into a room were soldiers were sitting around tables to eat. As I looked for a place to sit, I suddenly heard someone shouting my name. As the whole room of men looked up and stared at me, I heard two more men shouting, "Jozef!" A moment later three soldiers jumped up from their table and started to come in my direction. I couldn't believe my eyes when I saw it was Josef, Adam and Richard! I think I almost cried when I saw those three guys. We four embraced each other and for a few minutes there was happiness in that dining room as if a long lost brother had come home. They also were staying at the castle but in a different section. They had been wondering whatever had happened to me and told me that when we somehow got separated in France on that road as they were trying to get to the coast, Richard and Josef somewhere had turned south on another road, thinking that if they could not find a ship going to England, they would try to go to Spain. They made it to the French port of Bordeaux in southern France. Adam, who had lost me after the fighter plane attack, had gone on another road in a southern direction and had met Richard and Josef again in a field when they were looking for a place to sleep close to the city of Bordeaux. Together they had found a coal ship which left with other soldiers and civilians going to England. The port of Bordeaux is located in that part of France which was never occupied by the Germans during all of Word War II. Josef, Richard and Adam had arrived in England a good week later than I did.

Together we had many a conversation at the castle. All of us were trying to cope and to accept the fact that our lives had taken an unexpected turn. Here we were in England and the war against Germany had not ended with the surrender of France, as we had thought. Instead of going home to Poland, we had landed in England with the war in Europe getting worse every day. When we four came together, we talked mainly about Poland and wondered how our families were doing. Not much news came about Poland and its fate through the English broadcast news on the radio in our large dining and entertainment room. A few weeks after arriving at Westerly Castle, Adam who was a corporal, was now in charge of artillery cannon. Josef and Richard went to Officers' School. But whenever possible we would come together and go to one or another Scottish Pub for a drink and talk.

In the meantime more and more soldiers arrived in England. They came from Australia, New Zealand, from the British colonies of Africa and from Canada and South America.

The Polish Army was in charge of the section of the east coast of Scotland where we were located. More to the north the Canadians guarded the coastline. England had established a defense line of radar stations and artillery cannons along the whole coast of eastern and southern England and up its western coast in defense of an eventual invasion by the German Army.

I was in the communication platoon, assigned to the Communication Headquarters Regiment. We built and maintained telephones lines to and from the observation posts and to the places where our artillery cannons were positioned on the coastline with their muzzles aiming at the sky. Some of our artillery was placed in an area on the coast where nobody lived close-by. It was an area where many rabbits had made their living quarters in the grassy hills. When we first came to that area, thousands of rabbits were hopping around, but by the time I left after nine months, there were no bunny's jumping anymore. I think there were none left. Since our Army chow was not the greatest, I am sure many a soldier had eaten a good rabbit meal!

St. Andrews, which lay on the East Coast of Scotland on the North Sea, was a nice town which had a University and an Air force Academy. Most of the soldiers now took English lessons which were taught at our castle. Not only did we want to speak to the Scottish people, but also we especially wished to talk to the girls we met on Saturday nights at the local dance halls. Many of the girls had boyfriends who were in the Army, Marines or Air Force and who were stationed somewhere else in Scotland, England or abroad. Since the girls loved to go dancing, we were more than willing to take care of their girlfriends.

A girls' dormitory was located near the castle. There must have been about 200 girls living there attending the Westerly University. Many a time they played tennis on their tennis courts and always were looking for a guy to play a match with them. Whenever I could I went to the courts and played tennis with one of the Scottish girls. Even though I had never played tennis before in my life, it did not take me long until I could hit the ball as good as many of the girls.

The beaches of St. Andrew were wide and very pretty. When it was ebb tide and the sea pulled back the beaches seemed a mile wide, and I would walk on my bare feet for a long time before reaching the water. I loved to walk there on the beaches by myself and, while looking to the far horizon of the North Sea, my thoughts would go back to Poland and to my family. While walking there on the white sand I soon noticed that not many Scottish people enjoyed this. I think the North Sea is so very cold that even during summer times it is impossible to go into the water. Only on a rare warm sunny day you saw people on the beach. Sometimes a whale became stranded on the shore. A special unit of the coast guard was called in and removed the enormous body, which was quiet a job and difficult to do. Also many a dead sailor was swept onto the beaches. Every day a patrol would gather dead navy men, to be buried in a special section of a cemetery. In those war years many ships sunk off the coast of England and Scotland by the magnetic mine fields which the Germans had laid in the North Sea. Also many ships were sunk because of heavy fighting on the sea between German and British warships.

Close to the beach was a large, well-kept golf course which was used not only by the local golfers, but also was (and still is) the location of the famous St. Andrews International Golf Tournaments. We had established an observation post close to the coast and on the side of the golf course. Every fourth day I was assigned to go there with two other men from our observation crew to observe the sea for possible enemy ships.

One day when I had nothing much to do and was walking on the golf course, an older Scottish gentleman asked me if I would like to try my hand at golf. So I did, but it was the first and last time I ever played. Golf is just not my game. More than anything else, I played soccer. Not only did I like to play the game, but also it was an escape for me. I was still depressed sometimes which I tried to escape. So my outlet became soccer.

The first six to eight weeks when I was stationed at Westerly Castle in St. Andrew, I played soccer with the men from our company. We had formed a small group who liked to play. One day I had an appointment with the military dentist. While I was sitting in the waiting room, I noticed a captain who was also there for an appointment. I saw that he was staring at me, but I did not know the man. After we sat there for a while the captain said, "Don't I know you from Poland?" Surprised I said to him, "I am sorry, sir, I don't remember you, but yes, I come from Poland." He then said his name was Captain Pruss and asked if I had played soccer in Poznan, Poland. When I answered him that I had, he asked on what team I had been on. We started to talk about soccer in Poznan and about the teams in that city. He said that he had seen me playing there and remembered me. He then asked if I would like to give it a try to play for the brigade's soccer

team. Of course I said yes. He then said I should be ready for next Tuesday afternoon practice

You have to know that Colonel Krueger, who was commander of our regiment, was a fanatic about soccer. When he was younger, he himself had played
on a well-known soccer team in Poland. So when the following Tuesday came
(Tuesdays and Thursdays were the teams training days) a sergeant took me in a
truck to the practice field which was located just out of the city. There I went
through training that day with the men of the brigade soccer team. That evening
before I left the practice field to go back with the sergeant to the castle, the coach
said to me, "We will see you on Thursday!" It was then that I knew he was interested in me.

After two weeks of training the coach told Colonel Krueger that I was
accepted in the brigade team and that I would be playing the coming Saturday.
This was my first big game. After that, I practiced twice a week and most Saturdays. We played in different cities against other soccer teams from the Army, Air
Force and civilian teams. Even though I say so myself, I was a good soccer player
and made many a goal for our team. Colonel Krueger loved it and seldom missed
a game. He did not want me to be assigned regularly for guard duty, especially
not on the day before we were to play a game. Our Major Kapelinski did not like
this and cussed many times about it. He needed many men, not only Castle
guards but also needed men to guard the cannons which were positioned along
the coastline. But the major could do nothing about it, he had to follow orders
from Colonel Krueger.

We had been at St. Andrew for a few months, when word was received that
King George and Queen Mary of England and their two daughters, Princesses
Elizabeth and Margaret would visit the newly formed First Polish Brigade. The
Polish Army was the first of all the other armies that were forming in England
and Scotland in that time. A big parade was planned, and everyone in and around
St. Andrew was excited about it. The people in town talked about nothing else
but the parade and the King and his family who were coming to their city. However, I disliked marching in parades and everything that was connected with it. So
I thought of a way out. I went to our doctor and complained about my knee. The
week before, I had hurt myself while playing soccer, and the bruises still showed.
The doctor told me to take a week of rest including no playing soccer and no
marching in the parade. Of course major Kapelinski was angry that I had gotten
out of the parade. Not only I had gotten out of many of my guard duties because
of soccer, but now also had gotten out of the parade. The major must have been a

100% soldier. Anyway, during that whole week, I and some other men who gotten out of the parade, had to peel potatoes for the entire week. We joked a lot about it and had a good time. We watched the parade from the sidewalk and saw the King of England and his family.

I had been at Westerly Castle nine months when word was received from the Headquarters of Artillery under command of our Polish General Niemira that our regiment had to supply twelve men to that office. The Polish Army was still forming and was short on men. Now it happened about the same time as that order came from the headquarters, that I had guard duty from Friday noon until Saturday noon. I knew I had to play soccer that same Saturday, so I shouldn't have been sent on guard duty. But I thought orders are orders, and went on guard at the main gate which was located in front of the castle grounds, in the meanwhile wondering what was going on. The major should have known that I had to play the next day. The next morning about 9:00 there came our Chief Keszak with another soldier to the guard house where I was standing guard. Walking up to me he said that I was released and that Colonel Krueger would pick me up at 12:00 for the soccer game. He then said that I first should go to sleep. I think that Chief Keszak had forgotten to tell my major that I had to play soccer and so I should not have gone on guard duty that day before.

It was about 12:00 that afternoon and I was fast asleep in my bed, when Chief Keszak woke me up and said to me, "What are you doing still lying in bed? Colonel Krueger is waiting for you!" I turned myself around in my bed and said loudly to the chief, "What in the hell, I did not sleep the whole night because of guard duty, and now you want me to play soccer!" The colonel who was staying in the hall below my room heard the argument and was all upset. Of course I went with the colonel and played a good game. But that incident was my death warrant, because it made the major even more mad at me. After he had received that order to contribute to the twelve men they needed for the Polish Artillery Headquarters, he sent me on my way as fast as he could. I think he was glad to get rid of me. One other man and I were the only soldiers of our company to be sent to the headquarters of General Niemira.

I was sent to the city of Dundee which is located just north of St. Andrew. I landed there with eleven men in a house close to General Niemira's office. As it turned out we were the only occupants of the house, which was great of course, as we had complete freedom. The eleven men were a great bunch of guys who loved to joke a lot. All but one soldier and myself had gone through Officer's School in

Poland and gone through similar war experiences as I had before coming by ship to England. We talked a lot about the future which hopefully would be back in Poland. We still believed that the war would soon be over and that not to long from now we all were going home. The eleven men all had come from different cities and towns in Poland. When the war had started in 1939, many Polish officers had escaped to England. Most of them were officers from the reserve units. Because of this the newly forming Polish Army now had many more officers than the Polish Army needed, and so they were used elsewhere wherever men were needed.

It was there in Dundee that my depression finally left me. Probably because of the many laughs we had and the jokes that were told there in our house. The first few weeks we did nothing much. The headquarters of the general office was not complete yet, so we had to wait until they were finished. It was there that for the first time I heard the bagpipes playing. One of our neighbors was a older Scottish man who, as a real Scot, must have loved to play his bagpipe. Every morning until night he was practicing that darn thing which drove us nuts. One day we decided to have a talk with him. After first listening to our complaint, he said that he was sorry that his playing seemed to bother us. "It takes time to get used to this music," he said, "but it is the most military, the most fighting music in the world." We looked at the old man and said we believed him and went home. Even though the harsh music continued, he played less. I never could get used to the sound of a bagpipe which many men played in Scotland.

Not far from where we lived was a very nice, large and new YMCA. Many times we went there to play table tennis and other games. There were also pool tables and a library where soldiers and civilians alike could sit to read books and newspapers and catch up on the latest war situations, which many soldiers did, while drinking coffee or tea.

One man from our group, his name was Waldek Gierek, a lanky, tall, cheerful guy about my age, liked to play table tennis. He always challenged me for a cup of coffee with cake at our canteen, which was located close to our house. One day as we walked to the YMCA for a match and went across the street to go to the other side, who came with arms outstretched toward me—Chaplain Kaminski! I was happy to see him again; many times I had thought about him. We had not seen each other since we had landed in England and the truck brought us to our first camp. Because he was an officer, we had gone different directions. He told me that he was now a chaplain for our infantry and was stationed in another town. We talked for the longest time over coffee in the canteen before we each went on our way, hoping to meet again some day. But I have never met, seen or heard from him again.

◆          ◆          ◆

*Summer of 1941.* Before moving into General Niemira's office, I wanted to ask him for a ten-day leave pass since I never got one before, and I had already served more than a year in the British Army. So one day I told the general that Waldek and I wanted to go to London. First the general was worried that we didn't have enough money, but after I said to him since we didn't smoke or drink or gamble our money away on poker, we had enough money saved for a ten-day leave in London, England. After the general's approval, Waldek and I made our plans. We got our leave passes and another pass for free train transportation and we were on our way to London.

We took the express train going from Edinburgh-Scotland to London-England, which is about a 450 mile train ride. The landscape was flat with farm fields. Here and there we passed towns and sleepy villages with neat small houses with gardens, where families raised their own produce. Sometimes we passed little ancient towns, and patches of woods. The express stopped only two times on its road to London to let passengers out and others in. As soon as we arrived in London, we booked into the hotel "The Lion's Club." It was a hotel reserved only for the military and was located close to Buckingham Palace. London is such a large city and has so many interesting places to visit that a week would be hardly enough. Parts of London had been destroyed by German bombers, especially the harbor and the industrial areas. Later in the war the whole of London would lay badly damaged.

Waldek and I took in those places which were most interesting to us. We learned that the history of London was started by an early British tribe more then 2000 years ago. It became the capital of the Great British Empire and in 1941 had a population of 8.700.000 people. It had more influences in shaping the destiny of the world affairs than any other capital. Waldek wanted to see the Bank of England which is the oldest bank of England and is located with other large banks and the headquarters of the industrial concerns which transact the business of the Empire. It sure was an impressive place. From there we went to the Stock Exchange Building which Waldek was very much interested in (I don't think he had money in stocks). Before going back to our hotel we went to Buckingham Palace and saw the changing of the guards.

The following day we walked beside the Thames River and saw the hustle and bustle of the many ocean going freighters moving up and down or being loaded or unloaded by tremendous cranes. The smoke and fog often blanketed the city there. We also saw some of the burned-out houses, and the piles of rubble where the bombs had fallen, and the other destruction left by the German bombers. Special workers for this job were cleaning up. One day we visited Westminster Abbey, which is a very old and large church where the kings and queens of England were crowned. From there we took a walk to the House of Commons which is the house of free speech.

Another day we decided to go to Hyde Park which was famous for its "soapbox preachers" who were standing on boxes to tell the world their ideas. One preacher was standing on his box and was yelling about the politics and said not to vote for the mayor. Another screamed at the top of his lungs that the world was coming to an end and God had sent Hitler to do just that. A man in a strange kind of robe told the people about a new religion, and another man with a long beard tried to convince people about the need for a park for dogs. One women on a high box a little farther on yelled that they should behead all man who were unfaithful. Those soapbox preachers stayed on their boxes throughout the park in all kinds of (sometimes very strange) clothing. Women and men, young and old, were telling it all to the many people around them who watched and listened to them. It was very amusing for Waldek and me to see and hear all this. We had a good time just listening to all those preachers. Only in London's Hyde Park was there anything like this.

On the way back to our hotel the air raid sirens sounded over the city. German bombers were on their way and plunged on toward London. Everyone had to go off the streets and into the shelters. Soon the English fighters (Spitfires) took to the air and the anti-aircraft guns fired, and the tremendous system of alarms and defenses went into action. Since we were close to a subway station we went with many other people down there for safety. The subway in London is a tremendous underground network of trains that run in every direction from all under London to far out of the city. During the war years those underground tunnels were a blessing. The people felt safe there and many spent their nights rolled in a blanket on the floor of the subway. In that time when Waldek and I were there in London the military started to send all women and children of the soldiers who were in the service and other people who were not needed in London, to other cities around London and other towns throughout England and Scotland.

A year before, the Air Force had hung large barrage balloons all over the city. I think there were hundreds and hundreds of them hanging over London. Those barrages were large hydrogen filled balloons that were raised and lowered by long cables. Many of the balloons were then placed near and around important ground targets, such as aircraft and weapon factories. Unsuspecting German bombers would fly into the balloons at night and crash. At night London was blacked out, as were all cities and towns in England and Scotland. Not a sign of light was to be seen, and London looked asleep but was well guarded by thousands of the mechanical radar eyes on the coastlines. The RAF fighters destroyed dozens of German bombers who were shot down over the English Channel before they could reach their targets in London and other large cities.

About 45 minutes later the sirens sounded again that everything was clear. The German bombers, many of them chased by the Spitfires, had left leaving behind destruction in the city or in one of London's innumerable outlying districts. When we came out of the subway a thin smoke filled the sky over the city. While we walked to our hotel, the streets filled again with the hurrying crowd. Even though London was tense the people calmly went about their daily business.

Every night there was a dance in the ballroom at our large hotel. The dance hall was open not only for the military but also for the citizens. It was a pleasant and nice place, and we enjoyed going there which we did every night, drinking a beer and dancing with the English girls. The hotel had, as did almost all hotels, a very comfortable underground shelter where hot tea and coffee were always on hand in times of air raids. Many Canadian soldiers who were on furlough were also staying at our hotel.

On the last day we went to the Tower of London. It is one of the oldest buildings and is a large and impressive fort with four towers which were built circa the year one thousand. Later in the war the House of Commons, Symbol of Speech, and Westminster Abbey, Symbol of Faith, were bombed and heavily damaged. Later after the war they were rebuilt again.

Our vacation had been great and we had enjoyed it very much, although sometimes we had to go into a shelter or subway because of an air raid. We had seen many of the great places of London but also the destructive force of the bombings. Many buildings and houses were destroyed or burned out. While walking back to the railroad station, I said to Waldek, "I don't see how the people of London can take it. How long will it be before this all will end, and they can live a normal life again?"

When we came back from our trip to London, we moved into the new Artillery Command Office. I worked at the central telephone and at the Headquarters of General Niemira. After we worked at the office for about six weeks, word came that all twelve of us were going to Sterling, which is a small town to the west of Dundee. We asked our captain about the move to Sterling, why we were going there. I know as soldier you don't ask, you just follow orders. But our captain being a nice fellow said that the Polish Army was forming an armored division and needed men. The new artillery office would probably be closing. Why, he didn't say.

Our new camp was about three miles outside of Sterling. We went there with about 200 men to the newly established School of Instructors where they taught us everything that had to do with tanks and other vehicles. They taught us how the vehicles worked and how to operate and drive them. It was a very rigid and interesting course. Every day we had theory and practice. We practiced with the tank by the name of 'Matilda I.' The British were using those tanks in the war in Africa, but soon found out that the Matilda I had a much shorter shooting range than the German tanks. Later the American Army came out with the Sherman tank which was a much better tank with a longer cannon barrel and a farther range. It was the Shermans they eventually drove into battle in Europe. In those tanks there was room for five soldiers. Each man had a specific job to do. Three men—an officer, a radio man and a gunner—sat in the top position of the tank which is called a turret. Two men—the driver and the machine gun operator—sat in the lower front of the tank.

At the end of the two-month course we went back to Dundee. When we arrived there, our captain told us that the newly established Artillery Command Office was closing. I do not know exactly why they were closing it down, but I think the English or Polish government in England thought that our Artillery Command Office was not needed. We stayed there ten more days; then they closed up. In the meanwhile my diploma had arrived. I was happy to see that I had good grades. I now could operate and teach other soldiers about tanks and armored vehicles. I was placed with the other eleven men in the newly formed 'First Polish Armored Division' where I would stay for the rest of the war.

**British Army**

Full Army:  200,000 soldiers
Full Division:  20,000 soldiers
Full Regiment:  12,000 soldiers
Battalion:  350 soldiers
Company:  200 soldiers
Platoon:  36 soldiers

Because there were fewer men in our Polish Army than in the British Army, our Divisions, Regiments, and Battalions were smaller. Only our Companies and Platoons were about the same size.

On December 7, 1941, the United States was plunged into World War II after Japan unleashed a surprise air attack against six U.S. military installations on the Hawaiian Island of Oahu. Chief among those bases was the giant Pearl Harbor Naval Base. On December 8, an angry United States declared war on Japan. Japan's allies, Germany and Italy, then declared war on America. And so the war was again extended and now engulfed most of the world.

# 8

## COSSFORT HOUSE

The twelve of us were sent to the military camp which was called Cossford House. This camp was about eight miles south of Edinburgh on the North Sea. Cossford House was originally a large mansion with many acres of ground around it. The house belonged to a bachelor who was in the military service and who had given his house and land to the military for the duration of the war. They had built a huge camp there with many barracks, a hall for entertaining, a church, a small hospital, a library, a YMCA and bathrooms with showers. There were about 2,000 soldiers in that camp, all Polish. Our officers were lodged in the large, old but very nice mansion which stood in the middle of the camp. In each of the many barracks were eight soldiers sleeping on cots, each with his own hanging closet on the wall behind our beds. It was a very nice camp, separated from the North Sea by a main road.

Many a time I would sit on the boulders at the side of the sea in a pale sunshine which peeked once in awhile through the low hanging clouds. My thoughts would drift back to my childhood when once-upon-a-time I lived the magic years of a child hidden from the world of turmoil and pain. My family was my world and my universe expanded into the large yard with my animals and chirping crickets. I thought about the large house we lived in with the dark-toned paintings on the wall. And the kitchen which was a different world commanded by my mother. How well I remembered the washdays when my mother hung her wet clothing on the laundry line where the warm wind would take it and play with it. And my parents' bedroom where you had to knock on the door to get in. It was their own private place where we children only could come in on Sunday mornings. In wintertime we would jump into the huge bed under the warm thick blankets to warm our cold feet. And I still could hear the laughing and shouting of my younger brothers while they played outdoors. I thought about the town where my family lived and how the storks build their nests on top of the barns. There were so many of them during the spring and summertime. Yes, it was magic years too soon gone. Here I was a soldier in a strange country hoping that this war would end soon. But it didn't; it only got worse. The war seemed so far away—here in Scotland. I felt it was such a waste of my young years to be living my life in a soldier's camp. I was worried about my family wondering how they were surviving the German occupation. It had been a few years now since we had heard from each other. I knew that they were worried and must be wondering what had happened to me and where I was. How I wished I could let them know that I was all right.

Many times while sitting on those boulders looking over the turbulent sea, I thought about Jan and the cousins and our ordeal in the mountains. I thought about how this war had become a total war, an inclusive war, not just a war of one country against another, but one way of life poised against the other—a battle of outrage. I could sit there on the boulders for the longest time while the wind blew salty spray against me which had a relaxing effect. While I watched the shrieking seagulls around me, I soon felt somewhat better and returned slowly back to the barracks and to my soldier's life.

◆     ◆     ◆

*Spring of 1942.* For the next year and a half, the camp at Cossford House would be my base. My daily duties were to work on telephone communications. One day to our surprise we received a new radio communication system from America. This radio system turned out to be a great improvement over communication by telephone. To learn the new radio system, how to operate and repair it, I went to a school that had been formed not too far from our camp. Each morning we had instructions, and in the afternoon we would board the English land carriers. Those carriers were small open tanks with four men in each carrier and were used by the infantry for the transportation of soldiers to and from the front lines. They also were used by the flame-throwers with their equipment. With the heavy battery operated radios, we drove around to see how far we could hear each other and communicate. Sometimes it was frustrating when we could not find the exact wavelength that we all should be on. I guess we had trouble because it was a new invention and was not always working the way it was intended to. This course, in which we had to practice many times, took four weeks. One day a week we went on field exercises.

In America and Canada the factories were beginning more and more to produce all the material that would be needed to win a war. Tanks, trucks, warships, airplanes, all kinds of war equipment, bulldozers and armored cars, jeeps and ambulances, and immense quantities of clothing and medical supplies, food, etc. It became a huge lifeline of convoys coming from America and Canada to England protected heavily by English destroyers, Spitfires and the fast flying Hurricanes. The German torpedo boats were hunting those convoys and destroyed many a supply ship. Also many new airplanes, such as bombers and fighters, came from America. England produced now about 400 airplanes a month, which was great, but there was still one huge problem for the RAF. There were not enough experienced pilots. Many young inexperienced pilots were shot down by the violent encounters with the much stronger famous German Luftwaffe (air force). But this problem was slowly solved by the many new men who came to England from Australia, New Zealand, South Africa and South America.

Our Polish Army got an addition of about one thousand ex-soldiers who had been in Russian prison of war camps since 1939. They were set free because of an agreement between Stalin, Roosevelt, Churchill and the Polish government in England, when Germany invaded Russia, and Stalin became America and England's allies. Most of those men came with the help of the Polish General Andersen to Syria, Iran and Egypt were they formed an army. Later they were sent to Italy to fight the Italian and German troops, especially in the battle of Monte Casino. Others were sent to Scotland.

I thought that the ancient city of Edinburgh was one of the prettiest places in Scotland, not only because of its rich history but also because it was very modern with trendy bars and boutiques. The entertainment in that city was great with its many movie theaters, dance halls, dog-races, opera house etc. In the time I was stationed there, the dance halls of that city were always full of sailors and Canadian soldiers. Not only on the weekends but every evening of the week.

Almost every Saturday some army buddies and I went to Edinburgh. After mess we took the Army bus, or we walked if the weather was good, and went into town. It was there where the action was. We enjoyed going to one of the many large dance halls where the great big bands played dance music. There were always good singers who sang the favorite songs of that time as *Good Night Sweetheart, I'll Be Seeing You, You Are My Sunshine,* and my favorite—*Begin the Beguine.* Or we would see one of the many American movies that came to England in those war years. I liked to see Bing Crosby with Bob Hope and Dorothy Lamour in the series as Road to Morocco and Road to Singapore etc. My favorite big screen stars were Clark Gable, Tyrone Power, Orson Wells, Maureen O'Hare, Dorothy Lamour and Betty Grable.

Many a time when we were ready to go back to our camp after seeing a movie, or from just going out into the city of Edinburgh, the last bus had left. A thick mist had formed in the meanwhile, and it was difficult to see where we were going. It became especially bad when we came outside the city and walked the road on the side of the sea. Most of the time we had to feel our way back by touching our hands against the stone wall which lined the road to our camp.

It was there close to Edinburgh that I met Bessie, the first Scottish girl I really liked. I had become friends with Stanley Moskwa, a easy going fellow about my age who in 1939 had escaped from East Poland. He was in the same barrack as I was and was also in our radio crew. Every Saturday night he and his girlfriend Nancy went out in Port Seaton were she lived. Port Seaton was a fishing village where the paving stones are worn smooth and the sidewalks are grooved by ages of strollers. It was located a half-hour walk south of our camp.

One Saturday night Waldek and another friend from my barrack by the name of Stanley Gurkle and I decided to go to Port Seaton for some fun. It was the first time we went there and looked around for some place to go. Since the village was small and the streets narrow, it didn't take long until we saw a dancing place with a bar. We went inside and ordered a drink at the crowded and noisy bar, where the barmaids were drawing beer as fast as they could. It was a strange tasting beer were most of the alcohol had been taken out of to make munition. It was not cold and was named token beer—a gesture rather than a drink. When I looked around the place, I saw Stanley with Nancy and another girl sitting at a table close to the dance floor. I went to them holding my pale yellow fluid in my hand and, after introducing ourselves, I found out that she was Nancy's girlfriend Bessie. They asked me to join them at their table which, after looking Bessie over, I did—of course, after first telling my buddies good-bye. Since Stanley did not much care for dancing, I had a great time that night dancing in turns with Nancy and Bessie.

The last bus had left, and a strong wind was blowing from the north when Stanley and I walked back to the barracks that night. While finding our way I said to Stanley how pretty and pleasant a girl I thought Bessie was. After that evening we four would go out in Port Seaton or in Edingburgh on Saturday nights. We went mostly to movies or to a bar where there was dancing. Usually the large dance halls in Edinburgh were full of soldiers and men from the navy dancing the evenings away with the girls to the great band music. Most of the time there were two bands playing. They took their turn on the rotating platform that turned around every 1/2 hour.

Bessie's mother and one of her four brothers, who lived in Port Seaton, operated the family fishing business. Her father had died and her other three brothers had gone into the navy at the beginning of the war. While Bessie's brother took charge of the fishing boats, her mother with 12 other women took care of the packing and shipping of all fish. Since most of the men in England and Scotland were in the service, the women and girls had taken over the work force which they seemed to do very well. They worked hard and never complained, determined to help side by side with their men to win the war. After a whole day of hard work the girls would go home, eat, get dressed and go to the dance halls, which were open seven days a week.

In the fall of 1942 Stanley and Nancy got married. It was a small church wedding which was attended mostly by women since the men were away in the service. It was there at the party afterward, that Bessie for the first time introduced me to her mother. You have to know that in that time in Scotland you just didn't get to meet your girlfriend's family until you became engaged. But with Bessie being her girlfriend's maid of honor and her mother a guest at the party, we met. She looked me over and soon we drank a whole bottle of sherry together. It sure was a good party! After Stanley was married, he lived most of the time off base with his wife.

It was about that time that two regiments of artillery went by truck for field exercises to the area by New Castle, which is located in England. It was a large heather covered area with larger and smaller sandy hills. There we trained with real ammunition. The maneuvers simulated actual combat, helping the participants sharpen their skills and get a taste of what true combat could be like. Stanley and Frank Bajerski, who was also in our communication platoon, and I had built a observation post. We were there mostly to communicate with the artillery the distance they had to shoot to reach the enemy. The Forward Observers, which I belonged to, is a communication platoon in which the men are placed up front with the infantry to find out where artillery fire is needed to help them. The observers radio back to the gunners which then provide the fire as quickly and accurately as they can. At night after dark there was not much to do, and everyone was glad when after two week of training we went back again to Cossford House and our routine, girlfriends and me to Bessie.

◆    ◆    ◆

*Christmas of 1942.* All the soldiers of our camp received a package from America. Since it was the only package I received during the war years, I can still remember what was inside of it. Besides gloves there was candy, an orange, dried figs and Christmas chocolates. The days of Christmas, New Year's, and Easter came and went as any other day. The only time we would notice it was Christmas was on Christmas morning in the church, if you happened to go to church that is. Many of the soldiers had guard duty or just didn't go. The Chaplain would tell us that it again was Christmas and that peace in the world was nowhere to be found except in our hearts. But the peace in our hearts that the Chaplain was talking about, was sometimes hard to find. Especially when mail came in and the Polish soldiers from Canada, South America or Australia received letters and packages from their families and home towns. We who came from Poland were just left wondering about our families back home. Not knowing anything about them made it difficult for many men, especially the married ones who had wives and children there.

That Christmas I was invited to Bessie's house for Christmas dinner. Since all the factories were working 24 hour a day, many of the people of England worked hard those two Christmas holidays (England, as all countries in Europe, have two Christmas and Easter days). But Bessie who worked at the Navy office was free those days and she and her mother made a dinner for Bessie's married brother, who was not in the service, and his family and me. I remember how good the dinner was, for sure a far cry from the Army suppers in our camp. The English and Scottish way of cooking their vegetables was different than we were used to. They usually boiled the daylights out of their vegetables to a sticky pulp and the flavor gone. But everything else was great and I left the veggies alone. The home was beautifully decorated with Christmas ornaments but I did not see a Christmas tree, maybe because of the war. There were probably not enough men to cut down Christmas trees in England (Scotland has few forests).

Of course the family wanted to know everything about our Christmas in Poland and how we celebrated those days. I told them that when I was a child and Christmas came, my father and I went to the forest looking for the best Christmas tree we could find. It usually took awhile to find the tree we wanted. While Father chopped the tree down with his sharp ax, I looked on. After shaking the snow from the branches, we carried our prize home walking through the snow. The day before Christmas, we decorated the tree with little red apples and cookies in shapes of wreaths, and Santa Claus. There were also bells and shiny balls in many colors. We made paper garlands ourselves. A pretty homemade paper angel, usually made by my sister Irene, crowned the top of the tree. Later when the first star peeked towards the earth, Mother would put her special Christmas dinner on the table. This is an old Polish tradition. After a dinner of borsht (beet) soup, carp with fried potatoes, a vegetable, noodles with poppy seed, a dessert and, of course, Mother's special Christmas bread, we went to the living room. There in all its glory stood our Christmas tree. My father would read a Christmas story out of a very old and treasured book. After the reading, we sang Christmas songs and then we opened our presents. Usually we got some clothes, books, games, and a toy. "I always asked for tin soldiers to add to my vast collection," I said to Bessie's family who listened on. "My friends and I battled with the foot soldiers and the soldiers on horses. When we got older, we went to Christmas mass at midnight." I then told the family that I especially missed the snow that crunched beneath my feet as we walked to church for midnight service. In Scotland just once in awhile a little snow fell in the wintertime.

As I walked back to my barrack that night a heavy gray mist had formed. It was cold. I turned my overcoat collar up and shivered and thought how miserable the weather was in Scotland. While trying to find my way back in the dark to the camp, which was about a half-hour walk from Bessie's home, my mind filled with memories of past Christmases. I longed for the happy times with my family in our home in Miedzychud. Sometimes it seemed a lifetime ago when I was the last time home for Christmas, other times it was like yesterday. How all had looked so uncomplicated back then. And I thought about my Christmas vacations from school when going down a hill on my sled in the deep snow while steering my sled with my feet trying to avoid the trees that always were in my way. And I wondered after all those years, that I never had an accident going down those tree-lined slopes.

◆     ◆     ◆

*Spring of 1943.* One day a year was a special day for all the men in the Polish Army who had the name of Jozef. You have to know that in Poland no one celebrated a birthday but always their name day. Every day of the year is named after a saint. So a child celebrated each year on the day of his or her saint's name day and not on the day the child was born. I was born on September 3 but my name day (St. Jozef Day) is on March 19. So all boys and men whose name was Jozef celebrated on the 19 of March. But Jozef was the only name which was specially mentioned. As a child I liked this because at school on St. Jozef Day all the children got a sweet roll with their milk in the morning. This special name day started not only with a saint but especially when a Marshal from the Army in Poland liberated Poland from the Russians in WW I. His name was Jozef Pilsucki and he became one of Poland's heroes. So that day we soldiers by the name of Jozef had to step forward after the morning call and got a handshake from our commander and were dismissed from duties for the day.

Since we didn't have a regiment soccer team at Cossfort House, I just played some soccer for fun with the guys from our camp whenever I had time, that is. Or I jogged around the campgrounds. I wanted to keep myself in shape, I guess. You didn't see too many guys jogging around as I did in that time. Our captain would look at me and shake his head. Poker, bridge and other card games were the favorite game of many, too much so, I think. But many other soldiers were reading books that they got from the library. Some, as Waldek, were always with their noses in books and studying for when the war was over and they would return home again to their jobs or start a new career. Josef and Richard who were in another company had gone a different way. They had different work and social lives and friends. But sometimes we met each other and caught up on the latest news. I did not see Adam much anymore. He had asked for a transfer to another artillery regiment where his brother was serving. His brother had also escaped from Poland and the two brothers had met each other in Scotland. I heard from him just occasionally, but we were always happy to see each other again.

Life in camp went on in the spring of 1943. They send Frank Bajerski and three other men from our battalion to a commando training school. Frank was a little older than I was and a pleasant quiet guy. His father who was an officer worked in London for the government. I don't know exactly what work he was doing there. Frank and his father had escaped from Poland to England in 1939. They came from the city Krakow were his mother and sister (hopefully) still lived. I knew that Frank sometimes missed them. When Frank and I had received the order to go to that commando school, we were wondering why they choose him and me for this again.

I think this was the worst training I ever had to go through. It was in a school close to Aberdeen, Scotland. There we were with about 80 men together. They came from everywhere—English soldiers, Canadians, Australians etc. We were divided into two groups of 40 men each. The first week our instructors were

Gurkhas, who were a special group of soldiers from India. They trained us how to move on our stomachs at night in the dark from one place to the other. They taught us the fastest and best ways to kill with knives and ropes. I sure didn't care for the every night training, being left alone in the black of night outside, and having to find my way to the enemy crawling on my stomach, overpowering my enemy (dummy) and knife or strangle him to death without a sound.

The second week we got the English instructors from a special commando group. This course was about land mines. We had to learn about the different sorts of mines, how to find them and dismantle them, and how to find our way through a minefield without stepping on a mine. The last week was a training session for special assignment. They taught us how to silently overpower your enemy and bring him back alive to your side for interrogation. We also learned when and how to escape etc. This three week course was just a fundamental session. The men who would become commandos in the British forces had many months of training ahead of them.

When we drove by truck back to our camp, I thought about the last three weeks and wondered why they always sent Frank and me to the training camps. Even though some soldiers went to the paratroops training school and others learned mechanics, transportation, paramedics, etc., most didn't go for special courses. Not that it bothered me much because it gave me something to do. I hated to be bored. I knew that our Major Makuch always watched me as I ran around camp. But I did this for myself, for when I went back to Poland. I wanted to play on a soccer team again. Maybe, I thought, he could use me later for something, as going with commandos on a special mission, and I was not very thrilled by that thought.

Our Major Makuch was also the only one who knew about my escape from the Russian prison camp. About a year before, the major and I once had a long talk about home and what we had experienced in the past. I had told him about the Russian prison camp and how I had escaped from there and how I got to England. Major Makuch had been a professional in the Polish Army. He was not married and about 42 years old. He was a fine man with a optimistic outlook and always wanted to be close to his men. I liked him very much.

Meanwhile Russia had been under attack by the Germans since 1941. After two years of bitter fighting in Russia and after the battle of Stalingrad, the German Army was pushed back. Exhausted by the severe Russian cold in the winter of 1942 and 1943 poor food and clothing the German Army, thousands of them starving from cold and malnutrition, fled back to the west and were now not far from the Polish borders again.

During the months that the invasion "Overlord" (the secret code name for the invasion into France) was being planned, England and Scotland became one huge crowded military camp. Some 1.5 million US troops poured into those countries and began to train for the invasion. They joined 1.75 million soldiers from Britain and its commonwealth nations. Also on hand were more than 40,000 fighters from France, Norway, Poland, Belgium and Holland who had fled their countries in 1939 and 1940. A flood of supplies, coming mainly from America, poured into Britain along with the men. About 40,000 British workers got the job of constructing giant concrete caissons, which were great blocks with hollow centers. Those caissons stood as tall as five story buildings. They were to be towed across the English Channel with the invasion for makeshift harbors so the army could bring in the great amount of supplies that would be needed for the troops.

# 9

# *THE WAITING*

It was the summer of 1943 when our whole regiment went by trucks to Wales, which is an area west of England. There we were going to exercise in a life-like combat with live ammunition. West Wales is a rugged mountain terrain area with small coal mine villages here and there where people spoke their own language, Welsh. Sometimes when we drove through such a village, the natives came out of their small stone houses waving and smiling at us. They were very friendly people, but we could not understand the strange language they spoke when we tried to have a conversation with them. Wild horses in large herds roamed free over this beautiful area. Sometimes they got killed when they came too close to our firings. Even though the place where we played war was in a specially designated area, we could not control where the horses roamed.

Since there were no camps with tents to sleep in at night, we soldiers slept wherever we found a comfortable place to lay down on the ground or we slept in our vehicles. Our communication platoon always had three vehicles assigned to us, a Sherman tank, the carrier and a half track. The tank was used for when in battle and we needed to find enemy points for our infantry. After finding the enemy points we then called the artillery who would destroy them. A half track is a vehicle that has wheels in the front and tank tracks in the back and is mostly used for transporting soldiers over rough terrain. For sleeping at night Stanley, Eddy Novak our driver, and I used the half track where we also had stacked away our clothing. For two weeks our regiment trained there in the hills of Wales. Stanley, another men of our crew and I were, of course, mostly at the observation post which we had constructed from small boulders and tree branches on a hill overlooking the enemy positions. Or we were driving around in our carrier talking into my 2-1/2 foot radio to our artillery or infantry.

Toward the end of our training one of the eight men from my barrack at Cossfort House was ordered to bring a message on his motorcycle to our commander who was about three miles away. As he drove on one of the narrow sandy roads, he came into the path of a herd of wild horses. He tried to escape, but there was no way to outrun or hide from the wild running animals. A little later they found his body stampeded to death.

Before we had left for Wales, a rumor had gone around camp that we would not return again to our camp at Cossfort House, but would stay in England. We thought that probably the invasion into France was close at hand, since we had to take everything with us and clean out our barracks. We all had said good-bye to our friends, girlfriends or wives in Scotland before we had left for Wales. When our training was over in the beautiful hills of Wales, our whole regiment went to a camp about twenty-five miles south of London and settled in.

As soon as we had arrived at that camp, I was ordered to go to Major Makuch where I was told that I would leave the next morning to an American camp for instructions. Here we go again, I thought, another school. As it turned out Frank went also. Together with some other soldiers from our regiment we went by truck to an American camp near Oxford, England. There they taught us the latest American artillery surveillance technique, which was a new improved way for us to learn about the distance of enemy targets and the adaption of mile to the European km on the larger table-maps.

How we loved that camp! The American food was fantastic. We started out in the mornings with scrambled eggs, bacon and sausage and bread. It was something we never got in the Polish Army, and had not eaten since I had left Poland. The suppers especially were a treat for us with schnitzel or other meat and all the trimmings. And we could eat as much as we wanted which we were not used to. Everything was so well prepared, and there was always plenty of coffee. We learned that all the food the soldiers in that camp were eating came from America. We had fun watching the young recruits who came fresh from the boot camps of America. They were marching and singing with great discipline under their sergeant's watchful eyes. It was something we did not do in our camp. With so many older men, many who had gone through a war already, no sergeants or officer would ever yell at us, or make us march anymore.

After two weeks of eating our stomach full and learning about the latest American technique, we went back to our battalion. I sure had liked this course. Our regiment stayed two more months at the camp close to London. We did nothing but wait there. Sometimes in early evenings or on Saturdays Stanley and Waldek or Richard and Josef and I together with some other guys would go to the outskirts of London to go to a bar or see a movie. But everywhere in movie theaters or bars and dancing places it was overcrowded with soldiers, mostly Americans.

Sometimes we were just girl hunting to fill the evenings or Saturdays. But on weekdays we were bored and most of the guys played cards the whole day or just hung around and told each other horror stories. Then to our surprise our regiment went back to Scotland and Cossfort House.

◆    ◆    ◆

It was only five days after we returned to Cossfort House when I was called to the office of Major Makuch. When I arrived there, the major told me that I had to go to a school in Clam Castle, which is located on the west coast of Scotland. Looking at him I said, "Major, I need an explanation. Why do I have to go to a school again. I have noticed Frank Bajerski and I seem to be the only ones from our platoon who are sent to so many schools." Major Makuch looked at me and said, "Jozef, you will have no regrets. Just trust me." But the major said nothing more—no explanation or anything. The next day Frank and I got our things together and went to West Scotland, wondering what kind of a school they sent us to this time.

The school was located in a wing of a very large and old castle. Its name was Clam Castle. It belonged to the grandfather of the Queen of England who lived on a side wing of the castle. In the time that Frank and I were there, the two princesses, the now Queen Elizabeth of England and her sister Margaret, were spending vacation time at Clam Castle with their grandfather. Even though their private wing of the castle was closed by barricades, many times we saw the girls riding their horses with their escort. They were then 14 and 17 years old.

There were about 120 other soldiers in that section of the castle where the small group I belonged to also was staying. They got instructions from the Polish Corps of Engineers about how to lay bridges, build roads etc. In another section of the wing our 30 soldiers, chosen from four regiments, got lessons in communications, analyze situations, spy situations etc. It was an interesting course and the weeks went fast.

In our class was a Polish soldier from Chicago who had come via Canada to England. He had received a one hundred dollar bill from his sister from America and wanted to take five of us out for a nice dinner. So we went to a very nice looking restaurant. When we were seated and the waitress came, he said to her, "I'd like to order six chicken dinners." The waitress looked at him and said, "You mentioned chicken dinners? I haven't seen a chicken for the last two years!" Our friend was surprised. "No chicken!" I don't think he had been in England very long and must have thought that chicken was as plentiful in England as in America. We ordered fish and chips, the famous English supper. The people of England and Scotland were on rations. They needed coupons for everything—for food, shoes, coal for heating their homes, clothing, etc. I think there was not much that was coupon-free.

After four weeks Frank and I went back again to our regiment at Cossfort House. I was there a week when I got the order to come to Major Makuch's office. "Oh no, not again," I thought as I walked to his office. As soon as I opened his door I said to him, "I am not interested, Major."Looking up from his desk the major said, "Jozef, I want you and Frank to go to Officers' School." "He is crazy," I thought. "I don't want to become an officer. I am a corporal and that is just fine with me." The major, seeing that I was not too happy with this whole idea of me going again to another school, finally started to explain. "Jozef," he said, "when the war is over and we come back to Poland, we need men who know how to help with the new Polish Army we will form there—to teach them new skills and methods the way we do here in the West. We need a lot of good men who have enough knowledge to help out not only with the new army, but also in many other places. You will have a good future, Jozef, in our new Poland."

I can't say that I was thrilled about the whole idea. I had my own plans, and they did not include the military. That was the farthest from my mind. I wanted to go home, start my own bakery business and play soccer. And maybe get married, but not to a Scottish or English girl as many Polish men had done in the last few years. Of course I had to follow orders and off I went with Frank to the Officers' School which was luckily not too far from Cossfort House. I could stay at night in my barrack and in the evening I could go to my girlfriend Bessie or go out with the guys.

The Officers' School I attended was interesting, although a lot of courses they taught there I had gone through already in the last few years in other instructor schools, and sometimes it was a little boring to me. But, since I would be "home" in the evenings, it was better than hanging around in the barracks during the day and I learned something new again.

After I was out of Officer School, I stayed one more week at Cossford House before our whole regiment moved to Whiteburgh, which is west of Edinburgh and is one of the small coal mining towns which are located there.

It was Christmas 1943. A few days before Christmas the priest of a small Catholic church in Whiteburgh (there were not many Catholic people living in Scotland) had asked our major if he could send some of his soldiers to his church for a Christmas dinner. He explained that the families of his church wanted to invite soldiers over for a nice Christmas Eve. "Maybe you can send us ten men," he had said to our major. Stanley and I were two of the lucky ones chosen. That Christmas Eve when I walked into the little church made festive with Christmas decorations, I felt really good. The people had cleared the middle of the church and tables for eight were set up. Surprisingly we saw a large, decorated Christmas tree, which stood in all its glory in a corner of the little church. Each of us was brought to a family who were sitting at one of the tables and introduced to them. My adopted family for the night was a family with three grown daughters. Another of our soldiers was also sitting at our table.

After a nice Christmas dinner and singing Christmas songs, they cleared the tables away, and we danced the rest of the evening. I danced especially with one of the family's daughters by the name of Berta. She was a very pretty 22-year-old girl and knew how to dance well. Before leaving for my barrack that evening, I had to promise the family that I would come for Christmas dinner at their house. I promised, and did not regret a minute of it. Not only was the food good but also the family was great. Berta played Polish Christmas songs on the piano that I knew by heart. I don't know from where she got the music, but since she worked at the opera house in Edinburgh she probably knew where to get it. After Christmas Berta and I would sometimes go to the opera which I enjoyed very much. Or sometimes her mother would invite me over for a dinner on a Sunday. I liked Berta very much, but found out that she was married and her husband was stationed in Burma. I felt a little awkward about going out with her, and I soon dropped out of sight.

In the meantime the war in Europe and in the Pacific raged on. The assault on the Gustave Line in Italy continued, and allied bombers hit Monte Casino. The Allied losses were heavy. On the Russian front the German forces were falling back more and more everywhere. But the Pacific fighting brought a deep sense of dread to Americans. After vicious fighting the British and American forces won control over most of Guinea (Indonesia) where they would be able to embark for the Philippines. They fought off heavy enemy counter attacks all along the way. The fighting was not only heavy on land but also in the air and by battleships and submarines.

Even though Scotland had never been bombed by the German Luftwaffe during WW II, many military accidents did happen during that time. I remember too well the few I saw in Scotland when stationed there. An anti-aircraft training field from the Navy was located close to our camp. Every day the navy men were practicing with their anti-aircraft guns, aiming at a balloon which a navy plane was pulling. One day after a whole day of practice, the small plane came in too low for landing and hit the tops of the trees which were located on the edge of the field. The aircraft went down and exploded. The two men in the plane were killed and some soldiers on the ground burned or wounded.

Another time when we were on field exercises on one of the hilly areas of Scotland, we saw a bomber from the R.A.F.coming from over the water of the North Sea flying much too low. It probably had been hit by German fire somewhere in Europe and had lost altitude. When the bomber came over land it hit some trees and exploded, killing all aboard and burning a group of soldiers on the ground. It was a tragedy that happened many times in Scotland and England during the war years.

◆     ◆     ◆

In Whiteburgh there was a professional soccer team. Earlier, the coaches of that team had seen our Army soccer team playing at different games when we were stationed at St. Andrew. They knew that our regiment had moved to Whiteburgh. A few days later after we had moved into our new camp, one of their assistant coaches came up to Ted and me and said that he had seen us playing before when we were in St. Andrew. Ted had been one of the men living in our house in Sterling. After some talk back and forth he invited us and a few other players to come to their team's practice and talk to the head coach—which we did. The head coach told us that his team had problems and that many of the younger players had gone away into the service. They had only the older ones left and were in need of younger players to fill in the empty places. He asked us if we would be interested in trying out. But first we had to have permission from our commander, he said. If we were going to play on the team, we would get paid one pound for playing, one pound for making a goal and ten shillings for an assisted goal. It sounded good to Ted and me and when we came back to our camp, we went first to Major Makuch who, after hearing us out, had no objections to us playing for a professional soccer team. So Ted, three other men our company and I went for practice once a week. Two of the other guys went out and the three of us played with the team almost every Saturday in and around Whiteburgh against other teams.

Our camp at Whiteburgh was adjacent to a very large and new hospital which was built for Whiteburgh and the surrounding towns. Ted had become good friends with a nurse from this hospital. One Saturday after a soccer game in which we both had played, he introduced me to his girlfriend and to her girlfriend Mira. She was a soccer fan, as I soon found out, and whenever possible came to see the games. Mira was a nurse in the children's wing of the hospital. After we talked for a little while, we four decided to eat a fish and chip dinner somewhere and see a movie afterward. Mira was a dark haired, slim and pretty 23-year-old girl, and soon we saw a lot of each other. She liked to bring me an orange or some other fruit, which was something we never got in the army. I never asked her where she got it from, but since she worked in the hospital I am sure she got it from there. Fruit was hard to come by in those years and was probably only intended for the hospitals. One day she brought me twelve pairs of socks. She had found out that we soldiers had only two pairs of socks. She must have thought that this was terrible. I still wonder where she got them, since you had to have coupons to buy them in the store, and then you could get only two pairs. I remember selling six pairs to the guys in my barrack. What was I going to do with twelve pairs of socks? They took up too much room in my small closet space.

When the weather was warm and sunny and Mira had a few days free from her work in the hospital, we occasionally went for a two day visit to her parents. How I loved to go there. The large ranch style house where her family lived was located on an island off the coast of West Scotland. To get there Mira and I first took a bus to Glasgow and from there we took another bus which brought us to a small fishing village. Located there was also the coast guard from where she would call her parent's home to pick us up. Since the island was about a hour away by motor boat from the fishing village, we would sit on a boulder by the shore and wait until someone came for us.

Besides the family's home there was also a farmhouse on the island. It stood further up, and was owned by Mira's family but was run by a sheep farmer, who worked for her father. He lived there with his wife and three young sons. They were the only two families on the island, which was about two by three mile in size. Mira's father ran two businesses, one was the sheep business and the other was two fishing boats. His love was the sea, as Mira said to me, and whenever possible he went with the fishermen sometimes for days fishing to the northern part of the Atlantic Ocean. They must have had hundreds of sheep roaming the heather covered island. As Mira told me, most of the sheep were sold to the Army in the fall. They paid good money for them, she had said laughed while running her fingers through the fur of a sheep.

Mira's mother grew vegetables and flowers in the large garden which was surrounded by a wall of stones. The house and walls were built by the great-grandfather who had come as a young men from Norway and had started the sheep business on the island. Inside the wall the soil was brought in long ago and was kept rich with the manure from the sheep and a cow. They sure lived very self-sufficient lives there on that island.

When I came back to the island with Mira one spring day, the large fruit trees were in bloom in the garden and spring flowers were growing against the wall. It happened to be the busiest time of the year with the young lambs. Mira's father showed me the whole operation there, which was quite a business. Special men were hired who castrated the young male lambs with their teeth. I never had seen this done before, and I wondered how they could do this so precisely. The older sheep were shaved and mountains of wool were put in large sacks to be transported to the mainland. It sure was a very busy place there, and I enjoyed seeing a different way of life. The house, with its many rooms, was build on a hill close to the beach. Mira, her younger sister and I liked to sit there and watch the overfat large chickens pick everything from the beach such as small crabs and other small sea creatures. Their ducks were swimming in the sea close to the shore between rocks eating tiny fish. I didn't know that ducks eat from salty water.

It was very pretty on the island with the heather and golden dunes. Mira and I would go for long walks in our bare feet. We walked in the water of the cold Atlantic Ocean, and through the dunes where the only sound came from the many seabirds who nested there and from the waves of the ocean rolling in on the sunlight beaches. The island was such a beautiful and peaceful place, and the war with soldiers in overcrowded places seemed far away. After a two-day visit with Mira and her family, I hated to back again to my life in the barracks.

I would come back to the island a few more times during my stay in Whiteburgh. One day while walking through their garden Mira told me how in late summer they picked the grapes from the vines which grew in the garden on the stone wall which protected the garden and house from the harsh winter wind. And how everything in late fall was prepared for the long cold winter ahead. The northern part of Scotland, which lay quite far north, has only four hours of darkness during the summer. But the winters are long with only a few hours of light during the day. As Mira told me, the winters have cold harsh northern winds which sweep over the island with little or no snow. She said, sometimes as child, she couldn't go to the mainland for weeks and not to school.

Too soon the visits with Mira and her family came to an end when, after the morning roll call on the 6th of June 1944, our major told us that the invasion into France had begun.

◆        ◆        ◆

The invasion into Normandy was the largest and most complicated operation ever undertaken. For more then a year now the Allied airplanes had heavily bombarded German targets around the clock. Their targets were enemy airfields and war factories, railroad tracks and crossing points. Hundreds of the Lufftwafe airplanes had been destroyed in air and on the ground. Two months before the invasion, General Eisenhower set U.S. airplanes to attacking rail lines and bridges in France and Belgium, and airfields located 100 miles from the Normandy beaches, so it would be difficult for the German troops to move from one place to the other and bring in supplies for their troops.

The Allies knew that the German General Rommel had organized a bloody welcome for the Allied troops. Never in the history of modern warfare had a more powerful and deadly array of defense been prepared for an invading force. The Allied generals also know it would be the most dangerous and critical operation of the whole WW II. It was the only way that the Allied powers could destroy the German Army in Europe. In the early morning hours of D-day, 2000 Allied airplanes bombarded the Germans behind the beaches of Normandy to destroy the Atlantic Wall. There had never been a bombardment anywhere of such a size and intensity. The Allied mine sweepers had finished clearing ten separate paths through the fields of floating mines that the Germans had sown in the English channel. British, Canadian and US paratroopers took off late at night on June 5, flew to France and plunged through the darkness to points behind the German defenses. Once on the ground, they destroyed bridges, cut telephone lines, and took over roads, all to keep the Germans from quickly sending reinforcements to help defend Normandy shores.

Slowly, ponderously, the great armada of 5000 ships moved across the English Channel. It followed a minute by minute traffic pattern of a kind never attempted before. Ships poured out of British ports and the sea teamed with ships. It was the most impressive unforgettable sight ever seen. The invasion sites were Sword, Juno, Gold, Omaha and Utah beaches in Normandy. The fighting was very bitter and by the end of the first day of D-day, 10,000 soldiers and officers had died, were missing or were wounded by machine guns on the Normandy beaches while trying to go from their boats and ships onto the beaches. Or drowned in the high waves as their boats and ships went down on the beach obstacles or at sea by the firings from the German fortifications.

It was an exciting time. We had expected the invasion to begin for a while now. I knew that I again would go to war but was excited and hopeful that I finally would go back to Poland and my family. We knew that our First Polish Armored Division would land in Normandy later on, but we did not know when. Everything depended on the success of the first phase of the operation in France which was the taking of the beaches and then the enlargements of the beachheads.

It was about the 12th of July when word came that we were moving out of Scotland and would go to a holding place in Hull, England for further orders. When we left Scotland that morning, I could not believe that I had been there most of the last four years. It had not been bad years, sometimes there had been good times, which I always will remember. Other times had been not so good, especially in the beginning when I had come to Scotland, and I had been depressed and had wondered what I was doing there. I also had learned that life was very unpredictable and could change any moment. I had learned a great deal about another culture, which in the beginning was strange to me. Before coming to Scotland I had known nothing about that country or of England and its people. All that I can say is that basically all people are the same, and that only the culture is different. After a few years of living in Scotland and understanding their way of life, I liked the people who lived there and was comfortable talking to them. I had said goodbye to my girlfriends Mira and Bessie. They knew that the day would come when I had to leave. Both hoped that I would return some day. Both of the girls would write to me for some time, but I never saw them or Scotland again.

◆    ◆    ◆

Hull was a vacation town on the east coast of England. In and around that town were soldiers staying in the many small hotels that were located close to the beaches. They were empty of tourists, and all set up for the many soldiers who were waiting there. We slept with eight men in a room of a small hotel. In that time there were about three million soldiers from many countries from all over the world in England, and as they would say, "England would submerge in the sea by all this weight if it would be not for the many balloons holding it up." It must have been a tremendous organization talent from many generals. Not only to organize and assemble the many troops but also to send them over the Channel to the beaches of Normandy. There were about 280,000 men in the Allied Expeditionary Force. It was not only the men they had to transport over the Channel but also armored vehicles, trucks, weapons, gasoline, food, medical supplies etc. which had to follow the fighting soldiers closely. With all this, many more men were needed behind the front lines than actual fighting soldiers. Without those men and women no war could be fought.

We were in Hull about 2 1/2 weeks when orders came that we were leaving for Portsmouth, a harbor port in South England. In the early morning hours under a gray dark sky our whole division left Hull for Portsmouth. Our infantry had left the day before. Our tanks were followed by trucks that were loaded with gas for our tanks which we needed on this trip. Armored vehicles and trucks loaded with food supplies followed us over the crowded roads. Slowly we moved forward in sections. I saw convoys on every road, and congestion became a major problem. I was with Eddy Karlick, our driver, and Stanley in our Sherman tank. Eddy was a quiet fellow, who had been in a war prison camp in Russia in 1939, (the same as I had been,) and had been sent to Siberia to work in a coal mine. One day he had told me about the hunger and cold Siberia winters and the many men who had died there. Later when he and other Polish soldiers were set free because of the agreement between Churchill, Stalin and Roosevelt, he came to Iran and from there to England.

Driving in our tanks on paved roads was not the most comfortable way, since they have tank-tracks instead of wheels to drive on. The tanks have large openings on the bottom and that makes them very cold and dusty to drive in. Because of this, many men who had lung or sinus problems could not drive in a tank. During this trip I mostly stayed half way outside the turret opening, which is the opening on top of the tank. At the end of the first day of stop-and-go travel on the congested roads, we ate our ration which we had in our tank. We then rested for a few hours as good as we could sitting on the small seats in the tank, until the first morning light came over the horizon. I don't think too many of the soldiers slept that night.

The next day we drove further again in the long column, slowly section by section. By the end of that second day late in the afternoon we reached the harbor city of Portsmouth, which is a town that had been bombed many times in those war years. The harbor was especially set up for the enormous amount of trucks, tanks and armored vehicles to be transported over the English Channel to Normandy. I looked around over the tremendous amounts of war equipment and said to Stanley and Eddy, "Modern warfare, I think, is a matter of science, invention, and factory production. It is an army of steel." While rubbing his behind, Stanley replied, "Jozef, this moment I wish I had a live warm horse to sit on instead of this small cold hard seat I have been sitting on for days."

That night we slept in our tanks again as good as possible, with thousands of other soldiers and officers close to the harbor and the many ships which were anchored there. In the early morning hours after our breakfast in our tanks, our division prepared to go on board in the larger and smaller transport landing crafts. The large harbor which was full with war and troop transport ships, was a fantastic sight to see. Above our heads the R. A. F. protected this enormous undertaking with their fighters. Slowly we drove our tank to one of the smaller transport crafts which was opened up on the front and, while a soldier was guiding us, we drove slowly into its space. There was room inside for 8 tanks and 24 men. As soon as we were inside, the hatch was closed and we were on our way to Normandy over the turbulent sea and under overcast gray skies.

The interior in those transport ships have no windows so we could not see how many carriers, warships and supply ships were going with us at the same time to Normandy. We spent our time talking, smoking cigarettes or playing cards. Others tried to read or relax. Some of the men were nervous, especially one who told me he had a feeling he would soon be dead. A few days later he was killed when he and five soldiers tried to rescue two Red Cross men. All six were gunned down by German soldiers.

It didn't take long until our landing craft landed on the beach of Sword in France. It was the most northern landing beach in Normandy and not far from the ruins of the city Caen. When the hatch of our landing craft opened up and I looked at the beach of France, I thought that it had been more than four years when I had left France from the burning city of St. Nazaire. Now I had come back, and God willing I would finally go home, back to Poland. It was the end of July 1944.

# 10

## *FRANCE, NORMANDY*

One after the other our tanks drove out of the landing crafts right onto the beach of Sword, where on D Day the first wave of British and Canadian soldiers had come on shore. On the other beaches of Normandy, American and other British troops had landed. The first days of the invasion had been very rough, and there had been terrible bloodshed. As I was leaning halfway out of the top of the turret, I noticed that behind us came the Second Canadian Armored Division which was under the command of Marshall Montgomery. Our First Armored Division was commanded by General Maczek and was part of the Allied Armored units.

As we drove slowly forward on the beach, I looked around and saw everywhere tanks, armored vehicles, ambulances and jeeps. The whole beach area was covered with many cargo trucks to assure the constant flow of ammunition, food and medical supplies to the fighting forces. There were special trucks to bring the enormous amounts of Jerry cans filled with gasoline and water for the troops. They brought it all by the many ships, large and small, which were coming and going to and from England. They also were unloading soldiers and weapons, and reloading wounded soldiers, taking them back to England. As we drove slowly further I looked over the dark gray sea, and saw everywhere sunken ships and wreckage of small landing crafts and other debris sticking out of the water. It was an unbelievably sad sight to see and impossible to describe this adequately. Too many of those crafts and ships had been destroyed and sunk carrying their soldiers below with them.

Jozef standing on his tank, France, 1944.

About 3/4 mile of the beach Sword was cleared of the German General Rommel's maze of mined anti-invasion obstacles which had made the landing of the Allied troops difficult. Those mined obstacles which had been anchored half way under water along the shore line had sunk many smaller landing crafts or small boats loaded with soldiers. They had sunk and many soldiers drowned in the high waves. They drowned not only by the heavy strafing of the German guns, but also because of the loads of equipment they carried on them when their crafts sank. The steel and concrete structures of the German erected obstacles that once stood, were now high piles of junk in gruesome heaps on both sides of the beach opening.

As soon as we landed on the beach and started to drive, we noticed that they had made some sort of a road. When we drove about 200 yards we saw a sign saying to switch over to the right side of the road, as we were accustomed to drive on the left side in England. This was not difficult to do since it wasn't much of a road anyway. There was such a traffic jam on the beach that they needed traffic controllers to keep everything moving. While driving further I saw the silenced destroyed German fortifications which had dotted the entire coast from Holland to the south of France. Because of the intense aerial bombardments before the invasion, the whole area had become almost one flattened-out space.

After leaving the crowded beach area behind us, we drove about three miles further. We passed two small, completely destroyed seaside villages and stopped. As I jumped off the tank and touched the French soil, I suddenly felt elated and thought, "I am going home! Finally after more then four long years I am on my way to my country." An officer who passed looked at me strangely; he must have wondered what it was I was so happy about. I noticed that there were no trees standing anymore, just splintered tree trunks, hard dry grasses and weeds. Only some shrubs dusted by warm white soil stood in the earth plowed by bombs.

There in that area of the town of Caen, which was about 8 mile inland, our whole regiment came together and would stay there that first night in France. We talked, laughed and joked, but I don't think any of us slept very much that night. We knew that the times of waiting were about to end, and that the times of that for which we had waited was about to come. We were going to help put an end to Nazis and to this war. We tried to sleep that night in our tanks or armored vehicles, wherever we could find a place to lay down.

After the invasion of the Allied forces into France and the holding of the beaches of Normandy, the Allies very slowly expanded their toehold. While reorganizing themselves and building up their strength they now were ready for a bold powerful attack further into Normandy and France. In the eyes of the Germans generals the city of Caen was a key to their defense of France and they focused enough power to hold off the British for weeks, but finally they pulled out and left Caen in total ruins. The Germans were now holding in and around Falaise which is a city about 12 miles northeast of Caen. In the meanwhile the American Army under General Patton had spend the last weeks, after the invasion and holding of the Omaha and Utah beaches, in an encircling move. After capturing the city of Nantes, he swung back toward Normandy and headed toward the town of Argentan. His dash had formed almost a giant oval shaped pocket. Caught inside were 15 enemy divisions. General Patton planned to close the pocket and prevent a German escape by taking the nearby city of Falaise. But the American troops were weakened—not only had they suffered serious losses by the savage fighting of the Germans, but they also outran their supply lines.

In the meantime Germans General Von Kluge (General Rommel had been wounded) had seen the strange situation unfolding on his map and had asked Hitler to withdraw his Seventh Army out of the forming pocket. But Hitler's orders were to fight and hold, not to pull out!

It was now expected that the British forces, which included not only the English troops but also the Canadian, Scottish and Polish divisions would come from the southwest, as the American forces would come from the east in and around Falaise, and close the German Gap, with hundreds of thousands of German soldiers inside as well as great amounts of Panzer tanks and weapons. This battle which was about to come would last thirteen days.

Early in the morning after we had arrived in Normandy, our regiment came together for a short field mass which was attended by all the men. Our Chaplain spoke about that finally after four long years of waiting, the day had arrived that we were on the way back to Poland. He had a good speech and said, "Be strong and of good courage," and tried to raise our morale high. After mass I talked to Josef, Waldek and other buddies from Scotland; we joked and had some laughs. We then wished each other good luck before each of us went on to his own company. I wish I had met Adam also, but he was in a different regiment, and I did not see him.

When we had come back from the field service that morning and had our first breakfast chow on French soil, we received heavy enemy artillery firing and had our first casualties. That day we moved slowly up toward the front lines and passed the ruins of Caen which the British had been trying to take for weeks. Looking at it I wondered why they had been so anxious to capture it. The city was in total ruin as far as the eye could reach. The sun shone down on the ruins and the burnt out tanks and other war equipment that was left behind. It was quiet and nothing moved, not even a poor animal looking for water. As we drove a few mile further, we came under heavy enemy fire. Some men were killed and others wounded. Later that day we learned the truck with our six kitchen crew men, which always follow behind the front lines, was hit. All of them were wounded and send back to England. I cannot remember if we got our supper that night, but then we always had rations in our tanks. The following day we got a new kitchen crew.

For the next few days under heavy German firing, our division prepared for a breakthrough in the general direction of Trun, an important road-junction about 10 mile east of Falaise. The heavy fighting swung back and forth, we attacking them and the Germans counter-attacking us. Then after a whole day of intense battle with a German panzer division, Waldek was killed. While he was sitting in his tank sending messages to the artillery, an antitank grenade came through one side of the tank, went through the stomach of Waldek, took off the arm of his officer and went out through the other side of the tank. While dying Waldek still was able to finish an important message to his commander. That day had been hot again, and the air had been filled with dust that smelled of burning tanks and the stench of men and animals which were killed that day and the day before. The earth had trembled, and we all became exhausted from the constant noise of the shellings. That evening when the shellings had almost stopped and the sun was setting in the Western sky, I was sitting beside my tank and my thoughts went to Waldek and the good times we had together in London on our first furlough in England. I thought how he always had been reading books which he borrowed from libraries. He had hoped, someday back in Poland, to be somebody up there on the corporate ladder. He had been a easy pleasant guy, and I always had liked him. While settling for the night under our tank, I thought on how he had died and how nothing made sense, the whole rotten war.

Early the following day, when the earth was still warm from the hot sun the day before, another friend got killed. He was Anton, one of the guys from when we twelve where living in the house in Sterling and we all worked for General Miemira's office. Anton was killed while driving a jeep in the early morning hour to deliver a message to Major Makuch. A German fighter plane came over and fired, blowing up him and his jeep.

That same day after a couple of hours of intense fighting the Germans pulled back about two miles. Because of this movement, the lieutenant, our driver Eddy, two other men from our crew and I were assigned to go by carrier to prepare the new position for our battalion's cannons which would be about two miles further inland. Since our carrier did not have a km or mile reader, we got a field map from our commander for some orientation points to look for. Finding the right position for the heavy cannons is very important in war, so the shells will not fall on your own troops. We drove our carrier through the flat torn up field, to the area where we were supposed to find the right place for our cannons, and mark the ground for each cannon precisely with a few colored poles. While driving we were looking for the tower, or ruins, of a small church which we should be seeing in a close distance but was nowhere to be seen, as were the other points the commander had talked about. The lieutenant looking on his map started to curse, saying that there were no more orientation points left anymore in the field. As soon as he had said that, he realized that we had driven too far. Suddenly we heard machine gun fire coming from the front of us, and we knew that the Germans had opened fire on our carrier. Instantly we realized that we were in an area between the German Army and probably the British infantry. We were in no-man's land, and no soldier ever wanted to be there. Eddy, suddenly understanding the danger we found ourselves in, drove under a rain of bullets as fast as he could to a ruin which we had seen about two hundred yards to the left of us, and what looked like the remains of a large farm house.

There we were, safe for the moment behind the ruins, but what now! The Germans were still firing and to our misery our lieutenant, an otherwise great guy, lost it and developed a nervous breakdown. While wringing his hands, he blamed himself that he had got us in that dangerous situation. That was not what we needed right then. Something had to be done but we couldn't think of anything, at least not right then at that moment. I got on my radio and told our captain what had happened. I gave him my position and told him about our lieutenant. The captain asked how the rest of us were, if we were all right and said to stay put, they would cover us and try to get us out. He told me further to take the command and do the best I could.

In the meanwhile the Germans had stopped their firing. But not trusting the silence I told the crew to get out of the carrier and to go inside the ruin of the farm house with their tommy guns, then to spread out and watch the Germans. After the men were gone into the ruin, I turned to the dazed and shocked lieutenant and told to him to stay put in the carrier, and that everything was going to be all right. I then got out of the carrier and, while staying close by, I watched intently in the direction behind us. As the Germans were in front of us, I thought, then one or another Allied infantry should be behind us. Then about 200 yards or more from me I noticed an infantry all dug in behind low growing hedges. I could not see which company they were from. I saw only that they were waving as to tell me to stay where we were. I waved back to let them know that I understood. While finding my way into the ruin to tell the guys about the dug-in infantry, I thought about what would happen if the Germans came before help arrived. Would I be a prisoner of war again, this time by the Germans? I didn't want to think that way and said to myself that I would do everything I could to get us out of this situation and back to our company.

It was unusually quiet and a sense of desolation came over me as I found Eddy crouching behind a crumbled wall with his tommy gun at the ready. I told him that I had no idea who the infantry was I had seen all dug in. While looking in the direction of the Germans, Eddy asked me if I thought we would come out this alive. Looking at him I answered, "There are two ways out—either the devil will be hungry or he will not be! But we will not be an easy prey for the devil, I promise you."

We were in that miserable position for about three hours when suddenly I saw behind us about twelve soldiers in our direction crawling on their stomachs with their rifles in their hands. As they came closer I saw that they were Scottish infantry men. They waved their arms and shouted to come toward them. I raised my hand in the air as if to say I understood and then signaled the guys from our crew to go back into the carrier. Our lieutenant was still sitting there as if in a trance, and I wished he would snap out of it. When the with dust-coated men were in the carrier, I told Eddy to get the hell out of there and go as fast as our vehicle could go. Under a rain of German bullets, and lying as low as possible in our carrier, we went like crazy and in minutes we were at the Scottish position. Believe me, I breathed a sigh of relief. A Scottish Captain waved his hand and said, "Go, and good luck!"We then drove further toward our company. In the meanwhile I had talked on our radio to our captain, and had told him that we were on our way back.

As soon as we had reached our company, all the men there started to applaud. I think they were happy to see us. Maybe they must have thought we would not come back anymore. Our regiment doctor took care of our lieutenant and, after examining him, ordered him back to England. Later I thought how lucky we had been that the Germans hadn't used their artillery (or maybe they did not have artillery there) or we would have been a perfect target. Meanwhile another crew had been assigned to take our place to prepare the cannon positions.

The accidental driving of a vehicle into no-man's-land happened more. It was a week later when the same thing happened with one of our tanks when, after an all out fight with the enemy, the tank with five men inside became lost. They were overpowered and the men where left with their throats slit, probably by the fanatic German SS troops who were well known for their cruel treatments. This did not happen much by the regular German troops.

◆    ◆    ◆

*August 8, 1944.* As I recall, it was about 11:00 in the morning on a day which would become one of the worst days of the war for many of our soldiers. It was again hot and sultry as it had been every day since we had come to Normandy. As I looked up into the cloudless sky in which the sun revolved in its ever-circling circles, I thought how much different the climate was here in Normandy than in cool Scotland. Some guys and I had shaved all the hair from our heads that morning because of the heat and dust, and our helmets didn't help matters either. It would be much better and easier to wash the sweat and grime from our bald heads using the water out of our Jerry can. There are no showers on the front—that luxury we left behind in Scotland. Sometimes we washed ourselves in a lake, river or stream. But that did not happened too often, and then only between shootings, that is if we got the chance.

That day our First Armored Division together with the Fourth Canadian Armored Division would start its frontal attack along the Caen-Falaise Highway. The Allied headquarters in England had decided to use bombs first by using hundreds of airplanes, so as to soften the German defense line which the enemy was holding tight there.

We were standing and leaning against our tanks, talking, smoking and joking and checking things over. As we stood there waiting for orders, sometimes our faces turned to the westward distant horizon. Stanley, Eddy and Felix (a soldier who also was a forward man) had been telling jokes with some other guys from our platoon when we heard from afar the heavy droning sounds of Allied bombers coming. As we looked up, I saw a long line of bombers stretching back as far as I could see. They were flying low with incredible slowness as if held on invisible rails. We just stood there and stared at the unbelievable sight of the coming of hundreds of heavy "Lancasters" and "B 17" bombers, which were going to crush the enemy lines. As the first string of planes where droning almost overhead, I saw suddenly to my horror that the first bombers were releasing their bombs which were falling in clusters toward us. For one second, time seemed to stand still as I stared blankly at the following four-engine monsters which also released their bombs which where falling downward in a slowly lengthening curve. Then all hell broke loose. The whole world turned upside down.

It is difficult to describe the next hours. Soldiers were screaming in disbelief at the bombers with their arms up in the air, as if to tell the pilots of the planes that they were bombing their own troops. Polish and Canadian soldiers where running in all directions. It became a chaotic situation. The bombers kept on coming and coming and releasing their bombs on their own soldiers. It became dark with smoke and dust and flying soil and an unending sound of explosions all around which did not diminish but went on and on. The ground trembled as in an earthquake. My feet were nearly knocked from under me. Automatically I began to run. The volume of noise shut out all thought. There was no lull—no second in which to breathe. The sky grew darker and darker as the dust rose. I could hardly see. I fell down, got up, stepping over fallen comrades. I leaped into a foxhole which a German soldier probably had dug for himself the night before. It was just a shallow pit and my body was barely below ground level. Lying low, I looked up and saw airplanes which seemed like ghosts through the clouds of dust and smoke releasing their bombs eleven at the time. I thought, "God, what a stupid waste if I were to die now, finally on my way going home. Or maybe He wants me to see

Hell first before He sent me off to Heaven." Then a bomb exploded close to where I was lying and nearly buried me. My mouth was full of dirt. My mind automatically told me that I had to get out of the hole, that another bomb explosion close by could bury me alive. I started to run but there was no place to run to. It was a nightmare! I felt I was about to collapse, when the deafening thunder of crashing explosions suddenly ceased. It became deeply quiet. It was over; the bombers had left.

It is not easy to describe the hours which followed. I did not know where I was. I only heard the anguished cries for help from the wounded and twitching not quite dead. The scene was horrible. Unable to help, I staggered further on. I was horrified at the destruction that had been wrought in a matter of such a short time. Soldiers who had lost their minds were walking around like zombies. Others, as I did, walked in a daze, looking for familiar faces. I came to a Canadian Major who after seeing the destruction of his regiment by the bombers, knelt and cried and said over and over again, "They have killed all my soldiers, they have killed all my soldiers." I walked further, hoping I would find my way back to my tank, destroyed or not.

I don't know how long it took me, but somehow I found my way back to the area where I was before the bombing had started. A little later I found my tank which was still in good shape, but I saw none of my crew. After I waited awhile hoping that some of the crew would appear, I decided to go further. Now men began to come out of the smoke and dust. Medics had arrived and were working among the wounded soldiers. Sometime later I saw the armored car which I had driven earlier that morning. Some of the soldiers of our platoon were standing beside the damaged vehicle with blood-streaked faces. No one said anything and just stood there staring at each other with hollow eyes. Our uniforms were gray from the dust and dirt, torn and in many cases bloodstained. Soon more soldiers arrived walking in a daze. But how lucky were the ones who came out of this alive.

Not until later in that afternoon did we start to come out of our state of shock. Officers arrived and reorganized our company immediately with new troop and equipment replacements. By then I had found out that many of the men I had known so well, and some of my platoon buddies, were killed, wounded or were missing. Stanley and Felix where hurt but not bad enough to be sent back to England. They had walked around in a daze as I had, and had finally found their way back to the area we were before it all had started. And all this by our own planes!

As we discovered later, the mistake came when the pilots of the bombers in England got their orders when and where to drop their bombs. The Germans had fallen back a few miles and we, the infantry and tanks who happened to be in the wing of our division, had moved further forward. On that late morning, out of the one thousand airplanes that were supposed to destroy the German lines, about half of those bombers had targeted their own troops. Somehow they had not seen our large nylon signs we always placed on the ground for our airplanes to see. So our own planes by mistake, because of movement, had attacked their own troops. It was one of those terrible mistakes, those that happen in all wars on both sides.

The next day arrived with heavy fighting as we continued our frontal attack. I think as bad or worse than the front lines were the German masked pockets which were situated in the region and opened surprise attacks. This happened to us when our armored company moved across some fields and without warning there was a sudden roar of gunfire on the left side of our tanks. We could not tell whether we had run into German tanks or if the firing was from anti-tank guns. The only thing we had seen around us were rolling wheat fields, some trees and shrubs, nothing else but the hot sun. But the firing was accurate, fierce and at close range. We realized that we had fallen into a trap and were caught in a devastating fire that knocked out our lead tanks which blew up in a fire red explosion, without having fired one shot. Fire and smoke bellowed up. One after the other our tanks were being knocked out. Some exploded into an inferno with all the crew trapped inside. Other tanks where heavily damaged and some of the crew escaped with or without injuries. In ten minutes time we lost 10 tanks. We halted our attack and were forced to withdraw from the German cannon range. We had discovered that there was a strong pocket of camouflaged German tanks dug in. With their hulls low and with only their turrets showing they were difficult for us to detect.

In the meantime the colonel from our armored regiment called in for artillery and air force support. As soon as the artillery received the exact position of the German pocket, they opened fire. We knew that the artillery could not destroy them, but could hopefully damage them enough until the fighter planes could finish them off. It was only a few minutes later when we saw in the sky about four Spitfires coming. They were from our Polish Air force which always was on standby and supported the troops when and where they were needed. The fighters thundered overhead, circled a few times and then dove in a near-vertical dive full speed and attacked the pocket of enemy tanks with rocket fire and destroyed them. I was amazed how precise and fast those planes were in destroying their targets. After the violent attack the German tanks went up in smoke. Most of the German soldiers were killed, but some had tried to escape by running away as soon as they saw the Spitfires coming. It did not take long until our infantry surrounded the German soldiers and took them prisoners of war. Later we learned that the pocket had held six Tiger tanks. The German Tiger and Panther tanks were superb and were much better than our Sherman and Cromwell tanks. Theirs had a much longer shooting range and much heavier metal plates.

A few hours later replacements of men and tanks arrived for our company. As we continued our assault and fanned out across the field, we passed our demolished tanks. Small grass fires were still smoldering. The stink of the smell of charred bodies and burned out tanks was hanging in the air. Some of the black burned bodies of men were hanging from the burnt-out tanks' turrets. When I saw the destruction of our tanks and soldiers, an overpowering anger came over me. At that moment I could have killed any German that would have been there. I thought how could our company lose so many men and tanks in only two days. First by the bombing of our Allied bombers, and now this. About 75 of our soldiers were killed or wounded in those ten minutes by the pocket of German tanks.

For two days our troops fought without a break—we attacking our enemy or the enemy counter-attacking us. The fighting was bitter and exhausting. Snipers were hidden everywhere, mostly in the stacks of wheat which were standing in the fields. Their targets were our officers. But our infantry learned quickly how to take care of the snipers and destroy them. But the pockets with wheat camouflaged machine gun nests took some more work. Our soldiers fought them without pity to break all their savage resistance and many of them were killed. Many of our own soldiers and officers also were killed or wounded by those wasp nests of German defenses.

After two days our crew was relieved by another crew of our forward communication platoon. After sitting for more than two days in the Sherman tank, and reporting the enemy targets to our artillery, I was glad to go back to my battalion and my half track. The half track was always with the artillery. The radios which were located there, were always in contact with the forward crew at their observation posts or in their tank. The half track was Stanley and my 'home' in which all our belongings were stacked away. When I was not assigned to our tank battalion or to our infantry, I was to report the location of enemy targets, which I received from the forward crew on the front line, to the artillery from out of the half track.

After two days of being "home" and eating my meals from the field kitchen instead of my rations from out of the tank, I relaxed a little. I then was assigned again to go with our crew to relieve another of our crews who were with the infantry.

We always had four men in the tank. It was usually Lieutenant Barski or Lieutenant Belinski, Eddy our driver, Freddy our gunner and me. When going with the tankers, we stayed inside our tank where I received the messages from their tank commander to send through to our artillery. When going with the infantry, I usually went out of the tank and took my radio to a hidden place were I had a good observation of enemy targets. I reported those enemy targets to our lieutenant in the tank, who passed it on to our artillery. In open fields the relays on my radio were pretty good, but behind a wall, farmhouse or trees the sounds were poor. Many times I got German transmissions on my wave length.. They always tried to bother us with loud nasty noises. But then, we did the same to them.

The fighting was continuous with repeated attacks and counterattacks. The enemy was fighting for every foot of ground for the top of the Laison River Ravine, which was a river in the vicinity of Falaise. To push the Germans to the other side of the river was very important to us because of the connection we had to make with the units of the American Fifteenth Corps and the British forces, which where attacking the enemy from the south-east, and together we would close the Gap. But not until after bitter fighting, heavy artillery and cannon fire was the enemy pushed back to the other side of the Laison River, leaving behind many casualties from both sides. We took many German soldiers as prisoners of war. But now the enemy was establishing a second line behind the river that we had to cross. Before we could do the crossing, we had to destroy the German infantry units that were dug in on the other side. Scores of our fighter planes started to blast everything that moved, and all the while gunfire was plowing up the area. Slowly the Germans retreated.

Since the bridge over the Laison River was destroyed one of our infantry battalions received the assignment to cross the river by assault boats, which was done under fire from the enemy. After cleaning up the last German resistance, our infantry crossed over the Laison River in their boats. In the meantime a battalion of engineers had laid down a pontoon bridge. It took about three to four hours before our whole division crossed the Laison River. When I was going over the pontoon bridge I looked into the shallow water where the destroyed bridge had fallen. The scene was horrible. Army men, horses, vehicles and equipment had crashed from the bridge into the river and lay there together in gruesome heaps.

When we came to the other side of the river, the ground looked like a deep plowed farm field. The trees which once stood were pulverized, the trenches were filled with dead enemy troops, blasted either by our artillery or by the merciless airplane shellings. Because of the heat the decomposing corpses were ballooning double their size, and the smell was sickening. I remember well Eddy saying, "Holy Moses, Jozef, those krauts are stinking like Hell!"

We had noticed that the famous German Luftwaffe was nowhere to be seen in the daytime. I think that they were greatly outnumbered by our Allied Air force and they knew they had no chance. Also the German Luftwaffe was probably unable to supply their planes with the required fuel or defend themselves against the continuous attacks of the Allied Air Force. It was only at night that a few would come over to harass us, and then mostly aiming at our artillery. The heavy Allied artillery had fast become a headache for the German troops.

From the Laison River we moved slowly up. We crossed the Dives River near Jord without much resistance and attacked in the direction of the town of Trun, an important road junction about 12 miles from Falaise. On the way our troops captured several villages. For the French farmers, who where living there, and who were caught up in the battle, it was hours of chaos, terror and elation. The people where hiding in shelters in their villages or homes. Their houses were heavily damaged and in many of the ruined houses were nests of resistance by the hard pressed German troops. When we moved through the French villages, small groups of people came out their hiding places and would wave and shout, "Viva les Anglais."

Our infantry and armor pushed further and advanced across the meadows in the intense summer heat. Falaise was taken by Canadian infantry on August 17 with considerable losses on both sides. Only a narrow corridor between the town of Trun and the Gouffern forest remained open for the retreat of the German Seventh Army. To capture this area it was necessary to conquer Mount Ormel, which had an elevation of 262 ft. Because of its characteristic shape, it was called "Bludgeon." Our First Armored Division, together with the Fourth Canadian Infantry Division, was given the order from General Montgomery to seize this region and to help to cut off the German escape route from out of the pocket. With the hilltop in German hands they were in a position to paralyze any movement by any force for several miles in almost any direction. They also had the area widely mined. Possession of the hill was a key to the success of our assignment, which was the closing of the Gap together with the American forces.

In the meanwhile the German withdrawal through the Gap became desperate, and what they had never done before happened now—mass movement in daylight. Because of this, Allied fighter bombers struck at the packed roads hour after hour, while the artillery poured thousands of shells into the killing ground. In those bright summer days one of the mightiest armies ever that had terrorized Europe was perishing miserably.

Our intense battle opened up with a roar against the Second German SS Armored Corps. The fighting lasted the whole day and night from August 17th. to August 18th. Under fierce exchange of firepower the enemy wavered and began to fall back. Then after hours of bloody fighting by infantry and tanks, we took the "Bludgeon" and Chambios. Although our division had reached and held onto our assignment to close the pocket, the American forces were late. By not reaching their geographical objective on time, they made a most serious mistake. Hitler had made the mistake of not pulling his Seventh Army out of the then-forming pocket a few week before. Now American forces made the mistake of not closing the gap in time with the Polish forces, and they let thousands of German soldiers escape through the small opening left. Not only were the American forces late, but also the British and Canadian troops were late. They had to give us support and did not reach their objectives in the time they were supposed to.

While we attained our assignment, our division suddenly found itself in a very difficult situation. We were attacked from all sides by overwhelming enemy forces who tried to keep the narrow escape route open for the German troops. The German Seventh Army, which was pushing through to the northeast and out of the almost-enclosed pocket, attacked us from the south. From the other side we found ourselves fighting the Adolf Hitler First Armored Division, the Twelfth SS Hitler jugend Division and other top German divisions. We now found ourselves completely encircled by the enemy. While holding on to our assignment, we fought for two days and nights. We were cut off from supplies and all possibilities to evacuate our wounded soldiers. As soon as our division found itself encircled, orders came from our General Maczek to split our division into two separate evenly-divided fighting groups. One was defending the south and the other the north side of our encirclement. The general tried to keep our morale up by saying, "The situation will be short lived, stay on defense!" Then the general said further, "We are waiting for the American First Army to come from the east and the Canadians from the south. They are gathering strength and are moving in our direction and will relieve us from our predicament." He then went further, saying, "Men, let us give it one hundred percent. We survived many situations and we will survive this one too!"

Every man and gun was needed now. Everything and everyone who could shoot was put into position for defense. So what I had not done before in this war, I started to do now. Alone with our platoon Officer Lieutenant Barski, a quiet man of short statue and in his mid thirties, we started to operate our tank's cannon. The lieutenant would tell me the distance, and I would load the shells into the gun chamber and fire. The loading of the shells was done inside the tank which is a narrow area where also the rest of our ammunition was. We shot at random. Any place was as good as the other just as long as they landed on enemy territory. Because of the continuous loading of the heavy shells I remember how very heavy the grenades became after a while. I sure was not used to such hard work anymore.

General Maczek must have asked for airplane support, because after just a short time the fighter planes showed up and started to attack the German troops. We all were standing there and grinning at the sky. It gave us a comforting feeling to see our air force. But the enemy artillery fire went on and on and all that we could do was defend ourselves from the severe pressure. Between the shootings we tried to keep our mind off the situation and started to talk to each other about our lives, our girlfriends or wives, and homes. While the shells shrieked over our heads, Eddy would tell us again stories about his imprisonment in Russia. Later Freddy told us about when he lived in France where he was born from Polish parents. He had gone into the French Army when the German troops had invaded Holland and Belgium in 1940. He had escaped to England on an English warship. He was about 30 years old, tall and skinny and never had been married. He loved to joke around a lot.

After a sleepless night, daylight came. The sun was low in the east and hiding behind the thick smoke which bellowed up from the burning tanks and other vehicles. While the bursting shells ripped the soil apart and debris was flying everywhere, I tried to close my mind to the screaming of the wounded and dying soldiers who were being transported by jeeps to the center of the circle. There were not enough medical supplies anymore, and soldiers went around collecting the heavy emergency bandages the tank crews always carried with them in their tanks. We also did not have enough medical help and some of our officers and soldiers became medics in those days. They gave the casualties a shot of morphine and did the best they could.

The weather was hot, and the smoke and smell from burning vehicles became intolerable and burned our eyes. Water and food supply were rationed, and we got the order to slow down on our firings. Our ammunition was getting low. Our captain had said to fight it out and not to surrender whatever it would take, and we all knew he was right. Surrendering would not guarantee our safety; we could be killed either way. The Germans SS troops did not have the reputation for being especially kind to their prisoners of war, as we had seen before.

Firings went on the whole day and by evening there was still no relief from the pressure around us. We all had become very tired and weary. Our officers moved as though they were drunk while doing the best they could. I was sitting at the side of our tank, and I thought it looked as if the sun had fallen out of the sky. It seemed to me that the sun had been sickened by the nauseating endless day.

That night our infantry troops, who were in front of us, were attacked, and they fought man to man. I heard the exploding hand grenades and the rattle of rifle shots in the dark. It had become a measure of survival for all the men.

The following day arrived in a yellow-gray thick haze. Maybe, I thought, maybe help will come for us today. I was bone tired and could hardly keep my eyes open. I crawled under the tank saying to myself, "The hell with everything" and went to sleep. I think it was more a collapse than a sleep. After about three hours I woke up and for a few seconds everything looked and sounded unreal to me. Ones again I said to myself that I would come out of this Hell and make it home. As I crawled out from under the tank I told Freddy to take my place, close his eyes, ears and mind, and try to sleep for a while, just to try to get some relief from the miserable situation we had landed in. I thought it could be the last time he would get a chance to sleep and wake up at the end of it. While putting out his cigarette Freddy said, "Well, all right then, Jozef, I will give it a try." He crawled under the tank, closed his eyes and tried to sleep, but could get no rest. Only a very few of the men were able to sleep for even a short time in those days of encirclement. They more of less collapsed for awhile.

The battle had been raging on, and no one knew exactly what was happening on the huge battleground. The only thing we knew was that it was time that we got out of this. Not only we were low on everything as ammunition and water, but the constant noise of shelling, the smoke and dust, the heat and nauseating smell and the droves of flies didn't help matters either. Then early that morning we suddenly heard the droning sound of airplanes coming, and to our relief we saw scores of Allied fighter bombers attacking the German troops. This brought new hope that finally the American and British troops were on their way.

It must have been later in the morning, when I was sitting in the tank that I suddenly heard my code number coming across through the headphones. It said, "Are you receiving....calling....over...." It was from our Battalions Headquarters with the message that the American, Second British and Canadian Army would reach us in a matter of a few hours. Finally they were coming!

Suddenly, greatly relieved, I brought immediately the good news to our Lieutenant, and told the other guys that it almost was over. I then went back inside the tank and started to listen further on my radio. Lieutenant Barski and Eddy, followed by another soldier, had come inside our tank and were now listening to every word I repeated from the radio messages I received. A little later I overheard conversations in English back and forth among Allied tank crews. They sounded far off and not clear. I guessed that they must have been about seven miles from where we were. As time passed, the relays became clearer. I knew the American troops, although they were moving very slowly, were finally on their way. Together with the Polish troops, the two armies would close the Gap which we had held on to so tightly.

On that morning, August 19, contact was made between the American Ninth U.S. Infantry Division and two of our Polish Regiments and together they closed the pocket. It was a historic moment. The battle was over.

The German General Von Kluge, who had been well aware of the situation of the Seventh German Army in the now-closed pocket, gave the order to surrender. The other German troops, which had been outside the pocket and had encircled the entire Polish Division, began to retreat before the massive Allied and American thrust.

While listening further on the radio, I received a message from our Headquarters that the Second Canadian Tank Division had rolled into the northern section of our encirclement and would reach us soon. A short time later the Canadian tanks, followed by about 200 Red Cross vehicles, arrived in our section to take away the wounded and dead.

The German prisoners of war now poured in by the thousands. It was pitiful to see them in shambling dusty files. They were bowed with fatigue, although many had nothing more to carry then their ragged uniforms and their weary, hopeless, battle-drugged bodies. Along with them came General Otto von Elfeld, who was the commander of the Eighty-Fourth Corps, and four colonels. First we took away their weapons and after separating their officers from the soldiers, they were loaded in trucks and sent to the coast. Many of the German prisoners where relieved; for them the war was over. But others we could not trust and we had to watch them carefully with our guns in the ready. The German prisoners of war would bury their own dead. During the carnage of the pocket and the Gap, eight German Divisions had been destroyed plus 2000 tanks and other vehicles. Our division paid with 2200 dead, missing and wounded for the closing of the pocket.

With the Failaise pocket crushed, the battle of Normandy was over. The battle had been bitter and savage and difficult to describe. It had lasted 13 days. The battleground of the pocket had been covered with human and material debris. The German Army had suffered the greatest disaster in modern military history, and it would be remembered as "The Hell Of Failase." And we—we got a break for a week, to fill in men, tank and other armor replacements.

The Germans were now in full retreat. The American and Allied forces pushed the Germans further into France. While the British Army went north, the American forces went northeast toward Paris. On August 25th, an overjoyed Paris was liberated by American and French units.

The French resistance had been very active in all of the war years and of great help to the American and Allied Armies. During the invasion they blew up bridges, railroad lines, trains and trucks, making it difficult for the Germans to move men and supplies to the front lines. The French underground had made it not easy for the Germans in those occupation years.

For most of our soldiers the first days of our rest were very difficult. Even after we had washed ourselves clean from the grime and smell of sweat and smoke, had finally been able to remove our shoes from our hot feet, and had shaved our beards of several days, we could not relax. We had eaten a good meal hoping we would feel better, but nothing helped much. I think those 13 days had been just too much. Many of the man were just sitting around incoherent, or they cried, or as I did—tried to take deep breaths in an effort to relax. But nothing helped much. We had become like zombies—numb and hardened to the suffering around us. So many men of my original regiment, which had been formed in Scotland, were not here anymore. They were killed, missing or send back to England because of being wounded or a nervous breakdown. Some more of my army buddies from Scotland were killed, as two from our former barrack in Cossfort House, and also Ted who had played soccer when we played in the professional team in Scotland. So many good men—gone.

Early in 1944, the German General Staff warned Hitler that his armies on the Russian front were spread dangerously thin. Germany had been unable to replace all the losses of the three previous terrible years of fighting, while the Russian Army had grown enormously in numbers and had greatly improved in fighting qualities. Hitler insisted his armies must hold on to every inch of Russian territory they occupied. Instead of building a deep defensive zone, as his generals suggested, he threw most of the German reserve forces into the front lines with orders to hold on at all cost. Then in late June Germany suffered one of its worst defeats when the Russians struck north of the Pripal Marshes and the Carpathian Mountains. He scraped together the few remaining reserves, withdrew troops from all other parts of the front and build a new German line just east of Warsaw, Poland. In violent counterattacks he slowed the Russian advance in east Poland and finally in early August he halted the Russians on the banks of the Vistula in sight of Warsaw.

On July 20, at the height of this terrible bloody fighting, Hitler paid one of his frequent visits to the eastern front headquarters in East Prussia. There one of his staff officers, Lieutenant Colonel Claus von Stauffenberg, tried to kill him by exploding a bomb concealed in a briefcase near his chair.

Stauffenberg was one of a group of German officers who had conspired to end Hitler's tyrannical and disastrous rule over Germany. Those men were disgusted by Hitler's gangster methods and by his mass murders of the Jewish people. But most of all, they were aware of the terrible losses of German soldiers. They knew that Hitler's refusal to listen to military advice would mean the ruin of Germany. They had planned to kill him, to seize control of the government, and to make peace with the Allies. The explosion of the bomb was to be the signal for the uprising. By chance, Hitler left his chair just before the bomb was to explode. At the moment of the blast he was partly protected by a table and some other furniture. He was injured, but lived, and immediately gave orders to put down the conspiracy. The plotters were seized and tortured before they were put to death. Germany's popular Field Marshal Rommel, who was in on the plot, was allowed to commit suicide instead of being shot.

# 11

# *THE PURSUIT*

After a week of rest and with many new replacements of men and weapons, our First Armored Division joined together with other Allied forces under General Montgomery. We were in pursuit of the enemy, slicing through any German units that attempted to stand and fight. We came through villages that were badly damaged and looked deserted and empty, and we wondered what happened to the people. Slowly we drove northward along the coastal plains. The plan of the Allied generals was to capture the large sea harbors of Belgium and Holland. They knew it would become impossible to bring enough supplies over the Normandy beaches and through the hastily reconstructed harbor of Cherbourg to furnish the great American and British Armies. The generals realized that if the troops failed to receive enough supplies, they would have to stop their advance.

On September 6 1944, we crossed the French-Belgium border and went toward the town of Ypress where we encountered strong German resistance. The enemy was bunkered down, and they had to be brought out by flame-throwers. Most of the German soldiers came out of their bunkers with their hands up, but some of them chose death instead of surrender and were burned alive in the red and yellow flames. After a day and night of hard fighting, we liberated Ypress and took many Germans prisoner. From there we moved slowly in a northern direction to the city of Gent, while leaving behind only dust and rubble from destroyed enemy positions.

Our assignment was to take Gent, one of the larger cities in Belgium, and for us the largest city so far. We noticed little resistance when our infantry and tanks moved into the town. Only small pockets of resistance and snipers gave us some work. Soon the city of Gent was cleared of the enemy and the people came out of their homes and hiding places and shouted, "Viva La Belgium." Flowers and kisses welcomed us when we drove through their town. I think it was the first time since we had landed in Normandy that we felt good. Smiling, we looked at the crowd from our slow moving rattling tanks. The people of Gent danced and sang their patriotic songs and climbed onto our tanks. After more than four years of occupation by the Nazis, the people were free again from tyranny and wanted to thank us for their liberation. After a few hours of driving and stopping in this thankful city and seeing the excitement of the people, we began slowly to move further and out of the town.

From Gent we moved further north toward the river Schelde, which the Allies so desperately needed for bringing in their supply ships to the large harbor of Antwerp. On the way going in the direction of the river, we first did not encounter any resistance until we had to cross a canal by the village of Zelzate. This canal starts at Gent and spreads to the broad Schelde river between the North Sea and the seaport of Antwerp. British paratroopers had captured the city of Antwerp on September 4. But the perfect seaport was of no use to the Allies, because the Germans still held on to the 50 mile long Schelde river which flows from Antwerp to the North Sea, as well as to the Dutch coastal inlands that overlook the entrance to the ships channel. The Germans knew that as long as they controlled those areas the Allies would be unable to use Antwerp as a seaport. They also had mined the very wide Schelde from Antwerp to the North Sea and were defending the river's mouth with a formidable concentration of 67 big naval guns. So the Germans held on to their positions as long as possible. The network of waterways and the channels were easy for the enemy to defend because the Allied tanks were useless in such terrain.

The German troops at the canal by Zelzate where dug in, and for three days we encountered intense fighting. The enemy fought desperately to hold onto the north bank of the canal. Finally they began to fall back and retreated, leaving behind many casualties on both sides. The Army of engineers constructed a pontoon bridge, and we crossed over the Belgium-Dutch border. When we came to the other side of the canal and I saw all the destroyed war equipment, I thought, "More tanks and more broken cannons and wagons going to the blast furnaces to make more tanks and weapons."

Another one of my buddies from Sterling, Scotland, was wounded seriously. A grenade fragment pierced his spine and left him paralyzed. I always had enjoyed him. He was a great guy who loved to joke and had hoped so much to go back soon to Poland and his family. They took him to England and I never heard about him again.

It was now about September 15, 1944. Because of the soft conditions of the low-lying fields, the maneuver to go from here to there was slow and difficult. It soon became impossible to drive our tanks and other vehicles on the land, and we were forced to stay on the narrow roads, driving one after the other. Many of the German soldiers had fled to the Dutch coastal inland and had abandoned their weapons and armored vehicles, many of them still burning. Other Germans surrendered and had to be transported by trucks, which made it all the more difficult on the narrow roads.

We drove about five km further when we stopped. It was almost evening and we had not encountered any enemy resistance since we had left the canal behind us. It looked like a good area for us to stop and fill our tanks with the needed gasoline. The road was between two sugar beet fields. I remember how high the plants where and how pretty, green and fresh everything looked there in northwest Belgium after the hot and dry conditions of the last weeks. We jumped from our tanks and some of the men went into the beet field to do what nature told them to do. But one of the men went a little farther, probably to have some more privacy. While walking between the beet leaves, he loosened his belt and unbuttoned his pants, holding onto his rifle with the other hand. Suddenly, he must have stepped on a German soldier who was hiding in the beet field. That same moment we saw five German soldiers jumping up with their hands up in the air. Our buddy seemed confused, because he threw his gun down, raised his arms, and stood there with his pants down. Then suddenly, looking at the Germans and realizing the situation, he quickly picked up his rifle, then put it down again, pulled up his pants, and then reached for his rifle again. It was such a hilarious sight, that all of us roared with laughter. In the meanwhile, other soldiers had already jumped into the beet field, encircled the five Germans, and took them prisoner. I think the poor guy never got his relief that evening. The situations concerning normal body functions are almost never mentioned in books or movies, but it is one of the unpleasant things of war when nature calls—especially on the front lines.

After the little incident our company drove farther until we reached a large farm with barns, close to the town of Axel. We decided to stop there for the night. While some other tanks drove to the nearby buildings, we drove our tank to a large barn close to the farmhouse and hoped, for a change, to spend the night in a barn under a roof, stretched out in the hay. As we jumped down from the tank, the farmer, his wife, two young sons and a girl around 20 years old, came from their farmhouse to greet us. First they looked us over and wondered what nationality soldiers we were. They had heard us speak a strange language which they could not understand. When I said something in English, the girl looked at me and answered in broken English. She explained that they had expected to see Canadian soldiers because they had heard that they were moving into the area. They never had expected to see Polish soldiers! For the last few weeks, she said, they had German soldiers on their land who had slept in the barns and on haystacks in the fields.

When the farm family recovered from the shock of seeing Polish soldiers on their property, they shook our hands and said how thankful they were for finally being released from German occupation and for bringing back their freedom. Sometime later that evening, while I was sitting on a bench near the farmhouse, the same girl came out of the house, walked over to me and started to talk. She said that her family lived in the city of Den Haag (The Hague) in Holland. Since there was not much to eat back home, she had walked to her uncle's farm for food.

For the first time I talked to someone who had experienced German occupation, and I realized how bad life had been for those people in the German-occupied countries. I had not talked to a girl since I left England, and I sure enjoyed this conversation. She was pretty and her hair was long and blonde and smelled so fresh and good to me—a far cry from the dusty, sweat-smelling soldiers I had been living with for the last two months. I saw that her feet were raw and asked her about them. It brought memories back to me from four years ago when I had walked over the railroad tracks. She then told me that there was almost no transportation anymore. She had walked most of the way from The Hague to Axel, which is more than 100 miles, while sleeping at night in small hotels. Too soon for me I had to say goodbye to her, and under a bright starry night I walked to the barn where most of the men were already sleeping. While I stretched myself out in the soft hay, I thought how much better this was than being cramped up in the tank. Soon my thoughts went back to the night when I had escaped from the Russian prison camp and we had come to a village and found a barn stacked full with hay. How very cold and wet we were, and how good it had been lying there in the soft warm hay. Five long years had past since then.

Early the next morning I woke up to sounds from the battalion kitchen, and soon the smell of coffee drifted into the barn. I jumped up and went outside and saw that most of our platoon were already eating their breakfast chow. Since the crew and I were separated most of the time from our battalion and the kitchen, we carried our own rations with us in our tank. Our rations were always cans of food and Army tea, a most obnoxious fluid called powdered tea. Usually when we were gone from our battalion, we never had a certain time for eating. We just ate whenever we could or were hungry enough to eat the stuff we carried with us. What a treat to eat breakfast from the kitchen with the men from our platoon. The fresh coffee, the large slices of white bread with big hunks of cheese and butter and jam was a treat for me and my buddies of our crew.

Another special treat had come that morning in the form of letters from my girlfriends in Scotland. The letters were for my birthday which had been September 3. I was 27 that day. At that time I had been somewhere in France not thinking about a birthday. It sure was good to receive mail—something I never got. Stanley was happy to receive many letters from his young wife. The rest of the day he was in a good mood and carried a big smile on his face. Eddy got letters from his many girlfriends from Scotland and was happy with a letter from his uncle in America. Felix received a letter from his family who lived in Australia and sometimes sent him money. Yes, it was a good morning.

Soon our tanks where grinding, and we were on our way again—destination unknown—route unknown—life even for an hour ahead unknown. It was a bright day and the sun was warm. The weather had now become much cooler than in France. Later after a short stop we got the assignment to go to the town of St.-Niklaas, Belgium. A few hours' drive later we came upon the wide waters of the river Schelde which the Allies so badly needed for their cargo ships. The Germans still controlled the entrance to the seaport of Antwerp.

In the meantime with Eisenhower's approval, General Montgomery decided to try a very daring plan. They felt that to be able to use Antwerp as a seaport, they had to seize the Ryn (Rhine) crossing at Arnhem in Holland and cut off the German Army there. While one British and two American Airborne Divisions would parachute into Holland and capture the crossing of the bridges of Schelde (Scheldt) and Maas (Meuse) near Nymegen in south Holland and held the road open, another American Airborne Division would hold the bridges over the River Lek at Arnhem. In the meantime the British and American land troops would drive north and link up with them.

The operation, named "Market Garden," began on September 17. With many hundreds aircrafts of large troop transport pulling towering gliders full of soldiers, it was to be the biggest airborne operation in history. It got off to a good start, but soon things went wrong. The Germans, who had been informed by their intelligence (spies) in England about the Allied plans of the operation Market

Garden, knew the exact time and place were the parachutists would be coming down. German tank troops were waiting for them. The enemy reaction was quick and violent. The paratroopers were shot in midair while drifting down in their parachutes. Others were immediately killed when they landed on the ground. After a week of bitter fighting and with most of the paratroopers killed, the remaining ground troops surrendered. "The Battle of Arnhem" was over. Once again the Allies had to continue their step-by-step advance along the river Schelde and across the now-flooded Dutch islands.

While driving on the narrow roads, we crisscrossed further between farm fields and small towns but encountered no enemy resistance. By early evening we reached the town of St.-Niklaas which is close to Antwerp. As we stopped at the edge of the town, we were told that our company would stay there for one whole week, waiting for supplies to arrive, of which we had a great shortage. Also we had almost run out of fuel for our tanks and trucks. We parked our vehicles in an open field, where our soldiers took turns guarding them. We then were instructed to go to the town square where our company assembled. When we were all together, our Chief Sergeant told us that we would be staying in the homes of the people of St.-Niklaas. We looked at each other. This was new to us, staying in a house, sleeping in a bed! It was not much later when our crew was taken to the houses in which we were going to stay for a week.

The addresses were of people who were willing to take one or more soldiers into their homes. I was assigned to a large, old house. How well I remember the huge bedroom with the large soft bed where I would sleep for a whole week and, after I got used to all that softness, I felt great. It brought memories back to me of when I was in Hungary staying with those wonderful people. I had never slept in a bed like that since then. The lady of the house where I was assigned, was a motherly soul who could speak some English, which was helpful. I looked around the spotlessly clean living room and looked for the least clean chair in which I could park my grubby self. But not feeling comfortable I soon retired to my room.

That same evening, the lady's married children came over—probably to look me over. It didn't take long until we had a tea-drinking ceremony. The tea, served from a gold trimmed pink teapot, had been saved from five years ago for this special occasion, I think. The family was very thankful that the war was finally over for them. They spoke Flemish, a language I could not understand. But luckily for me a granddaughter (Leah), about in her early twenties, could speak English.

Even though I understood the happiness of those people and that they felt proud to have a Allied soldier in their home, I did not feel at ease. I went outside and hoped to see some of my crew buddies who were in one of the other houses close by. As soon as I came outside, I saw Stanley and Freddy and some more guys of our platoon standing on the other side of the street. They too had felt the same way as I had. I guess after two months of harsh living it was difficult to be in a civilized world. I think also that we soldiers, after being together for a long time and going through so much, had become close—always looking out for each other. We decided that the next day we would all go together and investigate the town of St.-Niklaas.

It was the first time since Scotland that I had walked in a city—passing by stores, movie theaters, dance halls and the like. But we were puzzled that there was so much merchandise in the stores. In France, we knew, it had been a different situation. Later when I asked the lady of the house about it, she said that the merchandise I had seen was from four years ago. She explained that Belgium had learned a lesson from the War of 1914-1918. That was to hide everything from the enemy and take it out later after the war was over and the enemy was gone.

For one great week we stayed in St.-Niklaas. I went to the bars with the boys, and to the movies or dancing with Leah. The whole town was in a party mood that week and celebrated their liberation. Too soon our break was over as new supplies had come in. We had to say good-bye to everyone, especially to the girls. We climbed on our tanks and trucks and, after some orders, were on our way. We drove in a large circle around Antwerp to the town of Mickelen where the enemy previously had been, and then further to the north—close to the Belgium-Dutch border again.

Finally we stopped at an area close to the village of Turnhout, which was near the front line. To the east of our division the American troops were dug in and to the west were the Canadians. The victorious Allied Armies had stretched their supply lines to the breaking point. Though our troops got some more supplies in, gas and rations were in short supply and ammunition stocks were dangerously low for all the Armies. Each Allied division required an average of 500 tons of material every day. Only a fraction of that amount could be delivered by truck convoys from the port of Cherbourg some 350 miles to the rear. We all had to wait to build up enough reserve to start our offensive into Holland. As it turned out, we would stay there for four weeks in a fighting position with nothing else to do but to wait.

By mid-September 1944, the Allies had liberated most of the German occupied areas in Western Europe, except Holland and some scattered regions in Belgium and France where pockets of German troops were holding several coastal areas.

◆    ◆    ◆

A month before in August of 1944, the Polish people in Warsaw had been given new hope by the approach of the Russians, who would set them free of the Nazis. The Poles had secretly organized, collected weapons, and prepared to rise against the Germans when they thought the time was ripe. Then, when they heard the Russian guns and saw the smoke of battle to the southeast, they struck. Once the Germans recovered from their surprise, they reacted strongly. While they held off the Russians to the east, other German units, such as the SS Storm Troopers of Gestapo-leader Himmler, attacked the Polish patriots. The revolt of Warsaw was suppressed in a few weeks of hard street fighting, and were only ruins were left of the city. The Russians, in sight of Warsaw, made no effort to help the Polish patriots. The herotic but unfortunate Poles soon learned why. They were still loyal to the old government that had fled to England after Poland's defeat by Germany and Russia in 1939. Since then, Stalin had set up a puppet government composed of communist refugees. He wanted to get rid of all the Poles who were loyal to the old government, and he had decided to let the Germans do it for him before he tried to capture Warsaw. Few countries have ever been treated so cruelly as was Poland in the terrible years from 1939-1945.

A few days later while remaining close to the village of Turnhout, our Lieutenant Beliski came to Stanley and me along with a few other men saying that he brought us bad news. From a sheet of paper which had come from the Headquarters out of England, he started to read the latest news from Poland and said, "All our plans and dreams to return to Poland have gone up in smoke. The Polish communist puppet government, which Stalin had organized, declared that the Polish fascist government in England and all people connected with them, were not welcome in Poland."

The dreams our lieutenant was talking about were, that all of us, as an army, would march into a free Poland, our homeland, after the war with Germany had ended. Maybe we should have already been worried with the signing of an agreement about the political future of Europe in May of that same year in 1944, between Churchill, Roosevelt and Stalin at the Yalta Conference. (Yalta was a resort in the Soviet Union) At that time was decided that Poland was to be taken from the German Army by the Russians as were other Eastern European countries. We should have known then that the Russian 'Liberators' would never set Poland free—that the moment they came into our country Poland, all important positions would be run by Communist Russia. They had already clearly shown that Stalin would not allow Poland to be set free by anyone except Communist Russia. They had no interest in humanity; Communism stood above everything.

It was a slap in our faces. We were stunned and started to discuss the situation. Here we were called "fascists." The war was not over yet, and already we were not welcome in our own country. In the days that followed there were long discussions about the new situation for the Polish officers and their soldiers. We all had fought in this war for freedom and peace so we could return home to a free and democratic country. We had lost friends and suffered with our wounded buddies, and now to be advised not to return to our country was hard to accept. I always had said to myself that I soon would be going home. It was the only thing that had me kept going during all those war years. Suddenly my dream seemed blown away. I had not counted on this! If this situation would remain after the war was over, I said to myself, what then? Where will I go?

For the following few days all that we talked about was where we would go if we could not or did not want to return home to a communist dictatorship which as we knew was nothing better than the Nazi leaders. Some of the men decided that as soon as the war was over they would go to Brazil. Others were going either to Australia, New Zealand, America or Canada, but many of them said they would return to Scotland or England where they had been married and where their wives were living. Some of the soldiers couldn't or wouldn't believe or were not sure of the fact that, as soon as the war was over, the communists would not change their mind, and we could return to Poland and be left in peace. Or maybe, we hoped, our country would be free again in a year or so. They held on to their hopes that everything would turn out all right for the Polish men. After a few days of analyzing the situation, I decided I would never go back home as long as this situation would stay as it was now, and Communist Russia was in my country. I couldn't live in a country without freedom. Maybe, I thought, I would return to Scotland when the war was over and start a new life. But I guess the Lord had a different plan for me.

◆　　　◆　　　◆

Three weeks later, we were still close to the village of Turnhout when one day I was going to the observation post with Lieutenant Barski and Eddy. First we stopped at the company's headquarters where the lieutenant had to get some information. While Eddy stayed in the carrier, I waited outside for the lieutenant's return. When looking around I noticed that three soldiers were butchering a pig on the side of a small road not far from us. I went over to them and asked jokingly if I could have a ham. All three guys started to laugh. Then one of them said, while pointing his finger at a pig that was standing a little farther away, "Look, you can have all the ham you want. There are plenty of pigs around here!"

The pigs, cows and horses were probably all set free when the farmers had abandoned their farms because of the oncoming troops. The animals were now roaming around the fields. One of the soldiers asked me, "You want one? I'll get you one. You want a small, medium or a big one?" Not believing he actually would get me a pig I laughed and said, "What about a medium one!" So the soldier took his rifle and shot one of the pigs in the head. The three men pulled the pig to me and said, "Here is your pig!" I stared at the dead animal and, while I saw a vision of pork shops before my eyes, I said thanks to the soldiers. I then went happily to the carrier where I called Stanley on my radio and told him to send the small truck to transport a pig which I got for dinner. At first he didn't believe me and asked if I had found a dead pig that was killed a week ago by the German artillery. I said to him that the pig was killed a few moments ago and was still warm.

A little later here came the small truck, and there went my pig. I had told them before they left not to eat the whole pig, but to leave a piece for the three of us, for when we came back the next day from our observation post. They took the pig to the battalion's kitchen and a lot of soldiers had a feast that night. In the meanwhile, the three of us had gone to the observation post, where we stayed for 24 hours, watching the Germans—their comings and goings.

The next day when we arrived back at our battalion and parked our carrier, I saw Stanley leaning against the half-truck yelling at me on the top of his lungs, asking if I had brought another pig. First, I didn't know what he was talking about. Then he started to laugh saying that the whole pig was gone. "But there is some bean soup left over from yesterday for you guys!" he said. Not believing him I went to the kitchen and asked the cook about the meat. The man looked at me and said, "What meat? The meat is gone!" The whole pig was eaten! When I told him that I had given special orders to save meat for three men, he answered that nobody had said anything to him about saving meat. Then he rubbed it in on how good the pig's liver had tasted, and that he and the other cooks had fried and eaten it. That evening Lieutenant Barski, Eddy and I ate bean soup for dinner.

Every time our crew was assigned to observation duty we watched the Germans through our binoculars from a hidden place in a ridge of woodland. From there we had excellent observation of the enemy. We had noticed that every day at the same time after dark, their kitchen came and, when the moon was bright, we could see their soldiers coming out from their trenches and other places. Then they would go to their kitchen and we could see them eat. Sometimes when the wind was from the north, we could hear them talk and laugh. So, for the last two weeks, we had numbered the exact distance of targets around the gathering place. Then we waited for the right moment. In the meantime, the supplies for our division had arrived and now we were waiting for the orders to start the offensive into Holland, and go on with this war.

One night, it must have been two days before the offensive and the weather was clear, we saw our chance to destroy the gathering place. I had observation duty that night and, in the pale light of the moon, I saw with my binoculars the German kitchen coming. It didn't take long until about two hundred of their soldiers got their evening meal and were sitting around on fallen trees or wherever they found a place to eat their meager meal. We knew it was the right time and informed the major. When our artillery received the message from our major to shoot, it was a ten minute Hell in the German dining place, and for many it was their last meal. The German artillery, probably thinking we had opened our offensive, started to fire. But after a while everything was quiet again with only fire burning in the destroyed German dining place.

All that we did now was wait for our orders to finally start our attack into Holland. The order came two days later. We started our offensive with heavy artillery fire. The Canadians attacked in the direction of the town of Rosendaal, the Americans toward the city of Eindhoven and our division toward the city of Breda. We had about an hour of intense fire before the infantry moved up. After a short fight we broke the front line and the enemy began to retreat. When we moved forward, we passed the place where the German kitchen had been. It sure was a mess. Somehow I couldn't help feel pity for all those soldiers who had been killed there while they were eating their supper.

We soon noticed that the Germans had left the area mined when everywhere there were explosions. It didn't take long until our tank drove over one, but lucky for us it was not a mine which could destroy a tank. Besides a sudden loud explosion which made us jump, the only damage done was two broken tank treads. We couldn't go further and while Eddy cussed about those lousy krauts, we had to stop. It was not much later when men of a special repair group came with their truck and fixed our tank, and before long we were on our way again.

We became aware that the Germans were weak in their defense, which probably was due to a shortage of weapons and ammunition. In the last couple of months the Allied Air forces had been busy destroying bridges and roads in France and Belgium. That made it difficult for the Germans to transport their soldiers and weapons from one place to the other. This had been good news of course, but now after the Germans were pushed out, it had become also difficult for our own troop and weapon transportations. We now couldn't use those railroads and roads either.

# 12

## *HOLLAND, BREDA*

*October 28, 1944.* Soon we crossed the Belgium border into Holland and advanced with little resistance from the enemy. Orders came to capture the military airfield of Gilse-Reyen which is located just east of the city of Breda. I went with a unit of our armored task force. Together with an infantry battalion we moved to the airfield, while the other units of our division moved toward Breda. When we approached the airfield we encountered heavy anti-tank fire. Our colonel called in for air assistance and, after a powerful airplane assault of rocket fire, the infantry encircled the airfield and the tanks moved in for an attack. After a short fight, it was over. The Germans came out of their bunkers with their hands up and surrendered. When the lieutenant and I looked at the German soldiers, we noticed that besides the older ones there were many very young soldiers. They could not have been older than sixteen or at the most seventeen and their young old faces were lost under the deep rims of their helmets. They were very scared of us, and we wondered why they were so afraid. It was evening before every German prisoner was searched for weapons and sent on their way in trucks. We decided that we would stay at the airfield that night and try to get a little rest in our tanks or wherever we soldiers could find a place to lay ourselves down for a few hours.

Early the next morning we moved toward Breda. For me it was just another city which we passed through on the way to somewhere else. How little I knew then that later I would live for seven years in that city of Breda. As we reached the town, most of Breda was already liberated by other units of our division. Only small pockets of snipers were left which the infantry was cleaning up. Only on the north side of the town were the Germans still resisting.

Our crew was sent to the train station which is located just in front where the enemy was holding on. We climbed onto the roof where we had a good observation of the German infantry which was dug in that neighborhood. I was tired and figured I had been in action for the last 48 hours with little sleep in between. As soon as we got to the top of the station, I told Stanley to call the kitchen chef on my radio to send us some food because we were hungry. And also to tell Lieutenant Barsky we were waiting for another crew to relieve us.

After two hours of watching the Germans from the rooftop and reporting their locations and activities, the new crew finally came and took our place. But still no food. Our lieutenant, Eddy and I went into our carrier and drove through some streets in the direction where our battalion was located. A few minutes later we saw the small truck of the kitchen coming with our food. We halted the car and asked the kitchen help what had taken them so long. They said that they had been unable to find us. Anyway, we finally had our food plus some extra and were looking for a place to eat. We stopped on a side street by the side of a factory named of "Teolin Verf." I later learned it was a paint factory. As soon as we had settled ourselves to eat and enjoyed our first bite, suddenly there people came from out of nowhere, most of them children. They were staring at us with hungry, curious faces. They did not ask us for food but we saw the hunger in their eyes. Even though we ourselves were hungry, we could not eat anymore and gave all our food away to the children. They grabbed the food with both hands while saying, "Thank you, thank you." After our food was gone, we got into our carrier and drove away.

In the meantime our battalion had gone into a Dutch military camp which was on the edge of the city and not far from where we had been planning to eat our food. After some driving we found the camp and first thing I did was to investigate the buildings for a place to sleep. But nowhere was there a bed, mattress or other furniture to be found—just a layer of dirty straw over the floors and outside. We soon wondered what those Germans had been sleeping on. After looking everywhere I finally found a place on an office floor that was the least dirty. I laid my things down and, after I got something to eat, went outside where I saw Stefan Ratke.

Stefan was a soldier I first met in Hull, England. He was born in Poland from a Polish mother and a German father who had been a fisherman. Stefan had lived all his life in a fishing village on the Baltic Sea in Poland with his family. Because his father was German, Stefan had been forced to fight with the German Army in Africa even though he himself was a Polish citizen. After the surrender of German General Rommel's Army in Africa, Stefan became a prisoner of war of the British Army. There he and other Polish soldiers who had been in the same situation were segregated from the rest of the prisoners. After a thorough interrogation by Polish Officers he was sent, together with other Polish men, to Scotland where he became a soldier in the Polish Armored Division. The Polish Army gave him a new name, Stefan Ratke. It was for his and his family's protection in case he ever would become prisoner of war of the Germans.

Stefan was staying outside the barracks smoking a cigarette and after seeing me asked if I wanted to go with him looking for a bar. Maybe we could get a drink, he said. I was tired and had not much ambition to go, but thinking I could not sleep anyway because of everyone walking over the floor in that office where I wanted to sleep, I said that I would go with him.

We noticed that the whole camp was surrounded by a high fence. Since we did not want to walk to the gates, which were on the other side of that camp, we looked around for another way to get out. I saw a hole in the fence close to where our carrier was parked, and Stefan and I climbed through it. We came into a neighborhood street and from there we started to walk to, which we hoped, the main street. In the meantime we looked for a bar. It did not take long until we saw on the corner of a street a nice looking large bar. As soon as we walked through the door, we noticed that no one was there. We only saw a man who was working behind the counter. Puzzled we asked the man if we could get a beer. He looked at us and started to laugh saying that he had not seen an alcoholic drink for a long time. He then suggested a "surrogate" beer—it was the only drink he had, he said. So Stefan and I said we would try one. We never had heard of that brand name. After we drank one sip we looked at each other. Then after another sip, we put our glasses down. It tasted sour and awful. We never had tasted imitation beer. We wondered how anyone could drink this stuff and what it was made from. We talked to the bar owner who was thankful we had liberated his town. In broken English he told us about the difficult war years in Holland and how little there was to buy. Stefan wanted to talk some more to the man, but by now I hardly could keep my eyes open any longer. I went outside and soon Stefan followed.

While crossing the street to go back to the military camp, we saw two Dutch girls coming from the opposite direction. They must have come from the downtown area, going home. Even though snipers and small pockets of the enemy were usually left in the towns we liberated, many of the people of those places soon came out of their homes and shelters and walked around. As we passed the girls, Stefan said something to the tallest of the two while I walked further on and then stopped. I looked at the girl who also had walked further on and then stood still while saying something to her girlfriend. I was very tired, but I remember exactly what she was wearing and that I thought what a pretty girl she was. A few minutes later Stefan and I were on our way again. While we walked to the barracks, Stefan told me to go to sleep but just for two hours because, he said, he had told that one girl that we would meet again by the fence, early that evening. While we slipped through the hole in the fence, I told Stefan, "O.K. I will go, but let me sleep at least a few hours!" That one girl got my attention, and I wouldn't mind seeing her again.

Exactly two hours later Stefan woke me and suggested to get some food from my tank for the girls. Half awake I got up from the hard office floor and walked to the tank to gather some cans of meat and chocolate. We went through the hole in the fence again and waited there wondering if the Dutch girls would show up. It was a short time later when we saw the two girls coming and went to meet them. After we first introduced ourselves I learned that the girl whom I thought prettiest was named Eef. The name of the taller one was Chiel, and I guessed both were about 19 or 20 years old.

After the short introduction, the girls took us to the house where Eef lived. This was close by and in the same neighborhood where we had tried to eat. While carrying the cans of food in my pocket, we walked the short distance and entered Eef 's house. The house was damaged from the grenades the night before, which had blasted out all their windows. As soon as we entered Eef's house, we were introduced to her family.

Her father, a military man as I later learned, took my arm and lead me to a table. He had a map of Holland-Belgium spread out. He wanted to know exactly where the Germans were holding out. He would do this for the following few weeks, always asking us where the front-line was. Because Stefan spoke the German language fluently, and the family could understand and speak some of that language, he did most of the talking. I remember how glad that family was with all the cans of food we had laid on the table. While sitting in a comfortable chair I thought what a nice family it was, and I thought about my own parents, brothers and sisters. How much I wanted to see them. Looking at the youngest brother I thought how my own brothers, except the youngest, all had become almost adults by now. They were not the young boys anymore as the last time I saw them back in Miedzychud.

Eef's oldest brother, by the name of Jan, was a light blond pleasant young man in his early twenties. He could speak the English language, and so the conversation was a mixture of Dutch, German, English and a lot of hand gestures. The younger brother by the name of Henk was all excited to see two Allied soldiers in his living room and tried to understand those different languages we were speaking. He was tall, very thin and about 15 years old.

We were there about a hour when Eef's brother left, and the two girls decided that they would walk us back to the hole in the fence. Arriving there they said goodbye, and I thought we would not see them again. Who knows where I would be tomorrow, I thought. But the following evening we were still in Breda, and

Stefan and I decided to go back to Eef's home. We enjoyed the family and it was better then hanging around in the camp. And besides that, we liked the girls and hoped they were home.

◆          ◆          ◆

After two days we drove the Germans completely out of Breda and over the Wilhelmina Canal. This canal was about 6 or 7 miles north of the city. It was there where the Germans were dug in and were holding on. Even though the canal was about 60 feet wide, it was about 45 miles long connecting one waterway to the other. The canals in Holland were built not only to keep the low land from flooding, but also as a waterway used by farmers for transporting their grains, produce and potatoes by ship or barge to villages and towns. Many of the man-made canals in Holland have a 5 to 6 feet high sloping dike or dam of earth on both sides, which was thrown up in digging the canal to prevent flooding.

It had been a bad situation for our infantry at the canal while trying to cross over to the other side. Many of our soldiers were killed or wounded by the resistance of the enemy there. Since all the bridges over the canal had been blown up by the Germans, we had to go over by rubber rafts. But the dug-in enemy was waiting for us on the north side of the canal and destroyed everything that moved.

One night I was with the infantry, carrying my heavy radio on my back. After a whole night of our artillery fire, our infantry tried to cross over the canal by rubber rafts to establish a foothold on the other side. It was dark, and a light misty rain was falling. While I was sitting on the foot of the dike busy reporting to my company, a soldier with his machine gun on his shoulder was trying to go over the dike to get to a rubber raft. He was almost on top of the dike above me when he was shot. As I later would find out, the shells hit him right in his face. When he fell backward, his machine gun hit my head and back. I must have been knocked unconscious because I cannot remember anything after that.

Hours later when I woke up with a sharp pain in my back and a dull pain in my head I felt sick. The dead soldier was lying beside me with half his brain hanging out and his face gone. His blood was all over me. I tried to understand what had happened. All was strangely quiet now. I heard only the sound of the water flowing by in the canal. The rain had stopped and the sun was just rising over the treetops of a forest which was a short distance from where I was lying. I remember how very cold I felt. I moved my legs and got some feeling back in them. It had me worried at first that maybe I had broken my back. I think after lying for a long time motionless in an awkward position my body had gone numb. I looked around me. I knew that something had gone wrong with the crossing of the canal. The infantry had withdrawn and only the dead were left behind.

While I lay there behind the dike in some gravel and grass, I tried to get my senses back. Suddenly I saw in a short distance a large farm horse. It was alone by itself walking toward the forest. As I looked more intently, I saw a soldier on one side of the horse. His uniform was torn and bloody. He was hiding behind the horse from possible German machine gun fire while trying to get to a safer place. While watching this strange sight I thought I also should try to find a safer place and wait. Or maybe I could crawl to the forest and hide there until, hopefully, our soldiers would come back.

Slowly I crawled away from the corpse beside me in the direction of the wood. I did not got far until I felt nausea coming over me and had to rest. Lying there in the wet grass, I suddenly heard a sound coming from the forest. As I looked up, I saw that it was a carrier moving toward in my direction. With all the strength in me I tried to get up, but I couldn't. I saw the carrier coming closer and when it reached me, I saw two men jumping out of it. I recognized them as our Lieutenant Barski and Eddy. How thankful I was to see them. They got me in the carrier and drove quickly back into the forest.

Later Eddy told me about that night. He said it must have been at the same time as I got hit, the Germans had opened a fierce counter attack. They had probably waited until our soldiers crossed the canal in their rubber rafts. Only a few of our men, who tried to get a foothold on the other side of the canal, came back. Our offensive had failed and the rest of our infantry retreated from the canal and went into the forest where they reorganized themselves. In all the confusion they probably had overlooked to make sure if I had survived or not. They thought that I had been killed because of all the blood that was over me and how I was positioned. Later, when Lieutenant Barski found out that I was missing, he had taken Eddy with him in the carrier and wanted to go back to the place were he saw me the last time. He wanted to be sure and had taken a chance.

I must have lost consciousness again when riding in the carrier because I remember only when I woke up and was lying in a hospital bed with a doctor checking my back, and a nurse standing at his side. I remember how very tired I felt and was glad when the doctor and nurse left. My head pounded and I was glad that it was so quiet in the hospital. All what I wanted was to sleep. I closed my eyes but could not keep them closed; there were too many bloody sights behind my eyelids.

After a few hours of lying in the bed, sometimes sleeping and other times awake, I tried to get up but was too weak. The doctor had told me that I would have to stay in the hospital for at least a few days. In the afternoon a nurse came into my room to bring a new uniform and new underwear and laid them in a small cabinet. After waiting until she left I tried to get carefully out of my bed. While holding onto the bedrail, I slowly got dressed and, while holding on to the wall, walked on wobbly legs out of my room and out of the hospital.

It made no sense, of course, but then nothing did. I think I was afraid I would not be able to stay with my company and my buddies if I was left behind in a hospital, and they would go further on. I went back to the barracks which was almost connected with the hospital and which was only a few minutes walk away. As soon as I got to the barracks I had to lay down as I sure was not feeling very well. After a while our regiment doctor walked in saying that he had received a call from the hospital that I was gone. He was very angry with me and called me a name which I would rather not repeat. But then, he was right. Because for years afterwards I had bad headaches and pains in my back, which I could have probably avoided by doing what the doctor had told me to do. When our company doctor had left, I rested a few more hours until evening. I then got up and started to walk to Eef's home. I thought seeing her would make me feel better. Halfway there I saw Stefan walking with Eef and Chiel in my direction. The only thing I remember was that we went to Chiel's house, which was closer by, and I sat down on an easy chair. The next thing I remember was that I woke up the next morning in my sleeping quarters and feeling somewhat better.

Eef told me later that Stefan had brought me back to the quarters the evening before because, as she said, the way I looked and acted was not very good. Every day for the next week the doctor examined me and ordered me under bed rest, which I did, but only in the morning. In the afternoons I was over at Eef's house usually together with Stefan who was my interpreter. If I went alone to her house I tried to talk to Eef and her mother using a lot of hand gestures. When I felt much better I went with Eef for walks while we told each other the names of things we saw.

In the meantime the Allies, at the cost of 13.000 casualties, gained complete control of the territory on both sides of the Schelde, and which could open the waterway to Antwerp. Because of the flooded low-lying land, the infantrymen had been slogging through the flooded fields, and it soon was called the nastiest campaign of the war. Scottish infantrymen had been fighting building to building in the small towns to gain control of the island Walcheren, Holland. Then on

November 3, after bitter fighting, the British and Scottish forces finally gained control of the badly needed waterway to Antwerp. More than one hundred Royal Navy mine sweepers began clearing the 60-mile-long Schelde Estuary of the magnetic mine fields, and twenty-two days later de Schelde was declared safe for shipping.

◆      ◆      ◆

After three weeks of staying in Breda, we moved northward. While I had been recuperating, our infantry battalion had finally crossed the Wilhelmina Canal. Together with the Canadians to our left and the American troops to our right we had driven the Germans back over the broad river Maas and into North Holland. The principal rivers of Holland are Ryn (Rhine), Maas (Meuse) and Schelde (Scheldt). The German Army also was driven to the north side of the long and very important Moerdyk Bridge. This bridge which lay about 17 miles north of Breda, connects south and north Holland over the wide river Maas. Even though there was fighting over this great bridge in 1940 and again in 1944, it was never destroyed. I think this bridge was just too important for both sides, for the transportation of their great Armies.

One day our regiment moved out from Breda to take position just south of this river. Together with the Canadian and American troops we were now guarding the long and important river Maas. This great river begins in France and empties into the North Sea in Holland. While our battalion moved to the village of s'Gravemoer, which is about 18 mile northeast of Breda, other battalions went to other villages in that area. We all were staying in the homes of the citizens of those small farm towns. Eddy and I moved into an upstairs room of the home of an older couple in the village of s'Gravemoer.

During the Battle of Arnhem the Germans had destroyed many dikes between the network of Holland's rivers and canals. It also had brought some flooding further west unto the area we were staying. The low-lying land of Holland and the flooding had made the use of our tanks impossible, and we were only able to drive on the roads. Because of the many waterways, the Allied forces could not make further advance into Holland and were now in a holding position south of the great rivers.

The whole area where our division was staying was farmland. Here and there were farm villages which were connected by a few narrow roads which made driving our military vehicles difficult. Our company had an observation post established in one of the hastily evacuated German bunkers. Those empty bunkers were made from wood and located in a bank of the river Maas. It was about half an hour drive from where I was living in s'Gravemoer. The area of the river where our observation post was located was normally not as wide as it looked when we were there, as we found out. Because of the floodings it was shallow and just looked very wide. It was close to a nature area with islands and waterways where the Dutch went boating and fishing for their pleasure in better times. This area was called the Biesbos and, I am sure, must have been very pretty. To the north, not far from our side of the river, was a larger island where the enemy was dug in wooden bunkers. How many soldiers there were on that island we did not know, but we expected at least 3 to 4 hundred German soldiers. Every day the German artillery would start shooting in our direction, not aiming at anything, but just for the Hell of it. Soon we were doing the same, just to bother them. After a few weeks it became more serious on the river when almost every morning we found some of our soldiers killed lying in their bunkers. No one ever saw or heard anything, not even the guards. We suspected that it was German commandos specially trained for this kind of warfare. They came and left over the water without a sound.

Once in every four days I had 24-hour observation duty on the Maas river. From the bunker I had to report all German activities which I observed on the island and then reported to my headquarters. Usually we were with our three, our Lieutenant Belinski or Lieutenant Barski and another man from our crew.

When I was free from duty, Stefan and I sometimes went for a ride with one of our trucks which happened to go to Breda that day, and we visited our girlfriends. Or on weekends, when possible, I hitchhiked Saturday mornings to Eef's house and went back on Sunday afternoon. Many times on Saturday nights, there was a Red Cross dance in a school not far from Eef's house which was open not only for soldiers, but also for the public. Those dances were fun. There was always a good band playing, and a lot of soldiers and British army nurses danced to the latest American dance music. The people from the neighborhood were happy finally to have a good time, and they loved the American dances which were new to them. For the last four years, ever since the German occupation, they had not heard American or English music. Also in the last year before the liberation, all dances and other places where people gathered were strictly prohibited by the Germans.

Usually we went with Stefan and Eef's girlfriend Chiel to those Red Cross dances. I always had a great time and forgot the war for a few hours. Those Saturday nights I stayed over at Eef's parents' house and slept in her brother Henk's bedroom. Her oldest brother, Jan, who had been with the underground, had gone into the Dutch Brigade as soon as the south of Holland was liberated. After that he was not home much anymore.

On those Sunday mornings before I went back to my battalion, Eef and I always went for a long walk. Usually we went to the Wilhelmina Park and walked back to her home on small farm roads behind their house. While walking and laughing we tried to learn each other's language. The Polish language is difficult and not easy to learn, but soon Eef could say a few words in Polish. The Dutch language, on the other hand, was not difficult for me to learn since I had learned the German language as a child at school, and also from my mother. Every day I learned a few more Dutch words, and soon Eef and I were better able to understand each other, even though we needed a lot of hand gestures.

After the weekend at Eef's house, I hitchhiked back to the small town where my company was stationed. While thinking about Eef, I walked to my quarters back through the narrow dark streets which were lined with tanks and trucks. I always thought how pleasant the weekend had been. I almost had forgotten the peace and quiet hours of a day, and I thought that there were still such things.

◆       ◆       ◆

One evening Lieutenant Beletski, Felix and I left for observation duty on the Maas. The weather had become cold with early freezing temperatures, too early for the time of the year. It was only the beginning of December. It was cold and a light snow was falling when we came to our observation post in the bunker. Even wearing our white snow overalls, we felt the cold coming from over the water. I remember how quiet it was, maybe a little too quiet. No gunfire or anything, just a cold dark night at the river Maas. I had no enemy activity to report to my headquarters of our battalion. All seemed quiet. The lieutenant tried to make something hot for us to drink on a kerosene heater we had brought in. Since it had been so cold, they had given us a bottle of rum, probably to keep us warm. But it tasted bad and we left it alone. While we were watching the Germans on the island through our binoculars, we talked about the war and when it all was going to end. But in spite of everybody being alert and wide awake the whole night, when the first morning light came, there also came the discovery of the killing of seven of our soldiers. Five soldiers inside a bunker and two of the patrols outside.

Again it seemed the work of German commandos; noiselessly and with great skill. No one of us or the many guards had seen or heard anything that whole night. Af course we were all upset about this. We all had known the men so well.

The following day we heard from our headquarters that General Montgomery wanted to make an end to all the killing at the river Maas. He was going to get rid of all the Germans on the island. The American and Canadian troops had experienced the same problems at the river as we had. Many of their men had been killed the same way as our men had. That same week, The Second British Army brought in a Canadian battalion of artillery and two battalions of Canadian and Polish infantry. After a long intense artillery fire, the infantry moved in on assault boats and finished the last of about 400 enemy soldiers on the island.

It was a few days later when I walked careful over the partly frozen water to the island and checked it out. It was swept clean of everything alive. The whole island looked like a plowed farm field with all bunkers gone but one. I entered the bunker and looked around. There was a gauntness and darkness in that place despite the sunlight which came through an opening made by a shell. The former occupants must had been killed or had left in a hurry, since some of their personal belongings were left behind. Besides the regular soldier things, I found also a wallet with pictures and letters from children to their father. I looked at the pictures, but put it back where I had found it. As I was leaving the island, I saw further away a barge halfway under the ice. It looked as if it was on the edge of the river and the flooded land and had coal on board. I thought it was probably wrecked by an earlier air raid.

On the way back to s'Gravemoer, I talked about the barge to an infantryman I knew. He told me that for the last few nights, the Germans from the north bank and our soldiers from the south had taken turns taking coal from the barge without firing at each other. I guess that the soldiers of both sides had problems with the cold! It was like a silent agreement between us and the German soldiers that we would not shoot while either side was taking the coal. Thinking about this it gave me an idea, but to work this out took me a whole night.

A few days later, I put my plan together and told Eddy and Jurek about it. After hearing me out they said that they would help me. That same day I got two large jute sacks from the kitchen. I then told Lieutenant Belinski that we needed some coal for heating the house in which Eddy and I were staying, and we would not be gone long with the tank. We would take the coal early the following morning, we said. The lieutenant told me to be careful, but had no objections further. Taking a tank for private use is against army regulations, of course.

It was still dark when we got our tank and Jurek, Eddy and I were on our way on our little adventure. The early morning was cold with a pale sun coming up through a thin fog. An icy mist was hanging over the frozen water. We jumped from our tank and quietly slid into our snow overalls, which made us look like ghosts. We then started to move on our bellies over the frozen shallow floodwater toward the coal barge with our empty sacks. Carefully we listened for any sounds coming from the German side of the river. It was very quiet. As soon as we had reached the barge and were sure there were no German soldiers on the other side of the vessel doing the same thing as we were doing, we filled the sacks full of coal. As it turned out the coal was anthracite, which is the best coal of all. We worked fast while all the time listening for any sounds which could foretell disaster. When the sacks were full, we gave each other a sign and slid as quickly as we could back over the ice again. As soon as we reached the place from where we had started, we threw the sacks of coal on the tank, took our overalls off, got into our tank and drove to Breda. I'll never forget the faces of Eef and her mother when we drove our tank up to their house, jumped down and deposited the sacks of coal into their front yard.

For the people, coal and especially anthracite for heating their homes, was a luxury few people had that winter. Most people were using wood and many were burning wood from their homes, just to stay warm. After the coal delivery we went immediately back to s'Gravemoer and drove the tank through a side entrance back in its parking place, hoping no one had noticed anything. When I came back to the house where Eddy and I were staying, I saw that the windows of the house were blown out. A German V-I rocket had gone wrong and had landed not far from the house, shattering the windows.

The V-I was a real pain. They were launched somewhere in west Holland for the destruction of Antwerp. But many times on route, they malfunctioned and came down sometimes destroying farms or houses. The German V-2 rocket went much higher and was aimed mainly at London. The V-I and the V-2 rockets were one of the secret weapons on which Hitler increasingly pinned his hopes of victory. However, the V weapons were developed too late to change the course of the war.

A few days later, a sergeant from my battalion woke me up. It was midday and I had come back from my 24-hour duty on the river a few hours earlier. The sergeant told me to report to Major Makuch as soon as possible. A little later when walking to the major's office I thought, "What does he want now? It must be urgent because he knew I just came back from my duty." Major Makuch always sought me out for special duties. But then, he always gave me special favors too; such as giving me a pass whenever possible.

As soon as I walked into his office, the major told me the situation and said that we had to supply artillery support in case it was needed, to a group of English commandos who were going over the river on a mission. Major Makuch continued further saying, that they needed a forward observer in case the commandos would run into difficulty. They would shoot pink flares off in the sky if they encountered serious problems. When seeing the flares, it was then my duty to report this by radio to the artillery. They in turn would put up a screen of artillery fire in front of the commandos, so they could return back to safety. The major said that the captain of the artillery was already informed about the distance etc. Then he continued on telling us that before reaching that area of the river from where the commando's mission would start, we had to go first through a minefield. That minefield had been laid by our engineers in case of a German counter-attack. We were to follow our engineers who knew the mines locations. Major Makuch said, "Jozef, if you are willing to volunteer for this, then take another man you can trust with you for helping with carrying the radio. Lieutenant Barski will go also." I answered the major that I was willing to go and would take one of my buddies who would be free of duty that night. He then told me to be back as soon as possible with the other man for instructions. While leaving the office, I knew I would ask Freddy Karlik—he liked action. Not much later I was back at the major's office with Freddy for instructions.

It was dark, and heavy low hanging clouds foretold not much good. We had driven our carrier and arrived about one hour later at our meeting place on the edge of the one-half mile long minefield. The commandos, dressed in camouflaged uniforms, were already there. I counted twelve men. After some time the two engineers arrived in their jeep, got out and joined the waiting men. The group of commandos got their last minute instructions from their commander and then we went on our way. First came the two engineers who would pave the way for us, carrying their maps and mine detectors. They were followed by the commandos, then the lieutenant and then me with my radio and last of all came Freddy.

It was the first trip for me into a minefield, and it was nerve racking. One after the other, the men moved slowly and silently into the cold night, sometimes going straight sometimes in a curved line, toward the river. Freddy and I took turns carrying the heavy radio when the line had to stop. The reason for stopping was usually for a mine. I don't recall how long it took us to go through that minefield, but finally we reached the river bank. The river must had been very wide and deep there, and not completely frozen over as I saw the dark water glistening in the light of the moon which peeked once in a while from behind a cloud. Later I learned that on that area two rivers came together. As soon as we had reached the water, the group of commandos immediately inflated their rubber boats which took only a few minutes. Their commander then told us that they would be back shortly. We wished them good luck and, without a sound, they disappeared over the water into the dark of night.

The engineers and the three of us tried to make the best of it, staying or sitting on boulders on the side of the broad water. We waited and waited. One hour passed, then two hours, no sound, no flares, nothing. We listened to every rustle in the dry bushes. We said to each other that maybe the commando group came a little further down the river when returning. So we started to take turns scouting up and down the side of the river, but no sight of them was to be seen. Three, then four hours went by and still no commandos. By now, we were very cold. Even in our heavy white winter overalls with caps, we could feel the icy north wind from over the water. The strain of waiting started to get to us, and we felt weary.

When the darkness gave way to the first morning light, the lieutenant decided I should call the captain of our artillery and ask him if we should wait any longer or go back. The captain answered that he was going to send someone over to Major Makuch because he could not make that decision. After a while we got the answer, which was to wait until full light, and then to look once more on the river's bank. If we found nothing, then we were to come back. After a hour or more of waiting and searching for any signs of the commandos, we decided to end our mission.

I took one last look over the river—now blanketed with fog. It was very still, and I knew that something had gone wrong for the 12 men on the other side of the river. We followed the engineers back through the minefield again. Our line was short now with only a few men. It was much easier going in daylight than the night before. Even so, I was glad when we walked out of that minefield. Soon we drove off to our company; the engineers in their jeep and we in our carrier. The commandos truck left with only the driver. A few days later, when I asked the major about the commandos, he said that they had never heard from them again.

# 13

## "THE BATTLE OF THE BULGE"

The worst winter in fifty years had settled over Europe bringing with it heavy snows and icy winds. It was then that the Germans struck back with a surprise blow that Hitler believed would end the war in his favor. It was Hitler's greatest gamble—an all-out attack aimed at Antwerp. The attack came on December 16, 1944. Without warning, a massive enemy force burst out of Germany and hurled itself at the American and the Allied troops stationed along the Belgium and Luxembourg-German borders. The assault marked the start of the offensive that the Americans soon nicknamed "The Battle of the Bulge."

The situation in the Ardennes was serious, even desperate. It was a nightmare for the tens of thousands of young inexperienced American soldiers who came fresh from the boot camps out of America and were stationed there. The snow was deep and the temperature low. Tanks stalled on icy hillsides. Trucks and antitanks guns jackknifed and collided. Bridges everywhere were out.

On December 18, while the Allies teetered on the brink of disaster, our whole division went to the vicinity of the city Den Bosch, which is about 40 miles east of Breda. I think because of the bad situation with "The Battle of the Bulge," we and other Allied troops were sent to that vicinity in case something went wrong with the battle and the German Army would break through. American troops, who had been already stationed in the area of Den Bosh and further south, and the many other troops who came in, were waiting now for further orders.

For four weeks I stayed in Den Bosch in a house with a family. We soldiers would do nothing more than come together, then play cards, or sometimes go to the movies. For most soldiers waiting was one of the most frustrating aspect of the war. It was something I never got used to. In the time I was in Den Bosch I learned a lot of the Dutch language from a newspaper I sometimes found laying in the house where I was staying. I wanted more then anything else to be able to have a conversation with Eef when we were together. I knew I had fallen in love with her, but did not always understand her feelings about things.

It was Christmas of 1944 and I wanted to go to Breda to be with Eef and her family. Because of the serious situation in the Ardennes with the battle, we soldiers could not get passes. So I went to our sergeant-major (he was usually the one who gave the passes) and asked him of he thought if I could go for a few hours to Breda to have dinner with my girlfriend and her family. He answered me that since there was no news from the Ardennes battleground, he thought I could go but had to be back before dark. This gave me enough time to see the girl I love, I thought, even if it was only for a little while. Stefan, I and another soldier who also had asked to go to Breda for a few hours, jumped in a jeep. It didn't take long until we were on our way.

That winter there were no Christmas trees in the homes. I guess life was too difficult for everybody. Bad news trickled in from north Holland, which was the area still occupied by the Germans. People there were living under extremely difficult conditions, and many were dying from hunger, cold and disease. Eef's parent's family were all living in that part of Holland and naturally were very worried about them. Communication with north Holland was non-existent anymore. It was a hard, cold and worrisome winter, that winter of 1944-'45. But for a few hours Eef and I were together and that was all that mattered at that moment for us. I ate Christmas dinner with them; it was simple but made with love. Food was still scarce for the people in the liberated areas. From the tank I took a few cans of food for the family. It was the only gift I was able to bring for Christmas. Too soon, the guys came again for me in their jeep. After saying good-bye to the family and kissing my special girl goodbye, hoping I would soon be back, I jumped in the jeep and went back to Den Bosch.

In the meantime the battle in the Belgium Ardennes forest became the most confused battle on the western front in WW II. The front-line broke up into an unsolved jigsaw puzzle, and there were days when nobody was sure which side held a given town. More than a million soldiers were now involved. The weather was bitter cold and many wounded men froze to death in their foxholes.

On New Year's Day, Stanley, Felix, Freddy and I decided to go sliding on a frozen field that had been flooded. There were many people on ice skates or, as we, just sliding and having some fun. Sometime later that afternoon, we suddenly heard a V-I coming over. It was very low with its flame coming out of its tail. It must have been not much higher than the treetops which were growing on the side of a road. The V-I went over the frozen area where the people skated, then it turned around and went back from where it came. Then it turned again and went in a circular movement. In the meantime the people were in panic. They ran or skated in the opposite direction that the V-I was going. Soon everyone went in every which way, depending on the direction of the missile. I could not help but burst out laughing. It was such a funny sight to see. Finally, the "drunk" missile went in the direction of Antwerp and disappeared out of sight, leaving the people frustrated behind.

End of January 1945. The month-long bloody battle in the Ardennes was over when surrounded American soldiers made a heroic stand at Bastogne, refusing to surrender in the face of what looked like impossible odds. The third American Army, under General Patton, stopped the great German thrust. The Germans were pushed back with 170,000 of their men dead, wounded or captured. The American and Allied troops had lost 75,000 of their men.

After "The Battle Of The Bulge" had come to an end, we—the Polish Division—went back to the vicinity of Breda again. As the war raged on in Italy, the Russian Army was only 35 miles east of Berlin. There the German troops resisted so fanatically, that they completely halted the Russian advance. Unable to move further westward, the Russians moved north into East Prussia. On the western front, the wide waters of the Rhine River flowed before the British and American Armies; a formidable barrier.

In the meanwhile, our whole division was kept on hold until further notice. Our company was staying just north of Breda in a small town named Oosterhout. When our division had left in December for the area in and around Den Bosch, the Canadians had been assigned to take our place on the river Maas. They would stay there until the end of the war.

I could not have wished for a better holding place, so close to Breda and my special girl, Eef. We saw each other a lot in that time. During this time, I had helped a soldier that I knew well, to get a pass to France where his parents lived. When he returned from his furlough, he gave me a civilian suit for helping him get his pass. It had been hanging in a closet at Eef's parent's house. I always disliked a soldier's uniform, for never in my heart was I a soldier. It was against army regulations, of course, to wear anything else. But now that I was here in Breda, I thought I wanted to feel and look like a civilian again for a change. Especially when Eef and I were going out. It sure was very strange, after wearing an army uniform for five years, to see myself in a suit. I remember it was a dark blue striped suit with a white shirt. The tie I borrowed from Eef's brother. After looking at myself in the mirror, I felt great and ready to go out on the town.

Eef and I enjoyed dancing in the bar of a hotel which was located on the edge of the forest. It was always crowded there that winter with Canadian and Polish soldiers who were stationed in the area around Breda. The bands which were playing in that bar were always good, and the atmosphere was great. Sometimes when we did not want to walk so far to that hotel, we would go to a dance place in downtown where the young people from Breda came to dance. But wherever we went, it was very crowded. The American and English soldiers were stationed further to the east of Breda. Even though they came to Breda, we never saw many of those soldiers.

On Sundays we usually went for a long walk. We both loved hiking and I think I've never stopped walking since I met Eef. In that cold winter when the air was frosty and clear, we hiked for hours through the forest in the snow. Thick snow would be laying on the evergreen branches, which made it look like a postcard. It was beautiful then, and it brought me back to my childhood when, as a child, I loved to look for deer in the snow covered forest. When Eef and I would come home after our hike in the forest, Eef's mother had hot imitation tea ready for us.

Of course, we went to the movies many times to see the latest films from America. I think the American movies must have followed closely behind the soldiers. Finally the language had become less and less of a barrier for Eef and me. I had learned the Dutch language quickly, even though I had still much more to learn. Especially when Eef teased me and I didn't understand the words she used.

My thoughts went back to Poland a lot in that time. For five years I had heard nothing from my family. Communications with Eastern Europe were still none existent. I was anxious to know about my parents, brothers and sisters. What had happened to them and were they still living in our house? Would I ever see them again? I knew the war was coming to an end soon, and if I would make it, what would I do then? Would I go back to my country? All these questions went through my head. But then, when I saw Eef again, she lifted me out of my depressing moods, and everything was better for awhile. By now, Eef (Efka, as I would call her) and I had become close in our feeling for each other. We enjoyed each other's company when we were together and understood each other's moods when things were difficult.

◆    ◆    ◆

Meanwhile, the Allies prepared for the final drive into Germany. The harsh winter had left Europe and the snow was gone. It was the first week of March when orders came from General Montgomery that our division was going to move out from the vicinity of Breda toward Germany for a massive offensive. The good times with Efka were coming to an end. We both had known this. We had known that someday I would be moving on. But it did not make it any easier when we said goodbye to each other. I had taken her in my arms and said that wherever I would go or whatever would happen, I would never forget her, and always would love her. I was not sure if I would be coming back. In war you take one day at a time; that was all you could take.

Two days later our whole division rolled over the highway from Breda toward the city of Den Bosch. The going was slow and many times we stopped before we drove slowly further again. Most of the time I was staying half way outside of the tank turret opening for some fresh air. From Den Bosch we went to the city Nymegen where we slept that night in our tank. The following day we drove between the rivers Maas and Rhine where some of the worst fighting terrain in Europe is located; flooded, waterlogged fields. From there we crossed the border into Germany without resistance from the enemy. As soon as we drove on German soil, a strange feeling came over me. Here I am, I thought, in the country of the enemy I had been preparing for so long. It was difficult to believe I was actually on German ground, the ground of the Nazis. But it also was the ground where I was born and lived the first few years of my life.

We passed a small town which was completely destroyed. We saw no one; it seemed to be empty of any life. We went further and were now close to the famous Siegfriedline, (Westwall) which is a German defense line of large bunkers and heavy artillery. They are connected with each other by underground tunnels. This Siegfriedline, which ran from north to south close to the German border, stretched from Holland, Belgium and France to Switzerland. We encountered weak resistance at the Siegfriedline which surprised us greatly. After a short fight, it was over. We took German prisoners and weapons.

After a few days of soaking rain we swept forward to the Rhine River, the mighty river, the last great barrier protecting Germany in the west. Some of the villages and isolated farmhouses along the way had been transformed into fortified strong points which we had to destroy first. The German troops which were well dug in on the opposite bank of the Rhine, had dynamited and destroyed all the Rhine bridges, as far as we knew. They fought bitterly to hold the Allied troops from crossing, and bombarded us with heavy artillery.

When our division had taken position, our crew and I went up a high hill overlooking the Rhine to observe enemy positions. There I saw, for the first time, the mighty river Rhine before me. It flowed from its Alpine sources in Switzerland 450 miles through Germany before joining the Old Maas river at Rotterdam in Holland, emptying into the North Sea. At some points the river had served as a major artery of commerce for carrying the products of industry to the North Sea ports for transshipment to the world beyond. I thought back for a moment when I was a child in school and had learned about this mighty river. I thought who could have dreamed I would be fighting a war on its bank someday. There were now more than 1 million soldiers ready to attack. Besides American, English, Canadian and Polish divisions, there also were the Scottish—ready for the assault over the Rhine and further into enemy territory. It was very crowded everywhere with soldiers of many countries waiting for the final thrust into Germany.

The following day in the early morning light Lieutenant Barski, Felix, Eddy and I looked for a good location for an observation post. After a whole night of showers the rain had stopped. There was a haze as well as smoke hanging in the air. From our high place we saw below us a wide, long-destroyed bridge laying in the water. It had connected the east and west banks of the river before being blown up by the Germans. Somewhere there in that area, I thought, we will be going over to the other side of this mighty Rhine River. "It will be a hell of a job to lay a pontoon bridge down here," I said to the lieutenant, who was staring at the fast streaming water of the Rhine. He fully agreed. Across the river the German guns were responding desperately to our assault, and their shells flew low over our heads. Allied fighter planes were attacking the enemy everywhere, and smoke and fire filled the air over the German land.

It must have been mid-morning as I stood talking to an infantry man when a shell exploded nearby to the left of us. Shell fragments shrieked though the broken trees. Deafened by the explosion and shaken by the blast, I picked myself up off the ground and shook the dust and debris from me. I was fine, but fragments of the shell had struck another infantry man who had been standing near us. He was hit in his upper body. The infantry man and I tried to help and made him as comfortable as we could. But he was bleeding heavily, and in agony he soon lost consciousness. A little later he was taken away by stretcher-bearers.

Heavy bomber attacks and intense artillery fire went on for days. Sometimes it was so noisy I could not get my messages to our artillery. Then one early morning when we were at our observation post, we suddenly saw many British and American planes coming from the west toward our direction. Many of the planes were towing gliders behind them. Moments later they flew over us and the water of the Rhine. It was an airborne assault planned to help Allied ground troops establish a bridgehead across the Rhine. Almost at the same time we saw hundreds of black dots jumping from the planes, and the sky filled with drifting parachutes. They came down a few miles behind the enemy lines where they fought the enemy from behind. Many of those parachutists would be killed before the sun was down. Some of our planes were hit and came down in smoke and flames.

Meanwhile, hundreds of combat engineers braced themselves for what they knew would be one of the sternest tests of the war; the crossing of the Rhine river. Great amounts of bridge building material, pontoon and assault boats had been brought in by hundreds on enormous trucks during the last days before the crossing. I don't think I ever had seen so much war equipment together in one place as there at the Rhine. In those early morning hours, when the attack began, hundreds of engineers and infantry men pushed out into the river's rapid current aboard assault boats, under artillery fire from the enemy. Many of the engineers and soldiers were washed downstream when their boat was hit and sunk, and they were never found.

Not much later the infantry had established a foothold on the other side of the Rhine. It took only a few hours until the engineers had laid down a pontoon bridge over the water. I was amazed how quick and precise those bridges were laid in the fast-running water by those men under such a bad and dangerous situation. The paratroopers soon headed toward a rendezvous with the Allied ground forces. The battle for the Rhine was over at that place in the wide long river. Later we learned that only one bridge was saved. The bridge of Remagen, which was about 100 mile south of us, was captured intact by American troops.

It was later in that same day when our tankers and then the rest of our division began crossing the Rhine. When we came to the other side, our regiment regrouped again before going further. For the following days there was an unbelievable concentration of different army troops pouring into Germany, all coming from over that one bridge. A week later there would be 16 more pontoon bridges across the river Rhine. The fight for the crossing of the river at that area of the Rhine where we were, had taken five days. Since the Germans had only a small air force left and it was probably very short of gasoline, we did not see any German airplanes in those days of fighting for the crossing of the Rhine.

*March 28, 1945.* Allied troops were now pouring across the mighty Rhine River, Germany's last natural defense, for the final assault into their homeland.

A few days after the crossing, our Polish and Canadian Armored Divisions got orders from General Montgomery to go northward in the general direction of Emden, north Germany. On the way we would liberate the northeast Dutch provinces still occupied by the enemy. The idea from the General was to cut off west Holland by the Yselmeer (former Zuider Zee) Automatically the whole of western Holland would fall without the necessity for a large-scale battle. While the British went in a northeast direction in Germany toward Hamburg, American troops were sweeping deeper into central Germany. The Russians pushed ahead on the eastern front.

Hitler's Germany had not the slightest chance to survive much longer. Their cities were in ruins; their transports were at a standstill; railroads, bridges and factories were tangled masses. They were short of weapons and ammunition and their once famous Luftwaffe (air force) was destroyed. Yet amazingly, the Germans still held on grimly, and were fighting for every meter of their home ground.

While we went north, we passed the Reichwald Forest where for the last three weeks some of the bitterest fighting of the war had taken place. The bombardments and solid mass of explosions had destroyed the forest where thousands of soldiers from both sides had lost their lives.

Going north, our division crossed back over the Dutch border near the town of Enschede. Orders came from General Montgomery that our Polish and a Canadian infantry battalion were to go north to the Orange Canal. Two French paratrooper battalions and a Canadian infantry battalion had encountered heavy resistance from the enemy who were dug in on the north side of that canal. The French and Canadian troops made very little progress there and needed the help of an armored battalion. After two days of heavy artillery and plane rocket fire, we succeeded in crossing over the canal.

From there, we liberated the Dutch town of Emmen, where I slept that night in a large farmhouse for a change and not in my tank where I had slept and eaten for the last ten days. The following day we went further north. The enemy was now in retreat, and although we encountered pockets of resistance, the overall fighting became less intense. After liberating the town of Assen we soon were on our way to the city of Groningen, the most northern city in Holland, and close to the North Sea. I remember well how thankful the people of that city were to be liberated. As we passed through their town, people came out of their houses many waving their Dutch flags. They wept and danced and sang their patriotic songs. The years of oppression and waiting were finally over for them.

We soon left the city of Groningen behind and advanced toward the German border, where we linked up again with our other battalions. Passing the border, we went further in a semi-circle to the German harbor city of Emden. As soon as we had driven into Germany, we encountered pockets of fighting German soldiers everywhere. But even though they were a pest, we advanced rapidly to the north of Germany. Before we reached Emden, we encountered fierce resistance from the enemy who was dug in there. After a few hours of heavy artillery fire, we broke through the German defense line and captured the city. Because of years of Allied bombardments, which had left the city of Emden in piles of rubble, the inhabitants had fled their homes long before we entered their city. The houses if not completely destroyed were left naked and exposed, with their furniture and portraits showing, and bathtubs dangling from pipes. The Canadian infantry cleared the city of snipers and took care of the many German soldiers who surrendered.

We moved further north and passed long columns of prisoners of war. We came through towns where ruins bordered ruins, the streets gouged with shell holes, and we breathed the smoke of the rubble. Those cities which had nothing of importance were usually spared by the Allied bombers as were most of the smaller towns and villages in Germany.

The liberation of the cities of German-occupied countries was over, but now we had to occupy the German cities. This was done by the Allied infantry until later special occupation troops would move in. I think that we had become accustomed in the last months after liberating a city or town in France, Belgium or Holland, that the people came out of their homes or hiding places and embraced and thanked us with smiles and open arms. But here in Germany it was different. There were no happy crowds in the streets and no flags waving and flowers stuck into our guns of our tanks. We saw few German civilians. They had fled, or maybe were hiding from us. I don't know.

One day, our Lieutenant Barski, Eddy, Felix and I were resting in a village which looked empty and deserted. We felt tension in the air, but saw no one. We were sitting by our tank, when two old men came into the dusty street and passed us. They looked at us with fear in their eyes. Then some children came. They looked at us soldiers and ran away. But a little later they returned and some of the smaller boys, still trusting in the goodness of adults and, above all curious, came close to our tank. They stared in awe at our big machine. Their bare feet in dust, they looked with bright eyes from small peaked faces at our resting crew. We knew they wanted food. Then a woman ran from her house into the street after one of them. She took a little boy up in her arms and went inside the house. We knew then that the people of that village were watching us from behind closed curtains. We sure were not used to such a (un) welcome. We wisecracked a little and went further.

But I think those children, even though they were hungry, were the lucky ones in that time in Germany. They still had their mother or other family members to take care of them and a home. It was worse when we came to the larger cities. Many of the children from destroyed towns who had lost their families or got separated from them during air raids, were left alone without family or a home. They grouped together like small animals and roamed around looking for food. At night they hid in the ruins of the city, packed together for warmth and support. Those packs of dirty, tattered children, some of them carrying for a little brother or sister, didn't care who we were. They only knew that we had food. When we rested someplace they came and would hang around us until we drove further. It was a terrible, heartbreaking sight to see them, so young and small, hungry and alone. I remembered Major Makuch saying back in England, "Jozef, this war will be incomprehensible, not only for men, but everyone will suffer, even the children."

◆     ◆     ◆

Orders came for our division to move to the large harbor city of Wilhelmshaven. We followed the North Sea coastline in north Germany toward that city. One night, after a whole day of driving and cleaning up enemy defenses, our battalion decided to stop for the night. It was somewhere between Emden and Wilhelmshaven. Slowly our company was driving on while we looked for a place to rest. It did not take long until we came to a large damaged farm from where the people and animals were gone. Since it had many outbuildings where our soldiers could sleep, we decided to spend the night there. All around us was an unsteady rumble of machine gun and heavy weapon fire. Sometimes the shells were screaming overhead.

When we had finished our evening chow, our crew and I went to the farm's kitchen for instructions with Major Makuh and Captain Dobalski. I remember that in the middle of the kitchen floor was a long heavy wooden table with benches on each side. After cleaning the table and chairs of debris we sat around the oak table discussing the next day's assigned action. Early next morning we had to relieve another crew which was with our infantry. The captain had taken out an action map which he just had unfolded and spread out over the table. At that same moment, as we later discovered, a heavy 105 mm artillery grenade came through the kitchen wall. It must have gone over our heads, because we were pushed from our seats onto the floor from the tremendous air pressure. The grenade then went out the other side of the kitchen wall and came down about 20 yard further in the ground without exploding. Things happened so fast that we did not know what had happened until it was all over, and we suddenly found ourselves lying between broken stones and other debris. In the utter silence which followed nobody spoke or moved. In spite of the flying stones and other debris most of us had only a few superficial scratches. Believe me, we all blessed our guardian angels that this large grenade had not exploded. We all would have surely been killed. The major later had the grenade dismantled and dug up. It turned out to be a France-made grenade. Later he took it with him as a souvenir.

Meanwhile the battle for Berlin, the German capital, was raging on. There was no more bitter fighting than that which now took place. It raged from street to street, from house to house. Hitler himself had stayed in Berlin to take personal command of the German soldiers there. He ordered them to fight to the last man. With no thought for his people, he had decided to die in a terrible last battle that would bring his country and his capital down in a final ruin with him. Early in the morning on April 30, 1945 after giving poison to Eva Braun, his bride of one day, Hitler shot himself. He left instructions for his closest cronies to have his and his wife's body to be burned. And so the end of Hitler had come.

Our Polish and Canadian divisions had reached the outskirts of the harbor city of Wilhelmshaven, where Germany's navy was located. Here desperate enemy resistance stiffened and a bitter fight began. The German soldiers were bunkered down and dug in and fought hard. They were racked by close range fire to get them out of the bunkers. Some of the enemy soldiers came out with a white flag and their hands up. When I saw the action of those flame-throwers and the German soldiers coming out of the bunkers, I said to Eddy, "Why in heaven's name are those damned Germans still fighting so hard? Don't those fools know the war is lost for them and is almost over? What senseless bloodshed!" It took a whole day of fighting before we could advance further into the city. Wilhelmshaven was bombarded by Allied planes for years and was in rubble. Most of the people of Wilhelmshaven had left their city a long time ago or had been killed.

The enemy resistance was bitter and the infantry and tanks fought street for street and building for building. I think there was not a house standing anymore in that big city that was not damaged. It is impossible to describe the terrible sight to see of that once great city. After the German's last desperate fight, Wilhelmshaven was finally captured. The infantry and other special units captured many warships which were docked in the harbor, along with three cruisers and 18 submarines. Besides the 3500 German soldiers and navy men who surrendered in and around the city, there were two admirals and a general. We also took in a great number of weapons. Many soldiers were killed, missing or wounded in this confrontation on both sides. And that all so close to the end of the war.

In a warehouse near the harbor of Wilhelmshaven was discovered a great amount of food which was probably meant for the German Navy. It happened that the week before a section of our division had discovered and liberated a Polish women's concentration camp. It was located close to the Dutch border in Germany. In that camp were 1700 Polish women who, after the battle of Warsaw, were captured by SS troops and sent to that camp. When our soldiers liberated that camp, they found a terrible situation. The women were lying on dirty, rat-infested straw. They had no food and were sick from hunger and disease. As soon as the food in Wilhelmshaven was discovered, General Maczek told our soldiers to load all the food in trucks and take it to the women's camp.

I was very tired, as were most of the other soldiers. I noticed that I did not know anymore if it was morning or night. The fighting had been hard the last couple of weeks, with very little relief in between. Most of the man looked ashen, dirty and unshaven. Because of losses, we now had a serious shortage of man in our regiment. Many a time I had double duty, being a communication man and now, also the driver of our tank or carrier. Eddy had been seriously wounded when grenade fragments entered his lower body. I was not there when it happened. He had gone with another crew that day to an observation post when suddenly, without warning, a German tank came out of a grove of trees and fired pointblank. The other two men were killed and Eddy was wounded. I felt very bad. We had been together so long, and now on the last days of this stupid war Eddy had been badly hurt. Everything was so senseless to me. They took Eddy to England; I sure missed him for a long time. None of us ever heard of him again. But then so many of our comrades lay wounded in England or had died. Somehow you do not pay much attention anymore. It is no use thinking about it too much when you are in the middle of it.

During the last days of the struggle many of the German soldiers surrendered. Even though many threw their weapons down, many more fought desperately to hold on until the last moment. Some of their officers disappeared while others shot their soldiers if they tried to surrender. It was a savage bloodshed. We knew the end was coming and all that we had to do was survive this final stage.

# 14

# *THE SURRENDER OF GERMANY*

It was May 5, 1945, when early in the morning I drove our carrier with Lieutenant Belinski and Freddy to a point just outside of Wilhelmshaven where we had observation duty with the infantry. It had rained, but now the sun rose steadily in the clearing morning mist. The place where we had to go was on the roof of a large damaged building overlooking a wooded area were German troops were grimly holding out. Just before our small crew had left that morning, our major told us that at noon the fighting would cease; the Germans had surrendered. The war was over. Then the major went further saying that after the ceasefire I had to contact the infantry commander for further orders.

Even though the official signing of the surrender came May 7, we and many other troops in and around Germany had stopped fighting earlier than the official surrender date. So for the last time in this war I left for observation duty.

While driving to the building where we supposedly had to go, we said to each other how senseless this fight was anymore. "Why didn't they stop this slaughter as soon as Hitler killed himself?" I said to our lieutenant who was looking at his map. "Yes, Jozef, they should have," he answered me grimly. "But we have to go on until everything is documented by the generals. It has to be done in a correct manner, even though German troops are crumbling away everywhere."

The whole area where we drove through was totally destroyed, and the litter of war was everywhere. The smell of burned out war equipment filled the air. We passed a column of German soldiers who were captured or had surrendered. Beaten and tired they were scuffling down the shell torn road. Others were sitting beside the road bewildered and glum in their dusty, sometimes torn uniforms. It was a chaotic scene. "There they are," we said to each other, "Hitler's great Nazi Army." When we reached the building, the smoke in the sky from the fires of Wilhelmshaven was still hanging over the city. "Just a few hours more," we said, "and this war will be finished." It was difficult to comprehend that finally the end had come. In the meanwhile the Germans and our artillery were firing at each other as ever, as if to use the last of the shells, which were exploding left and right.

We were on our observation post a few hours when suddenly without warning a lone enemy fighter plane appeared. It came over fast and low and started to fire. As suddenly as it had come, it disappeared, leaving behind one of our infantry soldiers with both his legs cut off. I will never forget his screaming before he left on a stretcher in the blessed sleep of unconsciousness. While grinding my teeth I was asking myself, "Why?" How bad it was to be killed or wounded in the last hours of the war. To give up your life just before this moment of freedom. The moment of freedom which for many came too late.

Noon came, and suddenly there was no more gunfire, no more the whistling sounds of artillery grenades, no more explosions, just an eerie quietness. I felt no joy, no sense of victory, for too many times I had seen death and had seen too much suffering. Towns were in rubble and deserted. So many homeless people and worst of all children whose families had been killed in bombardments and now roamed the countryside in packs looking for food. No, I felt no victory, just sadness for all the people who had died in this terrible war. "It's funny, is it not, how you can't feel anything," said the lieutenant. "The war is over, and I thought I would feel happy about it, but I feel only relief, nothing else." Yes, we felt relief that the war was over, finally over, and thankfully we came out of it alive and unhurt.

After the ceasefire, I called the infantry commander for further instructions. He told the lieutenant we could go back to our battalion—that we were dismissed. As we drove back to the location where our battalion was, we passed Canadian troops moving into the totally destroyed city of Wilhelmshaven for occupation, while our Polish and the Canadian infantry and tanks were moving out.

Everything was already packed when we reached our battalion. We then withdrew about 18 miles to the west of Wilhelmshaven. When our communication platoon came together, there were mixed emotions besides being glad and thankful that the war had ended and that we were alive. Some of the men were excited and happy. They were the ones who came from France, Canada or Argentina or Australia where their families lived. They would go home as soon as possible after their demobilization from the army—back to their countries and towns where they lived. Or the soldiers such as Stanley, who had married a Scottish or English girl and wanted to go back and stay in that country. But it was a different situation for the soldiers who had fled Poland in 1939 and had served in the French Army and later escaped to England. Or the ones who had suffered in Russian prison camps and had via the Middle East come to England. Or also for the men who had been forced to fight in the German Army in Africa and had, after their capture or surrender, come to England. They were the men facing a big problem. After our demobilization all we wanted was to go back to our families and homes and our country Poland, but now we were strongly advised by our commanders against this. We would face an unsure future under the Russian-occupied Poland, its regime and communism. They told us it could have serious consequences. Our commanders also said not to be worried; we all would get the help we needed from the government in England. Our officers and we soldiers talked with each other for the longest time about this situation. I think it was worse for our officers. They thought they would have good jobs waiting for them when they returned to Poland. Many of them had always been in the military in Poland before the war. All their dreams of marching into a free Poland were blown away. When the time for our demobilization came, we said to each other, each of us had to make his own decision for the future, and where to go from there—which as it turned out, would still take some years.

The war in Europe was over. The stark horror of the concentration camps was revealed. The Allied troops were greeted by throngs of starved and tortured human beings. The American and British medical teams took over the camps to care for the living and bury the dead.

On May 8, 1945, the German commander-in-chief signed an unconditional surrender to the representatives of America, Britain, France and Russia. The war had taken the lives of many millions of people from many countries in many different ways—by bombs, on battlefields and sea, or in concentration camps. Millions more were missing or wounded. More than 14 million people were without a home. And for most of the people in Europe their lives were forever altered. The war in Europe was over, but there was little rejoicing by the American and Allied forces in the Pacific and Asia. They were still fighting a war against Japan, just as Germany had fought until the bitter end.

◆　　　◆　　　◆

Our battalion withdrew to and around the village where we would stay until further orders. How long this would be nobody knew. The village had escaped the ravage of war. Besides a few bombs which had come down on some farmhouses, there was not much damage in the small town. We soon moved into the houses of the German people, into empty houses and other buildings of the village. I moved into a home of the village dentist who, as it turned out, was a very friendly man. He and his wife were happy the war was over. He even fixed my teeth for a pack of cigarette. As I soon would find out the German people were more than thankful that finally the war was over, and they could begin with rebuilding their lives.

No more war, no more fighting and no sound of grenades! It was strange for all of us, for all the soldiers and their officers. We had to get used to a life without danger and noise. No more moving forward and for me no more observation duty to spy on the enemy and report their targets. No more reading the action maps and no more sleeping in or under the tank or in open fields. We all had a feeling of being lost and being bored. We didn't know what to do with ourselves. Many of the men got depressed. Now that the fighting was over, we took stock of who was killed, missing or wounded. From my original company which I had started out with in Normandy, about half the men were gone. The rest were replacements. Many men of our communication platoon were also gone. They were either killed, missing or were lying in England in a hospital. Now we had too much time to think.

We were in the village about a week when I decided to write to my family in Poland. "The war in Europe is over," I thought, "and even though there is a big mess and confusion everywhere, maybe the army is able to send my letter through." "I can try" I said to myself. "Mail should be established as soon a war is over." But I was not sure if my family was still living at the same address as when I had left our town of Miedzychud in 1939. Thinking about it for awhile I decided to write not only to my parents' address, but also to write to the addresses I still remembered of different family members and my parent's close friends. If the army is able to send this through, I thought hopefully, then some of them in Poland surely will get one of my letters. In case my parents would be living somewhere else, they then could write back to me about my family whereabouts. It was about five years ago now, I thought sadly, that we had last heard from each other. They must have been wondering all those years what ever happened to me, and they should know as soon as possible that I am alive and well.

After I finished the letters, I gave them to my Division Post Office who, as they said, would take care of them. All that I could do now was hope and pray that I would hear something from my parents or my brothers or sisters. Or that someone else in Poland would receive one of the letters and could send a note back to me.

When I returned from the battalion post office, I went to Major Makuch and asked for a pass to Breda. I wanted to see Eef. It had been two months now since our division had moved out of the vicinity of Breda for the massive offensive into Germany. We had written each other many letters. Sometimes I wrote to her sitting in my tank or in a hidden observation post. But in the last weeks I had not written to her. The fighting in Germany had become difficult and exhausting and nothing had seemed to matter anymore. Now that the war was over, I longed to see her. I longed to see her smiling face and hold her in my arms. I wondered if she was still thinking about me, but I would not blame her if she had found a new love. Her former boyfriends, who would by now be coming back from their ordeal in Germany where they had been forced to work in the war factories, had probably taken her mind off me. But I had to find out.

Major Makuch gave me a three-day pass, and the next day I was on my way to Breda. I was lucky that a truck from our company with some soldiers were going to Brussels and would go through Breda on its route to Belgium. The truck left early in the morning and for seven hours we drove over roads which were overcrowded with military vehicles such as trucks and jeeps. Many a time we slowed down to a halt when we reached a pontoon bridge over one of the rivers that we had to cross.

It was mid-afternoon when we finally arrived in Breda close to Eef's home. I gave the driver her address, as they would pick me up two days later. It was strange but good to walk through the familiar neighborhood again. A few minutes later I walked through the front yard of Eef's parents home and rang the doorbell. Eef's mother opened the door and seemed puzzled to see me. Behind her stood her husband. I think they were surprised to see me back again, especially so soon after the war had ended. But they were happy for me that I had come out of this war in one piece, as so many had not, and that the war had finally come to an end in Europe. I couldn't help but feel a little disappointed when Eef's mother told me that her daughter was not home. She was gone with Chiel, her girlfriend, she said. Where they went she didn't know.

Later in the afternoon while I was having a conversation with Eef's father and her mother was making supper in the kitchen, I heard Eef's footsteps coming from the front yard. I jumped from my chair and went to the hall. A second later Efka walked through the door and right into my arms. Later she told me she had been wondering what had happened to me when she didn't receive any more letters. She had been worried that something terrible had happened. I couldn't tell her all the bad and difficult times we soldiers had gone through in the last months—that could wait until later. Now everything was all right. The war was over and the girl I loved was in my arms again.

The liberation of the rest of Holland where the family of Eef's parents lived, had brought relief to the family. They had heard about the hunger, the starvation from cold and disease and the Nazi brutality in North Holland during that terrible last winter. Now Eef's parents waited for news about their relatives. I was sure mail would trickle soon into the south of Holland, and we all hoped that it would be good news.

Jozef in the back yard of Eef's family in Breda, Holland, 1945.

The day after I had arrived at Efka's parents' home I took out my civilian clothing and hung my uniform in the closet. What a good feeling, I thought, to wear light pants with a shirt instead of the uniform. The people of Breda were celebrating the end of the war. Everywhere was music and every evening everyone, adults and children alike, were dancing and singing in the streets until well into the night. I think Efka and I never danced so much as in those two nights that I was in Breda.

The following day after breakfast we took a walk in the forest. It was May and the forest, which was close to Eef's home, was full of promise of a new spring and summer. While we walked on the narrow roads between the tall trees of the vast forest, we talked about our hopes and dreams and what the future would bring for us. We also talked about the difficult situation we Polish soldiers and officers found ourselves in. I had told Eef that I probably would not return to my country Poland. "I can't live under the Bolshevism regime and communism as it is now," I said to her. "For now it is just not safe to go back to my country." As Efka looked at me not understanding, I told her, "I know, it takes time to understand something like this. Bolshevism is not the enemy for us alone but of all of Europe."

Those were truly happy days for us which came to an end too soon. On the afternoon of the third day the truck came to pick me up, and there I went back again to Germany and my company. I had promised Efka that I would be back as soon as I could. I loved that girl more than anything in the world and wanted to marry her. Even though I knew that her feelings for me were mutual, I had hesitated to ask her. "It is too soon," I said to myself, I have nothing to offer her. The war has just ended, and where do I go from here!"But by the time our truck reached Germany, I knew I had to ask Eef to be my wife. If I could not go back to Poland after my demobilization, then I did not want to stay in Europe which was forever at war. I had to know if Efka was willing to take that step with me when the time came. Whatever decisions I had to make in the near future, I knew that Eef and I could work them out together.

As soon as I came back to my battalion I went to Major Makuch and told him why I came to see him. I said that I wanted to marry Eef, and that I wanted to go back to Breda again as soon as possible to ask her. The major grinned. He had met Eef from when we were stationed close to Breda, and had said he thought she was a pretty and lovely girl. The major said to come into his office were we could have a talk. We already knew each other so well, back from when we were that first year in Scotland. The major had been like a father to me all those years. Finally he said, "Jozef, I will give you another pass, so you can ask that girl to marry you. I hope she will say yes!" So believe it or not, two days later I was at Eef's doorsteps again, this time to ask her to be my wife.

We decided to get married as soon as the situation allowed it. When this would be, we didn't know. First we had to see how things were going in Germany. The war had just ended! Since I had only a pass for two days, I had to leave again the following day. After saying goodbye to Efka and her parents (who were not too happy with their daughter's decision). I said, "I will be back again in no time!" This time I had to hitchhike back to Germany, which was not so difficult to do with all the Allied military vehicles on the roads. There was always room for another soldier in their truck. It did not matter what their skin color was or from which country they came. It made no difference.

As soon as I came back into the village and told my buddies the news about Efka and me, Stanley, Stefan, Felix, Frank and all my other army buddies started to slap me on my back. Of course they had to tease me first. Then they all wanted to know when the wedding was. Most of the guys knew Eef from the time when we all were staying near Breda. They had met her at dances or when she had walked me back to my battalion office.

A few days later our whole Division moved out of north Germany and went south, close to the Dutch border in Germany and about 125 miles from Breda. My company settled in and around a small town by the name of Frerren. Most of our soldiers moved into the town's empty apartment houses, and others stayed at farms around Frerren. I was staying with Frank at a large farmhouse. The farm was run by two unmarried sisters. Also living there, were three of their brothers who had been crippled in the war. One of them had lost both legs in Russia, a second brother who had fought in Africa was always sick with malaria, and the youngest brother was shot up in Italy and was paralyzed on one side of his body. I think there was not a healthy young or middle-aged man left anymore in that time in Germany. Just old men, cripples, children and women. All the work had to be done by women and children. You have to know that German soldiers became prisoners of war not only during the war but also after the war had just ended. They were sent to England, Scotland and America to work in factories or on farms, and were paid for their work. The reason they were send overseas was so the German soldiers could not in any way interfere with the Allied occupation, or form groups and attack Allied troops in Germany. Many of the German officers could not be trusted. It would take quite a long time (sometimes years) before they were sent back to their country again. By then everything in Germany was under control and calm.

Almost every night, in the first weeks when we were stationed in Frerren, if we expected German officers to be hiding in one of the farms near the town, we surrounded that farm. First we would go inside the farmhouse and ask the farmer and the rest of the people who were there for their identifications and we asked questions. We then searched the house and the outside buildings, especially the barns with hay, for escaped officers. The first few weeks we got quite a few of them. Some were still wearing their uniforms. Others were in civilian clothing which they got from the farmers. They were mostly officers who, just before the ceasefire, had deserted their units and were now in hiding. They were probably hoping to stay in hiding until it was safe for them to come out or to form groups. After we had taken them prisoners the military police took them away.

Major Makuch had asked me if I wanted the job of taking care of the mail in our post office. Of course I wanted that! Doing nothing was not for me. So, a week later I became our battalion's 'postmaster' with another guy from our communication platoon. Together we were soon handling all the mail which came in or went out.

It looked as if Germany had become a country of traders. Stanley, Frank, Felix, Stefan and I would come together smoking a cigarette while talking to the other guys of our company. Usually we were sitting in front of the apartments in the short street were many of our soldiers were housed. The farm where I was staying was a little further up on a gravel road. When we came together, Wincek would play on his guitar. Wincek was a replacement soldier who had come to our battalion in Holland. He was a mild and peaceable young man who loved to play his guitar. He had also a girlfriend in Breda. While he was fiddling on his guitar and we talked and smoked our cigarettes, there they came. They were people from bombed out cities, carrying with them suitcases full of merchandise. They came to the places where the soldiers were, and wanted to trade their goods for food and cigarettes. They carried silver, crystal, linens, clothing and whatever more they could carry with them. The merchandise was probably taken from the damaged houses of bombed cities where the owners had fled or were killed. Or, as many times was the case, the goods came from the houses of Jews who were taken away to concentration camps by the Nazis. Wherever all that stuff came from, all they wanted was trading their ware for food, especially cigarettes. They then in turn would take the cigarettes to farms to trade for food, any kind of food. I traded a lot of my cigarettes for some nice things, as linens, silverware and cloth materials, which I then took to Eef on my next leave.

Also homeless people started to swarm into the village. They were hungry with nowhere to go. They knew they could find food where soldiers were. The American Relief Organizations and Red Cross was pouring into Germany and other countries just liberated from the Nazi tyranny. The homeless children who were roaming the destroyed cities and the countryside looking for food, were now rounded up and sent to places where there was shelter and care for them. The names of the children who were in those shelters were printed on paper and hung outside on the shelter door. Anyone how was looking for their child would only have to read the names of the children in that shelter. The children would stay in those shelters until hopefully a relative would find them in the near future. So many people had lost their homes and families.

The work camps and the concentration camps were now open. The German people who had been imprisoned by the Nazis because of their resistance against Hitler, and the ones who were forced to work in factories away from their homes, were now looking for their family members. When they had gone back to their city from prison or camp, many times they found their house bombed out, and didn't know if their family was still living. Many citizens were killed. The ones who had survived the air raids had gone somewhere else and now, of course, they could not find each other anymore. They would look around, their eyes always searching and asking if someone had seen this or that person while holding up a picture of their loved ones. It was a total chaotic situation in that time all over Germany. Everywhere people were looking for people hoping they would find their child or other members of their family. The borders of Germany were closed tight. No one could come in or go out of Germany. Only military with a pass were allowed to cross the border. In the meanwhile American troops poured food into Germany for the starving masses. Food which came not only from America but also from South America, Australia, New Zealand and Canada.

After a month of waiting I received a censored letter from my mother. As soon as I saw my mother's name on the return side of the envelope, I knew that my father had died. My mother wrote how thankful she was to have received a letter from me telling her that I was alive and well. She had never given up hope that I someday would come back to her, even if it was only in a letter. She wrote she had also heard from the other relatives and friends I had written to, and that everyone was very happy for her. She then wrote that our father had died in April of 1942 while working in a Nazi work camp. Everyone in the family was all right, she wrote, and I was not to worry. She was sending me her address from the place where she was living now and would send me another letter as soon as she had received a letter back from me. She ended her letter saying to be careful what I was writing because all mail was opened and read by the Russian censors.

Immediately I wrote back to my mother, and soon received her next letter. She wrote about how she was put out of her house and that German officers had occupied it until the Russians came and occupied it. My two brothers Stanley and Marian had to work for German farmers during the war years. My oldest sister Irene had to sew German uniforms in a factory. My youngest sister Victoria had been the luckiest during the war. She had to work for a German dentist who was good to her and sent her to a dental school. Kazek my youngest brother was too young to work at the beginning of the war, and stayed with our mother until he became older and was sent to a German farmer who had treated him with terror. My mother wrote that life had been difficult and food had been hard to come by. Some days she had lived only on memories of a happier time when her family was all together.

After reading her letter, I felt depressed and longed to see my family. They had gone through so much and had suffered a great deal during the war years. I was glad that my mother did not have the added burden of worrying about me anymore. They all had wondered where I had been during the war years. Nobody had dreamed that I had been in England all that time. Most of the family had thought that I had gone to France in 1939 and had stayed in that country, since I had an uncle living there close to Nantes.

In later years I came to know that my father had been a prisoner of the Nazis for political reasons. In day time he had to work for the Germans and at night he was in prison. My mother and her children never would find out exactly how he died. The Germans had told my mother that her husband fell down a shaft and broke his neck. Later some men who had worked with Father told another story. They said that German guards pushed hem down the shaft. What really did happen we would never find out.

◆     ◆     ◆

It was June 1945. Anyone who had a ten day leave coming could get a pass. Stanley who had not seen his young wife for a year now, not since he had left Scotland, was all excited. He could not wait to leave and board a train to the

Dutch port of Hoek van Holland. From there he would go by ship to England and then further by train to Scotland. He packed and repacked his duffel bag, which drove me nuts. I was happy for him and his wife that finally he was going home, even it was only for a short time.

While he was gone, I went with Stefan to Breda on a three-day pass. Stefan had a new girlfriend in Breda, and he and his girl would come to Efka's and my engagement party, which would be that weekend. Eef had sent out engagement invitations and, besides her family, a lot of her friends and neighbors came to our party. Since I knew that there was not a drink to get in Holland, I had traded my cigarettes for a few bottles of drinks in Germany. We have to have a toast, I thought. I got also some food, from the farmer where I lived, to take to Breda. The weather was great that weekend, sunny and warm, and our party lasted well into the night. The following day when I asked Efka about all the flowers we had received, she explained to me that it was the custom in Holland to bring flowers to an engagement party as well as to many other occasions. Holland is truly a flower country, as I learned.

The Allied occupation troops had moved into Germany. The American and British fighting forces, who had helped liberate Europe, were now slowly returning back to their countries. The French-Polish soldiers in our battalion who lived in France wanted their demobilization papers and their discharge out of the Army, but it was refused them. They had gone home earlier on a leave pass, but now they wanted to go back to France to stay. Quite a few of those soldiers later went on a pass to France and never came back to their company in Germany. They just disappeared, and stayed in France.

It was toward the end of July that we heard that our whole division would withdraw from Germany and go back to England. No one knew when this would be. When our soldiers and officers heard about this news, they were happy and glad. Going back to England was far better than staying in Germany. But I was not happy with the idea of being further away from my Efka. I was already far enough from her. How could I leave the girl I loved behind. The following days I thought about this situation and came to the conclusion that the only thing to do was to get married and take Efka with me to England as my wife.

It was a few days later when I went hitchhiking to Breda, and discussed the situation with Eef. After long talks back and forth we finally decided to get married as soon as we could get everything arranged. Eef's parents were not very happy with the idea of a wedding so soon and their daughter going to England and tried to talk us out of it. At the insistence of her mother we went to the reverend (woman) of her Church who gave us another long talk. The end was that she could marry us August 30. "This give me enough time to get everything ready," Efka had said. I think she was not only excited about a wedding, but also the prospect of going to England. Now in case our company would leave for England before that date, I would then take a ten day leave, which I had coming at that time. I would then return to Holland and take Efka to England with me.

When I came back to my company in Germany I went first to our major to ask his permission to get married. I also needed the necessary papers for marriage, which were given only by the Chaplain of our battalion. This is an Army regulation. Permission to get married was not easily given. All my buddies were happy for me and they all promised, if possible, to be there in Breda for my wedding day.

In the meanwhile, the war on the islands in the Pacific had raged on since December 1941 after America had declared war on Japan. After the terrible battles and the taking of Reyte, the Philippines and Burma, the American Generals hoped Japan would surrender. But the fanatic Japanese generals would not think of it. Only after the American Marines, under great losses, took the island of Iwa Jima, it had become possible to attack Japan from the air.

It was in that time that the American scientists had succeeded in exploding an atomic bomb in the desert of New Mexico. President Truman, Churchill and Stalin sent word to Japan's premier to surrender or face complete destruction. But he defied the Allies to continued the war. Japan's refusal left President Truman little choice but to use the only method of ending the war. On August 6, 1945 the first atomic bomb was dropped on Hiroshima, Japan, killing 75,000 people. On August 9, a second atom bomb was dropped on Nagasaki, killing 40,000 people. Two days later most of Hiroshima was in ashes. It had become clear that Japan was now in a state of collapse, and on August 10, the Japanese government offered a surrender. It was not until September 2, 1945 an official surrender was signed on the battleship Missouri in Tokyo Bay. The war in the Pacific had come to a close. The long awaited victory over Japan had arrived. World War II was over. The blackest five years in human history had ended with millions of people killed and missing, and millions more wounded.

# 15

# *THE WEDDING*

It was a few days before my wedding when Major Makuh said to me, "Jozef, as you know we have a great shortage of men in our communication platoons. If we go to England or not, we have to have more communication men. I want you to train new men for our regiment's communication as soon as possible. The cold war situation with Russia is serious enough to have this justified." The major saw that I was not too happy with his idea of me going to train new communication men. I tried to get out of it and said, "Major, what about my upcoming wedding? Everything is already arranged." He looked at me and probably tried to bribe me because he said, "Jozef, I will give you one whole month leave for your wedding if you agree to go as an instructor for six weeks after you come back." One whole month with my Efka, I thought, how lucky can you get! So I said to the major, "All right, Major, let us agree on this: I will go as an instructor and you give me one whole month of leave." It was the best trading I had done so far, and happily I walked to the canteen.

By the time my wedding day came around I had a suitcase full of bottles of drinks. I think that all my buddies who had gone to England, France or Belgium on a pass in the last few weeks, had come back with a bottle of drink for my wedding. They all knew that there was not a drop of drink to get in Holland. I remember Lieutenant Barski, who knew about my wedding and had gone to Italy to visit his brother, came back with four bottles of whiskey for me. A few days before the wedding Felix somehow got hold of half of a calf which he then cut up, wrapped in sacks, went to Breda and delivered it to Eef's home. Another delivered a few pounds of butter to her home the day before the wedding. Earlier, Lieutenant Belinski who had gone to England on a leave and had asked me if I needed anything from there, had come back with plain golden wedding rings for Efka and me. I had given him about the size of the rings and, as I later learned, were the exact size we needed. Golden wedding rings were hard to come by in that time, even in England.

With a heavy old suitcase on my shoulder I started to walk to Eef's home. A military truck with which I had gone from Frerren to Breda had dropped me off about two miles short of my destination. I had taken a shortcut to Eef's home which led me through a sugar beet field and narrow farm roads, and which finally would bring me close to her home. The old reed suitcase which I got from Eef's mother when I had told her that I had to carry a lot back to Breda, soon became heavier and heavier. I think that in the last mile I had to stop every ten yards, and move the suitcase from one shoulder to the other. The cows in the fields were looking at me, probably thinking what in heaven's name was I doing there on their road.

Halfway to Eef's home I passed a farm that was at least 200 years old. It had a low-hanging reed roof that almost covered the tiny windows and front door. While setting my suitcase down again, I looked at the very pretty small chickens and roosters who where running free around the fields and gardens of the picturesque farm. They were of many colors and breeds. It did take not long until they chuckled around me, while pecking at the suitcase. A mixed-breed dog, which had first watched me from a distance, had come slowly over, sniffed me out and wanted to be petted. A goat, luckily on a chain, would bleat at me while a few small pink piglets with their tiny eyes looked it all over and decided to come on over too. It was such a pretty sight and it brought memories back to me when I was a young boy and had gone with my father to visit the small villages where his family had lived. After some rest I lifted the heavy suitcase on my shoulder again and went further leaving behind the picturesque scene. When I arrived at my destination at Efka's home, no one of the family could believe how I could have carried the suitcase so far all the way home. They couldn't even lift the suitcase from the floor.

Eef had rented a black tuxedo for the wedding for me. Not that I liked to wear a "monkey suit," but there was no other way around it. I didn't wanted to wear my uniform for my wedding, and Efka wanted me to wear a tuxedo, since she was wearing a wedding gown. The house was full of wedding guests when I arrived. They were family members from the north of Holland who had arrived the day before. It had not been easy for them to come to the wedding since transportation was still very difficult. Many bridges were out and there were few trains.

Even though the distance from Amsterdam to Breda is only 80 miles, it had taken them many hours before they had arrived in town.

I had been invited to sleep the night before the wedding at a friend's home—people I knew from since I had come to Breda. Efka had instructed me that evening to be ready at 10:00 in the morning, as a horse and carriage would pick me up to bring me to her home. She had been busy with what a girl is busy with before her wedding day, I guess, because she had not much time for me with all the things she "still had to do"as she said. She had given me a hug and said, "Sweetheart, I think your friends are waiting for you, I'll see you in the morning." Then, after I had some more conversation with the family from the north of Holland about the bad times they had gone through and the now improving conditions, I had left.

When I finally went to bed that night I couldn't sleep. It was quiet and a cool breeze was coming through the open window, billowing the curtains. The bedroom was small, my tuxedo was hanging on a hanger on a knob of the dresser. While I lay there on the bed looking at a bright moon which peeked through the window, I thought about my life and how things were changing again for me. This time I would share my life with another person, with Efka, the girl I loved so much. Maybe later, after my demobilization, we could leave Europe where there always seemed to be war, and find a more peaceful existence. I knew together we could make it, wherever it would be. It sure will be strange, I thought, to have a normal civilian life again after all those years. I didn't know what that was anymore. I was lying on my bed a long time thinking about my family back home and how I wished that some one of my family could be here for my wedding, and could meet my beautiful bride. My eyes were closed but I couldn't sleep, so many things went through my mind. Finally I must have fallen asleep, for when I woke up a new day had come. It was Efka's and my special day.

*August 30, 1945.* After a hearty breakfast served by my host, I got dressed in my monkey suit. When I looked in the long mirror which was hanging on the bedroom door, I thought that I didn't look so bad after all in a tux. I was eager to see my Efka, but had to wait until the horse and carriage came to bring me to my bride's parents' home, where she would be waiting for me, according to the old Dutch tradition. Finally the white carriage came, pulled by two white horses with plumes on their heads. Two riders in ornate white uniforms were sitting on the riders' seat, driving the horses. When I stepped into the carriage in my tuxedo, flowers for my bride in my hand, I felt at least to say very strange. I was sure more comfortable in a tank, in my dusty uniform with my radio on my side, than in this white silk fairy tale carriage. Later together with my lovely Efka, sitting in the carriage, I thought how romantic this was and we enjoyed the long ride.

First we went to the courthouse where we signed our names in the Book of Marriage. Our family and friends were sitting behind us and looked on. They had also come by horse and buggy, only their carriages and horses were black. The church ceremony was held in a small and very pretty 100-year-old church, which was located in downtown. After the beautiful ceremony, we went together in the carriage to the photographer. While our wedding pictures were taken, the rest of the family and our friends went back to Eef's home.

Jozef and Eef on their wedding day,
August 30, 1945.

The festivities and dinner were held in Eef's parents' home, as it was the custom in those years. Many of my army friends had come from Germany for the wedding, which made it all the more happy for me. Eef's brother Henk had made a dance floor in the back yard, where we danced to well into the night. I still wonder where he got all that wood! When a rain shower finally made an end to the outdoor festivities, some of the gasts went home and others went inside the house where Vincent played his guitar. The party lasted until the early morning hours with everyone singing and drinking.

I was happy when finally Efka and I left on our honeymoon in the morning. The place was in southeast Holland in an area of hills and forests named Valkenburg. There we stayed for two weeks in a small but very nice hotel in a wooded area, overlooking the hills of South Limburg. We went by train—the windows were still out because of former air raids and not replaced yet. Sometimes we had to go out of the train and walk over a river on a narrow pontoon foot bridge to the other side where another train was waiting to go further. Since there were not many trains running yet, it was very crowded everywhere, and it took us many hours to reach our destination. Inconvenience was just a way of life in those times during and following the war years. After two great weeks in Valkenburg we went back to Breda where I stayed another two weeks. Then after four weeks of honeymoon which we wanted to last forever, my leave was over and I had to return back to Germany to my battalion. It was not easy to say goodbye to my love that day, and put on my uniform again. I had to hitchhike back to Germany.

The housing shortage was a big problem in Europe in those years and would last for many years after the war. Young married couples could just not get housing and were happy to get a room any place, anywhere. Eef's parents, who lived in a four bedroom house, gave us two rooms to use for the time being. Her brother Jan had left for the Dutch East Indies with the Dutch Marines to fight the Indies Freedom War. The Dutch East Indies had been a colony of Holland for a few hundred years and wanted, after WWII and the war with Japan, its independence from Holland. Dutch military were sent to the Indies to hold on to their colonies which Holland finally had to give up to the people of the Dutch East Indies a few years later.

When I finally got back from my long leave, I found out that there were still no orders received for us to go back to England. It was especially a great disappointment for those officers and soldiers who were married in Scotland and England. A waiting period started now not only for Eef and me, but for every Polish soldier who was stationed in Germany. There was not much more to do except play cards, tell each other stories or play soccer. As soon as I came back to

Frerren, Major Makuch said to me, "Jozef, after tomorrow you will instruct new men for our battalion's communication. It will be in a school in another town. Lieutenant Belinski will pick you up." So for the following six weeks I was living in a town, which was about a half hour drive away from Frerren, teaching new communication men. In the meantime the other guy, who had taken over my post office duties for the last weeks, was going to continue to do so until I came back or until we would leave for England.

◆    ◆    ◆

*Summer of 1946.* A year had passed and most of the Allied fighting forces were demobilizest and had gone back to their own countries. Except of course, the occupation troops which were going to stay in Germany for many years. We Polish soldiers were still hanging around in Germany and were now also used for the occupation of that country. To great disappointment, we never heard anything again about us leaving back to England.

Since I had a ten day leave coming, Eef and I decided to go on a trip to Amsterdam and Haarlem. We would be staying with family. The only transportation was by trains which were still not running at normal times and routes. I remember how very crowded it was at Breda's train station, which was in that time not very large. When our train finally arrived and came to a screeching halt, we saw that it was packed with people. The passengers were sitting or standing on top of each other, it seemed there was no room left anymore. Not giving up, we finally found a place in a freight car just before the train started to move out of the station. Between boxes of all sizes and sorts we sat on the floor of the freight car with other people, who also had not found a place in a train car. Since many bridges were still out, it took a long time before we finally reached our destination—Amsterdam.

I had gone on our trip in my uniform since it was easier to travel this way. The military got much better and easier access to everything and everywhere in that time. Except the trains! Not that I wanted all the privileges they bestowed on us, but in case of difficulties, it would be better if I was in uniform. The family in Amsterdam was doing much better now that there was food again. Also life had become less stressful now everything began slowly to come back to a more normal living.

We stayed in Amsterdam with Eef's grandmother and Aunt Dien. They were from her father's side of the family and lived in an apartment in the middle of that city. I thought how pretty Amsterdam was and how much different it was than the other large cities I had seen in Europe. It was more compact with many canals and bridges and houses build close to the side of the water, especially in the older section of the city. Of course Efka had to show me the famous shopping places where she and her cousin Coby used to shop. Sometimes before, Eef had told me about the times when she had gone on vacations to Amsterdam to be with her cousin Coby. They were of the same age and always had a lot of fun together.

Jozef on top of a bunker,
Holland, 1946.

While walking through one of Amsterdam's well known shopping streets, Eef saw a few very pretty coats hanging in a boutique They were of the same color and style. Of course she had to see them from close up, since this had been a rare sight in the last years. The store owner probably had bought them from a store in England, which in turn got them from America or Canada. Anyway, half a hour later Efka walked out of the boutique wearing one of the coats which had been hanging there. She didn't care that it was a little to warm to wear a winter coat in the summer. She probably had to show the world her new bought possession.

For the first time in my life I was eating the famous Dutch Matjes Herring. It is a raw fish salted in brine and sold at one of the many fish stands which are located on many a street corner in Holland. At first I wanted no part of the herring. Raw fish, I thought, not for me! But after seeing Eef eating them, I had to try one. Believe it or not, ever since that first bite I love to eat those raw salty herrings called 'matjes haring', especially with chopped onions on top. Now whenever we visit Holland, first thing we do when coming from the airplane, is to look for a fish stand and eat herring with chopped onion.

We also visited the quaint fishing villages which are located just north of Amsterdam on the coast of the Zuider Zee. The Zuider Zee is now called Ysel Meer. In that time when Eef and I visited those quaint fishing villages, the natives still wore their colorful clothing and wooden shoes. Also for the first time I ate smoked eel in one of those small special restaurants which were located on the island of Marken. Smoked eel tastes very good, and many people in Holland like to eat them. The Dutch love their many different kinds of fish fresh from the sea, and they know how to prepare them! After a great week in Amsterdam talking with the family and learning many different things and a different way of life, we went to the city of Haarlem.

Haarlem is a city just south of Amsterdam and close to the North Sea Coast. In that city we visited Eef's other grandmother who lived there with her daughter Nel. For five days we stayed with them in their apartment which overlooked a wide river. One day we went to the coast where once there were busy beach resorts and now large bunkers stood. In time those bunkers would disappear and the resorts would be busy with vacationers again. The Germans had built those bunkers during the war years for an eventual Allied invasion into Holland. It was not long until we were strolling on one of Holland's beautiful beaches. In our bare feet we walked for the longest time through the cold water until the sun was setting in a red blaze in the far horizon of the North Sea..

Before we left for Breda, Efka had seen a ring with a blue stone in a jewelry store. I had wanted to give her a nice ring beside the plain golden wedding ring but had not been able to find one in Breda or in Germany. When we passed this store, there it was—sitting in the window between a few other items, looking at us. After all those years, she still wears it every day.

It had been an interesting trip for me, and I had learned some more about Holland and its people and of course the family. Too soon we had to say goodbye to Eef's grandmother and her Aunt Nel. They all had been so good to us. The trip back to Breda in the crowded trains was not much better then the one we had come on. The following day I went back to Germany; hitchhiking again. More and more I hated to go to back to Germany without Efka, my wife.

◆      ◆      ◆

Frank's father, who still was in England, had been able to get his son out of Germany and back to England. Of course Frank was happy to go to London to be with his father. It didn't take him long until he had packed his military duffel bag and said goodbye to all his buddies from the army. It was strange to see him leave for good. I missed the guy who I had known for the last five years. We had gone to so many courses together back in Scotland. Sometimes we had complained about it, and other times we were glad when it had been an interesting course. But always happy when it turned out we had to go together.

With Frank gone, I was now alone on the farm with the German family. One day I thought how nice it would be to have Eef on the farm with me. The large furnished room which I had was nice with large windows overlooking the fields. A cooking area was in the corner of the room which would do for making some simple meals. Another small room, which Frank and I had used for closet and storage, was beside the entry door. The only question was, how to bring Eef to Germany. The country of Germany was still closed to the outside world. The chaos which had existed in Germany for more than a year after the war, had now subsided. All the people without shelter and food, and the ones who had been looking for lost family members, were gone now. They had been helped by the American relief organizations and the Red Cross.

For days I was planning and talking to my best buddies about how to bring Eef to Germany. To be able for her to come into Germany, she needed to be in the military service. Finally, we put the whole plan together. One of the men's girlfriend was in the Polish Army and was about Eef's size. She had said that she would lend one of her uniforms to Eef—it would be no problem. We then thought about the best way for Eef to come into Germany. We figured out that the military express train, which traveled between the harbor of Hoek van Holland and Berlin in Germany, would be the best way. This express was the only train going into Germany and was carrying only military who were going or coming from England. On the road to Germany it would make one stop, which was in the city of Utrecht in Holland. It would be the only place for Eef and me to get on the train. Next I had to find out what time the military express would leave from the terminal in Utrecht. Then I planned with my friends how to get us from the train station in Germany where the express would stop just over the border from Holland.

The problem was, that in and around that small border station everywhere the military police were inspecting the papers of every passenger. What I needed was good timing, good friends and a jeep to make it work. After I had worked it all out with my buddies, there were only two things still left. First, if my Efka wanted to go with me to Germany and stay for a while on the farm. Second, I needed train passes for both of us which only the major could help me on. So I went to Major Makuch and asked him again for a favor. First he heard me out and shook his head, then he said calmly, "Jozef, I hope you will not bring us all in difficulties." He then ordered his secretary to get the papers in order.

When the whole plan was put together, I went to Breda and told Eef about it. I think we both were young, in love and maybe foolish. But then that is being young, things you would not do if you are older. It was two days later when we were on our way to Utrecht. As soon as we had arrived in the large train terminal, we looked for the platform from where the express would leave. After finding it, Eef went to a ladies room where she changed into the military woman uniform which I had borrowed for her. In the jacket's breast pocket were "her" papers. A little later when she walked out of the restroom in her uniform and black beret on her curly hair, I thought she was the prettiest military woman I ever had seen.

We had not waited long at the large and almost deserted platform when the express train from Hoek van Holland arrived. Only a few military men entered the train—no one went off. Eef and I had to be separated, with her going in a section of the train for officers and military women only, and me into a section of only soldiers. Before we left that morning, I had told Eef exactly where to get off the train and than stay where she was so I would find her.

A few hours later the express stopped at the train station in Germany, just over the border from Holland. There everyone had to get off from the train for inspection. As soon as I came from the train, I spotted Eef standing by some military men and women. I went to her, took her arm and led her quickly away across the railroad tracks to the other side of the train station. Everything had to be done fast. There the jeep with Jurek and Stefan was waiting for us, as planned. As soon as we were in the jeep, we sped away.

It took us over an hour's drive before we reached the small town where our battalion was stationed. Jurek drove straight to the farm where I was staying, and after I thanked them, they left. Before I had gone to Holland, I had told the farm family that I probably would bring my wife over, and that she would stay for a while. Later, after we had arrived at the farm and Eef had changed into her dress again I introduced her to the German farm family. I knew they would be good to my Efka.

We had a good time while Eef was staying at the small town of Frerren. Not far from the farm was a forest where we always went hiking for the longest time. Or we went for an afternoon hunting for mushrooms. They grew plentifully under the tall trees of the forest. At first Eef didn't know much about mushrooms, which were eatable and which ones to avoid. She was a little afraid to eat them. But soon she lost her fear after I taught her the difference between the poisonous and the good ones. We always came home with a bucket full of white and brown mushrooms. Eef would fry them with fresh butter from the farm on the small gas stove. We ate them with dark German bread, which we got from one of the farm women.

Since we had no German food coupons to buy food, many times Eef would eat her dinners over at the officer's mess hall, which she was allowed to do, while I ate my suppers with the soldiers. On Saturday nights there was always a dance organized by our soldiers for the women from the former concentration camp. Those dances were held in a school, and many Polish women came to dance. Those women now lived in a village about half an hour drive from Frerren. All the German people, who had lived in that village close to where the concentration camp had been, were removed from their homes. They had been told by the British military to find a place somewhere else. The Polish women also could not go back to Poland, as we, and soon moved into the vacant village.

The people at the farm were helpful and good to Eef, and my friends spoiled her. When I had to work at the post office, sometimes Efka went to the forest by herself to paint. She loved painting and always found a picturesque place she had to paint on her canvas. She had taken her painting supplies with her when she decided she was going with me to Germany. Other times when she was alone at home she wrote up a storm; letters to her family and friends.

After we lived at the farm in Frerren for almost two great months, good news arrived from our headquarters for the Polish officers and their soldiers. It said that those men who were married in Holland, Belgium or France, and wanted to stay and live in those countries, were accepted by the governments of those countries to stay permanently. The governments were also willing to help the men find work. This of course was no problem. In that time in Europe every country needed much more help as they had to rebuild homes, factories, destroyed bridges and roads. Many of these facilities were destroyed during the four years of war. I knew that Eef and her parents wanted me to stay in Holland after my demobilization. To go and live in Holland would be the best choice for now, we said. We expected our first child, and we wanted it to be born in Holland. Also I knew the Dutch language well enough to find work. I also learned to understand the people of Holland, their customs and habits. Yes, going to and staying in Holland would be the best thing for us, we reasoned. Going back to Poland and living under Russian rule and communism, if it would stay as it was now, was out of the question. Maybe in time, I thought, Efka and I could leave Europe.

I had to bring Eef home again, which was as not as difficult as bringing her into Germany. Also going out of Germany was not as risky as coming into that country. A few times a week a truck from our company went to Antwerp to bring or pick up soldiers who were on a furlough. "To take that truck would be the best way," my buddies and I had said to each other. A few days later Eef packed her belongings and said goodbye to the farm family who were sad to see her leave. She also said goodbye to some of the Polish women who had always been helpful to her. The last of her good-byes she said to my buddies who were not planning to stay in Holland.

When the truck arrived and waited to take soldiers to Antwerp, Eef dressed herself in my military overcoat and put her hair under the black beret. Together we went into the waiting army truck which was now full of soldiers. None of them paid any attention to us, and if they did, they did not show it and said nothing. A hour later we passed the German and Dutch borders without difficulties. Soon we walked on Dutch soil again.

Eef was home in Breda once more, and for the last time I went back to my company in Germany. Two days later I had a medical check up. Our regiment doctor asked questions about my health, looked me over and signed papers. The following day I had to go to another town for my demobilization papers. Those papers were very important to me because for every year I had been in the military, I would receive money. I had served six and a half years in the British Army.

As soon as I walked into that office who did I see sitting on the desk, but Josef, my friend from Sambor with whom I had gone to France by train. Together we had served in the French Army, had fled over the terrible road south to escape the German Army and had landed in England. In Scotland we both had entered the Polish Armored Division. Since the invasion in Normandy we had not seen each other, as he had served in a different company. We talked for the longest time; much had changed since the last time we had seen each other. While looking at him, I thought how slow the days had gone for us in France in 1940, and how fast the years had passed since then. He was now a second lieutenant. He hoped to go back to England soon, and from there would try to go to America where his uncle lived. He told me further that our other friend Richard had never come with the troops to Normandy. At the last moment he had been called to London where he and many other architects were needed for the rebuilding of London as soon as the war was over. When I asked Josef about Adam, he told me that he too had lost contact with him and had not seen him anymore since Normandy. He knew only that Adam's brother had been killed in France.

When all the paper work was done and in order, I got my demobilization papers and civilian clothing. They told me I could keep all the military clothing—probably for souvenir. Josef and I said goodbye to each other. We both knew we never would see each other again. But the memories of our adventures would remain for always.

The following day our truck, with the soldiers who wanted to stay in Breda and vicinity, was leaving for Holland. Those soldiers who did not want to go to Holland, Belgium or France would still remain in Germany for another half a year, until finally they all went to England. From there they went to their different destinations. Many stayed in Scotland or England, others went to Australia, Canada or America. Stanley finally went to his wife in Scotland to stay. Felix went to Australia. Wincek and Stefan also went to Holland, where they had girlfriends and wanted to live there. Jurek went to Canada to an uncle who lived somewhere on the west coast. And as I later learned Major Makuch had taken twelve men with him to Argentina to start a ranch there. A few soldiers went back to Poland and risked freedom. Lieutenant Barski also went to America, but I do not know anything about Lieutenant Belinski. Our General Maczek went to Edinburgh, Scotland, and lived there until his death in 1994. It was his wish to be buried in Breda beside 'his boys' as he would call us. He is buried there in the Polish Military Honor Cemetery. Most of the Polish soldiers and officers who were killed in Breda and vicinity are buried in that cemetery.

In that early morning hour, standing on the side of the road by the truck, we wished each other good luck. Major Makuch had come, shook our hands and had left. We all had been so close during the war; now destiny would spread us all over the world to start a new life in a new country. As the truck left I looked once more at my buddies who were left behind. They waved goodbye, and I wished in my heart all the best in the world to them. As the truck went across the border and left Germany behind, I thought back to all those times during the war years when I had said to myself, "Soon I will be going home." Now I had another home, my own home with Efka, my wife, and our soon-to-be-born child. I knew it would not be easy to adjust myself to civilian life again—a life of the same everyday routine. It scared me a little, even though I had confidence in myself that I would adjust. I had served for more than seven years in three different armies and went through battlefields, had seen death many times, and yet I survived. But now I had to fight another war, a war within myself, a war to bring me back to a normal life again. Now one life was over, and another life would begin.

# PART II

# THE LOWLAND
## (Eve's Story)

# PREFACE TO PART TWO

I often dream of the town where I lived and the home I grew up in. It is for me a memory where I go back every few years. The journey brings me from Omaha to Chicago by plane and further to Holland, my country. The small house in the small street is still there in the city of Breda. Like many people, I guess that I tend to romanticize the good old days. Yet I am the first to admit that times were sometimes frightening to a child like me, who was very aware of the seemingly constant shortage of money in every household. Yes, times were hard in the thirties, the years in which I grew up. But I always felt secure and loved. In the forties the war years had been horrible with food and goods very scarce. Yet it taught us to share during those hard times, and it had created a truly united Holland, which I will never forget. The war also had brought me the man I would marry and the new world we would find together.

Eef's parents, Jan Jansen and Cornelia (Cor) Breeuwer, in Amsterdam around 1920.

Father with Eef, Henk, and Jan in Breda, Holland, 1930.

# 16

## *CHILDHOOD YEARS*

Holland is a small country about 1/5 the size of Nebraska. It borders the cold North Sea on the west and the north; Germany lies on the east and Belgium to the south. It has been said that "God made the world, but the Dutch made Holland." Truly this little country has been made by men, for its history tells the story of a constant battle with the sea, always threatening to inundate the land. The famous dikes and the picturesque windmills have been the weapons that the sturdy Dutch have used for hundreds of years to keep back the waters of the North Sea. But many times she became angry and broke the dikes to steal the land back again, drowning men and animals.

Holland has no great natural wealth except the rich soil left in the wake of the floods. It is entirely a lowland country with much of the area below sea level and no elevated sections except in the Southeast. The famous windmills which once dotted the countryside are mostly gone with only a few left. They pump the water from the marshy areas and some are used for grinding the wheat to flour. The principal rivers of Holland are the Ryn (Rhine), the Maas, and the Schelde. The climate is cloudy most of the time, and the land is swept by northwest winds. The temperature is cool to moderate. Because of the sea it is almost never too cold or too warm.

Holland is noted for its flower bulbs, particularly tulips, which are exported in large quantities all around the world. Also important is the dairy product export, mainly cheese. Holland has rich pastures and many cows.

When I was a child, the population of Holland was 7 million people with 97 % of its population Dutch. There are now 16 million people living in Holland. Many of them are emigrants from Eastern Europe, who discovered Holland as the land of milk and honey. The language is Dutch. Many different dialects are present in this small country.

Holland's history started more than 2000 years ago when the first settlers came down the river Rhine. They settled the land which they named Holtzland, meaning woodland, which became Holland. Later the official name became Netherland meaning—low land. The history of Holland is rich with its many Kings and Queens and its wars against overpowering countries and tyranny. After her dramatic days of struggle for independence, first from Spain in the mid-1600s, and later from France in 1815, the republic of the Netherlands was free again. After their freedom Netherland had a period of great progress and development and became the leading maritime and commercial nation in the world and one of the most stable and prosperous countries in Europe. It is one of the few countries left which is a kingdom.

Holland is a very pretty country where in springtime as child, I loved to pick the little buttercup flowers and daisies or the scarlet poppies in the field. I then took them home and gave them to my mother. She loved the wild flowers from the meadow and arranged them in a small glass vase.

I was born in that small country not far from the Belgium border in a town by the name of Breda. It was March 6, 1925. My parents named me Eefje after my grandmother, the mother of my mother. All through my childhood years I was called Eefie. Both my parents came from Amsterdam. My father, Johannes Jansen, was born July 14, 1895 and was the son of Marten Jansen and Jacoba Krabshuis. Father was the oldest of three children, two boys and a girl. My mother, Cornelia Breeuwer, was born also in Amsterdam. She was born January 7, 1896. She was the daughter of Hendrik Breeuwer and Eefje Breeuwer who were cousins. Marrying one's cousin was still allowed in those years; there was no law against it yet. Mother was one of five children—two boys and three girls. Both my parents grew up in the same well-known neighborhood by the name of 'Jordaan.' They met each other on a bicycle trip to the tulip fields with friends when they were 19 years old. Seven years later, in May 1922, they were married in Amsterdam. At that time my father worked at a weapon factory outside Amsterdam. A year after their marriage their first child, my brother Jan, was born. Soon after his birth, my parents moved to Breda where my father became a rifle repairman for the Dutch Army in one of the 200-year old kazernes (barracks). Not much later he became a professional in the military. In later years Father became an inspector of military weapons.

Breda, the town where I grew up, is an old historic town. Its first people settled there more than a thousand years ago. The settlement was nestled between forests and rich meadow land and south of the large rivers. Breda is a very pretty town with red roofed houses. The architecture of the older and more prominent homes has ornately framed windows and scrolled woodwork. The inner city is very compactly built, as are all older towns in Europe. When I was a child, the town had about 50,000 citizens. The older narrow streets were paved with cobblestones and were not so easy to ride your bicycle on. By now those old cobblestone streets are almost all gone. The Grote Mart (city square) and connecting streets with their many shops was, and still is, the life of the city.

The Grote Kerk, which is a church standing in the middle of Breda, was built around 1300. This magnificent large church in Gothic design took more than a hundred years to build. The remains of the wealthiest and most distinguished citizens of early Breda are in large tombs lining the perimeter of the walls of this church. Those tombs have elaborate statues of angels and saints. The lesser important citizens' tombs were built into the floor of the church. The carvings on those flat gravestones have been worn down because of the many footsteps of people who have walked over them as they came to church. Although the words are faint, they still are readable. As the inscriptions are read, you realize how much the Dutch language has changed in the last few hundred years. Those people of lesser importance were buried outside the city walls.

Breda was a military town with a military academy, a large military hospital and three large kazernes (barracks). Also located in the city was a police academy. I still see the cavalry on their horses riding through town when I was a child walking to school. The platoon sat high in their saddles with drums hanging on the side of their horses. While some soldiers drummed on their drums, other soldiers blew their trumpets. The drum major rode on a horse at the front of the troops, swinging his baton with a mighty swing, which made me always wonder how he could ever hold on to the horse and swing his baton at the same time.

Our town was always full of military, and as I grew up I didn't know any better. My father was a military man and so were most of the fathers of our friends. So growing up among the military was a normal way of life for us kids, and I always thought that all towns were this way.

◆　　◆　　◆

When I was almost four years old, my brother Henk was born. But it was my older brother Jan and I who were close as children. Together we walked to and from school which was a half hour walk from our home. Our school was a newly built public school and had seven classrooms, grades one to seven. It had a large gym which was my favorite place in the building. Our school hours were from 9-12 and from 1:30 until 4:00. Wednesday and Saturday afternoons were free from school. For lunch time we all went home as lunches were not served at school. Those children who lived out of the city could bring a sack lunch. Every morning we had a milk break which was provided by the school. Those children who could not pay for the milk got it for free. There were about 40 children in each room, two students together at one school desk. There was one teacher for each room. Beside the principal and an office worker we had a custodian and a nurse who came only in the morning.

The method of learning was very disciplined from first grade until the last, which was the seventh grade. There was no excuse for misbehaving and we better not have complained to our parents about our teacher. Teachers and parents were as one unit and we kids better listen to them. We always had to speak with two words as ("Yes, Teacher," or "No, mother") to everyone who was older than we were. And it was a sin if we dared to speak with a forward voice to our teacher, parents or anyone older. Giving your seat on the bus to someone older was just expected. We were raised to have respect for authority. If we did something wrong, then we got a spanking, beng, beng, beng, and there was no one to help us out.

From third grade on we always had a great deal of homework to do. We were graded from 1-10 on our work, with 10 being the best grade. A 5 was a failing grade. Besides the regular lessons as mathematics, geography and language etc., the girls of the third grade and above had lessons in knitting, embroidery and mending two times a week. In the fourth grade I learned how to knit socks. I still remember that the first socks I knitted were made of yellow cotton yarn and that I wore them many times. In the meantime the boys went to a class for shop. Also twice a week we had gym in our large gymnasium which also was used in the evenings by Breda's adult gymnastic clubs. I loved gymnastics and when I became older I was pretty good at it and thought that the gym lessons were way too short. The only thing I didn't like was that I was the tallest girl in my gym class. As a child I was tall for my age but later I stopped growing at the age of about 14 years. I was five foot five inches tall, had dark blond hair, blue eyes and was always slender. I also loved to draw and read. Many times I was chosen to read my compositions in front of the classroom, but I was a little too shy to enjoy it.

On our way to school Jan and I had to walk through a park which was named Wilhelmina Park. The many tall growing elm, ash, cottonwood and willow trees and flowering shrubs made it a very pretty park. Geese, swans and ducks lived year around in the two ponds which were separated by a road which led to downtown. In the fall on the way to school, we gathered the wild kastanjes (chestnuts) which had fallen in the moist grass during the night from the very old chestnut trees, and we hid them under some bushes. We then ran to school and we better be there before the bell was ringing, because to be late meant that we had to stay after school—and that was no good! At the end of the school day we hurried back to the park and gathered the kastanjes which we had left under the bushes and took them home. They were so dark, shining and beautiful. We must have gathered hundreds of them each fall. We played with them or strung them together. Later as interest waned, Mother would throw them out.

When there was no school, or after school, we always played outdoors—weather permitting. All the children of our street played games together as jump rope, ball games and games with glass marbles, tops and others. In spring it was kite flying. Jan and I always made our own kites from store bought colored kite paper, that is if Mother could afford to buy some. Or other times when money was very tight, we made our kites from newspapers. But a kite made from newspaper tore so easily, which was no fun. Then Father would always say to us kids, "In this world one did the best one could with what one had."

Many times on our free afternoon from school all the children, young and old, came together and played "hide and seek" for hours. Or, we got our ropes out and everyone played jumping rope, snake or were high jumping. The street was our playground. A car seldom passed through since most people didn't own a car yet in that time in Holland. Our street was a small street not more than a block long, with rows of small houses on both sides, one built against the other—side by side. The houses of our street had no front yards, only a sidewalk. In the back of our homes were small tidy yards which were connected with a wide alley. The houses were locked only at night. During the day people were always rushing in and out of each other houses to borrow things, to gossip, to boast a bit or complain a bit, or tell a joke. Almost all of the married women were not working outside their homes. It was just not done in that time. The men were the breadwinners and the women's work was never as important as his.

On the corner of our street was a small grocery store where I spend the penny I got sometimes from my father or mother for a caramel or some salty licorice which is a favorite "candy" in Holland. I also went to that store to buy the groceries which Mother had forgotten to buy on Saturdays in a larger grocery store where the prices were lower. Or as many times happened, if there was no money to buy groceries, Mother sent me to that neighborhood store to buy the food on credit. Mother would give me a small booklet where the store owner wrote in the groceries I bought on credit. After Father received his next paycheck from the

Army, Mother went to the store and paid her bill. I think that most people bought their food on credit at the end of the week or two weeks, depending when a man got his paycheck.

Every morning the milkman and the baker came through our street with their hand pushed wagon to see if the housewives needed anything. The groenteboer (vegetable and fruit man) came through our street in the afternoons with his horse-pulled wagon to sell his wares. Sometimes Jan and I were hanging on the back of his wagon when he was going from one customer to the next through our small street. Hanging on the vegetable wagon was fun of course, but it was something the groenteman didn't like and he always scolded us, telling us to get away from his wagon.

I must have been about eight or nine years old when the groenteboer bought himself a truck from which he sold his vegetables, potatoes and fruit from that day on. One day Jan, I and two other kids were hanging on the back of his new truck. But this time the veggie man didn't stop at his last customer in our street, as he always had done, and where we always got off before he turned into the next street. This time the veggie man got even with us kids and he was not fooling around. We knew we were in trouble as soon as he drove further without stopping at the house of his last customer. This time we got a lesson none of us kids would forget. As soon as the truck drove out of our street and turned into another street, the two kids who were hanging with us on the back of the truck let themselves fall off. At that point the truck was not going fast yet and I too should have let myself fall. But somehow I couldn't, I thought that maybe the veggie man would stop. Jan screamed at me to let go, but I didn't. So Jan stayed, or rather was hanging with me, and together we were holding on for dear life while the truck sped away. A few streets further Jan pulled himself up into the truck, walked over the vegetables and fruit, and started to slam as hard as he could on the roof of the cab, while yelling to the veggie man to stop. But the man had seemingly a deaf ear for Jan's screaming. I remember how terribly scared I was hanging there, knowing that if I would let go I could easily be killed. Finally after the wild drive which seemed to last forever, the truck stopped in the downtown area. Jan jumped down from the truck and I finally let go of my hold. My arms and hands were hurting badly and we both were shook up. The veggie man came out of his truck and looked at us with a grin on his face. While Jan yelled something to him, we took off for home. We never dared to hang on the truck again. I cannot remember if we told our mother when we came home, but I don't think so. She had warned us a few times before, but we kids had not listened to her.

Now we had paid for it and learned from the consequences of our actions. Luckily everything had turned out all right. The two other kids, as we later learned, had scraped and hurt their knees when they let themselves fall from the truck.

◆   ◆   ◆

On Tuesday and Friday afternoons the fish man came to our neighborhood with his wagon selling fresh fish, such as mussels, herrings, eel and other seafood. The Dutch people eat a lot of fresh fish for lunch or dinner. Usually the fish was caught during the night out of the wind-swept waters of the North Sea, or from the Zuider Zee, which is now called Ysel Meer. Since the fish was sold as soon as the fishing boats came in, they were always fresh and many times still alive. The fish was then sold in the many fish stores or, when I was a child, at the fish market. The fish market was an open place where on large granite tables different kinds of fish was sold very inexpensively by making bids. Many times one bucket full of fresh fish sold for as little as 80 cents. We then took them home in a bag made specially for carrying fish from the fish market.

As children we loved it when the aliekrieken man (snail man) came. He would push his small cart full of little cooked black snails, still in their shells, always to the middle of our street. Then while yelling at the top of his lungs, 'Aliekrieken!'(snails!) he waited for his 'customers' to come. We children would run inside the house, asked Mother for a penny, got a small plate for the snails and a pin from Mother's sewing basket. We then hurried back to the aliekrieken man who was patiently waiting beside his cart. After we bought our snails for the penny, we sat ourselves down on the curb of the sidewalk. With the pin we then took out the little salty snails from their shells and ate them. Since it took some doing to get those small snails out of their shells, it always took a long time before we had emptied our plates. Henk, my little brother, always wanted more. But one penny for each of us was all that Mother could spare.

The month of August was vacation from school. We kept ourselves busy with high jumping, running and other sports in the alley behind our home. Sometimes Jan, I and a few neighbor friends put on a circus show. Usually I was (or maybe I choose myself) to be a Gypsy dancing girl. Jan was the strongman and other kids performed as clowns, tight rope walkers and lion tamers. Henk was the usher, and it was his part to bring the neighborhood kids to their seats. The seats were made by laying boards over flat large stones which had been in our shed. Later, Henk, dressed in a brown fur coat from a neighbor mother's closet, performed as a dancing bear. After a week of rehearsal and some squabbling, it was show time in the alley behind our home. Our yard was our dressing room, our 'costumes' were old clothing from our parents and our friend's parents. The make-up came from one of the mother's kids. The audience were kids from our neighborhood and the adjoining neighborhood. The neighborhoods were small in that time in Breda. What fun we had! Later after our show was over, other kids also tried to put on a show, but it was never as good as our circus show, which made us very proud. After the performance, or when we came in the house after an afternoon of hard playing, Mother made poffertjes. They were baked in a round pan with little hollows. Those little round pancakey things all covered with butter and powder sugar—we couldn't eat enough of them.

On a warm summer Sunday afternoon we occasionally went to the speeltuin 'Waranda' (café with playground) with the whole family. Since the speeltuin was located outside Breda, we went there by steam-tram which was in itself already an adventure. A whole afternoon at the playground was great! There were swings and a merry-go-round, slides and seesaws, swinging boats and best of all we could use them as much as we wanted. There also were funny long mirrors which made you look long and skinny or short and fat. Later when we were thirsty, we sat outside around a table and Father ordered drinks. There was raspberry or lemonade fizz with a straw for us kids, a beer for Father and for Mother a drink of (for me) unknown origin. How very special this was! The playgrounds as we know today in parks and everywhere were unknown when I was a child.

Going on a trip on one's vacation was not done much since most families had no cars yet. To go by train and also sleep in a hotel was for most families too expensive—there was just no money for that. This was true unless they had family living in another town so they could stay with relatives at their home. Traveling to another country as we know today was almost unheard of; only the rich could afford this. Other countries were just far away places we learned about at school or read about in books. But I remember well the few times when we went on our summer vacation for a week to Haarlem.

Haarlem is a town just south of the city Amsterdam. My mother's younger sister Ann, her husband Gerard and their two young sons Ken and Henk lived there not far from the North Sea. Since old people who were alone lived with their children, my grandmother (Mother's mother) lived with them. We had gone by train which was, for my brothers and me, a great adventure of course. I loved to go to Haarlem because when the weather was right we went altogether for the whole day to the beach. The adults rode their bikes and we kids were sitting on the back seats holding on to whatever had to go to the beach with us such as picnic lunch, balls, shovels and small pails. My uncle Gerard even took his tent with him on his bike! Usually I sat on the back seat of my father's bike holding on to some play stuff.

After about twenty minutes riding we reached the sand dunes where, between low-lying dunes, I could see the North Sea glistening in the sunlight. It always gave me such a happy feeling. I always have loved the sea as far back as I can remember. When the tent was set up on the wide beach and we all had changed into our swim suits, I would go by myself to one of the high beautiful sand dunes which line the white beaches of Holland's seashore. There in the warm sunshine, while looking out over the restless sea to the far horizon, I dreamed of far away places. Later, together with my brothers and cousins, we made sand castles as high as we could reach and played in the cold salty water until we shivered. After a whole day on the beach we went home where grandmother had dinner ready for us. She never went with us to the beach but rather stayed home and, as she always would say—made dinner for the family. As a child I never could understand that grandmother would rather stay home than go with us to the beach.

◆     ◆     ◆

Our family enjoyed going to the forest which was about a half hour walk from our home. This large, mostly very tall stately pine, forest which stretches out into Belgium is called 'Mastbos'. It was always fun to go there. When we went there for the whole day, which was usually a few times on our vacations, Mother made a large picnic lunch which consisted of broodjes (buns) with ham or cheese and krenten broodjes (currant buns) with butter. We also had apples and cookies and peanuts in their shells. For drinks we had lemonade and milk. After our picnic we picked blueberries which grew plentiful in August. Later we made a water pit with the sand shovels which we had brought with us. Since the people in Holland live almost on top of the water, it took us kids only about two feet of digging until the water came into our hole. After playing in the hole with water for a while we played hide and seek in the forest behind the tall trees until it was time to go home. Since we didn't have a car, we always had to walk wherever we went. Now walking to the forest was one thing, but going home was another story. I still can remember how tired I was sometimes and Mother always was saying, "We are almost home, just a little further." Going home and with the picnic stuff gone, Henk was sitting in the stroller which we always took with us for all the things we needed that day. He would sit on the picnic blanket while holding on to the ball and shovels. Looking at my brother and feeling envious I always thought, "How lucky can you get!"

Once in awhile on our vacation Mother and a neighbor with her two young sons took us to the forest to play. But those times we never stayed very long. The oldest boy always liked to tease me, which made me mad, and then I burst out in tears, which made Mother nervous.

The Dutch Queen Wilhelmina's birthday was on the last day of August. This was, in the old Dutch tradition, a day of celebration. Flags were waving in the wind everywhere. There were parades and in the evening a big fireworks display at the kazerne grounds. We kids liked that day, watching the parade and especially the fireworks in the evening. You have to know that as children we never were allowed to play outside after sunset. "No good comes from playing in the dark," my father would say. So of course, it was exciting to walk to the fireworks in the dark with my parents and my brothers. At the kazerne grounds there was always a special place set aside for the officers and NCO's and their families to sit and watch the fire displays. All other citizen of Breda had to stay further up, behind a roped off area from where they watched the fireworks. Because our family was permitted to sit on chairs in a special section of the field, I always thought that we were very special.

It was as if all the mothers from our town had a silent agreement that every Monday was the day they had to do their weekly laundry. The ceremony of washday started the evening before when, after supper, Mother sorted the white from the dark laundry. After the sorting she put the white wash in a large water kettle. She then filled it half full with cold water and added a few handfuls of soft green soap before the kettle went on the gas burner where it was further filled with water. In that time we didn't have the large hot water heaters as we know today. Mother turned the gas off under the kettle before she went to bed. Early the following morning when I got up, Mother was already busy with her laundry and had removed the small table and chairs from the kitchen. A large tub stood on a wooden stool with the clothes and hot water from the kettle, and Mother was busy washing the linens and white clothes with a scrubber on a washboard.

By the time we came home for lunch, Mother was washing the dark laundry while the clean white wash was soaking in a tub of bleach water. Because Mother's temper was short and cranky on wash day, we better stay out of her way. With a frown between her eyes, Mother made our lunch with hands which were wrinkled from the water. We used the dishes from the breakfast table which were still on the table. Father had never much to say on those days. He knew it was better not to talk when Mother had her wash day. As soon as Jan and I had finished our lunch, we took off. Wash day was the only day of the week when we kids were at our school very early.

In summer time when the weather was sunny and we came home in the afternoon from school, the dark laundry was fluttering in the breeze and Mother was almost done. But in wintertime it always took her longer. Mother's hands were always very red from the ice cold rinse water. When dusk came I had to help her bring in the frozen stiff laundry, which hung on the outside wash lines. Reluctantly I would help mother with this job of bringing the stiff laundry two flight of stairs up to the attic, were we hung the frozen laundry on the wash lines. Some of the laundry she hung to dry on a rack around the hearth. Yes, washday was the least pleasant day of the week for everyone, especially for the women with large families. It was very hard work. Tuesday or Wednesdays was a day set aside for ironing the laundry. This was done with an iron which was heated on the gas stove. If the iron was too hot the ironed article was scorched—something that happened many times.

Almost every neighborhood had its "scary" people. They were just ordinary people. But because they were oddly dressed, walked or talked differently, we children labeled them "scary." The scary people in our neighborhood were two old women who lived in a small dead-end street. From their small front room which they had made into a store, they sold different kinds of potatoes. Occasionally when Mother came for dinner too short on potatoes, she sent me there to buy some. In the time of my childhood the Dutch people att, besides vegetable and meat or fish, boiled potatoes for dinner almost every day. I did not like to go to that small potato store. It took a lot of courage for me to open the door and walk into the dark looking room which was full of wooden crates filled with different kinds of potatoes. The two old women in their long grimy dresses and with their dark scarves covering their long gray hair, looked like witches to me. As soon as I had my potatoes, I ran out of the store back home telling Mother (again) that I never wanted to go there anymore—ever!

Another 'scary' person was a woman who was divorced. Since divorcing was not a common thing to do in that time, we kids didn't know what the word *divorce* meant. We never had heard about the fact that fathers and mothers sometimes separated. But we had heard our parents talking about a women who lived in our neighborhood and that her husband had left her. Not understanding any of this, the neighborhood children thought it sinister and scary. She was not to be trusted! Whenever we saw the divorced woman coming down the street, we went to the other side so we didn't have to pass her.

♦        ♦        ♦

Jan loved to tease me and was always ready to make me mad. Sometimes I would take a swing at him, and then we were in the biggest fight till Mother came between us. Even so Jan and I were buddies and were always together, fighting or not, especially when in the fall our yearly kermis (fair) came to town. Our school was located one block from where the fair was held. The week before the opening of the fair, workmen came to set everything up. The kermis always lasted one week, but for Jan and me the excitement lasted two weeks. Every day after school we went together to the fairground to see how much those men had done that day. Mother didn't like it that we went near that area when they were setting up the fair. But every day after school, forgetting Mother's warnings, we hurried to the fairgrounds to inspect everything, and then we would run all the way home. Most of the time Mother knew that we had been there, and she would be angry with us. Jan and I never could understand how she knew. She always told us that she knew everything because she had eyes in the back of her head.

The first day of the opening, which was always in the evening, our family went to the kermis. But because that opening night was so very crowded, we went only to look at everything first. The sweet smell of oliebollen (sort of donut without the hole) and poffertjes filled the air long time before we even reached the fair-grounds. What wonderful things we saw. There were so many great rides and show tents. In front of some of the show tents were girls in skimpy costumes dancing to the tune of music. I always thought how beautiful those girls were. Later when we came home from the fair I always had to practice all those steps I had seen the dancing girls made.

It was a large kermis which also had a circus with tigers, horses, elephants, and clowns. As we went further over the crowded fair, we stared at sword swallowers, fire eaters and dancing bears. Then at the end of the evening Father bought each of us a fresh fried oliebol, and for us kids also a lekstok (candy stick.) My brothers always wanted a cinnamon, and me a peppermint stick. Eating them was a sheer delight! I never could take my eyes off the refreshment stand which was fabulous. The decorations were beyond belief. The wagon was as large as a good size mobile home of today. It stood on wheels because after the fair it was pulled to another fair in another town. The top half of the front was raised and became a roof for us to stand under while we chose our goodies. The bottom half was painted with colorful scenes. On the counter were large glass containers which held candy sticks of all sorts and sizes, large pieces of nougat and drop (salty licorice). On one side of the wagon behind glass, were the just-fried oliebollen and appleflappen (apple oliebol) waiting for the hungry fairgoers. The smells were wonderful and permeated the whole fairground. The inside walls of the wagon had small shelves attached at different levels. Those shelves held statues and figurines, some moving as the music played. Small pieces of mirrors were hanging by strings from the ceiling and moved in the night breeze and caught all the lights and colors of the fair. By today's standards it was gaudy, but viewed through a child's eye, it was the most wonderful snack wagon in the world.

As we walked back home in the dark, eating the goodies and talking about all we had seen that evening at the kermis, I always squinted my eyes while looking up at the lamp posts. The lights became long and skinny which danced with every step I took. On Wednesday or Saturday afternoon we went to the fair again with Mother, and we could ride many of the rides. Later when Jan and I got older we were allowed to go by ourselves, and we always had a great time, especially sliding down from the very high and wide large covered slide.

◆    ◆    ◆

Winter came slowly to Holland. Now it comes even slower and sometimes not at all. When my grandparents were young, winters were much colder. In those times the people from Holland used the many waterways large and small, to go to work, to school or just to visit. It was easier to skate to a destination than to go over the country roads. The frozen rivers and canals made for a speedy thoroughfare. Many times children would rather skate than walk. So the Dutch grew up with ice skates. It was a way of life which disappeared with improved roads, warmer winters, and later the cars.

I remember as a young girl going ice skating with my best girlfriend Mies in Wilhelmina Park where a lot of our neighborhood friends also came to skate. In outdoor stalls, which were staying on the ice, we could buy hot cocoa, anise milk and other goodies while a colorful draaiorgel (barrel organ) played our favorite tunes. Boys and girls watched each other, skated together and made dates for the next weekend. Yes, Mies and I always had a great time, especially when we got older and skated with the boys from our neighborhood. The Dutch still like to ice skate and, if the winter happens to be cold and rivers and ponds are frozen over, young and old can still be seen skating on the ice.

In winter time after school when the weather was bad, we played indoor games. We also did a lot of reading. I think that every neighborhood had its own library which was well used by adults and children alike. We would rent a book for ten cent a whole week. Children books were 5 cent. In the evenings after a simple prepared meal of vegetable, potatoes and fish or some meat, our whole family sat around the large table which stood in the middle of our living room. Above the table a lamp hung from the ceiling and was covered with a pretty lampshade. While we sat around the table, each doing our own thing, such as reading or homework, Mother made tea. Usually it was made with a little sugar and a little bit of milk, and we drank it with a biscuit-like cookie—only one.

Sitting in his favorite chair at the table, Father always played his game of chess in the evenings. Many times he smoked a cigar, or rather the half of a cigar, the other half he saved for a next time. Father belonged to a chess club in Breda and was always involved in State and National competitions. He won many trophies playing against other chess clubs. Of course, he wanted his children also to become interested in his favorite game of chess, and he taught us how to play. But none of his children became a chess player as he was. Father believed that children should be encouraged to collect things, and it didn't matter what it was. So Father started me on a collection of cigar bands, which I then glued in an album. Over the years I got a real nice collection. Father brought also, from the canteen, movie star cards for me. They came out of packages of cigarettes which most of the military men threw away.

The radio was as important to us for news, commentary and music, as the TV is today. Every Friday evening Father listened to the "Weekly World News"on our radio, which was half an hour of mostly political news. During that time we kids had to be completely quiet. But that was also the time we had supper at our home. During our dinner time we always talked about the events of the day or school friends and the things we had seen or heard and learned. Being silent while eating our supper was not the easiest thing to do, and many times Father, who was all ears for his half-hour of politics, reprimanded us kids when we were not completely quiet. I still wonder why Mother did not serve our dinner later or earlier. But then, I think, in those times the days were planned with the precision of a railroad clock schedule.

For special evening programs on the radio we all sat around to listen. Mother and I were always doing some knitting or mending. There were always things to mend such as socks, hosiery, and underwear. There was never an end to those! I was still young when our parents taught us never to waste our time—there was always something that had to be done. The "I'll get it done tomorrow" attitude was not tolerated. While Jan was sitting at the table, half reading and half listening to the radio, he was eating peanuts out of the shell. Henk played with his small cast iron cars on the table, and Father would as always play his chess game while listening to the special program.

After a special musical evening of the "Bonte Dinsdag Avond Train" ("The Tuesday Evening Variety Train") everyone sang or whistled the tunes of that evening the following day. How I remember walking to school and hearing the housewives singing while they cleaned their homes—windows always wide open. Or the bread boy on his bicycle with, on his steering wheel, a breadbasket full of bread which he had to deliver to the customers in our neighborhood. While pedaling, he would whistle the tunes of the radio show we all had heard the evening before.

On Friday evenings everyone listened to the weekly horror story of "Dodenhuis" (House of Death). Not many people missed this scary show in Holland! On the radio on late Sunday afternoons, there was a very popular children's show by the name of "Ome Keesje" (Uncle Kees). It was an adventure story of a older man going to the moon or going to China, etc. Those adventure story programs, which we always listened to, continued throughout the winter months.

December was the month of excitement. Every year on December 6, St. Nicholas' birthday was celebrated in Holland. The month before this special day, all stores were full of toys and gifts and goodies. Everyone was happy and excited, and the singing of St. Nicholas songs was heard everywhere. Two weeks before the big celebration, St. Nick and his servants, (black helpers) came with their horses on a big ship from 'Spain'. The ship was richly decorated with many flags which were waving in the wind. As the ship slowly entered the harbor of Breda, hundreds of children with their parents started to sing the St. Nicholas songs along with the military band. Soon the ship anchored and after a welcome speech by the mayor of Breda, St. Nicholas came ashore leading his beautiful white horse. He was followed by his black helpers who were riding on black horses. Since there were no black people living in that time in Holland, St. Nick's servants were young man with their faces painted black. They were dressed in beautiful silk and velvet costumes with plumes atop velvet berets. Behind them came a horse-pulled wagon full of packages for the good girls and boys. At the end of the parade came black servants carrying large jute sacks to put in those children who had been bad that year.

For two weeks every night before bedtime, the younger children, the ones who still believed in St. Nicholas, put one shoe in front of the hearth. In the shoe was a carrot for St. Nick's horse and a glass of water for St. Nick himself. While singing a St. Nicholas song in front of the hearth, we hoped that St. Nick would come that night to bring us some candy. Sometimes the following morning, to our excitement, the carrot was gone and the glass empty. In its place there would be a chocolate or a few sugar candies in our shoe. It took very little to make us happy.

Soon the big night of December 5 arrived and families came together to open packages. Many times the gifts were accompanied by a self written poem, most of them very funny. Then after the opening of the gifts, there was a feast of almond pastries, speculaas, and chocolates. If the family had young children, St. Nicholas came during the night while the children were sleeping. In the morning of December 6 they would find their presents displayed on the table. There were toys, and games and books, and a new dress or sweater. Every year we got our initial in chocolate and a large speculaas (spice) cookie in the form of a doll. Sometimes when my parents could afford it, we got also marzipan made in a pretty shape which looked like a work of art. That day we were free from school, which made it a extra feast. In order to enjoy such a special day one had to be awake, which was sometimes hard to do in the afternoon after getting up so very early in the morning.

A few days before Christmas (which is a two day holiday in Europe) our family went together to buy a Christmas tree in an open area close to the marketplace. Because the living room of our house was quite small, it never was a large tree. They were fresh cut and the smell of pine filled our home. The short needle evergreen trees were always decorated one or two days before Christmas and kept up until after New Years Day or until the sixth of January, Three Kings Day .

Every Friday our house, which was shined up by Mother from top to bottom, got an extra special cleaning before Christmas. While I decorated the living room with holly and greens, Jan and Henk hung the glass blown ornaments, glittering garlands and tinsels on the tree. The decorations were always stored in our attic. When we kids were done with the decoration, we hung the chocolate and cookies in the form of wreaths on a red ribbon from the tree branches. The top of our Christmas tree was decorated with a large bell which, as I remember, we had for many years. When all was done, Mother put the small white or colored Christmas candles in their holders and then on the tree. They were lighted only on the two Christmas nights in the evenings after dinner.

Every year Father bought a very pretty Christmas ornament for the tree, as the lovely butterfly I remember so well. As Father was taking the ornament out of its paper and was hanging it on a branch, Mother always said to him, "Oh, you shouldn't have, Jan,"and she would tell him how extravagant he was. But I think she enjoyed this little special tradition of my father. Presents were not given on Christmas; those were strictly for St. Nicholas on December 6.

The first day of Christmas was mainly for church activities and family togetherness. There was always a lot of special food to eat for Christmas, such as stollen (Christmas bread), buttercake and flaky almond pastries. Christmas dinner was made special with rabbit and pork roast, mashed potatoes and vegetables in a special sauce. For dessert there was usually vanilla pudding with a fruit sauce. After we had eaten our Christmas dinner, my father would light the candles on the tree. They burned only about 20 minutes. The more expensive ones would burn about half an hour. We children always had fun betting which candle would burn the longest. When the small candles were burned out, we could eat a cookie and a chocolate wreath which were hanging from the branches of the tree.

The rest of the evening our family played games together or played cards. Those customs were repeated on the second Christmas Day, which was also a day for family and friends visiting each other. Or as young people did, going to the afternoon dance in a hotel in downtown. We had no family living in Breda, and on those holidays I always thought how great it must be to have grandparents, aunts and uncles and cousins to help celebrate those special days. Sometimes the ground outside was covered with sparkling snow which crackled under our feet, but most of the time it was just cold and dry. In my childhood years no one in Holland decorated their homes on the outside. The first time I saw this done was when we came to America.

I remember well one special Christmas Eve. I must have been about eight or nine years old. That night it was the very first time that I went to a church service. Religion was just not practiced in our home, not even talked about. I don't think Father believed in a God. Or maybe he had his own private God with whom he communicated. I don't know. Much later I would learn that Father did not care much for churches, not for any kind of church. He believed that the churches were ruling and domineering the people of all walks of life. Mother came from a Baptist family. Even though she seldom set a foot inside a church, she believed there was an Almighty God. Mother, who loved to sing, sometimes sang a religious hymn which she probably remembered from her childhood. But that was as far as it went with the religion in our home. As a little girl, church was a strange place for me where only other people went, but not my family. I saw the churches only on the outside but never saw the inside. Sometimes when a church door was open and I happened to pass by, I wanted to peek inside, curious as to what that mysterious place looked like. But I never made it further than three feet from the entrance and I hurried further on.

One day a neighbor girl, who was my friend and a year older than I was, asked me if I wanted to go with her to her Sunday school and learn about Jesus. Even though I didn't know anything about Him except that Jesus was born on Christmas Day, I wanted very much to go with her and learn about Jesus. Sometimes before she had told me about a man named Jesus who had lived a long time ago, and I had become curious. After talking to Mother about it, she said that I could go. So for the next year and a half I walked together with my friend every Sunday morning to the school of her church, which was a Dutch Reform Church. There for the first time I learned about God, Jesus, Heaven and Hell and about praying. Every Sunday we got from the Sunday school teacher a small religious card with a prayer or verse printed on it which we had to learn for that following week. This I faithfully did.

Mother, who wanted to go with me that night to the Christmas program of my friend's church, was sick in bed and couldn't go. After some talking it was decided that I was going alone with my friend and her parents. As it turned out it was the most beautiful experience for me. I remember that as soon as we came inside the church, I saw the largest Christmas tree I ever had seen. It was decorated with all sorts and sizes of glass angels which were hanging from its branches. They caught the lights from the many burning candles in the church and they twinkled like stars on a clear frosty winter night. I was in awe over the beauty I saw, and it brought a great feeling inside of me. I never had thought that it was so pretty inside a church. When the choir started to sing a Christmas song and the people joined in, I wished that Mother was with me so we could have enjoyed this wonderful night together.

When the Christmas program ended, each child received cookies with a pretty paper angel on top of each of them. It was very cold as we later walked home. The cookies, which I saved for Mother, were deep in my coat pocket while my hand was protecting them. I knew that the cookies would make Mother happy. Later when I didn't attend Sunday school anymore, I saved the little religious cards which I had received from the Sunday school teacher. I especially loved the one of an evening prayer and saved it for many years.

On winter Sunday afternoons when the weather was cold and dreary, Father, Mother and we kids would play those afternoons away with games like Chinese checkers, checkers, playing cards, shuffleboard or table tennis. Or with Father we would put together a large puzzle which he had bought at a bookstore in downtown. While we were busy, Mother made tea with a cookie or a chocolate. The many junk foods as we know today were not invented yet. Another treat came occasionally on a Sunday morning, when Father and I walked to the pastry shop and bought there for each of us a gebakje (pastry). Father always let me choose the pastries, which was difficult because there were so many different ones. One was more delicious than the other, and it was not easy to find just the right ones. But finally I had five of them. For Mother a 'Bosse Boll', which is a cream puff filled with real cream and iced with chocolate. She loved those. For Father a 'Tompoez,' (Napoleon) his favorite pastry. My brothers always told me to buy for them the largest pastry in the store and it didn't mattered which one. And for myself I usually choose the chocolate cup filled with real cream and a piece of pineapple on top. I carefully carried home the box with goodies, where Mother had coffee ready for Father and herself. We children got milk.

In Holland, a New Year's Eve party was, and still is, strictly a home affair. That night everyone is at home with family and/or friends usually playing cards. Or just talking while eating the New Years Eve traditional oliebollen and appleflappen (oliebol with apple inside) dusted with powdered sugar which the women of the house had fried that day. It always took Mother hours of work. We children would watch with excitement the large bowls getting fuller and fuller of all the oliebollen and appleflappen. Besides the hors d'oeuvre there was also the pastry named 'banket letter' (puff pastry filled with an almond paste filling) in the form of a letter. It was a favorite for that night in Holland.

Then toward midnight the radio told the people the exact time and, when midnight arrived, the fireworks in the streets went off with a big bang. After first wishing each other the best in the new year, people went outside—that is if the weather was not too bad—and wished each other a prosperous new year. Back in their warm homes a priest spoke on the radio to bless each and every one. In the meantime the coffee was ready. While we ate worstenbrood, which is a long bun made of a flaky dough with hamburger inside, the party went on for hours. By that time we kids had been sleeping already for hours. On New Year's Day all stores were closed and no one was working which is still the case until this day. Family and or friends came together for some more oliebollen and appleflappen which were fresh fried or left over from the night before. The women drank coffee while the men emptied the leftover bottles of drinks.

Each season had its special delights, and Easter, which also is a two-day holiday, was a time for rejoicing. For me it was also made special by the fact that each year I got a new dress, which I wore even if the weather was still cold and somber. Sometimes, when money was not too tight, Father bought a pretty Easter basket, a large chocolate bunny and a chocolate chicken for us kids. We could choose which one we wanted. They were large and pretty and delicious to eat. I remember that my brothers gobbled their chocolates in a few days, but I just couldn't bring myself to eat it so soon, and it always took me at least a week before I ate the last bite of chocolate.

◆     ◆     ◆

My childhood years went on, mostly with school of course. When free from school and if the weather was good, I played outdoors with Jan or with friends from our street. Occasionally on a Wednesday or Saturday afternoon, Jan and I rented a scooter with large wheels in a small store around the corner of our street for 5 cents an hour. Since we got money for one hour only we rented just one scooter and divided the time between us. It was fun, but a half-hour each was always too short a time.

My best girlfriend was Mies, a girl who lived in our street. We had known each other ever since we were toddlers. She was the same age as I was and together we went to the same school. Mies was talkative and had a way of laughing at herself, which made her company stimulating. Her father was also in the military and was a drum major with the Cavalry. For my tenth birthday I had received roller skates from my parents. Mies and I liked to skate on the 'teerweg' which was a tar road just around the corner from our street. It was one of the first stone streets in Breda which was replaced with tar and it became a great place for kids to roller skate. Most kids were on the tar road as soon as they came home from school. Many times that spring and summer I could be found on the teerweg skating with my girlfriend Mies.

Then in late summer I lost my brother Jan to soccer. He now played on a soccer team, and in his free time he was found on the soccer fields. Our Wednesday and Saturday afternoons of running and jumping or just playing were over, and I missed him. I was used to having my brother, who loved everything which was sport, being around me. Together we always had races—which of us could run the fastest and who could jump the highest. He had taught me how to ride on our father's bicycle with one leg under the bar, in the alley behind our house. Jan was never bored and came up with the best games. Besides Jan having not much time for me, my best girlfriend Mies moved away to a new neighborhood and we didn't see much of each other anymore. It was dreadful, and I was quite lonely and unhappy for a while. I thought my brother Henk was too young to play with. He had his own little playmates who were, in my eyes, just little kids.

When there was no school, my mother kept me busy with all kinds of jobs around the house, something she was very good at. I enjoyed gardening in our small backyard and, even if it was small, it was always full of flowers. Father liked roses, especially tea roses, and we always had a lot of them growing in the summer. Mother's favorite was a red climbing rose which grew against and over the roof of our shed and down the other side. Every summer it had hundreds of fragrant smelling flowers which Mother would give away in late summer to the neighbors who lived around us.

We had a cat and, as I remember, we had a cat most of the time. But this cat was special—it was gray striped and a very lovable cat. It had babies every spring which I loved but my mother did not. She liked the cat but not the eight or more babies she always produced. To have a dog or cat neutered or spade was not a common thing to do in that time. The money was probably needed for other things. So, every spring it was the same problem, what to do with all those young kittens. Sometimes Mother took a pail of water and would drown the little kittens as soon as they were born. She always said that they were "gone" as soon as they touched the water, which did not make me feel any better. Mother always left one or two kittens for the mother to nurse. Later she would give the little kitties away. One year Father got an idea. He took the eight-week-old kittens to his kazerne and set them free. The soldiers loved all the young kittens and gave them food. Many of them would take a kitty home on their leave. But I don't think this was a good idea from Father, because he never did it again. Sometimes we had a dog, but I think we were not very lucky with them. As I remember we never had them for very long, or Mother would call the humane society one day, and we never saw the poor dog again. But a cat we had always for many years.

Mother and I liked to go shopping in downtown. Occasionally, at the end of the afternoon before going home, we went to a restaurant which was located above a department store. It had the name of the "Hema"where Mother ordered a 'tea-complete' for both of us. This was very special in my eyes since going out to eat, especially with the family, was almost never done. The 'tea-complete' consisted of hot tea in a delicate teapot with dainty little cups. On a silver tray was the most delicious finger food, almost too pretty to eat. This was something that only Mother and I did together. It was our special secret and I thought it was just great! I never told my brothers of this little adventure of Mother and me.

◆    ◆    ◆

When I became 12 years old, we moved to the neighborhood where Mies lived, and we became the best of friends again. The houses were, as children used to say—on the end of the city. Our house was a nicely built house which was in the last street of a new neighborhood. From the back of our home we overlooked the farm fields with here and there a farm with outbuildings. During summer time I loved to hear the farm children singing while they were milking the cows in the field, or later in the fall, as they were picking the apples in their orchards. I think that most of those children belonged to a church choir because their singing was not only in tune with each other, but also very clear and pure. Especially in the evenings when nature became still, the sounds of those children's voices over the fields was truly beautiful to hear.

The houses in our street, which were built one against the other, were larger than in our old neighborhood. Besides a larger living room and kitchen, we now had four bedrooms, two of them were small. We now also had a large attic where we could not only store all the stuff we didn't need, but where we kids could play. Because of Holland's high water, basements were never built in the houses. Besides a small back yard with a shed, there was also a front yard. Father, who liked birds, had told us that he was going to built a large birdhouse in the back yard now that he had room for one. The year before he got a canary from a bar owner. The man had told Father that he wanted to get rid of the bird because it sang too much and too loud in his bar. Some men threw things at the cage to make the bird stop singing. The canary was not pretty, too much brown, but its singing was unbelievable. It sang the whole day with a most beautiful trilling warbling. Sometimes when its singing became too much in the evenings, it sang even with a cloth over its cage. Later when the birdhouse was finished, Father said that the canary now could sing as much as it wanted to. That summer he bought many pretty birds for his large and grand birdhouse.

Mies lived on the Molengracht Straat. This street went from our neighborhood west to Wilhelmina Park and further to the downtown area. The Molengracht Straat was the main street of our neighborhood and started just around the corner of our street, which was named Zeisstraat. Beside houses the Molengracht Straat also had some stores and a bar. Just outside our neighborhood, going to the Wilhelmina Park, stood the paint factory 'Teolin'. On the other side of the Teolin was a large klooster (cloister) where many nuns lived, but who we never saw. Going to the east from the Zeisstraat, the Molengracht Straat came to an end, ending at a clump of very old and large cottonwood trees. From there, on both sides of those beautiful trees, started two winding paths. One went to the right and went not only to the entrance of boer (farmer) Backx large farm, but also further to a large Seminary named 'The Ypelaar' which stood about half a mile further to the east. The other path was winding through meadows and farmland with here and there a farm which we could see from the backside of our house.

On rainy Saturday afternoons when Mies finished practicing on her piano, we would go to the attic of her home. It was a large attic where we played theater, and where we dressed ourselves in all the old clothing which was hanging on a long rack. We curled our hair and used her mother's make up. We then fantasized we were famous movie stars. I still remember how much fun we had and how it made us explode into giggles. In that attic was also a large album of photographs of grownups in what we kids called, 'their clothes of olden times' which send us into laughing for the longest time.

Mies and I sometimes went to see a movie. For 29 cents we spent the whole afternoon at the movie theater. Besides a double feature, we watched a Mickey Mouse cartoon and a newsreel. We especially loved the Diana Durban movies. When going with Jan to the movies, we usually went to see one or another cowboy movie.

Sundays after I had washed the lunch dishes, I took my bicycle which I got from my parents for my twelfth birthday. My bike was a second hand one, as was that of Mies, but they were as good as can be, and happily we would ride on our bikes together to the Mastbos. When the weather was nice, we usually went to the 'Seven Huiveltjes' which was an area in the forest where seven hills were close together. We rode on our bikes up and down the tree-lined hills until we were tired of it. We then pedaled further into the forest to a swampy area where thousands of kikkers (frogs) lived. The sounds of their croaking in spring and summer was deafening, but fascinating. We always stayed there for a short time. But it was fun just looking at the leaping frogs with their long legs. After the swampy frog area, we rode out of the forest to a tennis court which was located on the edge of the Mastbos. While we watched the rich play tennis, we dreamed we were going to marry a rich boy someday so we could afford to play tennis too. Also on that same road was located a small but very pretty castle which looked as though it came right out of a storybook. The castle was named 'Kasteel Bouvigne'. Even if it was very old, it was well kept up and still in use. A wide moat surrounded the castle and gardens. It was accessible only by a drawbridge. Mies and I always stopped our bikes there on the way home, just to look at the pretty picturesque sight. Yes, it was all so free and uncomplicated, and we were always looking for new adventures.

On a free afternoon from school, Mies and I sometimes had a bike race with all the boys and girls from our neighborhood. It was fun and I always won the girls' races. I guess I probably had strong legs from all the running I had always done with Jan. Most of the time we all would wind up at the bakery at the corner of our street to buy some goodies. We liked to hang out there, boys and girls. And while sitting or hanging on our bikes, we talked and joked together for the rest of the afternoon.

# 17

# TRIP TO AMSTERDAM

The happy times of my early childhood passed. When I became fourteen years old, Jan and I planned to go together on our first big bicycle trip. We decided to go to Amsterdam first, and then before going home, we would go to Haarlem, which is a city south of Amsterdam. We planned to spend some time with our families and also go to the beach in Haarlem, where we had gone before with our parents a few years earlier. In both cities we had grandmothers who lived there with our tantes (aunts). They wanted very much that Jan and I came for a visit. So one summer day on our vacation, very early in the morning and with our bicycles in top shape, we started our 80 mile bike trip to Amsterdam.

Holland is a flat country and bicycle paths are everywhere which makes it for easy riding. It is truly a bicycle country where almost all people own one. But Holland is also windy and if a strong northwest wind is blowing, the going is slow. Our mother had seen to it that, besides our clothing in the suitcase, we had plenty of food—fruit and snacks to take with us on our trip. The containers of drinks were hanging in a bag on our steering wheels. In Holland in that time, there were no fast food places yet, and eating in a cafeteria took too much time and money. With our bikes loaded, some money and a road map in Jan's pocket, we were on our way to Amsterdam.

The sun was just above the horizon as we rode through the typical Dutch landscape of flat green fields and roads lined with willow trees. With its black and white cows grazing in the fertile and rich pasture, we passed windmills and drove through sleepy toy villages. Our first stop was beside the river Maas, which is a beautiful wide river coming from the north of France and emptying into the North Sea in Holland. A few years later many soldiers would be killed on its bank or drowned in the water. Little did we know then that the horrors of WWII were soon to come.

On the side of the river in a small park where ducks played in the early morning sun, Jan and I had our breakfast which Mother had earlier made for us. Our plan had been to go to Amsterdam via the city Utrecht, and then later after we had passed Utrecht, we planned to stop at Soesdyk. It was there in that small town where the palace of Princess Juliana and her husband Prince Bernard was located. The Royal couple expected their second child any day and Jan and I thought that maybe it would be born that day when we drove by. We would be swept up in the excitement of the happy occasion which the Dutch people were looking forward to.

When we had finished our breakfast in the small park, Jan studied his road map. He told me that we had to go on a ferry over the river Maas. The location of the ferry should be somewhere close by. For me it was the first time I was on a ferry and I thought it was exciting. It took about 15 minutes before we were on the other side of the river, and soon we were on our way in the direction of Utrecht. We rode further through winding tree-lined roads and villages where the apple and pear trees stood heavy with fruit. Sometimes we rested and Jan would look on his road map to see if we were on the right road. Then we went further again riding through golden wheat fields sprinkled with bright blue cornflowers. We soon passed the city of Utrecht on our way to Soesdyk. When we reached the beautiful white palace which lay in a grassy area with many trees and lovely flowers, a large crowd, especially reporters, was gathered before the closed gates. As we stopped our bikes at the palace gates, we heard that the baby was not yet born. It started to drizzle and Jan and I decided to go further to Amsterdam. It was the following day, August 5, 1939, that Princess Irene was born.

We reached Amsterdam early in the evening and, after first some searching for the right street, we arrived at Grandmother and Tante (aunt) Dien's house. Grandmother, my father's mother was born July 8, 1863. Her maiden name was Jacoba Crabshuis. She was a pleasant old lady who liked fun and joked a lot. Her long gray hair was worn combed back and tied in a chignon. She wore simple dresses with long skirts which were covered by a dark colored apron. Her husband, my grandfather Martin Jansen, was born on November 8, 1869 and died on March 4 of 1929. At the time of his death he worked for a gas company, laying and repairing gas-pipes. Tante Dien, my father's only sister, had never been married and lived together with my grandmother. She always tried to marry her daughter off, but Tante Dien never had been much interested in men. Mother told me one day, that Tante Dien sometimes would mutter to herself how bad all men were, and that she never would give one the time of day.

Grandma loved cats and always had two of them. Grandmother also liked clocks. Everywhere there were chime clocks in her home—from a Big Ben to small cuckoo clocks. Because they were running at all different times it took a long time before they all had their chance to chime. Now in daytime this was not so bad but at night, especially at midnight, it drove Jan and me bananas. We couldn't sleep! In our family, as was in most families of that time, old people were treated with special reverence. But Jan thought this chime business went too far. The end was that grandmother and Jan compromised and two clocks, the Big Ben and a little cuckoo clock in her kitchen were going to stay working. The other clocks were silenced.

Our cousin Coby was a tall girl who was blessed with a lovely shade of dark red hair. She was three weeks older than I was and very outspoken. She and her younger brother Max lived with their parents not far from our grandmother and Tante Dien. They lived above their lamp and electricity store which was located in the old neighborhood, the 'Jordaan.' Oom (uncle) Max was my father's younger brother and one of the first men to bring electricity into the city of Amsterdam. His store, by the name of 'Max Jansen—Lamps and Electric,' dated from 1928 and became well known throughout Amsterdam. They sold many lamps and lampshades which they brought from all over Europe.

Every morning after our breakfast Jan and I walked to their store to pick up Coby to go somewhere. During vacations, she usually had to work in her parents business, but because we were in Amsterdam, she could go. Coby knew all the right places to go to, and we three always had a lot of fun.

Amsterdam was once a marshland. It began as a small fishing village when fish traders settled there on a sand bank a thousand years ago. Later it grew into a small town and expanded after 1100, and became an official chartered city in 1300. During the 1600s, Amsterdam played a major role in Holland's golden age. Trade and new territory made Holland a world power and Amsterdam became the largest city. They called Amsterdam a 'Mokum' meaning a safe city. The houses and other buildings in Amsterdam are build up out of the water on piles. The Royal Palace alone stands on 13,659 piles. There are many museums and theaters where Jan, our cousin Coby and I spent many a day. There was so much entertainment and things to see and to do for young and old that we never had enough time. Amsterdam with its stately houses and its many canals was then a most pleasant city. We loved the croquettes from the automats or herring sold in one of the many fish stalls, which were open until late in the evenings. After a day of adventure we went home where grandmother had dinner ready for us. Grandmother and Tante Dien always spoiled us with the best meals. Yes, Jan and I always had a great time in Amsterdam, a time I will never forget.

After about three weeks of exploring Amsterdam and enjoying our family, we rode our bikes to the city of Haarlem, where our other grandmother lived with

Tante Nel. Grandmother was born on March 3, 1865. Her name was Eefje Breeuwer. She came from a windmill family and grew up in the vicinity of Haarlem. When her mother died, Grandmother was young and had no sisters or brothers. She married Grandfather when she was 17 years old. His name was Hendrik Breeuwer. It was a happy but short marriage. Grandfather was born in 1861 and died in 1903 of blood poisoning . At the time of his death he was a salesman in chocolates, leaving behind his wife and five children with little money. In those times there were no social services or any kind of government help for a widow and her children. People in those situations depended on their churches for financial help. To make ends meet Grandmother started to sew for other people. Some of her children were very young when Grandfather died. The others were only in their early teenage years, and had to quit school. They had to start working long hours to bring in the money for living.

Later when all her children were married, Grandmother moved in with her youngest daughter, Ann. Tante (aunt) Ann and her husband Oom (uncle) Gerard and their two young sons Ken and Henk lived in Haarlem. We had been there on vacation before, the time we all had gone to the beach. In the depression years, it had become difficult for Oom Gerard to find work anymore. Seeing great opportunities for his trade as a carpenter in South Africa, he took his family and emigrated to the city of Bloemfontein, South Africa. After their move from Holland, Grandmother Breeuwer moved in with her oldest daughter Tante Nel. Her husband had died after they had been married only a few years, and she had never remarried. Her only son, my cousin, also had gone to South Africa as a young man.

Grandmother Breeuwer and Tante Nel lived in a house overlooking the Spaarne. It is a river which had formed a wide lake where they lived. From their living room window you could see the many ships, such as barges and tugboats, going up and down the river. During summertime there were always many sailboats on the water. Grandmother was always happy to see us. She was a very gentle and kind woman. Her eyes were always looking at us with loving tenderness. She had a heart condition and was always sitting in front of the window looking over the wide busy river. Especially in the evenings was the river a wonderful sight to see. Tante Nel took care of her and the household which also included a man in his mid-thirties. His name was Wim Stein. He was a painter, a nice quiet man, who lived in Tante Nel's home as a son for many years. Even though his paintings were dark, he became well known, and some of his paintings can be seen in museums. A few years later, when I was seventeen and on a visit in Haarlem, he asked me to pose for him . He painted one large painting of me which he sold. Another smaller one, a bust, he gave to me to keep.

On our bikes it was about a twenty-minute ride from Tante Nel's home to the beautiful wide beach of Bloemendaal. On the warm sand we enjoyed lazy hours in the sun and played in the waves of the sea. If the weather was too cool for us to be on the beach, we went on bicycle trips in and around the city of Haarlem. While we were enjoying ourselves in Haarlem, we heard one evening on the radio at Grandmother's home, some disturbing news about a possible war in Poland. I had no notion of war; I was young and on vacation. I think I had more interest in where was the best place to go, and where was the most fun. When you are young, the important thing that matters is the moment. A thought of a possible war some place far away was the farthest from my mind. It was a few days later when we said goodbye to Grandmother and Tante Nel and rode on our bikes home to Breda again. We went back over the same roads that we had come from a few weeks before. It was a windy day but a warm sun was shining brightly in a cloudless sky. Nothing foretold the dark clouds which were forming over Europe and the horrible war years ahead.

◆     ◆     ◆

My parents were worried about a serious developing situation in Germany. For the last few years I had heard them talking about the economic depression in the world and the difficult time for many people who were without work. Because we lived in Breda, a military town, we didn't feel this depression as much as other people in Holland. For some years now, my parents had talked about Adolf Hitler, a social extremist who came to power in the thirty's and became counselor of Germany. Later I heard about the anti-Jewish demonstrations in Germany and how the Jews were singled out for cruel persecution. So many had fled their country and had come to Holland where they felt safe. I did not always understood why this all was and why my parents listened to the radio and became more and more worried about Hitler who made such upsetting violent speeches. My parents also were worried about the Nazi attacks on Czechoslovakia during the last year. Sometimes I wondered why everybody was so excited—it was all happening so far away.

Then one day something became clear to me after I had come upon a parade of NSB-ers (National Socialists Organization) during a walk with Mies on the edge of the Mastbos. During the thirties this Nazi party was formed in Holland and had grown to a few thousand members. That day the Dutch Nazis held some sort of a parade and demonstration. Most of the men were dressed in black uniforms. They told the onlookers, who were standing on the side of the roads and watching them, that all the Jewish people should be exterminated, and also all the Gypsies, the rich and many others. I suddenly understood that Nazism was bad, very bad, and Hitler did not look funny to me anymore. What before had been a clownish figure with a silly little mustache and strangely cut hair that looked like a bad fitting hairpiece slipping on his forehead, was suddenly something very sinister, capable of destroying our freedom and happiness. That evening when we sat around the table eating our supper, I said to my parents that I couldn't understand why the people of Germany had chosen Hitler as their countries leader. Father looked at me and said, "We need to remember that no country is immune to the lures of a warped genius."After thinking about what Father had said to me, I decided that we were blessed in Holland. We had our Queen Wilhelmina to take care of our country and not a man like Adolf Hitler.

Holland did not fight in World War I (1914-1918). It declared itself neutral and hoped to stay neutral in any future war. But that August of 1939 the situation became serious enough to mobilize our entire Dutch Army. Men left their homes and families and reported to their regiments. On the first day of September the German Army attacked Poland without any declaration of war. Hitler's pantzers smashed into Poland from the west while the Russian Red Army attacked from the east, requiring the Polish Army to fight on two fronts at once. The fighting was fierce and bloody. The Polish people had no chance. On September 3, 1939 England and France declared war on Germany and mobilized their Armies. But surprisingly they did not attack the enemy but stayed behind the Maginot Line. This strategy did not help Poland. And so World War II began its rein of terror.

After the fall of Poland everything was quiet again. The winter of 1939-1940 brought icy weather; people skated along the frozen canals and on park ponds. Life seemed as peaceful and orderly as usual, but the Dutch people were uneasy. We listened closely to our radios, waiting for the latest news. The Dutch complained that their small country was 'caught between the devil and the deep blue sea'. It was a troubled winter in Europe.

◆     ◆     ◆

Schooling continued, and my interest in social life increased. My parents sent me to a school of domestic economy, where I learned how to sew, cook, and keep house. Besides these domestic skills, the students were taught language, mathematics, nutrition and manners. Parties were held at the school and occasionally we attended a social function in the city. It was not unpleasant.

My parents loved opera, especially my father. Before they were married, Father and Mother went almost every week to see an opera in Amsterdam. But in Breda there was not always a opera in town. So whenever there was a opera on the radio or a tenor singing operatic arias, my father tuned the radio up loud and sang along. Father had a good voice, and I think he knew all the famous Italian opera singers of that time by name, and also all the arias they sang from the operas. We teenagers had a different taste in music and Father never could understand how we could call our 'Jazz'-music. I think in that way there has not been much changed in the world.

When I was growing up, I heard so much about opera in our home that I became fond of the beautiful, dramatic music which my parents listened to on the radio. That winter I saw my first opera with my parents. It was "Tosca" and was performed in our opera house in Breda. It was very glamorous. I wore a lovely blue silk dress and my hair was all in curls. My mother looked so pretty and young that night with her light blond hair all made up. Mother's hair always had been very light blond, even in her older years. She never used cosmetics, only on special occasions like her rare evenings out with Father. I remember exactly what she was wearing that night. It was a pale green dress with lots of fragile lace in the same color. Father looked handsome in his good suit (he never wore his uniform when going out) and his dark wavy hair all shining. After that night I truly learned to appreciate the opera with all its drama.

Thoughout the winter there were rumors that Hitler would invade Holland, despite its neutrality. Fears rose in April of 1940 when Hitler invaded neutral Denmark and Norway, yet the month of May arrived in Holland without incident. Our country was in bloom with tulips, hyacinths and daffodils. We were concerned, but never really believed that the situation would get out of control or that we were in any danger. We could not believe Hitler would dare attack us, nor did we think the German Army was as strong as it later turned out to be. A few days before the crisis deepened, Hitler addressed us with one of his sardonic, rambling speeches, and it sounded as though he was trying to scare everyone. We hardly understood what Hitler wanted from us. But the Dutch people feared that they would be engulfed in the ever widening war. Though we all tried not to think about it, darkness was falling over Holland, and our country prepared for war.

It was May 10, 1940, when Holland awoke in a changed country, destined to suffer through five years of Nazi occupation.

# 18

# *DARK CLOUDS*

*May 10, 1940.* The war came like none was ever seen before in Europe—terror, extermination, nothing like it had been experienced by civilized man. That Friday about 6:00 in the morning I was awakened by strange noises. When I rose from my bed and went downstairs to our living room, I saw my father dressed in his uniform, turning the dial on the static-filled radio. My mother in her robe, looking all upset, stood behind him. My heart began to pound and in an instant I knew something was terribly wrong. "What is it,"I yelled to my parents. Mother answered almost crying, "We are at war. The Germans have invaded our country!" Father got up from his chair by the radio and said to Mother, "I have to go to the kazerne. Hitler is ready to swallow us." He kissed Mother and said, "Don't worry, I will be back." He then turned to me and my brothers who had come down from their bedroom and told us to take care of each other and Mother. He then left for his kazerne to await orders. We did not not see him back for a few weeks.

Still in their night clothes, many of the neighbors were out in the street, standing in small groups, talking and comforting each other. Others were listening to their radios to hear the latest news about the war. We came to know that Hitler and his Army had invaded Holland, Belgium and Luxembourg at 4:45 early that morning without even a declaration of war. It was the second time in the last two weeks that we were shaken from our beds. Because of the war threats of Nazi Germany, the tension had been high. Two weeks earlier our neighborhood had been awakened by explosions, and we had thought the worst. The night sky had been red from the fire of the paint factory just three blocks away. The large barrels of paint, which exploded, lit up the night sky like fireworks on Queen's Day. That night all the neighbors were out on the street to watch the fire, but later when the fire was under control, we all went home and to bed. But this time it was different. We didn't know what to expect. No one went to school or work, and people where glued to their radios which continued to send out the latest news reports on the situation.

War! It was impossible to believe it. This day was to have been filled as any other day with small matters of living such as going to school and making plans for the weekend. This coming Sunday was not only Pinkster day (Pentecost) but also Mother's Day. I had wanted to buy something pretty for Mother. All of this suddenly lost its sense. The world turned upside down! Later, that same morning, Mother told us to stay close to our home. An old complaint of my mother was that I was always disappearing—always running off. But Mother allowed me to go to Mies' home, which was around the corner and two blocks away. Her father also had gone to his kazerne that early morning and her mother had been worried and cried a lot. Before the morning was over we heard that German parachutists had come down behind our train station, and that they fought against our troops for the Moerdyk bridges. In that time those bridges were the longest in Europe and connected north and south Holland over the wide rivers of Hollands-Diep and Maas. Those bridges, traffic and trains are about 15 miles north of Breda in the direction of Rotterdam.

When I was at Mies' house that morning, our first air raid alarm went off. The noise from the sirens sounded different this time to me than the other times when it just had been exercises. When Mies and I looked up in the clear blue sky, we saw about five or six airplanes. They must have been German and English fighter planes and were attacking each other. First they climbed high up in the sky and then suddenly with high speed swooped down while shooting. The sounds of their machine guns were frightening. It was the first time in my life I heard this terrible sound. I ran home. Home is where a person feels safest. I remember when I came to our house and stood in our living room, the ground suddenly trembled from explosions. It did not last long, but it seemed like an eternity. As it turned out, a German bomber had dropped its bombs when it tried to get away from its attackers. The war killed its first people in Breda when the bombs came down on some houses.

In the afternoon the air grew heavy with explosions coming from the military airfield, Gilse Reyen, which is about 12 miles east of Breda. Later we heard on the radio that the German Luftwaffe (airforce) had dropped parachutists disguised in Dutch military uniforms along with guns and equipment. Other German forces were attacking Dutch airfields, while their troops were driving into the southeast provinces of Holland. They were also advancing into Belgium and along the Ryn (Rhine) and Maas rivers. With few tanks and only 125 aircraft, Holland's armed forces were no match for the tens of thousands of well trained German soldiers with modern bombers, tanks and other equipment. The small countries such as Holland, Belgium and Luxembourg were defenseless, and they were especially vulnerable to the German attacks. Later that day Queen Wilhelmina issued a fierce protest on the radio calling the attack 'a flagrant breach of conduct.' The broadcast ended with the Dutch National Anthem. My mother was crying while Jan cursed the Germans. It was late that evening when everyone went into their homes. That night we went to bed with worries about the next day.

The following morning we woke up early and turned on the radio. There was no music, only announcements about the war. Hitler's attacks on Holland had continued throughout the night while our soldiers desperately defended their country against the invading German Army. But our ill-equipped Dutch Army was losing one battle after another. Announcements came about more landings of German paratroopers in Holland at strategic points. Later in the morning French troops arrived in our city to help with the defense. As I later learned, Breda was the most northern defense line point of the French Army. With their brown uniforms they were dressed differently than our soldiers. Of course since their language was French, most of us could not understood them. Some of those soldiers drove small panzer wagons; others were in cars or on motorcycles. "Is this the French Army who is going to help us," we said to each other. They looked tired and dusty, and it looked as though they had been on the road for days. Many times during that day the air raid sirens went off and German planes came over. A few were shot down and came down in a ball of flames just outside our city. But much further happened.

Mies and I stayed a lot at each other's house those days or on the street close to our homes, talking to our friends about the war and the hated Hitler. More French troops arrived and took positions in and around Breda. The radio reported that the German soldiers had taken the Moerdyk bridges and also were moving from the east toward our city. Later in the evening we got a notice from the French commander who instructed all the citizens of Breda to leave their city before 10:00 the next morning. The plan of the French commander in Breda was to form a defense line just north and east of the area where we lived, so they could hold the fast moving German troops for 6-8 days from advancing further. Because Breda was in the middle of the line, it was decided that our entire city had to be evacuated. The only direction which was still open and safe for the evacuation of 50,000 people was south in the direction Antwerp in Belgium.

At first Mother almost panicked and said she had no plans to go anywhere. She was not going out of her home and town and no one could make her, and this was the end of it. She was not going! After her angry outburst she started to cry and said that the whole world had gone insane! I am sure that many people in Breda felt the same way as Mother did that night and thought that the whole evacuation was a mistake. Evacuating 50,000 people on foot! But then in war things happen which are illogical and incomprehensible.

That night I went to bed with more worries than I cared to have, and I wished that Father was home. I couldn't sleep and thought morning would never come, and when it came I thought it would never end. Early the next morning when I went downstairs, I found Mother in the kitchen making sandwiches. She looked worried and told me to eat as much as I could because, as she said, "You never know when you will be able to eat again." She then continued saying, "After you eat, go to your room and gather some clothes together—enough for a few days, and help your brother Henk with his things." Until this day I don't know what had changed Mother's mind of not staying where she was, in her home, in her town. Maybe it was because everyone else in our street was leaving, and everyone feared that our city could go up in smoke during a battle. It had happened before in Belgium in World War One.

After forcing down my breakfast, I went to my room and began to pack and repack one bag, while thinking what would one need going on an evacuation to who knows where! My eyes caught sight of the small photograph album I always had in my room on top of a shelf with my books. It was an album of our family, pictures of all our good times together, our vacations in Haarlem on the beach, and pictures of other happy occasions. At once, this album became my most important possession and I laid it down on my bed along with my clothes. A little later when Mother came in my room to see if I was finished with my packing, she saw the album and said that we needed every bit of room for our clothes. After I told Mother that I wanted so badly to take my album along, she put it in my bag without a word. I think she didn't want to argue with me.

After mother had closed all the bedroom windows, we went downstairs to Jan and Henk who were already waiting for us. "We'll have to hurry," Jan said, "it is time for us to leave." I don't remember if we were allowed to take a bicycle with us. I know only that Jan's bike was all packed, and ready for our long walk to Belgium. We were used to walking long distances, but when I heard we were to walk probably as far as to Antwerp, which is more than 50 km, I thought how do we do that! I never had walked this far before! Since we didn't know where we were going and for how long we would be gone, Mother had opened the door of Father's birdhouse in the backyard. "Now the birds can fly out and find food on their own after they have eaten the food I leave behind for them," Mother said. She felt that she had to give the birds a chance to survive, in case it would be a long time before we would be home. Once again Mother went inside the house to be sure all windows and doors were closed, and the gas, water and electricity was turned off. And so the evacuation of Breda started on the third day of the war on May 12, 1940. It became a flight from which many never returned home.

The weather was beautiful that Mother's Day. The sunlight was golden, the sky without a single cloud. It was warm for that time of year, almost summery. It must have been about 10:00 that morning when we left our home. Jan pushed the bicycle. On the back seat was our suitcase and a large folded blanket, and on the steering wheel in a bag were sandwiches which Mother had made that morning. Mother walked beside Jan, and Henk and I walked behind them, each of us carrying a bag. As soon as we left our home we noticed that most of the neighbors from our street had already left. As we came around the corner of our street, we saw that the Molengracht Straat was full of people. Some of them were pushing small carts or children in strollers and some had, as we did, a bike on which a suitcase and blanket were secured. But most of the people were taking too much with them. The further we walked, the more people were on the road. I looked at the crowd around me—women, men, teens and children, city people as we were—a worried mass flowing south. Occasionally there were French soldiers who grew in number when we reached the edge of the Mastbos. From there we had to walk about two miles on the side of the forest before coming to the main road which led into Belgium and further south to Antwerp—Belgium's large harbor city.

As we walked on the side of the forest, I looked into the woods where I had picnicked so many times during summer vacations with my family or friends. I thought about the times Mies and I rode our bikes up and down the Seven Hills and the fun we had doing that. And our blueberry trips in the woods, our hands and faces all purple. While walking in the midst of the mass of fleeing people, I wondered where Mies and her mother and sister were at that moment. A little later we left the forest behind us. Suddenly German planes came flying fast and low over the road which was crowded with people. At first I stared at the planes, not comprehending the situation and the danger we were in. The French soldiers, who shared the main road to Belgium with the fleeing civilians, started to fire at the German planes, which in turn released their bombs on the soldiers on the road. As I stood there close to some trees staring at the terrible sight, I felt for a few seconds as if the whole world was revolving around me. Then as more bombs were coming down not far from where we were standing, I suddenly saw people running for cover. I quickly ran to the nearest tree where I fell on my knees and hid my head between my hands. While I crouched down as much as I could, I prayed that we would survive this violence. It seemed forever before the German planes left. The people on the road, who had fled in all directions overcome by fear and confusion, continued further. I never will forget when I saw the first bomb crater and looked at a few people who were standing and kneeling there in the middle of the large hole. In the dust and debris of the crater, I saw a young woman lying down. She was ready to give birth to her baby. A desperate man, probably her husband, tried to shield her and the coming child with his jacket from the bewildered eyes of the fleeing mass of people. As the young women screamed in agony, two women tried to help with the birth of her baby. While holding onto my mother, I thought how awful it was to give birth to a little baby in a bomb crater. Somewhat further on the side of the road I saw a little boy who was lying in his own blood with half of his head blown away. Beside him was a young girl sitting as if she was in a sleep leaning against a tree stump. A small stream of blood had dripped from her head down her cheek. She was dead.

As we went further up the road which was broken up by bombs, I saw more bodies lying in the debris of torn trees and dirt. I never had seen a dead person before in my life, and suddenly to see this horror was very frightening to a 15-year-old girl as I was. A suffocating feeling came over me, and the hordes of fleeing people added to the unreality. I looked at Mother. Her face was blank and her eyes had a terrible strained expression as if she had been forced to look at more than her mind could ever accept. Years later Mother told me of that day, that moment when she saw those dead children. She said that the thought of having to leave her children behind, dead on the side of a torn up road in a ditch full of debris, frightened her so much that she almost panicked. The mass of people went further going south, trying to flee the bombing and strafing of the German planes which were meant for the French soldiers. The French soldiers, who supposedly came to help us, made the whole situation worse. Later we saw French soldiers retreating in a southern direction.

In the beginning the people talked to each other, but after the bombings it became more and more quiet. It soon became a silent mass, with now and then a child crying. After hours of walking, passing farm fields and small villages, I did not feel tired or hungry. I remember how a young woman, seemly in the last months of her pregnancy, walked with us carrying a heavy suitcase, which she said was full of baby clothes. At first we tried to help her, putting her suitcase on Jan's bicycle. But it became too much of a problem when the road became bad. Soon she had to leave her heavy suitcase behind in a ditch. That day many of the fleeing people had to leave their belongings and bags behind in ditches. They had become too much of a burden. I remember how sorry I felt for the young women. She was all alone. How sad I thought to be so alone and soon expecting a baby in this insanity of war. I tried to stay close to the young woman, but lost track of her when we came to a large farm which was engulfed in flames. Not only the house but also the stables were fiercely burning, fed by a dry wind that swept over the road on which we were traveling. We could not go further.

The farm probably caught on fire when low flying German fighters targeted the French soldiers who were holding their position there. Some people were going in a large circle around the burning farm and later tried to get back on the main road again. Jan looked the situation over and said to Mother, "Let's not go further over the highway. It's just too dangerous." Then, while pointing his finger to a narrow dirt road he said, "Maybe we should go on that farm road; it's probably a little safer." After a short discussion we decided to take the hard clay road and hoped to find a farm where we could stay for the night. Some people and a few families with children also went with us, hoping to find one or another farm where they could stay instead of going further south as first planned. As we started to walk, I looked around for the young women but she was nowhere to be seen.

We traveled about half a mile on the farm road when suddenly a few German fighter planes came over. They came fast and low and opened their deadly fire. I don't know if we were their target. I only know that everyone jumped into the ditch beside the road as fast as they could. It was full of shrubs and weeds and I remember how my new hose were torn up and my legs were scraped. It was frightening to see those planes turn around and come back again, flying low over the fields and over the main road, where we had come from. Again they spit their deadly fire, probably at the French soldiers. As suddenly as the German fighters had come, they were gone, and everything became quiet once again. We scrambled out of the dry ditch and got to our feet. None of us were hurt but some of the children were crying with fright and clinging to their mothers or fathers.

As we went further on the narrow road, we saw in a short distance a small wooded area and decided to rest there. But just before we reached the small forest, the fighters came back again. They flew just above the treetops at a high speed; then they circled around probably looking for a target. Our small group started to run as fast as we could into the protection of the tall trees in the wooded area. While Jan and Henk were hiding together under thick-growing small trees, Mother and I went a little further into the protection of a clump of tall trees. Other people had gone further into the woods. While the planes circled around, I looked at Mother who had started to cry in a disturbing way. I had never seen her like this before. Mother was hysterical. While pleading with her, telling her that everything would turn out okay again and trying to help her to overcome her hysteria, my eyes searched desperately for my brothers' help. As the planes left in the distance, Jan and Henk came to where we were hiding. Jan tried to talk to Mother who refused to go further. Patiently he said to her, "We can't stay here. Mother, we have to go further. Please, let us go." We gave a sigh of relief when Mother got up from the damp ground of the forest. She had become quiet, as if in a trance. Her eyes still held a look of shock, but she did consent to walk further with us. We got our belongings together and walked out of the small forest following the other people from our group. We heard the shootings from airplanes far away.

Mother's nervous breakdown brought her severe headaches which lasted for many years to come. Many a time she would tell me she wished to live no longer if there was nothing the doctors could do for her. Many a day her severe headaches robbed her of sleep and normal living. Finally after the war, new medicine came from America which brought her relief and healing.

It was early evening when we reached a large farm house surrounded by high trees and straw roof barns. The black-and-white cows were grazing in the spring-rich pastures and chickens chuckled around. A watchdog became alarmed to see all those unexpected people. When we reached the farmhouse, the door opened. The farmer, followed by his wife and children, stared at the tired looking and dusty crowd. A few men of our group talked to the farmer, and soon we were told that we all could stay in the barn for the night. Fresh straw was laying on the ground which we could sleep on. We had to share the barn with a few cows which were standing in a corner of the stall on some thick fresh straw. I don't know why they were there, maybe they were sick or were ready to calve.

When everyone was settled (no one was in the mood to be fussy) Mother divided the sandwiches which she had prepared that morning before we had left, but had not eaten during the day. We got water from the farmer's well. It was turning dusk when the farmer came inside the barn, carefully closed the barn doors and wished us a safe night. Everyone had found themselves a place in the straw. The children were restless and cried and wanted to go home. There was little conversation in the barn. I think we all kept our fears to ourselves. We did not know what to expect from one minute to the next. In the distance we could hear the thundering of cannons. For a long time I listened and wondered about our town and home. I tried to sleep; it had been a long day.

I must have dozed off when suddenly I awoke because of some sort of explosion. I remember Mother kissing us as if to say goodbye to her children. How hard it must have been on her without Father, alone with her children in this miserable situation. Most people in the barn were awake. Someone coughed; someone else swore; others were talking to each other in a worried low voice. A few children were crying. Jan was awake but Henk was in a blessed peaceful sleep. I didn't sleep anymore for the rest of the night. I tried to understand what was happening to us and to comprehend the horrible things that were hanging over our land.

The whole night through there were sounds of shootings and the roar of motors. We knew that the German Army had invaded the region where we were, and it was very frightening. I think we expected the barn doors to be opened any moment, and German soldiers to come in with guns pointed at us. Finally daybreak came and the sounds of war quieted down. A few of the men opened the barn doors to see what the situation was outside. They soon came back and closed the door behind them. They told everyone that German soldiers in armored vehicles were on the farmer's land and we should stay inside the barn and wait. After awhile Mother and a few other women decided to go to the farmer to ask if we could buy some food from him. The barn was connected from the inside to the farmer's house by the kitchen door. Most of the older farms in Holland were built this way.

A little later Mother and the other women came back carrying sandwiches, but looked very upset. They said that they had heard on the radio that the Germans had bombed our harbor city of Rotterdam with 54 Stukas and had destroyed the inner city. There were hundreds of deaths and thousands of injured, and Nazi Germany had threatened to bomb other Dutch cities if Holland did not surrender. A few hours later another news bulletin came which left many people in the barn surprised and dejected. Our Queen, her family and the Dutch government, had escaped from Den Haag, (The Hague) the Dutch seat of government, to London aboard British warships. For a moment it looked like desertion to us. But then as some men said, the struggle against Hitler will be carried on from inside England. If our leaders had remained in Holland, the government itself could have been taken captive by the Nazi invaders. It was better that they ran a government in exile.

After long discussions in the barn about the bad situation in our poor country, some men went outside again to investigate the situation around the farm. When they came back, they said that the German soldiers were gone. We all felt much better. Later that afternoon the farmer came into the barn with tears in his eyes and said that the Dutch radio station in Hilversum, (a town not far from Amsterdam) was in German hands. The Dutch broadcaster had said, "God bless the

Queen, Holland and all its people. Goodbye until we meet again." The Dutch National Anthem was played and after it ended the radio went silent. Some people in the barn started to cry, others expressed shock, anger, sorrow and fear. Our country, our Holland, how uncertain was our future. The rest of the day we stayed in and around the farm. We did not see any German soldiers. The sounds of war we heard now were far away.

Two of the men of our group planned to go to Breda on bicycles early the following morning to see if our city was still there and if everyone could safely take the walk back home. That second night in the barn everyone slept much better. Toward the morning I woke up and didn't feel very well. I had developed a fever. "Just what I don't need now, getting sick here in the barn," I said to myself. Not that a fever was anything unusual for me. A strep throat at the age of eight had left me with rheumatoid fever. Many times I had fought the sudden onset of high fever, which always landed me in bed for a few days. Later when I was about 18 years old the sickness disappeared and never returned.

That morning I stayed in the barn rolled in our blanket in the straw. Mother was worried. She was worried about Father and now she was worried about me too. When the two men who had gone to Breda came back, they brought the good news that our city was still the same as we had left it. There was not much damage done, as they told us, and it was safe to walk back home to our city. They said further that there were many German soldiers on the roads and Breda was occupied by the Nazis, but everything seemed safe enough to go home. It was not long thereafter that we gathered our belongings and said goodbye to the farmer and his wife. As soon as we left the farm behind, we saw the first German soldiers. An armored car and two large tanks with the Nazi swastika sign painted on its sides stood in a field beside the road. A soldier with his gun across his knees and a cigarette drooping from his mouth was sitting on a boulder. A small group of other soldiers were eating. Some were naked from their waist up, shaving and washing themselves. We were all nervous but the soldiers paid no attention to us when we passed carefully. We soon came to the bend in the road which would lead us to the small forest where a few days before we had hidden from the German fighters. I looked at Mother, who looked strained but determined to make it back to her home as soon as possible.

Heavy clouds were hanging in the sky as the people walked in silence on the narrow road, past the forest and fields toward the highway that runs from Breda to Antwerp. Here and there we passed German tanks and soldiers. As soon as we came to the highway, we saw the German Army in long columns of heavy large tanks. With their powerful engines roaring and the noise of the clatter of tank treads on steel rails, they moved in a southern direction. We saw the soldiers of the infamous SS Panzer Division in black uniforms with white crossed bones emblems on their collar, standing tall half way out of their tank turrets. Regiment after regiment of German panzer and infantry were driving over our highway into Belgium. They looked well organized, and enormous strength was felt coming from the endless flood of uniforms and weapons. It was heartbreaking and frightening for us to see them. It is hard to express how we felt—what it meant to see those Nazi uniforms. I thought about my father, where he was, and of all our soldiers who had fought a losing battle against those masses of enemy soldiers, and the many who had lost their lives.

As soon as we reached the highway, Mother took her shoes off as her feet bothered her. With the extra socks from Jan on her feet she walked at full speed past the columns of the mighty German Army. With her lips tight she kept her eyes on the road in front of her, showing only contempt for the Nazi soldiers. She told us three kids to walk as close to her as possible. She was like a tiger protecting her cubs After walking a few hours I felt the fever becoming worse. I tried not to think about it, but I surely was not feeling very well. The dust on the road, which billowed up from the tanks, didn't help either. I thought how good it would be to get home and take a bath and lay on my bed. Passing some trees we decided to take a break from our long walk home. We were all so tired. By now our whole group, with which we had been together in the last days, had disappeared. It's hard to stay together—some walked faster than others.

There were many other people on the road, going back home. They were, as we were, the lucky ones who had not gone too far from their homes in Breda. It was because of the fire which had swept over the road a few days earlier that many people had gone into side roads and had found farms where they stayed, as we had done. But thousands of other people had gone further that day, the 12th of May, and later they reached the area in the vicinity of Antwerp in Belgium. Because of the fast advancing German troops and the many fleeing Belgium citizens, many people felt pressured to go further. They were in the power of a flight psychoce, a phenomena closely studied after WW II. Many of the fleeing people went further and further through Belgium, some even into France and further to Spain. On the way many of the struggling people suffered hardships, others lost their lives or were injured. Many of the citizens of Breda didn't came home for weeks—even months. On May 17 a school in St. Nicholas, Belgium, where some of the fleeing people from Breda found refuge, was bombed by German dive bombers—Stukas. More than 50 people lost their lives, many of them children, and many people were injured.

After a short rest we continued on. Mother was driven by her concern for her home and to get away from seeing the endless columns of the enemy. Before evening passed we entered our city. The streets looked deserted. It was so strange to see the usually busy streets empty of traffic and people. Only once in a while we saw a German armored car, a few tanks and soldiers on trucks. Some dogs roamed the street, probably looking for food. We must have been the first in our street to come back home because we saw none of our neighbors. It was eerie to walk through our empty street. It was so quiet, no children playing or housewives talking to each other or cleaning their windows and sweeping their sidewalk. As we came home, everything was exactly as we had left it a few days before. Mother was happy to be home again. She opened the windows wide to let the fresh air flow in from over the meadow.

One of our neighbors had left their German Shepherd dog in its kennel when they left. The dog was barking in a urgent way. Jan went to him and let the poor dog out of his confinement. The animal then sped like crazy through his back-yard and over the fields behind our houses and disappeared for some time before he came back. The poor dog had not done his duty when nature called and had been in misery. Luckily for him we came home early because his master didn't come back until 8 or 9 days later. On May 12 when the citizens of Breda were told to evacuate, they were warned not to take any animals along, but to destroy their pets. Of course few people had done this, because no one believed that they would be gone longer from home than a few days. I think most people left their pets in their yard or in the kennel with the door ajar. Some of Father's birds had flown away out of the aviary and we never saw them again. Others were staying in and around the bird house close to the bird food which Mother had left for them. The canary which had always been singing had left also and never came back. We sure missed its wonderful warbling sound.

We were home, but soon found out we had no electricity, gas or water. Because of Pentecost, a holiday in Holland which had been a few days earlier, Mother had bought extra things to eat for that special day. Now that everything was closed and there was no gas and water, we had enough food and drink in the home. The warm bath I had looked forward to had to wait. I was happy to be in my bedroom again where my wallpaper continued to sprout its tiny rosebuds and where my books were still on the shelf waiting for me.

# 19

# *OCCUPATION*

Our war with Germany was over. With their overpowering warfare and strength the German troops overrode Holland, Belgium and Luxembourg. A formal surrender was signed on May 15, 1940 just five days after the German invasion. There was some panic among the Jews, the German refugees and well-known anti-Nazis. They were terrified at the prospect of Nazi control, and some of them committed suicide.

We could not imagine life under occupation. Our Holland always had been independent. All my memories were of a life that was happy and above all free. Now all that was gone. Many German soldiers swarmed everywhere. Our armed forces were now formally dissolved and sent home. Their army took our army's equipment, motorized vehicles and guns, then moved into our barracks and army buildings. Hitler issued orders that the leadership class of the Dutch people was to be arrested as quickly as possible. The nation was to be stripped of its prominent intellectuals. An order was issued that all arms must be delivered to the authorities immediately. From then on, anybody found in possession of a gun would be arrested and sent to prison camp or executed. We were now under German law and order. As long as we abided by their laws, they would leave us alone. But those who resisted, or who were suspected of resisting, would be sent to a prison camp or put to death. And if they didn't like a citizen's religion or politics, he or she could be killed without a trial. We would no longer be free to speak openly about our thoughts and ideas. The Germans occupied the best hotels and villas in our town, giving the occupants only a few hours to leave. Throughout Holland, Nazi soldiers lowered the red, white and blue Dutch flags and replaced them with the red and black Nazi swastika flags. German soldiers marched through the Dutch streets, singing songs that had words I didn't understand. After the first shock was over, we knew what to expect from those German conquerors

Father had come home two weeks after the fall of our country. All that time he had been stationed in a kazerne in Haarlem. This area which is located in the northern part of Holland never experienced the invasion of German troops. When Holland capitulated, all of Holland automatically fell. And as Father said, those Nazi bastards had done it so easily and quickly. For some time Father stayed home, angry and irritated with the situation in Europe and with the German occupiers. Then one day he got orders to work in a metal factory in Breda. He worked there for the rest of the war years hating every minute of it.

The first week of June the BBC (British Broadcasting Corporation) radio station announced that British troops had lost a horrendous battle in Belgium. Thousands of Allied soldiers had been stranded on the beaches of Dunkirk, helplessly awaiting the Germans. Many English Naval and civilian small crafts managed to rescue 337,000 of the men and evacuate them to England.

Life continued with the superficial appearance of normality. The people of Breda resumed their daily activities such as going to work and school while German planes flew overhead. Mies had come home with her mother and sister after eight days in Belgium during the evacuation. Her father also had returned home.

One day Mies and I went shopping in downtown. Mies wanted to buy a new pair of summer shoes she had seen before in a shoe store. As soon as we came into the store, we were greatly surprised to see so many German soldiers there. The saleslady we both knew said to us that the Germans were buying up everything. She warned us to buy everything we might need, or it would be gone. She then continued saying, "Soon there won't be anything left to buy, they are snatching it all and sending it to their families in Germany. It had been bad there for many years."

Wherever Mies and I went that day, we saw German military men buying food and other goods. Later when we stopped in our grocery store, there were German soldiers gobbling down boxes of chocolates and cookies. Foods, goods, raw material, anything and everything was going to Germany as if pulled into a gigantic vacuum. At first the small business people were happy with the many sales they made, and they sold everything that was on their shelves to the German soldiers. They thought the war would not last long. Then the German invaders would be gone, and they would have made good money. But later when there was nothing to sell anymore and new merchandise did not come in, it became a different story.

The city was dark at night, no street or commercial lights would shine anymore for four long years. Inside the houses the lights were dim and the draperies were closed very tightly. Every night a patrol walked through the streets and knocked on the door if there was a glimpse of light to be seen from the outside of the house. All throughout the war years Mother, who always loved a lot of light in her home, complained in the evenings how miserably dark it was inside the house. Father always answered her saying, "Not long anymore, Cor, then the war will be over, and the lights will go on again."

July brought more restrictions. It was illegal to listen to any radio station except for the official German one. This station was our own radio station from Hilversum but was controlled by the Germans for the news, and it played only German, Dutch and French music. Nevertheless Radio Orange, a Dutch radio station, began broadcasts from London in July. Soon people from Holland began listening regularly in secret to a short wave radio for the latest news about the war. Father, who had a short wave radio, had hidden his in the attic behind a wooden wall. All through the trying years of occupation, he listened to London at 7:30 every night. It was our only direct link with the free world and our only means of obtaining true and unbiased news reports on the international situation. The German newscast from our own Dutch radio station in Hilversum with their loud introduction, "From the Furher's Main Headquarters," were propagandistic lies. Occasionally the Gestapo or green police came for a house search. If they found a short wave radio, the householders were immediately arrested or sometimes shot. The green police were the Dutch Nazis, betrayers to their own country and bloodhounds for the Gestapo. Our movie theaters now showed only German, French or Italian films with Dutch subtitles. The newspapers could print nothing negative about Germany.

◆    ◆    ◆

That summer Jan and I wanted to go on our bicycles to Amsterdam again to spend some time there. At first our parents were not very happy with our plans and said that it would be better if we stayed home on our vacation that year. Jan and I understood that it was hard to be peaceful in a time when there was no peace. But remembering how we had enjoyed our vacation last year in Amsterdam and on the beach of Bloemendaal, we wanted to go. Although we knew things were different now with the German soldiers everywhere, Jan and I hastened to assure our parents before they might have other ideas, that everything was safe on the roads that we were to travel, and they were not to worry. We would be careful, we said. It was a few days later that we got permission from our parents to take the trip and to see the family up north. Jan suggested that we would take a different road this time going to Amsterdam. We were going first to Rotterdam, the city which was bombed by the German Luftwaffe a few months before, and then through Den Haag (The Hague) further north to Amsterdam.

It was shortly after 6:00 in the morning when we left Breda behind us. The morning air was cool and fresh as we pedaled our bicycles briskly down the roads, singing some old Dutch folk songs. After riding a few hours we came to the complex of wide rivers which separate north and south Holland. They are connected by the long Moerdyk Bridge. There are actually two bridges. The train bridge was built in 1871 and spans 1432 meters, while the car and footbridge was built in 1937 and is 1350 meters long. It was those bridges the German Paratroopers first captured in a surprise attack the moment the Nazis invaded Holland. Four years later with the coming of the Allied troops the two Moerdyk Bridges were saved again, but many soldiers lost their lives on its banks or drowned in the water. The Moerdyk Bridges were very important for all the armies for the fast transportation of war materials and men.

It was quite an experience to ride with our bikes on this great new bridge over the beautiful wide water of the Holland Diep. The dramatic Dutch sky with its almost always towering clouds and the many soaring sea birds added to the beauty of Holland's landscape. As we passed the town of Dordrecht going in the direction of Rotterdam, we noticed that some of the bridges which we had to cross over were destroyed and had fallen into the water. They had been blown up by the Dutch Army during the German invasion to make it more difficult for them to advance. Luckily there was a ferry going over those rivers for the people on foot or who were on a bicycle. It always took a while before we finally were on the other side of the water.

As we came closer to Rotterdam, we faintly could smell a stench which was drifting on a breeze from the north. The closer we came to the city, the worse it became. I never will forget the moment when I saw the inner-city of Rotterdam. The sight was terrible. Among those huge piles of rubble and dust we could hardly recognize a city that not long ago had been shops, apartment buildings and schools, all occupied by people doing their daily living. All around us were desolate ruins. Some decomposing human bodies were still buried under the rubble after three months, and the sharp acrid stench saturated the air. Luckily we had received shots against typhus and diphtheria a few weeks before when everyone in Breda had to take them. I don't recall why. I only remember that the typhus shot was very painful and that everyone was sick for a few days. Jan and I did not stay long in Rotterdam, it was just too terrible to see the devastation in that great city. Rotterdam had been one of the largest and busiest seaports in the world before WW II. Years later, after the rebuilding, Rotterdam not only became a beautiful modern city, but one of the largest harbors in the world again. But the terrible bombing and its destructive force remained a bitter memory for its citizens.

It was late in the day as we reached Amsterdam. This time we came into the city on a different road than the year before when we had come from the direction of Utrecht, and had quite easily found our way to Grandmother's house. But this time it was different. It was growing dark and it had started to rain, and somehow we just couldn't find the right way. After asking a few times for the right direction we finally arrived late in the evening at Grandmother and Tante Dien's home. They had been waiting for us and had been worried when it became dark outside. While we ate Tante Dien's homemade soup, Grandmother told us about the war and the strange uniformed men in her city. Turning to Jan she asked him if there also was war in Breda. Jan and I looked at each other and did our best to understand what she meant. Grandmother was born and raised in Amsterdam, and this was her world. Anything outside the city walls never had been of importance to her. She had never attended school and had taught herself how to read and write.

Our days in Amsterdam were great. With our cousin Coby we went by tram to Amsterdam's most famous shopping centers to window shop, eat apple pan-cakes or ordered croquettes at one of the many outside terraces. Or, as Coby would suggest, we took a bommel treintje (tram car) to the fishing village of Vol-lendam. Sitting on the dike, looking over the Zuider Zee and the many fishing boats, we ate the famous smoked paling (eel) and mussels. From there we went to the island of Marken, which was a small island about a 45 minute boat ride from the mainland. It was quaint, very pretty and well kept up. We walked around and talked to the friendly natives who still wore their wooden shoes and colorful clothing in those times. Later while the warm summer wind blew from over the sun drenched Zuider Zee, we went back again with the boat to Vollendam, and from there with the bommel train to Amsterdam.

In the smaller towns we had not seen much of the German Police, but in Amsterdam it was a different story. The hated Green Police were patrolling the streets and restaurants wherever people came together. We also saw many of the SS troops and the feared Gestapo in their black uniforms—probably keeping a eye on things. After our two weeks in Amsterdam and enjoying our family, we decided to go further to Haarlem to see Grandmother Breeuwer and Tante Nel.

And, if possible, we wanted to spend a day or two on the beach of Bloe-mendaal—which, as it turned out, was just great. The sun was shining, the wind was warm, and it was very quiet on the beach. It was hard to believe there was a war going on. From Haarlem we planned to go home, by the way of Den Haag.

◆    ◆    ◆

Mother was happy when we came home again from our trip. She told us that hundreds of German bombers had droned overhead the night before. Father had heard on his short wave radio from Radio Orange out of England, that London was being bombed repeatedly. Many a time during the first year of the war we heard the Luftwaffe droning over as they headed across the English Channel toward England.

Vacation was over and Jan, Henk, and I went back to our schools again. Henk was usually with two of his best buddies, and Jan was by himself most of the time walking with his nose in one or another textbook. I don't know how he could learn anything this way while walking to and from his school. People always thought that he was studying to become a priest.

Mies and I attended the same school which was a 20 minute walk. Usually we went together on our bikes to and from school. One day while riding to school we met our first 'boyfriends.' They were boys from our neighborhood, and we had seen them before when we had our bike races. But since there were always so many boys around at our races, we never had paid much attention to them. The boys had followed us one day while they were going to another school. Since that day the boys always pedaled about a fourth of a mile behind us, while Mies and I giggled on our bikes all the way to school. After a few weeks they were brave enough to ask us to eat French fries with them. The French fry stalls were, and still are, very popular in Holland. They also serve croquettes, which is a Dutch specialty. The stalls, which are very nice, are usually located at popular spots or close to some busy street corner.

Laughing and looking at each other we ate our fries with piccalilly (mayonaise with chopped gherkins and onions) while hanging on our bikes. One day while talking with the boys at the stall again, suddenly out of nowhere German and English fighter planes were above us and started to attack each other. They went first way up almost above the clouds and then came down fast in a swoop. First we watched them, but after one of the fighter planes came down like a fire ball, leaving a tail of black smoke behind, the air raid sirens went off and we all had to go off the street. Since we were near an underground shelter, we hurried to the place of safety. Later in the war I would hate those underground shelters. I always felt as though I was buried in a tomb. After that day the boys and we girls became good friends for awhile. Little did we know then, that a few years later, those boys would fight together with Jan in the underground resistance.

Along with the end of our democratic government came economic restraint. Prices and various goods were fixed, and people needed special permits to use cars or motorcycles. The Nazis began exporting Dutch gasoline and raw material to Germany. Tens of thousands of cattle and horses, and poultry by the millions went eastward going into Germany. The Nazis began rationing certain foods and cloth goods. By showing identity cards people got weekly ration books. The coupons showed the specific amounts of particular foods that one could buy. At the beginning of the war we managed to buy almost everything that we needed, even on the ration coupons. But as the war progressed everyday simple necessities slowly disappeared.

The Nazi propaganda came steadily to Breda in the form of radio programs, newspapers and movies. Much of that propaganda was meant to divide the Dutch people along religious and political lines and to arouse hostilities toward Jews. It was also about that same time when the Nazi persecution of the Jews began in our country. They dismissed Jewish civil workers and other public officials including postal workers, teachers and professors. The Jews were ordered to sell their businesses at unfairly low prices and were forbidden to buy property. The Nazis considered the Jews as enemies of Germany. As the Jews were being singled out for persecution, our general living condition also declined.

Christmas came in a dark world. Father closed the draperies tightly, I think not only so that no light could be seen on the outside, but also to shut out the dark misery of a world at war. Mother had seen to it that we had our Christmas dinner with all the trimmings. While Father lit the candles on the tree, we sang Christmas songs and, as tradition, we each choose our candle and guessed which one would burn the longest. For New Year's Day Mother and I fried oliebollen and appleflappen as always, and friends and neighbors came over. While dipping the oliebollen in the powdered sugar they would discuss the news we had heard on Radio Orange. Optimistic news from out of England always made everyone feel better and more secure in the belief that soon the war would be over and we would be free again.

◆    ◆    ◆

It was March 6, 1941, the year I became 16 years old and I could start dating. For the last few years Mother had told me that I could not date before my 16th birthday. And here it was! Not that I had a boyfriend, but I could date if I wanted to. And next year I was allowed to go to dance lessons, which sent me into day-dreams of beautiful billowing gowns and handsome young men. Life never seemed brighter than at that moment. I had asked Mother if I could have a party with my girlfriends for my birthday. Of course Mies would be there and my girl-friend Chiel de Jonge. Chiel was a girl who lived around the corner of our street on the Molengracht Straat, close to where Mies lived. She was a happy go lucky girl our age, was tall with long legs and had very curly long dark hair. She had an older brother and two younger brothers. Her father worked for the customs office in Breda. Chiel's mother was very protective of her only daughter, and with the German invasion she had cut Chiel's hair as short as a boy's haircut. Probably she had done this to protect her daughter from hungry German soldier's eyes. Another girl coming to my party was Gina van Lierop. She was somewhat younger than we were, but she was a lot of fun. As I remember, her father had also been a military man and worked in the military hospital in our town. She had one younger brother who was about Henk's age, and he always wanted to know what we were up to. The two other girls who were invited to my party also lived in our neighborhood, and even though they were not my close friends, we went around with each other many times.

The minute I opened my eyes and saw my white curtains fluttering in the soft breeze blowing from the meadows, I knew it was going to be a great day. It was my 16th birthday! I took great deep breaths of air and wished the sun would hurry up and warm the day. When I came downstairs, Mother was busy setting the breakfast table. Usually our breakfast consisted of white and brown bread, peanut butter, jam, cheese, chocolate sprinkles and honey cake. The sandwiches were always eaten open faced. We got a egg only once or twice a week with our breakfast. With our morning meals we always drank tea or milk.

There was nothing like a birthday to make a student the star of the day in my school. It was something I quite enjoyed, and gave me the feeling of belonging. As soon as school was out, I walked home as fast I could hoping that Mother would not have one of her headaches on my birthday. Poor Mother, I thought, always those headaches. It seemed that the doctors could not do much for her. As soon as I walked through the front door, I looked at Mother and saw that she was her happy old self, and I gave a sigh of relief. On a pretty platter she had already arranged the pastries, and the raspberry fizz was ready to be served. Soon my friends came over, each bringing a small present for me, which was greatly appreciated of course. After the opening of the presents, it did not take long before the pastries were eaten and the drink was gone. We played games, and soon doubled over with laughter when we, in turns, sang Deanna Durbin love songs. We remembered them from before the Germans took everything American away from us. We talked about her hairdo, her smile and her walk. But mainly we talked about her clothes. When the war was over we said, we would all dress like Deanna Durban, and we dreamed on and on, until at last we got tired of it. It was already late when my friends walked through the blacked out streets back to their homes again.

On Sunday afternoons throughout the year whenever the weather permitted, and sometimes when it didn't, my friends and I walked to downtown. It was about a 25 minute walk from my house. In Holland all stores were closed on Sundays. Those laws still apply today, except for cafeterias, movie theaters, a few drugstores and pastry shops. I think all the young people of Breda were in the centrum of our city on Sunday afternoons, just walking around. First we walked to the city square, then through connecting narrow shopping streets to another square, and then on the other side of the sidewalks back again, like as in an oblong circle—just walking, talking and looking at one another. Boys looking at girls, and girls looking at boys. The cafeterias and ice cream parlors were full of young people, eating, drinking and sometimes making dates. Usually we walked four times around the oval while laughing at some of the funny hairdos, hats and weird clothing we saw. In the meantime, of course,we were eyeing the good looking guys. Later we went to our favorite place, a cafeteria by the name of 'The Hex' where we ordered their specialty—apple pancakes—before going home.

◆     ◆     ◆

One day Mother unexpectedly said to Jan and me that we both should have formal instruction in the Baptist religion. She said that when we turned eighteen years old, we then could be baptized and become members of the Baptist Church. Jan and I must have looked surprised because Mother began to explain that even though she herself did not go to church, she wanted it to be different for her children. First Jan and I didn't know what to say. Become members of a church? After first thinking about this and knowing that Mother wanted this so much for us, Jan decided to take the lessons and learn about the Baptist faith. The following year Jan and a few other young people were baptized and became members of the Baptist Church. Later when I became seventeen years old I also went to the same religion classes as my brother had gone to a year before. The teacher was a Baptist minister. He was a gentle and very friendly older man with an impressive long gray beard. Patiently he explained the old and new testament to me and to two other girls. When I became eighteen years old, I was baptized and became a member of the only Baptist Church in Breda. But Jan and I never practiced our faith much.

# 20

## *THE JEWISH GIRL*

One year had passed since the occupation began and no lights glowed on the horizon. Hitler and Germany looked stronger than ever. Conditions deteriorated for everyone, but the Jews faced much graver problems. A series of new laws came for the Jewish people. The children could no longer attend school or go swimming. Everywhere were signs posted "Forbidden for Jews "as on busses, trains, stores, restaurants, theaters etc. The tensions were high when Nazis attacked Jews living in Amsterdam. Angered by the violent attacks, Christian neighbors fought back to help the Jews. The Germans retaliated by viciously arresting 425 young Jewish men in Amsterdam in a razzia (a Dutch word for roundup) and shipping them by truck to a prison camp in Germany called Mauthausen. The men's families soon heard that they had died of illnesses or heart attacks—stories the Dutch did not believe. It was clear that the Dutch people showed themselves to be strongly opposed to the Nazi system, and that the Nazis were going to treat us severely if we were not cooperative. Many people throughout Holland were soon arrested and imprisoned. Violence appeared and spread.

Food was no longer plentiful at mealtimes. There was less to eat and food cost more, often ten times what it had cost before 1940. Real coffee and tea were more and more difficult to get—even with coupons. Soon we got coffee and tea substitutes which were horrible inventions. The coffee was made from roasted barley and the tea from potato peels and bramble leaves and was bitter tasting. But somehow we got used to not having the real thing anymore. Our family was lucky to live close to a farmer where Mother always had bought her milk and eggs. Although we got less and less of everything, we could still get enough milk and eggs from our farmer.

Every week as long as I can remember, rain or shine, there were two market days at our city square—Tuesdays and Fridays. Every woman went there shopping at least once a week. Before the German occupation the canvas-roofed open stalls had sold about everything. Piles of linens, underwear, coats, pots and pans, books and paintings were waiting to be bought. Stalls with many different sorts of fish—stalls with produce, cheese or flowers and everything else under the sun could be bought at the large open marketplace.

Sometimes when I was free from school, Mother and I went together to the market. It was always alive with people not only from our own town but also from villages around Breda. With everything becoming more difficult to come by, Mother now went to the market twice a week. She hoped that she could buy something extra, such as cheese or meat without coupons. The black market flourished by now, and Mother knew she had to pay more money for her wares if she had no coupons. But mostly Mother went to the market to buy fish for her family. Fish was still plentiful in Holland and took more and more the place of meat. Oil for frying the fish also became scarce, and the butter we got we needed for other things. Soon we ate only boiled fish, which I liked anyway, especially if Mother could afford to put a small pat of margarine on top. At the end of Mother's shopping spree at the market, and with her large linen shopping bag full of stuff, we went to the flower truck. Mother always had to buy a bunch of flowers from one of the flower trucks which stood on the very end of the market. Especially at the end of the market day, people could buy an armful of flowers for just a few dimes. Mother always said that flowers in the house were like bringing the sunshine in.

One day Mies and I were walking to the Wilhelmina Park when a regiment of German soldiers marched through the Molengracht Straat, probably on their way to one of another kazerne. With their heavy black boots on, they were marching to the German hit song "Wir fahren gegen England. "(We are going to England). Mies and I had heard the song before on the radio, and it had us made sick to listen to it. We all were very worried that the Germans might in fact invade England. The fall of Britain would spell the collapse of everything; it would be the end of the world for us. The German bombers continued to drone over almost every night on the way to England. And every night the German radio station would tell us gleefully of English cities that had been wiped out. Of course many of those statements turned out to be lies, as Father would tell us after he had listened to Radio Orange in the evening. The news from England brought us not only news but also hope and most important—the truth.

◆     ◆     ◆

It was September and Jan had gone to a dance school with his girlfriend. When I grew up, the dance lessons were 'the thing to do' for young people. The dance schools which were located throughout our city were usually not large and had about 20 students. Mother always had told me that I could not attend dance school before my seventeenth birthday, which was something I didn't agreed with. Mother and I had been arguing about it the way teenagers and parents do. She thought that I was too young because, as she tried to explain to me; when you go to dances you will be dating. Mother always had wanted me to double date first with Jan and his girlfriend before going to dance school. This reasoning from her made no sense to me. Here I was sixteen and I could start dating, so why couldn't I start dance lessons together with Jan and his girlfriend. The end was that Father said to Mother that in this miserable war I should be allowed to have some fun because as he said, things looked bad enough as it was and who knows what tomorrow will bring. So two weeks into the dance course I started the lessons which lasted throughout the winter months.

Throughout the fall of 1941 we heard nothing but bad news. Hitler, driven by his successes, had attacked Russia in June and had almost reached the Caucuses with its great oil deposits. Once seized, it could fuel the German war effort indefinitely. We also heard that in North Africa, where General Rommel fought the British Army, the Germans gained one victory after another.

One evening as Father listened again to Radio Orange on his short-wave radio, the broadcaster announced that the English city of Coventry was total leveled by German bombers and that there were thousands of casualties. It made Mother upset and Father said that the Germans fought for world domination and the English fought for the defense of England. Everything was insane and senseless. He then cursed Hitler and wished that all the Nazis were locked up in Hell. Since Father worked in the factory, he had started to curse—something that had never been permitted in our home, and it scared me. A few days earlier one of Father's former colleagues from the military, with whom he always had been in contact, was arrested by the Gestapo. In his house they found an underground press stowed away. He was arrested and tortured for not telling the names of the people who helped him with the printing. Later he was taken away, destination unknown. He never returned. The underground press, which had been expanding since 1940, was distributed in secret at night to give people advice about hidings from the Nazis, upcoming restrictions and every day practical advice. Another illegal newspaper by the name of 'Het Parool "was read in secret by many people in Holland and survived the four years of Nazi occupation.

My parents, together with most of the Dutch people, held on to their belief that Hitler could not win and that Holland would be free again. One night in December of 1941 we were sitting around the living room table and, as usual, we kids were doing our homework from school and drinking our substitute tea. A cold wind was blowing outside which rattled the windows. I was struggling with my homework while my brothers were reading and writing. Mother was mending socks. Suddenly Father came running down the stairs from the attic and tensely told us that he had just heard from Radio Orange about a terrible Japanese bombing on an American Naval Base in Hawaii, and that America had declared war on Japan and Germany. "Now that the United States has joined the Allies in the fight against not only Japan, but also Hitler, the war would not last long any-more," Father said hopefully. "Maybe a year at the most, then it will be all over!"

The following day the news about Pearl Harbor was in our newspaper and, of course, the Germans blamed it all on America. All the occupied countries in Europe were happy that America was now going to help, and new hope arose. I think that after the declaration of war from the United States, the Nazis went insane. Because of our happiness many people became careless and the Nazis arrested people left and right. One could get arrested for saying something, even vaguely, against Hitler. A mild word against the Nazis in a public place could be the last word spoken outside a prison camp. In all our misery of the war years, America was for us a symbol of light in the darkness and of hope in a world gone insane.

The Saturday evening dance lessons were fun. All students were 16 to 19 years of age. There were as many boys as girls. We learned to dance to the fox-trot, slow waltz, tango and waltz, which were in that time the most popular dances in our country. Our dance instructor was a short man in his forties with a receding hairline. He was not the friendliest man, but he was a fantastic dancer who seemed to be floating over the dance floor with only his legs moving. His dance partner was a pretty young women, always wearing the loveliest dresses. She helped him with the dances and was as good in a dance as he was.

In the beginning quite a few boys didn't know the right foot from the left, but we managed to have a good time and somehow it didn't matter how we danced at first. Our dance teacher didn't want us to have the same dance partner all the time, because as he would explain, you will learn your steps better if you dance with different partners. Of course we didn't always like doing this, especially not when a boy and a girl liked each other. Many young romances began there at the dance school. Our dance lessons always started early on Saturday nights. Since the German invaders had come to our country, we were under a curfew and everyone had to be off the streets by 11:00. Our dance teacher always told the boys "No girl should walk home alone through the darkened streets. See to it that all girls get home safely." Usually the girls were home before the curfew started, but for those boys who had their girlfriends living further away, it was a race with time. They would run through the streets and hoped to make it home safely before the street patrols came.

Poor Jan, who always stretched his goodbye to his girlfriend too long, had to speed through the dark deserted streets to be home before eleven. I don't think he ever made it home in time, always worrying Mother. That winter I made dates with boy's from the dance school quite a few times, but they never lasted longer than a few weeks. Then I got tired of the boys. I rather liked to hang out with my girlfriends. We always had a lot of fun together.

◆        ◆        ◆

The cold of winter passed and the spring of '42 arrived with soft spring rains. Crocuses and daffodils were blooming everywhere. In the fields behind our home the pussy willows showed their fuzzy heads, and the summer birds arrived from the far south of Portugal and Northern Africa. It was a day in May when my girlfriend Gina told me that she had heard about a store in downtown, which always had sold very nice coats and dress materials before the war. The store had received a supply of rayon dress materials. She told me to be at the store as soon as they opened up at 9:00 in the morning to be sure I would get some material for a dress. Gina and I loved to sew our own dresses. We thought that they not only fit much better than the store bought ones, but also were exclusively our own design. The fabric stores received less and less materials and, if they came in, there was not much in fabrics, color and designs for us to choose from. The dresses which I had hanging in my closet from the last two years and which by today's standards were few, had become too tight for me. I had grown in certain places and needed a new dress. Since one of my bike tires was flat that morning I decided to walk to downtown and hoped that I did not have to wait too long in the line at the fabric store.

It had become more and more of a problem with the tires. The inner tubes started to look like patchwork with one patch over the other. New tires were hard to come by. Sometimes, if you were lucky, you could buy one on the black market, but they asked outrageous prices for them. I knew that if I would ask Father for new tires he would say, "My dear, take your legs and start walking; that's what they are for!" Beside the bus, our bicycles were our only means of transportation.

As I walked further through the Wilhelmina Park enjoying the fresh spring breeze, I watched some geese swim toward the edge of the water. My thoughts had gone back to when, as a child, I loved to go with Mother and Henk to the park to feed the ducks and swans. There were always so many of them. As I went further the air raid sirens suddenly started to wail, and everyone scurried away out of the park. Since there was not a shelter around where I was, I walked further hoping that the Allied planes would not come over our town. Suddenly anti aircraft fire started to erupt which sent me looking for a place of safety. When alarms went off and there was no shelter, people went into houses for shelter.

On the east edge of the park stood a row of stately homes with lovely yards in front. I saw a few people entering one of the houses and thought that I should go there also and find shelter. As I reached the house a young man, who had placed his bike against a fence, entered the house at the same time as I did and waited in the hall with other people until the safe alarms went off again. It did not take long until I felt the boy's eyes looking at me as though I were a great curiosity. Even though I was always called pretty, I was not a movie star. My first impulse was to look away. I never had seen him before and I wondered who he was. From the corner of my eyes I guessed he was about 18 or 19 years old, medium tall, well dressed, dark hair and, as I thought, good-looking.

After the safe alarms sounded, I left the hall of the house together with the other people and walked briskly further. As soon as I was out of the park, the boy with the bike came alongside me and asked where I was going and if he could walk with me. I said I didn't mind; he looked a nice guy. He introduced himself and said his name was Piet van Hagel. By the time we reached the fabric store, we had already made a date to see a movie on the following Sunday. He then left.

A long line of women were waiting for the store to be opened up. I went to the end of the line and still had to wait more than 2 hours before I got inside the store. Luckily they had some material I liked. It was a rayon fabric and had a lilac flower print. I gave my coupons to the clerk, paid for the material and went happily home. How well I remember the dress which I made in a pretty design and wore for many years.

After a few years of living in our street, I think almost everyone who lived there knew everyone else. At the end of our street lived a young family with three small children who played with the rest of the children of our street. I enjoyed watching the oldest, a girl by the name of Saartje who was about 8 years old. She was a pretty and fun-loving child who always protected the smaller children (and sometimes the older ones too) and tried to keep peace when things went wrong. I didn't know they were a Jewish family until that day when I walked home with my dress material in my shopping bag and came into our street. It was Wednesday afternoon and the children were playing outside as usual. Looking at Saartje I suddenly saw a yellow star on her clothing and also on the shirt of her younger brother. It read JOOD (JEW). I had heard that the Nazis had announced another rule for all the Jewish people. All Jews over the age of five must wear a Jewish star (Star of David) on their clothing. It had to be made of yellow-colored cloth with the word JOOD printed in black. It had to be sewed on their clothing on the left side of their chest and be visible at all times. Not until I saw Saartje with the star on her dress did I realize that to be a Jew meant to be branded like cattle by the Nazis. A few months later the mass deportation of the Jewish people in Holland to destinations unknown would begin.

◆    ◆    ◆

*Summer of '42.* After our first date to the movies, Piet and I saw each other mostly on Sunday afternoons. Usually we went on our bikes together with his friends and their girlfriends. On narrow sandy roads, we pedaled our bikes through a heather covered area to a restaurant with an outside terrace. Around small tables we ate spumoni ice cream, which was not as good as it had been, or ordered something to drink before we rode our bikes through the forest back home again. If the weather was sunny and warm, we went with the whole group to the 'Leemputten' which was a favorite swimming place a half hour ride from Breda. Originally it was large dugout sand pits which had formed small lakes and white sandy beaches. Especially on warm summer Sundays it was crowded with sun worshippers trying to tan. If the weather was rainy or gloomy, Piet and I saw a movie in one of the theaters in our city and went to a cafeteria afterward.

Piet lived in a new neighborhood behind the railroad station and quite a long way from where I lived. He was 19 years old and was a great guy with a lot of great humor. After he had graduated from high school he started working in Dordrecht, a town 20 minutes by train from Breda. He worked there for a shipping firm. One day, before I met his parents, Piet had told me of his only brother with whom he had been close and who had served on a submarine. During the first day of the war his ship was sunk with all men aboard by a German torpedo just off the coast of northern Holland. He had been twenty years old. It had been a terrible blow to his parents. When I came in their home, a life size portrait of their lost son was hanging on a wall in the living room.

That July of '42 Mies and I graduated from our school. Mies went to a beautician school, something she always had dreamed of. When not at that school she worked as a helper in a beauty shop. I had decided that before starting to look for work, I first wanted to go to Amsterdam. Jan, who had graduated from high school, was working as a bookkeeper at a firm for welders supply by the name of Gils and Co. This firm was also a depot for the Electra Oxygen Factory from out of Amsterdam. Gils and Co. received large steel bottles of oxygen, carbide, nitrogen and acetylene from that factory. Because of his work, Jan told me, he could not go on vacation that summer. So I talked with my parents about my plans to go by train to Amsterdam by myself for a short vacation and also visit Grandmother and Tante Nel in Haarlem. It was a few weeks later in that August that I took my suitcase and left for a two-week trip to the family up north. After a three hours ride in a crowded train I arrived in Amsterdam where Coby was waiting for me at the very large train terminal.

Even after two years of occupation Amsterdam was still a nice place to visit, that is if one knew where to go and what places to avoid. Vondel Park with its old trees and many flower beds was as always a popular spot with the people of Amsterdam who were looking for a little relaxation and a stroll. One day Coby and I took a tram to Amsterdam's famous Ryks Museum. I had been there many times but never saw all of it. Many of the famous paintings were stored in archives during the war, but many other works of art were still there to admire in the very large and beautiful museum.

The food shortage in Amsterdam was worse than in our city Breda. Many of the food stands, which were always such popular places to eat a snack, were almost all closed up. It was not only the food shortage I had noticed, but also other goods such as shoes and clothing. But what was the most dreadful was the mass deportations of the Jews in Amsterdam. The Gestapo came into the Jewish neighborhoods with vans, and the victims were forced out of their houses at gunpoint and cruelly pushed into the vans. They were taken to the train station for an agonizing trip to a Nazi concentration camp.

Slowly we heard of the concentration camps. We didn't know what was happening there, but now and then a family would receive news that their husband or son, who had been arrested and taken away, had died in one of the Nazi camps. Why and how nobody knew. Some of the Jews and other hunted people had fled to farmers and begged to stay in their sheds. But I think most of those hunted people sought help from friends or resistance workers who helped them find a "safe house."

After two wonderful weeks with Coby and the family in Amsterdam I went by train to Haarlem. I had stayed a day or so with Grandmother Breeuwer when Tante Nel told me about a girl, who was staying with her Tante Marie for a while. Tante Marie, as she said, was Tante Nel's late husband's sister. And, as Tante Nel continued, the girl who was staying with her was a little lonesome, and it would be nice if we two would come together. Her name was Hetty Berthan. Since there were no young people at Grandmother's house, I thought it would be fun to meet someone my own age. Little did I know then that she was a Jewish girl in hiding and not at all related to the in-laws of Tante Nel. As I later came to know, Hetty's father and mother had decided to go into hiding just before the deportation of Jews began. To reduce the risk of being caught, none of them knew where the other was. Hetty had no sisters or brothers. She and her parents hoped they would meet each other again after the war was over at a place only they knew about. Hetty had come to Tante Marie through the resistance workers who had helped her on Aryan and other false identification papers.

When I met Hetty for the first time, I had no idea who she was and I didn't ask. Deep down I knew something was different about her. In war time no one asked many questions, so many people were in hiding. We also knew that the ones who helped hunted people risked being imprisoned themselves—or even shot. Thousands of people faced those dangers in the war years.

Hetty came over to Grandmother's house for a visit the following day together with her Tante Marie. Hetty was a pretty 17-year-old girl and soon we talked and talked, as all young people do, about boys, books, music and the latest movies, wondering of we ever would see the American movies again. Before Hetty left we promised each other to come together before I would leave to Breda again. It was two days later when Tante Marie came over and asked me of I wanted to go sailing. She explained that the husband of her girlfriend was a avid sailor who, on his days off, loved to sail over the Spaarne in his sailboat. Hetty and another girl by the name of Stien were going also. It sure didn't take me long to think about it. I was ready to go! I never had sailed before and it sounded just great.

That Saturday, together with Hetty, Stien and Mr. Van Meerdonk, I sailed the whole day over the wide water of the Spaarne. The weather was great with just enough wind to make our sailboat slide with calm speed through the water. We all had a fantastic day, and that night we came home sunburned and tired. I wonder if Mr. Van Meerdonk came home with a headache from all that chatter of three girls the whole day, or that he had enjoyed that day as much as we had. Two days later I hopped on the train back to Breda and wondered if I ever would see Hetty again.

On the way to Breda the train stopped at the Rotterdam train station without opening its doors to let passengers out or to enter the train. At first I thought nothing about it until I saw a train directly besides ours being loaded with Jewish people. Surrounded by shouting German soldiers who were pointing their guns at the bewildered and shocked people, they were bullied inside the waiting train. Nazi SS officers were looking on and yelled orders. As long as I shall live, I will never forget the faces of those Jewish people. With their eyes full of fear they were holding on to one another. I saw mothers with their babies or small children close in their arms as if protecting them from harm, while other children were holding on to each other for dear life. The men were being pushed by the soldiers and were crowded together like cattle. Dry-eyed, grim and in despair they were looking around for their family members. I don't remember how long it took before the train with the human cargo started to jolt and then move away out of the train station with the destination of one or another concentration camp. As we later came to know, the destinations were the gas chambers.

When they were gone, I sat in silence staring out of the train's window at the now empty platform. This is what the Nazis loved, I thought, the power to dominate, the power to destroy and to kill. I tried to put it all out of my mind but I couldn't. Why, I thought, why hadn't the Jewish people opened their mouths when it still counted some years back. And why had the people not denounced Hitler. Now it had become an unstoppable avalanche. When will it end? It was not only the Jewish people who disappeared to places unknown, but also many non-Jews.

# 21

## *PIET THE SABOTEUR*

A few days later, after I came home from my trip, I went to a Houte Couture fashion business which was located in the centrum of our town. I always have been interested in sewing dresses and everything that has to do with fashion. It was the only shop of its kind in Breda and served the well-to-do ladies of our city and places around it. Before the war they had sold exclusive materials, and the rich ladies had ordered their dresses and suits at the Houte Couture House. Live models (mannequins) walked around and modeled the latest in fashions. I knew, of course, that the clothing business was not the same anymore as it had been two years before, and they probably needed no help. But I had to find out. And besides, I wanted to see the inside of the place. So far I had seen it only from the outside. Bravely I entered the richly decorated showroom and was greeted by a fashionably dressed young woman. After I explained to her why I came, she took me to a sort of office-workshop. There I saw many drawings of dresses hanging on a wall. Behind a desk, piled with other drawings, was a women sitting. She was about in her late forties. Her very light blond hair was fashioned in a bun on top of her head, and her trim figure was in a beautiful light brown colored dress. As it turned out, she was the boss and owner of the Houte Couture House. Her name was Mrs. Van der Pol. I must have stared at her because she started to smile and asked me if I was interested in a drawing or in her hair. Eagerly I told her that I wanted to work in her shop, and it didn't matter where she wanted me—drawing, sewing or modeling. I didn't care where she wanted me to work, I said. As long as she would give me a chance, I would do my best to learn wherever she needed me. After I answered some questions, she told me that her business had changed since the war, but that there was still plenty of work. She now designed dresses made from two or even three older garments, and the remodeling of those gowns kept the shop busy. As Mrs. Van der Pol started to work again on her designs, she told me to ask the girl at the front desk to show me around. I was to come back on Monday morning at 9:00. Then looking at me she said, "I am sure we can find some work for you."

I think I went home on wings. I could work at the Houte Couture House! On my way home I went first to the flowershop were Gina worked and told her my good luck. She gave me a carnation and I had to promise to tell her all the secrets of the House, especially the designs. Later after I came home and had told Mother the good news, she asked me how much the shop would pay me. For a moment I stared at her and muttered, "I don't know!" I had not thought about the money, only about the fact that I was going to work there.

It was great working at the House of Mrs. Van der Pol. There were eight girls working in the sewing room—two ladies for the cutting table and fitting room, two models who worked only when needed and an office desk girl. Mrs. Van der Pol drew sketches and talked to her customers and the salesmen who sold her material which now came mostly from the black market at incredibly high prices. I started to work mainly in the sewing room and learned many things, which also included a lot of gossip about the rich ladies of Breda. One of the girls who already worked there for some years would mimic one of the eccentric customers. We would laugh so hard that Mrs. Van der Pol came running in and asked us if we wanted to go home and stay there. For the following two years I worked at the Houte Couture House and learned many things which had to do with sewing, fitting and the fashion business.

It was the beginning of September of that same summer when Mies came running through our backyard into our home. Without a word she fell down on Father's chair and while crying she said, "I don't want to go, I don't want to leave here!" Looking at Mies I asked her what she was talking about. The last time I saw her so upset was when her mother almost had died of food poisoning a few months back. Mies sighed and, while wiping her tears, she told Mother and me that her family was going to move away from Breda in about three weeks. Suddenly I remembered that she had told me a while back that her father was offered a music director position at a school of music in the city of Deventer. Since we had not heard further about it, Mies and I hoped that her father had not gone further into it. Her father was a very musical man and ever since the capitulation of the Dutch Army, he had worked as a music teacher at a high school in Breda. Mies always had played the piano, but was not as gifted as her father was. She had told me once that on the day she was born, her four-year old sister had died of pneumonia. She had been a highly talented child, who already played the violin well. I still remember the small violin specially made for her and a portrait of her sister hanging side by side on the wall of their living room.

My best friend was going to leave. We had known each other since we were small children. We had played in our street together, had fought and cried together. When we were growing up, we had made big plans together, had our first boyfriends together and hoped, after we were married, we would have our first child together. All our plans surely had not included Mies moving away from our town.

The last weeks before Mies moved away to Deventer, a town about 100 mile northeast of Breda, Mies, Chiel, Gina and I spend long hours in each others company. Too soon the day came that we had to say goodbye, promising each other to spend our vacations together. The following weeks I missed Mies a great deal. I missed the talks with her and the sharing of our secret thoughts and dreams, and I felt rather lonely. Sure, I had my other friends and there was the great guy Piet. But no one could replace my best friend Mies.

It was a few weeks later that I went to a school of gymnastics and became a member. I always had loved sports especially track but, except for a few Catholic schools, track for girls was not offered yet in that time in Breda. So I thought gymnastics would be the next best thing for me. I liked the sport and for the following few years I spent a lot of time on the bars, horse and ropes. I also enrolled again at the dance school for the winter of '42-'43. Piet had said he was not interested in the dance lessons anymore, and I had not gone further into it with him.

One Saturday Mother asked me if I wanted to go to the meat store. She had heard from the neighbor the store had received fresh meat and sausage. As I was standing in a long line in front of the store, Truus, the girlfriend of one of Piet's friends was standing in front of me. After we talked for a few minutes, she whispered in my ear and asked if I knew about her boyfriend Joop. When I said, "No, what happened to him?" she answered, "Meet me at the coffee shop terrace after we are done here." The coffee shop terrace was located not far from the Wilhelmina Park. Before the war it was a nice place to drink tea or coffee and eat a pastry. As I was standing in the line, I wondered what it was all about. Two hours later I finally got my meat and sausage. While asking myself what the sausage was made of, I walked to the coffee shop where Joop's girlfriend was waiting on the terrace. After we had ordered our imitation coffee, I said to Truus, "Tell me what happened to Joop." Nervous and with a low voice she told me that Joop had not come home last week after he had left her house. Nobody knew where he was. Then a few days ago, she continued, his parents got a notice that their son was arrested by the Gestapo. His father went to the SS office in Breda to seek information about his son. There they told him that Joop was arrested for sabotage and was being held in a prison in Fught (a Dutch prison about 40 miles northeast of Breda). His father was told that Joop was not allowed any visitors. He had gone anyway to Fught but was sent away without seeing his son. None of the officers there wanted to talk to him and had told the poor man to go home and forget about his son. "Please, Eef," Truus said sadly, "do not talk about this to anyone. You know what big ears those Nazi informants have, and I don't know if Piet is in any way involved in this or in any other sabotage." A little later when I said goodbye to Truus and walked home, I suddenly felt very tired. It had dawned upon me that Piet was never home very much, not even on Saturday nights. Most of the time we saw each other on Sundays, but I always thought he liked to be with his friends. So many things suddenly fell into place. Sometimes Piet had been gone a whole weekend. I did know that Piet cared about me, but I never had asked him what he was doing in his free time. One year later I came to knew what he had been doing. He had been in the resistance in Dordrecht, where he worked, and was working with a sabotage group blowing up bridges, destroying railroads and freeing political prisoners whenever possible. Maybe Piet had sought revenge for his brother's death, I don't know—I would never find out. A few weeks later I learned that Piet's friend Joop was interrogated by the Gestapo and when he did not cooperate, he was brutally tortured and finally shot.

Sabotage was difficult because the Nazis were at their peak of power in 1942 and retaliated brutally when they were provoked. Sometimes when a car with German officers inside was ambushed or a high ranking officer was shot dead, it would drive the Nazis insane. They then would line up a group of well-known people of the town, or the nearest town where the ambush took place. If no one came forward and took responsibility for the ambush, the well-known people of the town would be executed within 24 hours. The following morning the names of the innocent victims were printed in the newspapers all over Holland. This was one way for the Nazis to keep the occupied countries under their control.

There were different resistance organizations. In addition to the sabotage groups there was the underground printing organization for falsifying papers, I.D's, food stamps, publications and so forth. Then there was the group that helped Jews to safer places. This group also helped the Allied pilots who were shot down over Holland to hiding places and or found for them a way back to England. Some people worked on the coding and decoding of messages that were to be sent to or received from England and deliver them to members of the underground forces. Again another group received weapons delivered by airplanes from England which were then distributed amongst the underground resistance. Life in hiding presented many problems, but more people chose to go underground as the Nazis became vicious. Those who were helping people in hiding had to be especially careful not to show hostility openly and risk arrest. The resistance provided food stamps for the ones who had people stowed away in their homes. Despite the care taken by those in hiding and their protectors, about 20,000 hidden Jews in Holland were found and deported before the war ended in 1945. The same number of non-Jews in the resistance were arrested. Some were found by accident; others were the victims of Dutch-Nazi informants.

Life under oppression was not easy, especially for a generation that had been raised in the sunny side of democracy. In all the darkness of that time there was one bright spot—there was a feeling of trust and togetherness I have not experienced since, and helping each other became the most natural thing to do.

Many comforts of everyday life that had been taken for granted were gone, and we had to learn to cope with shortages which became worse every day. Grain had become scarce, so the bakeries no longer sold the tasty rye or wheat breads of the past. Now, potatoes and other flours were mixed with extra water, resulting in sticky black loaves. As we ate less and less of other foods, Mother peeled more and more potatoes. Peeling potatoes carefully with thin peels became one of my daydreams of the high life. Besides foods, other household items including soap were scarce. The soap that was available hurt people's skin and did not get things clean. Living without adequate food, fuel or cleanliness led to much higher rates of illness and death. Contagious diseases, such as influenza, dysentery, diphtheria and especially tuberculosis, increased greatly.

It was a cold rainy day in the late fall of '42. My poor mother, who was having one of her headaches, muttered gloomily that it was so cold in the house. We had received our coupons for buying coal for heating our house, but it was not much, and we had to save coal for the winter. One never knew how cold it would get. Father had said to Mother that there were small wood burning stoves available which could be placed in the corner of the living room in front of our hearth and was also meant for cooking. "This way," he said to Mother, "you not only heat the room but also can cook the meals all in the same time." Mother, like most Dutch housewives, was very fussy about her house. She had said to Father that she did not want to live like a farmer with a stove in her living room. I think that Mother first had to get used to the whole idea of not cooking in her kitchen. After Father bought one of the small ugly-looking stoves which happily spread its warmth throughout our living room, Mother soon found out that comfort was more important than looks. The rest of the house stayed without heat, as it always had been. Sometimes the bedrooms were unbearably cold during cold spells, and the water pipes in our bedroom washbasin would freeze up. How well I remember the many times I had ice cold feet in the winter while trying to sleep.

Stockings were another worry, we almost could not get them anymore. Nylons did not exist at that time, only silk stockings. It was a disaster when I came home from dancing or had gone out with friends and found a run in my hose. But people were inventive. In Breda many small businesses that could repair those runs with the help of a small cleverly designed machine started up. After the treatment the stockings looked like new again.

◆    ◆    ◆

Winter of 1943 came, and soon the rivers and park ponds froze over and people were skating. One Sunday evening Piet and I had gone to the piano bar for some fun and a drink. The piano bar was a place located in mid downtown. It was popular with young adults and the older teens who gathered there on Saturday and Sunday afternoons and evenings. The piano player, who was very well liked, was a man in his mid twenties. He not only played well, but also knew how to sing. By now, the third year of the war, the drinks in the bars had become sour tasting liquids. But we were out with friends and had a good time that night. It was always too bad when 10:00 came around the corner, and we had to start going home so that Piet could be home before the curfew which started at eleven. This was no fun, especially not for young people. When we came home and kissed goodbye, Piet and I made a date for the following Sunday to go ice skating. That is, if everything was still frozen over, we said.

Next Sunday came with a great day for skating. The rivers and the ponds in the Wilhelmina Park were still frozen over, and the weather was just right with only a few clouds in the blue sky. I was dressed in my warm coat, skates in my hands and ready to go. Piet had said he would pick me up at 2:00 sharp. But Piet didn't come. It was unusual for him not to come at the promised time. He never let me wait, he never disappointed me. Sometimes, if for one or another reason he could not make it, he always had sent a friend over with a note from him (we did not have telephones yet in our houses). After waiting for more than a hour, Piet still wasn't there, and I could not understand where he could be. Then, when looking out the window, I saw one of Piet's friends Nick, coming to the house. When I opened the front door he gave me a note from Piet in which he wrote that he was sorry but he was sick and could not make it for our skating date together. When I asked Nick how sick Piet was, he said that it was serious but he could not tell me more. After he left I said to Mother that I was going to Piet's house on my bike, and I didn't know what time I would be home. It depended a lot on my bike tires, if they were not giving up on me, and I had to walk. When I arrived a twenty minutes later at Piet's home, his mother opened the door and asked me not to stay too long. Piet was lying in his bed and asked me not to come too close to him. Then, full of tension but with his voice down, he told me that he was seriously ill with tuberculoses. For a moment I thought a stone had hit me. At first I couldn't believe it. He always looked so strong. Maybe a little thin lately, but then we all had become that way. Piet told me not to worry, he would come out of this, and when this shitty war was over, he said, he had some real living to do. I didn't stay long. His mother said that he needed all the rest he could get. It was dark when I rode my bike home that evening. The streets were deserted and a cold wind was blowing from the north which made me shiver. The blacked-out city was lightened only by the moon which peeked once in awhile through the clouds. Further away search lights from the military airfield slashed through the dark, looking for a wounded airplane. I thought about how unfair this all was. We were all so young and wanted to go on with our lives. It felt as if there was a wall in front of us. It felt as if we were not allowed to plan and dream and look ahead toward the future. When I came home, I told my parents what had happened to Piet. "He had been just fine," I said to Mother, "just some coughing, not even much. A few days earlier he had gone to the doctor when he had coughed up some blood."

I visited Piet a few times before he went to a sanitarium in the Veluwe. The Veluwe is a beautiful forest area about a two hour train ride northeast from Breda. He was there in a room with twelve other young men, all sick with tuberculosis. I wrote to him often and sent pictures which, as Piet wrote me back, were enjoyed by all the guys on the floor. Sometimes I received a letter written by all the guys. In the summer of '43 Piet got an operation on his lungs, but it must not have been successful because a few weeks later he came home to die. I saw Piet one more time. Since I was not allowed to go any further then the screen door of his room, I could not come close to him. It was so sad to see the once young strong guy, who had been so full of life and fun, now too weak to speak and so very thin. He whispered my name, but said nothing more. I stayed for only a few minutes. I didn't know what to say. How could I tell him to hold on to life, and that someday everything would be great again, and we would have swimming parties again and go to the piano bar. We both knew that this never would come again for him.

A week later Piet was buried. He was 20 years old, the same age as was his brother when he had been killed. Piet and all the young men from his floor at the sanitarium had died because of war—innocent victims of the Hitler regime. In the years that followed I sometimes saw Piet's mother in one or another store or on the bus, and we talked. Piet's father had died of a broken heart a year after his youngest son was laid to rest.

# 22

# *RAZZIAS AND ABDUCTIONS*

The winter of 1943 was the year of Germany's first major defeat. The German Army had penetrated Russia as far as Stalingrad. While German troops were battling the Russian winter, their losses, especially at Stalingrad, were enormous. They also had one defeat after the other in Africa, especially after the United States entered the war and the big American war production machine swung into action. Even so, we no longer believed the war would end soon. Every evening Father still always listened to Radio Orange on his little short-wave radio at the attic which kept us informed about the war efforts.

Mother who ran out of ways to prepare potatoes, tried new ideas which were not always successful without butter, meat, or cheese or anything which make a dish tasty. Mother was worried about Henk, my younger brother. He was in his young teenage years and had grown tall. He did not get the food he needed for his growing body and became very thin and pale in his face. He was always hungry and devoured every morsel he could get his hands on. Not only Henk needed better food, but his beaten up leather oxford shoes became alarmingly too small for him. Shoes were a real problem, especially for families with growing children. It was a fight to keep children in shoes. Mothers would cut out the front of their shoes to make room for their toes. When going by bus we saw more and more of the seat coverings cut out. By the end of the war most of the leather materials were gone from the busses and transformed into shoes. But the materials were too stiff and thick for comfortable shoes. Women were sold shoes with wooden soles, and strips of material or straw on top, for which fewer coupons were needed. Because we walked so much, our older shoes with leather soles were repaired and repaired until there was nothing to repair anymore. I think that every Saturday Jan was working up a sweat to mend the one pair of shoes he had. He was always repairing his leather soles and heels with one or another piece of leather from an old pair of shoes which were beyond repair.

More and more Allied bombers came over at night on their way to Germany where they bombed the German war factories in the Ruhr region. From our house we could see the searchlight from the military airfield, Gilse Reyen. In their crossing searchlights the Germans tried to hold a Allied bomber and then, after heavy anti-airplane artillery, tried shoot one down. One morning after the Allied bombers had come back from Germany, a lone wounded airplane came over, probably trying to make it back to its base in England. Suddenly a roar of anti aircraft artillery erupted from the airfield. Looking at the slow flying large airplane, I saw to my horror it suddenly plummeted to the earth in streaming flames and dense black smoke. The bomber came down in a field not far from our row of houses. I did not go to see it. As I later came to know, it was a bomber from the American Air Force. None of the plane's crew had come down by parachute. They were all killed.

Beb, the girl I worked with in the Houte Couture shop, and I had gone a few times on Sunday afternoons to an ice cream shop which was located in downtown. Beb was a pretty light blond and good natured girl my age. Her boyfriend Ken worked on Sundays selling ice cream, together with his friend Jon. Jon's father was the owner of the popular ice cream shop. It was a very busy place year around. In the front of the store they sold take-out ice cream. In the pretty back room the customers could sit and eat their ice cream around small wrought iron tables and chairs. Before the war the shop had served different kinds of ice cream—creamy and delicious. But in '43 the ice cream had become a substitute, an imitation of the real thing. It was full of air, with a little sweet taste. But people enjoyed it anyway, since there was not much else to eat for a snack. The ice cream was made by Jon's father, and after a few times coming to the shop on Sundays, Beb and I could eat as much ice cream as we wanted from him. When it was freshly made, it tasted pretty good to us, and we always gobbled a lot of it right out of the containers in which it was made.

The ice cream shop became a hangout for Beb and me and a few friends of Jon and Ken. We were there whole Sunday afternoons, especially when the weather was miserable and the rain pattered down. While Jon and Ken served the lousy ice cream to the customers from behind the counter, we were laughing and talking with friends of Jon and Ken who came into the back room. It was not long until we all became good friends, but it was mainly in the shop where we gathered. When the shop closed up on late Sunday afternoons, Ken, Beb and Jon and I sometimes went to see a movie or we went to the piano bar. Jon was a few years older than I was. He was a nice guy but talked incessantly and left me with nothing to say. It was fine to go the movies or to the piano bar with our four, but I didn't much care to go out with him alone.

In March I turned eighteen, a birthday considered a milestone on the road to adulthood. I had a birthday get-together with my girlfriends Chiel, Gina and Beb. Mother had talked to our baker about baking something for my birthday and had given him some of the coupons for next week's bread. A letter came from Mies for my birthday in which she wrote that she was coming in July to see me and would stay with us for a week. Also a letter came from Hetty and Tante Marie. She wrote that if everything was good, they where planning to go camping in August and asked me if I wanted to go with them. Mother was not too happy about the camping idea, although she didn't say much about it. The situation in our country was deteriorating more and more, but my parents did what they could to keep our lives as normal as possible. Danger was always around, vacation or not.

The beautiful Dutch sky, which was always changing, had brought dark clouds in April and it rained for days on end. But now the weather turned balmy even if it was still only May. Father had decided that we should try to get some bunny rabbits and raise our own meat. We got very little meat with our coupons and rabbit meat would help us for the next winter. So Father came home one day with six small bunnies, just a few to start out with, he had said. As Henk gathered some grass from the field behind our home, Father put the small bunnies in a cage which he had made earlier. Mother, who was watching, asked father sarcastically if this was the meat for five people—for next winter. It had become more and more difficult for Mother to put a meal on the table for her family.

One morning a few weeks later, two of the bunnies were laying dead in their cage, and we could not understand why they had died. Some of the neighbors said the bunnies had too much grass, and another told us not to give much water. We never had raised bunnies before, and I think we didn't know how to take care of them. Father knew everything about chess, rifles, guns and opera, and Mother about her household and books, but raising bunnies was another matter. The end was that for the next two years we did our best to raise bunnies, but for one or another reason some of them always died. Later as soon as the war was over and we got meat again, the adventure of raising bunnies came to an end.

◆　　◆　　◆

It was one night in June when I suddenly woke up and heard a faint cry in the darkness outside. I then heard shouting and harsh commands in German, "Snell einsteigen, snell einsteigen, wir gehnen…….." (get in quickly, get in quickly, we are going…). I could not hear the last words, but in the dark in front of the Jewish family house, I saw German soldiers. By the light of a flashlight which was held by a policeman, I saw the members of the Jewish family pushed into a truck. For a second the light paused on a girl's face. It was Saartje. The neighbor's young daughter, the little girl who always wanted peace among her playmates was now harshly pushed into a truck. I swallowed hard as I was staring through my window. When the truck left, my tears flowed silently as I looked up into the dark night. I asked God why this all was happening and pleaded with Him to somehow save Saartje, the little happy girl. Two days later a truck came and took all the belongings out of the house of the Jewish family. A week later a new family moved in, and it looked as if Saartje and her family never had existed. But I would never forget the large brown laughing eyes of Saartje and her two small brothers who lived and played in our street.

One day when I was walking home from the Houte Couture House and was passing Chiel's home, I saw her standing by the front door. She said to come in; she had been knitting something and had to show me. Most women and girls knew how to knit in that time. When I came into their living room, Chiel said proudly that she had been knitting a top for herself from hospital gauze. Her father had gotten a large quantity of gauze and she asked me if I wanted some for a top. How her father got the gauze I did not know or care to ask. The same evening I went to Chiel's home and together we knitted until curfew time and I had to go home. When the top was finished a week later, Mother looking in amusement said that it was nothing less than a miracle, and I did fully agree with her. The gauze top looked very pretty, but after a few times of careful washing it was falling apart.

In the last weeks we had heard through Radio Orange that in North Africa the American and British forces were pushing steadily ahead. Then on May 11, 1943 Father came excited down from the attic with the news from England that Field Marshal Rommel's 'Afrika Korps' had capitulated. Rommel himself had escaped back to Germany that morning. In Russia the German Armies were in constant retreat, and their positions were deteriorating. Of course the German radio made announcements of 'strategic withdrawals,' which the Dutch people gleefully translated as yet another defeat.

A new fear had been added for the families with men between the ages of 18 to 45 years old. The Nazis had made a new law that every able bodied man in that age group must work for the German war effort. The only exceptions being married man with children and the ones who had special permission, Aus weis (green card) to stay, because they were needed for their work in their towns. Those employers who ignored the law were in danger of execution. But most men including my brother Jan ignored the new law and went on with their daily lives.

It was the end of July when Mies arrived for a week vacation in her old town of Breda. When the train slowly came to a halt, I saw that the windows of the train were shot out probably by the strafing of one or another Allied fighter plane or an air raid. It was something that happened all the time. There were not too many trains anymore with unbroken windows. After we hugged each other, Mies said happily, "Luckily it is a sunny day, because I forgot to take along my umbrella, not thinking I would have needed one if it rained while sitting in a train."

After days of rain the weather had turned great, and the sun was brightly shining while a balmy breeze was blowing from over the meadows. I had taken a week off from work, and everyday we walked, as good friends did, arm in arm together to old familiar places. We visited Chiel and Gina and told each other the latest gossip and talked about the boys she had known. Gina had a steady boyfriend and, of course, Mies had to meet him we said. One day Mies and I went (for old times sake) to the kikker place in the forest. We walked the Seven Hills and the narrow paths between tall trees and visited the place where many kikkers still lived. On the way home we passed Castle Bouvigne and the tennis court. On the last day of her visit to Breda we four girls went downtown and drank imitation coffee at the piano bar. Mies missed her old town and all her friends and hoped that maybe her family would move back to Breda when the war was over. The following day as the train was leaving to take Mies back to Deventer, I promised her that I would visit her as soon as possible.

Eef (Eve) Jansen in Breda,
Holland, 1943.

Eef (on the right) with her best friend,
Mies, in the Jansens' back yard, 1943.

It was the end of August 1943 and time for our planned camping trip. The train had taken me and my bike, which Father had repaired as well as he could, to the small town of Putten. There at the train station I was going to meet Hetty, Stien, Tante Mary and her girlfriend Elly. They had written to me that they were coming on a later train from Haarlem, but as it turned out, they were already waiting for me with their bikes. From the station we left for a camping place in the forest where we would camp for ten days. Soon we were riding down hilly roads and through forests until we saw the camping place.

That part of mid-Holland, which is called 'The Veluwe', is a most beautiful area of deep forest and large areas of heather covered land. The camping place consisted of a cluster of buildings each with six units. After we registered at the office, we went to our unit which had two small bedrooms and a sitting room with a cooking area. It was clean but bare, but then it was meant to take the place of a tent. Showers and bathrooms were in another building. A water pump was outside in front of each unit. About a few minutes drive away was the small town of Putten. Never will I forget the moment I saw Putten for the first time. It looked so pretty and quaint, so full of charm, laying there in the tall green forest. The people who lived there were friendly and helpful. When we came into their store with our food coupons for the groceries which we needed, many times they would give us something extra such as milk, which we greatly appreciated. While camping there we rode our bikes a few times through the beautiful forest to the Zuider Zee which was only a hour drive from our camp. There we enjoyed happy hours lying on the beach or playing silly games in the water. Other times we drove our bikes on the narrow sandy paths through the heather-covered areas while taking deep breaths of sweet smelling air and enjoying the beauty of this unspoiled place. Other days we were for the longest time just lying by tall birches on the side of a stream. It was a place where a person could do her dreaming, and it made us forget all the worries of the war. (I think here especially about Hetty, her worries about her parents and her own life). Even though Hetty walked around free, she was always careful, prepared to run, her eyes and ears had to be sharp and her reactions quick.

Four boys were camping in the unit beside ours. They were a little older than we girls were. In the evenings after we were done with our many times very late supper, we three went outside and talked for the longest time to the boys. Tante Mary didn't like this late gathering very much and told us girls to leave those boys alone. I think since we got up so early every morning she wanted us to go to sleep on time—which we didn't, of course, but talked and laughed with those guys until late at night. The day came too soon when we had to leave this great place and the lovely small town. How little we knew then the terrible things that would happen to Putten and its people.

These terrible things happened in that following year of September 1944 when a German Staff car, traveling at high speed in the vicinity of the village of Putten, was ambushed by a Dutch resistance group. The English intelligence, which expected papers of great value about the war effort in the car, had informed the Dutch resistance about this. A heavy fight developed between the resistance group and two other cars filled with German military who happened at that moment to pass over a bridge and saw what was happening. From both sides men were killed and wounded. But the Dutch resistance got away with the valuable papers and a map of the headquarters of Hitler. The captured information was sent to England and from there by radio codes to America and Russia.

The revenge that the German Army Commanders took was terrible. After the ambush the lovely town of Putten was immediately surrounded by German soldiers. Those people who tried to escape by running away were shot and killed. They then rounded up all men between the ages of 18 and 50 and transported them to a concentration camp in Germany. From the 600 men and boys sent there, only 40 came back after the war. The rest of the citizens of Putten were forced to leave their homes. The Nazis then set fire to the small town and burned it down to the ground. Many times before, the Dutch resistance had ambushed

German Staff cars when they expected to find documents which were of importance to the Allies. Never before in all the war years in Holland had the Nazis taken such a revenge as this one because of an ambush.

◆    ◆    ◆

By the end of September I registered again for the dance lessons and for my gym school for the winter of 1943-44. I was now taking gymnastics twice a week with about eight other young women. I loved to go there, but not especially the walking home alone by myself. A few weeks before when I had left on my camping trip, Father had put his tires on my bike so I could use my bike for my vacation. But when I came home, he had taken his tires back again for his own bike. From then on I had to walk wherever I wanted to go. Mother sure didn't like it when I was going to the gym in the evening. Before I left I always told her, "Mother, you worry too much. I will be just fine." Father who understood that I was young and could not be locked up, sometimes picked me up from the gym lessons. But other times I walked home by myself and when the moon was hiding behind low hanging dark clouds, I almost could not see where I was going. I had to find my way home carefully, which was normally a 20 minute walk, but on those very dark nights it took me much longer. Very few people would be on the street and the pitch darkness and the cold or rain were miserable. On the way to my home I always had to pass a building were German officers and soldiers were staying. I never was worried about passing there because we seldom had heard of any German attack on girls or women. The German soldiers kept mainly to themselves. I am sure they were warned by their commanders to stay away from the citizens. But on those very dark nights I passed the German place on the other side of the street, just to be sure.

It was a few weeks later and the dance school had opened up again when a young man by the name of Wim Lambert walked in. We had met before at the ice-cream shop when he was there with one of the other guys of our group. I had liked him, but never really had the chance to talk to him. Seeing him there at our dance classes made my heart go flip-flop. Everything about Wim was great. He was tall with blond curly hair, blue eyes and an easy smile and 19 years old. When he walked in for the dance lessons, he recognized me, and it did not take long until we two danced the whole evening together, which our dance teacher didn't like. He told us to take a different dance partner, which we sometimes did, but most of the time did not. After our dance lessons Wim walked me home, and in the alley behind our home we talked and kissed until curfew time—and sometimes after. When I went into the house, Wim would run all the way to his home, which was a ten minute sprint. That winter the curfew time was set at 10:30.

Wim worked for a large department store and in his free time he played in a band. On Sunday afternoons I went occasionally with Wim to a place where his band practiced. They had six guys in their band. Since there were not too many parties or other celebrations going on as before and many bars were closed, they played now mainly for their own pleasure. Wim played guitar, accordion and mouth organ which he played very well. But I thought that the practice and the repeat and repeat of the same tunes too boring, and I did not go there very often. If the weather was great, Wim and I took walks which usually ended up at a park. There we sat on a bench at the waters edge where he would tell me amusing stories. Or we walked through the forest to a restaurant which had served poffertjes with butter and powdered sugar before the war, but now had no more then imitation coffee and tea, and the lousy airy ice cream. Wim was always fun to be with, and I enjoyed his sense of humor.

By the fall of 1943 the Jews had completely disappeared from our city of Breda. There also were less and less German soldiers in our town. After their great losses in Russia their armed forces were probably short of soldiers and needed every man on all fronts. Sometimes I saw German soldiers who were, I think, as young as sixteen and other men who looked at least sixty years old.

When the forced labor law had failed, the German police started razzias (raids). They began abducting men off the streets, from homes or at work. Those employers who had men working for them without an Ausweis were now in danger of the death penalty. Many men, including Jan and Wim, were now without work. Some of them started to work at farms or went into hiding and stayed at homes of relatives to wait out the war. But many of the men, as Jan, Wim and some other guys I knew, stayed home and became experts in their intuition for danger.

It was about in that time that Jan joined the resistance through some friends of his. Both fathers of those friends were long standing members of the Breda Police. As soon as Jan had entered the resistance, that organization took care that Jan would be completely erased from the register of population. So, officially Jan did not exist anymore. Because of this, it was not long thereafter that Mother didn't receive food stamps for Jan anymore. But since the resistance did occasionally raid the building where the food coupons were stored, those people who were underground or those who had people in hiding, received food stamps from the resistance. Usually Jan got more coupons than he would have normally received. Many times Mother was puzzled about the fact that there were more food stamps in her small wooden container than she thought she had. In the beginning my parents didn't know that Jan was with the resistance, but finally he had to tell them. They kept it a secret from Henk and me for safety reasons.

Through Jan's soccer organization N.A.C. he got work at an expedition business. This business took a great risk by hiring Jan. If the German police would have caught Jan in a razzia, the company would have been severely punished. Jan always was warned in time by his friend's fathers, who knew about the expected searches when the Germans were hunting the addresses of suspected hideaways—(which sometimes was the work of a traitor). The only danger was an unexpected razzia by the German police, or running into a razzia by the Gestapo. So even though Jan freely walked around town, he always had to be careful and be prepared to run at the first sign of trouble which happened to him three times. Two times it happened when there was a surprise razzia by the SS police in our busy shopping street of downtown. At the moment just before Jan entered the street where the razzi took place, a few people, seeing a young man, warned him. Jan immediately turned around and disappeared into another street. The third time he had to run for his life when unexpectedly some Gestapo men came toward him in a building. Luckily he escaped. How I remember the ladder which stood in our backyard against the house. It was there in case of a visit by the German police. Jan then could quickly climb out of his bedroom window down the ladder, disappear over the fence into our neighbor's yard and run further on through other yards into the street. But luckily this never happened. Of course Mother was always worried, especially after she saw the ladder which Jan had set up against our house. Mother muttered to Father that it was something else to worry about. One day Mother was upset about something and said to Father, "Jan, (Father's name) when will it all end? It looks as if it is becoming more horrible by the day." Father looked at her and said with his usually calm voice, "You better believe it, Cor. The worse the war goes for the Nazis, the more vicious those bastards get!"

While thousands of Dutch men were forced into munition plants in Germany, Hitler was giving one of his public speeches and told the world about his secret weapon which would destroy England and America. The Nazis were always talking or writing about their secret weapon, but we did not take it seriously and considered it to be Hitler's propaganda. The Allied air raids on Germany were getting more and more frequent. Many a night I was kept awake not only by the hundreds but many times by a thousand heavy Allied bombers flying over us en route to Germany. There they released their bombs on the German factories and on the cities of Munster, Essen, Dusseldorf and Berlin. Those nights I also couldn't sleep from the anti-aircraft artillery at the airfield. The Germans always went crazy there trying to get an Allied bomber in their searchlights and shoot it down.

◆          ◆          ◆

It must have been the beginning of December '43 when one day as I was going home from standing in a line for some soap, I met Chiel and her mother in the Molengracht Straat. They both looked upset, and Chiel's mother was crying. Chiel explained that when her oldest brother and his friend were on the way to a farm to get food, they were pulled off their bicycles by German police and taken away in a truck. Like Jan, Chiel's brother was hiding from the Nazi labor law. Chiel's parents later learned that after the abduction they were sent to Ebenswald labor camp close to Berlin. There he worked in a steel factory for the rest of the war and barely survived. Many men who were forced to work in Germany died from sickness and exhaustion; others were killed by the Allied air raids.

It was also during that time when the Houte Couture House closed. Mrs. van der Pol promised us and herself that one day she would open up again. She said we must always be optimistic and believe that the evil which had come over our country would never succeed. She then gave us each an extra weeks wages and closed the shop. A few years after the war she started anew and her business prospered again.

Some friends and neighbors had always asked me if I wanted to sew a dress for them. Even though I had only a very few dresses, they never saw me looking shabby during the war years. Many a time I wore a pretty dress made out of a few old garments which had been Mother's or from Tante Nel. Now that I was without work, my friends all hoped that I would sew for them. Mother said that I should stay home for now and forget all that sewing for other people. She herself had never learned to sew and, as she had told me many times, it made her nervous. Mother's headaches became worse. The emotional stress was worse for her than the hunger we now always seemed to have. But doing nothing was not for me and so, besides helping Mother, I started to sew for other people. Mainly I made one dress from two old dresses, or dresses and shirts for children from old clothing.

# 23

# THE LONG-AWAITED INVASION

Winter of 1943-44 arrived, and with it came the long cold dreary days. Food was the topic of most conversations; it seemed the only thing on everyone's mind. All of us had become hungry—always wanting food, always thinking about food, always dreaming about the food we once had. We ate boiled potatoes two times a day now. For a vegetable we usually had winter carrots, cabbage or turnips. Once in awhile we had a little piece of meat which had to be divided into five portions. We still could get fish once a week which we also boiled and, if we got a little piece of butter on top, it became a special meal. A real treat came that winter in the form of mussels. Many times I stood for hours in the line for a half-bucket of mussels, but it was worth it and the same evening we had a feast on our table. We were lucky that we lived so close to the farmers because sometimes Mother got a few eggs or some skim milk from our farmer where she always had bought the milk in the last few years. After Mother boiled the eggs and divided them, she always sighed and said, "We have too much food to die, but not enough to live." Many a time I saw Mother giving her portion of her supper to Henk when no one looked, and it broke my heart to see my young brother devouring it.

I think that the worst thing for me was the cold. I could get used to about everything else—as to the whole lousy situation with the food, clothing and shoes, transportation and curfews—but I could never get used to the cold that winter. I was always cold—constantly cold. I am sure that it was because of the persistant lack of good food. Also that winter we had less heat. Our Dutch coal was shipped to Germany, and what was left for us was a bad grade coal which burned up fast. Also there was not much wood. We were forbidden to take wood out of the forest. Not that we didn't try, but it was too difficult to do.

One day the wind came from the northwest and whipped over the fields. The cold rain had came down relentlessly for days. It was chilly in the house, and I had come down with a cold again. It was miserable. It was late in that afternoon when Jan came home through the alley behind our house with a delivery push-cart full of wood. He didn't say much while he stacked the small cut tree trunks into our shed—only that he had gotten them from somewhere. I remember Father telling him to be careful. A little later Jan split some of the wood and put it in our small stove. Soon the room filled with warmth, and it took the chills out of me. How thankful I was that my brother, I am sure under difficulties, had brought the wood. Much later Jan told me about that day. In a forest, which is somewhat further away from Breda, he had seen a lot of sawed up small tree trunks. He had been sure that the wood was intended for the German Army, and that it was ready to be transported. Jan had thought about a plan how to get some of the wood. He got lucky and with three other guys they got hold of two delivery push-carts. They then went to the forest and stacked their wagons full of wood. Pushing the carts home had been very difficult. The first time they were lucky and no one saw or stopped them. But the second time when they tried again, a forest ranger halted them and wanted to know where the wood was going. Jan told him that they had paid a lot of money for it, and the wood was needed for heating and cooking for a children's home. The ranger let them go with the wood, but they had to come back to his office the next day, and tell him exactly who and where it was they sold the wood. Of course they never went to that office, and the ranger probably didn't care about the wood. But for a while we had extra heat in our living room. Later Jan transported guns in the same push-carts. Luckily he never got caught.

I hated to stand in lines. I remember another cold miserable morning standing in a long line for some dried beans and sugar which the grocery store got in that day. As I stood there in that damp penetrating cold waiting with other people, mainly women, I noticed that almost all of them had lice in their hair. The eggs could be clearly seen on the end tips of their hair. This was nothing unusual because we all got lice in the last year from time to time. We did what we could to get rid of the miserable itchy creatures, but whatever we tried to do, they were gone just for a few days, and then they were back again. It was just something we tried to live with. Maybe I was so cold or felt depressed that day, but at that moment I suddenly saw clearly what had become of us. Because we could get so very little soap, we were not clean anymore. We had become constantly hungry, cold and many people were sick. At that moment I prayed silently for this misery to end, that a miracle would happen, or a sudden victory by the Allies or maybe the assassination of Hitler. "Please Lord," I pleaded, "let this whole lousy war be over, and let me not be so cold anymore." It was then that I promised myself that if life ever became normal again, I would never, never and ever again wait in a line for food.

◆    ◆    ◆

Christmas of 1943 was a silent Christmas. Two days of no American or Allied bombers flying over and no aircraft shooting from the airfield. It was Christmas, even in war. Mother prepared her Christmas dinner as good as she could with what she had. Father had killed the largest rabbit we had, and Mother had saved some butter from the last few weeks coupons to fry the rabbit in. The potatoes tasted delicious with the rabbit gravy, and together with the vegetables we had a good meal. Father had put some extra coal in the little stove, and that Christmas I felt warmth returning to my body. It felt cozy and safe inside our living room, and we played cards until we went to bed. It had been a good Christmas. We hoped with our whole heart that by next Christmas the war would be over and we would be free again. That night when I was lying in my bed, my thoughts had gone back to the sounds and smells of Christmas past. I remembered Mother singing; she always had loved to sing before the war had come. Usually they were songs from her childhood, and it always had given me such happy feelings. I thought about Mother's Christmas cooking and baking. The sweet aroma of Christmas tulband, which is a moist cake with large golden raisins, and the butter cake filled with almond paste, were delicious. My mouth was watering just thinking about it. And I yearned for the time in which peace and beauty would reign again.

Jan got more and more involved with the resistance. He never talked about it. It would have been too risky for everyone. Much later he told me some of the stories. Jan knew the addresses where his former boss (the firm van Gills) had always delivered barrels of carbide. Because of this it was possible for the resistance to know how to obtain carbide. It was well known that if you put carbide and water together in a closed-in space, it forms a gas which then explodes by itself. So one night in February '44, Jan and three other resistance workers went with their carbide to the village of Lage Zwaluwe which was in that time an important train crossing about 16 mile north of Breda. There, not far from the train station, they went to work and blew up the railroad tracks with the carbide. It was another headache for the Germans, and for a few days the damage delayed the Nazis from delivering weapons which went through Breda to Belgium and further south.

It was a week before my 19th birthday when Beb said to me that she and Ken and the rest of the group were coming to my home for my birthday. I looked at her in surprise and said, "That will be great, Beb, it will be fun! But what will we do about food or drinks. We should have something!"Cheerfully she answered, "The only thing we need is a good time together and have a laugh or two."

A few days earlier Mother had gone up north by train. Every year she visited the family in Amsterdam, and then on the third of March celebrated her mother's birthday in Haarlem. As long as I can remember she always had done this. Mother had never skipped Grandmother's birthday. Whatever came along, she would be there. The day before my birthday she always came home again from her yearly trip to her family.

All my friends from the ice cream shop would be coming for my birthday, and I was excited about it. Also Wim, Gina and Chiel would be there. When Mother was home again from her trip, I told her about the party and said that all my friends were coming. Distressed, I said to her, "Mother, what will we do? What will we eat? We have to have something!" Mother smiled at me and answered, "Don't look so gloomy; I will make something special. It is the latest delicacy from Amsterdam, and I ate it with the family in Haarlem." When I asked mother what it was, she smiled and said—a potato torte!

My birthday party was great. Besides me, there were four other girls and four or five boys. First Wim played on his mouth organ and we all sang along loudly, especially when he started to play Dutch patriotic songs. Soon we pushed the furniture to the side turned the radio on and danced. Father complained that the music we played was too loud and left for his chess club. There was a little rivalry between Wim and Jon. They were a little jealous if I danced with one more than the other. We had a great time and, after everyone sang Happy Birthday, we ate the 'potato torte' which, as everyone said, taste good and we drank our substitute tea. (I think everything would have tasted good to a bunch of young people who didn't get much to eat anymore) Too soon our party was over and everyone had to leave again by 10:00 to make it home before curfew. When they all had left, Mother and I talked about the party and, of course, laughed about the boys. My father and brothers came home hoping there was some torte left over. But not a crumb was left anymore and Mother promised to make another one for Easter. The potato torte was made from boiled potatoes, some sugar and two eggs.

It was about a week after my birthday party when Wim, Ken and a few of their friends were abducted in a razzia at the ice cream shop. At gunpoint they were pushed into trucks and taken away to an unknown destination in Germany. In one or another munition factory they would work the rest of the war as slaves for the Germans. Jon had a permit to stay in Breda because of his father's ill health. He had to earn the money for the family. But soon after the razzia he closed up the ice cream shop and worked here and there, odds and ends.

It became a rather dreary situation for us girls. No more boys and our hangout closed up. I missed Wim and his sunny smile. I was worried about him and prayed that he would come out of this war and not be hurt or worse. I began to stay longer at my gym, even though there were few less girls there than before. Father would shake his head and thought that I was becoming too skinny doing all that 'jumping,' as he would call it, without enough of the right food. "I'll be fine, Dad. Really, I will be fine," I would always answer him.

◆　　　◆　　　◆

In the meantime Germany was in the process of developing two new powerful weapons which they called the flying rockets VI and VII. The first flying bombs, the VI, were launched by the hundreds at targets in England—mainly in and around London. At the beginning of 1944 an even more deadly rocket was put into use—the improved VII. They flew high, silently and undetected; the rocket cut its engine at a high altitude came down and hit its target. But the secret weapon the Germans were hoping for, and which had been discussed so much, we still couldn't believe in. We never had believed in Hitler's secret weapon which would destroy the Allies. We did not think that anything could be invented that was so powerful that it could destroy the whole of England and could also reach America. What we didn't know was that German scientists were working feverishly in laboratories on the development of the atom bomb. Those laboratories, which were located in Peenemunda on the Baltic, were destroyed by highly trained English commandos in the winter of 1943 '44. The Germans had been very close to success, but luckily for the world their plans had failed.

For some time now the headquarters of a German tank division had been located in our Castle Bouvigne. Jan told me later that in the early spring of '44 the resistance in Breda had received orders from London to destroy the electric centrale of the castle. "At the same time we received that order," Jan said, "an electric company in Breda received orders to go to the castle after the blast. Then when that electric company was replacing or repairing the damage, one of the resistance men, working as an electrician, was to install a listening device. This device would be in direct connection with the resistance. This way they hoped to be able to get information and send the enemy conference plans from the German officers at the castle through to England."

Castle Bouvigne is surrounded on all sides by a moat about 60 feet wide filled with water. In front of the castle is a road and across the road is the forest Mastbos. The only means to get into or out of the castle was by a bridge across the moat. This bridge was guarded day and night by German soldiers. That night the German officers held one of their many parties at the castle, and extra guards were posted at the bridge. Under heavy clouds, which were hiding the moon, Jan and the small group of men walked first through the farm fields which were located on three sides around the castle grounds. As soon as the men reached the cold dark water, they silently began to swim to a place of the castle which had been explained to them earlier. Under the sound of music and laughter which came from the castle, the men placed the carbide in two rows at the electric centrale without much difficulty. As soon as they had completed their mission, the men silently swam back to shore to the place where they had entered earlier. No sooner had they reached the bank of the moat when there was a heavy explosion from the inside of the castle where the centrale had been. In their wet clothes Jan and the other men began to run as fast as they could into the forest where they separated. Each went on his own to a house in the Dillenburg Straat where they had changed their clothing before going to the castle. The house was the location of the resistance group. They left their wet clothes at the house and would pick them up again at a later date. Jan and the other men never learned what did happened after the explosion in the electric centrale of the castle.

On our little short-wave radio Father heard more and more about an expected coming invasion by the Allies, and we could hardly wait. Then on June 6, 1944 came the long-prayed for invasion of Europe. Father came down from the attic that evening and said almost shouting, "Finally, finally, they are coming, and it will be the end of those Nazi devils."With his voice full of excitement he said, "Six months and it will be over; the Nazis will be finished."We all hoped he would be right! Then Father continued saying that the Allied and American troops had landed in Normandy, France. First the Allies had sent 2000 heavy bomber planes to destroy the areas where they were planning to land. Then came hundreds of ships and landing vessels with ground troops. But the fighting was very severe and the losses were high.

It was an exciting time for all the occupied countries of Europe. We knew this was the beginning of the end of the war in Europe, and it became a nervous wait. In the following weeks the only conversation was about the invasion in Normandy and about food. Nothing else seemed to matter. The streets were quiet—many German soldiers were gone from Breda. I think they were sent to Normandy or to the Russian front. There were almost no cars or bicycles on the streets anymore. We saw now many more Allied fighter planes overhead, which were shooting up trains and German targets.

After the Normandy invasion Hitler made fewer and fewer public speeches. On July 20 we heard in disbelief that an attempt had actually been made on his life. Some of his Army officers had grown disgusted by Hitler's conduct of war. At one of Hitler's hideaway staff conferences, a briefcase with a time bomb was placed under a table. Unfortunately Hitler escaped with only light wounds. The German officers who were connected with the conspiracy were executed often in a barbarous way. General Rommel, who was part of the conspiracy, was forced to take poison. Since he was such a popular general in his country, they did not want to execute him.

The summer of 1944 was unusually warm. All of Europe was flooded with bright sunshine. The war in Normandy inched forward under terrible bloody fighting and with great losses. More than ever we listened to our little radio and followed the day by day situation. People fell silent more often and most conversations and thoughts ended with the words "…when the English come…."

◆    ◆    ◆

It was on a warm day at the end of July, when I said to Mother that I was going swimming. The swimming place by the name of Prinsen Plassen was about a one hour walk from our home and was located in the Mastbos. A few of my girlfriends were planning to meet me there. They left early that morning. Because there were some things I had to do first, I had told them that I would meet them later at the swimming place. As I was walking alone on the narrow paths of the forest, I saw no one—not even a squirrel. A light breeze was blowing through the tops of the tall pine trees. It was so silent and peaceful there in the cool woods and a great quietness was around me. While walking steadily on, I planned to take a short cut which brought me deeper into the forest. Going this way I would reach the swimming place sooner.

Suddenly from further away in the distance, air raid alarms were shrilling. The sounds came from our town Breda. Not much later heavy explosions erupted in the far distance. I had no idea from which directions they came. In the forest the sounds carry differently than in the city. The bombardment seemed heavy and at first I did not know what to do—to go to Prinsen Plassen, which was not too far anymore or go home. I stood still and listened to the heavy explosions but did not hear the droning sounds of bombers. Suddenly I felt very alone in the deep woods of the forest. Then being concerned that maybe something had happen to our neighborhood or to our house where Mother was alone, I turned around and walked the long road home. As I was coming out of the forest, the all-clear sounded over our city.

A little later when I was walking through our neighborhood and turning into our street, I saw thick black smoke coming from the direction of the military base Gilse Ryen. The allies had bombed the airfield. Luckily nothing had happened to our city of Breda. When I reached my home, I found nobody there. Mother must have gone someplace. The door was locked, and I had no key. I walked to the backyard and sat down on the cement of the patio with my back leaning against the house. What now I thought. It is only 1:00 and too early to stay home. Staring for a while at the heavy smoke which went high up in the sky, I got up and walked back again to the forest. A hour later I finally reached the swimming place where my friends had wondered what had happened to me. It was too late in the day to get a good suntan. So I decided to take a short dip in the water with my friends and then together we all went the long road home again.

It must have been about 11:30 on one of those quiet, dark nights when the bombers did not come over, that Jan got up from his bed. Quickly he dressed himself and silently went downstairs so as not to wake our parents. If they had known where their son was going, they would have been very worried. Jan left the house through the back door and walked quickly over the fields and along small dark farm roads which stretched out behind our house. About a hour later he reached the Cadetten Kamp. The Cadetten Kamp was a large and very pretty wilderness area of sandy hills and some low growing vegetation, located northeast of Breda. On the north edge of the sandy area was a forest of lush large trees and tall pines which seemed to reach to the clouds. Much later Jan told me about that night.

There in the dark still night ten men of the resistance had come together in a low-lying area of some dunes. "Patiently we waited," Jan said, "for the sound of a low-flying English airplane which was going to drop weapons and munitions by parachute. The time and place of the drop was known only by the resistance. It was so quiet and dark there that night that you very easily could lose your sense of where you are," he said. "The only sounds came from the wind which rustled the leaves of the trees in the distance. It was exciting and nerve wrenching at the same time. We sat hunched together and whispered information to one another. Excitement grew when we finally heard the sound of a low-flying plane. Quickly one of our resistance men got up and shot off a flare. After a short wait we heard the plane circling. We stared into the black sky but couldn't see anything. When we heard the plane coming in our direction again, we shot off another flare." Until this day Jan cannot believe how on that exact place where they were hiding, two parachutes came down silently within minutes. Rolled in blankets were tommy guns and munition. "First thing we did," Jan continued, "was hide the parachutes in a hole which we had dug before, and cover it up with the white sand. Everything had to be done quickly. If any German had seen our flares, they would be on their way to investigate. We left Cadetten Kamp as fast as we could with the guns, the munition and the blankets. When we entered the city, we quickly and silently went through the dark streets. It was a risky and dangerous business. We peered through the darkness and listened to every sound. About an hour later we reached Breda's School of Agriculture where we delivered the weapons and munition. It was 4:00 in the morning," Jan said, "when exhausted from tension, nerves and running, I finally reached home." As we later came to know, many weapons and munition were hidden in that agriculture school during the war years.

August was the beginning of an increasing amount of Allied plane activities in and around our area. Through Radio Orange we heard that the Allied troops had finally broken through in Normandy and had made rapid advances from France into Belgium and further on north. It was about at the end of the same month when our hope was renewed for an early liberation. It was one day when unexpectedly many German soldiers were coming through Breda. They came from the south-going north. As we learned, their Army which had suffered great defeats in France, had been driven north. They were not organized and probably needed to regroup.

That day when my brothers and I went to a road which was located besides the Wilhelmina Park to see "The Great German Army," we saw columns of war-weary men. Looking at them Jan said smiling, "There is sure not much left of the great victorious German Army that conquered Europe!" He then added, "The great Adolf's time is running out, and our time is rushing in." Most of the soldiers we saw were tired and dusty and were sitting or lying on wagons pulled by sweating horses. Some of the men were drunk; others had French women beside them. Some walked in small groups and did not talk amongst each other. We saw no cannons or other weapons. Many of the soldiers were young and in their own despair shuffled on in their dusty uniforms. Looking at them I remembered the arrogant, boisterous German soldiers who had marched into Breda in 1940. They had believed the world was theirs and showed it. I wondered how many of the original invaders were alive on this day more than four years later to witness this sad ending of Hitler's imperial fantasy. Yes, it was a day of laughing for us. That day had looked good. It was late in the afternoon before the sounds of the last German horse pulled wagons faded. As we later learned, the German soldiers who came through Breda from the south, were from the 711 Infantry Division which had fought hard in France and had suffered great losses.

As the great American and Allied Armies were making rapid advances toward us, rumors had now began to circulate and wild stories were added daily to the earlier ones. Everyone was getting excited and happy. Not too long anymore we said, and then those Nazis will be gone!

In the afternoon of September 5 heavy explosions were coming from the military airfield. The sky turned red, the ground was trembling and the windows rattled in their frames. That same evening as we listened to Radio Orange and heard on their news that English soldiers were on the outskirts of Breda, our happiness and excitement escalated. But this statement from London was false, and events turned nasty for us—the people of Breda. The consequences of this false statement was that some people on the side of freedom, started to sing wildly and openly and were waving the Dutch flag. Some of the men of the underground who felt the end was at hand became careless. Many men and women who were in hiding from the Nazis and who had spent time worrying about their chances of survival, now couldn't wait. Many people carried small Dutch flags inside their coat to be taken out as soon as the English troops moved in. I still wonder where all those little flags came from. The following day Father told us not to go out on the street because it was too dangerous. "The Germans are still here!" Father said. "Don't be in such a hurry!" But Jan couldn't stand it being cooped up and left our house. It was not much later when he was back again saying, "There are too many German Police around."

This liberation party mood would prove very bad for everyone. Dozens of people got arrested by the Gestapo and the Green Police. Many others were shot and their bodies left behind. No one went to work, and schools were closed.

Everyone had to be inside their homes at 7:30, and the curfew was strictly enforced. We got no newspaper or mail, and the food situation became still worse. We got only a few hours of gas everyday and electricity only in the evening hours. We heard rumors that the mistake made in London about the war situation in Breda was that, instead of Allied soldiers, only a small group of Allied scouting patrol was seen on the edge of Breda that day—the 5th of September. But Radio Orange never corrected this serious mistake they had made.

A few days later we tried to go on again with our lives. Schools opened up, and people went back to their work. Also we got some food again. Besides some hard black bread (which was impossible to eat) and a little skim milk, we also got herring. Even though they smelled bad, we ate them anyway and, surprisingly, never got sick.

One day our neighborhood butcher got hold of a war-killed horse, and wanted to share the meat with the people of his neighborhood. On the window of his store he had a sign put up saying, "Horse meat for sale starting at eight tomorrow morning." This news went like wildfire through our neighborhood, and people stood in line long before his store opened up. Later, after standing in line for hours, I went home with a nice piece of horse meat, which Mother simmered on the small iron cookstove with some potatoes and a winter carrot. We had a good meal that day.

# 24

## *PLANES AND GLIDERS*

It was September 12, 1944. Every day we prayed that the tense situation in our city would end and that the English soldiers would come to set us free. Surviving under stress and living with bare essentials gave many people a sense of inner strength, and we went on as good as we could. German soldiers moved back into our city which gave us a nervous feeling, and we asked ourselves—what are those Germans planning. Also more Allied aircrafts were flying over and around Breda, attacking the trains, railroads and bridges, which killed some of our citizens.

In this drab world in which we lived came a day of new hope and excitement. It all happened on the Sunday of September 17 when, after a few days of rain, the morning mist cleared and the sun rose steadily in a cloudless sky. It would be a beautiful late summer day, we said. After we had eaten our meager breakfast, Father went outside into the yard to look at the rabbits. We had two rabbits left which Father did not want to kill because, as he said, "We will save them in case there is nothing else to eat anymore." Father never gathered the rabbit's food and always left the feeding of the rabbits to Henk. But that early Sunday morning I got the small pail from our shed and went to the field behind our home to gather some greens for the rabbits. While I picked large fresh clover, and other kinds of leaves, I muttered to myself, "First we spoil the bunnies, and then we eat them." I felt sorry for the white fluffy rabbits with their large eyes which always seemed to stare at me.

As I filled the pail full of greens and walked back to the house, there was a steady drone of airplane engines. Looking up I saw that the airplanes were coming from the west and were flying low. They were so low that when they came over I could easily see the markings on the bottoms of their fuselage. When the first American and English aircraft had flown over, I ran into the house and shouted to my parents and brothers to come outside—something was happening! Everyone stopped whatever they were doing and went as fast as they could to our backyard where they stared at the sky. We couldn't believe what we saw! The sky was filled with airplanes. We also saw that some of the planes were pulling gliders which, as we thought, were probably full of soldiers. A little later we went to the alley behind our house which overlooked the farm fields and where we had a perfect view of the airplanes and the gliders. After the first aircrafts had come over, others followed close behind. With waves of noise they soon filled the sky as far as the eye could see, until I thought there could not be anymore airplanes left in the world. Still they came over in an endless parade of planes and gliders. It was an unbelievable sight to see which I will never forget.

All our neighbors, who had first watched the parade of planes from their backyards, soon went in their homes and came back with a chair. Behind our houses sitting in the field, we would watch for hours the spectacle in the sky. While looking up, we all wondered what was happening and where all those planes were going. No one knew the answer. We did not hear German artillery or see any German soldiers. It was strange and very exciting. Chiel had come over and together we sat in the grass looking up at the sky. As we watched the endless parade, Chiel sighed and said to me, "This stupid war has all the boys, good and bad, taken away from us. And now look there, just above our heads are thousands of handsome American and English boys. Who knows, maybe they can see us but we cannot see them. It just is not fair!" Suddenly we saw a glider coming lose from the plane which pulled it. It landed further away in a field. The soldiers who were inside the glider were later taken prisoners of war. They would be after all, the lucky ones as we later sadly would learn. For two and a half hours the planes and gliders came over. When the last ones were gone, the first airplanes already came back and were flying to their bases in England.

We couldn't wait until the evening, when we could listen to Radio Orange. When 7:30 came, we all sat glued around our little radio at the attic, which told us that Americans and British divisions and a brigade of Polish paratroopers had come down at Arnhem and vicinity, just over the river Ryn. The 20,000 airborne troops under Field Marshal Montgomery was called "Operation Market Garden." Their mission was to seize crucial bridges across the Ryn (Rhine) and Maas (Meuse) rivers while American and Allied land troops would link up. The area where the paratroopers came down is about 85 miles northeast of Breda. A few days later we heard via Radio London that the attempt to capture the bridges and cut off the German troops who were holding northwest Holland was not going well. The Allies had been betrayed. A concentration of German panzer troops were waiting for them. Many of the paratroopers who were coming down, hanging from their parachutes, were killed while they were still in the air. Forty years later America made a movie about that terrible bloodshed by the name "A Bridge Too Far."

That same night, when all the airplanes were gone and it was quiet again, German soldiers walked side by side through the streets, their rifles at the ready. I think they were looking for Allied soldiers who had escaped when their glider came lose from their plane and had landed in our area. Shot-down pilots or other Allied soldiers were, if possible, rescued by the resistance fighters and brought to a safe place. The following day no one went to work or school again, and people were staying inside their homes and waiting. The curfew was now set at 7:00 in the evening and it would stay this way until after our liberation.

The atmosphere grew tense when the situation accelerated with more arrests. A few days later, it must have been the end of September, I had gone one morning to Gina's house. It was a beautiful autumn day and the trees were a glory of yellow, orange, rust and red. The trees of the apple orchard at boer Backx, (a farmer who lived on the end of the Molengracht Straat and not far from our house) were heavy with yellow and red apples. Every year boer Backx was ordered by the Germans to supply a definite amount of apples to the German Army. If he refused, he would be in danger of arrest. But, of course, boer Backx took quite a few apples for himself and for some of his old customers who had always bought his fruit. The last few years, Mother had gone to his farm just before the apples were ready to be picked. She then bought as many apples from him as he would sell her. Of course, this was great, and for a while we all had an apple a day. It had been a healthy supplement to our food ration.

That morning I had gone to Gina, who lived around the corner of our street in the Molengracht Straat. She and her brother had been busy gathering wood in the area of some large cottonwood trees which were growing close to boer Backx's farm. Gina's brother Frans told me he had been trying to steal some apples from boer Backx but, he said laughing, "Those dogs of his which are running in his orchard are mean, and I sure don't want to be a dog's meal. But I will try again!" As we walked slowly through their yard the air raid alarms went off, and suddenly a few English fighters came over. First they circled around and then climbed high up in the sky before diving down with a high shrill sound, as fast as a rocket. They attacked trains which were staying on some railroad tracks at our railroad station. The attack lasted about eight minutes and then they disappeared and the all clear sounded.

Later we learned that after the Spitfire attack, German soldiers took boys from the street to help with the clean up of the debris which was laying everywhere on the tracks and railroad station. Not far from the station a small group of boys, ages 14 to 16, who had been playing ball before the plane attack, were ordered to help with the clean up. But three of the boys refused and tried to run away to their homes. Before they were twenty feet away, all three were shot in the back, and their bodies were left for others to see the consequences of disobeying orders.

A few days later when Chiel and I stood in the front of her home talking to each other, we suddenly heard again the roaring sound of Spitfires overhead. The sirens screamed their warnings and, before we knew what was happening, the air was filled with sounds of rocket explosions. Three Allied fighters had seemed to come from nowhere. With great speed they climbed up in the sky and then swooped down faster then anything I ever had seen. The attack took no longer then a few minutes. When it was all over and the fighters disappeared, they left behind death and destruction. Later we came to know that at the time of the attack a meeting was taking place between high ranking Nazi officers in a large mansion. That mansion was a German officers' headquarters and was located on the edge of Mastbos. Located on one side of the Nazi office was a home for old people. Many times when I had passed the very nice large home, I always thought how very pretty it was there laying between the large gardens full of flowers on the side of a fast running small stream. Somehow that fateful day the instructions from England to the fighter pilots were not understood correctly. And instead of destroying the Nazi place, they completely destroyed the nursing home. Many of the old people were killed or wounded. The high-ranking Nazi officers saved themselves by running into the forest.

◆    ◆    ◆

It seemed as if everyday something else happened in our town, and the intensity grew with every passing day. It was about that time when one morning while waking up, I thought I was still dreaming. It was early in the morning and everyone in the house was sleeping. While lying in my bed I listened to a constant mumbling sound. By now we were well used to the droning sound of airplanes above our heads. Almost every night hundreds, and sometimes a thousand, bombers came over on their way to Germany, which was now under constant air assaults. At night it was the heavy English Wellingtons and Lancasters and in daytime it was the American bombers who dropped their loads of destruction on that country—especially the Ruhr region. But this time it was different. I left my bed and opened my window a little more. In Holland our windows were always half open at night, even in winter time. I think the Dutch like cold fresh air.

There was a cool breeze coming from over the meadows, and the sun had just risen above a clump of large elm trees which grew further away in the field. Some blackbirds were looking for their breakfast, while in the meantime picking on other smaller birds. As I stood there by the window listening carefully, I heard a constant rumble in the distance like a remote summer storm—oppressive—ever present. It sounded to me as if it came on the wind from a southern direction. Listening intently now my heart started to beat faster. The far away sound which I heard was from thundering cannons. "Yes," I uttered to myself, "yes, they are coming. They are finally coming!" A mixture of excitement and an uneasy feeling started to come over me. Then after listening to some more distant sounds, I woke my parents.

Finally the English are coming, this time for sure! Maybe in a few days, even maybe tomorrow! But the sounds of cannons which we heard now continually was going nowhere. Every day it was the same thundering sound in the far distance, day after day after day. We asked ourselves many times, "Why are they not coming, why are those English or American soldiers staying where they are."Radio Orange could not give us any answer either. Much later we learned that the Allied troops, which had run out of gasoline and were short of food and ammunition, had to wait for supplies before their assault on Holland. It was a difficult task for the Allies to supply the great Armies with a constant flow of supplies from Normandy. One tank alone used two gallons of gasoline a mile.

For almost four weeks the British and American troops would remain on the Dutch- Belgium border line and about 15 to 20 miles from our city Breda. Everyday, especially if the wind was from the south, we could hear the cannons in the far distance. Small American scouting planes buzzed above our town every morning, but nothing else happened with the war. Father thought, the military man he was, it was strange with all those German soldiers in our city and the cannons set up in and around Breda, there should be much more heavy German artillery pointing south, if they were planning to hold on and defend their position.

The following weeks were trying times. We grew uneasy and had no idea what to expect. People got arrested for no reason at all. I think the Nazis got nervous themselves and couldn't figure out why the Allied troops didn't move. Many of the NSB-ers, the Nazi sympathizers and German citizens living in Breda, had now left. They had gone to Germany by small groups to find safety. They were afraid the Dutch people would take revenge for all the suffering and hardships they had endured in the last four years.

In the meantime more citizens of Breda lost their lives, which also included my doctor. Dr. Vennekamp and his wife were both physicians. Mother had gone there for her headaches at the recommendation from our family doctor. For the last three years I also had visited their office when I needed some medicine for one or other ailment. Mrs. Dr. Vennekamp knew that I sewed and had asked me about a year earlier if I wanted to sew for her four young daughters. Sometimes she received material for dresses for her girls from an out of town patient who paid her this way for her medical service. Not only did I like to sew for the girls, but also sometimes there was enough material left over for a top or skirt for myself. Her husband, Dr. Vennekamp, had more than once criticized Hitler and expressed his discontent with the Nazis to Mother and me, and we had been worried about his safety. Then one day, just one week before our liberation, the Gestapo went to search his house and found a loaded handgun in his library. He was shot immediately in the back of his head in the hall of his home while his wife and his four young daughters had to witness the crime. Mother and I felt very bad. All those years he had so longed for his country to be free again, and now he was killed so close to our liberation. Not long after the murder of her husband Mrs. Dr. Vennekamp moved out of their large home and went with her children back to the city where her family lived before she had married the young promising doctor.

The situation with food was bad enough, but now for the last couple of weeks we had not seen any kind of soap anymore. There was also no more salt which made the boring two-times-a-day-potatoes even more tasteless. For the last few months we ate the potatoes with peels from the boiling water. Luckily though, we always had potatoes. We tried to keep our spirits up by believing that soon the English would come to set us free, free from this sad life we lived. Until then we just lived from one day to the next and were wondering about the Allied troops who were so close, yet so far.

# 25

## *LIBERATION*

*October 28, 1944.* It was a quiet fall day, and a serene cool sunshine in a cloudless sky seemed to tell us of better times to come—free to live and free of violence that had held us more than four years. It was Saturday morning. My parents and Jan were in the living room where the radio was playing one or another of Germany's favorite songs. As I was busy in the kitchen trying to sew one of my shoes which was falling apart, the front door flew open and Henk, followed by his long-time friend Tjue, came in the house. While running into the living room he shouted, "They are coming, the English are coming! Don't you hear the cannons? Come outside and you can hear the cannons clearly!" We all stopped what we were doing and excitedly we ran after Henk and his friend through the hall and into the street. Some of our neighbors were talking to each other on the sidewalk and were listening to the heavy artillery which was now much closer to our city. This time the sound was different than it had been in the last weeks. It was still far away, but we knew that finally the day that we had been waiting for had arrived.

Henk told us that he and Tjue had seen a lot of German soldiers in the Molengracht Straat, and a large cannon was at boer Backx's farm. Full of excitement, Henk told us that there were more German soldiers with another cannon further up to the left. Mother went into the house. I think she felt that this gun business was a little too close to her home. Somewhat later that morning I said to Mother that I was going to see Chiel for just a little while. I needed to talk to my friends on this exciting day. I was too restless to sit at home. Chiel's parents, who had been waiting and praying everyday to hear something from their abducted son, were now full of hope that the war would soon be over and that their son would return home. It must have been about 2:00 in that afternoon as I left Chiel and her family. We wished each other good luck. We knew that the hours ahead of us could be difficult. We didn't quite know what to expect.

The streets were deserted as I walked back home. I saw only German soldiers moving in an eastern direction. People were now staying inside their homes and waiting for things to come. Suddenly there was an explosion followed by a second one which sent me running. I knew I needed to get out of the streets quickly. When I came home out of breath and entered the living room, Mother asked me angrily if I was out of my mind to walk on the street in this situation. "It is too dangerous!" she almost shouted. Suddenly there were rolling explosions which seemed to come from the airfield. It sounded like a battle, and black smoke billowed up in the sky. Even though the Allied troops were still far away, we knew it was a matter of time and they would enter our city.

It was about 4:00 in the afternoon when we heard more and more grenade explosions from everywhere. A few weeks before Jan had decided we needed a shelter. "In case we need to get out of the house to a safe place," he had told us. In all those war years Breda never had experienced a serious bombing attack. But now with the coming of the Allied troops, an attack on our city was a possibility. So Jan had started to dig one under our shed. It was large enough for five people to sit in. It was covered with boards from our house. Over the boards Jan laid a thick layer of dirt which came from the dugout. After he had finished the shelter, we all had to inspect it. It looked good enough to us, but when Mother shivered said, "I hope we never have to sit in there," we all had agreed with her.

When dusk came, Father told us that he had to leave soon. We understood. He probably had secretly received orders from the former Dutch military to report himself that day. Where he would go—we didn't know. Father had been puzzled, for it seemed that the Allies planned a night attack on our city. "This is not done much," Father told us and he wondered why. Before he left he said we should take our pillows and blankets from upstairs and sleep in the living room. He explained that it would be a little safer in case we needed to get out of the house in a hurry.

After Father left, Mother found out that we had no electricity anymore. She thought that it would be wise to eat something before it got too dark and have something in our bellies before the night came. Mother had been brave during the war years and had kept her worries and troubles mostly to herself. She always had seen to it that her family had something to eat. Many times in the last year Mother had given her own portion of food to Father or to us kids. She had never complained that she was hungry, but I knew that she had been very hungry many times. Mother, who always had been a little chubby, had become thin during the last year, as Father had. They both looked strained from all the worries.

When we had eaten some of the tasteless, coarse, black dry bread and an apple, we took our blankets and pillows downstairs to the living room. Each of us made our own little place on the floor. I laid my things down in the corner behind Father's easy chair and thought it was the best place for me. Maybe I felt protected there. When done with my "bed," I went to the front door, opened it and peered down the deserted dark street. The air was filled with the thunder of cannon grenade explosions which were now much closer, but not yet too close to our own neighborhood. I remember, when looking up at the cloudless sky, how the stars looked so bright in this strangely frightful night. High in the sky was a VII which probably was going to London to bring more death and destruction to that city.

As I was standing there outside the front door, looking up at the sky and thinking about Father and about all the boys I knew who were so far away in Germany, I noticed that it was turning red behind the house. I closed the door as fast as I could and quickly went through our house to the backyard. There I saw that the large seminary, which stood less than two miles behind our neighborhood, was engulfed in flames. Large tongues of red and yellow flames reached high into the sky. In peacetime it would have been exciting to watch this large fire but at that moment, between the heavy shell explosions in the not far distance, it was frightening. As I stood there I suddenly got a sense of complete unreality.

Later we learned that the First Polish Infantry troops had surrounded the seminary where enemy soldiers were trying to hold their position. Then, while the Germans tried to escape, they had set the seminary on fire with hand grenades. As I came back into the house, Mother and my two brothers were looking through the window at the enormous fire which had turned the sky red in this intense night. Suddenly we heard artillery fire from not too far away and saw German soldiers going through our street pointing their guns.

The front had reached Breda. All that we could do now was wait it out and pray for the best. We thought that we should lay down for safety and also try to get some rest since there was nothing else we could do. I laid myself down in the corner of the room and wrapped the blanket around me. But I was unable to close my eyes as the air grew heavy with sounds. Time passed slowly. The whistling sounds of cannon grenades became closer, and the cannons at boer Backx were firing. They were probably firing at each other I thought, while wrapping my blanket tighter around me. It was very frightening. It must have been about midnight when suddenly I sat up as shells came whistling overhead followed by heavy explosions. The screams of an approaching shell is an appalling sound. It is worse than anything I had ever heard before, and have ever heard since. In terror

I heard glass breaking and stones falling. The whole house seemed to rock with each explosion. Some pictures fell off the walls and ornaments toppled off shelves. Then there was another loud explosion, and our home was engulfed by a violent sound. The room filled with acrid smelling smoke. Glass was everywhere. I jumped up and then I heard the terrible whistling sound of another grenade coming and again an explosion. Sharp shrapnel penetrated our home. Suddenly someone took my hand, and we ran out of the house, through the backyard, into our shed and down into the shelter Jan had dug before. It was cold, damp and uncomfortable in our small shelter, but for now we felt safe and thankful for the dugout. The attack continued for hours, one explosion merging into the next. It was a nightmare. After each explosion I thought surely that had been the climax and that it would be the end, but many more followed. As the night wore on I was able to detect, by the sounds of screaming grenades, where they would hit—further away or close to our home. While sitting in our shelter shivering and shaking, we wondered what had happened to our home and to our neighborhood.

Toward the early morning the shellfire diminished a little—then a little more. It finally became quiet and daylight came. Carefully we climbed out of our shelter and to our great relief we saw that our home was still there. Suddenly we heard quick footsteps in the alley behind our yard, the backyard door opened, and there was Tjue. Excitingly he told us that there were soldiers all over the neighborhood who looked English but were speaking a strange language. He didn't know who they were. Soon we would find out that the soldiers who had finally came to set us free were from the First Polish Armored Division and had come with the Allied troops through Normandy from England. After some protest from Mother that it still was too dangerous, Henk went with his friend to see the "strange soldiers." Being fifteen years old, it was the only thing on his mind—to see the soldiers in English uniforms, our liberators, his heroes.

Soon people came out their hiding places. We were free, finally free! For four long years we had longed and waited for this moment, the moment of freedom and free from terror. And here it was! We were still shaky from the long stressful night, but we were so very thankful it was over, finally over!

What a mess everywhere! Rubble had been flung across the yards and streets by the explosive force of the grenades. There was not one unbroken window left anymore in our home and in the houses of our neighborhood. The curtains were hanging out of the windows in shreds. Red roofed stone tiles had toppled down, and some of the houses received more damage. One of the many grenades which had been aimed at our neighborhood had landed in our large sturdy willow laundry basket. It had been full of potatoes and stood against our house in our back-yard. Just a few days before Mother got hold of the potatoes. They were from the farmer from where she always had bought her vegetables, eggs and milk. She had placed the potatoes in her laundry basket, and for the time being had set them outside against the house. Of the basket full of potatoes there was nothing left except than a paste on the back wall of the house and on the fencing. Later we found only here and there tiny fragments of the heavy basket. The potatoes had smothered the many grenade fragments which are so dangerous with a explosion. Some of our family could easily have been hurt or killed if that basket with pota-toes would not have been there in that exact spot. Our family had been protected by our guardian angel that night. How very blessed we had been.

Inside our home we could still smell the smoke left from that exploding shell. It was such a mess everywhere. Glass and debris was over and in everything. And our heavy closed draperies, from the back room where we had been sleeping on the floor, were riddled with grenade shrapnel. A year later we still would find the small fragments in our home.

While Henk and Tjue were behind our house trying to talk to some of the Polish Infantry men, Jan had left. He probably had to get in contact with other men of the underground. Mother and I could hear the artillery in our town and, even though our neighborhood swarmed with Polish soldiers, we knew we were not free yet. As we tried to clean up the glass and other mess in our home, a sud-den loud explosion made Mother and me jump up. Then it was quiet again, except for the sounds of artillery somewhere further away.

Mother and I tried to go on with our sweeping. It must have not been much later when Henk, followed by his friend, came back in the house saying that a German cannon grenade had just killed some people around the corner of our street. A little later we learned that the grenade had killed Gina's brother Frans. Frans had gone to some Polish soldiers who were staying not far from his home. Just a few minutes before, he had said to his parents that he wanted to shake their hands and see their tank. Suddenly an enemy grenade, which came from a Ger-man cannon not too far from our neighborhood, landed between him and the two Polish soldiers. All three were killed instantly. I felt very bad for Gina and her parents and I began to cry from exhaustion and frustration. When Father came home later that morning—I don't know where he had been that night—he told us not to go out of our street. "Even if our neighborhood is free of those damn Germans, it is still not safe," he explained. "The rest of Breda is not cleaned up yet from German resistance."

Early that afternoon I said to Mother that I was going to Chiel to tell her what had happened to Frans, Gina's brother. Mother understood and, since Chiel lived just around the corner of our street, I promised her I would be home soon, and she was not to worry. As I came around the corner into the Molengracht Straat, there were two dead German soldiers lying on the sidewalk, while Polish soldiers were walking in the direction of the Wilhelmina Park. Quickly I went to Chiel's house. She and her family had survived the night in the basement of the convent in the Molengracht Straat. It had been open that night for everyone who needed shelter. Chiel told me about their neighbor who had been killed by a grenade fragment while he stood in the hallway of his home. Chiel and I felt bad for our friend Gina and talked about it. We planned to visit her and the family the next day. A little later as I went home, tanks rolled into the Molengracht Straat and people came out of their homes to greet their liberators. The German occupation had been endless and suddenly it was over. In spite of being hungry and tired, we were happy, and people embraced each other and were laughing and slapping each other on the back. We clasped hands with the Polish soldiers or embraced them. Small Dutch flags came out of the closets, and we sang our freedom songs. No more darkness! No more curfews! We were free and it was exciting!

But it was not so exciting when I came home and saw that Polish troops had placed guns in the fields behind our row of houses. They were shooting their guns at the German enemy who were resisting further up in our city. Every time the guns went off, our house shook and chattered. It was such a loud noise that my poor mother had a terrible time to stay sane. While I had gone to Chiel's house, Father had been in the attic and had torn some of the wooden boards from the attic walls to board up our blown-out windows. It had become miserably cold in the house. Jan came home for awhile and together with Father they boarded up the downstairs windows before dark. That evening we got some water again and were happy not only to be able to drink, but also to wash our faces and hands. But we still had no gas and electricity yet to make something hot to drink which we longed for.

After a night of fitful sleeping I woke up early in the morning to the roar of guns from behind our house. It was terrible! While holding my hands over my ears I thought, probably those guns would stay there until all the Germans were gone from our town.

Although the guns would stay behind our house for some time, they would not shoot anymore after that day. The night before, Jan had told me, that they (the now former underground) were going to be busy with the rounding up of collaborators, NSB-ers and the local traitors in our town. Happily he said to me, "Eef, we are going to burn the Nazi flags and hang our own Dutch flags again. We will burn Hitler's portraits and all that belonged to those Nazis!" Jan had longed for this moment with his whole soul. The day of revenge! That day he saw his future opening up again, which before had looked like a wall in front of him. Jan had left the house the evening before, and we would not see much of him anymore for a long time. As soon as we ate our meager breakfast of one slice of black bread with water, I said to my parents that I was going with Chiel to see all the excitement in our town and didn't know what time we were going to be back.

It was still early in the morning when Chiel and I went first to Gina's house. The body of Frans, or rather the pieces of what was left of him, was taken to a hospital mortuary. A few days later we would attend his funeral. It was a terrible tragedy for Gina and her parents, and they suffered for years to come.

Chiel and I hurried down the street to the building in our town were the Gestapo had been living for the last few years. As the flames of the high pile of books, portraits of Hitler, the hated swastika flags, furniture and everything the Gestapo had left behind, shot high in the cloudy fall sky, people around it cheered loudly and danced around the flames. There would never be the Gestapo, the SS or Green Police again! From this day on there would be democracy and freedom! After the burnings we went to downtown where the headquarters of the police of Breda was located in a street just a block from the city square. There we saw the former underground with guns in their hands, busy with bringing in the Nazi collaborators and other local vermin. People shouted at the traitors. It was a cry for vengeance. I think people needed to express themselves for the years of oppression. Later we watched the roundup of those girls and women who had been friendly with German soldiers and officers during the occupation years. The women's heads were shaved bald, and they then were pushed through the streets while people shouted at them. But I didn't care too much to watch this. Sometimes there were small frightened children, who were holding onto their bald shaven mothers and were crying in fear. I felt sorry for those innocent kids who didn't understand what was happening.

It was later in the afternoon when Chiel and I decided to go home. We both were tired, not only from the excitement of that day but also from not much sleep in the last few nights. We could hear rifle shots while we were walking home. German snipers were still hiding at some places in town. But it had not stopped the people from going out on the streets and celebrating. Chiel and I were both hungry. The only food I had eaten that day had been my breakfast. Potatoes would fill me up again, I thought, hoping that mother would have some since the basket full of potatoes was now porridge paste on the wall and fence. And if we have gas and electric again, I thought hopefully, then maybe I could get something hot to drink.

As we were going home and walked in the Molengracht Straat on the side of the closed Teolin paint factory, two Polish soldiers who had just crossed the street were walking in our direction. I didn't pay attention to them because so many Allied soldiers had now come into town. As they passed us, one of them, a tall guy with a broad smile on his face, said something to Chiel in German. As I walked slowly on, Chiel stood still and answered him. Even though I wanted to go home I stopped. While turning around I said to Chiel, "Come, let's go." While I was waiting for her, I looked at the other soldier. He also had walked a little further and now stood still while waiting for his friend. He looked very tired and probably wanted to take a rest, as I did.

A little later when we walked home, Chiel said to me, "Eef, I will pick you up in about two hours because we are going to meet those soldiers again." I protested and said to her that I had no interest in going out again and meeting those soldiers. But when she said, "Eef, those guys will bring us food. We will meet at the fence at the side of the barracks. Because your parents and probably your brothers are home, we will bring them to your house. Then later, since the barracks are so close by, those soldiers can walk by themselves back to the barracks again." Well, the word *food* had a most magical sound, and I told her that I would go with her.

A few hours later we went to the barracks where the two soldiers were waiting by the fence with their pockets bulging with cans of food. We shook hands and the tallest of the two started to speak in German. He introduced himself as Stefan Ratke. He was a tall, dark-haired fellow with a pleasant grin on his face. The other one was of medium height and smiled at me as he shook my hand warmly. With his blue eyes he was looking me over with obvious interest. He had removed his black service beret, and I noticed his very short blond curly hair, and I thought how cute he was. His name was Jozef Otto, and he spoke English. Both men looked to be about in their mid-twenties. Since Chiel and I couldn't speak English and, of course, not a word of Polish, we talked mainly with Stefan. After the introduction we walked to my home where the two soldiers unloaded their cans of food on the living room table. The cans with Canadian bacon, ham and corned beef and the bars of chocolate were worth more than gold to us. It was the most delectable food I had ever seen. We almost could not remember anymore how real food tasted. Father first looked the soldiers over, and then he shook their hands. He tried to talk to them but neither soldier could understand our Dutch language. He then took out the road map of Holland and wanted to know about where the front line of the Allied troops was. Luckily we could understand and speak some German, which we had learned during those last few years of German occupation. Jan, who was home for a few hours that evening, started to talk with Jozef in English. Soon the conversation in the room was a mixture of four different languages.

It was about a hour later when the two soldiers stood up and planned to leave. Since they seemed to be a couple of nice guys, Chiel and I decided to walk them back to the fence at the barracks again. After thanking them for all the food and wishing them good luck, we turned around and went home, thinking we would not see them again. Soldiers at the front were here today and somewhere else tomorrow. But for the following days they came over to our house almost every night to bring food. One day Jozef came alone and brought bread. It was one slice, but the whitest and largest slice of bread we had seen in years. On top of the bread was a large piece of butter, a hunk of cheese and a scoop of jam. It was delicious, and wonderfully real to my hungry eyes. Later we learned that the bread with the trimmings had been his breakfast.

Many times in those early days of liberation, Jozef would bring his breakfast to our house. I think the two soldiers enjoyed coming to our house where a family lived, which was a far cry from the barracks and, of course, where there was two pretty girls. Even though we could not speak much with each other, it was home for them and gave them a few moments of sanity in an insane world. Sometimes we went to Chiel's house where we visited for a short while, and then they were off again. Jozef tried hard to learn some Dutch words. He wanted so much to be able to talk and understand the Dutch language.

# 26

# *A SOLDIER NAMED JOZEF*

No peace came with our freedom. Two days after our liberation, the First Polish Tank Regiment rolled into our neighborhood and parked their tanks one after the other on one side of our street. Other Polish troops settled in other parts of our town. Breda became a city right behind the front line. The Polish Military Police moved into a house, which was a few houses down from us, and parked their jeeps on the sidewalk. Soon Polish officers came knocking on the door of every house in our neighborhood, telling people that one or more soldiers were going to stay in their homes. When they came to our house and told Father that there were two soldiers going to stay in our home, Father protested and said that there was room for only one. After the Polish officers went through our house and Father talked some more to them, one of the officers said that they would sent only one soldier to our house.

When they left, father told me that I had to move out of my bedroom and sleep downstairs in the back room. I sure did not like this. A strange soldier sleeping in my room—in my bed! But I didn't argue and did as I was told. I hoped that this arrangement would last for only a few days, no more than a week, and then they would move further again. Then thinking about it I thought—those soldiers are willing to give their lives for our freedom, so let me not complain and move to the sofa downstairs. It was the least I could do to help. A few hours later Waldek Wieck, a tall handsome Polish soldier in his early thirties walked into our home. He looked friendly enough and shook hands with Father. He then bent down and kissed Mother's hand which made her smile. We had to get used to this Polish custom of hand kissing which was done by many Polish soldiers as we later would find out. Mother thought it was very nice, but I didn't care for it.

Waldek turned out to be a nice and pleasant man. Besides his native tongue he spoke German and English. He came from the city of Krakow (South Poland) and had a wife and young son living there. He had been called for military duty when Russia invaded Poland in 1939 and was taken prisoner of war by the Russians. When Germany invaded Russia in 1942, he and thousands of other Polish military prisoners were set free because of pressure by America and England when the three nations joined hands. From Russia he went to Iran and further on to Egypt. From there he and many other Polish men were sent by ship to England where they joined the First Polish Armor Division which was forming at that time in England.

Our neighborhood became crowded with all those soldiers living in our homes. The loud noises of tanks and cars was something we had to learn to live with. We were just not used to traffic on the streets. Many an evening there were six to eight soldiers in our living room. Waldek would say to Mother, "Mamma, clean up the table and bring us some glasses." Soon his army buddies came with drinks and food. They smoked their cigarettes, drank, ate and sang until late in the evening or until they went to the front-line.

Because of the soft ground in Holland which made the use of tanks impossible, the Anti-Tank Regiment which was staying in our neighborhood, was of no use at that time. Their soldiers were now used as infantry men in the area of the Moerdyk bridges.

My parents became increasingly nervous with all the soldiers in and around the house. They became very protective of me, even when I told them many times not to worry so much. Nothing was going to happen to me! But then I couldn't blame them. I was a pretty 19-year-old girl, and it worried them greatly when sometimes the soldiers in our house had too much to drink. But never in all that time did a soldier bother me or make a pass at me. Even though the time they lived in was rough and harsh, most of those Polish soldiers were good and civil men who knew their place.

Along with the Allied troops came the food for their soldiers. And what food! A Polish army kitchen now stood at boer Backx's farm, and I think that all the kids from our neighborhood gathered every afternoon around that place. With their eyes big as saucers they watched as the cooks were preparing the army meal for that night. They never had seen or smelled such food, not in a long time anyway. Later in the afternoon the soldiers who came to eat there gave most of their meals away to the children who crowded around the kitchen

Aside from the tanks in our street and my bedroom being taken away from me, something else came along which was in the form of a VI, the flying bomb. The Germans, who were holding northern Holland, were now firing the VI missiles at Antwerp for the malfuction of that city. In the beginning of September

Antwerp had finally fallen into Allied hands. While on route the missiles sometimes dysfunctioned and came down on farms or houses, bringing death and destruction. The VI's, which came over mostly at night, looked like a cross with a flame coming from its tail. They were flying very low and made quite a noise. As long as we heard the rattling buzzing sound, we knew we were all right. But as soon as the sound stopped, we knew the missile was coming down and we waited in fear. Many people could not sleep at night and were glad when the weather was bad so the missiles wouldn't come over.

It was a frightening situation, but somehow I had told myself that there was nothing that I could do about it. If it would happen—it would happen, and somehow I found acceptance in the situation and most nights I could sleep. The only nights when no one could sleep was when a thousand heavy Allied bombers came over on route to Germany which happened more and more often. Sometimes we wondered if there was one stone left on the other in that country. On those nights I would lay awake and think about Wim and the other boys I knew. I wondered where they were and if I would ever see them again.

About a week after our liberation we got soda crackers and powdered milk from America. It came with the Red Cross to the liberated areas. The crackers held vitamins and minerals, something we needed badly. Later as the months passed, more and better food came very slowly into the empty stores. But it would take many years before our stores were finally full again and the ration coupons were gone.

It must have been about a week after our liberation when I went to Chiel to tell her of an American movie which was showing in our town. The first American movie had come to Breda. After four years of seeing mostly German movies with Dutch subtitles, we were going to see an American film again. Not that there was anything wrong with those other films, but nothing was as exciting as an American movie and, of course, we had to see it. While staying in Chiel's front yard talking to her, we saw Stefan coming down the street walking toward us. He was alone. As soon as he reached us he said that Jozef had been wounded and was lying in the hospital. How bad he was hurt Stefan didn't know. Jozef had gone with the infantry to the Wilhelmina canal that night, but more he could not tell us. Then Stefan asked us if we wanted to go with him and see Jozef, maybe we could do something for him. Chiel went inside her house, grabbed her coat, and we were on our way to the hospital. We walked about one block when, to our surprise, we saw Jozef coming. His step was unsteady and his face was gray, yet he smiled at me as he walked toward us. Stefan said something to him in Polish and shook his head. Puzzled Chiel and I looked at each other and decided to take Jozef to her home which was a little closer than my house.

As soon as we arrived at Chiel's home, Jozef slumped down in one of the easy chairs and lit a cigarette with trembling hands. By the look on his face we knew that he was not feeling well. He didn't say much, only that he had been hurt in his back and head. He had walked out of the hospital and was not feeling too good, but that it would pass. But Jozef didn't act like himself and Stefan decided to take his buddy to his sleeping quarters since, as he said—Jozef didn't want to go back to the hospital again. As I watched Stefan disappearing with Jozef in the misty rain of that dark November day, it was the first time that I felt afraid for Jozef—afraid that the next time he could be killed. Much later Jozef told me about that night when he was with the infantry on the river. They had tried unsuccessfully to go to the other side of the water and he was left behind wounded.

For the following week Jozef came over our house every evening. During the day he was in his bed at his quarters recuperating, but in the evenings he came over to learn more Dutch, as he would tell me cheerfully. For years to come Jozef had bad headaches due to the concussion he had received during this failed crossing at the Wilhelmina Canal. Also his back hurt him for a long time. After his recovery he worked at the Battalion Headquarters Office where I met some of his officers, as Major Makuch who looked like a tough but good man to me.

By the third week of November most of the Polish Battalions had moved out of Breda and had gone about 20 km further north. There they positioned themselves in and around the villages south of Holland's great rivers. The German troops who held the north and eastern part of Holland were now bunkered on the north side of the rivers. It was a formidable barrier for the Allies. The many smaller waterways between the great rivers and the waterlogged plains made the use of tanks impossible. The Allies who were in position on the south side of the rivers were laying many minefields in case the Germans decided on a counterattack. In the southeast of Holland and in the East of Belgium the American troops slowed down their advances just west of the Ryn River and the German border. Now a waiting period started.

The battalion of Jozef and Stefan moved out of our town and stationed in and around Gravemoer, a village northeast of Breda. Chiel and I thought we would not see them anymore and went on with our lives such as standing in lines for food, trying to stay warm and going to the theater to see an American movie.

Because of the war situation in September, the school of gymnastics and the dance lessons had been canceled until further notice. Occasionally we went to the coffee house together with Gina for a talk and, since there was nothing better to drink, we drank the cheap imitation coffee. The loss of Gina's brother Frans was hard on her and her parents.

Even though the Polish Anti-Tank Battalion had not moved out of our neighborhood, the cannons behind our house finally were removed. When the German troops were driven completely from Breda, those cannons had been left there. Hundreds of pure copper shells and a mountain of jerry cans were left behind. Heavy military trucks came later to take it all away back to England. I wished sometimes that I had taken many of those shells and had saved them, because later they turned out to be worth a lot of money. I took only two of the shells for souvenirs. Later before going to America I gave them away; they were just too heavy to take along.

◆    ◆    ◆

My brother Jan was seldom home anymore since the day of our liberation. The world was again promising to him, and he was eager to help the Allies liberate the rest of his country and drive the hated Nazis to defeat. The first week after our liberation Jan and the other men of the resistance slept on the floor of a café which was located on the edge of the Wilhelmina Park. After the traitors had been rounded up, the former resistance workers were used day and night for the guarding of bridges.

Jan, Eef, and Henk with Mother and Father after Breda's liberation.

It was a week later that Jan went to Den Bosch, which is a town about 40 km east of Breda, to enlist in the newly forming Dutch Army. There he was placed in the Dutch General Staff Office. Prince Bernhard, who had come from England with the Dutch Brigade "Princess Irene," now had his office in our province Brabant, and it would remain there during the winter of 1944-45. With the Dutch insignia on his sleeve Jan proudly wore his new British uniform. A few times Jan acted as translator for Prince Bernhard when there was a meeting or conference of high ranking officers in Breda or elsewhere in the south of Holland.

After four long years my father also wore a uniform again. Only this time not his Dutch, but a British uniform as all the Allied troops were wearing in that time, with exception of the American and Australian forces. Father was thankful to be finally free again. Not only could he speak openly without being worried about imprisonment, but now he didn't have to go to the metal factory every morning anymore. All those years he had hated to work there. The very moment we were liberated, Father had taken his short-wave radio from the attic and finally had placed it in our living room. Since the Dutch radio stations were located in the northern part of Holland and were in German hands, we still had to listen to Radio Orange from England for the latest war information.

The Red Cross began to organize dance evenings for the troops, but they were also open for everyone who wanted to come and dance. The dances were held in the gym of a school which was close to our neighborhood. There was always a great band playing and they were attended by many British, Canadian and Polish soldiers with their dates. Also Dutch men with their wives or girlfriends came to dance those nights. One evening, when Chiel was over at my house, Stefan and Jozef, who felt much better again, came over and asked if we wanted to go dancing and have a good time together. It sounded good to us. Finally to go dancing and have a good time again was great! Soon we walked together to the school where we were welcomed by the music of the popular American Rock and Roll. Of course, Chiel and I had never heard or seen those new dances. For the last four years of German rule, open dances had been banned in the occupied countries. The only exceptions were the private dance lessons like the ones I had attended. The first time when Chiel and I saw the Canadian and English soldiers swinging the Army nurses and other military women to the Rock and Roll music, we stared in wonder at such wild dancing. Especially the English soldiers and nurses were fantastic in our eyes. Chiel and I were used to dancing at a much slower pace. Of course not everyone danced as those English did, and there were a lot of other dances in between for everyone to dance to. Yes, those Red Cross dances were fun. The soldiers were able to put the gnawing stress of war aside and forget their worries for the moment. The following days Chiel and I tried to dance as those English did, but the Rock and Roll was not as easy as it looked.

After that evening at the first Red Cross dance, Jozef came to our house many times. If he had no duty on the river Maas, and it was possible for him to go for a few hours to Breda, he came over our home with or without Stefan. Sometimes we went together to the movies or went dancing in the bar of one or another hotel. Most places were crowded with soldiers, but we always managed to have a good time. When the weather was good, Jozef and I took long walks. He liked to walk as did I—especially through the fields on the small winding roads behind our house. They seemed to go on forever. Or we walked through our beautiful old forest Mastbos. Jozef was learning the Dutch language quickly. He wanted more than anything to be able to talk with me and to the family. It did not take long until we all were able to understand him. Maybe it came easily to him because he could understand German, which in some ways is similar to the Dutch language. I liked Jozef more and more and had decided he was a nice guy. There was something about him I liked very much. He always thought about my comfort first before he thought about himself. Nothing seemed too much for him to please me. He was a man who had gone through many things but yet could laugh at my sometimes silly girlish ways.

How well I remember that day at the beginning of December when the weather had turned bitter cold with icy winds and dark clouds. The wind blew from the north and made our boarded-up windows in the house rattle and shake. It was unusually cold for Holland with its moderate climate. We sure didn't need this, especially this winter when every household had not received much coal for heating their homes. "If this weather stays so, and we don't receive any more coal," Father said to Mother, "it could be the worst winter yet."

It was dreary and cold that day. Mother had the watery potato soup simmering on the little stove. There was not much coal in the stove, not enough to warm the living room. Waldek had left with some soldiers in an armored car and probably had gone to the vicinity of the Moerdyk Bridges, the area where he usually went when he was on duty. Mother and I were alone at home when suddenly we heard the clanking sound of a tank. We were well used to that sound, but this time it sounded different. Mother and I went to the front door to see what it was all about. When we opened it, we saw the largest tank ever driven in our street. It stopped right in front of our house, and two soldiers jumped down from their high seat. They were dressed in white winter overalls. At first I could not see who they were. Suddenly I looked in the face of Jozef and, while giving me a smile, he deposited a large sack of coal in our front yard while the other soldier carried another sack. Without saying a word they immediately jumped back on their tank and with clanking noise disappeared around the corner of our street. Mother and I went outside at once to see from up close the treasure which had landed in our front yard. It was anthracite, the best grade of coal. While Mother and I looked in disbelief at the blessing in the form of anthracite, a few neighbor women came over and envied us at such good luck. Mother and I soon dragged the sacks of coal to our shed in the back yard. Then Mother took a scoop full of coal and went inside the house where she carefully deposited the black gold into our little stove.

A few days later Jozef came over and said that he had a few hours free before going to the river Maas. It was Saturday and we decided to go to the Red Cross dance where a military band was playing that night. Stefan did not come that day, so we went together. For a few hours we had fun and were laughing at ourselves when we tried to dance to the Rock and Roll music.

After a few hours of dancing, listening to the big band music and to an American crooner singing, Jozef had to leave for duty. When we came outside, a tank with some of his platoon buddies was already waiting for him at the school's gate. Quickly he put a snow overall over his uniform, kissed me goodbye, climbed on his tank and disappeared through the opening of the turret before it took off for the river Maas. There in a bunker he had to report on his radio to his battalion the activities of the Germans, who were on the other side of the Maas. As soon as the tank had disappeared in the dark, I walked home. The night was cold and the moonlight pale and clear. An icy wind was blowing in my face which made it tingle. While walking through the streets, I saw a VI coming just over the houses with flames shooting from its tail. I thought what a strange world I lived in, and how uncertain life had become in the last year. It was the beginning of December and St. Nicholas time. The most wonderful, magical, warm time of the year before this war had started. It had been the time of the year when stores had been full of gifts and toys and the bakeries had smelled of the most delectable pastries. And everyone had been happy, and the sounds of singing and laughter had been all around. There had been bright lights everywhere and excitement—and I was longing for those times to come again. The VI had gone over and had disappeared out of sight. It was dark and blustery and I missed Jozef's arm around me keeping me warm while we walked home. I thought how miserable it must be on the river Maas in that ever-present danger of being killed. I shivered while I turned into our deserted street.

In the dark and cold before dawn of December 16, 1944, German forces struck with a massive surprise attack at the American Army which was stationed at the Belgium-Luxembourg and German border in an area called Ardennes. When I got up that morning the sun was hidden behind heavy clouds. I found my parents in the living room talking about a German assault on American troops in the Ardennes, which the Nazis earlier gleefully announced on our Dutch radio station. For the last weeks we all had wondered about the seemingly quiet situation on the front lines. After the liberation of south Holland, there had been no further advancements made by the Allied or American troops, or by the troops which were at the German border lines in the southeast. The north of Holland had been cut off, and its people were suffering from malnutrition and cold. All connections with north Holland had been broken, and it had worried my parents greatly. Both my parents had their families living there and both grandmothers were too old for this kind of suffering.

Soon everyone was talking about the situation in the Ardennes. Everyone believed that the Germans had been greatly weakened and did not have the war equipment anymore to pull off a breakthrough. As we later learned, the plan of Hitler had been to recapture Antwerp. In doing so, he would cut of tens of thousands Allied and American soldiers who were stationed in the south of Holland and north Belgium. It became a very bitter fight which the Americans soon nicknamed "The Battle of the Bulge."

Two days later on December 18 all Polish troops which were stationed north of Breda got orders that they were going to leave for the vicinity of Den Bosch and further southeast. They would be there in a holding position until further orders. The situation in the Ardennes became quite serious after the unexpected breakthrough by the German forces. They had recaptured an area of the Ardennes and were advancing west. All passes and furloughs of the Allied soldiers and their officers who were stationed in the south of Holland were canceled. Later in the afternoon of that same day Waldek told us that his battalion was going to leave in about one hour, and he didn't think they were coming back to Breda. He gathered his belongings and said goodbye to us all and thanked my parents for their care. He then turned to me and said jokingly that my bed was the best he had slept on in years, and he would always remember it. He then gave my mother a kiss on the back of her hand and said, "Some day we will meet again." He then left. Soon our street filled with the peculiar tank sound which we had come to know so well, and they started off, kicking up the dust. The tanks pulled out of our neighborhood and our street became uncommonly still. When the tanks with the soldiers had disappeared, I went to my bedroom which I immediately started to clean and happily placed my own things back in their place again. That night I finally slept in my own room—in my own bed. For the following days we missed Waldek. Even though he had always been gone a lot, we had come to know him quite well in the weeks he had been staying at our house. We hoped that he would make it through the war and finally go home to his country and family.

The following morning Jozef unexpectedly came over to our house. He had come by jeep with Officer Belinski who I had met before when Jozef was working in the office of his Battalions Headquarters in Breda. Jozef could stay only for a short while, just to say goodbye before he left. He and Officer Belinski had gone to Breda for something that had to do with their communication system. Their battalion was the last to leave for the east. While the last Polish battalions were leaving, Canadian troops came in and took their place at the Moerdyk bridges and Maas river areas. There they would stay until the end of the war

When the Polish Tank Battalion had moved out, life in our neighborhood settled down once more. In the last four years since the Germans had taken everything away from us, there were almost no materials left anymore for repairing. The houses were repaired only to the extent necessary. Our windows still lacked glass. Father had put some larger pieces of glass here and there between the boards and this had given us some light in the house. A few days after our liberation, and to our great relief, the street lights had come on again. I guess it was now safe again to have lights on in the city. The German Luftwaffe which had suffered great losses and was short on gasoline could not afford to bomb us. But to conserve energy the bright commercial lights had to wait until much later. Poor Mother—she never had gotten used to the blackout shades and the dim lights every night during the grim war years. Only now she had to live with dim light in her home during daytime. But she was not complaining. The war in our town was over and the glass in the windows would ultimately come to let the sunshine in, Mother said to herself many times. She had been thankful and happy when the streetlights had come on again. Our town was still full of Allied military, mainly Canadians, but the people of our neighborhood were relieved that they could go back again to living as normal as possible.

Christmas and New Years Day of 1944-45 came and went. For most people the holidays had been very difficult with shortages of coal and food. It had been a Christmas without a Christmas tree. Jan came home from the Dutch Headquarters for one day, which made my parents happy. As soon as he came home he went first to his girlfriend, but later brought her over to our home for the rest of that day. In the early afternoon there was a knock on our front door and when I opened it there stood Jozef, smiling broadly, beret in his hand. He told me he could stay only a few hours, until early evening, when a jeep would come for him. While Mother made imitation tea and Father deposited some more of the anthracite in our little stove, we all played cards until dinner time. Henk, who was never far removed from his best friend Tjue, decided he could live a day without him and stayed home. When we had eaten our rabbit dinner (our last bunny), Jozef and I went outside. We wanted to be alone for awhile before he had to leave again. The frozen snow crackled under our shoes as we walked through the very quiet Wilhelmina Park. The sky was heavy with clouds and it looked as if more snow was on the way. It was unusually cold and snowy that winter. Jozef told me in his broken—but improving—Dutch, that he was stationed in Den Bosch and that it was very boring to have nothing else to do except wait. The situation in the Ardennes looked bad for the American soldiers who were fighting there he said, but he didn't wanted to talk about it further. He then told me proudly that every day he learned some more Dutch words from a local paper he had found in Den Bosch. It gave him something to do, he said. When early that evening the jeep came and left with Jozef and a few other soldiers, I watched them disappear into the frosty Christmas night, I knew I had fallen in love with him.

# 27

# *END OF THE NAZI REIGN*

The weather continued to break records of cold throughout Europe that January of 1945 and didn't get any better as the days slowly passed. As I recall, one afternoon when I was going to Chiel, I opened their front door and there was a lot of noise coming from the upstairs. I asked her what all that commotion was about. Then when she said to me, "My dad is pulling the wood from the attic to burn for some heat, "I couldn't help but laugh and said to my girlfriend, "It sounds so funny to saw up your house to heat it."

It must have been about the first week in January when one night many VI, (flying bombs) came over on their way to Antwerp. I don't think many people were sleeping that night. Suddenly toward the first morning light our house shook from an explosion, and I knew a VI had come down someplace not far from where we lived. A few hours later we learned that a VI had come down on the farm which was not far from our house. Before we had boarded up our windows, we always had been able to see the farmhouse in the open field from our bedroom window.

The farmer who lived there with his wife was retired from a life of hard work on his large farm. Before the war he owned many cows and large fields of wheat. Their son, who had taken over the farming of his father's land, also lived there in the large farmhouse with his wife and four children. Many times I passed the farmhouse when riding on my bicycle or when I went walking there on the narrow paved roads. On one side of the road was a quaint small building where they baked their bread for themselves and the workers. A large water well (where I always peeked in) was between the house and the road. A few years earlier many chickens, ducks and geese had been running free around the grounds. But in the last two years I had not seen them anymore. A few weeks before, another farming couple with their four young children had found shelter in the farmhouse when their own house had been badly damaged by a VI in December.

In that early morning hour when all the children and the grandmother were sleeping on one side of the large house and the parents and grandfather were on the other side of their home, the VI came down. With explosive force it destroyed that side of the house where the children were sleeping. It killed all eight children instantly as well as the grandmother. After finding his dead little girls, the farmer's son searched through the rubble for hours looking for his four-year-old son while calling his name before he found him. The boy had been his only son and was the apple of his father's eye. A few days later Gina, Chiel and I attended the funeral. All eight children were laid to rest in a mass grave with the grandmother's grave nearby. That night I cried for them and for the continued destruction of lives in this senseless, seemly never-ending war.

The Battle of the Bulge raged on. The fight was bitter and the losses enormous. The snow in the Ardennes turned red with the blood of American and German soldiers. The Germans had first penetrated quite a way back into Belgium, but then the tide turned and the American forces under General Patton stopped the German offensive. The German troops slowly withdrew back to the German borders.

The news, which sporadically trickled in from above the rivers of northern Holland, was bad. Sometimes during that winter we heard about young people who had escaped from the north through the maze of waterways and danger to the liberated area of Holland and freedom. They would tell of the desperate need for food and the suffering of the people in the bitter cold without heat. In that time my thoughts went not only to our family in Amsterdam and Haarlem, but also I wondered about Mies and her family—of how they were doing and were surviving the bitter cold. And I thought of Hetty—was she still walking in streets that were forbidden to her, or had she vanished into one or another concentration camp and no one would ever hear or see of her again.

To escape from the bad news around me I started to read a lot of books. During that time I always was looking in our library for novels in which stories were set in far away warm and happy places, stories of love and romance. But I also loved to read the novels of Pearl Buck and Jules Verne. Sitting beside the little black stove I forgot for a few hours the war and my longing for Jozef.

By mid-January Jozef was able to come to Breda. Only to say goodbye again after a few hours, when a jeep came to pick him up. The wind was biting cold, and a light snow started to fall when the jeep went around the corner of our street—and he was gone again.

Toward the end of January 1945, The Battle of the Bulge was over. The German Armies were defeated. The carnage left 76,890 American soldiers dead, wounded or missing in that terrible bloodshed. In later years Jozef and I visited this area in the Ardennes and the beautiful large war memorial at Bastogne. This war monument is a high open structure in the form of a star. In the middle of the star is the tomb of an unknown soldier. Around the tomb are high columns with all the names of the battalions which had fought there. As I stood on the flat roof of the large star and looked over the beautiful Ardennes where it was so peaceful, it was hard to believe that there once was a terrible battleground where so many men were killed, many of them so very young. On the side of the hill where the war memorial is located is a very pretty chapel for all religions. Also located there is the world's largest war museum.

◆     ◆     ◆

It was toward the end of January when one evening there was a knock on the front door. When I opened it, there was Jozef. Happily I fell into his arms. While he kissed me, he said cheerfully that his battalion was going to stay in the village of Den Hout which is located close to Breda, and maybe they would be staying there for a few weeks. "With this snow and cold," he said, "I don't think the Generals are going to pursue the Germans any further for now. Probably they will wait until spring comes around and things warm up and dry out."

To everyone's surprise the Polish battalions came back to our city again and settled in the villages northeast of Breda. For the following few weeks Jozef forgot his worries, and we spend a lot of time together. Many times we went dancing or went to the movies and, when the weather was not too bad, we went for long walks in our peaceful forest Mastbos. Jozef came to know Breda as his own town. As his Dutch improved he told me about his boyhood, his parents, sisters and brothers. He had not seen them in years—not since he had left his family and hometown as a nineteen year old, going to the east of Poland. I knew that he was lonesome sometimes for a time past, a time before this all had started with the war. I learned that he had left his youth and innocence behind on the battleground with Russia in 1939 and in the Russian prison camp. Little by little I learned about the roughest times of his life. Some of it took years for him to tell me.

A few days later after Jozef's battalion had moved to the small town of Den Hout, he walked through the front door with a grin on his face. Hanging over his arm he had a dark blue pinstripe suit and a white shirt. I must have looked at him with puzzled eyes, because he started to laugh and said to me, "Put your red dress on Efka (his pet name for me). We are going out tonight."I knew that he didn't enjoy being a soldier and being part of the war machine. But he was a soldier and to wear a civilian suit during times of war was, as I knew, against army regulations. Before I could say anything he went to Henk's bedroom, changed into the suit, borrowed a neck tie from my brother and came downstairs into the living room. When I saw Jozef, I almost did not recognize him. He looked great! I had seen him only in uniform. My father, who was listening to his favorite opera music on the radio, looked at him and with a blank face said, "Civilian garb—the war is over?" While Mother straightened Jozef's tie, she told him how handsome he looked in his suit. But she was concerned that if he wore the suit in public and there was any kind of difficulties, he could get into trouble if they found out he was a soldier. But Jozef shrugged off the idea of any problem.

Soon we were on our way to downtown to have a good time—Jozef handsome in his dark suit and me in the red dress. First we went to the piano bar for a drink, and then we went to the hotel on the edge of Mastbos, our favorite dance place. As Jozef ordered our drinks, the waiter who had served us before a few times, looked at Jozef with a strange expression on his face and said carefully, "I know you—you are a soldier." Jozef looked him in the eyes and sternly answered him, "Not anymore I am!" The waiter turned around without a word and came back a little later with our sour drinks while the man at the piano loudly played Boogie-woogie. We had a great time that night and it reminded Jozef about other times, other places back in Poland before the war.

The following weeks were pleasant; it was a time for laughing for Jozef and me. Many times he came over our house, usually for a few hours, but on Sundays he would stay the whole day. When he arrived on those Sunday mornings, he almost always went straight to Henk's bedroom and changed his uniform for the pinstriped suit. When he came down the stairs, he always would say how happy he was to be out of his uniform and to be a civilian again. Chiel and Stefan had not continued their friendship after he came back from Den Bosch. Since it was crowded everywhere on Sundays that winter with Polish, Canadians and English soldiers, we went for long walks and stayed away from the crowded places. We loved to take long hikes in the snow through the forest under the gray winter sky. The peace and serenity that the forest brings, especially in winter, was wonderful, and we walked for hours. But sometimes as the winter wind was howling outside which enhanced the coziness inside our living room, we stayed home and played cards while listening to music on the radio.

After the bitter battle in the Ardennes the fronts remained relatively quiet for a few months. Only the Russian forces moved slowly further west toward Germany. There was a constant assault on Berlin and other large cities, harbors and the war factories by the Allied bombers which came over almost continuously.

March 1945 came with strong winds that smelled of coming rains. The snow and ice had left Europe, and the American and Allied Generals were ready for a massive assault on Germany. It was about the second week in March when the weather finally turned calm. One day a soft wind was rustling the brown dry bushes in our front yard where I was standing, talking to Chiel. A little later just as she was leaving to go home, I saw Jozef with his always quick step, coming around the corner of our street. As soon as he reached us he took my hand, and while looking at me with his usual loving expression in his eyes, he asked me to come for a walk with him. Suddenly I knew what he had to tell me. I had been waiting for this moment for the last week. I knew that the armies were ready to go further with this war, and that Jozef had to leave.

We walked the narrow farm road which ran behind our house, passed the gaping ruin of the half-crumbled large farmhouse until we came to a small park where we sat down on a bench. We talked some but not much. Finally turning to me he said gently that he would like to say so many things. He loved me, he said, but it was no use to talk about it. "Tomorrow I have to leave," he continued. "I have to go further with my battalion and division into Germany and finish those Nazis." We both had known that this day would come but had never talked about it. Later when we kissed goodbye to each other, we knew without saying it, that it was not sure if we ever would see each other again.

It was two days later when the whole Polish Division began to roll over the roads of southern Holland, going east toward Germany. It was in the afternoon of that same day when I went to Chiel and asked her if she wanted to go with me to the highway which connected Breda with the town of Tilburg. I knew it was this road that the Polish troops were going to take, going eastward. Since I had not seen Jozef anymore, I thought that maybe I would see him there on the road, on top of his tank or in one or another armored vehicle. Perhaps I would have a chance to say goodbye again and wish him good luck.

As soon as Chiel and I reached the highway to Tilburg, we saw an endless column of military vehicles and tanks slowly driving past us with their engines roaring. Sometimes they stopped for a few minutes and then went further again.

Large troop transport trucks—full of soldiers—passed behind armored cars or other military vehicles. It brought memories back to me when in 1940 I saw such a military column for the first time. Then it had been the German Army's highly trained elite regiments which had passed us on the road between Breda and Antwerp while we walked home from the farm. But now almost five years later, people were standing on the side of the roads and waving goodbye and good luck to the men who had liberated us from those Germans, our enemy.

When Chiel and I stood there on the side of the road together with many other people who were watching the convoy passing by, we saw Waldek. In his white overall he sat on top of his tank waving at us while he passed. Not much later as the endless column slowed down again and almost came to a halt, I saw Jozef standing on top of his tank. At the same moment as I saw him, he saw me and jumped from his tank. Quickly he came to us and gave Chiel and me a hug. Holding me for a moment he whispered in my ear, "Efka take care. I shall be back." He then turned around and jumped on his slow-moving tank while his buddies grinned and waved at us. A short time later they were out of sight, going further in the long convoy. Chiel and I waited some more but we did not see Stefan. Probably he was sitting in one or another troop transport truck.

I remember as clear as yesterday how I once more looked over the unbelievable, powerful and mighty sight of that endless slow-moving convoy which was creeping eastward like a dangerous snake. And I looked at the thousands of men passing in the dust and the roar of engines—men who the war had brought so close together that they were willing to risk death for one another. Standing there in the setting sun, I could almost imagine what it must be like when those mighty forces came together in battle. Chiel must have felt the same as I did, because silently we walked home each with our own thoughts which somehow we could not express. When we reached Chiel's home we said goodbye, while I walked further. As I went through our street I thought about Jozef, and I knew he would be living from one moment to the next until the end of the war.

It was not only the Polish battalions which moved eastward over the highways, but also the English and American troops and the Canadian infantry had left our area. One day Chiel and I walked to her aunt's house. Her aunt was not feeling well, and Chiel's mother had made something for her to eat and had asked Chiel to take it to her. While walking on a main street to her aunt's home, which was on the other side of town, we saw four large military trucks. They were the largest trucks we had ever seen. They were empty except for the soldiers who drove them. The trucks drove past us and then stopped. When we passed the parked trucks, two drivers jumped from their very high seats just in front of us. They were Canadian soldiers. One of the soldiers asked us something in Dutch and, surprised to hear our language from a Canadian, we stopped to answer them. As it turned out, one soldier was from Dutch parents who had emigrated from Holland to Canada before the war. Soon they took pictures from their pockets and showed us photos of their family and their girlfriends back home. I think they were homesick and tired of their dusty life on the roads. Ever since they left Normandy, they told us, they had been driving all day and night, sometimes in long slow moving columns. They couldn't wait until the war was over and could go home to family and a normal life again. A little later as they climbed back on the high seats of their transport trucks again, we wished them well and good luck. With roaring engines the enormous vehicles left the side of the road and disappeared from our sight. When Chiel and I walked on, we hoped that they would make it back to their beloved Canada, their families and girlfriends.

It was about in the beginning of April when after a ring at the door I ran to opened it and there stood my cousin Ken from South Africa in his British uniform. After some hugs and kisses, especially from Mother, we sat down and talked over a cup of surrogate coffee. Ken told us all about how he had been drafted into the Army in South Africa and had gone by troop transport ship to England in 1942. After the invasion of Normandy he had come with the African Corps to France and from there to Belgium and further to southwest Holland. He was stationed on the island of Walcheren. He told us that there was not much more for them to do except cleaning the beaches from the dead navy men, pilots who were shot down, and soldiers who had been on troop transports and drowned when their ship was torpedoed and had sunk. He told us further that sometimes many cases of powdered milk and egg whites washed ashore from sunken ships. While slapping his bulging belly, he said laughing that almost everyday he and his buddies made pancakes from the powdery stuff.

Ken then told us about life in Africa, and how he couldn't wait to return to the warm climate of South Africa. Of course Mother wanted to know everything about his mother—her sister. She told Ken that not since 1940 had there been mail or any other communication with Africa. All those years Mother had been left to wonder about her sister and her family. Before Ken left again for his island on the North Sea, he told us sadly about my other cousin, Tante Nel's son, who also had lived in South Africa. He had gone by troop transport from Cape Town to England, but the ship never arrived. The ship with a thousand men aboard was presumed torpedoed by German warships and sank. Neither ship nor men were ever heard of again. Tante Nel would not know about her son until later when the war was over.

In the following weeks Ken came over to our house a few times more. He always brought some powdered milk and egg whites for Mother, which she greatly appreciated. Occasionally Ken and I saw a movie together and afterwards we had a drink and talked for the longest time about Africa. When the war in Europe was over, he went back to his warm place in the sun in South Africa. There he married his love who had been waiting for him all those years. Ken never returned to Europe again.

◆    ◆    ◆

The American and Allied troops, which had fought hard for the river Ryn, were now advancing across Germany itself. After Jozef had left with his battalion, we wrote each other frequently. The letters were short, of course, since it was difficult to read each other's writing, but somehow we managed to understand what each of us was writing about. As long I received letters from him, I knew that he was all right and tried not to worry. It was about in the second week in April when his letters stopped coming, and I was afraid that something had happened to him. Maybe he had no chance to write, I told myself, maybe he is tired or too busy with the war in Germany. On our little radio we heard from out of England that, at some places, the fighting was bitter and hard against the enemy soldiers in Germany. The Nazi commanders had told their soldiers not to surrender but to stand and fight until the very end. We also learned about the chaos in Germany and the destroyed cities and hungry children without home or family who lived in the ruins. Also for the first time we heard about the concentration camps which the American and Allied soldiers came across and where they found unbelievably horrible situations.

While the war raged on, but with the end in sight, Wim had come home. It was on an afternoon and the ceaseless April rains had finally stopped. There was a knock on the front door and when I opened it there stood Wim on the doorsteps. Surprised and happy to see him I invited him in. I noticed how very thin he had become. After greeting Mother we sat down, and soon Wim told us about the last year after he was abducted that day in March of '44. He and his friends were taken from the ice cream shop at gunpoint by German soldiers and pushed into trucks. Later they were shipped by train to West Germany and had to work in one of the many war factories in the Ruhr region. There they worked hard and lived in poor conditions with little to eat. Many times the factories and the areas around them were bombed by Allied planes. Then, a few weeks earlier, they came to know that the American Army had crossed the Rhine and was moving toward their area. Then one night, just before the American soldiers came, he and one of his friends escaped during a bomb attack. Later, somehow and with great luck, they found themselves behind the American lines. The American soldiers gave them food and drink. Then after days of walking, and sometimes riding a bicycle they stole, they came to Holland where they were helped further to Breda. Wim didn't know anything about what had happened to the other guys from our former group. He felt bad that so many of the men, who had been abducted by the Nazis and had to work in the war factories, were killed. They would never taste the freedom which was finally coming.

The following day Wim came over our house again and asked me if I wanted to go for a walk with him. We walked through the Wilhelmina Park, where we had walked so many times before, and sat down on a bench. We talked and talked until the sun was setting in the West. When he brought me home I knew I still cared for him. But Wim had changed. I think both our worlds had been changed in that short but turbulent last year, and the Wim I remembered was not there anymore. I knew that what I felt for Jozef was so different than I had ever felt before. Sometimes Wim still came over to our house for a talk. Later he and his new band played here and there in our town and Jozef and I would occasionally go to hear them play.

◆    ◆    ◆

May of 1945 came with pleasant weather with crocuses and pussy willows in bloom. It was the first fine days of spring. Even though big clouds are almost always present in Holland's sky, the sun was peeking more than usual from behind a cloud. As we were sitting around the breakfast table that morning, Father said to us that he had some good news. The evening before he had listened to his static-filled radio to the latest news from out of London. He said that it seemed that we could expect a truce between America, the British and the Germans in the next few days. We knew that the Allied troops were steadily pushing further into Germany, and that they were fighting street by street in the city of Berlin. But finally a truce—the end of the war, was still difficult to grasp. Then on May 6 we heard that the Germans had capitulated, and a formal surrender would follow. Soon people gathered on the streets. People cheered and shouted, others burst into tears and some said prayers. We all hugged each other. The end of the war! Finally it was over.

Then on May 8, 1945 a formal surrender took place at Reimz, Germany and the horrors of the Second World War in Europe was over. The Nazi reign of terror had finally come to an end. Later we learned how Adolf Hitler and his new bride had died, and their bodies were burned by his Nazi friends in Berlin. Also more and more we heard about the tortures, killings and extermination of millions of Jews and non-Jews in the concentration camps. We heard also of the now chaotic situations in Germany itself. Millions of tired, hungry uprooted people were now forced to wander homeless—looking for lost family members torn apart by the storm of World War Two.

While the liberated countries in Europe were celebrating the end of the war and while our cities were ablaze with lights and people were dancing in the streets, the war in the far East against Japan raged on. The American troops fought hard on the islands in the Pacific and suffered great losses as they slowly recaptured the islands back from the Japanese invaders.

# 28

# *THE ATOM BOMB AND THE END OF WORLD WAR II*

*The end of May 1945.* After a short visit to his family and girlfriend, Jan had gone back to Den Bosch. Before he left, he told us that he would be back for a few days before leaving with the Dutch Command Stoottroepen Corps (shock-troops) for England. From there they were going to the Dutch East Indies to help bring normalcy back into the islands as soon as the war with Japan was over. Indonesia, (the 'Dutch East Indies' as the islands were known before their independence in 1949) had been a colony of Holland for 350 years.

Two weeks later Jan came home on a three-day pass before leaving for overseas to England. When he left that morning, he said not to worry, and that he would be back in no time. I still see him walking through the front yard with his duffel bag over his shoulder and headgear in his hand. His short light blond hair looked almost white in the sunshine. After an emotional goodbye from our family, Jan left. Mother had gone into the kitchen and acted busy cleaning the kitchen counter as I walked in a few minutes later. She hid her face from me, but I knew she was crying. I went over to her and put her head on my shoulder and tried to comfort her, telling her that Jan would be back before she knew it. Together we wept. After all the difficulties she had gone through in the last years, I thought, now her son is leaving for a far away war in the jungles of a strange land.

A few weeks later we received a letter from Jan in which he wrote that he was not going to the Dutch-East Indies yet. They were leaving for Australia and would stay there for some time, how long he didn't know.

During the first days after Germany's surrender and the following end of the war in Europe, people had wildly danced in the streets. Then about a week later the celebrations in our city became more organized, but not less enthusiastic. Each neighborhood now had its own party and the people danced and sang for many night in the streets. Breda was bursting with happiness and joy. The dark war years were over! Music played and our red, white and blue flags waved from the houses and other buildings. Everyone was wearing orange (the color of our Royal House). The entire population of our town seemed to be dancing in the streets—celebrating.

My brother Henk and his friends were gone every evening and thoroughly enjoyed this party mood in the blazing lights. Chiel and I had gone out and together with other friends from our neighborhood danced and sang in the streets. But with all the joy and fun we had those days, there was something missing inside of me. Many times I caught myself thinking about Jozef—where he was—or if he was all right, or if he was coming back. Instead of truly enjoying myself in those early days of freedom and the end of war, I felt lonesome sometime, and missed the man I loved.

It was early afternoon when Chiel came to our home and asked me if I wanted to go with her to her aunt's house. Her mother had made something for her sister again, something which resembled a casserole, Chiel said jokingly. While we were walking steadily on, Chiel told me that they had not yet heard anything from Paul, her oldest brother who was abducted in late 1943, and was sent to one or another labor camp in Germany. Chiel said her mother often looked out of the window every day in the hope of seeing her son return home. They knew from a letter he wrote to his family that he had been working close to Berlin. That was far away from Breda, especially now with no trains, cars or any other transportation left in the whole of Germany. I carefully said to Chiel, "Now that many people who had been in concentration and labor camps are free and want, one way or another, to get back to their homes and families, it might take weeks before Paul could be coming home." Sadly, I wondered if Paul would ever be coming home. When we had delivered the greatly appreciated casserole to Chiel's aunt and talked for awhile with her while drinking the surrogate tea, we left.

Since the weather was delightful, we decided to make a stop at the Wilhelmina Park. After the long cold winter, wild ducks and swans had come again to our ponds. As we looked at the many beautiful birds, I said to Chiel, "I hope no one eats them this year!" In the last years of the war the birds in the ponds and rivers had been a good meal on some hungry people's table. Chiel answered me pessimistically that she thought there would be no swans or ducks left anymore in the ponds before the end of summer, the same as it had been in the last few years. "But who knows, Eef," she said, "maybe next year everyone will have food enough again and leave the birds alone."

It was already evening when we reached Chiel's house where we made a date for the following day to go downtown. As I came a little later to our home and opened the front door, I thought I heard Jozef's voice. It came from the living room and it sounded like he was talking with my parents. I stood still and my heart suddenly went into overdrive. I was not sure yet if it was Jozef's voice I had heard. Then unexpectedly the living room door opened and there he was—my love. He had come home. In an instant we were in each other arms. He said to me, that he had been too exhausted to write in the last weeks before the end of the war. At times it seemed as if the war would never end. How long we stood there in the hall I don't know. I remember only that Father thought that it would be a good idea for us to come into the living room. I know that my parents had mixed feelings about Jozef. He was courteous and caring enough, Father had once said, but he was not a Dutch man.

The following three days Jozef stayed in our home, and Henk shared his bedroom with him for the nights. Jozef had changed his uniform for his suit again. He always said, "It makes me feel good." The days which followed were magic for us, and life seemed exciting. We took long walks in our forest where buds had sprouted new leaves. We enjoyed walking over the thick springy soft layers of old leaves and brown needles while a warm spring sun was shining through the branches of the tall pine trees. Jozef told me funny soldier stories, but also serious and painful ones. Although he skimmed over parts of those stories, I could sense the pain beneath it. He could not bring himself to talk about the last weeks of the war. It had to wait for much later, I thought, that is if he ever could talk about it.

It was on the last day of his leave when he told me that he had written letters to his family and their friends. He hoped so much that he would hear something from his parents, sisters or brothers. In case he didn't hear anything from his family, he hoped that maybe one of their friends would write back to him. Even if it was only from one person who could write him something about his family. He said further how he wished the war had not stopped at Berlin, but that the Allied troops had advanced into Poland, and then had pushed the Russians out of his country and back to their own borders again. I answered him that Father had said the same thing—that it was wrong that the Russians were staying in the Eastern European countries. No good would come from this situation. "The way I see it at this moment," Jozef said sadly, "is that I will not go back to my country and family." When I answered him that maybe the situation with Russia would change in the near future, he said, "I don't think so. Our commanders are urging us not to make plans to go back to Poland, but that the government in England would help us." I felt bad as he explained to me what it meant for him and the other Polish men not to go back to their country—to have fought a war for other countries to be free, but now they were left without a country of their own.

Jozef and I spent the evenings in downtown where it was crowded with celebrating people. We danced in the streets, and I think we never did so much swinging as then. But too soon our time together came to an end. That morning when Jozef came to the breakfast table in his uniform he said that he had to get used to the idea that the war was over. "For so many years I was a soldier," he said. "It was an existence which spanned too many years of my life." As the military truck came to take him back to his battalion in Germany, he said to me, "I will be back as soon as I possibly can." I still cannot believe that a few days later he was back again.

It must have been after midnight and I had just fallen asleep when something woke me up. While listening carefully I heard a tick from a small object hitting my repaired bedroom window. Wondering what it could be, I got out of my bed and looked through my window. At first I didn't see anything but when I looked closely, I saw Jozef standing in the dark front yard looking up at my bedroom window. Through the half-opened window and with my voice down so not to wake my parents, I told him that I would open the front door for him. I grabbed my robe and went downstairs as quickly and as quietly as possible. In the meanwhile I wondered what brought Jozef back to Breda again so soon. And in the middle of the night! As soon as the front door was opened, Jozef walked in and whispered that he didn't want to wake the family so late at night. He had found some small stones to throw against my window to waken me. There we stood in the dark hallway, me in my robe, bare feet, my hair in a mess and he in his soldier's uniform which smelled of gasoline and truck dust. It was then that Jozef said that he had come back to ask me to be his wife.

The following day after we told my parents about our plans of us getting married, there were long discussions. They were not thrilled with the idea of me getting married to a Polish soldier. They didn't know much about him nor about the family he came from. Finally after long talks, it was decided that we would wait with our marriage until Jozef got his demobilization papers and knew what he was going to do because he probably was not going back to his country. Since the war had just ended, my parents felt it was better to wait until everything had settled down. We agreed and said that it had not been our plan to get married straight away.

The next day Jozef went back again to his company. Since there was at this time no truck from his company going in the direction of North Germany, he had to hitchhike. After Jozef had left that morning, my parents talked to me again. They wanted to know if I was sure that I wanted to marry a soldier from another country. They were worried and said to me that I knew so little about him or of his family. Yes, he was always considerate of me and seemed to be a good man, but for me to marry him, that was a different story. Their dreams for me, their only daughter, had been different and had not included a stranger from a faraway country. They had hoped that I would marry a respectable Dutch boy from a good family. I answered my parents that the only thing I knew was that we loved each other, and that I knew that he came from a good family in Poland, and that Jozef was a caring and good person with ambitions and drive to succeed in life. "And the rest," I said to my parents, "will work itself out. You will see, trust us!"

◆     ◆     ◆

Life in Breda was very slowly trying to come back to normal that spring. It was a time of great joy, but for many people there was also a tearless grief of which some parts would remain forever. Father worked again in his kazerne and was busy with the new weapons which came in from America and England. Also his chess club had opened up again for its members now that life was settling down. It made Father happy and every Thursday night and Saturday morning he played his favorite game at his chess club.

Mother's headaches were still there, but now new and better medicines were coming which gave her relief from most of her pain. Even though the war had been terrible, it somehow had accelerated the progress of new wonderful medicine, which had brought healing and new life to many people who were sick from serious infections and diseases.

Mother missed Jan terribly, but regained her zest for life. She enjoyed telling me about the old days when she was a young girl, and we both would laugh about her stories. I think she regretted the passing of the old days, the days when she was young and life was much different. Mother cooked less potatoes now since we got more and better bread. Henk who was still in school remained very thin, but there was more color back in his face now that he got more food.

Even though the food situation remained scarce and monotonous, it was better than it had been. It would take years before many things were on the store shelves again The materials for repairing or building new houses also came in very slowly. It was going to take twenty years and longer before the house shortage problem was solved. The Dutch public transportation (which is government owned) was in that time very poor due to little or no repair materials available. Busses and other vehicles had been taken away throughout the last years by German military, and there was little left for our own country. There was also no material for the repair of the many bridges, trains and railroads which had been blown up during the war. So many countries were plundered empty or destroyed by the Nazis and the war.

Our little short-wave radio which had served us so well throughout the war years and always had given us new hope, and sometimes tears too, was now put away. We again had our own Dutch radio station from out of Hilversum. After the formal surrender of Germany the whole of Holland had finally become free from war, anguish and Nazi brutality. In the winter of 1944-45 more than 20,000 people died from hunger, cold and disease in northern Holland. My parents had been very worried about their families there and had been anxiously waiting to hear from them. Finally in the beginning of June the first letters arrived from the north with news that they all were happy that the war was over. Even though they had become very thin, they had made it. They wrote that almost every day for the last weeks before the end of the war, English planes had dropped hundreds of food packages for the starving masses. Now that food and medicine were pouring into the cities and towns by the truckloads, hunger would soon be a thing of the past.

This good news took a load off from my parent's minds, especially from my mother who always had been close to her family. She was ready to go north and see her and Father's families. But there was no way yet to get into the north of Holland. This had to wait until later. At the same time we received letters from my parents' family, I received a letter from Mies. She wrote that her family also had gone through a bad time. Her father had become seriously ill, but hopefully with better food and medicine he would be back to health again. Mies and her family also had wondered about us, how we had come through the terrible winter. They knew we had been liberated but they had never heard from us again since all communications were out after our liberation in October 1944.

It was about in the beginning of June of 1945 that Jozef came to Breda on a three day leave. He told me that the whole Polish Division had moved more to the south in Germany and had settled in and around the small town of Frerren in West Germany. It was not far from the Dutch border and about 175 miles from Breda. He was staying with Frank Bartkowski, an Army buddy, at a large farm house just outside of Frerren. Jozef told me about the people of the farm and how there seemingly was not one healthy man left in Germany anymore. All the work was done by women and children.

Jozef had brought from Germany very pretty new white damask table linens and materials for summer dresses for me. It was something I was very happy with, especially the dress materials. I must have looked puzzled at him, wondering where all that stuff came from, because he explained saying that it was a crazy situation all over Germany. He then told me about the many Germans, mostly women, many with children, who came to the places where the soldiers were staying. Some of them were begging for food; others carried suitcases with them full of all kinds of goods which they wanted to trade for food or cigarettes. They then in turn took the cigarettes to the farms to trade for food. Jozef told me that he had traded his one-week ration of cigarettes for the things he had brought and would do some more trading when he had cigarettes again.

During the months that followed, Jozef came home with many nice things, as silverware, materials and more. No one knew, or cared to know, from where the German traders were getting all that nice stuff which they carried with them. Jozef said one day that everything probably came from the bombed out houses in the larger cities, where the owners of all that stuff were killed or had left. Or maybe, he said, maybe it came from one of the many Jewish families who had lived in Germany and were now gone. In the war, especially toward the end, nothing mattered much to whom it belonged. All those goods meant nothing to the hungry people—all they wanted was food.

Jozef was always glad to be in Breda again, even if it was only for a few days. It is so depressing there in Germany, he told me a few times. Besides all the suffering people in Germany without shelters and food, and the masses who wanted to go back home to their own countries, now also many of their own soldiers had become depressed. They had too much time on their hands now. They were not only thinking about the last difficult months and about their buddies who had lost their lives, but also they asked themselves—what now! This was a question which was on many men's minds. No one had a clear idea yet as to what they might do next when the time of demobilization came. I said to him that I was happy that he was again back in Breda, even if it was just for a few days, and that we should make it as wonderful as we possibly could. "This way," I said cheerfully, "you can think about something pleasant when you are back in Germany." He put his arm around me and started to sing—" You are my sunshine, my only sunshine." It was a song popular in that time which Jozef loved to sing.

That evening we went out with Stefan and his new girlfriend Truus, and Vincent with his girlfriend Toos. Vincent was a young Polish soldier who loved to play his guitar. I think his guitar was more important to him than the whole war where in he had been forced to serve. Occasionally when we all came together in the home of Toos, Vicent played on his guitar while he sang the melodies of their country, with Jozef and Stefan joining him.

One evening I said to Jozef that I wanted to plan an engagement party for us and asked him if he could get a pass for the last weekend in June. "It is going to be just a small party with family and friends," I said to him, "and maybe a few of your friends would enjoy coming too, that is if they could get a pass." Jozef answered that he would try. It was the custom in Holland to give an engagement party when a couple planned to get married, even though it sometimes took years before they had their wedding.

◆ ◆ ◆

A few weeks after the war had ended, the first boys of our former group came home from working in the munition factories in Germany. They arrived tired, thin and hungry in our home town, but thankful that they had made it back to their families. One day Beb's boyfriend Ken also had come home. He was exhausted and in ill health when he arrived in Breda. He had walked for many days, living only on little food which he stole here and there. But in the loving arms of Beb and his mother and with food to eat, he soon was stronger again. In June Chiel's brother Paul finally came home. One day a military car stopped in front of Chiel's house, and to everyone's relief and happiness Paul stepped from the vehicle. He was thin and weak and was walking with a limp, but he was alive and home. Later he told his family about the trying times and constant bombings in Germany. Paul had been wounded during a bombardment, but fortunately it had not been serious enough that he lost his leg. But it still took at least a year before Paul's leg was healed again.

When Jozef came home for our engagement party, he brought food and drinks with him for the special occasion. He told me that in Germany he had exchanged cigarettes for these things and he still had some cigarettes left. Since there were no drinks available yet in Holland, they sure were welcome. Of course the food which he brought was greatly appreciated by Mother and me. We all had become so used to little or nothing to eat at a party, that something like a drink and a snack was just great.

Our engagement party was on a Sunday afternoon in our garden. The weather was beautiful and a warm spring sun was shining high in a blue sky. I had sent out engagement cards, and I think all my friends and neighbors came. Also Stefan with Truus and Jozef's friend Alfred came and, of course, my own family. Later in the day Henk's friends came by and wished us the best of everything. We received many bouquets of flowers and had to borrow vases from our neighbors to put them all in. It is the custom in Holland to bring flowers to a party whatever the occasion. Of course, in that time just after the war when we got engaged and later when we got married, there was not much of anything in the stores that people could buy for a gift. But even now to this day, no one goes to an occasion empty-handed. A present is not always given, but flowers are always brought. The flowers in Holland are plentiful and not expensive.

Later when everyone had left our party, Jozef and I took a walk around the block. The sun was setting as we walked and Jozef said to me that he was very happy, and that it had been a long time since he had felt this way. "To think, Efka," he had said gently, "to think I came all this way to Holland to find you." He kissed me and said, "I have to tell you something else that makes me happy, but at the same time sad. I received a letter from my mother in which she wrote that she and my brothers and sisters are doing as well as could be expected under the circumstances. My father died in 1942—from what or how my mother did not write. She wrote very little more about my father in her letter," Jozef continued, "only that everyone was happy and thankful that I was alive and well. They never had given up hope."

Jozef told me further that his mother would write again as soon as she received a letter back from him. "I have to be careful what I am writing," he said, "because the letters are censored. Just before I left for Breda I wrote another letter to my mother telling her about you, the girl I love and want to marry. Hopefully," Jozef said, "it will not take too long before I hear something again from her. I have so many questions, Efka," he said while putting his arm around my shoulder, "so many things I need and want to know after all those years." I answered him that I could understand that after such a long time he longed to know what had happen to his family and especially to his father. I felt bad for Jozef that he was so close, yet so far away from his family. He had served other countries, but now that the war was over he could not go back to his own country. How unfair and cruel, I thought, while we walked back home through our neighborhood. The following morning we said good-bye again as he left to go back to Germany and his company.

It was about in that same time, that I received a letter from Hetty Hamel. Hetty, the Jewish girl who had refused to hide behind closed doors and in dark places—the girl who had walked in forbidden streets. She had felt the wind through her hair and the sun and rain in her face. She had survived the four years of Nazi occupation and brutality. Hetty had written a long letter about the endless cold winter and how she and her aunt had held on to each other. She also wrote about the day when the war had ended, and how she and her father had found each other a few days later. Later she and her father learned that her mother had been caught in a street raid in the late 1943 and was transported to a concentration camp. No one had seen or heard from her again. Hetty knew her mother would never return home. But now, Hetty wrote, she was looking toward the future and hoped that she would find the peace in her heart she was looking for. "As soon as things are better again, Eef," she wrote, "we have to come together again." It was a wish I promised myself to keep.

It was about the middle of July and I had just returned from a swim with Beb. We had gone to our city swimming pool. It was not the greatest place but it had a nice white sandy beach for just lying around. Beb and I had not seen much of each other lately, not much since Ken had returned home from his ordeal in Germany. He was doing much better but still was weak and not himself yet, she told me. Beb and I had a lot to catch up on, and the afternoon had gone fast.

I had just walked into the house when Jozef arrived from Germany. His battalion troop transport truck had stopped on the main road to Breda to let soldiers off. From there Jozef always took a shortcut over small winding farm roads which brought him close to our house. We had not seen each other since our engagement party, and I had missed him. Jozef was quiet during the evening meal and had not said much. After Mother and I cleared the table and washed the dishes, he came to the kitchen where I was folding the tablecloth and said, "Efka, I want to talk to you. Let's go for a walk." It was a warm summer evening and we walked to the Wilhelmina Park where the sweet smell of many flowering bushes filled the air.

As we reached the pond, Jozef looked at me and finally said, "Efka, our whole division is soon going to withdraw from Germany and will be sent back to England. When that is exactly, we don't know yet. But I know one thing—if we are going to England, I want you to go with me." He then continued, "What do you think of us getting married as soon as possible?" Now the whole idea of a wedding and going to England as Jozef's wife was very exciting to me. I answered him that there was not anything I wanted more! He then started to explain that in case his division went to England before we were able to get married, he would come back for me on a later date.

Not much later we walked back home and talked the situation over with my parents. They were not very happy with the idea of us getting married so soon and moving so far away. They tried to talk us out of this unexpected decision of a wedding. Finally Mother suggested that we should talk this matter over with the minister who had baptized me two years earlier. I knew I was not a devoted church member, but I always wanted to get married in a church before God and my family. Even though Jozef was Catholic, he was all right with the idea of us getting married in our small Baptist Church. The next day we walked together to the home of the minister, but soon found out that he was retired from the ministry and did not live in Breda anymore. We were told that the new minister would be happy to marry us and that we should come inside. The new minister was a very pleasant and understanding middle-aged woman. After talking with her for awhile about our situation, Jozef explained that since his division was leaving for England permanently, that it would make things a lot easier if we could get married as soon as possible. Looking at us she answered calmly, "Why don't we set the wedding for next month, August 30."

◆        ◆        ◆

In the meantime under heavy losses, the American soldiers had fought hard on the islands in the Pacific. They had achieved great victories in the Philippines, the Island Reyte and in Burma. But the Japanese generals would not think of surrendering and the bloody war dragged on. To finally end this bloodshed, American President Truman had no other choice but to use the newly invented atomic bomb. It was August 6, 1945 when over our radio we heard that an atom bomb had been dropped on Hiroshima, a city in Japan. It was another black day in the history of mankind. A few days later another atom bomb destroyed the city of Nagasaki. As the result of the destruction of the two Japanese cities more than 125,000 people were killed, and many more people had severe burns and other injuries. Those people close to the blasts had been instantly incinerated. It was on August 14 that a special announcement was made on the radio that Japan had surrendered. World War II was over. The most terrible years in the history of mankind had ended.

While America celebrated the end of World War Two Europe tried, under great difficulties, to get back to normal. Russia had settled in Eastern Europe after the Yalta Conference where America, England and Russia decided the future of Eastern Europe. Russia never left Poland. They established Communism and took away Democratic freedom not only from Poland, but also from the other countries which were occupied by Russia.

Also in August we got a letter from Jan out of Australia in which he wrote that he was going to leave for the Dutch-Indies. After the surrender of Japan and the end of WW II, the people of the Dutch-East Indies saw their chance to free themselves from the colonization from Holland, and they started their fight for freedom. Of course the Dutch government wanted to hold on to their rich colonies with their many plantations of rubber, coffee, tea, spices and oil and they sent troops in from Holland. Jan went from Australia first to Java, Dutch-Indies, and from there moved around to different islands. A year later he was transferred to the island of Sumatra. There Jan worked for the Dutch Command Administration until April 1948. Holland gave their colony back to the people of the Dutch East Indies in 1949, who gave it the new name of Indonesia.

# 29

# *THE WEDDING*

Although WW II had ended and there was still chaos everywhere, life went on. Our wedding date had been set for August 30, and we began to make plans for that day. After a few days of soaking rain the clouds finally left and a pale sun tried to come through. Mother and I had cleared the breakfast table when I asked her if she wanted to go with me to shop for a wedding dress. For the last weeks I had looked everywhere to find one, but I think they must have sold the last wedding dress in Holland two years earlier. I always had dreamed of making my own wedding gown, but nowhere was a inch of white dress material to be found. In the last year many brides had been married in their best dress or in a suit. But other girls like me wanted to marry in the traditional way—in a white wedding gown. I also had always dreamed that my wedding dress would be something like a fluffy white cloud, something very pretty, something beautiful in organza and handmade lace.

A few days earlier I heard about a place in town which rented wedding dresses. So that morning Mother and I went to that place where they not only rented but also sold used clothing. We had never heard of a store like this before, and soon found out that it was something new in our town. When I told the sales lady what I came for, she showed me a few wedding dresses which were hanging in a separate place in the store. She had three gowns in my size. All three were made of white rayon in a very simple design. Each gown was somewhat different. I tried them on and it took me no longer than five minutes to decide which one I wanted. The dress I chose had a short train. The veil came with it. It was not the fluffy cloud of the wedding dress of my dreams, but it was a white gown, and I felt happy that I had found one. Now the shoes. That was another thing. I had no white shoes and there were no shoes to be bought. But that was soon solved by Chiel who had a pair of high-heeled white summer shoes. They were a little scuffed but we took care of that with some white paint which I found in our

352

shed. The size was okay, maybe a little cramped—but, I told myself, I would be too excited to notice.

Since Jozef didn't want to get married in his uniform, I explained to him that he had to get married in a tuxedo because I was wearing a wedding gown. He was not too happy with the idea of wearing a "monkey suit," as he called it. After he thought about it for awhile we went the following day together to the tuxedo rental place to rent a tux for him and for Father. The high-top hat came with it.

Some of the family from up north wrote that if possible they would come for our wedding. The train transportation had improved somewhat but was still very difficult. Also the food situation was still poor, and Mother and I hoped that our baker and farmer could help us out. Our baker had said cheerfully, "Our liberators deserve the very best!"and promised us that he was going to see to it that we would have pastries on the table and also some extra bread. The wedding cakes as we know today were not known yet in Holland. For weddings specially made small pastries were always served. To serve our wedding guests a meal, Mother had been saving some of the food coupons for the last few weeks before our wedding. Our farmer had promised he would give us something extra, such as cheese.

It was a few days before the wedding when a jeep stopped in front of our home. To our surprise Filex, an army buddy of Jozef, jumped out and delivered, all wrapped in paper sacks, about half of a calf. I think Mother almost fainted! We had not seen so much meat in years! How I remember Mother standing there in the kitchen with her hands clasped together. While shaking her head she said, "What a blessing, what a blessing! We have enough meat to feed an army!" Another blessing came in the form of a few pounds of butter which another army buddy brought to our home the day before our wedding.

After many hours of traveling in different trains, the family from Amsterdam arrived the day before the wedding. The family from Haarlem could not make it, but hoped that we could come to visit them soon. Also my cousin Eef and her husband Joop from Zeist, a small town close to the city of Utrecht, came that same day. She had brought with her her sister, my cousin Anny. Finally in the late afternoon Jozef arrived at our house. I had waited for him most of the day and hoped it had not been too difficult for him to get a ride to Breda, which sometimes was the case. Or maybe suddenly something came up. When Jozef finally arrived he carried a heavy suitcase with him. He carried it into the kitchen and when Mother tried to lift it, he said laughing to her, "Careful—there is a tank inside." No one could lift it from the floor. And to think he had carried the suitcase at least two miles! To everyone's surprise, the suitcase held many bottles of drinks. Bottles which he had received from his army buddies for our wedding.

Since all the bedrooms in our house were occupied by guests, I was sleeping in a makeshift bed in the attic where my parents also slept that night. My wedding dress was hanging there, since it was the safest place for it. I don't think I slept much that night. The bed was not very comfortable, and I was too excited to relax and fall asleep. I thought about Jozef who was sleeping that night at some friend's house and hoped he would have no trouble with his tux. I must have finally fallen asleep for when I woke up it was early in the morning.

Everyone was still sleeping. As I was looking through the small ceiling window of the attic, I thought how this day was the day I was going to be married. It was going to be a great day, I was going to be Jozef's wife. I slipped out of the make-shift bed, wrapped my robe around me and went downstairs as quietly as I could. After opening the kitchen door, I went to the backyard. It is a beautiful day for a wedding, I thought happily looking at the early sun in a cloudless sky. I hoped it would stay this wonderful the whole day. While sitting down on one of the fold-ing chairs which Father had borrowed from his chess club for the party, I looked at the dance floor which Henk had been working on for the last week. How nice of my brother, I thought, wondering from where he got the flooring. I had been too busy to ask about it and to thank him for making it.

A little later I went behind our yard which overlooked the meadows and where I loved to pick the little field flowers and listened to the wind rustling the cotton-wood trees. I thought about the many times when I sat there in the tall grass while staring at the dramatic clouds drifting by in the huge sky. During the last few years of the war the future had looked so bleak. There had been no future anymore to dream about. Only hope had been left. But with the return of our freedom, I and all the young people could dream again about a future. Even though Jozef's future was still unclear as to where he was going, I knew in my heart that everything was going to be all right. Somewhere in this world he would start a new life for himself and me. Where and when this would be was only for God to know. Today, I said to myself, today is only the beginning.

As I walked slowly back to the house, I saw Mother already busy in her kitchen. She was taking the good dishes with the little gray and pink flowers out of the cabinet. While waiting for everyone to come for breakfast, she poured her-self and me a cup of tea. As we sipped the hot surrogate drink, Mother and I had a heart-to-heart talk. I was the first of her children to get married and, in spite of her smile, I knew it was not easy for her. Later after breakfast the hairdresser came to arrange my hair in loose curls which she set with a hot iron. She then fastened the veil on my hair and arranged flowers on top of it.

It was close to 10:00 when the guests, all dressed up, were waiting for the groom to arrive in the wedding carriage. I waited in my parent's bedroom with my best friends Chiel and Beb, who were putting the last finishing touches on me. By the time I was ready we heard the gallop of horses coming down the street and stopping in front of our house. Quickly my friends left the room and a few moments later I heard Jozef's quick steps coming up the stairs. He opened the bedroom door and there he stood, all smiling and handsome in his tuxedo. He held in his hand a bride's bouquet of white carnations all tied up with long white ribbons. My bridal bouquet was a wedding gift from my Oom Nick, my mother's brother, who had worked most of his working life in a nursery. He not only made the white carnation bouquet but also the boutonniere for Jozef and for the other members of the wedding party.

Together Jozef and I had a wonderful romantic ride in the white fairy tale carriage. The carriage was pulled by two white horses with white plumes on their heads and driven by two coachmen in ornate costumes. Behind us came four black carriages each pulled by a black horse. They were for the family and closest friends. First we went to the City Hall, which was a fifteen-minute ride from our house. There in the high ceiling room we were greeted by a primly dressed clerk with a large mustache which I remember well. After the official signing of our names in the Book of Marriages witnessed by family and friends, we drove to the small lovely old church where the minister was waiting for us. With her velvety voice she started, "Dearly Beloved, we are gathered here…." As Mother later told us the minister gave a very nice sermon, but I could not remember much of it. Tante Dien said to me that, since the sun had been shining through the stained glass windows of the church, this was a sign of blessings for us. The wedding ceremony was followed by the sitting at the photographer.

In the meanwhile family members and friends went in their carriages to our house for coffee and pastries. Later, after the taking of the photos and a wonderful ride in our fairy tale carriage, we arrived home. There was a toast to the bridal couple. While Jozef whispered something in my ear, there was another toast. The dinner was made mainly with Felix's calf meat, vegetable, potatoes and a lot of gravy, and there was white bread for everyone. It seemed like a banquet. Later when Jozef's army buddies arrived from Germany, the music started to play. After Jozef and I danced the first dance, everyone started to dance on Henk's dance floor in the back yard. When it began to get dark, Vincent played on his guitar and everybody was singing and drinking the drinks Jozef had brought with him. When later that night the rain started to come down, the party was moved indoors. It was early morning when Jozef took my hand and said, "It is time to change our clothing, and disappear."

With our suitcase and food stamps we went by train to the small vacation town of Valkenburg in the province Limburg. The train with its windows still out was terribly crowded. There were not too many trains running yet. Because the bridges were still out, we had to transfer to another train many times. It took us many hours before we reached our destination. Very tired but happy, we finally were alone for three whole weeks, just us, in a small hotel in the hills of South Limburg.

Our three weeks were wonderful. We laughed and sang and took long walks through the hills and forest of South Limburg. We carved our names on the wall of a well from a medieval castle named Valkenburg. A long time ago it was a large and beautiful castle with a rich, and sometime tragic, history. Although much of the castle is in ruins, it still is most interesting. We danced away the evenings in a nice nightclub or walked in the moonlight. Too soon the undisturbed first few weeks of our marriage came to an end, and the day came when we had to go home again. Jozef could stay one more week in Breda before he had to leave to go back to Germany. As he left wearing his uniform he had put his arms around me and said, "I'll see you soon, Efka, as soon as I can." He took his green bag and left. He had to hitchhike back to Germany.

Jozef and Eef on their honeymoon in Valkenburg, 1945.

After Jozef left, the days that followed were endless, and I missed him terribly. There had been no word received yet of the Polish Division leaving for England. My parents thought we should have our own private room in the house for when Jozef came over, which I fully agreed with. Everywhere the housing problem was bad. It was especially bad for the young couples who wanted to get married. There was not a house, apartment or room to be found for sale or rent. Most young couples had a room in their parent's house or a room with family or friends. The room was then made into a living room with a folding bed. Furniture was also hard to come by. But there was always someone who had things they didn't need or use anymore, and which they sold for a reasonable price.

Since work was the answer to many things, I started to transfer one of the upstairs bedrooms into a living room-bedroom for Jozef and me. It kept my mind from wandering to Jozef in Germany. It was great to have our own room, even though the room was not large and there was not much furniture in. But it was our own room, our own place. So when Jozef came home on his next three-day pass, he was happily surprised. "Our own private territory!" he said. While hugging me, he said that it was a cheerful place, and that I made it even more difficult for him to leave me.

I got a notice in the mail from the school of gymnastics. I was happy to read that the gym had opened its classes again for the fall and winter of 1945-46. Immediately I enrolled for two nights a week and, if I could use my bike again, then it would be just great. Anyway I didn't have to walk through the dark streets anymore or pass the German Officer's building when the nights were pitch dark.

At the same time as the notice of the gymnastics came, I also received a letter from Mies. She wrote that she got engaged to Jeff Uitendaal. Jeff was a student in the town of Deventer in a college for the management of plantations in the Dutch-East Indie. About two years earlier Mies wrote me about him. In the last year of the war Jeff had gone into hiding from the Nazi workforce. "Eef," she wrote me, "I want you to meet Jeff. Why don't you try to come down and see us. You and I have so much to talk about." Mies had been unable to come to my wedding. Her father had died. Even with the coming of new medicine he had not recovered from his illness. It had been too late for him. He died from an intestinal disease.

It was about a week later when one morning a jeep stopped in front of our house, and to our surprise Waldek Wieck jumped out. We had not seen or heard from him since he had left with the troops going into Germany. He had been promoted to First Lieutenant and was stationed a little more north in Germany than Jozef was. He told Mother and me how he had gone in disguise into Poland as soon as the war had ended and had smuggled his wife and son out of his Russian occupied country. He had brought them back to Germany, and they were now living with him. He hoped that they would soon go to England and start a new life there with his family.

Mother and I had a pleasant talk with Waldek, and we were happy that so far everything had worked out for him. He said that he was sorry that Father was not home; he would have loved to talk with him. As Waldek was ready to leave, I asked him when he was going back to Germany. He answered me that he would leave in about an hour, first he had to take care of something in Breda. I then asked him if he could give me a ride to Deventer. I explained that Deventer was the town where my girlfriend Mies lived and that it would not be far from the road he had to travel on to his company in Germany. Waldek looked at me and said that it was O.K. with him, but that there were two fellow officers traveling with him in their jeep. When Waldek left with the promise that he would return in about one hour to pick me up, I started to pack my bag with only the most necessary things I would need for one week. Since Jozef had been in Breda recently, I knew he would be not returning home in the following one to two weeks. A hour later I said goodbye to Mother, who was not too happy with this little adventure of mine, and I left.

In the jeep together with Waldek and the two other officers, we drove to Deventer over the busy highways crowded with military vehicles. The open noisy jeep was not the best place for a conversation, and most of the time we drove in silence while passing heavy loaded, slowly moving trucks which came from Antwerp, headed for Germany. We passed busy towns and went through small villages until we reached the area where the "Operation Market Garden" was fought. Soon I noticed that all the bridges were out, blown up either by bombs or destroyed by battle. Slowly we drove over the long or smaller pontoon bridges, which the Corps of Engineers had laid a few months earlier. The destroyed bridges were half submerged in the fast running water. As we were driving slowly over a long pontoon bridge, I thought about that Sunday morning a year earlier when I was sitting with Chiel in the grass looking up at the airplanes and gliders which came over. I thought about the many soldiers who had been killed that day, while coming down hanging on their parachutes. They were now lying in Dutch soil, far away from their homes and country.

After about a five-hour drive we reached the town of Deventer. It was evening and we had to look for the right street which we finally found after asking a policeman. We stopped in front of Mies' house where I said goodbye to the two officers. I thanked Waldek for the ride and wished him good luck for whatever the future would hold for him and his family. "Who knows," I said to him, "maybe we will see each other again someday in England." But we never met or saw Waldek again. Later Jozef heard that he had gone into communist Poland a few more times and had smuggled the wives and a few children of fellow officers into Germany.

When the jeep had pulled up in front of the house and I stepped from the vehicle, Mies came running from her home followed by her sister Greeta and her mother. Of course, they were greatly surprised to see me, especially in a jeep. They wanted to know who those officers were that I had come with, and where they were going. It was so good to see Mies and her family again after all those difficult times. They were mourning the loss of husband and father. A large portrait of him was hanging beside the one of their first child and the small violin. That week Mies and I talked for hours on end. We shared her bedroom and talked half the nights away about the men in our lives, my wedding and about our hopes and dreams. And, of course, we talked and laughed about the times when she was living in Breda, our bicycle trips and the places where we had so many happy hours together.

I met Jeff a few days later. He was a pleasant guy, tall and blond and a few years older than Mies was. He hoped to graduate from his college in the summer of 1946. They wanted to get married before leaving for the Dutch East Indies, which he said would probably be the end of the summer or in the fall. When I asked him if he was not concerned about the Dutch East Indies campaign for independence and the fighting there, he answered me that they were not fighting on every island. He was only interested in plantations he said, especially in the management of coffee, tea and rubber plantations, which were greatly in need of new people. So many plantations on the islands were neglected or destroyed during, and also after, the war with Japan.

It was the day before I was planning to go home when I said to Mies that I needed train tickets for my trip to Breda for the following day. We went to the station, but soon found out that there were no trains going in the direction of Breda or any other town in that area. They told us that all railroad bridges were out in the area of Arnhem, and that the trains could not go further than that city. Here I was—what now. Of course, maybe I could have gotten a train going northwest and then come over another way into Breda. But that was a lot of riding around, especially with the few trains which were in operation. When we told Mies's mother about it later, she said that an acquaintance of her late husband, a military man, went at least twice a week with his car to Nymegen, which is past Arnhem and the rivers. "Maybe," she said, "you could get a ride from him and from Nymegen you could hitchhike to Breda." She said she would talk to him. In that time after the war with many bridges out and transportation poor, hitchhiking was a normal thing to do by everyone.

After a great week with Mies and promising each other to write soon, I left one morning in the car with the Dutch officer for the city of Nymegen where he dropped me off on the highway leading to Breda. He wished me good luck and hoped I soon would get a ride. "Well," I said to myself, "I don't think that this sport is difficult to do, just put your thumb up and hopefully a car will stop." I found myself staying in an area of the highway where quite a few people were waiting, trying to get a ride. Soon I noticed that there were more people waiting than there were cars coming by, and not all cars stopped either. Looking the situation over for a while I thought, "Eef, you will never get out of here with all those people. Why not try to walk a mile or so further to an area where no other people are waiting for a ride and see what happens." Picking up my bag I started to walk in the direction of Den Bosch which was the next town. I noticed that there were not too many civilian cars on the road—only many military.

After walking for awhile the sound of a car came from behind me. I put my hand up, and to my surprise the car slowed down, stopped and the door opened. It was a young man who said that he was going to the town of Tilburg and did I need a ride to that city. Too bad that it was not Breda, I thought, but anyway it was in the right direction. The young man talked a thousand miles a minute about his work and his boss whom he didn't like. Most of the time I didn't know what he was talking about, but then—I didn't care. I was glad that it had not taken me too long to hitch a ride. When we reached Tilburg, he dropped me off on the highway to Breda.

But this time I had a much harder time to get a ride—maybe it was because it was already later in the afternoon. Some cars stopped for me but weren't going to Breda, or they went just a few miles further. After awhile I started to get worried that I couldn't get out of there before dark. I don't know why I didn't take the train from Tilburg to Breda, I don't remember. As I walked slowly further I heard an old jalopy of a car coming. It stopped and a friendly old man in farmer's clothing asked me of he could give me a ride, and where I was going. I told him I was going to Breda. He answered me that he could give me a ride close to that city, but that was as far as he could bring me. Well, I didn't mind as long as I came to Breda before dark, the rest of the way I could walk. The friendly old man didn't talk much, which I was thankful for.

About five miles before Breda he stopped and let me off. He waved a friendly goodbye and drove his vehicle into a narrow farm road where he soon was out of sight. I still could hear the sound of his engine as I was left alone in the now dark early October night. I knew that I was still quite a way from home and had far to walk. Then thinking about Father—how he would tell me, "Pick up your feet and start walking; that is what they are for"—I picked up my bag and started the long way home. About one-and-a-half hours later I finally reached my house. This was my first and last hitchhiking experience.

# 30

## *A GERMAN VILLAGE*

It was late spring of 1946. With the relentless spring rains gone and the warm days of summer almost here, I dreamed about a vacation for Jozef and me. He was entitled to a change of air, I thought, and maybe he would have a long leave coming and we could go somewhere. For the last months life had gone by quietly, but it had not gone in the direction we had hoped for. Those days when Jozef came home, had always flown by. They were our happy times together which were always too short. After a few wonderful days we had to say goodbye again. All other days seemed the same as the days before when he was gone. I filled the days with some sewing and art painting and going marketing. No one had a clear idea yet of what the government in England would decide to do with the stranded Polish soldiers and their officers in Germany. Instead of going to England, they were now used for occupation troops. For how long this would be, no one knew.

It was a day in June when Jozef came home for a few days. He had brought some more dress material with him from Germany and also a red and blue striped swimsuit with which I was very happy. While holding the swimsuit up against me, I looked in the mirror and said to Jozef, "Wouldn't it be great to go on a vacation together and wear this pretty bathing suit on a beach somewhere." Then I asked him if there was a possibility that we could take a trip before the summer was over. He put his arms around me and said that it was a great idea because he had a ten-day pass coming soon. For the rest of that day we talked about the trip we were planning and where we would go. Finally we decided on Amsterdam since Jozef never had been there. "Amsterdam is a great city," I said to him, "and we could stay at Grandmother's house." From there we could visit grandmother Breeuwer in Haarlem and stay with her and Tante Nel for a few days. And maybe, if the weather was nice and warm, we could go to the beach.

It was a day in August as we left Breda on our ten day trip up north. Jozef wore his uniform, "Because it would be better," he told me, "in case of difficulties." His soldier's bag was full of cans of lunch meats such as ham, corned beef and bacon which he had carried with him from Germany for the family. There was still a great shortage of meat in Holland, besides many other things.

When we arrived at our train station that early morning, it was already crowded with people young and old. The train transportation was not much better than it had been a year before, but finally at last, new windows were installed again in the damaged trains. Also the bus transportation to other cities and towns was still sporadic. As the slow moving train finally arrived and came to a stop, we saw to our dismay that the cars were packed with people. I think many of them were probably on vacation or on a visit to family for the first time since the war had ended. Jozef and I looked in every car for a place to sit or stand, but no such luck—every car was full. Then, at the last moment, we found a place in a freight wagon where we sat ourselves down on the wooden floor between people, luggage and large crates. It was a very uncomfortable and long train ride, and we were happy when the train finally arrived at the Central Station in Amsterdam. While carrying our suitcase and the bag with cans, we found our way to the tram terminal which was located in front of the Central Station. After first looking for the right tram, we were on our way to Grandmother and Tante Dien's house, where we arrived in the late afternoon. They both had been waiting for our arrival and were happy to see us. Because it was the first time Jozef was in their home, Grandmother had to show him all the portraits which were hanging on the walls. The portraits of the family members, which were staring at us, were of the late 1800s and early 1900s. They still were in their original dark frames.

Our plans were to stay in Amsterdam with Grandmother for five days. The first thing we did the next morning was to visit my cousin Coby and the rest of the family. As soon as we arrived at their home, which was above their store, uncle Mart had to show Jozef his electric and lampshade business. He told Jozef, now that new merchandise was coming in slowly and people wanted to buy something new for in their homes, his business was improving again. That same day I showed Jozef the "Jordan," which is the old inner city of Amsterdam. It has many canals, bridges and tall stately houses which line the canals. Jozef enjoyed it and thought it very picturesque. One day we went to Amsterdam's Ryks Museum and saw the works of the world's greatest painters, such as Rembrandt, van Meer, van Gogh etc. And of course we saw the many other treasures which are located there. We also visited Amsterdam's famous diamond cutting center which was very interesting.

One day while we were going back to Grandmother's house, we walked through one of Amsterdam's busy shopping streets. As I was looking in the window of a small boutique, I saw some gorgeous coats hanging. To see such coats was still a rarity in that time. There were only a few hanging on a rack, all of the same style and color. Looking at the beautiful brown coats, I said to Jozef that I just had to look at those coats from up close—just feeling the materials—not buying. The coats probably were imported from America or maybe England. It was not much later as we walked out of the boutique and, believe it or not, I was wearing one of the lovely brown coats. I am sure it was way too warm to wear a winter coat that day in August but, for a little while anyway, I just had to show the world my new beautiful brown treasure.

The fish stalls in Amsterdam where opened up again. As we walked past one of the stalls I said to Jozef, "Try one of the herrings!" I explained to him that they were called 'zoute haring.' It was raw fish prepared in brine. At first he didn't want to try one and said, "Raw fish—not for me!" But after he saw me eating one, he had to try one for himself—and liked it. Since then he enjoys eating them, especially with some raw onions on top. On the last day of our visit we went to Volendam on a slow train which stopped at all the small villages. In the quaint fishing village of Volendam we ate smoked paling (eel) in a typical seafood restaurant, which overlooked the Zuider Zee and fishing boats. Jozef had never eaten Holland's favorite paling before, but soon took a liking to the very expensive smoked sea creatures. He was amazed at the many kinds of 'strange' fish (as he would call them) we eat in Holland which they still sell everywhere.

As we walked further, we enjoyed the peaceful existence of the fishing village where the small houses, tidy and shiny, are built one against the other. In the time of our visit the natives still wore their colorful costumes and had their own customs and style. On a small island, which we reached by ferry, we visited the picturesque fishing village of Marken where we bought some souvenirs in one of the quaint small stores. We also took some pictures together with some of the native children in their costumes. The young boys and girls were dressed almost identically and had the same haircuts. How darling they were.

After five great days in and around Amsterdam, the day had come when we had to say goodbye to the family and had to promise to come back soon. Before we left for Haarlem, Coby suggested that we take the bus instead of the crowded train. Some of the busses were running again between Amsterdam and Haarlem. Of course this was a great improvement. Also an improvement came in the form of a real cup of coffee, which was served in the cafeteria of Amsterdam's bus terminal. It was my first real cup of coffee in years.

It was so good to see Grandmother Breewer and Tante Nel again. It was the first time they met Jozef and after I introduced him to Grandmother and Tante Nel, Grandmother looked him over and told Jozef to sit beside her. She said that she wanted to know all about his family in Poland. While Tante Nel was serving tea, Jozef told Grandmother, as well as he could make himself understandable to her, about his childhood and his family. He skipped over his most difficult times, and went on telling her how he had met her granddaughter. Since Grandmother's last heart attack a few years earlier, she never went outside her home anymore. Besides the pictures in the newspapers she never had seen a soldier in British uniform. She wanted to know all the emblems on Jozef's uniform, which he patiently explained to her. Finally Tante Nel said that it was time for her medicine and to rest for awhile. A year before Tante Nel had learned, that her only son who had been missing at sea since 1942, was presumed drowned. She believed with her whole heart and soul that one day she would be together again with her son in Heaven, and then they would never part again. Tante Nel told me about Hetty and said that she now lived in Den Haag (The Hague) and worked there in a government building. She gave me Hetty's address so I could write to her. Somehow we had lost contact with each other.

The following morning, as we were looking for a bakery to buy some pastries for the coffee, we passed a jewelry store. In the window were some beautiful gold rings each displayed with a different colored gem. Jozef stopped and while looking at the rings he said, "Efka, I have been looking around for the longest time to give you something special, and I think I found it. I would like you to have a nice ring, something besides the plain gold wedding band." While pointing to a gold ring with a aquamarine stone he said, "What about this one?" Later when we walked out of the store, I wore the gold ring with the aquamarine stone on my finger and have never taken it off after all those years, except twice for a repair job. It became, and still is, my most treasured piece of jewelry.

In the evenings Jozef and I took long walks on the side of the river Spaarne while looking at the sailboats sailing by. It was so very pretty walking there on the shore of the wide Spaarne in that time of not so long ago. Now fifty years later large cargo factories line many of the once beautiful and peaceful shores which then were dotted with windmills.

On our last day in Haarlem we went to the beach of Bloemendaal, where as child I loved to sit on one of the high dunes. I would just sit there for the longest time, looking over the North Sea to the far horizon and dreaming of far away exciting places. It seemed all so long ago. Jozef and I took a long walk on the wide white beautiful beach while looking at sea-going vessels. Later, when we rested between dunes, we talked about our baby we expected in February. We hoped that Jozef would be out of the army by then and maybe could stay in Holland. While we dreamed about that possibility, the seagulls screeched over our heads and dove into the cold water of the North Sea which was rich with fish. Even though the beaches were as beautiful as always, it was so sad to see the wonderful dunes of Holland dotted with concrete bunkers. It was a bitter reminder of WWII. In time those bunkers would slowly disappear under the ever-drifting sand. Some are made into a museum for future generations to see.

Before leaving the beach of Bloemendaal we ate ice cream (which tasted almost as good as before the war) in one of the many outdoor terraces which are so popular in Europe. The weather was nice and sunny that day, but it was not warm, and I never did get to wear my new bathing suit.

That morning before we said goodbye to Grandmother and Tante Nel, Wim Stein came over. He had been in Paris where he sometimes went and lived for months to paint the street scenes of that city. Sometimes he sold his paintings, but other times he came home once again poor—to Tante Nel.

We had decided to take the train back home through Rotterdam instead of Utrecht. This was shorter in mileage but, as we found out, it was much longer in time. Because of many train bridges out, we ended up going from one over-crowded train into another. With all the cans of meat gone, our luggage was now much lighter than when we came. We arrived late in Breda but were lucky to catch the last bus which was leaving for our neighborhood. Early the following morning Jozef had to hitchhike back to Germany again. Our vacation had ended way too quickly.

After ten great days together it was difficult to be separated from each other again. A few weeks later Jozef came home for a few days and said to me, "Efka, I want to ask you something. What do you think of you coming with me to Germany." Not understanding him I said puzzled, "What do you mean?" He answered me, "How would you like to stay with me for awhile in Germany?" He then started to explain that the chaotic situation in Germany had subsided, and it had became calm. His roommate Frank had returned to England. His father, who was an officer and worked in London for the government, had been able to get his son out of Germany. Jozef now lived alone in the room and, as he said, had already worked it out. I said, "I thought that the borders of Germany were still closed to civilians." He answered me not to worry, that he had taken care of everything. The worst that could happen to me was that they would send me back over the border into Holland again. He himself would take the blame.

At first I hesitated. Being pregnant, we first had to think about the baby. I was feeling great, that was no problem, and I had not experienced any difficulties. I also was still slim. Thinking about it some more and how great it would be to go with him to Germany I said to Jozef, "You really mean it, don't you?" He answered me, "Yes I do, Efka. The furnished room at the farm is waiting for us, and the people at the farm are very caring." He then told me about how Major Makuck had given him the needed papers without much difficulties. Jozef explained that since civilians cannot yet enter Germany, he had a military woman's uniform in his bag for me to wear in case I decided to go. While giving me the outfit he said, "I hope it will fit you, Efka." As I was looking at the uniform with the Polish emblem and I thought about it some more, I finally said to him that I would go, but not for too long. Maybe for a few weeks. The woman's uniform belonged to the girlfriend of one of Jozef's army friends. She was in the Polish military. When I tried on her uniform it fit me exactly. He then showed me the identification papers which belonged to the owner of the uniform and also the train pass with the signature of Major Makuch. Jozef then explained how we would travel.

I had very little time to pack my stuff. Not that I needed much to take along with me I reasoned, because I would not be gone for a long period of time. Of course my parents didn't think it was a good idea for me to go into Germany. But Jozef told them not to worry, that he would take good care of me. I said to them that I would be just fine and would write as soon as I had arrived at the farm in Germany.

Two days later Jozef and I left by train to the city of Utrecht where the military express train, which traveled between Hoek van Holland and Berlin, stopped to let military on or off. This express was strictly used for military and mainly for those who were on furlough going to or from England by ship. I had left home in my regular clothing—we thought it would be better. As soon as we arrived at the large train terminal in Utrecht, I went to one of the nice restrooms with my military bag and changed into the uniform. I then checked my papers, which Jozef had put in the pocket of the jacket, once more. As I put the beret on my curly hair, I looked in a mirror and said to myself, "Eef, you sure are getting yourself into something which is called an adventure." A little later when I came out of the restroom and walked to Jozef who was waiting, I felt strange with my military uniform on and the black beret on my head. Jozef looked at me and laughed. He then said, "How great you look in a uniform. I think I never have seen a prettier woman soldier before now."

After some searching we found the large platform where the express was to arrive. It looked deserted since no civilians were allowed on that section of the train station. We saw no one. It looked strange and unreal to us after all those years of crowded train stations. I still see myself in the uniform, standing with Jozef on that large deserted platform, waiting for a express train which was going to Berlin into a devastated and closed country. After some waiting the express rolled into the station and soon came to a stop. A few military men got on; no one got off. Before we left Breda Jozef had told me that as soon as the express stopped at the train terminal in Utrecht, I had to enter that section of the train which was only for officers and women military. He himself had to go to the soldier's section of the train. He had also explained to me where everyone had to get off the train, which was a small train station just over the border in Germany. I had to stay there by the train and he would find me, he said.

As I entered the train, with Jozef going into another section, I saw that beside a few military women, the express compartment (car) was full of American and British officers. While walking further I looked around for an empty seat. A few minutes later as the train was moving slowly out of the station, I finally found the empty place I was looking for. As I walked to the seat, I suddenly saw that the two officers, who were in an amicable conversation and were sitting on the opposite side of the empty seat, were Polish. Oh no, I thought, that is not what I need, Polish officers who maybe want to strike up a conversation with a "Polish girl"—me! I could not speak more than twenty words of Polish! The only thing to do was to look for another place, maybe in another compartment, maybe with some American or English women, so I didn't have to make conversation. I walked past the open seat and the Polish officers and had no luck in finding another empty place. As I walked further, I came to a sliding glass door which let me into the following compartment of the express. As soon I entered I discovered that I had come into the restroom area. Besides the restrooms it had a nice open area with large windows—but no seats. Looking it over I thought that it would be a good place for me, for now. I always could look for a seat in the next compartment later. Until then I would make myself comfortable standing in front of one of the large windows. I was determined to be careful.

It was not much later when two young women in uniform entered the restroom area where I was staying with my military bag. I soon noticed that they were Dutch. They settled themselves in front of the other window. One of the girls who probably had seen the Polish emblem on the sleeve of my uniform said in Dutch to the other, "She is Polish, I am sure she can't understand us." While I looked out of the window, I smiled and thought, "How wrong you are, girl!" A little later a young British lieutenant walked in. He looked nervous and started to smoke a cigarette.

The express sped through the Dutch landscape with its golden fields of grain and passed villages where people, working in small yards, looked up to see the train speed by. Looking at the flatness of the land under the gray sky, I thought how I always had dreamed about an adventure, and here it was. It was the first time that I was in a railroad express and was amazed at the high speed it traveled. Not only the ride was smooth and comfortable, but it had also roomy compartments with many seats and sliding glass doors which connected one car with the other. It would made only a few stops and on its way to Berlin.

After looking out of the window for awhile, I walked to the other side of the restroom area and peeked through a glass door into the next compartment for a place to sit. But as far as I could see, every seat was taken. I walked back and passed the two girls who were in a deep conversation. Having nothing better to do, I said to myself, "Since those girls think I can't understand Dutch, I am going to stay a little closer, and overhear what they are talking about." I soon found out that they were going to Berlin to a place inside that ruined city which seemed difficult for them to get into. I couldn't understand what kind of place they were talking about. The only thing I could understand was that one of them had a boyfriend there, and they had only three days time to find him before they had to return to their base. How little they knew I could overhear their conversation. I really got a kick out of it, and it made the time pass faster for me.

As the fast-moving express sped to the German border, two Dutch custom officers came into the car to check everyone's papers. It took them a while before they got to that section of the train where I stood with the two Dutch girls and the young officer. While first looking us over, the C.O.'s asked for our papers in English. My heart began to thump in my chest, and I hoped they would not hear it. As I handed my papers to one of them, he said something in German to me, but I acted as though I couldn't understand what he was saying. He looked at me and then looked again at the papers. It seemed forever before he handed the papers back to me and walked further to the next compartment. I gave a sigh of relief.

By now I had stood in front of the window for one and a half hours, while looking over the landscape and sometimes listening to the Dutch girls conversation. The young officer smoked one cigarette after another. Occasionally some military women or officers came in and used one of the bathrooms. Finally the train slowed down, and I knew we had reached the Dutch-German border line. Not much later the express stopped at the small station where everyone had to get off, as I remembered Jozef telling me about. I picked up my bag and followed the two Dutch girls out of the train with the young lieutenant following me. When I got off the train, the first thing I noticed was the many military police at the small railroad station. It was one of the few places of entry into Germany by train, and everyone had to be checked and show their papers again. It was also the place were many of the military men and women went by car, truck or jeep further into Germany. Others continued on with the express with the end destination of Berlin.

When I stepped down from the train, I saw in front of me some officers, male and female, talking to each other. Looking at the small group I thought it would be safer if I acted as if I belonged to the group, while waiting for Jozef to find me. As soon as I was standing close to the group of officers, I saw Jozef coming toward me. For a few moments we looked at each other in silence. He then took my arm and before I knew what happened he led me quickly to the other side of the train. We went across the railroad tracks and further on to a narrow road where a jeep with two soldiers, who I recognized, were ready to take off. Everything happened so fast that I don't remember much about it. As soon as we were seated in the jeep, it sped away.

After driving a hour or more through mostly farmland and small towns, we reached a village by the name of Frerren. And as Jozef told me, it was the place where his company was located. Soon the jeep stopped in front of a large farm house—the farm where I was going to stay with Jozef. After a short talk to his buddies, who then left, he took me to his large furnished room. It had big windows overlooking the farm fields. On the window sills were many pots of flowering mums in different shades of fall colors. I think they were placed there by the women of the house as a welcome to me which I thought was very nice. A few days before when Jozef had left for Breda, he had told the farm family that maybe he would bring his wife with him from Holland.

Later, after Jozef brought our bags into our room and I had changed into a dress, he introduced me to the farm family. The oldest of the farm women who lived there had the appearance of a worn stocky woman of about 45 years old. She looked me over without a smile on her round German face. Her name was Anna. She was not the friendliest person and never would be in the entire time I was there. The war had probably taken a heavy toll on her. Her younger sister Ingrid was a tall, thin and pleasant woman and very helpful in the weeks I was there. When I needed something, I always would ask her. I could speak the German language just enough to make myself understandable but not enough for a conversation. I don't know if the two sisters were single, had been married and their husbands killed in battle or were missing in Russia as so many were.

After the introduction the youngest sister and Jozef showed me around the farm. First we went to their large living room where a massive oak table with a vase of flowers and family pictures stood on a thick red carpet. On one wall there was an open fireplace with a painting of a landscape above the mantel. On the other side of the room was an old grandfather's clock and a cabinet which held china behind stained glass doors. A large sofa stood on each side of the fireplace, while other chairs were scattered around the room. It was a very impressive place which never was used during the entire time I was there. It probably had been used in better times—in a time past. From the living room we came to the large kitchen where all the cooking and baking was done. A long table stood in the middle with wooden benches around it. It was there where everyone gathered after the evening meal. I did not see the bedrooms which were located in the back of the house. From the kitchen we stepped into the barn which was connected to the house and where about eight cows stood on dry clean hay. Ingrid asked me jokingly if I could milk a cow. I said to her that I never had tried. She then told me I could ask for milk whenever I wanted.

A little later as we walked toward the orchard I saw many apple trees, their branches heavy with red and golden apples, ready to be picked. It was there that I met Anna and Ingrid's brothers. All three men (I don't remember their names) were crippled by war and, as I later learned, could hardly do any work. The oldest brother had both his legs amputated in Russia after the entire German Sixth Army was captured at Stalingrad in the beginning of 1943. Both his legs had been frozen. In the time I was there in Frerren, I saw him mostly sitting in front of the farm house, always hoping someone would pass by and talk to him. The second brother was in Rommel's Afrika Korps in 1943. After the surrender in Africa he came home sick and weak. He suffered from malaria. He looked pale and very thin and never talked much. The youngest of the three brothers, no older than maybe 22 years, was paralyzed on one side of his body. At the beginning of 1944 he was wounded during a battle in Italy. Most of the time he sat in the kitchen, and I did not see much of him during my stay.

Later as Jozef and I walked back to our room, I asked him if there were any children living at the farm or perhaps working. He explained to me that on every farm in Germany those people who were physically able worked on the land. This would mainly be boys and girls over the age of eight, old men and the younger ones who had been crippled during the war. They harvested and helped with digging the potatoes and, when able, they plowed the fields. He said that he never had seen children at the farm house. Soon after he came to live at the farm he noticed all the work was done by the two women. They milked the cows and took care of the cooking, washing, baking and cleaning, besides the care of their brothers. "As far as I have seen," Jozef said, "the only help they had was from old men and children during spring planting and summer until after harvesting." It didn't take me long to find out how hard Anna and Ingrid worked. Every morning at 5:00 I heard them already working around the house. I think all the women and children in Germany worked very hard in those years. Besides the women's work, they also had to do the work of the men.

A few days after I arrived, I began exploring Frerren. It was a small town nestled on two sides by tall green forests. The countryside of Germany was not changed much by war with exception of those areas where the battles were fought and, of course, the cities. The small town of Frerren had a shopping street with cobblestones of all sizes. It had some stores which sold mostly necessities, such as groceries. Since I had no German food coupons, I did not go in. The town square with a statue of one or another famous general in the middle was typical German. On a wall in the square I saw some old faded propaganda posters hanging which had been distributed by the former Nazi Party a few years earlier. One of them said—Germany Wins On All Fronts—and the other poster said—Adolf Hitler Stands For Victory. They must have been from 1942. Many of the small stores around the square were mostly empty or closed up, waiting for better times.

Because Frerren had escaped bombing, it harbored many refugees from bombed out cities. I learned the people of Frerren showed no particular interest in politics that did not directly affect their town. Not all German people had been behind Hitler by any means. The war was over and they had lost. They had heard about concentration camps, but not very much. In this small place the concept of war guilt did not exist much. Food, although not plentiful, was not a serious problem in an area that grew potatoes, grain and some livestock. Coffee, tea, spices, sugar, soap and a few other articles were seldom available. Because of the very little sugar which they got, I noticed that the children, not knowing much of sweets, were always running after the soldiers for chocolate.

Our room at the farm was spacious, comfortable and sunny. On the wall on one side of the room was a large bookcase full of books which I liked to look through. But it held only German novels and other books written in the German language. Our bed was against the wall on the other side of the room. A round table with chairs was in front of the window overlooking the fields. Since I didn't have German food coupons, I didn't cook much even though we had a small space for cooking. As I recall, we ate only breakfast together in our room, sitting in front of the large windows. A few times a week we got eggs, heavy dark German bread and milk from Ingrid. Since I was allowed to eat my suppers at the officer's mess hall, I ate my evening meal there almost every day. But without Jozef, who ate his suppers with the soldiers, it was not much fun. One day I met Major Makuck at the mess hall. Smiling he wished me welcome and hoped I would have a pleasant stay in Frerren. Jozef's friends were nice and always made me feel special. We were never short of company in our room and had plenty of laughter.

Once a week there was a dance night held in a school in Frerren. It was organized by the soldiers for the girls and women from the former concentration camp. Those nights were lots of fun, and we danced almost every dance until midnight closing time to the music of a military band. The many women from that former camp lived now in a village about half a hour drive from Frerren. They were eager to learn the swing steps and jitterbug which had come from America with the troops. We never saw a German girl at those dances; they probably were not allowed to attend. Other times we went with a car to another small town where we saw an American movie with German subtitles. But since I couldn't understand much English and could not read German very well, I soon lost the story line, and it became too boring for me.

Many times we went for long walks into the forest. Or we went on a hunt for mushrooms which grew plentifully under the tall lush trees. From Jozef I learned the different kinds of mushrooms, which ones were edible and which ones were not. I think I never ate so many mushrooms in my life as I did there in Frerren. When we came home after a whole afternoon in the forest, we fried the mushrooms in real butter and ate them on a slice of German bread.

When I had gone to Germany, I took my painting supplies with me. I needed something to do when Jozef had duty at his battalion's post office and I was left alone. Those days, when the weather was nice and sunny, I took my painting things and went to the forest by myself. The forest was only a short distance from the farm, and after finding a pretty area I sat down and painted for hours with only the birds and squirrels for company. I never worried about being alone in the woods by myself; I guess I was used to the quietness of the forest from back home. Before going to his post office Jozef always would tell me when he was going to be home. So I always saw to it that I was back home before he was, as not to worry him.

I must have been in Frerren about eight weeks when Jozef came home from the Headquarters one day and with a broad smile told me that the governments of Holland, Belgium and France had officially announced that the soldiers and officers who had married a woman of those countries, or the soldiers or officers who wanted to work and stay in those countries, could stay permanently there if they wished to do so. Those governments also would help each soldier to find work. Of course, this news made Jozef and me very happy. Finally Jozef was going to leave the service. Finally he would be demobilized out of the army. He had quite enough of this life without a future and was ready for a new beginning. Finally we would always be together, and I couldn't wait to make a home for him and our baby, which we expected in a few months. It was time go home.

That same night some of Jozef's friends came over to our place, and everyone was talking about this new opportunity to start a new life not too far from their homeland Poland. Stefan, Jurek, Vincent and a few other men also wanted to go to Holland to live and work there. Some of them had girlfriends in our country and wanted to get married. Again others wanted to work in Holland and hoped that the situation with Russia would change in the near future, so they could go home to Poland. But others wanted to leave Europe to start a new life somewhere else. I couldn't understand much of their native tongue (Polish) and their sometimes rowdy conversation, but I understood that the decisions they had to make were difficult. Nothing had gone easy for those men in the last years. They were hardened by war, but yet inside of them was a compassionate heart, as I had learned in those few short weeks that I had been there in Germany. I realized how hard it must have been for all those soldiers and their officers who had fought for freedom and now could not return to their homeland. They were deprived of their native land and now had to search for a new home. When they finally left our room that night, I knew that many serious decisions had been made.

But first I had to go back over the border again to Holland. It would be easier this time than when I came into Germany, and I trusted that Jozef would find a way to bring me safely back home to Breda. When the day came for leaving Germany, I said goodbye to Jozef's friends who were not going to Holland. Eventually many of those Polish soldiers and their officers would be scattered throughout the world. Also I said goodbye to some of the Polish women and girls I had met there in Frerren.. Especially I think about the young women who had given Jozef her uniform and papers to borrow. She was a very bright and lovely person and was very helpful when I needed help sometimes. With the Warsaw Uprising in 1944 she had been captured by SS troops while defending her city and sent with many other young women from Warsaw to the concentration camp in West Germany. It would take another few years until finally in 1949 they left for other countries. Some went back to Poland, but most went to America to start a new life—to marry there and raise a family.

The last people I said goodbye to was Anna, Ingrid and their crippled brothers. In spite of everything that the Nazis had done, I couldn't help but feel a sense of pity for them. They had paid a enormous price in this war. Maybe they had hated Hitler and his Nazi party as much as we had. I would remember most of the people of Frerren as friendly, hardworking and drab—a community very much in need of healthy young men. I did not see much of Germany and none of the destroyed cities there. I did see some of the hundreds of thousands of uprooted people without homes in search for a place to live.

Coming back into our room which was now stripped of our personal belongings such as my framed pictures, I combed my hair on top of my head and put on Jozef's black soldier's beret. He then helped me into his military winter coat. It was too large for me, but it had to do. The dark gray military truck was already waiting for us when we came to the Battalion Office. The truck was almost filled with soldiers who were going to Antwerp on a leave. We climbed in the truck and still found a place in the back of the rough vehicle. I don't think anyone paid any attention to us, but I am sure some of them knew they had a stowaway on board. Soon we left the village behind us where I had been for almost two months. The summer had turned to fall, and winter was not far off. We passed the forest where the gold and red leaves I had painted were now gone. We were on our way to the Dutch border.

The soldiers in the truck were talking, laughing or sleeping. I had not spoken a word during the trip. As we reached the border, the truck slowed down and stopped. While Jozef said not to be worried, I tried to hide behind him as much as I could while clutching the coat around me. A few of the M.P.'s came, opened the bottom half of the door and looked into the waiting truck. One of them said, "Just soldiers?" In chorus, the soldiers answered, "Yes!" The back half of the door was closed again and we continued on to the Dutch side of the border where the truck was stopped. This time it was the Dutch border guards who opened the door, looked around and said, "O.K., go!" When the truck drove further I could breathe again. I had left Germany behind me, the land of so much grief and unbelievable suffering. It was many years later when I saw Germany again. By then the cities were rebuilt and the scars of battle had disappeared. The extermination camps where inhuman suffering had taken place had become places of remembering. A new generation had grown up. When the truck drove further, I took my beret off and my hair fell down. All the guys in the truck started to laugh. I was in Holland once more.

The day after we arrived home in Breda, Jozef had to go back to Germany. Since it would take most of the day to hitchhike back to his company, he wanted to leave early in the morning. It had rained that night, and the early morning air was cold but clear. As Jozef was ready to leave with his duffel bag, which had held all our belongings from Germany, he took me in his arms and said, "Efka, this will be the last time I have to leave you. When I come back, I will be a civilian." He then left. I watched him go through our street with his quick step which had become so familiar to me. He then went around the corner and disappeared from my sight. As I went into the house, I thought about all those times he had hitch-hiked the long road between my home and his company in Germany. And how he had gone through many obstacles just to see me for only a few hours. It would be strange, I thought, but wonderful to have him home and have a life with everyday routine and soon a little baby in my arms to take care of. As I went into the house, I hoped it would not be longer than maybe a few weeks or so, and then he would be coming home, a home he had so longed for—for so long.

One day toward the evening I heard footsteps outside coming into our front yard. They stopped at the door. I looked out the window, and there in the twilight stood Jozef, my husband. He had come home—home to stay.

# PART III
# NEW BEGINNINGS
## (Our Story)

THINKING

If you think you are beaten, you are
If you think you dare not, you don't.
If you like to win but you think you can't,
It's almost a cinch you won't.

If you think you'll lose, you're lost,
For out of the world we find
Success begins with a person's will—
It's all in the state of mind.

If you think you're outclassed, you are;
You've got to think to high rise;
You've got to be sure of yourself before
You can ever win a prize.

Life's battles don't always go
To the stronger or faster man;
But soon or late the man who wins,
Is the one who thinks he can.

# 31

# *NEW BEGINNINGS*

*Breda, January 1947.* (**Jozef**) The time was a quarter past five in the morning. The streets were deserted and a cold wind was blowing from the north. The air was clear and frosty. Quickly I walked through the dark streets to the rayon factory the H.K.I. (Hollandse Kunstzyde Industrie) which was about a thirty-five minute walk from home. With my hands plunged into my coat pockets and my lunch bag under my arm, I thought about the last few weeks since I had been demobilized from the Army to remain in Holland. The week after my discharge I got work at the rayon factory where about 2000 people were employed. There I worked in a place where many machines were winding rayon strings on large cones. I had to see to it that the rayon threads were winding smoothly on the cones. If they were not, I had to stop the machine to straighten it out. It was clean but monotonous and dull work. No, it was not the kind of work I had hoped for. But the pay was not bad, and then—I had to start somewhere.

The very first week before I came to the H.K.I. I went to a few bakeries to ask for work, but they all paid wages that were too low. While walking steadily against the strong cold wind, I thought that maybe in the near future I could find something better. Or maybe in this large factory they would have different work that would be more interesting for me. Soon I passed the downtown area where businesses were still closed. Later in the day people would fill the streets looking for new merchandise arrivals.

I thought about my friends in Germany. I missed them. I missed the everyday camaraderie of the men of my platoon. Seven years in the army had been a long time—too long to forget. My life had changed totally again as it did in 1939 in East Poland when the war started. This time I had not only to learn to be a normal law abiding citizen in a country which was not my own, but also I had to learn about where and how things worked and how to act and deal with the Dutch. I also had to face the numerous changes and challenges that came along. It was not an easy time for me. I think the only thing that made me happy in that time was when I was with Efka, my love. Even though we lived in her parent's house, and I didn't have the freedom which I wanted and needed, I was at peace when I came home and Eef was waiting for me in our small, but private, place in the Zeisstraat. But many times I was restless at night. I would be lying in bed with closed eyes and the horrors of the war came suddenly over me. I could hear the whistling sounds of grenades and bombs and the screams of wounded men. Now a new kind of battle had begun for me, a battle to forget the horrors which I had seen. But it never really would leave me the rest of my life.

As I reached the factory and walked through the gate, I greeted two Polish ex-soldiers who also were working there. Both were farmer's sons from villages in East Poland. They were of a different culture, and it was difficult for me to have a conversation with them. Neither of the men were married, and I think they were hoping that the Russian threats would go away so they could return to their villages and their families. When I reached the area where the cone machines were located, I was greeted by my co-workers. They were all friendly and helpful to me. They had been wondering how I came to speak their Dutch language so well while the other Polish men who worked at the factory had difficulties. But even though I did my best to adjust to the men around me, it was not easy. I had never worked in a factory before.

Even though I did not want to make my living as a factory worker longer than necessary, the H.K.I. was a good company to work for. They did a lot for their workers. I remember how once every month there was an evening at the 'Concordia' for the workers and their spouses. The Concordia was a very nice theater in Breda where all the musicals, plays, operas and operettas were performed. Eef and I saw many great performances there in that time and seldom missed those evenings. The H.K.I. would carry most of the cost for those nights.

Another thing Eef was happy with was when sometimes I got coupons with my weekly paycheck, which was about 25 to 30 dollars in that time. They were coupons with which Eef could buy merchandise at the factory such as towels, linens and children's clothing for a low price—things which were still very scarce in the stores. The factory probably had bought the merchandise from America for their workers. I remember how happy Eef was when she came home one day with six cloth diapers, flannel material for pajamas and a few towels.

The H.K.I. had its own soccer club. As soon as they found out that I liked to play the game, they asked me if I would like to join their team when spring came. Remembering the pleasures of playing on a soccer team in Poland and later in England, I joined the H.K.I. team a few months later and enjoyed it very much.

Letters from Poland now came more regularly, even though it took up to three weeks for them to arrive. We had noticed that they were always thoroughly censored. Victoria, my youngest sister, wrote that she was getting married in May to Cheslow Krzyaniak. He came from Poznan and was an industrial engineer. He had been ordered to work on airfields for the Polish Russian Air Force. She wrote further that she hoped to go with her husband to Warsaw after their wedding and live there. Cheslow worked on a new airfield outside of Warsaw. My youngest brother Kazek was planning to follow them later in the summer. His plans were to enroll at the University of Warsaw. His interest was forestry.

Victoria, Irene, Mother and Kazek
in Poland, 1947.

At that time my mother and my older sister Irene lived together in Miedzychud. Stanley, the oldest of my three brothers, was now managing the large farm where he had been forced to work during the wartime. The Germans, who owned the farm and had fled with the coming of the Russian troops, had left everything behind. My other brother Marian had been called to serve in the Navy and was stationed at the harbor of Dansk in Poland. My sister Victoria wrote that every farm, every factory, every shop had become nationalized. No one owned anything anymore. Stalin's Russia which had settled in most Eastern European countries had begun its tyrannical communist dictatorship over the people of those countries. They became no less ruthless than the Nazis had been.

The political situation between the now powerful Russia, America and England was very unstable. In that time I thought more and more about emigration—to leave Europe and settle in Australia, America or Canada in the near future.

◆    ◆    ◆

(Eef) The nurse walked in and said that it was irresponsible for me to walk around so soon after the birth of my baby. Four days before, February 3, 1947, I had given birth to our first child, a baby boy. We named him Jozef after his father and grandfather and his great grandfather before him. He was the most beautiful baby I ever had seen and his daddy and the rest of the family fully agreed with me.

Five days earlier I had gone into labor. Late in the evening of that same day I walked with Jozef to the hospital which was a ten minute walk from our home. "It is good to walk," my mother had said, something I did not then fully agree with when I got labor pains during my walk to the hospital. But then I said to myself, hopefully Mother knows better than I do. In that time the process of childbirth was still very much kept a "secret" from a woman. Doctors and midwives didn't explain anything about childbirth to a young woman, or what was to expect during her nine months of pregnancy. If she was fortunate to have a mother who told her daughter the miracle of childbirth, she was lucky indeed. The rest of us were left wondering about the whole process. Also drugs to ease the pain and agony of childbirth were not given yet. The breathing techniques, so popular now, were not practiced in the time of my first babies. Midwives were preferred over doctors, so most babies were delivered by midwives in the hospital or at home. In case of a difficult delivery an obstetrician would be called in. After the birth of a baby, which I thought was a true miracle, the mother had to stay in the hospital for ten days. The first six days we had to stay in bed. Then for two days we were allowed to sit on the side of our bed in a chair. And the last two days we could walk a little around the room or hallway before going home.

But this lying in bed for that long was not for me. By the fourth day when the nurse was not around, I got out of my hospital bed and went to my baby who was sleeping in his crib at the foot of my bed. In the large room where I was lying, there were two other young women with their first-born babies. During the day the newborn infants were lying in a baby bed in our room. But during the night they were taken somewhere else in the hospital so mothers could sleep. Only when it was feeding time at night did the nurse bring us our babies. Most of the mothers were breastfeeding their infants, and we felt sorry for those mothers who, for some reason, could not do so.

The stay in the hospital was most pleasant. Not only did we three young women have a lot of fun together, but also we got spoiled by our families and friends. We received many flowers and also presents. Since there was not much to buy yet of baby gifts in the stores, the hand knitted or self sewn baby things were more than welcome.

While I was staying at the hospital, Tante Ann from South Africa came for a visit to Holland. She had not seen our family since 1937 when she and her family had left. When Tante Ann came to Breda to visit my parents for a few days, she also came to visit me at the hospital. It was so good to see my tante again and it felt like the years melted away. In 1945, as soon as the war had ended, Tante Ann had sent us packages from South Africa. The packages had held materials for sewing clothing, sweet-smelling soaps, spices, coffee and chocolate. I will never forget how everything looked and smelled so wonderful, as if it came from a faraway planet. We were very grateful to her. When I asked Tante Ann about Ken her son, she said that he never wanted to talk about the war and his time in Europe. Even though he was now happily married, she said, he had taken to drinking.

After my ten days stay in the hospital Jozef brought me and the baby home in a taxi. As soon as we arrived, the neighbors came to see our little boy. Mother made coffee which she served with 'biscuit met muisjes', which is a rusk that is spread with butter and then sprinkled with blue or pink anise sugar hail. This is an old Dutch tradition and is served to family, friends and neighbors after the birth of a baby.

The spring of 1947 arrived and beside mild breezes there came new tires for our only bicycle and for me a baby buggy. I had bought the buggy from a neighbor down our street who didn't needed it anymore. I now could take Josje shopping with me and go for a walk with him. Those new tires and a used baby buggy may not seem very exciting now, but as I recall it then was a great improvement in our lives. Jozef was now able to ride to his work and didn't have to walk anymore the long distance between home and work every day, which was many times in soaking rains. He had joined the H.K.I. soccer team and played early on Sunday mornings. Sometimes I went with Josje to see him play, but not often.

The soccer field was quite a walk away from our home, and the baby first had to be bathed and nursed. By the time I was done with him, it was sometimes too late to go. But Jozef enjoyed his soccer and never missed a game.

Once a month the Polish ex-soldiers who lived in and around Breda came together with their wives, girlfriends or alone for an evening out. Usually it was in one or another restaurant for dinner with dancing afterwards. They were always pleasant evenings which were well attended. I think those nights the ex-soldiers felt connected again in the early days out of the Army and living in Holland. Jozef and I still have pleasant memories of those nights.

Stefan was married that spring of 1947. It was a nice wedding, but it had taken a great deal of work for Stefan and Truus to put it all together. Everything was still scarce and difficult to come by. Truus had decided to marry in her suit with a white little hat and a veil.

Also Mies and Jeff got married in June of that same year. Because of our baby and the still existing transportation difficulties, I could not attend their wedding and felt bad about it. That following month in July, Jeff and Mies left for their plantation in the Dutch East Indies. I cannot remember on which island it was they settled. Before they left Holland, we wrote each other long letters. Mies promised to write as soon as they reached the plantation which would take about four weeks.

My brother Jan wrote to us regularly from Sumatra. He was doing good, but Mother missed her son a great deal and couldn't wait for the day when he would return.

It was in that summer of 1947 that Jozef and I had our first conversation about going to America. Jozef had mentioned emigration sometimes, and we had talked about it. It was mainly about Australia and New Zealand and Canada. But we never had talked about it seriously. But this time it was different. One of his old army friends had left for America, and I think it had made up his mind that this was the country he wanted to emigrate to. That day he said to me excitedly, "America is the land of opportunity and freedom where one can advance oneself with hard work and accomplish something. The opportunities in America for someday having my own business, my own bakery, are so much better than any place else. Too many years were lost for me; years I could have made a future for myself." I answered him that I understood but I had first to think about all of this. No one ever really wants to leave his own country. Sure, it sounded great to go to America, away from this continuous shortage of everything where we had been living in already for such a long time. America could offer us things we probably never would have here at home. But to live in a strange country for always, for the rest of my life, was another matter. Even though I knew in my heart that it would probably be better for Jozef and our son, and God willing, our future children, I needed time to think this through.

◆    ◆    ◆

The summer of 1947 was a beautiful summer with days of blue skies and warm weather. Many times that summer our little boy Josje was lying in his baby buggy outside in our garden. He was so brown, especially in his light blue baby outfit that was made without sleeves and legs. He looked so very precious. I remember how proud I was to walk with him through the Wilhelmina Park to go shopping in downtown. Since we had no refrigerators to store our perishables, I went to the fish market two times a week. Since the fishing fleet could go out into the North Sea again, there was plenty of fish for frying and cooking.

Besides diaper changes and shopping I started to knit. The yarns for knitting had come in the stores slowly but steadily. Every woman and girl knitted to their hearts content, from sweaters to skirts and even dresses. Sometimes I painted, especially when the weather was rainy and cold. Since there was not an inch of canvas for painting to buy in the stores yet, I painted on paper or made drawings. I had quit the gymnastics four months into my pregnancy. Even though many times I wanted to go back to the classes, I never returned again to my favorite sport.

On Sunday afternoons, with our baby Josje sleeping in his baby buggy, Jozef and I went for long walks into the forest. All three of us enjoyed this very much especially when the weather was sunny and warm. Sometimes we walked to the Cadetten Camp which was the area where in 1944 Jan waited for an English airplane to drop weapons. It always was so peaceful in the Cadetten Camp and very pretty with the dark tall trees of the forest behind the white sandy hills. Usually we were there the whole Sunday afternoon. Sitting on a blanket we ate our picnic lunch which I had made for us at home. We played with our baby when he was awake and spent lazy hours on the white sand. Jozef was happiest during those days. I had noticed that he was depressed sometimes and didn't talk much for days. Other times he was happy again and would sing his Polish songs which he had learned at his school as a boy. Jozef had a good voice and I loved to hear him sing, even though he sang the same melody over and over again.

When Jozef was at his work at the H.K.I., I took long walks with Josje over the narrow winding picturesque farm roads behind our home. Or I walked on the side of the lively stream, the Lyke, which was located not far from our home. In the summer time the brook was always full of frogs and salamanders and other small creatures. From the Lyke we walked further past the burned out seminary and over another farm road home again.

Even though the rebuilding was slow, the cultural life in Breda had come back with music, singers and performers. Many times Mother took care of her little grandson and Jozef and I went to see a play or a musical at our theater, Concordia. Or we went dancing alone or with friends.

My girlfriend Chiel had moved from Breda and now lived together with a young woman in Den Haag. She had found work as a typist in one of the large government buildings and enjoyed living in that city. About once a month she came home to Breda for a visit to be with her family. When Chiel was in town, we always got together and went to our favorite restaurant 'Hex' for a sip of tea and a piece of pastry. Even though pastries had returned to the bakeries and restaurants again, they were not as delicious as before the war. But it was progress, even if it was just a piece of sweet-nothing. Of course, when Chiel came to Breda we had a lot to talk about such as the latest news, gossip and all the things women talk about. Our other friend Gina was engaged to be married. I did not see her much anymore. She was always with her mother or over at her fiance's home and his family. But occasionally I walked with Josje to the flower shop and visited her. Beb and Ken also had wedding plans, but they had difficulties in finding a place of their own. Ken worked in his father's hardware store and hoped someday to take over his father's business.

The warm summer and fall of 1947 had turned into a cold and misty rain. Gone were the days of walking and playing with Josje outside. One day, while I was in my living room, Mother came upstairs with a letter in her hand and said to me, "Eef, a letter for you from the Dutch East Indies." While Mother took Josje with her downstairs, I opened Mies's letter in which she wrote about her voyage over the oceans to the Dutch Indies. She wrote that she had become pregnant by the time they had left Holland and, when sailing over the Indian Ocean, Mies was ill and very nauseated. The last week of her voyage she was spending most of her time lying in bed. By mid-August they had reached the island of their destination and their home. She wrote about their house in which they lived and which was located on the edge of the coffee plantation Jeff managed. Not far from their home was a small village where the natives lived. Mies and Jeff had met some Dutch families who lived somewhat further away on other plantations. They all came together on weekends which was fun, only there was too much drinking going on. "It come probably from the loneliness in this hot and humid land, Eef," she wrote. Mies then continued in her letter, "Can you believe it, Eef, I have two maids—natives who do all the work in and outside the house—even the cooking. They think white women just should not work here in this tropical land! Jeff and I have to get used to all those native dishes the maids are cooking for us. But this is not so difficult to do since we both like Indian cooking." Mies wrote that the nature was beautiful where they lived, but because Jeff was gone the whole day she was very lonesome. She longed for her family in Holland and the cool Dutch climate. She continued writing that she was looking forward to having her baby which hopefully would take away her loneliness. "So far, Eef," she wrote, "we haven't noticed anything yet of the fight for freedom here or trouble with the natives, and we hope that it will stay so." Mies ended her letter with greetings for everyone and was sending me her mailbox address so I could write to her.

♦       ♦       ♦

*April 1948.* Jan arrived home from Sumatra. Since his regiment had been the first one to go to the Dutch East Indies in 1945, Breda had planned a big welcome for the return of its first war heroes. A few days before when my parents received a letter of his returning, they had been on top of the world. Especially Mother couldn't wait to have her oldest son home again with her. When Jan arrived in Breda that day, tanned from the tropical sun and not expecting anyone but his family, half of the people from our neighborhood stood in front of our house to welcome him back home. Later that evening local officials came and gave an overwhelmed Jan a welcome speech and a plaque. When everyone had left and we were finally alone with him, Jan said that even though he had appreciated the welcome, they had made too much of a fuss over him. He never had expected his homecoming would be anything like this. Jan had brought some nice native handicrafts with him from the Dutch Indies for his parents, me and for himself.

◆    ◆    ◆

(Jozef) In the fall of 1948 I received a letter from my mother which later would set things in motion to enable me to emigrate to America. She wrote about my cousin Chelca whose mother was my father's only sister. Besides his sister, my father also had three brothers who were living in Poland. Another brother lived in France.

In the mid-1920s my cousin Chelca had married Anthony Szymanski in the village of Daleszyn in Poland. He not only owned many acres of land, but also had many cows and horses. As I recall one summer when I was seventeen years old and was visiting there, they had twelve horses. Many hired farmhands worked the land, the stables and the barns. Chelca, who had maids helping her in her household, never did much work outside her very nice large farmhouse. Her husband adored her and put her on a pedestal. He called Chelca his 'Queen'.

During my childhood years and later as a teenager, I had gone there many times during vacation from school. How I remember the times they called me 'a city boy' when I did things differently at the farm. I would walk in the hot sun without the wide brimmed hat as the village men always wore in the summer. Or I walked bare from the waist up, which no one else did at the farm—not even the farm hands. They thought I was crazy and said that I would burn myself in the sun. Anthony's younger sister Palasia also lived on the farm and took care of their three small children, two girls by the names of Halina and Cesia and a boy named Henk. Palasia, who was three years older than I, liked to tease me a lot. She knew the farm well and how to handle horses, cows and pigs. Now fifty years later when we come together at Cesia's farm in Wisconsin, I still have to hear about all the things she did to me—a city boy. The memories of those great summer vacations at the farm of Anthony and Chelca are still as clear in my mind as if they happened yesterday. In 1939 life started to change dramatically when the Nazis came to Poland.

It was in 1942 when Anthony, Chelca and their three children were sent to Eastern Germany where they were forced to work on a large German farm. They would work there for the rest of the war. In the meanwhile the Nazis had sent German farmers from Romania to Anthony's farm in Poland. Anthony and Chelca lost everything—not only the land and farm and livestock, but also their personal belongings. Since they were taken away from their farm by surprise, they had no chance to gather much of their belongings and hoped they could come back for them later on. But everything was gone, not even a picture of the family was spared.

After the American troops liberated them in 1945, they were sent along with many other Polish people, who had been forced to work in German factories and farms, to holding camps in Germany. In crowded camps they waited until the American and British governments decided what to do with the millions of stranded people in Germany. Soon after Anthony and his family arrived at the holding camp, Camp Mornouw, Anthony became ill. After suffering from tuberculosis he died in 1947. In 1948 Chelca, her children and Palasia were offered help from a Polish organization in Chicago. That organization helped displaced people in German camps who needed help. They offered them a chance to come to America and start a new life. Since Chelca had nothing left anymore in her now Russian communist occupied country, she decided for the sake of her children to take the offer of help from America.

My mother continued on in her letter that she now was waiting for some more news about Chelca's plans. After reading my mother's letter, Eef and I began to talk again about emmigration to America. We decided that I would find out more about it and also about emigrating to Canada and Australia. It was a few weeks later when we received information from the different Consulates. We learned that to be able to emmigrate to America we needed a sponsor who could, if needed, take care of the family financially for two years. A questionnaire paper was included which we had to send back to the American consulate. They wrote further that as soon as they had received papers from our sponsor from America, they would then place us on a waiting list and notify us when our number came up. We also found out that it was easier to enter Canada and Australia since those countries didn't request sponsors. Because of the strict limited so-called quota system for immigration at that time, we knew that it would probably take a few years before our number came up. After Eef and I talked it over at great length, I said that I would wait to fill in the questionnaire for America until Chelca came to the United States and I had her address. I then would ask her to send me the address of the Polish organization in Chicago which hopefully could help us to obtain a sponsor. I had my heart set on going to America.

◆     ◆     ◆

(Eef) When my brother Henk had finished grade school, he went to a trade school in Breda for courses in auto mechanics. Then in that autumn of 1948 he was called for military duty. After his initial basic training in boot camp he was shipped overseas to the Dutch East Indies together with other Dutch soldiers. For sometime now we had a feeling that our rich colony would be set free of colonization by our government. Even so my parents worried about their youngest son having to go to that far away country. Too many terrible things were happening there, as we were reading in our newspaper every day. After three weeks on board a troop transport ship Henk arrived on the island of Java (Jawa). Many times during his stay on that island he wrote home and telling about the hot and humid weather and the terrible monsoon rains. He also wrote about how the Java plantations were in ruins. One day when Henk came down with the dreaded disease malaria, his close army buddy was killed by a land mine.

At the end of 1949 Queen Wilhelmina granted the Dutch East Indies their independence which soon got the new name of Indonesia. A few months later the Dutch soldiers were shipped back home to Holland where relieved and thankful parents, friends and family members were waiting for them. The first year after Henk was home, he occasionally got an attack of malaria. While lying in bed he shook as if from cold while sweating as if from heat. His temperature went sky high and it was awful to see him suffering. The medicine for malaria as we have today was not yet invented, and all the doctor could do was give him medicine for fever which did not help much. The high fever lasted a few days before tapering off, leaving Henk weak and pale. The sickness then disappeared again for some time. Luckily Henk overcame this dreadful disease in our cool Dutch climate.

The autumn of 1948 was the end for Jozef playing his favorite sport—soccer. One Sunday morning he left with his soccer team for an out-of-town game. Later that day when he came home limping through the back door, I knew it was more than a scrape or a bruise. Nothing ever seemed to bother him. He never complained even though he was sometimes painfully hurt. But this time he was in great pain, and his knee was badly swollen. He could hardly walk. Since his knee was not much better the following day, he stayed home. In the afternoon our doctor came to our house and, after looking at Jozef's knee, told him to stay off his leg and rest. How long this would be the doctor couldn't tell, probably six weeks, he said. Jozef also had to notify his company doctor, who came the next day. After he examined Jozef's knee, he said to him that it would probably take two months before his damaged knee would be healed again.

There he was, being bored and limping through the house. He started to read a lot but was sometimes tired of that too. Then one day, a few weeks before St. Nicholas, Jozef came into the living room carrying some small pieces of wood from out of the shed. He said to me that he was going to make some wooden toys for Josje for St. Nicholas. Soon he was cutting and sawing, and he made a small toy train. This was followed by a little car, a wagon and an airplane which he painted in whatever leftover paint he could find in our shed. By the time St. Nicolas came along, Jozef had all the toys ready for his little son who was very happy with all those new toys, especially the small train. Once a week for the following six weeks, our doctor came to the house to examine Jozef's knee. After he was able to walk again, he had to go to the doctor's office for his weekly knee checkup. Finally after two months Jozef went back to work again, something he was more than ready for. And so was I. But it was the end of his soccer playing years.

◆          ◆          ◆

One year later, it was October 29, 1949—five years after the German troops were driven from our city of Breda. In an official ceremony the 'Liberation Monument' was unveiled in the Wilhelmina Park. Many ex-Polish soldiers and high ranking officers attended the ceremonies and the laying of wreaths. In a speech the Mayor of Breda announced that from this day forward the Molengracht Straat would officially be named 'Poolse Weg' (Polish Road). He said that it was this road where the first Polish soldiers came through to liberate the city of Breda from the Nazi tyranny. Since that first memorial ceremony there have been many more celebrations in the Wilhelmina Park. With the passing of the years less and less of the ex-soldiers have attended. Many went to live in other towns or went to far away countries. Some went back to Poland, others passed away; but the city of Breda never forgot its liberators, and every year flowers are laid at the foot of the Polish Memorial in the Wilhelmina Park.

In the fall of that same year my curves were disappearing again, and as Jozef would say—I was getting lush. We expected our second child in mid-March, something we were very happy about. Josje needed a little brother or sister to keep him company. He was such a active little boy and always wanted to go outside in our street to play with other children. Of course, he was still too young for such a freedom.

The housing shortage all over Europe was enormous. In early 1947, with the help of America, Dutch construction companies began to erect housing facilities mainly in the larger cities as Amsterdam, Utrecht and Den Haag. Because of the great shortage, large ugly blocks of eight stories high apartment buildings were constructed. Each block could house up to 300 families. The city of Breda also was beginning to build new apartments. But luckily for our town the apartment buildings were going to be only three stories high, and as we heard, they were going to be much better looking. Some of the apartments were going to be rented to families without children. As soon as my father found out about the new apartments, he went to the housing office in Breda. There they told him that only those people who had been living together with another family in the same house would be eligible for one. When Father learned that the apartments were going to be with large rooms and windows, he signed up for one—for Mother and himself.

It was about the beginning of March 1950 that I came to know that a family, who lived on the end of our street, was going to move out of town. Three years before, Jozef and I had signed up at the housing office for a house or an apartment. With hundreds of other young married couples we had to wait for housing on the long waiting list. As soon as we knew that the house on our street would become available, Jozef and I went to the housing office. There we asked if we could possibly get the house on the Zeisstraat Number 52 which soon would become free. We told the clerk that we expected our second baby soon and had lived for almost four years in my parent's house. The man took our papers out of his file, examined them and told us that we had a good chance of moving into Number 52 on our street. To our great surprise and happiness we soon got a notice in the mail that the house on the Zeisstraat was ours to rent. We could move in on May first.

Not only Jozef and I, but also my parents were more than thankful that we finally would have our own place. Even though Mother and I had always been close, it had become a strain in the last year for both of us. One kitchen and two women do not work out well. With an active little boy in the house and another child on the way, this living together under one roof was not ideal. My parent's house was not built for two families. Many times Mother and I had been on edge with each other and sometimes we started to argue. But now this would change, and finally Jozef and I could start a normal married life together, and my parents would have the peace they deserved.

On March 23 of 1950 our little girl was born. How happy we all were. We named her Cornelia after my mother, but we called her Lia. She was so small and sweet and had long dark hair which stood straight up on her tiny head. It did not take long until she stole everyone's heart. After ten wonderful days in the hospital we took our baby home. Of course the neighbors came over to see the new baby, and we had coffee and rusk with pink sprinkles. The first few days Josje constantly stayed beside his little sister's crib and just wanted to hold her. But his admiration for his baby sister soon wore off, and he became more interested in riding the tricycle he had received from his grandparents for his third birthday.

Our baby was seven weeks old when we moved into our house. Since we had little furniture, the moving was not a problem. It was wonderful to finally have our own place. The children now had their own bedrooms, and for me—freedom in the kitchen. Our own home—rented, yes, but then everyone rented their home. Few people owned their own house in Holland before World War II.

One day that summer I said to Jozef that I had to go to the store to buy some meat for supper. Our neighborhood butcher was located just three blocks from our street on the now Poolse Weg. I said to him that I was going alone and would soon be back. Josje was playing in the back yard with his toys and a old high military cap from before the war. It had belonged to my father but, since Josje loved the cap so much, he had given it to his grandson. Our baby Lia was sleeping in her crib. When I came home after twenty minutes, Josje was gone from the back yard. Jozef said that he probably was behind our house with some other children who were there playing. We looked there, but no one had seen Josje. We looked everywhere, but our son was nowhere to be found. We started to get worried.

About a half-hour later, I saw Greta (a girl I knew) coming to our house on her bike. On the back of her bike was Josje sitting with the military cap which covered half of his face. His Teddy Bear, his favorite stuffed animal, he held tightly under his arm. Greta told us that while she was riding on her bike through the Wilhelmina Park, she had seen a policeman talking to Josje. She said she had found that strange since she didn't see me or his pappa. She stopped her bike, went to Josje and asked him where his mom was. He answered her, "I am going to the store because my mommy is there." The policeman told Greta that he had seen the perky little boy with his bear and the military cap walking alone. The boy was walking in the direction of downtown he said, and he had followed him. He then told Greta that he had been ready to take the boy to the police station. When the policeman asked Greta if she knew the child, she answered him that she not only knew who he was, but also where he lived and that she would take him to his parents. She then placed Josje on the back seat of her bike and rode to our house.

Later Josje told me that he had wanted to go with me to the store. He had started to walk after he found out from his pappa that I had gone to the meat store, and that I would be back in just a few minutes. Josje probably had thought that I had gone to the downtown meat store where we sometimes went and where he always got a slice of lunch meat from the butcher. Even though we resolved from now on to keep a closer watch on this little traveler, Josje loved to wander. When he was a little older he liked to go off by himself through the fields behind our home. Those times I thought about my mother's complaint when I was a child, how I always was disappearing—always running off.

Almost every day that summer I took Josje and Lia, who was lying in her baby carriage, to the Wilhelmina Park to feed the geese, swans and ducks. Even though the food situation was not that great yet, no one now needed to kill and eat the birds who lived most of the year in our ponds and lakes. Many times when we went to the park I took a little boy, by the name of Peter, with me. Peter and his older brother lived next door. Their parents, Bart and Lena van der Westen, had moved to Breda from Utrecht. Our former neighbors had moved up North to be closer to their children, so Bart and Lena had moved in and became our next door neighbors.

Our new neighbor was a very quiet man who worked at a government building in downtown. In contrast, his wife was an exuberant red-haired young woman who loved to laugh and talk. They were expecting their third child in the fall. It did not take long until their three year old son Peter was over to our house all the time, and he and Josje became close buddies. You could find him in our kitchen especially on Saturday afternoons. It was then that I always made apple pancakes dusted with powdered sugar. I never could believe how much those little boys could eat. Jozef loved pancakes too, and so Saturdays became pancake day for our family.

That summer my parents received notice that the house they lived in was sold and the owner wanted to move in by September of that same year. Since some of the new apartments in our town were almost ready for occupancy, Father went to their office to see if he could rent one soon. There he told the clerk that he needed living quarters since the house they lived in was sold and he and Mother had to move out. After the man looked through their papers, he told Father that yes, he could move into one by mid-September. They were nice modern apartments built in light brown stone. Each apartment had a roomy balcony in the front overlooking a large open area with a fountain in the middle. It was a 25-minute walk from my house. My parents were very happy with this new and convenient apartment in this new section of Breda.

Not far from our home, and close to boer Backx's farm, was an open field. It did not seem to belong to anyone. It was just there between the babbling brook Lyke and the pastures where cows were quietly grazing. In spring I went there with Josje a few times to pick flowers which grew in abundance in the field. The sweetness filled the moist air while bumblebees droned from flower to flower. I always thought that nowhere was there a prettier place than that field. For one month during summer vacation the field was well used by children of our neighborhood. They were playing at the side of the creek, catching salamanders and small frogs, or just romping in its clear water.

One day I walked with Josje and Lia, who was in her carriage, on the narrow farm road which ran beside that field. It was crowded with children flying their kites. Josje was fascinated with the kites, which were in all colors and sizes and filled the sky that afternoon. "Mom, can I have one too?" he asked me excitedly. It was a few days later that Josje and I bought some bright color kite paper, sticks, glue and kite rope and made our own kite. It was pretty and I made it not too large, so Josje was able to handle it.

One nice afternoon, after the schools had started again and the sun shone warmly in the September sky, I took my son with his kite and Lia to the now quiet field. While Lia was sleeping comfortable in her baby carriage, Josje and I flew his first kite. I don't know which of us had more fun. After a few hours running with the kite, or repairing it, there was not much of a kite left anymore. It was time to go home. But before we left, we caught two colorful salamanders in the Lyke. I think there must have been hundreds of them. Together with some sand, water and greens we put the creatures in a small container. I always had something with me for Josje to use in which to save his new-found treasures Usually they were pretty stones which he found on the side of the farm roads. The salamanders we caught would always live for a few weeks in a large glass container.

In October we ate biscuits with pink hail again. This time it was at the house of our neighbors. Bart and Lena had became the proud parents of a baby girl. Her name was Ineke and later became Lia's little girlfriend.

# 32

## *LITTLE FRIENDS*

The days came and went. It was the end of November and that time of the year again when St. Nicholas with his knights arrived at the harbor of Breda to celebrate St. Nicholas birthday, December 6. I decided to stay home with Lia that year. We thought she was too young for the crowded lively mass. Because of their new baby, Peter's parents were not going either. Jozef said to me that he would take Josje and Peter to all the excitement at the harbor that Sunday. For the last few weeks Lena and I had taught the boys a few St. Nicholas songs. We wanted them to sing together with all the other children when St. Nicholas and his horse walked down the gangplank of the decorated ship. Jozef and I planned that after St. Nick's arrival we would meet at my parent's apartment.

Many times on Sunday afternoons we walked with the children through the Wilhelmina Park to my parent's home to spend a few hours. There we discussed the weather, the politics and the latest news. Then after some tea with cookies and playing with the children, we walked back home again. Most children were very young when they walked quite a far distance. But sometimes when we were halfway to our house Josje, who had become tired, turned to his father and said, "Pappa, I want to play horsey." Jozef then would pick him up and set him on his shoulders.

St. Nicholas was and still is a great feast in Holland. All the excitement of those days when I was a child, I saw again in the eyes of my child. Every night for two weeks our son sang his St. Nick songs before the fireplace. He would then put something in his shoe for St. Nick's horse to eat and a glass of water for St. Nickolas himself. Every morning, Josje came down from his bed hoping that there was a candy in his shoe. Sometimes there was, but many times there was not. Although he was young, he learned to accept the little disappointments in life. How excited he was when in the early morning of December 6, St. Nicholas brought him toys, books and candies which, as was tradition, were all displayed on the table.

For Christmas Jan and his girlfriend Gerda came home from Amsterdam. Gerda was a soft spoken pretty girl. She was my age, slender and had dark hair. Jan had met her at the A.G.A. office where they both worked. Quite a few times Jan had brought his girlfriend to his parent's home for a weekend, and we came to know her as a pleasant and bright girl. During Christmas dinner at my parent's house, they announced that they had decided to get married sometime in the summer of 1951. We all were very happy for them, and there was an extra toast for the couple. Since Gerda's family and friends lived in and around Amsterdam, they were going to be married in that city. It had been a wonderful Christmas.

On New Year's day of 1951, we ate oliebollen with our family and with Bart and Lena and their boys. It had been a good year.

It was on a Sunday in January when, after we arrived at my parents for our Sunday tea, it started to snow. All day the sky had looked dark. But since this is nothing new for January in Holland where the days can be dark for weeks on end, we decided to go to my parent's house anyway. If it was going to snow, we reasoned, it probably would just be a little covering the streets and then it would stop again, as it usually did. But this time it kept on snowing, the large fluffy kind of flakes, and it did not take long until everything was covered with a layer of snow. When we had finished our tea, Jozef said, while looking out of the large windows of my parent's living room, "Eef, we better get going if we want to make it home. It doesn't look very good." Since I had brought nothing extra with me for the children to stay over for the night, we decided to make a go for home. After first laying our baby far under her blanket in the carriage, we covered the baby buggy with its rain cover. We pinned a towel in front of the carriage's front opening with clothespins. We then took our winter coats and while telling my parents not to worry, we said goodbye and closed their front door behind us.

As soon as we came outside, we noticed how bad it had become. The wind picked up and when we came around the corner of the apartment the snow swept around the baby carriage. Our son was all excited and happily he jumped through the snow while holding my hand. A little further up, away from the apartments, was an enclosed bus stop where some people were waiting for the bus. When we came there, we found out that the next bus was going in the direction of our neighborhood. Talking the situation over, Jozef and I decided that Josje and I would go home by bus, and Jozef would pull the carriage home through the snow with the now sleeping baby.

While Josje and I were waiting for the bus, I saw Jozef disappearing—pulling the carriage behind him. Even though I was worried, I knew that he would be all right and would bring the baby safely home. Josje, who always liked to go with the bus, wanted to stay this time with his pappa. He thought it much more fun to plow through the snow than to ride the bus. The bus driver, not used to driving his vehicle in this kind of snow, had a hard time going and sometimes it looked as if we would be stuck in the drifts which were forming. The bus ride took forever, but finally we reached the corner of our neighborhood. When Josje and I got off the bus and started to walk the last three blocks home, I saw to my happy surprise Jozef coming from the direction of the Wilhelmina Park. He was plowing through the snowdrifts, with the snow-covered baby carriage behind him. When we finally reached home, Josje did not want to go inside but to play outside in the snow—for just a little while. For him it had been excitement of the best kind. Our baby had been sleeping—cozy, warm and dry under her blanket all that time. She was such a sweet child, almost never crying or being fussy. She was so easy to smile and love. It was too bad that we had no telephones in our homes so that I could have called my parents and told them that we had come home safely.

Spring of '51 came with tulips and daffodils in bloom everywhere. To the delight of Josje and Lia, Jozef had bought a few two-day-old little chickens and two young rabbits. First he had made a cage from the old cages which we had used during the war years, and which had been laying in our shed. Even though I had complained to Jozef that our yard was too small to keep chickens and rabbits, he had bought them anyway from the farmer who lived close to our home. He promised me he would slaughter them before winter came around. I think those small animals reminded him of his childhood—the young animals he always had loved so much. Of course Josje, Lia, Peter and another neighbor boy, by the name of Hans, enjoyed all that young, fuzzy little stuff.

Every morning, right after breakfast, there they came carrying some green leaves for the bunnies, and crumbs of bread for the chicks. While sitting on the ground, the children all excited and fascinated, looked at the little fuzz balls which hopped and picked around them. Lia would scream with delight trying to hold on to a little rabbit, while Josje tried to protect the fuzzy creatures from too much handling by his friends. After about two weeks of excitement, the kids became less and less interested in the little chickens and bunnies, and life came back to normal again in our backyard.

The parents of Hans were Jan and Geertje van Dort. They were about ten years older than we were and a couple very much to themselves. They had lived for a few years in our street, but I never had really talked to them. One day Hans brought his mother over to our yard to show her the little bunnies and chickens he had told her about. Geertje and I started to talk and soon we were sitting at the kitchen table drinking coffee. She told me that she was expecting a baby at the beginning of November. While sipping our coffee I felt that she was watching me closely. Then in one breath she said, "Jan and I are hoping for a little girl, Eef. It will be our second child and last one; we are getting too old for babies." Looking at her I said, "I don't think you are too old Geertje. You are surely not as old as our melk vrouw" (milk woman).

The milk vrouw was the farmer woman who came every day through our neighborhood selling fresh milk. The milk which came from their own cows was sold to their customers out of large metal cans. The push cart was not only pushed by the woman herself, but also pulled by a large dog who was harnessed under the cart. This was still done in that time. Now, because of the animal cruelty law, this is not done anymore. Every year the milk vrouw had been pregnant with another child. As far as we knew, the family counted already twelve children with another one on the way. The woman had told me once that she thought she would have maybe one or two more children, and that would be the end. She had accepted every baby that God had given her with love, but, she had said, she would be happy when He finally thought that she had enough children.

When Geertje and I were children, it was normal for families to have five children or more. But by now it started to change, and young couples thought three or four were more than enough. A little later when Geertje went home with Hans, I knew we would become friends.

Even though the automobile was the new form of transportation, most people were still riding a bicycle in Holland. Because of this, the traffic in our street was at a minimal. Josje was now old enough to play outside in the street in front of our house. But before he went out to play with his little friends or rode his tricycle in front of our house, I always said to him, while rubbing my hand through his curly hair, "Stay in front of the house and behave yourself or you will be in trouble." As soon our son walked out of the front yard, there came Peter and Hans. The three musketeers thought it a great adventure to play in our street. But their favorite place was a sandpit which was left from the time our neighborhood was built.

The sandpit was located in a field behind the last houses of our street and close to our home. Occasionally when the weather was nice, I took Lia there with me when I knew Josje was playing in the sandpit with his little friends. She loved the feel of the sand running through her little fingers or she sat in a sand hole her brother made for her. Lia's hair was as golden blond and curly as that of Josje, and with their true blue eyes I thought my children were the most beautiful in the world. I loved to play with them or take them on walks or feed the ducks and swans in the park. Lia was still in the stage that, while walking in our street, we were going five steps forwards and four steps backwards. Every front yard gate she had to open and close a hundred times.

Every summer for one week Jozef had a paid vacation coming from the H.K.I.. Father had given him his old bicycle after he himself had bought a new one. Jozef had fixed the bike and bought new tires which were finally for sale again at the bicycle store for a more reasonable price. Even though the bicycles were old, we now each had our own bike. We also bought a child seat for Lia. That summer during Jozef's vacation, we took long rides through our forest with Josje on the back seat of his pappa's bike while Lia was sitting in her child seat on my bike. One day we rode to the place were the kikkers lived. Josje was fascinated to see them and hear their croaking, but Lia did not like them. It was too much of a noise for her. We also tried to pick blueberries which grew in the forest. Of course Lia wanted to help us. While she picked them, she squeezed the berries which then stained not only her hands and face, but also her dress. "This has to wait for another year or two," we said to each other. This was too messy for our little daughter.

Sometimes during our vacation, my mother came over our home to baby sit so that Jozef and I could go out for the evening together. Those nights we went dancing at the hotel at the edge of the Mastbos. It was still our favorite place to go to for an evening. Or we went to the cinema and saw one of the latest movies. Stefan and Truus had become the happy parents of a baby girl. They lived now in an apartment on the other side of town. Besides the monthly Polish evenings, which we all enjoyed, we came together for a drink when possible. A year earlier Vincent and Toos had moved to Leiden, which is a well known university town not far from Den Haag. Vincent was now a translator at the University of Leiden. A few days before they moved away we had a goodbye party for them. We all would miss them, we said. Jozef and I never saw them again. But the young Polish soldier with his guitar, as I first had met him, I always would remember.

*September 1951.* After a rainy night the sun had come shining through the heavy clouds. It was early in the morning. My parents and I had left by train to Amsterdam for the wedding of my brother Jan and Gerda. A few days earlier Jozef and I had talked it over and had decided that it was not such a good idea to take Josje and Lia with us to the wedding. Jozef said that I should go with my parents to Jan and Gerda's special day alone. He offered to stay home with the children. Traveling by train had become much better now with most of the bridges repaired. It had become again a pleasure to travel especially with the new fast moving trains which Holland had received. It was disappointing that Henk could not attend his brother's wedding. When Henk was discharged from the Army, he had gone into a merchant marine school in Dordrecht to become a machinist. He didn't wanted to go further in the auto mechanics. After his schooling in Dordrecht he sailed the Seven Seas on one of the large freighter ships. On his brother's wedding day he was probably somewhere in South America.

I met Gerda's mother and her sisters for the first time. Her father had died some years before. It was so good to meet and talk to everyone of Gerda's family. The wedding, which was held in Amsterdam's city hall, was short but very lovely. Gerda was dressed in a light colored suit and a white hat with a short veil. For the last few years it was the most popular wedding attire. The wedding industry had not moved forward much, and the wedding dresses which were for sale were way too expensive. Also for the first time the automobiles were taking over the horse and carriage rides to City Hall and Church. To go by car was American, they said. Everything American was 'the thing to do' in that time. But the horse and carriage never went completely out. Today it is 'in' again in Holland. Only now it is very expensive.

◆   ◆   ◆

(Jozef) In the late fall of 1951, I received a letter from my mother in which she wrote that my cousin Chelca, her son Henk, her two daughters Halina and Cesia and my cousin Palasia, finally had arrived in America. They were now living in an all-Polish neighborhood in Chicago. Together with my mother's letter she also sent me the address of Chelca. After reading my mother's letter a few times, Efka and I talked at great length about going to America. That same day I wrote a long letter to Chelca. First I wrote her about the years since the war had started in 1939. I wrote how sorry I was about the death of her husband, and the loss of everything they had owned in Poland. I wrote how happy we were that she and her family were now in America and were given the chance for a new life. I then asked Chelca if she could send me the address of the Polish organization which had helped them come to America. I explained that we wanted to emigrate to America, but we needed a sponsor. Maybe, I wrote, the Polish organization could help us to find such a person.

After a few weeks of waiting and every day looking in the mail box, I received a letter from Chelca. She wrote about their coming to America and their lives in Chicago. She also was sending me forms from the Polish organization to fill out. "Jozef,"s he wrote, "there are plenty of rich Americans who are more than willing to help an ex-soldier who has fought for freedom. It should not be difficult to find one." I filled out the forms and immediately returned them back to the organization in Chicago.

It was a few weeks later when I got a notice back from the organization saying that our papers would be processed. They wrote that, together with the papers from our sponsor, our papers would be sent to the American Embassy in Holland. The embassy would notify us when our number came up. Finally we had a sponsor and a new hope for a better future in America! All that we had to do now was to wait until our number came up. When this would be, we didn't know.

◆          ◆          ◆

(Eef) *Spring of 1952.* The winter had been long and we had been staying indoors too much. The griep (flu) and colds had gone around, and sometimes it seemed that all I did was wipe noses. It had also been a snowy winter with strong north winds which did not help matters either. In those days when the children were not sick, and if the wind decided to take a rest and the sun came through the dark clouds, I took the kids outside for a little while to play in the snow. Of course they loved those times—especially when Josje's buddies came outside and they made a snowman together with a stick for his nose and coal for his eyes. Lia, as young as she was, tried to help the boys, but it always ended up that she and I made our own little snowman. But finally spring came. A warm breeze was blowing in from the South, and the small snowbell flowers peeked their little heads through the last melting snow to catch the sun.

That spring I received a letter from Mies in which she wrote about her worries for their future in Indonesia. The Indonesian people did not want Dutch people living in their country anymore. This also included the island on which they lived. In recent months many Dutch people had been murdered in Indonesia. The Dutch government advised all the Dutch people who lived in Indonesia to return to Holland as soon as possible. Mies wrote that some of the Dutch planters who lived not far from them had already returned by ship to Holland. They had left their plantations and homes behind. As I was reading further, I could feel the fear from her letter, especially when she wrote how worried she was about her husband. Added to her worries was the fact that she had become pregnant with their second child. After reading Mies' letter, I said to Jozef how sad I felt for both of them. For Jeff—to have studied for so many years and dreamed about owning his own plantation some day. And for Mies—her dreams of having a large family and a beautiful tropical house. Now they probably had to leave it all behind or take the chance of being murdered.

About that same time Jozef received a letter from his mother. Of course, because of safety reasons she never wrote about the politics in Poland. But from our own radio station in Holland we heard many times about people who dared to speak up against Communism in the Russian occupied countries. They either were killed or disappeared into Siberia. It was far from peace in the world of 1952.

It was a few weeks after receiving the letter from Mies that one day while I was busy in my kitchen, Lena walked through the back door into my house. With her dark red hair all messed up she excitedly said, "Eef, did you hear the latest news? You can now rent one of those new washing machines which came out not too long ago!" I did read about the electric washer in the newspaper before, but did not know that you could rent one. It sounded fantastic, renting an electric washing machine! That meant no more washing the laundry and diapers by hand in a washtub with a hard brush on a washboard, as women and our mothers and grandmothers always had done before us.

Finally our lives were changing and we would start living as the modern women in America did. While sipping our coffee Lena explained to me that the machines were for rent by the half or whole day. "The rental place will bring the machine into the kitchen and pick it up later again. They can be rented for four gulden the whole day, or two gulden and fifty cents for half a day." With determination she continued, "I am going to rent one, Eef, that is, if my husband thinks it is a good idea!" A good idea, I thought, it is a fantastic idea! No more washing all those diapers by hand (disposable diapers were not invented yet). No more scrubbing the laundry until my hands were wrinkled like prunes. Who wouldn't think this was a great idea? When Lena was going to rent one, I said to myself, I was going to see how it worked.

When a few weeks later the delivery truck stopped at my neighbor's house, I knew they were bringing the electric washing machine which Lena wanted to try out. Finally she had rented one. Bart, her husband, had probably come to the conclusion that it was a good idea after all. It was about a half hour later when I went with Lia through the yard to her kitchen. Lena was standing in the empty kitchen beside the washing machine. On the floor was some of her dirty laundry. She was leaning over the machine with a most serious face as if she looked at an operation gone wrong. When she saw me standing at the open door, she said puzzled, "Eef, come on in. I don't understand how come the wash water doesn't get hot in the machine. What could I have done wrong?" Soon I found out that after Lena had put dirty clothes and soap in the machine, she had filled it with cold water, thinking that the water would get hot after the washer was turned on. "Lena," I said to her, "I think you have first to heat the wash water in your wash kettle. Then after your laundry and soap is in, fill the machine with the hot water." Houses built before WW II did not have water heaters as we do today. Some people in that time in Holland had a geyser above their kitchen sink. It was a device which heated small amounts of water, just enough to wash the dishes or wash your face and hands.

Well, after a few hours of helping Lena, we sat down. While Lia and Ineke were playing, we drank a hot cup of tea and discussed the future method of washing our weekly laundry. We still had to heat our water in the large kettle, we said, and wring the wash by hand. Even though the machines were not big and could only hold small amounts of laundry, it was a great improvement over the washboard. Later when I walked with Lia though Lena's backyard passing the lines where her wash was drying in the wind, I said to myself, when the next washday comes, I will rent one too. For me the washboard era had passed.

As the old way of laundry washing slowly disappeared, a new era came in the form of television. There had been a story in our newspaper about the latest invention in America which they called 'television'. It was like a movie screen in a small box and, as the paper said, many people in America already had them in their homes. We had not paid much attention to it because there were still too many things that were needed more in Holland. But one day in that summer of 1952, this small 'movie in a box' changed the way we had thought about it and opened our eyes to the magic of television.

One evening when Jozef and I walked home after seeing a movie in downtown, we passed a store which sold radios. A small group of people were gathered in front of the store and were discussing something which was in the store window. Wondering what it was about, we stopped our walk home and looked through the window. There it was! A small strange looking black box stood on a display table with a sign saying 'TELEVISION.' An explanation about the soon-coming TV stood beside it. Over the screen was pasted a picture of a singing Mario Lanza (a well known singer in that time) to show the people how it would look when it was working. A man, who was standing besides Jozef, said to him, "You will see, this will never work." Jozef turned to him and answered, "Oh, one day you will probably have one in your house." The man looked at Jozef as if he was nuts. A little later as we walked further, I said to Jozef, "You really believe that some day people will have a television in their home? Maybe it would be great, but no one will go to the movie theaters anymore." It was not until we were in America that for the first time we saw a working television.

After a nice ceremony in Rotterdam my father had retired from his military career. He was home every day now. He loved wood carving and was very good at it. He made many nice wall hangings during his retirement years. Most were landscapes made from thin colored wood which he carved out and glued on a board. And of course he played chess. He taught Josje to play chess, and it did not take long until our son knew all the chess pieces by name and what to do with them. My parents loved their grandchildren—especially my father who spoiled them. I told my parents that in the spring of 1953 we expected another baby.

That summer when Lia was almost two and a half years old, Jozef and I planned to go to the beach somewhere in Holland for vacation. Sometime before, Jozef had heard a man, who worked with him at the H.K.I., talking about beach cabins which were for rent on the island Walcheren in the province of Zeeland. They were right on the beach of the North Sea, the man had said. He had gone there with his family the year before. After Jozef and I talked about it, Jozef said he would ask the man for the address of the rental cabins so that we could write to their office. It was not long thereafter that we got our suitcases packed and went by train to the island Walcheren and the village of Zoutelande.

It was evening when after a long walk and carrying Lia, the suitcases, beach toys and more, we arrived at our cabin with a tired Josje and a sleepy, fussy Lia. The cabin, one of about twenty, stood just behind a row of dunes away from the sea. The wooden cabin was roomy and had a large kitchen and two bedrooms with a bed for each. From our cabin we walked over the dunes to a beautiful wide beach, which was only a short walk away. Every day we spent the whole day on the beach, making castles, finding sea shells and playing in the salty water. It would have been a perfect vacation if the weather would not have been so hot.

A rare heat wave had hit Holland. Our cabin, which probably had poor insulation, was hot—so hot that Jozef and I couldn't sleep at night. Only the kids didn't have difficulties with sleeping, I think they were too worn-out every night from playing the whole day on the beach. Even though we were close to the sea and we had all the cabin windows wide open at night, it stayed hot inside. There was not the slightest breeze. During the day between playing, we took an occasional nap on the beach in the shade of a beach umbrella. But even though we didn't sleep much, we had a great time. That week we were mostly all together in the water. As it turned out it was the last vacation for us for many years to come. When we came home, sunburned and tired, a heavy thunderstorm broke the heat wave and it stayed cool and rainy for the rest of the summer.

◆     ◆     ◆

*September 1952.* Jozef and I decided to enroll Josje in a kleuter school (kindergarten) which was located in a Catholic school. It was a ten-minute walk away and on a side street of the Poolse weg behind the convent. Also located there was the Sacrament Church. Josje was a lovable child but fearless which got him in many situations. One day that summer in late afternoon Hans and Peter came running through the back door into my house. In one sentence they told me that Josje was on the top of the construction building, and he couldn't get down. The construction building that the boys were talking about was one of three new apartments which was being built in a field not far from our house.

As I gathered from the boys, they and Josje had gone inside in one of the buildings—just to look around. Later while Peter and Hans went outside again, Josje had gone further to the very top. The two rascals told me he was now standing on a shaft which was on the outside of the building. How well I remember grabbing Lia and, while praying that my son would not fall down, ran with her in my arms to the construction site as fast as my legs would let me go. I still can see him standing there on the outside shaft, three stories high, not knowing what to do. As soon as I reached the partly finished apartments, I yelled to him to stay back against the wall and to stay there. I would come and get him. I handed Lia to some older children who were watching and looking it all over. I told them to take care of her, and went inside. Till this day I still don't know how I found my way upstairs between all the construction material and the skeleton of rooms and stairs. When I finally found my son, who was leaning against the outside wall, I didn't know if I should be angry with him or to be happy to have found him alive. I guess I was both at the same time. Carefully we found our way back to the main floor and to the outside.

Even though that was the end for the three musketeers to come even near the construction site, it was not the end for Josje to climb to higher places. About a week later when I was walking with Lia, I saw my son climbing a tall tree while some boys watched him. First I called to him to come down and then I asked him what he was doing in that tree. Looking puzzled and pointing at the tree he said that he was getting the kites out which were stuck in there. I wonder how many times he had done this before I had found out.

Whenever Jozef came home from his work I always would tell him about his son's escapades that day. I had asked him a few times before if he had been such a fearless child when he was a boy. Jozef then would tell me the stories of his childhood. How he loved to go alone by himself into the forest to watch the deer and other creatures of the woods. And how it had made no difference to him what time of the year it was, summer or winter. I always enjoyed to hear those stories, especially the ones about his family. Jozef still had his difficult days, and I knew that sometimes he was longing for his family and country.

Jozef had made a swing for his son in the door of our shed. Josje not only loved to swing for his pleasure, but sometimes he used his swing to get even with his friend Peter. Whenever the boys were in a fight, Josje would swing high up and peek over the fence to see if Peter was there. Then, if he saw Peter, he yelled—my father is stronger than your father! Or he would yell—my father can run faster than your father! Peter, on the other side of the fence, would yell back—and my father's bicycle is better than your father's. Whenever I got tired of the yelling, I asked both boys which of them wanted the biggest cookie I had. Usually the fight ended right then and there.

When Josje started school, Lia missed her brother terribly. She always was running after him in the house, or in the back yard to play or romp with him. She was such a happy girl, always laughing and making fun. With her blue twinkling eyes she saw the world as one happy place. When our radio was playing she danced to the tunes for the longest time in the corner of our living room. As often as I could I took her to Wilhelmina Park to feed the ducks and swans. Or I took the stroller and walked to my parent's apartment for a visit.

*May 6, 1953.* After a long difficult delivery our third baby and second son was born. We named him Edward—'Eddy', as we would call him. It was a name Jozef and I both wanted for him. Mother didn't agree with this name and thought her grandson should have a family name, as it always had been, and not a strange name. We told Mother that after giving our first two children family names, we had decided that our third baby should have a new name.

My hospital room was the same one I had as with our other two children. The room with the three beds and large windows overlooking our city canal. On the other side of the canal where the hospital stood was 'Sportfonse Bad'. It was a large indoor swimming pool which was built before the war. Behind this building was the kazerne grounds and the large 200-year old kazerne where Father had worked so many years.

My hospital stay was pleasant again, the same as it had been twice before. One day, a few days after the birth of our baby, Chiel walked unexpectedly into the room with a large bouquet of flowers for me and a Teddy bear for Eddy. She wanted to surprise me, she said smiling while hugging me. A few weeks before she had asked her mother to write to her as soon as my baby was born. She then would take the train to Breda.

Chiel got engaged to a businessman who was working for an electronic firm in Den Haag. They had not yet set the wedding date. It was so good to see her again. She looked great—tall, slim and dressed in the latest Paris fashion. The last time we had seen each other was when she had been in Breda for Christmas to visit her family. One afternoon we had come together with Gina at our favorite restaurant. We talked and drank tea with pastry for old times sake, and we had a good time. Our conversation had been about Chiel's future wedding which would be in the spring of 1954. She and her fiancee were planning to live in Den Haag and were already looking for a place to rent. The housing problem was still serious, especially in the larger cities. We talked also at length about our emigration plans. Even though Gina and Chiel had different ideas about us going to America, they could understand that Jozef wanted to leave Europe and its huge problems now that he was not returning to Poland. "Nothing is for sure yet," I said to them. "As long as we haven't heard anything yet from the Dutch Consulate in Den Haag, things can change." While pouring another cup of tea we reminisced about past events, some hilarious and some sad. A few months before, Gina and Phill had become parents of a little boy. He not only was the happiness of Gina and her husband, but also especially of her mother who lived close to them. Gina and Phill were married in 1951 in a small private wedding. Sometimes she still worked at the flower shop.

When Chiel left the hospital after the promise to come soon to Breda again, Jozef walked into the room with a happy Josje and a dancing Lia. They came to see their mom and the new baby again, as they did every day with their pappa or with my mother. Mother took care of my little family while I was staying in the hospital, something I was very grateful for. A little later Henk and his girlfriend Annie walked into the room. Henk who had arrived on his ship from a long voyage to North and South America was happy to be home again for a while. He soon was telling us the stories about his life on board ship, and the harbors where they anchored. He then told us about the large dishes of ice cream they served in America. One of them was called 'Banana Split.' "You never have seen anything like it," he said, laughing. "First they put a split banana in a dish and on top of it comes three different flavors of ice cream. Then comes the whipped cream, and over that they spoon different flavors of syrup as chocolate, butterscotch or coconut. Then over all of this they top it off with nuts and fruit. What an invention; it is just fantastic!" At first we thought Henk had made it up. But when I said to my brother, "It sounds like a fairy tale, Henk," Annie said, "It is for real, Eef, believe me, it's all he is talking about."

Henk and Annie were a great happy couple who had met each other when they were very young. The first time I met her was on my wedding day when Henk brought her to our home and introduced her to us. Annie who worked at an office in town was a very slender pretty girl who adored my brother. She didn't like that Henk was gone so much and wanted him to find work closer to home, somewhere on the land rather than on the sea.

An infectious disease, not serious, broke out in the baby ward of the hospital and also had infected our baby Eddy. The day I left the hospital with Jozef, our baby was in a small isolated room, and the doctor told us we couldn't take him home—not until he was completely well again. I felt very bad to leave him there and go home with empty arms. For the following days I rode my bicycle to the hospital to nurse and hold my little boy a few times a day. Then one morning, about five days later, the nurse told me that I could take my baby home. As soon as I was done nursing him, I rode home on my bike as fast as I could. I then took the baby carriage and said to Lena that I would come for Lia as soon as I came home with Eddy. Lia and another little girl by the name of Anja, who lived across the street, were at Lena's house playing together.

The following day we had our delayed coffee and buttered beschuit with blue hail for friends and neighbors. Of course my parents were there and Lena and Geertje with their children. While we sipped our coffee, Josje and Lia proudly showed their baby brother to their playmates. But the new little baby couldn't care less about all that attention and was very content sleeping in his crib. The following days if someone asked Lia, "Did your mom get you a little brother or sister?" she always answered happily—"No, I got a baby!"

# 33

# *THE LONG-AWAITED LETTER*

The summer of 1953 drifted into fall, and the apple trees in boer Backx orchard were heavy with fruit again. The tall chestnut trees dropped their nuts, and children were gathering them just as I had done with Jan when we were children. It was on an afternoon when I was home alone with Eddy, our baby, who was sleeping in his crib. Lia was playing with Anja, the girl from across our street in our backyard. After a ring at the front door I opened it, and there in front of me stood a young priest. He looked like a young physical education teacher dressed up in a black habit and a wide brimmed black hat. For a moment I stood there and looked at him wondering why he was here. Of course I should have expected him since Josje had started first grade in the Catholic school in September, the same school as he attended the year before when he was in kindergarten. I invited him in and offered a seat.

At first I felt somewhat uncomfortable, a priest in our home was not a common sight. As a matter of fact, it was the first time. While looking at him, a little curiously, I could not help thinking that he was way too handsome for a priest. As it turned out he was a sincere young fellow and had come to get acquainted with Josje's family who he had not yet met. He then told me that he taught religion in the Sacrament School and knew Josje from there. We had a pleasant conversation in which he told me about the village he came from and about his family who still lived there.

Later he steered our conversation to Josje and the First Holy Communion which was coming up the following spring. He asked me if we wanted Josje to celebrate his first communion. He said he knew that Josje's father was Catholic but didn't know anything about his mom. When I answered him that I was not Catholic, he asked if I was interested in learning about this religion. I then told him that the Catholic religion was not strange to me, and that I had gone a few

413

times with my husband to his church, but was further not interested. Later when getting up from his chair he asked me permission to call back when Jozef was home. He wanted to meet him too, he said cheerfully.

Since Geertje belonged to the Sacrament Church and Hans was in the same school and classroom with Josje, I talked with her about the young priest who had visited me. Geertje then started to tell me that this priest was popular with the young people because of his new ideas of teaching. "This young man has a knack of making sense out of religion, so kids can find meaning and pleasure in it," she said. She then continued, "Eef, he is not drawn into local politics, but does what God wants him to do, and that is to teach love and understanding." After Geerje left I thought about what she had told me. It was so different than I had heard so many times about religious teachers who often miss the point of religion and dishonor God by teaching a God who is merciless and makes the children afraid of Him. Are the times finally changing—is the need for power over their flocks finally loosening up, I said to myself. How I remembered too well the forbidden friendships with other denominations.

The predominant religion in the southern part of Holland was Catholic. If a young man of Catholic faith was interested in a Protestant girl, this was immediately forbidden by the parents and priests. But since WW II this has greatly changed and now, as I write this book, many churches in Holland are torn down or used for other purposes than a house of prayer.

It was a few weeks later when the young priest came back. This time Jozef was home, and soon they were in a light conversation talking about soccer which both men enjoyed. Finally the conversation turned to Josje and the First Holy Communion. Jozef had told me already a few times before that his wish was for his children to be baptized into the Catholic Church and become members of his faith. At first I had mixed feelings about this. I wanted more then anything that our children would grow up in a family where God was in the home. I didn't want my children to grow up without a religious faith. I wanted my children to go to church with their parents as a family on Sundays and Holy days. Jozef who was a member of the Catholic Church would not consider another religion. So after thinking it through, I felt that it would be the right decision for our children to become members of his church. "For myself to accept this religion," I said to the priest who had patiently listened to me, "I need to know much more about it. It is a faith which is sometimes very difficult to understand." He fully agreed with me. The priest then suggested that I read books about the Catholic faith. The young priest came a few times more to our home and seemed to enjoy our young family. He gave me a book, bound in red leather, as a gift. The title was "Triptik of het Godsryk" (Journey through God's Kingdom).

In spring of 1954 Josje, Lia and Eddy were baptized into the Catholic faith in a private ceremony at the Holy Sacrament Church in Breda.

◆　　　◆　　　◆

The holidays of 1953 were pleasant and busy with our three young children, family and friends. Eddy, our sweet contented baby, celebrated his first St. Nicholas and Christmas which, I think, always is so very special for parents. Eddy's big blue eyes had looked at the lights on the Christmas tree, and his little hands grabbed at all that was sparkling. Lia had made up her own songs for St. Nick and at Christmas she danced around the Christmas tree. Jozef had taught Josje and Lia to sing a Polish Christmas song which they not only sang for Christmas, but also well into spring. For New Years Eve I fried, as I did every year, olie-bollen and appleflappen. Yes, they had been wonderful and busy days. They were days which I would remember for the rest of my life, as they were the last holidays I would ever celebrate in my country Holland again.

So far the weather had been sunny and mild, but now in January it had turned cold. For days on end the harsh wind whooshed over the fields and down the street. Not for weeks came a ray of sunshine through the low hanging dark clouds. Since most of the houses had little insulation and only single glass windows, it could become very cold inside the houses. The only rooms which were heated were the living rooms. During the winter when there was a cold spell, every morning it was the same problem with our kitchen pipes. Those pipes, which go from the kitchen sink to a small covered well in the backyard beside house, were frozen solid every morning. On those icy cold mornings my husband stirred up the fire and deposited some new coal into the hearth. He then took the fireplace poker, put it in the fire and made it red hot. Then, with some strong words which I would rather not repeat, he thawed out the kitchen pipes. Besides frozen pipes, our bedrooms also became unbearably cold.

One morning after a very cold night, Jozef took the temperature in Eddy's bedroom. It read one degree above freezing. Our other bedrooms were not much better, depending on which side of the house the room was located. Some nights Jozef took the bedding downstairs to the living room for the children and me so we could sleep in a warm room. But since there was no room for everyone, Jozef slept upstairs with a hot water bottle. Of course the children thought this camping in the living room was great and wanted to do this every night. One night, after I said to Jozef that I hated the thought of him sleeping in such a cold room, he said, "This is not so bad Efka, I have slept in worse conditions during the war. I remember well one night, it was in 1944. That morning I woke up in the bedroom of the house in s'Gravemoer. The windows had been blown out by a V II, and an ice cold wind had blown a layer of snow in the room and on my bed."A little later when Jozef went upstairs, we could hear the wind howling outside, and we hoped this cold spell would end soon.

I clearly remember that winter of 1953-54. It was not only that we had those cold spells but also many people came down with influenza and colds. When the winter finally left and life seemed to come back to normal again, the children came down with whooping cough. Almost no one knows now anymore how dreadful this disease was before the inoculation for whooping cough. The duration of this illness took about six weeks—three weeks up, and three weeks down—as people always would say. The coughing spells were terrible and explosive and ended in a high pitched whoop (from there the name whooping cough). Especially at night the children were coughing up thick salvia which made them choke and vomit.

Since the children didn't have a fever or feel sick, the doctor told me that they should be outside in the fresh air as much as possible if the weather was good. I, of course, followed his directions. Since this is a very contagious disease, Josje could not attend school. Also the children's playmates were not allowed to play with them. From Josje's school we received books, sheets of papers and instructions for our son so that he could keep up with the rest of his classmates on school work. Every morning we played school in our living room, and even though they were interrupted by coughing spells, Josje thought the home lessons were great. But after a few weeks he got lonesome for his school and classmates, and missed his buddies Peter and Hans.

For the duration of the sickness our children played together warmly dressed in our backyard, or we went for a walk in the Mastbos. Since Eddy was still so very young and his lungs so tender, we were thankful that he had only a light degree of this disease. Of course Josje was the worst of the three. He always got colds and sore throats easily. Because of this, his tonsils were removed before the age of four. But problems with his neck glands left him many times with an unexpected high fever. Lia was always a very healthy child and seldom sick. But after a bout with tonsillitis in summer of 1954, her tonsils were also removed. It seems to me that in that time doctors were eager to remove the tonsils of young children.

Finally after weeks of holding our children in our arms at night when they were choking on their thick saliva or when vomiting, it was over. Finally we had our first peaceful night, but it had left me exhausted. I had lost about ten pounds on my already slim body, and it took me longer than the kids to finally recover from this difficult time.

◆    ◆    ◆

May of 1954 arrived with balmy weather. The gloomy last months were gone and our spirits rose steadily with the temperatures. The buds on the lilac bushes were swelling, ready to open a display of lilac and purple. It was May 6, our youngest child's first birthday. He was round and chubby with eyes as blue as forget-me-nots. Like Josje and Lia, he had soft blond curls. His hair grew long and at first I didn't want to cut his hair, even though some people thought that he was a little girl. Finally I gave in and off came his curls. The day before Eddy's birthday I bought a bowl full of narcissus and displayed it on the table. It scented the whole room. "Today is his special day," I said to myself, "and also my special day."

In the afternoon my parents came with a big birthday hug for their little grandson and a soft stuffed elephant which played the tune of a Dutch lullaby. Later, when school was out, Lena and Geertje came with their children for the small party. Besides tea and lemonade, we had a plate full of pastries. We sang happy birthday for Eddy who thought that all that attention was a lot of fun and showed everyone a big smile. Lia helped her little brother with the opening of the presents, pretending that it also was her birthday. But Josje thought that his sister was too bossy and pulled her hair. Just in time, before the screaming started, I pulled them apart. Later when Eddy's pappa came home from his work, we had some more partying to do.

That following week we had another celebration. It was Josje's First Holy Communion. After a few days of drizzle the sun came through the clouds and it turned into a beautiful day, as if to bless one and all. It was Communion Day at the Sacrament Church and the bells were ringing. As long as I can remember, those church bells had rung every morning and every evening at 7:00 sharp. Since my parents strongly believed that young children should go to sleep early, I always had to go to bed as soon as the church bell were playing in the evenings.

Of course I didn't want to go to bed and started to sing as loud as I could hoping that Mother would not hear the bells. But my singing never did help. Later when I was older, I loved the sounds of the church bells. They always gave me such a peaceful feeling. But on this day they sounded more wonderful than ever; it was our son's First Communion Day.

In the early afternoon while the bells were ringing, for this special occasion, we went to church. When the many people entered, a choir was singing of God's love and blessings. The church was crowded with parents, family and friends of the young communicants who were dressed in their finest. Later when we came home, we had a small party for Josje. My parents did not attend their grandson's First Communion Mass. They had not been happy with the idea that their grandchildren became Catholic. Especially my father. But later in the day they came over to our house for a drink and brought a gift for Josje. When our son's special day came to an end, I tucked him in his bed and said a prayer for him. It was the little prayer which I had learned when I attended Sunday School as a child. It had been my very first prayer which I had always remembered.

It must have been the beginning of August of that same year when I received a letter from Mies. It came from Den Haag. In a long letter Mies wrote that she, Jeff and their two young sons had escaped from Indonesia under a difficult and dangerous situation. It had become impossible to stay any longer on their island, she wrote. The natives from the village had ganged up on them and had warned Jeff that if they stayed any longer, he and his family would be killed. Then one night, just a few days before they were planning to leave their plantation to go back to Holland, a group of natives came and set their house on fire. With their two children and a few bags of belongings, they fled. With the help of a native boy who had worked for Jeff, they found their way to safety and returned by ship to Holland. They lived now with Jeff's parents in Den Haag. Mies wrote they hoped to visit us in a few weeks.

After reading Mies' letter, I thought about the time when they had left for Indonesia—so full of dreams and hopes for a good life on their plantation. It was not meant to be, I thought, but what now. Holland has plenty of farms but no coffee, tea and rubber plantations. When Jozef and I talked about it later, Jozef said that maybe Jeff could emigrate to South America and start there anew in Brazil or Argentina.

A few weeks later I got a letter from Mies in which she wrote that she and Jeff were planning to visit us the following week. Even though we had written to each other the last years, it was the first time we were going to see each other again. I wanted to be sure that everything was going to be just great for their visit and dinner that evening. One day in early afternoon a car stopped in front of our house and there she was, my friend Mies with her husband Jeff. How good it was to see her again. She still looked the same as I always had known her, with her trim figure and unruly curly brown hair which she never could hold in place. How tanned they both were, even after all those weeks in Holland. I was only a little disappointed that they had left their two young sons at Jeff's parent's home. Mies promised that the next time they came they would bring the boys along. They wanted to take this trip in Jeff's father's car alone together. Soon we talked and laughed about the time when Mies lived in Breda, and our adventures on our bikes on Sunday afternoons, and the fun we had doing that.

Later after dinner, Mies helped me with the dishes in the kitchen. She told me that a few months earlier her mother had died suddenly of a heart attack, and how she missed her. Her sister Greta was getting married at the end of October. Later when the children were in bed, we started to talk about the situation in Indonesia and Jeff and Mies' last difficult months. When Jozef asked Jeff what his plans were now that they had lost everything and could not return anymore to their plantation, he answered that he had seen a possibility to go to Brazil and was working on it. He said that he did not want to stay in Holland since there were no opportunities for him, or he would have to start all over again in another trade. Mies hoped also that they would go to Brazil in the near future. "Eef," she said, "Our Holland is a very nice pleasant and wonderful country, but seems so chilly and rainy here, especially after we have lived a few years in a tropical climate. It is hard to live anymore in a crowded country like Holland." Jeff showed us pictures of their sons and their home and plantation in Indonesia. A place which had ended too soon for them. The following morning after breakfast when Jeff and Mies left, they planned to drive past her old home at the Poolse Weg and through Wilhelmina Park to the downtown area. Little we knew then that it was the last time we would see or write to each other ever again.

◆     ◆     ◆

It was the beginning of September. The summer vacations were over and Josje started the second grade in his school. Proudly he told us that he now belonged to the big kids. That early afternoon while I was busy ironing the laundry in the kitchen, Eddy was taking his nap. Lia was playing with Anja and Ineke in front of our house. Through the open window I could hear the vegetable man coming in our street with his horse-pulled wagon, selling his home grown fruits and vegetables. Every afternoon he stopped in front of the houses of his customers. His name was Janus—a big man in his mid-forties and the father of many children. He had a boisterous voice and loved to talk. Janus was also a very happy and friendly man. After taking care of his customers in our street, everyone knew exactly what kind of veggies their neighbor was eating that night. Vegetables were still the most important part of a dinner in Holland.

Janus finally reached our house and rang the doorbell. In his far reaching voice he told me all the vegetables and fruits he had that day. I went to his wagon and looked at his wares which were displayed in open crates. In the meantime Lia, Anja and Ineke were petting Janus's gentle horse who was accustomed to the admiration of the neighborhood kids. While I choose my fruit and veggies for that day, I saw the postman coming into our street. He delivered his mail through the copper mail openings which were located in the front door of the houses. When he reached our house, he handed me the mail and, while walking further, wished me a nice day. I told Janus which veggies and fruit I wanted and went back to the house while looking at the mail in my hand. Suddenly my heart skipped a beat. There it was! A letter from the American Embassy! Immediately I opened it. There were just a few printed lines saying that our number had come up and we were eligible to emigrate from Holland to the United States of America. If we were still interested, we had to reply to this letter immediately.

The rest of the day was a blur to me. I could hardly wait until Jozef came home from his work, and I could give him the letter he had been waiting for— for such a long time. Late in the afternoon when Jozef walked through the door, I handed him the letter without saying a word. He opened it and while reading the few lines, a big smile came over his face. He took me in his arms and danced wildly around the living room while the kids looked at us as if their father had gone temporarily insane.

That evening after cleaning up the dinner dishes and tucking Eddy in his crib with his little stuffed yellow bear, I read Josje and Lia a story as I did most nights. Sometimes it was a story out of their favorite book, but both kids loved it if I told them a story I made up myself. After they had fallen asleep, Jozef and I went for our walk around the block. The stars were out and the evening was still and chilly. I had drawn my hand through his arm which he squeezed and then, as always, he said, "I love you, Efka." It was during those times when walking together alone through the dark quiet streets in the evening, we felt so close, and we always talked over those things we needed or wanted to talk about. Of course all that we talked about that night was the letter we had received from the Embassy. Again Jozef asked me, "Efka, are you sure? Are you sure you can leave

Holland behind you, your parents and friends, and everything you grew up with and are used to? It will not be easy to emigrate into a strange country with three young children and start there all over again." How well I remember standing still for a moment in the middle of the now dark street and while I kissed him I said, "If this America is what you really want and you think it is the best place for our children's future, then I am all for it."

I knew in my heart that since he never would return to Poland that America was the new true home he longed for. With all its possibilities, America could offer him things he never could accomplish in Holland. Yes, I wanted to go to America for my husband and children's future more than for myself. Although Holland and the rest of Western Europe was now much better off than the years directly following WW II, there were still shortages everywhere. Also the political situation with the mighty Soviet Union, (Russia) developed into a dangerous state.

That night I couldn't sleep and wondered what the future would hold for me. Yet I felt excited about this adventure called emigration and living in America—the land we had heard about so much during the war years. To think I would really be going to the land of the free and seeing land that seemed to stretch forever, as they said. But I also realized that I would be leaving my beloved Holland. I still had a few months time to get used to the idea of leaving my country behind. The following day Jozef sent a notice back to the Embassy that said yes, we were still interested in emigrating to the United States.

The most difficult thing we had to do was to tell my parents about our decision we had made—to emigrate to America. They always had known that since Jozef could not return to Poland, his wish had been to start anew somewhere away from Europe. But my parents had hoped that this desire of his to emigrate would go away. Even though my parents always had understood that there was more hope for us for a better life in America, Australia or Canada, they had hoped that we would remain in Holland. I was their only daughter and our children their only grandchildren. When Jozef and I told them of our decision, father did not say much. I think he kept his feelings inside and showed little emotion. Mother went to the kitchen—to make tea—as she said, but I knew she was close to tears and wanted to hide her face from us. I had seen the pain in her eyes, and I wanted to hold her in my arms to comfort her.

Near the end of September we received a notice that Jozef, the children and I had to come to the American Embassy Building in Den Haag. It was for paperwork on our emigration papers and a general medical examination. A week later early in the morning we went by train with our children to Den Haag. We had told Josje and Lia a few days before why we had to go there, but had gone no further into details yet about going to America. We had decided that we would explain this to them at a later date. They were still too young to understand everything at once. The day of our medical checkup would turn out to be long and tiresome.

You have to know that in the years following WW II, many young people and families from Western Europe emigrated. They left their countries to start a new life in faraway lands such as Canada, Australia, New Zealand and America. Also displaced people, longing for a better life, saw the opportunities to go to those countries to start a new life. Most of the people were helped by sponsorship or churches. We all knew that it was not going to be easy, and that we would have to work hard in the first years. Even so we were willing to tear up the old roots and familiar ways and learn a different way of life. Even though there was a strict quota system for those countries, ships left everyday with people and brought them to their new world.

The waiting in the large hall for our physical checkup, which was done in a building not far from the American Embassy, seemed to last forever. Josje and Lia, with the easy camaraderie of the young, played with other children of future emigrants. Sometimes they asked for a drink or something to eat. But Eddy was cranky. That morning he had not only been taken out of his crib too early, but also now missed his afternoon nap. After a few hours of waiting, Jozef was called for his checkup and to the office for our emigration papers. A short time later the kids and I went in for our examination. Eddy cried the whole time while the doctor checked him over. When it was Lia's turn, she did not trust the doctor and tried to run back to me. She was caught by a nurse whom she fought off and then landed back in my arms. Josje looked it all over and did not think his sister was funny even though he comforted her later. When we finally were done and Jozef had come back, Eddy, who had become utterly miserable, had fallen asleep in his papa's arms. While we walked to the exit, Jozef told me that all the papers and checkups were O.K. We now had to wait for further notice from the embassy which we could expect within two weeks.

It was late that afternoon when we finally arrived back at the train station in Breda. Not long after that day we got a notice in the mail from the American Embassy that we were to board the ship "Ryndam" on November 30, 1954, with end destination New York City, USA.

Eef with Lia, Eddy, and Josje in Breda, 1954,
shortly before moving to America.

# 34

# *EMIGRATION*

How well I remember the goodbyes I said to all the familiar places in the weeks before our leaving. I walked with Lia and Eddy to the Wilhelmina Park where every spring the rododendrums were blooming in all their glory. I said goodbye to the swans, ducks and geese while the children were feeding them. I took the kids for a stroll past boer Backx farm where in the field his black and white Friezian cows were staring lazily at us. I said goodbye to his apple orchard where always his apples grew in abudance, and which had helped us survive the last winter of the war. All the tree branches were barren now but next year, I said to myself, they will again hold many bushels of fruit. From boer Backx farm we walked further to the creek Lyke where in spring and summer the frogs and salamanders played in the sunshine.

I said also goodbye to our city square and the market place where I always had bought fish for our evening meal and herring for next day's lunch. I said a special goodbye to the last stall—the stall which always had the most flowers and lowest prices—49 cents a dozen, depending on the time of the year. The stall where Mother and I, as long as I can remember, had always bought our flowers at the end of our market day before going home. They were those simple everyday places of sight and sounds which we took for granted, but which I later would miss in my new country.

One day we told the children that we soon were going to leave our home in Holland and go to a faraway country named America, and that we were going to live there. We told them that we would be going on a big ship and also on a long train ride after we arrived in America. Lia thought about it for a moment and then asked me if she could bring her baby doll with her. When I said that she also could bring her other doll, she was happy and didn't asked any more questions. As long as we were all going to America together, it didn't mattered to her. She was still too young to understand.

First Josje did not say much. He was seven years old and understood that going far away meant leaving behind his two buddies, Peter and Hans, and their adventures in the fields and sandpits. It also meant leaving his school behind which he enjoyed very much and also his oma and opa (grandma and grandpa). When he asked how far away America was, I took the world map out of the cabinet drawer. Together we followed the route which the ship would take over the ocean to the place named New York City where it would anchor. My finger then followed the direction to Chicago where we had to go to by train. After my son studied the map for a while he asked me, "Mom, can I show Hans and Peter the route our ship will take to go to America and the city where we will live?" I knew then in my heart that my child would be all right.

We started to go through our things. First what we had to pack were those things we needed for our journey to Chicago which would be for about two weeks. Those things which we would use later, I set aside because they were to go into a large crate. The rest had to be sold. Since our family consisted of five persons, we were allowed to take many household articles with us to America, such as dishes, linens, blankets etc. Even my sewing machine, some chairs and the baby crib with mattress went with us on board ship in a large crate which a moving firm packed and took care of for us.

The weekend before we planned to sell our furniture, Jozef and I went up north to say goodbye to the family. We left the kids with my parents. First we went to Tante Dien in Amsterdam. Since my grandmother's death in 1950, Tante Dien lived alone with her dog in the same apartment, and she would live there until the end of her life. She lived to be 92 years old. When we said goodbye to my cousin Coby and her family, she said that she hoped to visit me in the states. However since she was fearful of airplanes, she never did. Coby and her husband Jaap both have a deep love for their city Amsterdam. Except for vacations in Europe they never would leave their beloved city. When we left, they wished us the very best and hoped we soon could come back to Holland for a visit. From Coby we went to Jan and Gerda's home to say goodbye. Because of their work they could not come to the harbor in Rotterdam to see us off. We spend the night at Jan's home and talked about our upcoming emigration. The following morning after we ate breakfast together, we left for Haarlem. There we visited Tante Nel who also was still living at the same address as before my Grandmother Breeuwer's death in 1948.

As I looked out of Tante Nel's living room window and saw the river Spaarne, it looked as great as ever with the many ships and sailboats. It brought back memories to me of a sunny day when I was sailing over its water with Mr. van Meerdonk, Hetty and Stien. We also said goodbye to Wim Stein the painter who, as always, had his mind somewhere else. When I asked Tante Nel about Hetty, the Jewish girl, she said that she had not heard from her in a long time. She only knew that she was married a few years back. I guess Hetty and I, as it seemed, had been just too busy in the last years to stay in contact, which was too bad. A few year later after we went to America, Tante Nel died—she lived to be 73 years old.

◆     ◆     ◆

(Jozef) Finally after a few years of waiting, my wish to start a new life away from Europe was taking shape. In the last years the political situation in Europe had not become any better. While the Eastern European countries suffered under Soviet Union Communist dictatorship, in Western Europe—especially Germany—the American, English and French troops were stationed everywhere. They were afraid of an eventual Russian invasion into Western Europe.

It must have been about three weeks before our emigration when I went to the H.K.I. employer's affairs office. I had to let them know that in two weeks I was going to leave my work at the factory. When I walked into the office, a man at the desk, who I knew from the H.K.I. soccer team as our goalkeeper, helped me. After talking about soccer for a few minutes, I told him that I was going to emigrate to America by the end of November. He looked at me in a disturbed manner. He then became upset and said, "Everyone thinks America is so great. Don't think, Jozef, that the money is laying there in the streets. Be smart and stay here and you can work your way up as good as in America." Calmly I said to him that I had already made up my mind years ago and would not change it. Yes, I thought, the H.K.I. had been a good place, the people nice and friendly and I had in those few years worked my way up. I then said to the man, "Tell the bosses that I will not forget the H.K.I. and, even though it had been a good place to work, my destiny is somewhere else." The man then shook my hand and wished me the very best in America.

The following day it seemed as if everyone at the factory knew that I was going to leave for America. The Polish men at the factory with whom I always had lunch were unhappy that I was going to leave. We always had lively political discussions at our table. Since politics greatly interested me, I usually knew more about the world situation than any of them. When they asked me where they now should get political information after I had left, I told them to start reading the political magazines and listen to the political news on the radio.

Later that day when I was leaving the factory to go home, one of the Polish men came after me and said that he also was going to America. "No one knows yet, Jozef," he said, "but a cousin in the American city of Syracuse is helping me to come to the States." I gave him a quick, gentle tap on the shoulder and said I hoped that he would make it. Not knowing where the city of Syracuse was, I said to him, "Who knows, we may meet each other there in Syracuse!" While riding on my bicycle to go home, I felt elated and excited. Breda is a nice town, I said to myself, and I don't think I will ever regret having lived here all those seven years. But it is time to move on and hopefully be closer to my dreams of owning my own business, a bakery.

In September as soon as I knew that we were going to America, I wrote my mother a letter. I explained to her that I had taken the opportunity to go to America with my young family to start a new life there. I knew that she was going to be unhappy with the thought of me going further away from Poland. She also knew with this move I would never return home again to Poland to live there. I still held the hope that the cold war situation with the Soviet Union would end somehow, someday, and that I could visit my family in Poland. My family in Poland was doing all right and made the best with what they had. I think the family closeness and strong religion helped them to cope and survive. The last years Eef had sent many pictures of us and of the children to my mother . Also in the letter I asked my mother if she knew the address of my cousin who lived in New York and if so, would she send me his address. That cousin's name was Jozef Otto and was a son of my father's oldest brother. In the mid 1920's, as a young man of about 18 years, he had gone to America as a worker on a ship, and there in that big country he disappeared. Later he married a beautiful girl and opened his own grocery store. During the war years he butchered cows for the Army and made a fortune. After the war he opened a new large grocery store and butcher shop in the small town of Bedford Hills, which is close to New York City.

It was a few weeks later when I received a letter back from my mother. She wrote that even though she was sad that I was planning to go further away from her, she could understand why we wanted to go to America and hoped that I would find the life and peace I was looking for. Enclosed with her letter came the address of my cousin in New York. I wrote to him immediately. I explained in my letter that I had plans to emigrate to America with my wife Eef and our three children. I then wrote that, if possible, we would like to see him and his wife before going to Chicago where we were planning to live. I wrote that our ship would anchor at the New York harbor. Later I would send him the name of the ship and the time it would arrive. A few weeks later I received a letter back from my cousin in which he insisted that we should stay at his house for a few days before going further to Chicago. He also wrote that two of my other cousins lived not far from his house.

(Eef) Even though I was excited about going to America, the land of our dreams during the war years, it was sometimes difficult for me. Breda had always been my home, my town. I began to say goodbye to people I always had known—people who, even though they were not close friends—had been a part of my life in Breda. Jozef and I went to the Polish Club one evening and said farewell to all the Polish men who had been stranded in Breda and had made a new life for themselves in Holland. Some of the men were envious that we were able to go to to America; others were happy with their lives in Breda. But they all wished us the very best in the land of the free.

Josje had come down with a high fever just ten days before our departure. He was now at his grandparent's apartment where he got more attention than from his busy parents at his home. The doctor told us that Holland did not yet have the right medicine for Josje's neck gland problem. He said that it was available in America and that our son would be just fine after taking it. We hoped this was true.

How little time remained for everything. Besides the selling and the packing, we said goodbye to good friends. Chiel came to Breda the weekend before we left to say goodbye to us. I had to promise her not to wait too long before coming back to Holland for a visit. The last week before our leaving, Lia and Eddy were mostly staying at Lena or at Geertje's house where they got spoiled, of course. It was close to St. Nicolas and the children received all sorts of small gifts from family and friends to take along on their journey. One evening I wrote a short note to Mies about our departure to America. The last letter which I had received from her was some weeks back. She had written in her letter that they soon were leaving for South America, and she would send me her address from there. Jeff had unexpectedly received a notice from South America, I believe it was Brazil, that he could start working there at a coffee plantation. But after that I had not heard from her again, and it left me wondering if she had left or was still in Den Haag. Beside the letter to her I also included my parent's address. I mailed my letter to Jeff's parents in Den Haag hoping that they would give or send it to Mies, wherever she was.

After dropping the letter in the mailbox, which was located close to the Teolin factory, I walked home through the dark streets. While looking up at the moon I thought about Mies and the time when we were in our early teens and dreamed of far away places. We did not know that one day those dreams would become reality. I also thought about the time when Jan and I were children and were looking at the moon. Jan always saw faces in the moon and tried to scare me by saying that the moon could see everything, and I better be good. Later in my teens during the war years the moon had become so very important to us for its light when we walked in the blackened out city. Later I walked with Jozef in the moonlight, and we dreamed our dreams. Wherever I go, I said to myself, the moon will always be there. Later our own children will look up and dream their dreams, wherever they will be. They will see the same moon as I see now here, walking at the Poolse Weg in Breda—only at a different place and in a different time.

◆    ◆    ◆

It was the early morning of November 30, 1954. It was the day of our departure to America. A bleak sun was peeking through the heavy low hanging clouds as I woke up. Jozef was still sleeping besides me. Quietly I got up and went to the kitchen to make tea. Since our own house was empty, we had been sleeping the last night over at my parent's home. While sipping my tea in Father's easy chair, I thought about the last week. It sure had been hectic and sometimes confusing. But finally at last everything had been sold, the large crate gone and our suitcases packed. We had said goodbye to our neighbors, Bart and Lena and Jan and Geertje. Josje, who had recovered from his fever, had gone to his school and said goodbye his schoolteacher and classmates who promised him that they would write to him when he was in America and had sent them his new address from Chicago. Josje and Lia had said goodbye also to their friends Peter, Hans, Anja and Ineke.

Later in the day when we were ready to leave for my parents' home, Jozef started to talk to a neighbor in our front yard. While the children played around their father, I had gone alone into the empty house to say goodbye again. I wandered through the house, climbed the stairs to the children's bedrooms and to our own bedroom where we had laughed and sometimes had cried. I looked at the cracked windowpane of our room which we always had planned to replace but somehow never did. Looking out our bedroom window over the green fields behind the house, I still could hear in my mind the sounds of farm children singing while they milked the cows, or in the fall when they picked the apples and berries in their orchards. Those children had grown up since then and had gone their way. I looked at the very old and large cottonwood trees which stood close to boer Backx his farm. I loved the sound they made when it was windy or on a rainy day. And I thought about our oldest son when he went off into the meadow and wandered through the fields. He enjoyed picking handfuls of twigs from the pussy willow for me in spring when the pussies were at their softest and fluffiest. I looked at the farmhouses in the distance and the forest at the horizon. It looked like a picture postcard, so pretty, even now in almost wintertime. It will not be long anymore, I sadly thought, when the beautiful meadows behind our home will be gone and there will be new neighborhoods. They already had started building the first apartments and houses in the fields close behind our row of houses.

When I stood there, looking out of our bedroom window, I thought of the night when a VII had landed on one of the farmhouses where two families lived and had killed all eight children and their grandmother. I had cried that day and cursed the war. With a smile I thought also about the boys I had dated and kissed goodbye behind our yard during the war years, and how they ran home trying to make it before curfew time. I was interrupted in my dreaming by Josje who had come into the house to tell me that papa was waiting for me, and that he was ready to leave for oma and opa's house.

The whistle blew, the train jerked forward with the customary creaking and banging and began to inch ahead. The railroad station of Breda fell behind and soon the train sped through the countryside with its carefully tended meadows and grazing cows. The little towns were smiling and children raised their bright Dutch faces to the train and waved goodbye to the travelers. We were on our way to the harbor city of Rotterdam where we were going to board ship. Beside my parents, Henk and Annie had also come to see us off. Josje and Lia were full of high spirits, joy and laughter. For them it was a pleasure ride in a train with the family. Soon we reached Rotterdam. From the train terminal we took a taxi to the harbor where our ship, the 'Ryndam', was anchored. The port was crowded with people. They were not only emigrants from Holland, but also from other West European countries. Also many American women, some with children, were waiting to board ship. They had visited their American soldier husbands who were stationed in Europe, mainly Germany, and were now on their way home. While waiting on the wharf, my uncle Nick and his wife came to say goodbye and to see us off. But the waiting was too long for them and after hugs and kisses and wishing us the very best, they left.

After long hours of waiting, checking emigration papers and other documents, we finally could board ship. But first we had to take pictures—we all smiled.

Then the moment came to say goodbye. I hugged my brother and his fiancee, and we promised to write to each other often. Saying goodbye to my parents was the hardest of all. My mother tried very hard to be cheerful, as I did. My mask crumbled when I saw my parents saying goodbye to my three young children. With tears in my eyes I hugged my parents once more and went on board ship. Before we went on board, we had said to the family that since it would still take a few hours before the ship would leave, we were going to eat something in the ship's dining room. We were all hungry and our baby Eddy needed to take a nap in the baby crib which stood, as they had told us, in our cabin. The family said it was a good idea, because they also were hungry and were going to look for a restaurant.

After eating a hearty lunch Jozef took Josje and Lia on deck again while I took care of Eddy. It didn't take long until our little boy was in a sound sleep. I quietly closed our cabin door behind me and went to the deck were I found Jozef and my other kids. We waved to my family, who had come back after their lunch, and looked at all the people who were standing there on the wharf. Some of them were holding flags and others had signs waving with the message of "Best Wishes In Your New Country!" Suddenly the piercingly sharp sound of the ship's horn was the first sign that we soon would leave. A little later a second blast followed. After the third sharp whistle the anchor was pulled up and the ship moved slowly from the wharf. Two pilot ships would tow the ship through the large harbor of Rotterdam into the channel which brings the ships into the North Sea. After many hours of waiting we finally were leaving.

Sadness came over me and my eyes filled with tears which I did not bother to wipe away. Through misty eyes I saw my parents and my brother Henk and Annie waving at us, and we all waved back. As the ship moved further from the pier, the people on board all waved to their loved ones who stayed behind on the wharf. Dutch flags and the well wisher's signs kept on waving until they became a hazy blur. But still people from both sides kept on waving, as if to hold on to the very last moment.

As the ship went slowly through the harbor, Jozef pointed out to Josje and Lia all the different ships we saw anchored or were going somewhere. The harbor of Rotterdam always had been a fascinating place to me with the many ocean voyaging ships coming and going from all around the world. Jozef and I had been in Rotterdam's harbor sometime back when we were on a trip. I had envied the passengers who had been standing on deck, going to faraway places. But now standing on deck of an oceanliner myself, my mind was on the land which I just had left—my Holland—my own cozy little Holland.

It was not long until we moved out of Rotterdam's harbor into the river Waal which brings the ships into open sea. As I looked over the low flat countryside, a mist was forming and the dark low-hanging clouds seemed to touch the brown earth. By now most people had left the deck and had gone inside the ship. Jozef and I also decided to go below deck until we would reach 'Hoek van Holland', the small harbor and summer vacation town which lay on the corner of the river Waal and the North Sea. When I was a child, I had gone there with my family one summer vacation. I had played with my brothers on the wide beach and had watched the ocean liners disappearing on the horizon. 'Hoek van Holland' was also known for when, just after the war, Allied Military on leave were going to or coming back from England by ship.

Before we went to look around the ship, I checked on Eddy. He was sound asleep in his crib. Besides the dining room, where we had been earlier, we found a children's playroom. Of course, Josje and Lia had to check this out first. Lia thought it was fun, but Josje was disappointed and thought that it was for little kids only. From the playroom we went to the lounge where many of the travelers were sitting around tables in a conversation. In the middle of the lounge was a dance floor where some children were playing or sliding around in their stocking feet. On one side of the large lounge was a bar and in a corner was a place for the ship's band. As we later would find out, the lounge was used every evening for dancing or games and in the afternoons for just lounging or a drink. It was a pleasant place where we came to dance every evening for the rest of our journey. In afternoons we usually were sitting in the lounge around one of the round tables talking to fellow emigrants. These were people who came from different places and backgrounds, and who had different hopes and dreams for their lives in America and Canada.

Later, when I once more checked up on my baby, I found him standing in his crib looking around the cabin with his large blue eyes. While lifting him out of the crib I kissed his rosy cheeks—he was such a sweet baby. On each side of our cabin was a bunk bed with a baby crib in between. Besides a dresser and a small washbasin on a wall, there was not much else in the cabin. Each hallway had its own bathroom—each with eight showers, washbasins, large mirrors and closed-in toilets. Though the ship was not large by today standards, it was comfortable and clean

When I went back to the lounge with Eddy in my arms and I looked through a window, I noticed that the ship was ready to pass Hoek van Holland, the place which I wanted to see from the deck. In the lounge I found Jozef in conversation with a couple who were sitting at the same table. Josje and Lia were playing and sliding in their stockings with other children of emigrants. They had fun and didn't want to go on deck again when I asked them. When Josje said hopefully, "Please Mom, please can we play some more here," Jozef said to me, "Why don't you go by yourself, Efka? It is nice and warm here for the kids." I gave Eddy to his papa and went quickly to the upper deck. There I found myself alone with only a few other passengers who wanted to see where the river Waal meets the North sea. A few minutes later the ship passed Hoek van Holland where I still could see its great beaches. I think Hollands beaches are the most beautiful beaches in the world. As soon as the ship reached the North Sea, the pilot ships pulled away from the ship to return to Rotterdam's harbor. At that same moment that they pulled away, the ship's whistle blew as if to say goodbye to Holland. The sea was turbulent with gray water which rolled waves toward the ship. It was getting dark, and a chilly soft misty rain was falling. One last time I looked back only to see the fast disappearing Dutch coast in a dark haze. One more time I said goodbye to my homeland, my beloved country, with the promise that one day I would return.

As I entered the lounge I found Jozef and the children sitting at the table sipping hot cocoa and eating biscuits. When I had been on deck, I had felt sad and a little afraid of the unknown. But returning to the warm lounge and seeing the trusting and happy faces of our children and Jozef smiling at me, I felt good and knew that everything would be all right. Together we would start a new life. Together we would learn a new language, learn new ways of living, new towns, new friends, new food, new drinks and new holidays. I knew it would not always be easy and that many a time I would be longing for my country, my family and friends and the old ways I grew up with. I would miss my town and our forest, the timeless place where I loved to walk. I also knew it would take time. If destiny brought us to America, everything would turn out to be all right.

Our ship 'Ryndam' was built in the thirties for voyages over the Seven Seas. When Germany invaded Holland in 1940, most of Holland's fleet had gone to England where the ships were used for troop transport ships during the war years. Later they were transformed again for transporting the emigrants to the new world.

It was the following day that, after a hearty breakfast, we went on deck to look at the harbor of Le Havre, France. Our ship had anchored there at 9:00 that morning. A bright warm sun was shining as we looked at the hustle and bustle of the French seaport. As all large seaports are, it was busy with ships of all sizes and large cranes which lifted the merchandise in, or out, of the cargo ships. The warm sun felt wonderful as we walked around the ship to investigate. Even though it was early December, to everyone's pleasure we could leave our winter coats in our cabin.

Jozef and Josje went to the upper deck to watch as a shipload of large crates full of chickens were transfered from an cargo ship by large cranes. Lia, with her sunny disposition, had seen a few children playing on deck and soon she joined them in a game of snake. This is a rope game and popular with boys and girls alike. Not far from where the children were playing was an empty lounge chair where I soon sat down in the sun with my baby. Eddy was cranky and not himself. He missed his regular ways from home.

It was early in the afternoon when our ship left Le Havre to sail over the English Channel to Southampton, England. The trip over the Channel was pleasant with a moderate sea and sunny weather. It was dark when we reached Southampton where our ship anchored until midnight before going further over the Atlantic Ocean to Canada.

The dining room, where we had our three meals a day, was set up with long tables. Eight persons were sitting on each side. The food was good and plentiful, something we were not used to yet in Holland in the mid fifties. The food we got on board ship probably came from America. Besides our family there were two other families sitting at our table. One family had three young children who were constantly yelled at by their father—usually about little things the children did or didn't do. The kids were shy little lambs with a mother who was the same shy creature as her children. Many times we wondered how she ever could make it as an emigrant in a strange country. The other family had one son, Josje's age, and it was not long before the two boys became friends and loved to play ball on deck. His parents were our age and soon we enjoyed each other's company. Many evenings during our voyage to America, when our children had finally fallen asleep, we four came together in the lounge for a drink, dancing or for a game.

It was December 2 when our ship steamed into the Atlantic Ocean. The dark cold water of the sea became rough, and the ship's wild motion awoke me feeling nauseated. As the hours went by, it became worse and I became quite miserable. In between bouts of nausea I tried to comfort Josje and Lia who were also seasick. They could not understand why they felt so terrible. While clinging to me, Lia said over and over, "Mommy, can't you make it go away." Since I was not be able to help her, it made me feel even worse. Only Jozef and Eddy felt fine. When breakfast time came, I told Jozef to go alone with Eddy to the dining room. I couldn't stand on my feet by now. Josje and Lia felt sick but not as bad as I was.

Later, when Jozef came back from breakfast, he said that almost no one was in the dining room, and that he and Eddy had been the only ones at our table.

The wild and stormy weather continued throughout the day. Sometimes even now I think about how miserably sick I felt. I had never known anything like this before. Later that day when Jozef came inside the cabin after a stroll with Eddy on deck, he said that many people were sick on deck lying in lounge chairs. They all were wrapped in blankets with only their nose showing. "Maybe," Jozef said, "you also would feel better if you were on deck." But I did not want to leave my bed in the cabin. I felt as though if I were dying. The bouts of nausea were terrible; it felt as if it started in my toes and went slowly up until it reached my head. Jozef and Eddy never got seasick and, besides a few waiters and an older man, were the only ones in the dining room that night. As we later learned, that day many of the ship's crew also had been seasick.

The next day the weather was clearing and the sea became much calmer. Josje and Lia felt better and went for breakfast with their pappa. But I still did not feel well and stayed in bed the rest of the morning. By late afternoon, under pressure from Jozef and my kids, I went on deck. I felt weak but not nauseous anymore. It was not long until the cold sea air made me feel much better, and I was able to drink something. Many of the passengers were still lying sick in their lounge chairs and would stay there that way for the rest of their voyage. They never did recover from their nausea until the ship anchored and they set foot on shore.

On December 6 we had a St. Nicholas party for all the children on board ship. Besides St. Nicholas with his long gray beard and zwarte Piet in his knight costume holding a large sack full of presents for the children, there were candies, cookies and drinks for everyone. Josje and Lia were having a great time, and their singing was loud and full of excitement. Only Eddy, who did not understand what all the commotion was about, couldn't care less. He was the happiest just walking around ship with his papa.

The evenings on board were fun. Besides dancing there were games such as betting on races with small metal horses. One evening Jozef was lucky and won two dollars and fifty cents when his horse came in first. Compared to now it seems not much, but in that time two dollars and fifty cents was some good money. How I remember Jozef walking to the bar with the money and buying himself two packages of cigarettes—Camels—for fifty cents (25 cents each!). Laughing he took my arm and said to come on deck with him. There he took a half empty small package of tobacco out of his coat pocket. While walking to the ship's railing, he opened the small packet and threw its contents into the sea. He then said solemnly, "From this moment on I will never roll my own cigarettes again." He then opened a package of Camel cigarettes and lighted one. Seven years before when Jozef came to live in Holland, he could not afford the price of cigarettes. So, like everyone else in that time, he had bought tobacco and rolled his own cigarettes, swearing if he ever would go to America, Canada or Australia, he would never smoke self-rolled cigarettes again. In that time many women were smoking cigarettes, but I didn't care for them.

On the days when the ocean was rough or when it was raining, our ship looked so small and lonely on the endless sea. But on other days when the sun peeked through the gray winter sky and the sea was calm, we wore our warm coats and walked on deck. The children loved to run and play there. Josje liked to watch the sailors when they worked on deck, or he watched large fish which were looking for food, swimming behind the ship.

We Dutch women soon noticed that the young American women, who were on board ship, came to the breakfast table every morning with a different dress on. Then later for dinner, they would dress up again in another pretty dress. We couldn't believe how many dresses and outfits they had. All that we emigrant women had were two or three dresses for day and one dress for evening for the ten-day voyage. That was just the way it was and I don't think we ever would have noticed it, if it was not for the American women. Soon we felt envious just looking at them when they came into the dining room wearing yet another dress. The waiter, who always served us at our table, had probably overheard us Dutch women talking about it because one day he said, "Just wait a year or two and you will have as many dresses as they have." How right he had been.

On the seventh day of our voyage Josje became ill. His head was aching and his body burning up with fever. His neck glands were badly swollen. I knew that it would take four to five days before the fever would subside, and that was too long, for we had to disembark in a few days. I went to the ship's doctor and told him about my sick boy and asked if he could do something for him. Immediately the doctor went with me to our cabin and examined Josje. But all he could do, he said, was give him an injection for his high fever. The doctor then said to Jozef and me that there were medicines for his condition in America which could cure him. As soon as we were settled in we should take our son to see a doctor. "Do not wait longer than necessary," he said when he left our cabin. The shot which the doctor had given Josje took the high fever down. But our boy was not well and just wanted to lay in his bed, something which was unusual for our always active child, and it worried me.

The following day as Josje and Eddy were taking an afternoon nap, Jozef, Lia and I went on deck. The weather was cold and cloudy, but a pale winter sun was trying to peek through. As we walked around deck, I noticed seagulls which appeared from an unseen shore. As we watched the birds flying around ship and skimming the water, Jozef said to me, "We must not be too far from Canada." A young man, who stood beside us, suddenly pointed his finger to the horizon and shouted, "Land!—land!" We strained our eyes but saw only the endless sea. Then—there it was! A very thin line appeared on the horizon. We had crossed the Atlantic Ocean.

After the first outcry of "land", the many emigrants on board who were to disembark in Canada, became excited and soon they were all standing on deck. They were talking to each other and looking to the horizon—to the new land which was Canada. Not long after that we went below deck and ate dinner. It was a few hours later when we stood again on deck, looking at the lights which came from the Canadian shore in the distance. When our ship entered the harbor of Halifax, the emigrants for Canada were full of anticipation, anxious to start a new life in this vast land. It was dark as I watched the men and women, many with children, leave the ship. While I looked at them, I thought how they were going to scatter over this land, this part of our world, full of ideas and dreams. And I wished them well.

It was about midnight when the Ryndam departed from Halifax with the end destination of New York City. With so many emigrants gone, our dining room had now many empty seats. Our fellow travelers, the family with the three children who had shared our dining room table, had also gone off ship in Canada. Before they left our ship, they told us that they had to travel three more days by train before reaching their destination in Western Canada. After the Ryndam departed from Halifax, it first sailed close to the coast of Nova Scotia before going in a southwest direction toward New York City.

On December 10 Jozef, who had gone alone on deck that early morning, came into our cabin where I was busy with the kids and said to me to come with him. I dressed Eddy and, while Josje and Lia stayed in the cabin, I went with Jozef on deck. As soon as we came there he pointed to a strip of land on the horizon and said excitingly, "Efka, look! There it is! There is America!" It is hard to describe how we felt. This strip of land on the horizon was America! This was the land we had heard, read and dreamed about, but did not know. With cities and towns unknown to us. It was the new land where we would live and work, and where our children would grow up.

# 35

## *THE NEW LAND*

It was on the afternoon of December 10, 1954 that we entered USA territory. A few hours later our ship sailed close to the shore of Long Island toward New York's harbor. The voyage from Rotterdam to New York City had been 10 days. It was dusk by now, and everyone was standing on deck looking at the spectacular sight of tens of thousands of lights. They came not only from the many small towns and beach houses, but especially from the long winding lines of automobiles which were probably driving on a highway close to the shore. We had never seen anything like this before.

While Jozef was on deck with Lia and Eddy, I had gone to our cabin to check on my poor son who was lying alone in his bed, reading a book. His fever was high again. "Way too high," I thought while comforting him. "We are almost ready to leave the ship. What will I do now?" While giving him a kiss I said that I would be back very shortly. A few minutes later I came back with the ship's doctor. He took Josje's temperature and shook his head. While giving the sick child an injection he said, "This will do it. The fever will be gone in about one hour." The doctor, who was a very sympathetic man, rubbed his hand through Josje's curly hair and said to him that he would be just fine. Wishing me the best, he left our cabin. As I was tucking my child in, I told him that I was going on deck to tell his pappa that I was going to stay in the cabin. I would bring Eddy back with me. I had wanted so much that our son could have witnessed our coming into the United States, but it was just too cold and damp on deck for a child as sick as he was. Just as I came on deck, our ship sailed past the fantastic sight of the Statue of Liberty. It stood in a sea of lights, and it looked as if it was greeting all who came into the land of freedom and justice. A few minutes later we sailed into the harbor of New York where I saw the port with its dark buildings and the many ships and freighters with the American flags. I then went downstairs with Eddy followed by Jozef with Lia.

While our ship slowly moved forward to the pier, Jozef went upstairs with our emigration papers and to take care of the necessary formalities with custom officials. In the meantime when he was gone, I was going to dress the children and do the last packing. Josje's fever went finally down but left him weak. Even though he did not feel too good, he wanted to help me with the necessary things I still had to take care of. His usually easy baby brother had decided to be difficult at the wrong time. Eddy refused to be dressed and kicked and screamed until Josje came to the rescue. With his good-natured tactics he made Eddy giggle and cooperate again. Finally we were ready to leave—but where was Jozef? I couldn't understand what took him so long. "He should be finished with the paperwork by now and come downstairs to help me," I thought, irritated.

After some more waiting, I decided to take the kids and the luggage and go upstairs to the lounge where we all had to go before our disembarkation. I still see myself going with the children through the deserted hallways, looking in the meantime for someone to help me. But I saw no one. As weak as he was, Josje lugged a suitcase, my four-year-old little girl dragged a bag and her dolls, and I carried a now-sleepy Eddy on one arm and hip with more bags on the other side. After some difficulties going up the stairs, we finally came to the lounge where people still stood in line to leave the ship. At the same moment I saw Jozef, he saw me. It had taken some time he explained, because after he finally was done with the papers, they had taken him to another place in the lounge. There they asked him if he wanted to sign up for military duty—in case—they said. If he would sign up, he could become American citizen in two years' time. Jozef was surprised that they had the copies of his military papers there, and he couldn't figure out how they came to have those documents. Jozef didn't sign up, but told them if they ever needed him, they would know where to find him.

Finally we were ready to leave our ship. As I carried Eddy, I descended the wooden stairs to the concrete of the pier. How well I remember the moment I stepped on American soil and thought, "I am in America. I am really in America," and how a strange feeling came over me. As soon as we departed from the ship, we heard over the loudspeaker someone asking if Jozef Otto would take a phone call which had come for him in one of the pier offices. It turned out the call was from Jozef's cousin—Joe Otto. He told Jozef that he had been on the wharf waiting for us earlier, but because our ship Ryndam had been three hours late, he had left. It was Saturday, and he was busy in his store. His cousins Martin Otto and Edmond Kaczor would pick us up, he said, and they would bring us to his house. While Jozef spoke Polish to his cousin on the phone, he sometimes said something in Dutch to me. As he put the phone down, Jozef talked to an office clerk in English. A man sitting there, who probably was waiting for something, looked at Jozef and said to him, "Are you a Jew? You speak three languages at the same time!"

Not long thereafter Jozef's cousins Martin, and Edmund and his wife Marisha arrived at the large wharf to take us to the house of his cousin Joe and his wife Frances. They lived in the small town of Bedford Hills. First after a warm introduction we went all together to Martin's car which was parked at a parking lot not far from our ship. Before reaching the car I took one last look over my shoulder at the Ryndam. The ship was anchored in a flood of light, and it looked as if it wanted to say a last farewell. For me the ship Ryndam was at that moment the last connection with Holland.

When riding through New York City, Jozef and I marveled at all the bright advertisement lights. We never had seen such large colorful advertisements. To Josje and Lia's excitement and delight, they saw for the first time lighted outdoor Christmas decorations on the stores and other buildings. It was a wonderful sight to see. Not much later we drove through the suburbs of New York City. For the very first time we saw a live evergreen tree standing in a front yard decorated with Christmas lights. We never had seen this in Holland, and we all thought that it was very pretty. While Jozef translated from English into Dutch, Marisha told the kids that they would see many more of those decorated Christmas trees. "Christmas in America is very pretty," she said. In the meanwhile Eddy had fallen asleep on my lap. After about an hour drive we arrived late in the evening at the beautiful ranch style house of Joe and Frances Otto. The large brick home was nestled in a hilly forest area.

It was there that for the first time we experienced the good life in America. Besides the many rooms in the house, where I sometimes got lost, it had a very large kitchen with all the latest electrical appliances. Besides the refrigerator with a freezer, which its existence I never knew about, it had many small appliances which I also never had seen or heard about. It was a kitchen I could not have dreamed in my wildest imagination. We also saw a working television for the first time. It was small and black-and-white, but even though it was not working very well, we thought it fantastic. In a side room off of the kitchen stood a beautiful grand piano on which Frances played her music. Also in that same room stood a large radio which could get stations from around the world. Besides the radio, Jozef was interested in a few cars which were parked in their driveway and said that they were Cadillacs, which I never had heard about, of course.

For two whole days we stayed at the home of Joe and Frances. They were two wonderful people who were very helpful and pleasant. Even though they had no children of their own, four young foster girls filled their home with laughter and happiness. The next day, Sunday, they took us to their church and later to Joe's store and butcher shop. It was a large place and full of meats, groceries and drinks. Many of the items I saw were packaged, something I was not used to. In Holland most articles were still sold by the pound or ounce. When we came home from Joe's shop, the families of Martin and Edmond and some business people, came over for dinner. Everyone sat around a large table in the huge dining room with a fireplace, and talked and ate from large plates stacked with meats and other foods. Many glasses of wine were poured from the bottles which stood on the heavy oak table. Everything was very impressive to us. We never in our lives had we seen anything like it.

Joe and Frances wanted us to stay in Bedford Hills. They said they would help us, and Jozef could work in his business. Later Jozef and I talked this over. But since his family in Chicago had taken care of so many things for us and were now waiting for our arrival, we decided to stay with our plan and go to Chicago. We said maybe later we could go back to New York. In that time we had absolutely no idea that the distances in America were so enormous. Later when we lived in Chicago, we sometimes would regret this decision of not staying in Bedford Hills. How little we knew then that later our destination would bring us further into America and finally to a town we never knew existed.

Late in the afternoon of the following day Joe and Frances took us to a train station which was on the line to Chicago. It was already dark when our train finally arrived. We said goodbye to those two wonderful people who had welcomed us during our very first days in America. We would never forget them. Even though we wrote letters to each other for some time, we never saw them again. Joe died of a heart attack a few years after our coming to America. Francis sold the house and moved to her family in Baltimore where she came from before she had married Joe.

The whistle blew and the train started to inch forward. Once more we waved to Joe and Frances until the train left the terminal and sped away. Josje and Lia each got a window seat and enjoyed some candy they got from fellow passengers who, after hearing our language, gathered we were emigrants. Josje was feeling much better and was almost his old self again. But now Eddy had come down with a cold and was feverish. Since it was not warm in the train, I covered him with a extra baby blanket. Josje and Lia set themselves down with some coloring books they had received from Frances for their trip to Chicago, which would take about fourteen hours. It was not long until the movement of the train put all three children to sleep, soon followed by Jozef.

I settled myself down and also tried to sleep, but I couldn't. I stared out of the train's window into the dark night where I saw just here and there a light from a farm. I wondered where we were. It was too dark to see anything. While the train sped through the night, my thoughts went back to the last few hectic weeks. Our goodbye from Holland had been difficult. I wondered what time it was now in Holland—probably everyone was soon getting out of their beds for a new day. It would not be long until Christmas was here, my first Christmas far away from Holland. I wondered what kind of city Chicago was and where we would live. I must have dozed off to sleep because when I awoke the train had slowed its speed and came to a stop in a small town. I looked out of the window but couldn't read the name of the place where the train had stopped. A few passengers came in—no one went out of the train. A few moments later the train jolted and began to move and soon sped away. Eddy coughed and I took him in my arms and cuddled him until he was again in a sound sleep. It was quiet once more except for the sound of the speeding train through the dark night.

Late in the morning of December 13 our train steamed into Chicago's large Union Station. For the last few hours we had been looking through the train windows at the landscape which was dusted with snow and stretched endlessly with only here and there a small town, village or farm. I was a little disappointed when all that I saw was flat land instead of mighty mountains and virgin forests which I had seen in a magazine in Holland. But we loved the look of houses in the small towns we passed which were bathed in the early sunlight. They were painted in different pastel colors, something we never had seen in Holland where most of the houses are built in different shades of brown brick. When we passed another pretty village, Josje said to his sister, "Look, Lia, another sugarhouse town!" He must have thought about the St. Nicholas candy houses which are made from colored sugar.

Finally we were in Chicago and as the train came slowly to a screeching standstill, Jozef looked out of the window to see if he could see the familiar faces of his family, but he saw no one he recognized. As soon as we got off the train and stood on the platform with our children and suitcases, there she was. There was Chelca—Jozef's cousin. Smiling at us and with outstretched arms, she walked through the crowd with her son Henry following her. It was an emotional welcome. So much had happened since Jozef and Chelca had seen each other in Poland 17 years ago in 1937. Henry, a pleasant young man of about nineteen, introduced himself as her son. Chelca was a trim and friendly woman in her late fifties. With her black hair worn in a chignon, she must have been a beautiful woman when she was young. With the coming of WWII she had gone through some very bad years, and it showed in her face. Chelca greeted me and the children warmly, as if she had known us for a long time.

When we got into Henry's car and drove through Chicago for the first time, the first impression I got of that big city was of tall buildings, busy freeways and traffic everywhere. After about a half-hour drive, we came to a complex of old, but clean, apartment buildings where I saw signs, names and advertisements in the Polish language. We had arrived in an almost all-Polish neighborhood where the people lived in sometimes very small apartments with only one bathroom which had to be shared by two families. Many of the people who lived there knew each other from the displaced persons camps in Germany, or from German farms or war factories where they had been forced to work during WWII. They now lived in a community that often was unlike their hometown. But they drew emotional support and helped each other in their new country. In later years, after they could speak the English language and had saved some money, those emigrants would spread to other neighborhoods or towns and cities throughout America.

Chelca and her son Henry lived in a very small apartment with a bathroom shared with a neighbor. The plan was that we would stay at Cesia's apartment, which was larger and had more room for us. Later in the afternoon Cesia and Halina, Chelca's two daughters, came from their work to take us to their apartments, which were about a fifteen minute drive and in a less crowded neighborhood. Cesia, the oldest daughter, was married to Frank Radaszewski. He had been a former schoolteacher from East Poland. Frank had been called into the Polish Army when the war broke out in 1939. He was taken prisoner of war by the German Army and had been forced to work for the their war machine. He emigrated to America where a few years later he and Cecia met in Chicago. He was about 17 years Cesia's senior. When we arrived in Chicago, they had no children yet. Halina was married to Edward Maletski who also came from East Poland. He was still a young man when his father was killed in the war. Edward and his mother were sent to Germany to work on a farm. When the war was over, they also were sent to one of the displaced persons' camps. From there they came to America. Edward and Halina also met in America. The first time I met them they had three young daughters. That same evening Palasia, the cousin who had stood by Chelca's side all through the trying years, came to see us with her husband Kazmier, a barber. They had two daughters as Palasia told us, but they were home and we would meet them later. We would stay at Frank and Cecia's home for one week.

◆          ◆          ◆

(Jozef) It was so good to see Chelca again after so many years. Her children had grown into adults, and I didn't recognize them anymore. There was so much for us to tell each other which we did in the coming weeks. Frank and Cesia didn't want me to look for work that very first week in America. "First you need a place to live and some furniture," they said, and insisted we borrow money from them until we were on our own feet. While Cesia and Halina looked for an apartment which we could rent in the neighborhood where Chelca lived, Frank took me furniture shopping. We needed beds, table and chairs, a gas stove and a washing machine (something Eef was very happy with), which we found in a furniture store owned by a Polish Jew. He gave us a good deal on the things we needed and easy monthly payments.

Our apartment, which Chelca found, was located on Huron Street. It was a street which consisted mainly of old apartment buildings in Chicago's Polish neighborhood. The rent was 30 dollars a month. We lived on the first floor of a three-story apartment. It had a living room, kitchen, two bedrooms and a bathroom which was located off the kitchen. In the front of the building was a small yard which was securely enclosed and where only the landlord, who lived on the third floor, could come in. After a week of crowded living at Frank and Cesia's apartment, we moved into our own place on Huron Street. That same day we not only got our furniture delivered, but also our crate from Holland. The crate had been stored in a warehouse in Chicago until they received notice from us as to where they had to deliver it. Eef was thankful to see the crate since she needed some things from it.

Here I was in the land of opportunity! And those opportunities I wanted to tackle as soon as possible. I knew that they were not up for grabs in the fifties but in an industrial city as Chicago, work shouldn't be difficult to find. And, as in Holland, I had to start somewhere and I didn't care what work it was as long as it made enough money to live on for now.

The day following our moving into the apartment, I bought a newspaper and looked through the ads for work. I had already talked to Frank about the different places of work and how to get there by bus or tram. A day later I said to Eef that I was going to look for work and didn't know what time I would be home.

She told me that she was going to tackle her first grocery shopping adventure with the children in a small supermarket.

Later that afternoon when I came home, I had found three jobs. They were all located in the downtown area in the clothing factories. One of them sounded good and paid $1.35 an hour. The minimum wage in that time was $0.80 a hour. The factory would teach me how to grease the sewing machines every day, and later I would learn how to repair them. I thought this was pretty good. That same evening Kazmir came to our home and said to me, "Jozef, a friend of mine works in a foundry which pays well. He told me that you could find work in that factory. If you are interested in working there, he is willing to pick you up when you are ready. He lives close by." I told Kazmir to tell this friend to pick me up the next morning.

The foundry, by the name of Well's Mfg, was a place where about 600 men worked. It was located north of Chicago in a suburb named Skokie. They manufactured parts for cars and trucks. The work was hard and dirty. Starting pay was $ 1.65 an hour. My work was breaking the molds in which hot liquid iron had been poured a hour of so earlier. After taking the parts out of the molds I then had to put them into a metal crate. The crate with the car parts then went further for inspection. I took this job because of the good money it paid, but when I started to work there I many times said to myself, "How can I work here in this hell? I will not last a week!" The place where I worked was hot and dusty, and the men who worked there were dirty with sweat. The first time when I entered the foundry and looked around a foreman came up to me and said, "It seems hell to you now, but in three weeks you will feel different about this place. You will get used to it. Take your time, take a rest when you need to, and go to the large water container for a drink every so often. Also you must take a salt tablet before you start your work." So I started to work there in that hell of heat and dust while wondering how long I could do this.

Many of the men who worked for Well's were Polish. They were men who had known a rough time in a rough WW II world. Many came from backgrounds of working in offices and at better jobs, before the war in Poland. I enjoyed talking to those men. They were not the factory workers I had expected to find there. All they wanted was to make money and buy a house outside of Chicago as soon as possible. Most of those men were attending a school to learn the English language. Then, after they knew the new language well enough, they planned to find better work and go further with their lives.

I worked five days a week—from four in the afternoon until twelve at night. Saturday and Sundays were free. On working days I always walked to Woodstreet which was a five minutes walk from where we lived. There I waited for Kazmir's friend, Alex Novak, who brought me and four other guys with him to the foundry. We paid Alex one dollar a week for gas which in that time was 32 cents a gallon. And so I started my new life in America, while thinking sometimes about Bedford Hills and wondering if I had done the right thing to go on to Chicago. "We always can go back there later when I have saved some money," I thought, "but for now I have to work here and take care of my family."

(Eef) By the time we had lived in Chicago for only a few weeks, I had already realized that living there was such a world apart from what I ever had known before. I knew also that every emigrant, and that also included me, must develop survival skills to get through the difficult adjustment period.

Jozef's relatives were a close knit Polish family, and they did everything they could to help us. It was almost Christmas and we had no Christmas tree that year or any other trimming which go along with Christmas. But Jozef's family didn't allow us to miss out on this so special time, and our first Christmas in America. On Christmas Eve, while Frank's older aunt was babysitting our children, they took us to a very old, large and beautiful Catholic Church for midnight mass. The church was within walking distance from our apartment. I remember distinctly how everyone in the church was so well dressed. The ladies wore fancy wide-rimmed hats and many were dressed in a fur trimmed coat and high-heeled shoes. Since this was a Polish mass, I couldn't understand much of the sermon. My thoughts drifted to Holland where, as little girl, I had gone to my very first Christmas Eve Service. How I had adored the many small glass angels hanging from the branches of the large Christmas tree which stood in the middle of the church. And I thought about the small paper angels on the cookies which we received before going home. How special that night had been for me.

As the church choir was singing a Polish Christmas song, I prayed silently that I would get used to living in this strange big city called Chicago. I felt lonesome for my home in Holland.

On Christmas Day we had dinner at Palasia and Kazmir's apartment. There I met more family members as Olena and Ursela, their two young daughters. For the first time I ate the Polish Christmas specialties Jozef sometimes had talked about. Since we lived in a Polish neighborhood, many of the ingredients for those special dishes and pastries were obtainable there in the stores. It was a great dinner and I felt happy for Jozef. He seemed so full of enthusiasm—talking and joking and singing the old Polish songs with all his family around him. Since their lively conversation was in their native language, I could not understand much of what they all were talking about, even though Jozef tried to translate it for me. I knew that sometimes they were discussing the time when they all lived in Poland and remembered another life from before the war—a time when they were young and free of worries. Since I wanted Jozef to have a good time, I decided to play with the children who were all together playing games in another room. I said to myself, "Maybe those children can teach my kids and me a Polish game, and I can teach them a Dutch one." Josje, Lia and Eddy were playing with the other children without difficulty, and I thought how nice it was that in the universal language of children, they could understand one another.

New Year's Eve came with a grand celebration. While Frank's aunt was babysitting our children again, the family took us to an American-Polish New Year's Dance. Since I knew that everyone was going in evening wear, I sewed a long full black taffeta skirt for myself on my sewing machine from Holland. I bought the material in a fabric store which was located in the main street named Chicago Avenue. The street was located close to our apartment and would become my shopping street. When I was finished with my skirt, I got a white lace sleeveless top from Cesia to wear with my new skirt. The combination of the heavy black taffeta skirt and the white lace sleeveless top together with black high heeled shoes was lovely. Henry drove us to the ball that night, and Jozef and I felt great. In a large decorated hall where a big band was playing all the tunes of that time, we danced the night away. At midnight we embraced and wished each other the very best in the new year. We listened to everyone sing America's National Anthem and other songs we didn't know yet. We came home late that night. It was our first American New Year's Eve. The year was 1955.

◆    ◆    ◆

The holidays were gone, and Josje started school. The Catholic school, by the name of Holy Innocent School which our son would attend, was run by nuns and was within walking distance from our apartment. He was placed in the second grade—the same grade as in Holland. But since Josje could not speak the English language yet, he was placed in the first grade for beginning reading. Poor Josje, it was not easy for him, especially not during the first weeks. He didn't understood his teachers or the children from his new school. He was such a brave child and seldom complained. But sometimes he came home confused and in tears when children had teased him and he didn't know why. Luckily the nuns at the school, who were well used to this kind of situation, were wonderful and helped our son over the worst times. The first day that we took Josje to school, the principal said to us, "He will be speaking English in no time. For the first few weeks he will probably be a little miserable, but children are very resilient." She lent us some first-grade books and said, "These books are for your family to read. Read them together every night." Josje and I did that even though he became bored and playfully tried to get away from the repeat and repeat of the same words.

One day Josje came home from school all confused and told me that he had lost his gloves at school. He had said to his teacher that he lost his 'handschoenen' which is Dutch for gloves but sounds like 'hand-shoes' in English. He couldn't understand why the children had burst out laughing. After I explained it to my son, we both laughed about it. I tried as much as I could to make it into a fun game when he came home with a problem. Since I had the same problem with the new language as he did, Josje did not feel alone. Later when his English improved, he found that he was happy in school.

Jozef and I decided to send Lia to preschool. It was in the same school as where her brother went. We reasoned it would be so much easier for her if she would start early with the English language. By the time she would be in the first grade, she would not have the same language problem as her brother had. She was still young enough to learn a new language while playing with other children. Lia loved her preschool, and every morning she went happily to school. When I picked her up at noon from out the hallway, I always heard her giggling with other little girls. I knew that my daughter was going to be all right.

It was a culture shock. Chicago was not what I thought it would be. The American movies, which I had watched in Holland, had showed life as a glossy America of neat houses and happy people. Sure, I had known that Chicago was a big industrial city, but nothing had me prepared for this. Every day the newspapers were full of stories about people being shot or murdered in a most gruesome way. "Do we have to raise our children in this city?" I said to myself many times over. Also I was not used to life in a big city where you had to look straight up through the window to see the sky. The high buildings around me and our apartment, where never a glimpse of sun came in, were like the walls of a prison from which I could not escape. I, who had lived all of my life in open spaces, hated this. Jozef, who had to work until midnight, was never home before 1:00 in the morning. After the kids were put to bed, I felt lonely with no one to talk to, and nothing much to read in the long evenings. Those nights I took out our photograph album from Holland and for the longest time I looked at the pictures of my family and friends.

The first weeks in America, I think I cried most nights until Jozef came home. Since he had to walk home alone late at night from Woodstreet, I was worried for his safety and could not sleep until he walked through the door. Even though I was depressed many times and longed for the life I had left behind, there were happy times too. I think about the Saturday mornings when Jozef took care of Eddy for a few hours, and Josje, Lia and I went grocery shopping. After so many years of food shortage I had forgotten how good it was to go shopping and buy all the food we wanted. Even though things in Holland had been greatly improved since the war had ended, it still did not compare with America. How rich I felt when for ten dollars I could buy three bags full of groceries. For Josje and Lia there were many new exciting discoveries, such as the wieners they ate by the package full. Later we learned that those wieners were meant to be put between a bun with some other 'stuff' and were called 'hot-dogs'.

Sometimes I had a hard time finding foods I was used to in Holland and couldn't find it, or didn't know the English name for it. I think especially about the hot cereal Farina. I wanted this Farina ('Griesmeel' in Dutch) for Eddy. He was used to eating this cooked cereal since he was three months old, and always had enjoyed it. Since this is a packaged food, it was not easy to find out in which package it came. It seemed that instead of griesmeel, I always took the wrong package home as cornstarch, cake mix, powdered sugar etc. Finally I found what I wanted and learned that the name was Farina. In the meantime in seaching for the right package, I had learned the names of other merchandise which came packaged.

In the first weeks living in Chicago I found by accident many of the articles which I needed. I will never forget about the buttermilk (karnemelk) which I wanted one day. I just could not understand in which bottle it came. Many times I had the bottle with buttermilk in my hands but thought that it was a creamy buttery milk and had it put down. Until, by mistake, I found it when I came home with the buttermilk thinking I had bought my regular milk. When I opened the bottle and poured a glass of 'milk' I started to laugh so hard that Josje asked me if I had swallowed a laugh bug. "Never mind," I told him,"Your mother just found her karnemilk."

The wide main street of Chicago Avenue runs through Chicago, connecting many streets. A section of this avenue ran also through the Polish neighborhood and was located three blocks from our apartment. It had many large nice stores where I loved to marvel at the latest fashion in clothing, lingerie and shoes. Most of the businesses carried signs in their windows saying, "We speak Polish." All around me I heard people speaking Polish instead of English, which made it more difficult for me when shopping. But somehow I could make myself understood and bought whatever I needed in the stores. Jozef and the kids' favorite store was the Polish bakery where they carried many delectable Polish pastries which we all had to try. At an American bakery we tried cheesecake for the first time. We never had seen this pastry before and we had to buy a slice. It became Jozef and my favorite pastry while the kids loved the popular American fruit pies the best.

The winter in Chicago was cold; it was much colder than we were used to. Since the people of Chicago used oil for heating their homes, it left streaks of oily dirt on all outside stones and made everything grimy looking. We were in Chicago about two months when Josje got sick again with the same problem—his neck glands. Remembering the words of the ship's doctor who had told us about the medicine which was available in America for his condition, I knew we needed a doctor. But not knowing where a doctors office was, I went to the drugstore on Chicago Avenue and asked if they could help me. "My son is sick," I told them as well as I could, "and needs a doctor." I then gave them my address. In that time doctors still made house calls. One hour later the doctor came to our apartment and looked Josje over. He then said something in English to me and prescribed a medicine for him which was a bright pink liquid. After taking this medicine for only two days, Josje's fever was gone. It seemed like a miracle to us. It was only a few days later when his fever came back and our child became very ill again. His throat hurt him badly and, thinking it was a cold, I put him in bed. After a few days with a high fever a rash broke out, and I asked for the doctor to come again. When he saw Josje's strawberry colored tongue and the rash on his body, he said that our son had scarlet fever and prescribed some other medicine for him.

Since this is a very contagious disease, Lia and Eddy had to stay away from their brother, which is difficult to do in a small apartment. For the following week the doctor came every morning to our home to see how Josje was doing, and if the other kids were still O.K. Josje recovered three weeks later, and went back to school again. It was about two years later when Josje had another bout with his neck glands. Another doctor (we lived then in Omaha) prescribed the same pink medicine as the one in Chicago. After a few days of high fever from his neck glands the sickness left him, never to return again.

One Sunday afternoon when we had dinner at Kasmir and Palasia's apartment, Kasmir was telling me that one of his customers was married to a Dutch woman. He then asked me that, if I was interested in meeting her, he was willing to arrange it when his customer came again for his haircut. Excitedly I answered Kasmir that I would love to meet her. "It will be great to have a conversation with another Dutch woman." I said to him. A few weeks later we met. It happened to be a family who, before their emigration to America, lived close to my hometown of Breda in Holland. He was a Polish ex-soldier who had, as Jozef, served in the British forces during the war. He met and married a Dutch girl when he was stationed just north of Breda, and later emmigrated to the USA.

His name was Stan Makewski and worked for Oscar Mayer Company in Chicago. His wife Ellie was a tall and somewhat skinny young woman about my age. They had two young sons about the same ages as Josje and Lia. Since that first meeting we became friends and came together at their apartment many Sunday afternoons. They lived about a ten-minute ride on the bus from our apartment. While the men were talking politics or watching a game on the TV, Ellie made the best open-faced sandwiches in Chicago. The children played together with the many toys which were scattered over their apartment. I don't think our children had ever seen that many toys together in one place besides in a toy store.

When we lived in Holland, I thought that the English language would not be so difficult. Jozef already had taught me quite a few words and I had learned some from out an English book. But living in America, I soon found out that it wasn't enough for me to be able to understand people, or to make other people understand me. Not by a long shot. But that began to change after we had met Stan and Ellie, and enjoyed their nice larger siced television. It was not long until Jozef bought our very first television—an 18-inch black-and-white Zenith. Now the evenings were less lonesome for me, and it became a great help in learning the English language.

The TV was also a good learning tool for our children. They loved to watch the after school programs for children especially Mickey Mouse cartoons. While I made my Dutch tea (tea served with cookies and chocolates), I always watched the programs with them. I think the commercials helped me the most. After seeing the same commercial a few times I could not only understand what they were talking about, but also had learned a few more words of the English language.

Almost every week I wrote to my family in Holland about our life in America. Josje and Lia drew or colored pictures for their grandparents which they then sent to Holland together with a picture of themselves. One day we received a letter from my brother Henk. He wrote that he and Annie were getting married and were busy with their plans for emigration to Canada. This news came very unexpectedly. Not that they were getting married, because they had known each other already for some years, but that they were going to emigrate came as a surprise to us. I thought about my parents—how hard it must be for them to have to say goodbye to yet another child who was going to live in a far away country. Of course we wished Henk and Annie a wonderful wedding and a great new future in Canada. I wrote that we hoped that they would come to live not too far from us in Chicago so we could visit each other.

# 36

## *HOMESICKNESS*

The cold winter months finally left, and a warm breeze was blowing. It was the first springlike Sunday, and we decided to do some exploring and go to Lake Michigan. We had lived for a few months in the midst of the large city, walked between high buildings and heavy traffic, and now needed to go somewhere else—someplace which was called 'the great outdoors.' A place where our children could run and play and where we could feel the warm sunshine on our face. From Cesia we learned that there was a very nice park and beach located near downtown Chicago. I hoped it was also a place where I could shake the blues which didn't want to leave me.

We took a bus going east in the direction of Lake Michigan which we reached after a transfer to another bus. After a short walk we came to Chicago's beautiful Lincoln Boulevard. On one side is Lake Michigan and on the other side is Grant Park. This is a large park with excellent views of the impressive skyline of Chicago's business district—its large banks and museums . That area of Chicago is great and many tourists visit there. It felt wonderful to walk again on moist green grass between the tall old trees and shrubs which opened their buds in the warm sunshine. The kids were running to their hearts content, and they let out screams of delights. It was the kind of freedom we all missed since we had left Breda. Soon we came to the large Buckingham Fountain which shoot water high into the air. It was great fun for the kids when sprays of cool water blew our way. Of course, the children put their hands in the cold water of the fountain and then made themselves all wet. From there we walked to Lake Michigan's shoreline where the wide blue sky meets the water. Even as many of the sailboats and other pleasure boats were far out on the water, others were anchored in the large harbor. While overlooking Lake Michigan we walked further on the side of the boulevard and came to the Adler Planetarium and the Shedd Aquarium. They were wonderful places which we would visit with our children on a later date.

While we lived in Chicago, we would visit quite a few times the great large Chicago Natural History Museum which is also located there. Josje and Lia especially loved to go there and see the large glass cases where wild animals were set up and displayed in their natural habitat. The famous huge Soldier Field, which can seat 110,000 people and is also located close to the museum, we saw only on the outside.

After a few hours of walking or sitting on a bench on the side of the water and playing with our children in the park, we got hungry. While looking around for somewhere to eat, we noticed beside the planetarium a man standing with a snack cart. We walked to him and asked the man what it was he was selling. He looked at us and, while opening the lid of his cart, he answered loudly, "Hot Dogs! Very good hot dogs! Only 29 cents! "We took his word for it that they were good and bought only one—first we had to try it out. After we each took a bite from it and thought it tasted real good, we asked the man to give us each a hot dog—with everything on it. It was our very first hot dog in America.

**(Jozef)** After only three months of working at the Wells factory, I got a nice promotion. I now started to work in the inspection department—the place where they inspected the molded auto parts for cracks and flaws. I not only didn't have to work in the heat and dust of the ovens anymore, but now made $ 4.25 an hour. It sure had paid off for me, not only to already know the English language when I began working there, but also to be a hard and dependable worker. Now that I made good money, I wanted to pay back the money I had borrowed from Frank for our furniture as soon as possible.

I got a letter from Poland from my mother in which she asked if we could send her some coffee. It had been many years since they had tasted real coffee and tea. So for some time once a month we got a package together for the family consisting not only of coffee and tea, but also chocolate, spices, canned meats, soap and material for sewing clothing. The Polish Organization Office in Chicago, which was located not far from where we lived, took care of the packages with the guarantee of their safe arrival. About six weeks after we had mailed each package, we always received a thankful letter back from my mother, saying that the package had arrived. She wrote us that the whole family had come together for a coffee and tea party and had divided the spices and materials among them.

(Eef) "Three months vacation! The schools here have three months of summer vacation! Can you believe that?" I said to Jozef in disbelief while waving Josje's report card which he just brought home. "What do children do here in this big city with three months of summer vacation?" I repeated, looking at my husband. While Jozef shook his head, Josje said happily, "Just playing, Mom!" Josje had a reasonably good report card, considering the difficulties he had in the beginning with the English language. We were both proud of him. He had handled himself well.

This three months home from school, instead of the one month school vacation that Jozef and I had been used to in our own country, was a little too much to comprehend. "There is sure not much to do here every day for children to play," I thought while remembering the sandpit, the creek and wide open spaces behind our home in Breda. It was there in our old neighborhood that the children played to their hearts' content in the summer vacations. But here, I thought sadly, the only place the children from the neighborhood could play was on the steps in front of their apartments.

Jozef's family had told us that the weather in Chicago could be very hot during the summer months, and I had looked forward to this. The only hot weather I had ever experienced was sometimes a few days of a rare heat wave in Holland. So when we got our first hot days that summer, I thought it was great. But it was not so great anymore when the midday temperature reached well into the nineties day after day. The worst were the nights when the heat lingered between the tall buildings and there was no wind to blow the heat away. It was difficult to sleep and we felt sweaty and awful. I had never felt such a heat before and never imagined such discomfort. At that time we didn't see many window air conditioners for home use. Only some of the stores and bars began to install air conditioners. Those stores which had their places cool, proudly posted large signs on their windows saying "We have air conditioning!" On those days when it was very hot outside, it felt great to walk around in the air-conditioned stores.

During the summer months we took our children for the whole Sunday afternoon to the beach on Lake Michigan to play in the water. It usually was crowded with people looking for relief from the heat. Occasionally we went also to the beautiful Natural History Museum where it was cool and where the children loved to go. Because it was summer vacation I had decided to take the kids to the beach two days a week. To reach the beach area of Lake Michigan from our home, we had to take a bus and transfer to another one before reaching Lincoln Park. From there it was a ten-minute walk through the park before we came to the beach. Usually I stayed the whole day there with the kids who played in the cool water and made sand castles in the white sand. The beach was the best place to spend the hot summer days, and we enjoyed every minute of it. Sometimes I also took Palasia's two girls with me and we had a great time.

Although I enjoyed going to the beach with the children, it was always a hassle going back home. After a whole day on the beach without his nap, Eddy decided not to walk anymore. He was tired so I had to carry him through the park back to the bus. While I carried him, Josje and Lia had to carry the bags with the beach stuff which did not always go well, and soon they were in each other's hair. Waiting for the busses, which were crowded with people going home from their work, did not help matters either. When we finally reached home, all three kids were tired and cranky and after a bath they were ready for bed. But those days on the shore of Lake Michigan in the hot Chicago summer and the Sundays together with Jozef going places with the children were the times I felt good and could cope with my homesickness for my country.

It was the beginning of September and the school bells were ringing, calling the children back to their schools. It was the morning that Josje and Lia got out of their beds early, eager to go to school. Josje, in his new pants and shirt looking like a real American boy, asked me again, "Are you sure, Mom. Are you sure that I can stay now in the third grade all day? Do I not have to go back anymore to the first grade for my grammar?" When I assured him, saying, "No, you can stay all day now in the third grade, but remember, every night you have to read from your school books," he couldn't wait to go to school. I hoped my son would make some friends this school year. Since we came to Chicago, Josje and Lia had been playing mostly together with Eddy following them. The few children who lived around our apartment played inside their homes most of the time or were standoffish toward Josje and Lia. Josje had been lonesome for his friends Peter and Hans and their adventures behind our home in the fields. The boys had written letters to each other, telling stories about what they had been doing. Josje always bragged a little in his letters about the beach and all that he had seen in the museums.

I took Josje to his third-grade classroom, and then I went with Lia to her kindergarten room. She was wearing a new blue dress which I had sewn one day for the occasion. When we reached her room, she clutched my hand and asked me,

"Mommy, will you stay with me, please?"After having comforted her and assured my little girl that I would soon come back for her, I left. Later as I walked home with Eddy, I thought about the fact that it would not take long for our children to become Americans, and how they never would know the soil from which they came.

◆     ◆     ◆

It was late in the year 1955. With fall almost gone and the long dark winter months ahead of us, I dreamed about going to Canada to see my brother and his wife. Henk and Annie had immigrated to Canada in late spring and now lived in Toronto. I had studied the road map and came to the conclusion that Toronto could not be further away than 6 or 7 hours by train from Chicago. Maybe, I thought hopefully, I could go there for a few days and see Henk and Annie and their newborn baby. After first discussing it with Jozef, he said, "Efka, if you want to see your brother then go for a few days. I will take one Friday and Monday free from work and take care of the kids."I told him that he was the best husband ever and wrote immediately to Henk and Annie that I was coming for a visit.

It was two weeks later when on an early Friday morning, I kissed my kids and husband goodbye and left with my suitcase and passport. I took a bus going from Chicago Avenue to the La Salle Train Station, which was the closest to our neighborhood, and bought a train ticket to Toronto. After a short waith the express train arrived. When I entered the train car I noticed that it was only half full with travelers. It took not long until we left Chicago behind us and rode through the flat open countryside of Michigan. The train was fast and comfortable. While sitting in the speeding train, I looked out the window and my thoughts went back to another express train some years earlier. That time I had gone to Germany on an express which had been full of military people going to that destroyed country. For sure it had been adventurous. Who could have thought that years later I would be sitting in an express train—this time going over the border from America to Canada. It just seemed so impossible, that I would be here—sitting in this express, only now the world around me looked more peaceful.

A few hours later the train slowed its speed and soon reached Detroit where it stopped on an indoor platform which was separated from the main station. All the passengers had to leave the train. The ones who went further into Canada had to wait for a Canadian express which was coming from Toronto. It was about a half hour later when the express arrived at its end destination of Detroit. From there it was going back again to Toronto and further to Montreal and Quebec.

Again there were not many passengers aboard when a hour later the train left Detroit's train station. The Canadian landscape which we traveled through had flat open spaces and forests and was sparsely populated. So this is Canada, I thought, which we had also heard so much about during the war years on our little radio at the attic. I thought about the two Canadian soldiers who had jumped from their enormous military truck back in Breda. They had been lonesome for this country—their Canada. I hoped they had made it back home.

A food vender came through the car with a cart full of goodies and drinks. I decided to take some coffee and something sweet to go with it. Since I spoke more Dutch than English, the man asked me if I came from Holland. When I told him indeed I came from that country but lived now in Chicago, he said," My mother is Dutch. She came to Canada before the war with her parents." While helping a passenger with coffee he continued saying, "There are many Dutch people living in Toronto, most are immigrants who came to this country in the last few years." We had a pleasant conversation and before I knew it the train rolled into the train terminal of Toronto where Henk was waiting for me.

It was good to see my brother again. He looked good—tall and handsome as always. After a short drive through the beautiful city of Toronto, we arrived at their apartment. Annie, with new born baby boy Richard, was waiting for me with tea and Dutch pastries. How wonderful it was to see Annie and talk to her again. Of course, I first had to hold my little nephew who cooed happily as I cuddled him. Laughing I said that we now had a little Canadian in the family. Later over dinner that evening Henk told me that Father and Mother had plans to go to South Africa to visit Mother's sister and her family. Mother had mentioned this in a letter to me but at that time she had not been sure of it. I said to Henk, "I hope that they are going; they both need to go away on a long vacation. Our leaving to go so far away from Holland must have been very hard on them."

The time I spent with Henk and Annie was great. We talked until late in the night about his work at a car service station, and Jozef's work at the foundry, and also about the new life we all had to get used to. We reminisced about all the places we had loved when we lived in Breda, the innocent yesterdays and, of course, all the friends we knew. Henk and Annie had many Dutch friends, young immigrants all living in Toronto who had left friends and family behind to go to Canada. They were full of ideas and dreams to work hard and to make a good life in this big new country.

One evening we had a party at their apartment 'in honor of Henk's sister'. It was great and we had a lot of fun dancing. We sang all the Dutch songs we knew and talked about all the good food we were now able to buy. The following day

Henk and Annie told me that they were going to take me to one of the Dutch grocery stores which was located in Toronto. Of course, I had to buy all kinds of Dutch goodies items which I was used to eating in Holland but could not buy in Chicago. "Did you know, Eef," Henk said, "that there are about 10,000 Dutch people living here in this city? Since they all like to buy something Dutch, something they used to eat in our own country, the Dutch grocery stores are doing well here."

After a great visit, it was Monday morning and after breakfast I had to say goodbye to go back home again. The days with Henk and Annie had been wonderful which I remember well. The days however had gone too fast, and we hoped to see each other again soon. After I hugged Annie and their baby one more time, I left with Henk for the train terminal where my train was waiting for me. As the express slowly moved out of the station, we waved to each other until it went around a bend and out of sight.

As soon as I walked into our apartment, Lia came running. While hugging me she said excitedly, "Mama, I will be on the television next week with my class!" Laughing I said to her, "Let me first hug everyone, and then you can tell me all about it." A little later she showed me a paper which came from her teacher. It said that her kindergarten class would be on the TV such and such day and time. It was a popular children's program and every week the TV station showed another kindergarten class from Chicago. In the program the children sang and some children were asked questions. Of course, I had to sew a new dress for Lia for this special occasion. Her choice of material was a pink-and-white striped cotton which we bought in the Woolworth Store on Chicago Avenue. The following week when the children's program came on the TV, Eddy and I watched together his sister on the screen. In her new dress with her curly hair combed back she looked so sweet. She was sitting in a chair and smiling happily and singing loudly with the other children the songs they had learned for the program. The program's host, who asked the children questions, came also to Lia. He probably had been informed beforehand about her because he asked, "And what is your name? Can you tell me where you come from?" After telling him her name, she said, "I come from Breda." The host, not knowing what or where Breda was, asked her, "Where is that country?" Lia being a little smarty, giggled and said, "Don't you know where Breda is? It is in Holland!"

Christmas came with a dinner at Kazmir and Palasia's apartment. The whole family came together that day. After a great feast of many Polish dishes the family started to tell each other their childhood stories from back in Poland, followed by their Polish Christmas songs. Everyone was happy and gay and I truly was happy for all of them and envied them for their gaiety and closeness. Even though I tried hard to feel good among all those happy people who honestly wanted to give me a feeling of belonging, I could not help the terrible feeling of homesickness which had again come over me. In that room full of happy people, my heart was crying. I tried not to show my loneliness and laughed and talked with everyone as good as I could. Jozef who felt my unhappiness asked me if we should go home. "No," I said to him, "not yet." He and the children had such a nice pleasant Christmas, and I did not want to give in to those feelings which tried to make my life miserable.

On New Year's Day of 1956, we were invited for oliebollen over at our friends Stan and Ellie's home. Since some of their friends also were coming that afternoon, Ellie had fried plates full of oliebollen and apple flappen. Everything looked so delicious. A large and nicely decorated Christmas tree stood in their living room. First we toasted the New Year in with wine and beer. Then everyone sat around the table and sprinkled their fried goodies with lots of powdered sugar. It was a great afternoon with all of our children singing Dutch Christmas carols which brought Ellie and me back to our own childhood in Holland.

Christmas and the New Year came and went without a letter, note or any sign of life from my girlfriend Mies. I had asked Mother in a letter if she had received a letter from Mies, but there had been nothing. I think what had happened was that at the same time as we emmigrated to America, Mies and Jeff were moving to Brazil. Mies probably never received my letter which I had sent to Jeff's parents in Den Haag with my parent's address in it. Since I didn't know Mies's sisters married name and had no idea where she now lived, Mies and I somehow just could not reach each other. Later my parents moved to Amsterdam and over the years I forgot Jeff's last name. As the years passed I always have wondered about Mies and her family and where they are. Sometimes when I think about her, I have a feeling that at that same moment somewhere in South America she is thinking of me and wondering what happened to us. God willing one day we will meet again, and we will have an eternity to talk together as we used to do back in our town of Breda.

◆    ◆    ◆

I could not get used to Chicago no matter how hard I tried. The cold dark winter months only added to my dislike for that big complicated city. The environment of crime, the dark and dirty-looking places, neighbors I never saw—only by accident on the steps of the apartment—and then they acted as if I was air. It was so very different from where I came from. In that time the children were a great comfort to me when Jozef was gone to his work, and the TV helped me escape from the long lonely evenings. It was as if somehow the sparkle seemed to have gone out of life, and I prayed that some happy solution would be found for all of us.

In early March of that year, a cousin of Jozef, by the name of Toni Konzak, had come by car with his wife Ann from Omaha to visit the family in Chicago. It was something they did every year since their emigration in 1948 from Germany. Toni was Chelca's brother. Another brother of Chelca, Tadeus, who had emigrated from Belgium, had just arrived in Chicago. Since Belgium did not finance people who wanted to emigrate, Tadeus had left his wife and two small daughters behind in Belgium for the time being. His plans were to work hard and then, when he had enough money saved, he would bring his family over to America.

During the war years Toni and Tadeus Konzak, as so many other young men, were forced to work in Germany. When the war ended in Europe, Toni worked with the American occupation troops for two years before marrying his girlfriend Ann and later they immigrated to America. In that same time Tadeus got the opportuniy to work in the coal mines in Belgium. Rather than sitting and waiting in a displaced persons camp in Germany, he took his young wife and went to Belgium. In the meantime he tried to immigrate to his sister Chelca in America.

One day during their visit to Chicago Toni and Ann also came to visit us. They both were about ten years older than I was. Toni had the same dark brown hair and fair complexion as his sister Chelca. He was of average build and talked constantly. Ann was a pretty woman, maybe a little too heavy. She spoke good English and worked for an insurance company. They had no children. Since they both spoke German and English, I was able to talk to them. After they had given the children a box of chocolates, we talked about Holland, and how quickly Josje and Lia had learned the English language. Of course, our conversation was about the families and the situation in Europe.

Later Toni said to me, "Eef, what do you think about living here in this big city." While holding back my tears I said to him, "Toni, I can never live here for always with our three young children." Ann who had heard this turned to Jozef and said, "Why don't you come to Omaha? You will like it there so much better. Omaha is a good place to raise your children. It is conservative and there are no gangs and not much crime." Then Toni started to tell Jozef that he could easily find work in one of the bakeries in Omaha. Ann's girlfriend was working at one of the bakeries there, and she could probably get a job for him. We talked some more about Omaha and the possibilities of work there. Before Toni and Ann left they said, "Don't worry, we will help you. You both think about it and let us know before we drive back to Omaha." We said goodbye to each other and they went to their car which was parked in front of the apartment. While looking with envy at their long white Buick, Josje said, "They are rich, aren't they, Dad?" Jozef answered him, "Some day, my boy, some day we will have a car too."

In the following few days Jozef and I had some lengthy discussions about us moving to Omaha. We never had heard about that city which, as we came to know, was in the middle of America. We took our world map out which had been in the closet, studied America, and found Nebraska and the city of Omaha. "You know, Jozef," I said to him while reading the map, "that Nebraska is made up of rolling prairies and has only 1,325,000 people? Omaha is the largest city in Nebraska and has the second largest livestock market in the world. It looks to me that it is primarily an agricultural state. Maybe we can start a farm there!" I said, laughing, knowing how much he loved the outdoors and animals. Well, the end was that we decided that first Jozef would go alone to Omaha and investigate before we decided to move there.

(Jozef) When Toni and Ann had left that Sunday afternoon to go back to Omaha, Eef and I talked about me going to that city for a weekend. It was a week later I wrote Toni that I was coming for a two-day visit to see Omaha. It was on a Friday early evening that I took the night train and arrived the next morning in Omaha, where the sun was shining in a bright blue sky. Since it was Saturday and Toni and Ann were not working, they were both waiting for me at the train station. Before going to their house they drove me around Omaha which, compared with Chicago, looked great to me. I still remember how amazed I was at the many trees in that city and how green they were already, which was not the case in Chicago where the buds on the trees were just coming out. Except for the downtown area I saw no high buildings but there were a lot of open spaces and everyone seemed to have a yard around their house.

Omaha was built well spaced out. "Eef would like it here," I thought, "it looks like a nice clean town and it would be much better for the kids here than growing up in Chicago. As for myself I wouldn't mind staying in Chicago. I made good money, the people I worked with were nice and I enjoyed my cousin Chelca and the rest of the family. I did not want to stay within the city of Chicago itself, but hoped to save enough money so that we could move to one or another small town around Chicago in the future. I knew how unhappy Eef was living in that big city. It was not only for herself, but also for the children that she felt this way. Even living in the suburbs of Chicago she maybe would not have liked it," I thought, "and the sooner she was going away from there, the better it would be for her and the children. And this Omaha here was maybe a good opportunity. Chicago was not especially the promised land we had dreamed about, but maybe Omaha was."

I stayed at Toni and Ann's house for two days. As we drove around Omaha, they told me everything about the livestock business in that city, the Missouri River, the horse races etc. They also showed me the places where they worked. Toni and Ann probably colored Omaha a little too rosy, but that I understood. They had no children of their own and no relatives living here and, understandably, wanted us to come and live nearby. Before taking the night train back to Chicago, I said with a smile to Toni and Ann that we probably would be moving to Omaha. I would let them know.

As soon as I arrived back home in Chicago, I said to Eef, "Let's pack the suitcases. We are going to move to Omaha. You will be much happier there." Of course, Eef was all thrilled with the prospect of moving out of "jail" as she called Chicago. Since we had little furniture, moving to Omaha would be no problem. Two days later I went to a moving company in Chicago which would take care of it, as they said.

Telling people at my work that I was going to move to Omaha was another story. Soon after I had told my boss that I was going to quit because I was moving to Omaha, he said to me that I had to come to "The big boss's office" because he wanted to talk to me. A little later as I walked into the office, the big boss was sitting at his desk. Looking up at me he said, "Sit down, Jozef. I hear you are moving to Omaha." I answered him, "Yes, in two weeks." He then asked me, "Why?" So I told him that my wife could not get used to Chicago. She comes from Holland and lived there most of her life on the outskirts of a town. "Chicago overwhelms her," I said to him. "And we also want to move for our children. It is important to us that they live in a place where the air is clean and where there is not much crime—a place where they can roam and play and grow." Then in his husky voice the boss said that Omaha was not an industrial city and that I could not make as much money there as in Chicago. "You will regret going there,

Jozef!" he said. He then continued saying, "I think that before you make this decision you should go with your foreman in his car around here in Skokie and look at houses. He can show you around. It is a nice suburb and I am willing to lend you money for a down payment on a house. Take your wife and show her how pretty this little town of Skokie is." But when I told him that everything was already set in motion to go to Omaha, he said, "I hope you will change your mind; you will make a big mistake going there, Jozef." It had sounded good to me to live in Skokie close to the factory and make good money.

But somehow it was not meant to be. Even as Bedford Hills was not meant to be for us. But my luck and faith in the future had always been there, and I knew that somewhere I would finally find the place I could call my home with Efka for always.

# 37

## *THE CITY OF OMAHA*

(**Eef**) It was mid-April of 1956 when we left Chicago by night train. The Sunday before we had said goodbye to Jozef's family. Of course, they were a little disappointed that we left for Omaha, but they understood. They were great people who still struggled. But as many other Polish people from Chicago's Polish neighborhood, they ultimately moved out to settle somewhere else in the United States after they learned the English language. The feeling of isolation and bewilderment that they had felt in the first few years in America had left them, and they developed a sense of belonging to a nation that they could call their own. As the years passed Chesia and Frank started a farm in Wiscounsin, Halina divorced her husband Edward and moved her family to South Carolina. In later years Tadeus moved with his family to Wiscounsin also. Henry moved later to Arizona. Palasia and her family moved to a suburb of Chicago. Only Chelca stayed in the Polish neighborhood were she later died.

Stan and Ellie took us to the La Salle train station. We had become friends in the short time we lived in Chicago. Ellie especially had helped me sometimes through the difficult days. We promised each other to write soon—which we did. For a few years we wrote to each other often, then it slowed down and eventually stopped after they moved to a suburb of Chicago.

The night train was not crowded and soon the city of Chicago, where we had lived for a year and four months, fell behind us. Somedays there had been trying times but other days there was the enjoyment of seeing great museums and other interesting places, which we will never forget and remember often.

As soon as the train left Chicago each of us found our own seats to sleep on, and the children settled down. Pillows and blankets were provided to us by the train's conductor. Jos, who thought it a great adventure, was all excited and his nose was glued to the train's window. But since it was dark outside and he didn't see much it did not take long until he drifted off to sleep like his sister and little brother, probably dreaming of cowboys and Indians.

As the train sped throught the dark night, Jozef and I talked some more about Omaha and the new life which was waiting for us there in that unknown town in mid-America. Later when Jozef dozed off to sleep, I closed my eyes hoping to have a few hours of sleep and get some rest. But my thoughts went to Holland and the people I had left behind, and how much further Omaha was from Holland than Chicago was.

At daybreak Jozef woke up and got coffee in the dining car for himself and me. Together we watched as the sun was climbing up over the flat countryside which stretched to the horizon. Only here and there we saw an occasional small town. The name of the state that our train sped through was Iowa. We wondered how far our train had traveled, and when we would reach our destination. The children woke up and after some yawning and rubbing their still sleepy eyes, we got them ready for their new town. As their dad told them, Omaha was a city which was build on a wooded bluff on the west shore of the Missouri River, which was a well-known long river in America. "It will not be long before we are there,"he said. When looking out the train windows for awhile, Jos and Lia saw surroundings which looked like the wooded hilly area their father had talked about. It looked so pretty after the monotonous landscape we had traveled through. Then, to everyone's excitement we crossed the Missouri River and reached our destination—Omaha.

Sometimes even now I lay in my bed remembering how optimistic we were, and how life seemed exciting once again to me. The children were full of good spirits, and they were laughing and giggling as only children can do. As the night train slowly pulled into Omaha's Burlington Station and came to a stop, we noticed how very busy it was with coming and going passengers. While Jozef and Jos took care of our luggage, I carried Eddy and helped Lia from the train. Toni had written to us that he and Ann could not get the day free from work to pick us up and that we should take a taxi to their home.

Later while sitting in a cab, I looked out its window to see what Omaha looked like. The first impression I got was that Omaha streets were hilly. I never had seen streets that were that way before. Holland was as flat as a pancake and so was Chicago. I noticed the clean single houses with yards and the many flowering trees everywhere which gave it such a pleasant and pretty impression. After about a 20-minute drive, we reached Toni and Ann's home. It was located in a neighborhood in South Omaha at 40th and Q Street. The first thing the kids saw when we came out of the cab was the large yard around the small brick home. The children thought it great and soon let out their bottled-up energy and ran around the lawn from front to back and back again while letting out screams of joy.

For one week we stayed at Toni and Ann's home. Their house was very small and the sleeping was crowded. Luckily the weather was great and the children played to their hearts content the whole day outdoors in the large yard. In the evenings after supper we drove around in the car with Tony, looking for a rental place. Then, a few days after arriving in Omaha, we found a home at 42th and T Street, just off of Q Street. It was not far from Tony's house and close to the just-finished new Hitchcock Park. The new fish pond was in and the park was landscaped. The swimming pool and ice skating rink as we see today, came many years later. It was there at Hitchcock Park were Jos, and later Eddy, went fishing many times throughout their childhood years and caught many a large carp.

The house on T Street was a single house. It had a front yard with large trees and a small back yard. The rooms above us were rented to a couple without children. The house was not large but it had to do for now. The rent was 80 dollars a month.

◆    ◆    ◆

(Jozef) The day after arriving in Omaha I went to look for work. I wanted to start in a bakery and hoped that the bakery where Ann's girlfriend worked had an opening for me. I asked Ann where this bakery was, and how I could get there. She answered me that on her way to work she would bring me there. The name of the bakery was Rotella and was a large bakery in Omaha. She was sure I could find work there. Ann was right. I could start the next day if I wanted to, but after learning they paid $1.00 a hour, I walked out. The bakery thought that 20 cents over the minimum wage of 80 cents a hour was good pay.

Back in the car Ann said that on 24th Street in South Omaha, three bakeries were located and that I should ask there. Maybe, she said, I would be lucky this time. Since Ann had to go to work, she dropped me off at one of the bakeries. It was the Sopczak Bakery, which is a Polish name. Ann also told me that another bakery was located close by on the same street. She explained to me how to walk back to her home. After thanking Ann for her help and wishing her a good day, I walked into the bakery which looked very appealing to me with its many Polish pastries.

In that time many Polish families lived in South Omaha, immigrants who came after the First and Second World War. The baker of the store was not only the baker but also the owner of the bakery. Soon we were in an amicable Polish conversation. Mr. Sopczak told me that the pay in Omaha was not only low, but that good paying jobs were hard to come by. He then told me that he was sorry but did not need anyone at this time. He advised me to go to Johnny's Café, which was on 27th and L Street—only 4 blocks away from his bakery. He said that the owner was also Polish and had been living in America for a long time. His restaurant was located next to the stockyards. "Because of his location," Mr. Sopczak said, "he has a good business there with many cattlemen always coming to his place to eat. Maybe he will have work for you."

Later when I left his bakery and walked to Johnny's Café, I thought about my former boss in Chicago. "He was right," I said to myself, "Omaha's salaries are much lower than in Chicago and because Omaha is not a factory town, work is not as plentiful here." I had learned from Toni that many people in Omaha worked in the stockyards but, if possible, I wanted to stay away from that kind of work. "I know that I will find something," I said to myself. What I really wanted, and many times still dreamed about, was to make enough money so I could save and then later start a bakery of my own. "Never give up dreaming," I said to myself while looking for the restaurant. "Who knows, maybe luck is with me this time. And maybe this restaurant has something to offer me," I thought hopefully while opening the entrance door of Johnny's Café.

As I walked into the restaurant, I noticed it was busy with late lunch business. I looked around, saw the hostess and asked for the boss. She brought me to his office and said to wait there for him. A little later Frank Kawa, a stocky man of about 50 years, walked in. After I introduced myself in Polish, I told him that I just had moved to Omaha and was looking for work—preferably bakery work. He seemed interested and asked me what kind of baking I could do. I then told him about my bakery experiences which I had learned as a young man back in Poland and how life had brought me to Omaha.

After a long conversation in Polish, he learned that I also could speak English (which, as I knew, was always very helpful and a big plus in the American work force). Frank Kawa looked at me and said, "Jozef, I will hire you as a baker and also for helping out in the kitchen when we are busy. Your starting salary is $1.65 a hour with a raise in six weeks if I like how you work. Since you have not worked in a bakery for such a long time, why don't you start out in the morning together with our baker Edward Calas. This way you can learn again how it is done and get used to the bakery business. Also you then will learn the American pastries such as pies and cheesecakes which we sell a lot here in the restaurant. Later when you have more experience, I want you working as an afternoon baker while Calas does the baking in the morning." He then got up from his chair and said, "Jozef, why don't you start out tomorrow morning at 5:00." As Frank Kawa walked out his office into his restaurant, which was still busy with customers, I started to find my way out.

While walking home I said to myself, "Finally, Jozef, after so many years you will be in the bakery business again, and what a place to start! The money is not the greatest to start out with, but I am sure that in a few months it will be better." When I walked from Johnny's over the bridge at L Street going west, I looked over the bridge railing and saw below me a train coming in with livestock. The many cattle holding pens were full and men on horses with cowboy hats on were riding around. In the background which was Q Street, I saw the meat packing companies of Wilson and Armour. In the middle of this large livestock business stood the tall Livestock Exchange Building which I am sure was a very busy place in that time and where a great amount of money was handled.

And so I started to work for Johnny's Café at the end of April of 1956. In the beginning everything was strange to me, and I had again to get used to making the dough for the dinner rolls. The pies and cheesecakes took somewhat longer before I had them coming perfect out of the oven. Later when I was sometimes alone in the bakery, Frank Kawa would come in and talk about his life. Leaving his family behind in Poland, he had come to America as a 12-year-old boy with a uncle. One day I asked him why his restaurant was named Johnny's Café and who Johnny was. He then told me that he, his friend Johnny, and some other men had made money by secretly making whiskey in the years when alcohol consumption was against the law. The whiskey they made they sold to some gangsters in Chicago. When they had enough money saved up, he and Johnny started a small restaurant which was located just over the bridge on the north side on L Street. Not much later they opened a new Johnny's Café which was located at the present address. Soon Frank bought Johnny out but kept its name, "Johnny's Café" because in a short time it had become a well-known restaurant in Omaha.

After a few weeks of working at Johnny's Café, I thought that it was the best-run business I ever had seen. There were 140 people working in the respectable and pleasant restaurant. It opened its business at 6:00 in the morning for the many cattle truck drivers and the cattlemen who sometimes drove the whole night to bring their livestock to Omaha's stockyards. In the mornings four cooks made the breakfast of steak and eggs, and homemade pancakes in amounts that I never had seen before. The lunch business was busy with lunch steaks, prime ribs, swiss steaks and short ribs, roast beef, barbecue ribs and fish with all the trimmings. All sorts of pies and cheese cakes were baked for dessert. The many cattlemen who came in wore boots and cowboy hats, something which I never had seen before. As evening business came, it was not only very busy again with the cattlemen, but also with Omaha's public who wanted the best grade of meats for their dinner and first-class service. I thought the prices for the dinners were very reasonable:

Prime beef dinner $1.85
Swiss steak dinner $1.10
Petit Filet Mignon with mushrooms dinner $1.60
Half chicken with everything dinner $1.65
Salad $0.50
Coffee $0.15

Below the restaurant of Johnny's Café was the butchery where the cleaned and the "cut-in-half" cows were hung. It was the place where the finest cuts of meat were carved out for the customers. The cows had been bought at the packing houses and only the very best animals were good enough for Frank Kawa.

It was not only a very busy place but also the best and largest steak house in Omaha. Frank Kawa was a shrewd man with eyes in front and back of his head, noticing and seeing everything that went on in his restaurant. If his employees were not working to his satisfaction, he fired them. A bar was located in the restaurant with drinks from around the world. Frank always liked to entertain his best customers until late in the evening. In that time, especially on weekends, the cattle trucks were lined up for miles on L Street to outside of Omaha, which was then to 72th Street. There they waited until it was their turn to enter into the cattle holding pens. I think that the whole workforce of South Omaha was working one way or another at one of the six packing houses, with the three largest being Armour, Wilson and Cudahy.

Since I did not have a car, I walked the three miles to my work, which I thought was not too bad since I was used to walking. It was quiet on the streets so early in the morning. The air was fresh, and it felt good. Early one morning when I was walking at a fast tempo on Q Street to my work, a police car stopped me. The policeman wanted to know where I was going in such a hurry and what my name was. I told him that I was on my way to Johnny's Café where I worked and, since I had no car, had to use my legs. "Not everyone has a car," I said to him while walking along. Luckily the policeman believed me and, after looking me up and down, he drove off in his car. About half a year later, when I worked during afternoon and evening hours, Frank Kawa ordered a taxi to take me home.

◆    ◆    ◆

(Eef) After moving into the house on T Street, we enrolled Jos in St. Mary's School at 36th and Q Street. Since Lia was a kindergartner and it was so close to summer vacation, we decided to keep her home from school. Next school year in September we said she would have a fresh start beginning in the first grade. It did not take long until Jos made friends with two boys from across the street who were about his age. Every day he walked with his new friends the 8 blocks to and from school. Jos got a fishing rod and some hooks from his uncle Toni and, almost every Saturday, he was at the fishing pond at Hitchcock Park trying his luck. Since there was not many fish in the pond yet, he didn't catch anything. When I teased him saying that he just let his worms swim, he always answered me with, "Mom, I am just practicing how to use this rod."

When Jozef was at his work and Jos was at school, I enjoyed taking Lia and Eddy to the small Hitchcock Park. They loved to run around there and throw small stones in the water. While I was sitting in the grass and the warm sunshine danced on the water, I knew that in time I would like Omaha. The people were friendly and very helpful in the stores. Somehow I thought, they didn't seem to have a problem with immigrants and it made me feel welcome. Even though Jozef didn't make as much money as in Chicago, we both liked Omaha, as far as we had seen it.

Our next-door neighbors were a young couple with a little boy Eddy's age. The day after we had moved in, the young woman came over with some home-made goodies and introduced herself. She was a lovely person and, even though my English was not too good, we managed to have many a conversation using a lot of hand gestures. We talked mostly in the yard over the low fence. As I would learn over the years, she and other American people did not know much about my country Holland or where it was located in Europe. Some people thought that the Dutch still wore wooden shoes and windmills were everywhere. But my young neighbor seemed interested and said that she wanted to know more about that little country on the North Sea. So whenever we were talking, I had to tell her all about Holland and its people.

The little neighbor boy and Eddy liked to play together in our front yard. Occasionally a large long-haired black dog came to play with the boys. I didn't know where he came from or who he belonged to, but it was such a sweet animal and so good with the children, that I let the dog stay whenever the kids were outside. On the side of our house toward the back was a garage with some junk inside. There, stored on some high shelves, were cans of paint which belonged to the landlord. Since we had no car and no key for the garage door, it was closed but not locked.

One day Eddy and the neighbor boy were playing in the yard while I was cleaning the house. I had seen the black dog playing with the boys who gathered some sticks together. A little later when I looked again out of the window to see what the boys were doing, I saw to my horror the black dog dripping with paint. With its long black hair in colors of green, blue and orange, it was walking out of our yard. As fast as I could I ran outside and there were the two rascals, standing there with dripping painting brushes in their hands and their pants a mess of colors. I still don't know how they could have gotten those cans of paint off the shelves, but they did. Both boys had a paint brush in their small hands with which they had painted the dog.

Later I came to know the story one little piece at the time. After the boys had taken the cans of paint from the shelf, they had opened them with some sort of screwdriver. They then found the paint brushes in the shed. While the boys covered the animal with paint the poor dog, being a good dog, had stood patiently and quietly. After I cleaned up the boys as good as I could, both of them were sent off to bed for punishment. But I don't think they really understood what was so bad about painting a dog. After that day the garage door was locked by the landlord. We never saw the dog again.

On a nice warm day in May after church services Toni and Ann took us in their car for the first time to Peony Park which was located on 71st and Cass Street. Peony Park was a very popular place with the people of Omaha. Besides the large picnic area there was a swimming pool, a put-put golf and children rides. There were stands with hot dogs, hamburgers, ice cream, popcorn, spun sugar and soft drinks. In the middle of it all was a very nice building which was used for dancing, weddings, and meetings. With its crystal chandeliers hanging from the ceiling and the raised platform for an orchestra, it was a great place for parties and dancing in the wintertime.

Also in the park was a beautiful outdoor pavilion for dancing in the summer. Large bands played there and provided the "Under the Stars" music on Friday and

Saturday nights. On Sunday afternoons another band played and many people came not only for dancing but also just to sit and listen to the music. Yes, Peony Park was a nice place to be. That afternoon Jos, Lia and Eddy could not get enough of the rides and when we finally went home, the kids each with a large cotton candy, they said that it was so much fun there, and that they soon wanted to go back. Later, when we had our own car, we always would go there a few times with the children during summer vacations.

At about that same time I received a letter from my parents in which they wrote that they hoped to go to South Africa in November of that year. The sailing time from Holland to South Africa would take 3 weeks. They planned to stay for a half year at Oom Gerard and Tante Ann's apartment which was in the city of Bloemfontein. Father wrote that Oom Gerard planned to take a trip with them to "Kruger National Wildlife Park." That park is located in the northeast part of South Africa and along the border of Mozambique. Oom Gerard always had wanted to go there as long as he had lived in Africa, but had never found time for it.

The plans were to travel for one week through the park while sleeping at night in a specially designed area which is protected from wild animals. "It sounds good to your mother and me," Father wrote. Also in his letter he wrote that since their children were gone and they had no other family living in Breda, that when they came home from their trip they would probably move back to Amsterdam. It was the city where they both grew up and got married. They then would also live closer to Jan and his family.

After reading the letter from my parents I felt happy for them. I know that they needed to go away for awhile, away from home and Breda. They missed us and with this trip to Africa, and later moving back to Amsterdam, it would help to overcome the loneliness they must have felt since their children moved so far away. For Mother it would be great to see her sister Ann again with whom she always had been close. They also would see Ken and his wife and their children and my other cousin Henk. "Yes, it will be great for them to see everyone again," I said to Jozef when he came home that night.

One evening Jozef came home from a visit to Toni and Ann. While putting his arms around me, he said excitedly, "You know Eef, since we are planning to stay in Omaha, I think we should buy a house." Not understanding what he was saying, I said puzzled, "Did you say buy a house?" When he said "Yes," I said to him, "And where would the money come from?" He then explained that he spent

$80 a month on rent for the house we lived in and that this was like money down the drain. He then continued saying that Toni was going to lend us the money for the down payment on a house, and we could pay him back whenever we had the money. There was no hurry. Of course, we both were very excited about it. This was great! A house we could call our own! In Holland very few people own the house they live in. Most people rent their home. We were indeed very fortunate, and Jozef and I were thankful to Toni and Ann for wanting to help us.

It was the beginning of July when we started to look for a house. It had to have a large yard for the children and not be too expensive since we could not afford much. Then one day when riding around with Toni and Ann, we saw the house we thought would be just right for us. It was in an old neighborhood, not annexed yet by Omaha, on 52nd Street, just two blocks south of Q Street. Even though the street was not paved, it looked nice and well taken care of. Most of the houses were small and were built far apart from each other. They had large yards with flowers and tall old trees were growing everywhere.

The first time when we drove through the street and saw the white painted house with the "For Sale" sign, we noticed how nice and clean it looked. It was in a large well-kept yard with two tall weeping willows dominating the back yard. Besides an open fireplace we saw a picnic table in the back of the property. There was also a chicken coop, rabbit cages and a nice size fenced-in place for other small animals. A old garage was in the backyard on the side of the alley. In the front of the house stood a rare tall flowering tree with beautiful sweeping branches, the name of which I have never learned. Also in the front yard were many flowers in all shades of colors, their little heads turned to the sun. On one side of the house was a row of grapes growing and behind it was a vegetable garden. It was everything we wanted for a yard.

The second time that we went back there, we saw the inside of the house. It had three small bedrooms, a small living room with large windows and a nice large kitchen. A porch was built on the back of the kitchen. Since the yard sloped down, the porch was high off the ground and gave the feeling of living in a tree house. It was almost in the branches of the weeping willows. The only bathroom in the house was located in the basement which I was not too happy about. All the woodwork was painted white with light oak for accent. Also all the floors were oak, except for in the kitchen which was linoleum.

Even though we liked the house and the yard from the start and the price was right ($7,500), Jozef had hesitated. He thought that since he did not have a car yet, maybe it was too far to walk to his work. After going back to the house a few more times, Jozef said one day coming home from his work, "You know Eef, let us buy that house. It is sure the place I would like to live. It is so peaceful and I know you and the children will also love it there. I could have some small animals again, just as I had when I was a boy. Maybe soon I could buy an second hand car so I don't have to walk to my work. I know it is about 45 min. fast walk from the house, but it is summer."

It was July of 1956 when Jozef and I bought our very first house, the first house we ever owned. We were very excited, and we couldn't wait until we moved into the house on 52nd Street. The years that followed would become our most treasured years.

◆     ◆     ◆

When we were settled into our first home, life finally became for Jozef the place he always had dreamed about. A home of his own, a place to rest and live his own life with his family. Finally a place where he could find peace and stability.

It was still early one morning when I got up from bed and very quietly, so as not to wake up Jozef and the children, went outside to the backyard and sat down on one of the steps of the stairway which led from the porch down into the yard. The leaves on the trees rustled gently in the light breeze while the mourning doves were calling one another from a far distance. Pulling my robe around me I watched the early clouds break up and could already see the patches of blue sky. It was only a matter of time, I thought, and the clouds would be gone. I never had seen so many days of blue sky as here in Omaha. It was going to be another hot day, the same as the day before, and the day before that. But now early in the morning it felt wonderful and I knew in time I would be happy here

Even though the summer temperature was high and I couldn't sleep well at night, it was not as bad as Chicago where the heat hung between the houses and buildings. Luckily our home here had good sized windows on both sides of the house, which we opened wide during the night to let the cool night breeze in—that is if there was any breeze. Sometimes this was not the case.

But even though it was hot, we really enjoyed living on 52nd Street. It was all so open and free—no fences and almost no traffic coming through the street. It was a pleasure to eat our breakfast in our screened in porch where the leaves of the weeping willow brushed against the screen. The former house owners had sold us their table and small chairs for the porch because they did not need them anymore. Looking at the picnic table in the back of our yard I thought how much the kids loved to eat there beside the open fireplace.

One day Toni showed us how to eat our hot-dogs which we had to put on a stick and then brown them in our open fireplace. The marshmallows, which we also had to put on a stick and then hold over the flame, got burnt almost black. We never had eaten them like this before and the kids thought it very funny. Also the corn on the cob was new to us. In Holland the only corn we ever had seen was for chicken feed. Even though we liked many of the new things we learned, many others were strange to us and we stayed away from them. But with help from Toni and Ann, we slowly learned the American way of life.

Living so free was great, and we enjoyed our first summer in Omaha. The only thing which was not so great were the cockroaches. I never knew that there were such creatures, and they scared me out of my mind. It all happened one night in the first week after moving into our home. That night I needed to go to the bathroom which was down in the basement. After turning on the light in the kitchen I found myself in the middle of black creepy crawling things which suddenly scrambled away and disappeared. It looked to me at that moment as if there were hundreds of them. I must have screamed because Jozef came running out of our bedroom and asked what happened. While holding my nightgown tight around me, I told him about all the scary black things all over our kitchen floor which suddenly seemed to have evaporated. While looking at the floor he asked me if I had been dreaming because he didn't see anything. Irritated I answered him, "I swear they were all over the floor." Jozef, not understanding what it was that had scared me, said that he would ask Toni about it—what it could have been.

It was a few days later when Toni came to our house. After I told him about the black creatures he said, "They are common house pests here and named cock-roaches. They will be gone when the weather gets colder. Until then you have to live with them, but they don't bite! They come out only during the night, because they don't like light." This information did not make me feel any better. Even though I learned what those awful bugs were, believe me, the rest of the summer I did not go to the kitchen or the bathroom during the night without first turning the lights on in the living room. By the time I would enter the kitchen to go to the basement, they had usually disappeared. Finally one summer we decided to make an end to the cockroaches in our home and called an exter-minator. Since then, thank heaven, we never saw those black crawling bugs in our house again.

Another new thing we learned that first summer was about chiggers. They were another trouble maker we never had heard of before. It was especially hard on the children. Even though I put the kids in a warm soapy bath every night, they were itching and they scratched themselves all over, especially under their armpits. It was something we had to learn to live with, and we took it all in stride. But the insects which all of us truly loved were—the luminescent fireflies. When we were in Holland, we read in books about fireflies but since they did not exist there, we had never seen them. On warm evenings the children enjoyed catching those glowworms which were flying everywhere in our yard. They put the little beetles in a glass jar with greens and let them fly away the following day.

That summer a woman who lived in our street told me to take our kids inside the house after 4:00 in the afternoon. Because, she said, there are many children here who get sick with polio during the summer months. Especially, she said, when they got tired. The year before there had been a polio epidemic and parents had been warned about this dreadful disease. Jozef and I never had heard of polio and didn't know about this sickness and what to think about it. We decided to live normally as always, only we would see to it that the kids would not get too tired during the hot summer months.

Almost every Sunday afternoon Toni and Ann took Jozef, me and the children for a ride in their long Buick to show us around Omaha and the surrounding small towns. One day Ann took me in their car to the large stores in South Omaha on 24th Street. She said that many people always shopped there. She explained to me that I could reach those stores by taking the bus which stopped at the corner of our 52nd and Q Street every hour. Since Jos and Lia were going to start school soon and needed new clothing, maybe I could do some shopping there with the children.

The shopping street at 24th in South Omaha was a nice place to shop. It had large stores such as Pennys, Woolworth, Hesteds and the large department store of Philips which became my favorite shopping place. Many other shops and stores which were popular with the people of Omaha were located there.

Two blocks from our home at the corner of our street and Q Street was located a grocery store by the name of Stoysich. The owner of the store was a man who had emigrated from Poland to America with his wife after the First World War. They were both Polish and had a large family. Whenever I needed some groceries, I went to their store and always talked a few words with the older couple. For my weekly grocery shopping I walked to the Hinky Dinky grocery market which was located at 42nd and Q Street. Since we didn't have a car yet, I took a taxi home after I was done with my shopping.

One day, when walking in our street going to the Stoysich Store with Eddy, I passed a house which was being built. A women who was in her front yard came toward me and started to talk in broken English. She introduced herself as Nelly Latek and she said they had three young daughters and one young son. They came originally from Poland but had been in a German work camp during the war years. As so many people in that time they were given the chance to start a new life in America. She told me that since they had not enough money to finish their home, they were already living for a few years in the basement of their unfinished house. Later we learned that many people who were building their own homes and had, for one or another reason no more money to finish it, lived in their basements. Some years later, with the coming of a new law which did not allow people to live anymore in their unfinished homes, the 'basement houses' were a thing of the past.

A few days later when I walked with Lia and Eddy past the unfinished home again, Nelly Latek came out her house and asked me if we wanted a young cat. At first I said to her that I didn't think so. But when Lia saw the young black kitten, she took it in her arms and said, "Please, Mom, please can we have it." Then while looking at my daughter I thought, "Why not!" It had been awhile since we had a cat in the house and it would be cute to have one again for the kids. A little later we took the 8 weeks old black female cat home with us. Lia named it 'Minni'.

# 38

## *NEW EXPERIENCES*

It was mid-August when I went to the office of the Holy Ghost Church which was located on the corner of 52nd and Q Street. The church and connecting school were only two blocks from our house. Jozef and I wanted our children to attend school there, not only because it was a school run by the Catholic Church, but also because it was located close to our home. Every Sunday since living on 52nd Street we had attended mass there. As I walked into the office, I was greeted by a nun who was, to my surprise, wearing a black dress. The nuns in Europe always wore the traditional long black robes with large caps on their heads wherein their heads almost disappeared. We had earlier noticed that the priests in America did not wear the long black robes as was the case in Europe, but black suits with only a white neckband showing. Sometime before, when I had walked with Eddy past a field which was close to our church, I had seen two priests wearing T shirts and black shorts, playing ball. At first I couldn't believe my eyes and thought I had made a mistake. But when I asked Ann about it, she said yes that I had seen it right, the priests in America wear blue jeans and T shirts in their free time. "And in summertime," she said smiling, "they wear shorts when playing ball." It was hard to believe! I had to write to Geertje, my old neighbor in Breda about it.

After a friendly talk with the nun about Jos, Lia and Holland, I told her what I came for. She said that she was very sorry but there was no room in the school for two more children. She took our address and said that if there was a child who was leaving their school, she would let us know. I said to her that I did not want my children separated into different schools. I wanted both my children at the same school. At first Jozef and I were both disappointed but hoped that maybe there would be a place for Jos and Lia on a later date.

It was a few days later that I went to Ashland Park Public School to enroll Jos and Lia for classes. That year Jos started his fourth grade and Lia her first. Ashland Park School was six blocks from our home and located at 48th and Q Street.

Our children, who always walked to and from school, come rain or shine, would attend this school all through their grade school years. It was the following year that we got a notice from the Holy Ghost School that there was room that year for both our children. But in the meantime Jos and Lia had made friends at their school and wanted to stay there. After some lengthy discussion Jozef and I decided to leave the kids where they were at Ashland Park and not move them to another school again.

The hot summer finally gave away to more pleasant weather. The air was fresh and crisp, and it was a joy to be outside. When Jozef was at his work and Jos and Lia were at school, I took Eddy to Hitchcock Park. He loved to run around in the grass and throw little stones in the water. Or he played in the white sand which was probably left behind when they had finished the park. Later when school was out, we picked Jos and Lia up and went home together, where I made tea served with cookies and chocolates, the way we were used to in Holland. In that time I think that, though my head was in Omaha, my heart was still in Breda.

On those days when the rain pattered down and I was home alone with Eddy, I did some sewing. Usually it was a new dress for Lia or for myself. The years of scrimping, remaking old clothes and babying each garment so as to make it last longer, were finally a thing of the past. Even though money was tight for us in those first years in America, I could afford to buy nice new dress materials again, which I bought in a store in South Omaha for 39 or 49 cents a yard. Since the European measurements are different from the Americans, I made many mistakes when buying material in the beginning, which always left me frustrated. But as everything, I soon learned how much material I needed for a dress or another garment without coming too short or having too much left over.

Jos, who had mostly played with Lia and Eddy in and around the house that first summer in 52st Street, had made friends of his own. One day he came home from school and came into the kitchen where I was preparing something for supper that night. While holding his arms around the shoulder of the two boys, he said, "Mom, these are my friends. Their names are Billy Mc Laughlin and Chucky Poland." I remembered seeing the two boys when they sometimes had been playing in the alley behind our yard. Those boys and my kids had eyed each other and had spoken a few words together, but later the boys had run off. Now that they went to the same school and many times walked home from school together, the three boys had become friends.

It was not long thereafter that Lia also made friends. Every day since then, neighbor children were at our house. Even though I was happy for my children that they had made friends, I didn't like or understand their manners. Many times they came walking into our house without a greeting or even a simple, "Hi, Mrs. Otto."It was something I was not used to. Some even went to the refrigerator, opened it and looked to see if there was something good to eat or drink. This to me was very rude, and I told Jos and Lia never to behave like this in their friend's houses. Something else Jozef and I had to get used to was that everyone was on a first name basis. But in time I would learn that we are all people and in this world we all have our own ways, of course some are easier to understand than others.

After the first frosty fall days a spell of warm weather came which, as we learned, was called Indian Summer Days. October slid quietly into November and St. Nicholas was not far off. Jozef and I decided now that we lived in America where gifts were given only on Christmas Day, we had to do the same. "It is too confusing for the kids," Jozef said, "if they would not receive presents on Christmas and their friends did. You will see that soon St. Nicholas will not mean much to them anymore, after they know that no one else in America is celebrating it." Even though I did agree with Jozef that it would be the best for our kid's sake to give gifts on Christmas, I did not feel very happy about it. I told myself that Eddy was too young to remember St. Nicholas, and Lia would soon forget this day and not miss it anymore either. It was only Jos who would remember this very special day which he always had celebrated in Holland. Thinking about it for awhile I decided I had to do something. Not to celebrate St. Nicholas on the 6th of December was impossible for me. I had too many wonderful memories of this day.

So when the evening of the 5th of December came, I told the children to put their shoes in the front hall (we didn't have a fireplace) with some water for St. Nicholas and some bread for his horse. A few days before I had gone to South Omaha and had bought a small gift for each of the children for in their shoes for the following morning, December 6th. I had also baked an almond butter cake. That night we sang together the old St. Nicholas songs which we had been singing so many times in our country Holland. The kids just loved it and were laughing and joking. I think that evening I just could not break away from my country's hold on my soul anymore than I could have from my cultural heritage.

◆    ◆    ◆

The days marched toward the end of the year and to our very first Christmas in Omaha. Since we had sold all our Christmas decorations before our immigration to America, we had to buy new ones. One Saturday I took the kids to South Omaha by bus where we bought glass Christmas balls in all colors and shapes at the Woolworth Store. Beside the Christmas decorations and a top for the tree, each of the kids also could buy their own ornament. For the very first time we bought electric Christmas lights for our tree, instead of the small Christmas tree candles we used in Holland.

The days that followed were exciting for our children, and they couldn't wait until we would buy our Christmas tree. Since Jozef and I were not used to having an Christmas tree up earlier than a few days before Christmas the kids had to wait, but we promised them that we would keep our tree up until after Three Kings Day which is January 6. Since we had not bought a Christmas tree for the last two years, we thought this one should be special. Because our living room was small, we knew that a large tree wouldn't fit. We had to look around carefully.

The Sunday before Christmas we took the kids and walked to the Hinky Dinky store where we had seen some nice ones. Not having realized that the families in America buy their Christmas tree very early, we didn't find much of a selection anymore. Almost all the trees were gone. The only ones left were tall, badly shaped trees. Looking it over Jos said hopefully, "Dad, maybe you can cut one of those large trees in half and use only the top part which is straight." It was a good idea. We asked a clerk at Hinky Dinky how much money he wanted for the tree. When he said two dollars, we bought one of the tall deformed trees and walked happily the ten blocks home with Jozef and his son carrying the tree.

While Lia and I got all the decorating things together, Jozef and Jos took care of the short needled pine tree in the backyard. Believe it or not, after some cutting and trimming it turned out to be a good looking Christmas tree after all which fit just right in our small room. While I made tea, the children decorated our first American Christmas tree which, with some help and decorating directions from their mom, looked just great—especially when the presents were placed under the tree. Eddy, being only three years old, thought he could open the packages right away and was upset when he couldn't.

Finally Christmas Eve came and after a special dinner the kids opened their presents with shining eyes and smiling faces—taking turns one package at a time.

It was new and a little strange to us to open presents on the night before Christmas and not on St. Nicholas Day, December 6th. Even though we never had done this before and did not know much about the American Santa Claus with his reindeer, we were happy and enjoyed this first Christmas Eve in America with just the five of us. I remember that Jos received an Erector Set so he could build cranes. He had wanted this Erector Set for a long time. Lia got presents that only little girls can enjoy, such as doll clothes and a purse with makeup. Eddy was happy with blocks and a metal toy bus. We also had bought books for the children which we thought they needed. Besides the usual candy there were also two balls—a large one and a small. Yes, that night Jozef and I felt rich in our own home with each other and our children. Christmas Day came with unseasonably warm weather. The kids had hoped for a lot of snow with Christmas but no luck. Instead of snow the weather was sunny and warm.

When we came home from Christmas morning service at our Holy Ghost Church, Nelly and her husband, Joe Latek, came with their children to our house to eat my homemade traditional Christmas stollen (bread). Later while the kids played outside in our yard with the balls, we four talked about our countries, Holland and Poland, and our cultural differences in America. Joe Latek worked for a laboratory, a place where they made serum which was taken from the blood of small dead animals, mainly cats.

Later in the afternoon our family went to Toni and Ann's house where we had been invited for a Christmas dinner. As we walked into their home, we were happily surprised to find Chelca there. She had come by herself the day before. She had arrived from Chicago to have Christmas with her family in Omaha. Toni and Ann had kept the unexpected surprise from us so as not to spoil the fun. We loved seeing Chelca again; it was just great. She was planning to stay only for a few days—"Just for Christmas," she said. Ann had prepared a very nice Christmas dinner with all the trimmings some of which we never had eaten before such as turkey, sweet potatoes and pumpkin pie. Later, after coffee, we all opened presents which had been under the Christmas tree. To the excitement of our children they again got toys and books and also clothing from Chelca and Ann.

It was late in the evening when Toni drove us home. Even though we missed the Second Christmas Day, as we were accustomed to celebrating in Holland and Poland, our first Christmas in our new town would remain a very special memory. And the snow? Well that came down a few days later—after Christmas. There was enough snow so that Jos and Lia could make an igloo together with a neighbor boy. Eddy wanted to help too, but I think that he was more in the way than he helped. I went outside and together with my little boy we made a snow-man.

Later Uncle Toni came to our house with a sled, which was a real happy surprise for the kids and they just loved it. With loud laughing and shouting they sped down the sloping yard on the back side of our house. Especially Jos and his brother enjoyed sliding down a thousand times. Lia was usually more interested in making her own snowman and she always made them very pretty. Besides a carrot for its nose and coal for the eyes and mouth, she put a knitted hat on his head and a colorful scarf around the snowman's neck. In his hand he held a stick or one of my wooden spoons.

New Year's Day of 1957 came with oliebollen and appleflappen. We had invited Toni and Ann to our home to eat the traditional Dutch New Year Day treat with us. Toni enjoyed the powdered sugar oliebollen, and I thought he would never stop eating them.

◆     ◆     ◆

Christmas vacation from school was over, and Jos and Lia were back in their classes. The weather had turned cold in January and, as the newsman on the TV the evening before said, another snowstorm was on the way. It was early morning when I got up from bed after Jozef left for work, and I thought that it was very cold inside the house. I went downstairs to the basement to see if there was some fire left in our centrally located large furnace. Leaving the fire burning at night was something which we had to do—we had been told. This was nothing new; it was something we always had done in Holland. But this furnace was much larger and much more difficult to handle than our small hearth in the corner of our living room in Holland. When I came downstairs and opened the furnace door, there was not a spark of fire to be seen. "That damn furnace," I muttered as I went upstairs to wake Jos and Lia for school. To make it a little more comfortable for my children, I decided to let the four burners on our gas stove burn and close the doorway to the living room with a blanket to keep the warmth in.

A little later Jos came into the kitchen. Looking puzzled, he asked me what I was doing—if I was doing something new. I told him, "Never mind, just hurry up with your breakfast and go to school with your sister." I then put a warm sweater over Eddy's pajamas, gave him a glass of warm milk and went downstairs. I grabbed an old newspaper and some small pieces of wood which were laying in the basement, opened the furnace door and stacked everything into the cold monster. While I lit the paper with a large match and closed the door, I hoped·

and prayed the wood would catch fire and start burning, which was not always the case. When I saw small tongues of flames, I laid larger pieces of wood into the furnace. Then, as everything was burning well, I filled the furnace with coal.

In the fall we had bought a truckload of anthracite which was poured through the basement window and was now laying on the basement floor behind wooden poles. To my misery the coal which they had delivered had left coal dust all through the house, and it had taken me forever to clean everything. Because the whole process of making a quick and good fire was not always easy, sometimes it took a while before warmth filled the home. We knew that the trick was to keep the large furnace burning day and night which was not always easy to do. We had to learn and get used to many new ways in that first year of living at the 52nd Street.

Jozef had gone to Johnny's Café early that morning, and I hoped he would make it home before the snow came down. In the afternoon the air was still and the sky was heavy with low hanging dark clouds. While staring through the kitchen window at the trees in our backyard with their bare winter branches, my mind went back to Holland. During the holidays I had been too busy and happy, and my homesickness had left me. But now in January with its long cold days, Jozef gone to his work and Jos and Lia were back in school, the loneliness for my country and my life in Holland had come back. Even though I had my house-work to take care of, my busy three-year old around me the whole day, and a TV to watch, I was lonely. I was lonely for my family and the people I had known in my little country—people who I sometimes had taken for granted and now could not forget. I was homesick for the friends I had left behind even though they all had written me faithfully. I told myself many times that I shouldn't feel quite so depressed. Maybe I was sitting inside the house too much. It was too cold to play outdoors with Eddy and since we had no car, it was not easy to go with the bus every time to the stores in South Omaha.

It was later that afternoon when Jos and his sister came home through the kitchen door all excited, saying, "Mom, the kids at school are saying that we are getting a lot of snow tonight and that we don't have school tomorrow!" While Lia took her coat off she looked at me and said hopefully, "Yes, Mom, maybe two days. Wouldn't that be fun!" After telling them to put their shoes outside on the porch, I said, "We will see. Don't count on it yet. Let us first drink tea and eat your father's crumb cake which he made for you last night." The kids loved the Polish crumb cake which their dad occasionally made at home for his family. Especially our oldest could eat big pieces and never had enough.

About the time when Jozef came home from his work, the first snow came down. And what a snow! It all started with some wind and tiny flakes of frozen ice. Soon it turned into a snowstorm. Jozef and I had never experienced such a rage of nature with the exception of 'The Big Storm of 1953' which had broken many dikes in Holland and had flooded large areas of land. But this kind of a snowstorm was new to us and we didn't sleep too well that night. The storm howled around the house the whole night and our weeping willow branches swept against our porch as if it wanted to break it down.

The following morning when we got up from bed it was still snowing and blowing. We never had seen so much snow before. Everything was covered with heavy layers of sparkling snow which was most beautiful to see. The schools and stores were closed that day and, of course, the kids couldn't wait to go outside and play in the high drifts. Except for Jozef, it was the most snow the children and I had ever seen. Soon they were rolling in the white fluffy snow and making snowballs to throw at each other. Later, with a lot of laughter and screaming and pushing each other, the children came back in the house. "Just to warm up," they said while first having brushed the snow from their clothing. Five minutes later, while their little brother stayed inside the house, Jos and Lia went out in the snow again full of excitement.

Although the snow was deep and the temperature was bitterly cold, the mailman managed to get through the drifts and deliver our mail. It was our first big snowstorm in America.

One afternoon, when I came home from shopping, an envelope was in our mailbox. It was a letter from Africa. My parents had arrived in South Africa in late December after a long and interesting voyage on board a Dutch ocean liner. After three weeks of sailing over the Atlantic Ocean going from Holland to the furthest point south in Africa, they arrived at the harbor city of Cape Town (Cape of Good Hope). When Father and Mother descended from the ship, they were welcomed by mother's family who had driven for two days all the way from their town of Bloemfontein (mid-South Africa) where they lived.

Father, Mother and the family stayed in and around Cape Town to see the sights for a few days, such as the high Table Rock Mountain overlooking the Indian Ocean, before driving further to other places of interest. From there they drove back to Bloemfontain. Father wrote that the car ride to Bloemfontain had been interesting. After they left Cape Town they had driven through mountainous areas and later beside jungles. As Father wrote in his letter, "This was most beautiful." The second day they came to an area where they saw nothing else but endless dry grassland with here and there some shrubs or a small tree. The two lane road they drove on was endless and very lonesome with almost no passing cars and just here and there a native village. Then Father wrote further, "The soil here is red which is strange to us who are used to the black soil in Holland. This time of the year it is summer in South Africa and vacation time. The weather is very nice and we are gone many times."

Mother wrote about the family and the new nice apartment building which my Oom Gerard had built and owned. He lived with Tante Ann in one of the apartments which he had built especially for themselves. My parents had their own room in their apartment. She wrote that my cousin Ken now had four children, two boys and two girls. He and his wife were doing well. My other cousin, Henk, was a Civil Engineer. He was engaged to be married and also lived in Bloemfontein. The letter from my parents had taken five weeks to get here to my mailbox which was a long time. I decided to write back to them immediately. A letter from Omaha to Holland in that time took twelve days by airplane, six weeks by ship.

◆　　　◆　　　◆

Spring of 1957. It is impossible to have any thoughts about our first spring in 52nd Street without first recalling the thick mud. With the coming of the first spring rains and thaw, our street became an ocean of mud. To walk through it was like walking through ankle-deep molasses. Whatever we wore, boots or shoes, they got a layer of thick mud on them which had to be cleaned off after each trip or it became a hard thick crust. Soon our porch became the place for our shoes and boots. Maybe the kids had found some fun in this but Jozef and I did not. But, mud or no mud, the kids had to go to school, Jozef to work and I had to get my shopping done. I did this by finding the less muddy patches on the side of the road.

The year before when we had bought our home, the street had looked great. We knew it was not paved, but it looked well taken care of and we had not been worried. Once in awhile during the summer and fall the large city street scraper had come through our street and had made our road nice and level again with a new layer of gravel. They had worked on the road until the beginning of winter when they stopped coming. Now with the end of the winter, we were fighting the mud and had to learn just to be patient until the road would dry up.

One morning in late spring when our road was dry and level again, Eddy was playing in the home of a little friend from across the alley. I was busy ironing some clothes in the kitchen when Jozef walked through the front door. Earlier that morning a man, who also worked at Johnny's Café, came to our house and Jozef had left with him in his car. Before they left, Jozef told me that he soon would be home, but he did not say where he was going. This was unusual since we always told each other where the other was going.

A few hours later my husband walked into the kitchen with a strange expression on his face and said, "Oh, I see you are busy." He then said, "Put your shoes on, Efka, and come with me." When I followed him and walked outside the door, there in front of the house in the bright sunshine stood a shining light beige car. It was a 1953 Chevy. Our very first car! How proud Jozef was. When he opened the car door for me, I felt like a queen. After first telling our neighbor that I would be back for Eddy in a little while, Jozef and I drove around for the longest time. First we went to Ralston and then further to Papillion and back again over country roads. While he was driving, Jozef told me that the week before he had gone for his driver's license. He had brought his old Army driver's license along with him. He said that he first answered some traffic questions and then he had to drive around. He had no problems and after a short wait, they gave him his driver's license. He then went with the man, who also worked at Johnny's, to a car dealer and bought a used car. "A real good car and not too much money!" he told me happily. When I asked him why he hadn't told me about it earlier, he said that he had kept everything a secret because he wanted to surprise me. Which he sure did! It was wonderful to have our own car now. What a blessing for Jozef now that he didn't have to walk to his work anymore. And for me not to need a taxi every time when I was done with my weekly grocery shopping at Hinky Dinky. When we came home from our drive and went into the house, I noticed a faint scorching smell coming from the kitchen. I had left the iron on.

One day at the beginning of May Jozef said to Lia, "What do you think Lia, should we buy some little baby chickens?" This did not fall on deaf ears since Lia loved any kind of animal. It was about an hour later when they came home carrying a large box from which rose shrill cheeping noises. It were 20 new little chicks that had just popped their heads out of a shell and into the world. The kids were fascinated with the little puffballs and were sitting beside the box for the longest time giggling and holding them carefully. Since we had a chicken house with a nice run around it in our backyard, we put the chicks outside in the sunshine during the day. When the nights were cold we brought them inside in the box and set them in front of the heater in our kitchen to keep them warm.

Since that first spring at 52nd Street, Jozef bought one-day-old chickens every year for which he paid 10 cents each. He bought mostly little roosters which he slaughtered—one each week before winter—for eating when they were big and fat. He also bought a few hens for their eggs.

One day in May we received mail from my brother Henk from Canada. He wrote that he, Annie and their little boy Richard were coming to Omaha for a visit. They were planning to come by car in July and were going to stay for one week. After reading their letter I poured a cup of coffee for myself and sat down. My brother and his family coming to Omaha for a whole week! How happy I was. I couldn't wait until Jozef came home to tell him. First thing the next morning I wrote Henk back that we were more than delighted to have them. Jozef had decided to take his one week vacation when the family from Canada came.

Finally we had a telephone installed in our home. Our very first telephone. It was a black rotary one and rented, something that most people did in that time. From now on we could call Toni and Ann which made it much easier for all of us. Calling to Canada or other countries was not done much yet since this was much too expensive.

When Jozef bought the car, most Sundays we went exploring for places to spend an afternoon with our children. It did not take long until we found the best places to go. At that time Omaha was not developed further than 72nd Street and had not many lakes in or around the city as is now the case. The most popular places for the people of Omaha to go picnicking, fishing and swimming were Carter Lake, Lake Manawa in Iowa and the lakes in Fremont. But the place which soon became a favorite with our family were a few large sandpits which had formed lakes a long time ago and were located along Highway 75 beside the Platte River. One of the sandpit lakes which had a very wide beach was made into a swimming place by the name of Merritt's Beach. Besides the dressing rooms and snack bar it had swings, trampoline, water slides and other entertainment equipment. It was a wonderful place to go, but because we had to pay to get in, most of the time we went to one of the other sandpits which were free. Even though there were no trampoline or swings, I think we had as much fun there. A few times during the summer, especially during Jozef's vacation, we went to everyones favorite Merritt's Beach for the whole day.

Another place we enjoyed was Fontenelle Forest. One day I saw a story in our newspaper about the many deer that lived there in the wild. I told Jozef about it and we decided to investigate the area they had been writing about on the following Sunday. This strip of forest on the Missouri River turned out to be a great place—not only for the children who loved to run on the hilly paths of the forest—but also their mom and dad enjoyed going there. Usually our end destination was the Missouri River where we rested beside the churning fast running water. After their dad first taught his kids how to skip small stones over the water, we had to find our way back through the forest again.

One day I said to Jozef that I wanted to find out if there were other Dutch families living in Omaha. Even though we had some nice neighbors here, I missed the conversations with a Dutch woman. Jozef was lucky that almost every day he spoke his native tongue not only with his boss, but also with Toni and Ann and sometimes with Joe and Nelly Latek. I said to Jozef, "This town is large enough that there should be at least one family living here who came from Holland. "We talked some more about it and decided to ask our insurance man who had sold us an insurance policy. "He knows many families,"I said, "and maybe he knows a Dutch family who lives here in Omaha."

It was a few weeks later when the insurance man came to collect our monthly payment. At that time the premiums were paid by cash or by check every month at the door. I told him that I was looking for a Dutch family and maybe he knew a family in Omaha who came from Holland. He answered me saying that he didn't know anyone, but he thought that a colleague knew of a Dutch family who had come to our city. He would get information about it and let me know.

It was a few week later that we received a telephone call from our insurance agent saying that he had made contact with a Dutch family and, yes, they wanted to meet us. It was not long after that phone call that we met Henk and Coby Hendriks and their two young daughters, Joanne and Connie. They had immigrated to Omaha from Holland in 1957. To my surprise and delight the family we just met came from the same town in Holland as I came from—Breda. Coby, an attractive slim young women a few years younger than I was, had always lived in Breda and knew my brother's wife Annie from school. We soon learned that Henk's father, who also had been with the military in Breda, knew my father. Henk, who also was younger then we were, worked in the beginning at a cement factory in South Omaha but soon started to work for the telephone company, the ATT, as an electrician. Here we were, living in mid-America and coming from the same city and background as in Holland. It was like a miracle to talk to someone who not only spoke my language, but also knew all the stores, parks, schools and places that I knew in Breda. It was not long until we became friends—a friendship which lasted through all those years and hopefully many more years to come.

◆     ◆     ◆

It was again summer vacation from school. A family by the name of Joe and Rita Cizek and their three children lived on the other side of our street. Their children were about the ages of our children and sometimes they played ball together. Occasionally Rita and I had coffee in my or her kitchen and we talked. By now I had gotten used to the English language, enough anyway, to have a conversation.

One day Rita and I were having coffee in her kitchen when she asked me if I had any regrets about coming to America. Rita, who had lived on a farm with her parents before she had married Joe, was a bright small-built woman with blonde hair which she usually wore in a knot in the back of her neck. She always was baking or cooking something for her family. That day when I was over at her house, drinking coffee with a piece of her home baked peach pie and she had asked me that question, I said to her, "I am not sure yet, Rita." I then said that, even though I slowly was getting used to my new life in America, I still did not have the feeling of belonging here. "I think I need more time, Rita. I still think about Holland every day. Not only do I miss my family and friends, but also our way of life, such as the colors and sounds of the market place, the fish market with its just-caught fish from out of the North Sea, and the forest or park where I loved to walk and listen to the wind in the tall trees. I miss the evening church bells ringing, blessing the people with evening prayer and, believe it or not, Rita, I still miss the big loaf of fresh baked bread from our bakery on the corner of our street." While she stirred a large pan of soup on her gas stove, Rita looked at me and said, "Eef, I believe you and can understand that it must be very difficult to leave one's country. But in time you will learn the American ways and make your memories here in your new country. I guess living in two different cultures, that of your homeland and that of another country, must be difficult for anyone." A sudden strange sadness swept over me and I answered her, "I think, Rita, that is the price one has to pay for leaving the old country for a new one."

While pouring herself and me another cup of coffee and cutting a second piece of her pie, she said, "You will see, Eef, in time you will be happy here. Trust me, you will." I then told her about Jos, that we had noticed that children at school called him Joe instead of Jos. Not that we minded, because we were used to the fact that Jozef had been named 'Joe' already in Chicago. "For myself," I said, "I do not want to change my husband's name and would always call him Jozef. But for Jos it is different, he wants to be called Joe. Probably in time we will be calling him Joe too," I said to her smiling. I then continued telling her that because Jozef was not a Dutchman and was familiar with the English language, more and more we were beginning to speak English words in our house. "Maybe it is wrong," I continued, "maybe it is wrong for our children to speak only one language in the future. I try to keep the Dutch language in our home, but sometimes the kids refuse to answer me in Dutch now that English comes easier to them."

Many times when I came to Rita's kitchen in those first years in America, she taught me how to bake fruit pies, cook sweet potatoes, squash and corn on the cob. It was food which I never had seen or baked or cooked before in my life. I also learned from her about her life on the farm in Iowa when she was a child. She told me about winter time when she had to walk the long country road going to school through knee deep snow, and the grasshoppers which came in the summer and many times ate everything in the fields.

The chickens were growing as chickens do, and some of the roosters tried their first crow which made a funny sound. To our children's happiness, our cat Minni had a litter of kittens—six were black, as was their mother, and two were black and white. We planned to keep them all until they were older and then sell them or give them away.

One Sunday Jozef and Toni built a double swing from wood for the kids. Now two children could swing at the same time. It was a nice high swing, and I think that not only the kids but also their mom enjoyed sitting on the swing, even if it was just for dreaming.

After the swing was finished, Jozef started to paint our house on the outside. Since he never had painted a house before, it was quite a job for him. It looked great when the painting job was finished. He had painted it white as it had been before. Jos usually mowed our lawn with a blade mower which we got in a second hand store. Since we lived on the edge of Omaha and many people around us had large yards without fences with native grass growing, the only thing they did was keep it mowed whenever the grass, and the weeds, became too tall.

One day at the end of July Henk, Annie and little Richard arrived by car from Toronto. We had been waiting for them the whole day, and finally here they were. It was wonderful to see them again and have a whole week vacation together. The weather was great that week and besides going swimming at the popular sand pits on the side of Merritt's Beach, we also went swimming and picnicking at Lake Manawa. One day we went all together to downtown and, of course, did some shopping there in one of the large stores. Annie and I love to shop. The last day we stayed home and invited Toni and Ann over for a cookout in our backyard.

That afternoon while the children played, we talked about living here in America and Canada. Henk told us that some of their friends had moved back to Holland. "They just couldn't adjust themselves to a different lifestyle," he said. "They felt that they were pushed into changing and couldn't do it, or maybe wouldn't do it. Some of the immigrants in Europe think that money is laying on the street in America. When they arrive here, they are disappointed that they have to work as hard as they did in Europe, so they want to go back again from where they came."Jozef looked at Henk and answered him, "Nowhere in the world is there such a great opportunity for a good life as here in America and Canada. That is, if you are not too lazy to work."

While Toni helped himself to another beer he said, "Yes, look around you. These great countries, America and Canada, are made by immigrants. They all came from other countries—they came here like us. I am sure many felt like we did when we first came to this big country; many wanted to go right back home."I said that I thought that life here was so different than in Holland where our life was not so focused on materialism but on families. Annie answered, "Eef, people are people. They just have different ways of handling their problems and have different lifestyles, but we probably have the same goals." We then started to talk about the weather in Omaha and Toronto, and how in Holland hardly a day goes by when the weather was not mentioned. We all agreed that the weather here was so much better than in our cool rainy Dutch climate. Except, we said, for those days when here it is much too hot or too cold. It seems it never is good enough! We had a good laugh, and after a dessert of ice cream we decided to end the pleasant afternoon.

It was early in the morning of the following day when Henk, Annie and their little boy said goodbye to go back to Toronto. The time had gone by too fast. But the wonderful memories of our first vacation together in America would remain forever. When they left and the car drove slowly out of our street, I knew in my heart that my homesickness for my country and my life in Holland had left me. It was the beginning of my new life in America.

# 39

# *OUR NEIGHBORHOOD*

*October 1957.* One day when I was talking to Nellie Latek, she asked me if I knew about Halloween, which was coming up that following week. I said to her that I didn't know what it was and that I never had heard about it. She answered me that she thought so because, as far as she knew, in Poland it was not celebrated either. I must have looked puzzled at her because she said to me, "Eef, next week Wednesday, which is Halloween night, come to my house with your children at about 6:30. Give each of your kids a large paper sack and, since Jozef will not be home, close up your house. We will go around the neighborhood with our kids, and you will see what Halloween is all about.

When the following week came, I went to Nellie's house at the promised time. As we walked through our street, I saw lights on the front of the houses everywhere and many had decorations of pumpkins or were scary with ghosts and witches. The many children on the streets were all dressed up in funny or scary Halloween costumes. They went from house to house and knocked on the doors while shouting, "Trick or Treat!" The door was then opened and the owner of the house gave them a candy, chocolate, gum or an apple. After the children said in a chorus "Thank you!," they ran to the next house. It was not long until Jos and Lia understood and soon were running along with Nelly's children from one house to the next. With their faces all smiling and their eyes big with excitement they opened their paper sacks to receive their candies when the door was opened.

Only Eddy stood close to me and didn't want to go with the other children. He was four years old and didn't know what to think about all those scary looking people on the streets and the houses with all the screaming noises. He never had seen or heard anything like this before in his young life and was frightened until Jos took his little brother's hand and led him to a house where, after a knock on the door, a friendly older lady opened it. After first giving the older children their candy she gave Eddy, who stood halfway behind his older brother, his candy and then closed the door. Eddy, looking at the lone candy in his sack and probably thinking that this was a fun game, took his candy and with a big smile gave it to the lady of the next house. The lady must have understood the young boy without a costume because she gave Eddy his candy back and also two more from her candy bowl. My little son, all confused, just stood there looking from the candies in his sack up to the lady and to the candies again. It was time for some explanation from his mom who just found out herself about Halloween. Eddy seemed to get the right idea and without a word he turned around and ran happily with the other kids from house to house.

I will never forget the faces of my children when we later came home, and they emptied their paper sacks filled with candies in a big pile on the kitchen table. They never had seen so much candy in their lives—and it was all theirs. Jos and Lia looked at all the goodies, grinned, and said, "Mom, we have enough candy for a whole year."

Ever since that first Halloween our children always were dressed in Halloween costumes for that day, and our house was decorated with paper ghosts, witches and pumpkins. A plate full of candies was, and still is, always there for the kids who knock on our door saying "Trick or Treat! "Every year since that first Halloween in America, I have made costumes for our children and later for our grandchildren. I think as long as I am able to, I will be making them. Every year when Halloween comes around, I enjoy remembering the time on Halloween night when it started to get dusk and the children would say, "It is getting dark, Mom, can we go?"I think Halloween is a wonderful day for children because it is a magic kingdom where children can pretend they are someone else. The thing which I still can't figure out after all those years is, when is it that the kids become too old for running around for candies.

More and more I went downtown. I went there with Eddy when Jos and Lia were at school for the day. We took the bus which stopped at the corner of our street, and we transferred to another bus in South Omaha going to downtown. I loved to shop in the large four story high buildings as Brandeis, Kilpatrick and Pennys which were located within walking distance of each other. The stores and the wide streets of downtown were always crowded with people who were shopping or doing business. Because there were no gangs yet or much crime in that time in Omaha, people felt safe to be in downtown even at night. Eddy and I usually ate our lunch at the Brandeis Cafeteria which we both enjoyed. After a few hours of walking through the stores and looking at the merchandise, and also doing some buying, we went home on the bus. I always tried to be home before school was out.

When in January of 1958 the ponds in the parks were frozen over, Jos and Lia made a long ice slide beside our house. On the highest point of our sloping yard which started at our street, they left the water slowly running through the garden hose for the whole night. The next morning Jos moved the hose further out until the whole side, about 10 feet wide, was one frozen ice mass and which gave them a wonderful sliding place. Later that day when school was dismissed, the kids got their friends and, with their cheeks red from the cold, they all were screaming and sliding down the hill. Not only the kids had a lot of fun doing this, but also one of their friend's dog who thought it fun and went sliding down on his four feet.

In February Jos celebrated his eleventh birthday with a party. He invited his friends, sister and brother. By now everyone, including Lia and Eddy, called him 'Joe'. It was not long thereafter that Jozef and I also were calling him Joe instead of Jos.

May 1958 was a special month for our family. It was not only our youngest son's birthday on May 6, but also Joe made his confirmation at our Holy Ghost Church. We celebrated our oldest son's special day together with Toni and Ann. In the afternoon the Bishop of Omaha arrived at our church. While the organ played and the choir sang, the celebrants walked slowly down the middle aisle to the front of the church. For a moment my thoughts went back to Breda when Joe received his first Holy Communion. How fast the years had flown by, and I realized how lucky we were in spite of the first difficult years. I looked at my son standing there in front of the altar. He was such an active bright boy—always full of jokes which sometimes had gotten him in trouble. But now he looked serious as the ceremonies were ready to begin. Later when the solemn ceremony had ended, we took pictures of him with our family and Toni and Ann in the church yard. When we got home, the coffee and cake was ready to be served.

It was a few weeks later when our daughter celebrated her first Holy Communion. A few weeks before I had bought pretty white material and had sewn a lovely communion dress for her. I also had made the flower headband with a veil. Because Toni and Ann were planning to stay for brunch after the church ceremony, I got up early that morning to prepare some of the food which I wanted to serve later that day. It was sunny and quiet outside, and I decided to open the kitchen door which connected with the porch. Soon I found myself sitting on the stairs which go from the porch into the backyard. I loved to sit on those stairs, especially in mornings like this. Even though the flowers of the fruit trees in our neighbor's yard were now almost gone, the aroma of spring was in the air. I looked at the chattering birds in search of food in the early sunlight, and I thought how peaceful it was here.

After some doing, our family finally was ready for church. On Sunday mornings it always took awhile before everyone was dressed. Somehow during those mornings the kids decided to be lazy. Even though I tried to start early to get every one ready for church, it was always at the last moment when we left the house. Not being on time for church, or anyplace, was something which their dad did not like. But this Sunday was different and both boys didn't needed to be told to get ready. It was the day their sister had been waiting for. Lia's communion dress and veil was hanging in her room and she couldn't wait to dress herself. How lovely she looked when she came from her bedroom ready for church. When everyone was all dressed up, me in a light brown linen summer suit with a pretty matching hat, we were on the way.

First we delivered Lia to a side door of the church, we met Toni and Ann who were waiting for us in the entry hall. Inside it was already crowded with family members and friends of the communicants. When the organ began to play and the choir began to sing, the communion procession walked into the church. Eddy became excited when he was the first one to see his sister and waved at her. That day many boys and girls received their first communion. When I saw our young daughter with her sunny smile walking down the aisle in her white communion dress, she was to me the most beautiful girl in the world. As I looked at Jozef, I knew her daddy thought so too.

When the communion ceremony ended and we came outside, we first had to take pictures of Lia. Later we took some more in our yard with the family. After our brunch we went outside with Toni and Ann and the children. A few days earlier Jozef had bought 20 one-day old little chickens again the same as he had done the year before. Also Minni our cat had decided the week before to have a large litter of kittens. The children more than enjoyed all the young kittens and chicks and liked to watch and hold them. Later that day Nelly and her husband came with their children to congratulate Lia on her First Holy Communion.

For the last few months we had received cards and letters from my parents about their adventures in Africa. It looked as though they had a good time going to many places in South Africa. In their last letter they wrote that they were planning to leave the following day for the Kruger National Wildlife Refuge. It was the place which Oom Gerard had wanted to visit for many years, but he always had been too busy working and thought that someday he would go there.

It must have been in mid-June when we again received a letter from my parents. But this time it was a very sad letter. Father wrote that when they were on their way to the Kruger National Refuge Park with my oom, Tante and another couple who were their friends, Oom Gerard became suddenly ill. It happened in a restaurant in a small town when they stopped for lunch. Suddenly Oom Gerard did not feel well and could not see—everything had become black in front of his eyes. They soon found out that Oom Gerard had suffered a stroke. He was taken to the nearest hospital where they kept him for weeks. Tante Ann stayed with her husband while the others decided to go back home to Bloemfontein.

Father wrote that they felt very bad for Oom Gerard. Here he was so close to his dream and now this. Mother and Father were now alone in their apartment and, as I noticed from their writing, it had become lonesome for them without Oom Gerard and Tante Ann. After reading the letter I looked at the calendar and saw that it was already nearing the end of their vacation. It was the end of June when my parents had planned to go back to Holland. Such a sad ending for everyone, I thought. It is good we never know what is around the corner of our lives.

It was more than a month later when we received a letter from Holland from my parents. They wrote that they had arrived safely at their home back in Breda. It had been a long trip home for them. Oom Gerard would never see Kruger National Refuge Park. He died a year later at his home in Bloemfontein in South Africa.

◆     ◆     ◆

After living more than three years in America we still had many things to learn about our new country. When we lived in Chicago in an all-Polish neighborhood, we had not been aware of America's National Holidays. Now living here in Omaha it became a different story. I remember that day when I was busy with my weekly laundry, and Toni and Ann came over to our house. It was the Fourth of July and a gorgeous day. We had not realized that this day was an important national holiday. The day before Jozef had said to me that Johnny's Café would be closed because of some holiday, but he didn't know exactly what it was. The kids who had summer vacation from school were watching Howdy Doody Time on the TV.

As I was hanging the linens to dry on the washline in the backyard, a loud voice suddenly said, "What are you doing? Don't you know it is the Fourth of July today!" It was Toni who stepped out of his car. Turning around I said to him, "Yes, I know it is Wednesday, July fourth. What about it!"Jozef came out-side to see what the commotion was. Ann, who was waving her hand in greeting to me, followed Toni to the backyard. A little later as we were sitting on the porch with a cup of coffee Toni explained that the Fourth of July was a national holiday, a day of celebration. It was the day of America's freedom from the English and is called Independence Day. He then went on saying, "Since this is a national holiday in America and very much observed by everyone, no one is working today. Eef, you better not hang your laundry outside on a national holi-day. This does not look very patriotic."

Well, this taught Jozef and me a lesson to be more aware of America's national holidays. I still always remembered Holland's national days and I missed them, but now it was time to learn about America's national days and to remember and celebrate them as Americans do. To the kid's excitement Toni and Ann took us that evening to the fireworks in Ralston. It was very crowded with people but it was the best fireworks we ever had seen. It was the very first time we celebrated an American national holiday. Since then we went many a year on the Fourth of July to Ralston's parade and fireworks.

A few weeks later we went for the first time to the yearly Johnny's Café family picnic. We learned those picnics were usually held in a park or sometimes on the grounds of Frank Kawa's friend. This friend lived on a large wooded property beside the Elkhorn River and was surrounded by water on three sides. There were rowboats with paddles for everyone to use which was lots of fun, especially for the children. Besides the picnic with many wonderful foods to eat, there were games for the children and great prizes to be won. We had fun especially with one of Jozef's co-workers and his wife. They had a young son and soon Eddy and he played together. For a while we became friends until a year later they moved away to Boston. When the picnic and last game was over, we drove back to our home with our tired kids in the car. They were holding the prizes that they had won at the games. Every year since Jozef worked at Johnny's, we always went to the tra-ditional yearly Johnny's Café picnic.

Occasionally we went with Toni and Ann to a park in east Omaha which was named Riverview Park. It was a pleasant place for just a stroll or a picnic or for listening to the music of a band on a Sunday afternoon. There was a playground for the children, and a few cages which held a tiger, wolf and a bear. Also in the park was a lagoon with ducks and swans. And to everyone's pleasure a few pea-cocks and deer walked freely around. Every year the city of Omaha added a few more animals to the park for the enjoyment of its people. Of course, there was also an ice cream and popcorn wagon.

Riverview Park later became the Henry Doorly Zoo, and over the years we watched as the zoo expanded into a great place with many animals living as if they were in their natural habitat. In later years they opened the world's largest indoor Tropical Rain Forest and the beautiful Sea Aquarium. Also located in the zoo is the Crewcock Conservation Research Center for animal care and reproductive physiology, genetics and genome resource banking. As the years passed Henry Doorly Zoo became one of the finest zoos in America.

Eddy was now five years old and ready to start kindergarten. He was excited and asked me a thousand times if he could carry books to school like his sister and brother. Before the children went back to school I decided to take them for a whole day to downtown. First we went by bus to South Omaha and then with another bus to downtown. The bus rides alone were excitement for them since our children seldom rode the bus. When we came to downtown and stepped from the bus, we went first to the large stores and bought new school clothes for all three. When lunchtime came, we went to the large self-service cafeteria which was located inside Brandeis. This was very special for my children since going out to eat was not done very often in that time. After first carefully looking over the food section, the kids decided what they were going to eat. Of course, they always piled too much food on their tray and then couldn't eat it all.

From Brandeis we went to see a movie at a theater which was located in mid-downtown. Because it was the only theater in Omaha which had a very wide double screen, it was a popular place to see a movie. With a soft drink and a sack of popcorn we watched a funny or cowboy movie. After a wonderful whole day in downtown we went home again on the bus. For some years during their summer vacations, the children and I always would spend one whole day in downtown, going shopping, lunching and seeing a movie.

At the end of the summer we bought a puppy, our first dog. It was a brown haired cocker spaniel and we gave it the name of Trixie. It was the cutest little puppy and he soon followed the kids wherever they went—even to their school if we did not watch it carefully.

The summer turned into fall. As I looked outside the kitchen window, I noticed that the rain had stopped and saw the wet leaves which were plastered against the screens on the porch. My mind went to Holland—to my parents. Father wrote that his health was not good and wanted to move to Amsterdam as soon as possible and live there. Amsterdam was not only the city both my parents came from, but also where Father's sister and my brother Jan and his family lived. Since there were no houses to rent or buy anywhere yet in Holland, this decision of Father was not as easy as he was hoping for.

Father had gone first to the Housing Administration in Breda. When he learned there that the only thing open for them was to exchange their apartment with someone in Amsterdam who wanted to move to Breda, Father signed up. The man at the desk told him that if they knew of someone who wanted to move to Breda, the administration would let my father know. They also said that the list was long, and it could take a few years before his name came up. As soon as I read Father's letter, I wrote back and asked what was wrong with his health. A few weeks later I got Father's answer saying that he had arteriosclerosis of the heart, and there was nothing the doctors could do for him.

That fall Jozef decided that we should have a new gas furnace installed in our basement and get rid of the old coal furnace. I couldn't have agreed with him more. It was on a nice crisp day in the beginning of October when a furnace company came and took the old monster coal furnace out. What a mess! Late in the afternoon when they were finished with the installation of our new gas furnace, I couldn't believe how much more room we now had in the basement. The next morning as soon as the kids were at school, I began to clean the basement which took me at least two weeks before I got it all painted clean and shining. Finally no more fighting to get wood and the fire going, or a cold house in the mornings and—no coal dust anymore.

For Christmas we received mail not only from Holland, but also from Tante Ann in South Africa and a letter from Poland. The family from Poland was doing as good as could be expected under the circumstances. We had sent them a package with food and clothing a month before which they had thankfully received. Jozef's mother wrote that she and her family were going to be together for Christmas and wished we could be there with them. Together with the letter came also a few pictures from the family which we enjoyed very much. From Holland we received for the holidays a package from my parents with everything Dutch inside, such as our initials in chocolate, almond windmill cookies and their favorite salty licorice. There was also a toy for each of the children. It was always a happy surprise for our kids to receive a package from their grandparents from Holland.

From my brother Jan and and his wife Gerda came a long letter with pictures of them and their two children. The pictures made me feel happy and homesick at the same time. How I wished I could see them again. Also cards and letters came from our friends and neighbors from Breda. They all were doing well. Geertje van Dort my old neighbor wrote, many items such as food and clothing were returning on the shelves of the stores again. Only the inventions, as refrigerators, clothes dryers and other household electric appliances which they saw in American magazines, were still far from being available in the stores in Holland.

After reading her letter I realized how much I had already taken for granted in America. In the few years we lived here we got used to having plenty of foods and drinks which were sold in the stores for reasonable prices—not forgetting the clothes and shoes we now had. I also received a letter and pictures from my friend Chiel. She and her husband had become the happy parents of a little girl. Chiel wrote a sheet full about their baby and how beautiful she was. She was happy that everything had turned out well for us in the States, and she asked when I was coming to Holland for a visit. She wrote that, when visiting her family in Breda, she also had gone to my parents and had a nice visit with them. It was so good to hear from everyone. I made a teapot full of tea for the children when they came home from school. There was something special waiting for them from Holland from their grandparents.

◆        ◆        ◆

The cold snowy winter of 1958-59 left us early and our road was almost dry and hard again. But the drying mud had left deep ruts in the road and it was difficult to walk. We couldn't wait until the big scraper came through our neighborhood and the roads would be solid and easy to walk on again. Also my husband was more than ready to work in his vegetable garden. This spring he was planning to grow more spinach and some kale for the winter. He also wanted to buy a few young rabbits. The former home owners had left four rabbit cages hanging on the outside of the chicken house, but so far we never had used them.

I was sitting on the outside steps and let my mind wander. Soon my eyes followed a blue jay through the trees to our chicken house and, even though it was too early, it probably was already looking for a place to build its nest. Fascinated I looked at a few squirrels which chased each other through the branches of the weeping willow trees. It was something I never had seen in Holland where we saw squirrels only in the forest and then just once in a great while. Since living in

Omaha I never had seen so many squirrels, and I enjoyed watching them, especially when they were chasing and tumbling over each other.

It was midday when I got a phone call from my friend Coby Hendrix that they were coming over Sunday afternoon for a visit. I was always happy to see Coby and her family. We shared memories about the time we lived in our city Breda and talked about the latest news from Holland—news that we got from letters which we received from our families.

A few weeks later Jozef came home with a box full of day-old chickens, four little ducks and four baby rabbits. They were so precious and soft, but I couldn't understand why my husband had also bought ducks. Didn't he have enough animals yet to take care of. The little rabbits with their tiny wiggly noses and big eyes looked at me, and I could not help thinking how we ever would be able to eat them later, after we first fed them to be big and fat. Looking at them I remembered a time when Father raised rabbits during the war. I hoped Jozef knew more about raising rabbits than we had.

When the children came home from school that day, they were elated with all the young babies—fuzzy and warm. Immediately they made plans to make a small pond in the chicken run for the little ducks. When evening came, it was difficult for the kids to put the little rabbits in their straw-filled cages and the little chicks and ducks into the box with a lid on. They had to stay in the kitchen during the night close to the heater.

I think that Lia thought that we never could have enough animals. One day she came home from school and carried a small puppy in her arms. While she walked through the kitchen door she said full of excitement, "Mom, can I keep it please, can I? I know we have Trixie but can't we have this little puppy too, there is enough room in the basement for the two of them at night." Looking at her and the little animal which she carried, I explained to my daughter that the puppy was lost and that she had to take it back again to the place from where she had found it. "Its mommy will find her baby, or the puppy will find its way home to its mommy all by itself," I said to her. It was not only the puppy she had come home with, but other times it was a small kitten or even a bird which she somehow found along her way back home from school. After a few times of bringing a small animal back from where she had found it, it didn't take long before she understood that it was of no use to bring home a "lost" animal, and soon it became a thing of the past.

The mother of Joe's friend, Billy Mc Laughlin, called me on the phone one morning and asked if I would like to come to a Tupperware party. I did not know what a Tupperware party was and thought it was a party maybe with just the neighbors. So I said to her that I was sorry, but since my husband had to work evenings, we could not attend her party. Billy's mother began to laugh and said, "No, Eve, it is only for women." She then explained what kind of a party it was.

Of course, I went and had a good time at my very first "Home Party" and met some more of the women who lived in our neighborhood. The Tupperware parties were something new and soon became a great success. It didn't take long before other companies as Sara Coventry (jewelry), Avon (cosmetic) Home Decorating, Flower Arrangement and others, started selling their merchandise at home parties. In the beginning they were fun and many women attended and ordered the ware which was displayed on a table at the house where the party was held. As the years passed, fewer women came to the Home Parties and their popularity came to an end.

After I talked to Billy's mother on the phone, I went outside to the backyard where I saw our cat Minnie coming from the other side of our street. Slowly and with great difficulty she was trying to get home. When she almost reached me, she began to vomit and lay down. A few minutes later she was dead. Our poor Minnie, she probably had eaten poison somewhere. We all felt bad that we had lost our beloved cat so soon. We buried Minnie with honor beside the garage close to the alley. With the years it became a small burial place for pets and birds.

Even though it was still early spring, the children couldn't wait to go fishing. Fishing was both our sons' favorite pastime and since Lia was with her brothers most of the time, it became her favorite sport too. Usually we took them fishing at Lake Manawa or at a lake behind Merritt's Beach. It was Joe who especially liked to fish. During summer vacations Joe and his friend Billy slept on our porch or in a tent in our backyard with their fishing gear ready for the next morning. The evening before he made his fish dough which was his own 'special recipe' as he said.

As I remember, it was made from flour and some spices which he cooked for the longest time in boiling water in an old white cotton sock. Joe was very proud of his own recipe and would not tell his secret to anyone. The following morning as soon as the sun peeked over the horizon, the two friends got from their tent or the porch and walked with their gear to Hitchcock Park where they fished for hours. When they got hungry, the boys came home again with or without a fish. But most of the time they got one or more large carp which I then had to fry.

Since carp have many large bones, I was not too happy to fry them. But with a smile on my face I did it anyway and made my son happy.

During summertime our screened porch was our favorite place. Not only did we eat most of our meals there, but during the summer vacation when it was hot, the kids slept many a night on the porch floor with a blanket and a pillow. Sleeping outside was something they loved to do. I also enjoyed sitting there with a glass of lemonade and writing my letters to Holland. During winter months we used our porch for our snowy or muddy boots or shoes.

That summer of 1959 we went swimming at the lakes behind Merritt's Beach with Henk, Coby and their children. It was fun especially when we all went into the water together and the children splashed us as hard as they could and lapsed into peals of laughter. After a picnic we played games in the water and went home when the sun went down. Usually Eddy fell asleep soon after we started to drive back home while the other two kids were sitting quietly in the back seat too tired to start an argument about who got a window seat. Even though the kids had to rotate their seat, they still had to argue about it.

Besides fishing and playing in our yard or their friend's yard, Lia and Joe enjoyed to venture down our street. Our street ended on a back road where the kids loved to pick the wild blackberries which grew there in abundance on tall bushes. On that unpaved stretch of road, which ended in a wooded area, were a few houses and a small chicken farm. Next to the wooded area was a railroad track and beyond that the Papio Creek, which at that time I did not know existed or that the children went there. Growing up free as a child myself I was never worried about my kid's adventures to the berry bushes and the small forest. Eddy, who was now old enough, had joined his brother and sister and our dog Trixie a few times on their adventures to that area.

Then one summer day my three kids, Joe's friend Billy and our dog Trixie went together to pick berries. A few hours later while I was hanging some laundry on the washline outside, I saw them coming back through our street. They seemed unusually quiet, no laughing or loud and chipper voices. When they were close to our house, I saw that all four kids were upset. After I asked them if there was something wrong, they all told me that Trixie was killed by a train. When they where going home beside the railroad tracks a train came and Trixie, who tried to chase the train, was hit and killed. Not knowing what to do they had left Trixie on the side of the tracks on a hill. I told them to leave Trixie where he was—he would be happy there watching the trains go by.

At that moment I didn't realize the danger the children had been in until that night when Eddy got out of the bathtub and I saw that his behind had scratches. When I asked him how he got those scrapes on his bottum, he told me that they had gone to the Papio Creek where he had taken off his pants before he slid down the hill into the fast running water. When I asked Joe where that Papio Creek was he told me that it was beyond the railroad tracks. When they had walked back over the tracks it was then Trixie was killed. Even though the kids still went berry picking sometimes, their adventures over the railroad track came to an end.

It was toward the end of the summer vacation when one day, while I was busy cooking supper, I suddenly heard screaming which came from our backyard. As fast as I could, I ran from the kitchen to the backyard and saw four boys running away out of the alley. Two of the boys were my own sons and the other two were their friends—each running away to their own homes. I don't know which of the boys screamed the loudest. I knew only that my youngest son was in pain and hysterically cried, "It hurts! It hurts!" While running toward me, he clasped his arms around himself. Joe was not much better off and also screamed.

Little by little I gathered from him what had happened. He, Eddy and two other boys were playing in the alley behind our house when they decided to open the door of an old shed which was not used anymore, and look inside to see what was in there. What they didn't know was that the shed was inhabited by hundreds of bees which probably entered their territory on the other side from where the boys were. When they broke into the shed, the bees attacked the boys. Poor kids. Joe had seven stings and Eddy five. Immediately I put the boys in a baking soda bath and gave them aspirin. It took a few hours of misery before they felt somewhat better. Later, after they ate their supper, the boys told me the whole story. I don't think that they ever went near that old shed again.

# 40

# *THE NEBRASKA STORE*

It was September and the children were back in school. Eddy, who was now in the first grade, was happy to go to school and proud that he was now "a big boy." I always have enjoyed having my kids around and doing things together especially during their summer vacations. Now with them gone to school the house felt empty. One day after giving the whole house a good cleaning I sat down and, while looking at the floor, I thought how nice it would be to have the living room carpeted. Most houses in that time had oak wooden floors which was nice, but it was not in style anymore. More and more people now had wall-to-wall carpeting installed in their homes and, since I was always used to carpets in Holland, I thought it looked prettier and warmer. Because we always needed the money for more important things than for a carpet, I knew that there would not be a carpet coming soon. "Or," I said to myself, "or maybe now that the children are in school I could work somewhere and save the money for carpeting. But what could I do for work which would not require too much of the English language." Then it came to me that what I always had enjoyed, and still did, was sewing. Maybe I could find something in that line.

After Jozef and I talked at great length about my plan to work, he said, "If that is what you want to do, it is all right with me," I went downtown one day to look for work. First I went to the large Brandeis store and talked there with an older lady who was the manager of the sewing room. When I told her about myself and why I came, she said that they were always short on seamstresses and I could start working anytime. She then showed me around and said that the work was paid by what I sewed. For example, the store charged two dollars to shorten a straight hem—I would be paid eighty cents. Taking in the waistline was three dollars—I got paid one dollar and twenty cents. She then told me that, later if there was an opening at the fitting room, I could work there. It was also paid hourly. I noticed that it was a busy place with at least twelve women, young and old, working in the sewing room. Since women wore dresses or skirts and blouses in that time, those stores which sold ladies' fashions and did their customers' alterations were busy places.

When the manager had showed me around and explained everything to me, I thanked her for her time and said that I wanted to think this over first. What I really wanted was to see what other places had to offer me. On the way to the large Kilpatrick store (which in later years became Younkers), I passed Omaha's most exclusive women's and men's clothing store by the name of "The Nebraska Store." Many times I had walked past the large building and looked at the beautiful dresses which the mannequins in the windows were wearing. Knowing it was an expensive clothing store, I never had gone inside. But that day while standing in front of the store I said to myself, "Why not, who knows, maybe they need someone. I can try." As I walked into the store and went upstairs to the ladies floor I noticed, besides the regular priced dresses, the many exclusive dresses from well-known designers. I saw that some were from Christian Dior, my favorite French designer, whose dresses I had seen in magazines. I couldn't help but look at the labels for the prices. They were priced at $300 and up! This was very expensive in 1959.

It was not long until I saw the manager I was looking for and asked her if she needed help in the sewing room. She looked at me and asked some questions. She then told me that she needed all the help she could get. She explained, "The Ak-Sar-Ben (Nebraska spelled backwards) Coronation Ball is coming up and the dresses for the princesses and the queen of Quivira will be coming in soon from Italy. Most of the dresses usually have to be altered and there is a great deal of work to be done." She then told me how much the store would pay me, which was not much more than what Brandeis paid." You can start working Monday morning at 9:00 if you are interested," she said, while she walked to a fitting room.

And so I started working at the fashionable The Nebraska Store. Since Jozef worked from two in the afternoon until eleven at night he drove me every morning to 42nd and Q Street in his car. From there I took the bus to downtown and got off close to The Nebraska Store. Most of the ladies who came in the store and bought their dresses there were well-to-do. Many times they bought two or three dresses with color matching lingerie at the same time. If some alterations had to be done on the dresses they bought, one of the fitting ladies was called in for alteration.

There were about ten women working in the sewing room. The working conditions were very good, and the women were friendly. During our lunch break in the afternoon I always went with a few younger women to a small restaurant where we ate our lunch. In that time downtown was a most pleasant place to go for lunch or to shop. I enjoyed the hustle and bustle and the many people on the streets. It was a different place to be. When I came back to the store after lunch, I loved to look at the racks with dresses of Europe's designers. I was in my element there and soon copied some of the designs for my own use.

After I worked there for a few weeks, boxes and boxes full of dresses arrived from Italy. In the boxes were the gowns for the many princesses, countesses and the gown for the Queen of Quivira. The weeks that followed were very hectic on the ladies' floor. Not only with the fittings and alternations of the gowns which were heavy with beads and silver threads, but also with the alterations of other dresses. Many of the affluent women who planned to attend the Ak-Sar-Ben Coronation ball also decided to buy their fancy ball dresses at The Nebraska Store.

In that time this Aksarben Coronation, with a ball afterwards, was one of the most important social events in Omaha. It is an annual coronation ball which was founded in 1895 and held in the Ak-Sar-Ben Coliseum. Since it was televised every year, everyone in and around Omaha watched the glitter and glamour of the crowning of the new King and Queen of Quivira (mythical kingdom) that night. During the last days before the great event the women in the sewing room and the staff of fitters had to work overtime. I especially recall the day when the young future queen came for her last fitting. Besides her fitting she also had to practice walking with the beautiful heavy beaded train which was connected to her shoulders. This same train is worn every year by the new Quivira queen. After the coronation it is stored away in a large container. This long train is so heavy with beads that it is almost impossible for one person to carry it. When I saw the beautiful train, I thought how very difficult it must be for the young Queen to walk from the entrance of the coliseum to the other side while pulling this train behind her.

This Ak-Sar-Ben Coronation ritual is still an important affair for the prominent and affluent Omaha-area families and serves as a sort coming-out party for their college-age daughters. Even though this gala evening is not shown on the television anymore, every year the Omaha newspaper announces the names and shows pictures of that year's princesses and countesses. Later after the coronation, the pictures and names of the new King and Queen of Quivira are shown in Omaha's newspaper.

I worked at The Nebraska Store for nine months and always look back with pleasure at the time when I altered the beautiful dresses there. Because of the children's summer vacation I quit that following year. My wall-to-wall carpet was installed a year later.

By fall our chickens and ducks had grown large and fat and were ready for the frying pan. Almost every week Jozef slaughtered one or two of the roosters or ducks after the children had gone to school. When the end of December came around, we had eaten most of them—except for those chickens which Jozef kept for their eggs. The rabbits were usually eaten in the winter after they had grown large. Our kids knew from the very beginning that none of the animals were pets and had been bought for eating. When after the summer vacation the children went back to school, the children's interest in the animals waned. Later in the fall when the time of slaughter came, we never had a problem of hurt feelings. Since Jozef and I never talked about the meat which was prepared for supper, there were no difficulties.

It was a day in December when the kids came home from school and our youngest son walked into the kitchen announcing that our two leftover ducks were gone. The two large white ducks, which had outgrown the little pond Lia and Eddy had made in spring, sometimes waddled around our yard looking for food. They never had strayed far from the chicken coop. When Eddy told us that the two ducks were gone, we put our boots on and started to look for them. First we looked everywhere in our yard, then the alley and connecting yards and finally the field where the kids occasionally played ball. Wherever we looked, there were no ducks to be found. We then looked in our street but again—no ducks. Finally we decided to search in other streets and yards.

As I went back into the alley and walked to the street below us, I suddenly saw two black muddy creatures standing side by side on a street corner. With their neck stretched high in the wind and their feathers caked with mud, probably spattered by passing cars, they stood there—a picture to behold. As soon as they saw me they started to chatter as to say, "Hello, where have you been so long!" It did not take much to lead them back to their home into the chicken coop where they stayed to their end which came a few weeks later.

Every year Johnny's Café held a Christmas party for the employees and their spouses. Those parties were held at the downtown Castle Hotel. It was the first time that we had attended the big celebration. Jozef and I were sure that our children were now old enough to be left alone for the evening. We had taught our kids what to do in case of an emergency and what was expected of them. A few times before we had left the children alone for a few hours, just to see how they managed themselves. We also had told Lia and Eddy to listen to their big brother. Joe was good with his brother and sister, and it worked out just fine.

With my prettiest dress on and Jozef in his good suit we went to the Castle Hotel in downtown Omaha. It had been awhile since we had gone out together and had danced in a ballroom. The last time we danced was at the New Years Eve party back in Chicago. Since I didn't know many people at the Christmas party, Jozef introduced me to everyone including his boss, Frank Kawa, who I thought looked not only like a little round fire ball but was also very sharp. After a great dinner the floor was cleared, and everyone danced to the music of the big band orchestra. It was a wonderful evening. It was our first Christmas party put on every year by Johnny's Café, a party which Jozef and I would attend every year until the death of Frank Kawa in 1964.

◆     ◆     ◆

The cold winter of 1960 brought hard freezing weather. It was the kind of weather during which I enjoyed staying home. I wanted to do some sewing and catch up on my letters to Holland. It was Saturday morning and, as on every Saturday, Jozef had left early for Johnny's Café. He worked six days a week and never had a day off except on Sundays. The kids who had been sleeping late finally got out their beds and soon watched the cartoons on the TV. I told them that I was going to make their breakfast by using my very first toaster which I had bought a week before. I wanted to get my children to eat something different for their breakfast than always the dried cereals which most children in America like to eat. As all kids they did not always like the same breakfast cereal or cared for sandwiches in the mornings. Since my kitchen did not have enough cabinet space for the different kinds of large cereal boxes, it did not take long until I bought the eight small cereal boxes wrapped together in cellophane wrapping. I told the kids that they could now have any kind they wanted. Since then my children were happy, and I had no problem anymore, but I still wanted them to eat something different.

That morning I made toast in my new toaster and told them to put on whatever they wanted, such as butter with jam, cheese, ham or whatever we had in our refrigerator. This was something new and all three kids liked it. Joe, who had already eaten a few slices of toast, covered another slice with a mound of butter and jam and crammed it into his mouth. Lia looked at me and said, "Mom, this is gross. Why is he doing this?" With his mouth full, Joe answered her, "This is none of your business, sister!" Soon they were in an argument. Eddy came into the kitchen and put his penny's worth into the fight, and it did not take long until they were shouting at each other. It was during those times when I told them that I would trade them in for another set of kids and take them back to where they came—from under an apple tree. After they were settled down, I told Joe to sweep the snow out of our porch and Lia to start cleaning her room.

Our children were usually good with each other but sometimes, as all parents, we had our frustrating days. Later Lia and I baked cookies while Joe did his homework from school. Eddy and his friend were playing in the snow. Since it had thawed for a few days it was muddy in the street, but there was enough snow on the side of our house to slide down with their sled. Ever since Lia was eight years old, she and I baked cookies or cake on Saturdays. She loved to do this and since she was very young she became very good at baking.

In the spring of 1960 Lia celebrated her confirmation at the Holy Ghost Church. She was only ten years old. The children who celebrate their confirmation now are at least fourteen years old. It was a special day which Lia had been looking forward to. I had sewed a lovely dress for her which was made from a shiny light yellow colored material. I remember walking into the church and looking over the many people who were already sitting in the pews. In that time the women wore a suit or a dress with a hat and high heeled shoes when they went to church. The men always were dressed in a suit and tie. This dressing up had always been the custom, not only when going to church but also going to the theater or out for dinner. It was not until the 1960s when things started to change with unrest in America and the coming of the freedom of expression generation that people less and less dressed up when going places.

When the choir started to sing, the procession walked in, and we looked for Lia. We noticed that not only children but also adults celebrated their confirmation that day. When the formal confirmation ceremony ended, we took pictures of our daughter with the family. Toni and Ann, who had gone with our family to church to celebrate with Lia this day, went home with us after the ceremony for a nice lunch. Later Rita, her husband Joe and their children came to bring Lia a gift and congratulate her. It had been a good day.

It was about in that same time that the Holy Ghost Church announced that they had started an adult discussion class which was meant for non-Catholics who were interested in learning more about the Catholic faith. Many times in the last years I thought about attending such classes, but I had been too busy with our new life, and so I never had attended the class. There were so many unanswered questions and doubts for me about the Catholic religion. Most times I had pushed away the thought of learning more about this faith, but it never had left me alone—not since that day in Holland when our children were baptized in the Catholic Church. After reading again the notice of the Church's pamphlet, I decided that I would go and enroll for the studies.

For the following months I attended faithfully the discussions which were given in a classroom of the Holy Ghost School with about eight other men and women. When the sessions ended, the priest who had led the discussions asked me how I felt about the Catholic religion. He knew that every Sunday I went to church with my family. I answered him that after going to the Catholic Church for such a long time, I had become familiar with the religion. I then said, "The only thing that I find difficult to accept and have a hard time with, is the confession to a priest." He answered me that this was normal and that maybe I never could fully accept this. "To become Catholic sometimes takes years," he said.

A few months later after learning more about the Catholic faith, I became a member of the Catholic Church in a private ceremony at the Holy Ghost Church. Our friends Coby and Henk Hendrixs were my sponsors.

*Spring of 1961.* One day the mailman brought us a letter from my parents from Holland. They wrote that they were planning to come on a long vacation. First they were going for three months to my brother in Canada, and from there they planned to spend three months with us in America. I think I read the letter least three times over. How excited and happy I was. The last time I had seen my father and mother had been six years ago. I couldn't wait until evening came so I could tell Jozef the great news. When school was out that afternoon and the children came home, I told them that I had exciting news—their grandparents were coming to see them.

Many times in the last six years I had wanted to go to Holland to see my family again. But to take three young children along was just too costly and to leave them home alone with Jozef had not been possible. Joe and Lia asked a thousand questions, as when they were coming and if their grandparents would recognize them. Joe and Lia remembered their grandparents well but, of course, Eddy did not. He had been too young when we left. When we came to America, I always had seen to it that Joe, Lia and later Eddy colored, drew or scribbled something for my parents to keep the line of communication open. We had sent them many pictures of the children and had also received pictures from them so their grandparents would not be strangers if they saw them again. My parents wrote that they would stay at our home from the beginning of July to the end of September.

In that time the parents of the many families who had emigrated to America or Canada always went for long visits to their children. A trip overseas was too expensive to make it again soon, so they visited for a longer period of time.

It was May and First Communion day again at our church. This time it was our youngest son who was going to receive his First Holy Communion. He had just turned seven years old with a birthday party and now—he had another special day with cake and presents. It was something he truly enjoyed. Eddy, who liked to look well dressed when going to church on Sundays, was happy with his new suit and bow tie. As young as he was, he knew what he wanted and what looked good on him. He was an even-tempered and easygoing boy.

When Eddy received his First Communion on that Sunday it was a cold and dark day. With our warm coats on we went to the church where it was crowded as always. Later when our son received his communion, my thoughts went for a moment back to Holland and how quickly the years had gone by since the day I took him home from the hospital. There he was, our little boy, standing tall and proud, and I prayed that he always would walk with God and stay such a fine son. When the ceremony ended and the choir was singing, the communicants left the church. Since it was cold outside, I quickly took some pictures of Eddy standing outside at the church entry, and then we went home where the hot coffee and cake were waiting for us. As always Toni and Ann celebrated those special kinds of days with us.

A year earlier we had given Lia a bike for her birthday. Even though it was not new, it was in good condition. She liked her bike and enjoyed riding for the longest time around the neighborhood with her friends. One Sunday afternoon when I was in the living room and Jozef was busy in his vegetable garden, I heard one of Lia's girlfriend's mother stopping her car in front of our house. She ran to our front door followed by her daughter. When I opened it, I saw that she was all upset and, before I could ask her anything, she said that Lia was in her car and was hurt. Without a word I ran past her to the car and there was my daughter. She was semi-conscious and looked at me as in a daze. The first thing I noticed was a big bump on the side of her forehead that had gone inward. This frightened me because of the injury which she had received a few weeks before at about the same place on her head. That time she, her brothers and the neighbor kids had been playing baseball in the field which is close to our house. While they played their favorite game there, Lia got hit in her head by a baseball bat. When Joe had brought his sister home, she had been crying from pain and it had taken a week before she was over the injury.

When I looked at Lia in the car, I became scared, ran inside the house and called the rescue squad. Jozef, who came around the house to see what was the commotion about, went to the car, looked at his daughter and carried her in his arms inside the house without a word and laid her on her bed. It was not long until the rescue squad came and took the semi-conscious Lia to the Methodist Hospital which was in that time located in downtown.

Later we learned what happened. When Lia and her girlfriends were riding their bikes in the parking lot of our church, she must have hit her bike somehow on a rim of one of the church's window wells. Her friends, who didn't see the accident and did not understand where she had disappeared to, began to look for her. A little later they found her lying unconscious in the window well with her bicycle on top of her. The girls became frightened and went to the house of one of Lia's friends. The girl told her mother what had happened. They then went all together in the car to the church parking lot and helped to get Lia out of the window well. While the mother of Lia's friend drove our daughter to our house, the other girls went home.

For three days Lia was in the hospital with a concussion. For a long time after her bicycle accident Lia had headaches, especially when she was in the sun or when she got tired. Jozef fixed her damaged bike and, I am sure, from then on she was more careful where she rode her bike.

# 41

## *VADER EN MOEDER*
## *(Father and Mother)*

After weeks of shining up our house and working in the garden until it was full of flowers and vegetables, we were ready for my parents' visit. Since traveling by airplane was still a luxury in that time, they had left by ship in spring to Canada. After a three-month stay at Henk and Annie's home, they were on their way from Toronto to Omaha by train.

It was evening and we were ready to drive to the Burlington train station where my parents were going to arrive. Just before we left the house, a taxi stopped in front of our home and, to our great surprise, my parents stepped out of the car. They told us the train had arrived a hour earlier, and they had taken a taxi to our home. We were happy they had arrived safely and after long hugs and kisses, Jozef finally paid the taxi driver who had patiently been waiting beside his car for his fare money.

How wonderful it was to see my parents again and have them at our home for three long months. At first the children didn't say much, but just listened to our conversation. Especially our youngest son Eddy didn't understand much of what we were saying. Even though the language was sometimes a problem between the children and their grandparents, they soon learned to understand each other by using gestures and speaking Dutch words which Jos and Lia knew.

My parents enjoyed the warm, and many times very hot, weather. Sometimes Jozef and I couldn't understand how they could sit for so long in our backyard in the sun. Because my parents where used to the cool Dutch climate, they thought it was 'heerlyk' (wonderful) as they told us. Almost every morning we ate our breakfast on our porch which was 'hoog in de bomen' (high up in the trees) as my mother always said. After breakfast and while the children were feeding and playing with the young rabbits and chickens, my parents, Jozef and I talked until coffee time.

Joe, Jozef, Lia, Eve's mother, Eve, Eddy, and Eve's father during the Jansens' visit to Omaha in 1961.

Visitors from Holland and Chicago in front of the first house the Ottos purchased in Omaha.

Many times we discussed the political situation in the world. Dutch people are very much interested in everything that is political. The cold war between the United States and the Soviet Union was accelerating, and there was heightened concern about the nuclear missiles and other long-range weapons in Europe. As Father told us, American soldiers and pilots were stationed everywhere in Europe. Also many American pilots and warplanes were on the military airport close to the city of Utrecht in Holland.

My parents were happy with the election of President Kennedy in 1960 and hoped he could bring some peace in the world. We talked also about the housing situation in Holland which was still not good, and the food which was now much better and the store shelves which were now full. Even though Father felt good, he got chest pains when he walked too long or went up a hill. I had told my doctor in Omaha about Father but he had said that there was nothing that they could do for Father's arteriosclerosis.

It was Sunday and the first day of Jozef's vacation. We planned to go to Merritt's Beach and have a real America picnic for my parents. Toni and Ann said they were also coming. Early that morning I made the potato salad and the hamburger patties. Beside the hot dogs, watermelon and dessert, I had bought marshmallows. After first going to an early church service, we were on our way to the popular Merritt's Beach in our six seater car which, if necessary, could sit seven people. As soon as we arrived and settled down under some trees with our beach chairs, the children went swimming and went up and down the water slide. When we showed my parents the place and walked around the beach, we saw our kids jumping on the trampoline.

It was later in the afternoon when Toni and Ann arrived with some more food when we had our picnic. My parents looked at all the food, shook their heads and thought it way too much. How could we eat all this! They were not used to see so much food for a picnic. The kids, who had cut sticks from the trees for our wieners and the marshmallows, got a kick out of their grandparents when they had to put their marshmallow on a stick and then roast it in the fire. My father, who thought it dubious to eat a burnt sugar ball, said that he had never seen this done before—not even in Africa where they sometimes ate strange food. My mother, who was more adventurous than my father, asked Eddy to roast her a marshmallow which he did grinning. Later he had to roast another one for her. It had been a great picnic which my parents truly enjoyed, especially the hot dogs on a stick, and the watermelon which is a fruit unknown in Holland.

Father truly enjoyed America and the way of life. Many times during his stay he would say to Jozef, "I wish I was still a young man. I would try to come to America and live here." Father liked the friendliness and helpfulness of the people, the wide open spaces and beautiful large parks and the great wide wild Platte River. Besides going to the lakes in Jozef's vacation, we also went for one whole day to our Nebraska Capital—Lincoln. We visited the State Capital Building and the Lincoln Natural History Museum. Before driving home we walked through the large Pioneer Park.

One day I went with my parents to the downtown post office and had to wait in line for my turn at the window. A young black woman was also waiting in line in front of me. When I was done with what I came for, I went back to my parents who were waiting for me a little further in the hall. When I reached them, they told me that they were surprised to see a black woman standing in front of me at the same window as I was. When I said to them that I didn't understood what they meant, Father said that they had seen a quite different situation in Africa where the black people got a different treatment in public places. They were not allowed to use the same office windows as the white people or sit in the same bus or go to the same restaurants where the white people ate. I explained to my parents that many of the same situations existed in the southern states of America where the black people were not allowed to sit in the same restaurants and busses as the whites. "But this situation is changing," I said, "because after black men came home from WW II, and having fought for freedom for other countries, they now wanted freedom and equality for themselves. You will see, it will not be long anymore until the blacks will get what every human being wants and deserves, and that is freedom and equal rights."

Being born and raised in Holland where in that time no black people were living, we didn't know what it meant to be prejudiced toward the color of another person's skin. Not liking or even hating a person because of color was never instilled in us. I then told my parents that in Omaha the difference between black and white people was in the workplace. The black people were paid lower wages for the same kind of work, and they had a much harder time to climb the ladder of success and thus have a better living. Mother then told me that the black women in Africa, who worked for the white people as maids, got very little money. "Which is," as Mother said, "their own fault. In the beginning when Tante Ann came to Africa she gave the black maids more money for their work than they were used to, but then the maids didn't come back until their extra money was gone, which was sometimes a week later."

It was the end of the vacation week when Jozef said to me that we should take my parents to see the Omaha Stockyards and Livestock Exchange Building. With its 19 meat packing plants Omaha had become the largest livestock market and meat packing center in the world by 1955. In that year they slaughtered a total of 6,436,007 cows, pigs and sheep. Omaha also became the only city in the world where the slaughter houses such as Armour, Swift, Cudahy and Wilson each slaughtered all three types of animals. In that time a full one-half of Omaha was employed in some facet of the livestock industry. Armour, which had supplied American fighting forces with canned meat during World War II, had a walkway running throughout its plant for tourists and people who were interested in the livestock business.

From a walkway high above the ground, people could walk along and see the whole process from slaughter to sausage. Jozef, who had heard about this, thought it interesting not only for my parents but also for us. And, as it turned out, it was not only very interesting but also educational to view the different stages the butchered animals go through before becoming a sausage or cuts of steak. From that day on I sure have looked at a sausage in a different way!

From the large Armour plant we drove over the L Street Bridge with the railroad tracks below. Even though during the last years most of the livestock was brought in by cattle trucks, we saw cattle trains with cows which had been shipped from the west to the stockyards. The animals which they unloaded were brought into holding pens by cowboys on horses.

From there we went to the very busy Livestock Exchange Building which was constructed in 1885 and was in the middle of all the hustle and bustle. It had 40 offices and housed 25 commission firms. A seventy-room hotel for the many livestock men who sometimes came from far away was also located within the three-story building. After we visited the lobby where about 1,000 people daily poured through, we went to Johnny's Café for lunch. After having seen and having more understanding about the enormous cattle business in South Omaha, I understood why the place where Jozef worked was so very busy every day. Frank Kawa's restaurant was located beside the stockyards! When we were finished with our lunch, Jozef's boss Frank came to meet my parents. He invited us for dinner at his restaurant for Saturday night which was Jozef's last vacation day. He said that we could order whatever we wanted. Of course, that night we ordered the best Johnny's steak, a meat so tender you could cut it with a fork. My parents never had eaten such a tender steak before and talked about it for a long time.

It was the end of August when Tadeus with his wife Mary and their three children came from Chicago for a visit. Henry had come along also. They came for a few days and were staying at Toni and Ann's house. It was a very hot day that Sunday when they came to see us. Even though I had all the windows open wide, it stayed hot inside the rooms. In advance I had made bottles of lemonade and ice tea for the thirsty crowd. While all the children played in the backyard, we talked. Tadeus and Mary did well in Chicago but hoped one day to leave there for a more peaceful place. They also told us that Cesia and Frank had plans to move to Wisconsin and do some farming there. It was late when the family left. Not only it had been a great day, but also my parents had met more of Jozef's family.

It was August 13 when we heard on the morning news that the communists had erected a wall around the Soviet zone of Berlin. They were shutting off the flow of refugees to the West and by doing this, destroying any hopes of reunifying Germany. It had been a power struggle, as Father said, between President Kennedy and Soviet Premier Nikita Khrushchev. The cold war with the Soviet Union was increasingly becoming worse. When the Berlin Wall was built, President Kennedy significantly increased U S defense spending and forces in Europe.

It was toward the end of the children's school vacation when Mother said to her grandchildren that she wanted to buy something for them—but didn't know what. The boys had to think about it first, there were so many thing they would like to have. But Lia knew exactly what she wanted. Her heart was set on the new

'Barbie' doll and—a turtle. It was a few days later when we went to the Woolworth Store in South Omaha for Lia's Barbie and the little turtle and a turtle bowl. Since that first day Lia caught flies which she then fed alive to her turtle, and cleaned and scrubbed his shell every week. She made a little pond in the backyard and saw to it that he had everything a turtle could wish for. In wintertime when the flies were gone, she fed him hamburger and raw vegetables. As the years passed and her turtle grew out of his little environment, she bought an aquarium for him. Every day throughout her school years when she came home from school, she took care of her turtle. The turtle knew her well and stretched its neck out in full length when he saw Lia coming.

How well I remember years later, when she and her husband came back from their honeymoon and took home her turtle which I had cared for when they were gone. The turtle was so happy to see Lia that it was swimming and running with its head high up all through its aquarium. One winter day when Lia must have had her turtle about 25 years, he got sick. He was not eating anymore and its shell was beginning to get soft. Not knowing what to do she called Dr. Simons from the Henry Doorly Zoo in Omaha. After listening to her on the phone he said to bring her turtle to him because he wanted to see it, not only to see if he could help but also he never had seen a dime store turtle living such a long time in confinement. A few days later Lia went to the zoo and talked to Dr. Simons. While looking the turtle over, he told her to leave it with him. He would do his best to make him healthy again. It was four days later that Lia got a telephone from Dr. Simons that her turtle was healthy again and that she could bring him home. But due to heavy snow and bad road conditions Lia did not go to the zoo for her turtle. It was about four days later when she got a telephone call from the zoo telling her that her turtle had died. Until this day Lia believes that her turtle had died because he had been lonesome for her. Lia never forgave herself for not picking up her turtle sooner.

It was the end of August when we went with my parents to Aksarben to see the horse races. Aksarben horse racing was popular for the gamblers and for people who enjoyed something different in the summer months. Since the large stadium and tracks were located not far from our house, we had driven by the grand place many times. One time Jozef and I had gone there and had enjoyed the many horses which run the races. Not knowing anything about the horses and their jockeys who ride them, we didn't win any money. But it had been fun and we wanted now to bring my parents there to experience the whole excitement of horse racing at its finest. As it turned out Father and Mother enjoyed it very much. They never had seen such a large and beautiful racetrack with a stadium. They even won some money with a horse which had, as they heard a man saying, little chance of winning. That made it even more fun. It was altogether a great afternoon which my parents never forgot.

Summer gave away to fall and too soon the day came that my parents had to go back to Holland and their home in Breda. Early that morning I had tea with Mother on the porch. Father was walking in the yard and looked at the chickens and the bunnies. He loved it here; he loved the sunny weather and the free and easy living. He loved our large yard and the many flowers which grew there. Even though Mother was happy to be with us in America, I think that she was ready to go back to her own home. It had been a long time away from her house and everything she was used to.

It was early evening when we took Father and Mother to the Burlington Train Station. A night train was going to take them to Chicago and further on to New York. From there they would take a Dutch ocean liner back to Holland. When my parents boarded the train, we all went inside with them until the train was ready to leave. The children, who were sad that their grandparents had to go back to Holland, were curious about the inside of the train and looked around until we had to leave. After an emotional goodbye we walked out of the train car. As I looked one more time at my parents and saw my father sitting by the window, I knew that I never would see him again.

A few weeks later we received a letter from my father. He wrote that the trip home had been good and pleasant. Even though they missed us, they were happy to finally be home again after such a long time. He also wrote that there were a few people from Amsterdam who had written about a house exchange. Father wrote that they were going to Amsterdam soon to see about the apartments. It was a few weeks later that my parents wrote a letter saying that they had found the right house and would move soon to Amsterdam—the city which they had left so many years ago.

◆    ◆    ◆

*February 20, 1962.* It was the day that the eyes of the world were on Cape Canaveral, Florida as astronaut John Glenn took off on his orbit flight around the world. For the last few years the American space program had built rockets to fly around the globe and hoped eventually to send men to the moon. It was an exciting time and people all around the world listened and watched every time a rocket was sent up in space. The year before, on May 1961, the astronaut Alan Shepard made the first successful sub-orbit flight around the globe and became the first American in space. It had been fantastic and everyone was talking about it. Now in February 1962, astronaut John Glenn made the first orbital flight circling the globe three times. It was very exciting and everyone listened to the hour-by-hour messages from the spacecraft which was traveling high around the earth. Later with the "splashdown "of the capsule into the Atlantic Ocean near an island, everyone who watched the TV was hollering and applauding with excitement. In the stores, businesses, schools and everywhere there was a TV, people were watching this great event.

**(Jozef)** Two years before in 1960 when we had lived in America for five years, I said to Eef that since we were planning to stay here in this country, we should become United States citizens. A person has to live in America five years to be able to apply to become a citizen of the USA. Well, that was two years ago! Every time there was something that needed our attention, or we simply forgot about it. But finally I didn't want to wait any longer, and one day Eef and I went to the courthouse. There they handed us the applications for United States citizenship and a small book about the American Government which we had to study at home.

A few weeks later we received a notice by mail to come in for a examination which, as it turned out, was not difficult. Eef had been nervous about it, but when she was done with her examination and had made it with flying colors, she felt better. Then on July 19 of 1962 together with about 50 other people, we became American citizens. The special Oath of Citizenship Ceremonies was held in the Omaha Courthouse and, after a short speech, we received our American citizenship papers and a small American flag. We were now citizens of the United States of America.

When Eef and I drove home that day, we felt good that we had taken this step. Not only because I now had a country again, but also it was better for our children. Since they were still young, our three children automatically became American citizens with us. Even though we were now citizens of another country, our own birth countries would for always have a special place in our heart. Many times we would talk about the land where we grew up and lived when we were young. When we came home in the afternoon, we received flowers and cards from neighbors and friends. It had been a very special day.

**(Eef)** It was also in that same time that we met more Dutch people. Besides Henk and Coby Hendrixs and the Vredefelt family, who we had met a few weeks earlier, we also learned about some young Dutch women who were married to American pilots. Those pilots had been stationed in Holland, had fallen in love and got married before they were stationed back to America. Some of those young families lived now in Bellevue where their husbands were stationed at the Air Force Base. Especially I think here about Ken and Liz Culp. Ken was a Major in the air force and lived with his young Dutch wife Liz and their two young sons in Bellevue. Liz's sister Maria and her husband and their two small boys had emigrated from Holland and lived in Omaha. We all became friends and it did not take long until we came to each other's house for visits. Later we had the best parties which were held mostly at Maria and her Henry's house. With the years the American pilots moved away from Bellevue and Omaha with their families when they were stationed somewhere else in America.

It was in that same year that Toni and Ann moved away to South Carolina. Ann's sister, who had immigrated from Germany with her husband to America, were now living in South Carolina. The husband, who was a chemist, worked at a textile business in South Carolina. Another sister of Ann also came to America and settled in a small town not far from them. Since the three sisters always had been very close, Toni and Ann decided to move to South Carolina. Jozef and I felt bad about it but we understood. We stayed in contact, and a few years later we visited them in the town of Charlotte, South Carolina.

It was August of that same year that we went on vacation for the first time since arriving in America. Our plans were to drive to Chicago first, stay there with Chelca two days and then drive further to Canada to see Henk, Annie and their two children—Richard and little Ingrid. It was very early in the morning when we left our house with our suitcases of clothing, and other stuff, which we needed for the trip. The early morning sun rose in a cloudless sky, and it looked as though it would be a hot day again. Since there were no air conditioners invented for cars yet, driving far on a highway with all the car windows open was not very pleasant. But that was how traveling was in that time and we didn't know better. Soon we left Omaha behind and were driving over Highway 6 in the direction of Chicago.

Even though they were working hard in the east on Interstate 80, most states did not yet have an interstate. Since most of the transportation was done by trains instead of trucks in that time, the traffic on the two-lane busy road was not heavy and we made good time. The only thing which slowed us down sometimes was a slow driver ahead. One time I remember when two old ladies were driving very slowly and, because no one could pass, a long line of cars soon were forming behind them. Finally after about 20 min., the old lady turned onto a side road to a church.

After about a six-hour drive, some potty breaks and three children sometimes quarreling over two car windows (even though their father made them rotate at each stop) we stopped after we crossed the bridge over the Mississippi River for lunch. From there we went further to Chicago which we reached in the evening. As soon as we drove through the city, I got the same uneasy feeling that I had when we lived there. I was glad that we had moved out a few years before.

It was dark when we reached Chelca's house where the family already was waiting for us. It was so nice to see them again. Except for those who had visited us in Omaha, it had been seven years since we had the last time seen each other. There were many toasts that night and lots of Polish stories. We stayed for two days in Chicago before we went further to Toronto. Before we left we had to promise that on our return trip we would stay again with them for a few days.

Soon we traveled on a highway which was built above the city of Chicago with the streets and buildings below us. It was something which we never had seen before, and it impressed us very much. Another impressive sight was when we passed the factories of Chicago's blast furnaces. The many massive factories with their high towering chimneys, where smoke billowed high in the cloudless sky, left us in awe. Seeing this side of the world left me feeling small and not very important. As soon as we left Chicago behind us, we came on the Indiana Toll Highway. Later this became a part of Interstate 80. Driving on this new four lane super highway for the first time was fantastic. It had two lanes on each side of the highway which was separated by a medium of grass. It was wonderful to drive on a road with no cars coming from the opposite direction. The bridges we drove over were now an even part of the road.

While driving Jozef said to me, "So this is what everyone is talking about. This is how the interstate will look and how people in the future will travel! How fast you can drive on a road like this! And don't forget, people driving on the interstate don't have to go through the small villages and towns anymore!" Jozef continued saying that he read in the newspaper about the plans for building a 41,000 mile system of expressways and four-lane super highways and that they already were working hard on those roads everywhere throughout America.

Driving further we saw here and there on both sides of the interstate beautiful resting places by the name of 'Stuckeys.' Travelers could buy gasoline there for their cars and go to the restrooms which were modern and clean. There was also a restaurant which served the hungry traveler and a gift shop with many souvenirs, gifts and candies and nuts. After driving a few hours Jozef had to stop at one of the new resting places for gas. We all got out of our car and looked around the large place, especially the gift shop. Before we went further the kids had bought some sweets and I my first collectors ashtray which was of the Indiana Toll Highway.

A hour later we had to leave the new interstate and on to another new expressway, in the direction of Detroit where we had to go over the border into Canada. When we reached the city of Detroit we thought it looked old and dirty and drove straight on to the border where we had to stop. There we waited for a long time before we could go further. The problem was about my old sewing machine which I had taken with me in our car for Annie. The machine was in good condition but I had bought a newer one and, since Annie didn't have a sewing machine yet, I planned to give this machine to her. The trouble we had on the border seemed to be if this sewing machine was an old or new one, and that was holding us up. Finally we could go with our sewing machine and soon we were driving on a wide highway in Canada.

The traffic became very light and we passed some small farm villages and wooded areas. It started to get dark and the moon and stars were sometimes the only lights we saw. The children in the back seat became restless and started to quarrel since there was nothing better to do or see anymore in the dark. To try to keep them from being too bored I began to sing a popular song and soon the kids joined in. I think by the time we reached Toronto we had sung all the songs we knew. When we came to the city with its millions of lights, it was a most beautiful sight after we had driven so many hours in the dark. Two years before Henk and Annie had moved with their children to Aurora which is a suburb of Toronto. Not knowing where the town was we started to look for a sign which would tell us the right direction.

We drove for the longest time through Toronto on the now busy highway, but saw nothing which directed us to the small town of Aurora. Finally Jozef, who wanted to get off of the busy road, turned into a street and there to our great relief and surprise we saw a sign that said 'Aurora.' We were in Aurora! How lucky can you get! It did not take long until we were driving in their street and reached the home of my brother and his family. They had been waiting for us and wondered where we had been. Soon we all were hugging and kissing and telling each other how big the kids had grown. Annie's father, who had come from Breda for a visit, was also staying with them. Henk had taken his vacation, and the week that followed was full of good times for all of us.

One day we went all together to the mighty Niagara Falls which was not a far drive from their house. It was very impressive to see the Niagara River drop its water 315 feet down and pour the tremendous volume of nearly half a million tons of water into its basin every minute. We looked at the seething and churning water below us for quite some time. It was fascinating. From there we walked through a park where tourists can walk beside the water to the aerial cable cars which provide a thrilling ride over the Whirlpool. Of course we all, especially all five children, wanted to go on the cable car. It was busy and, after some wait for our turn, we saw the spectacular sight of the Niagara River with its churning from above. When the cable car returned, we ate lunch and then we went to the Flower Clock.

This clock, which is very large, is built on a slant and made from flowering plants in different colors. It gives the exact time and chimes every hour. Not only is the clock very pretty but also its surroundings of flower beds made in different designs. We took many pictures there in the park especially of the five children standing in a row in front of the clock. On another day we saw downtown Toronto which we thought a big beautiful and modern city. The last night we left the kids home in care of Joe and went to a well known topless night club in Toronto where we had a great time. It was the first time I ever saw such a show, and Annie and I giggled the whole night about those busty girls.

The week had gone too fast and before we knew it was time to leave again. After a long goodbye we drove back over the same road that we came a week before. It was late in the evening when we reached Chicago and the apartment of Cesia. We stayed in Chicago two more days and visited those places we liked to go to when we lived there. The places the kids enjoyed most were Lake Michigan's beach and Chicago's Natural History Museum. After two days we said goodbye again to the family and left very early to escape Chicago's morning traffic. Our first vacation in America had been great, and we think back to those days many times with enjoyment.

◆　　◆　　◆

As soon as we were back from our vacation, Jozef Latek came over to our house and asked Jozef if he wanted a couple of pigeons. Jozef who loved any kind of animal or birds said, "Of course, yes." It was the following day that my husband made a place in our large chicken house for a pair of pigeons and an opening for them to fly in and out. Jozef Latek had very nice and large pigeon houses in his backyard. It was a hobby of his. Even though he had different breeds, he had mostly the large white pigeons. A few days later Jozef came home with his treasure. It was a pair of beautiful large white King Pigeons.

After keeping them in the chicken house for a week, Jozef let them fly out and watched them sit on the roof of our house. When it became dusk, they flew into the chicken house again, and Jozef knew they would stay at their new home from that day on. Early the following spring the pigeon pair made a nest in the chicken house, and soon two white baby pigeons came out of their eggs. That same summer Jozef made separation hangers on the walls for next spring nesting. Over the years Jozef's pigeons multiplied and were very tame. Every day, when Lia came home from school, they would fly to her and sit on her head and shoulders. She loved to hold the tame birds in her hands, and they would not leave her until she gave them food. Lia and Jozef were the only ones in our family the pigeons would fly to. As her father, our daughter loved animals and beside her turtle she now had a guinea pig also which soon got a male companion. Also we got a dog again. Eddy wanted one. One day after looking in the newspaper, we found a cute little black mutt terrier with white feet and a white spot on his chest. Our son called him Star.

About that same time Julie Karasek, who was the mother of one of Eddy's friends and his Cub Scout leader, came knocking at my door one day and asked me if I wanted to take over her group of Cub Scouts. After telling her that I didn't know much that is expected from a Cub Scout leader, she told me she would help me the first weeks and would give me a book about the regulations and rules. So for the following two years I was a Cub Scout leader for my youngest son's group until he graduated to the Webelos when he was eleven years old. Every Tuesday after school nine boys ages 9 to 11 came to our home. We had our den in the basement where we made different things, played games, talked or went places. Once a month we had a group meeting at school where all the boys from different groups showed what they had made in that last month. Usually most of the parents came to those evening meetings, but some never came and never showed any interest in what their sons had been doing in their den. Once a year we had Derby races. It was something the boys always looked forward to. For weeks they worked on their little cars at home or in our den. They carved and painted and the fanciest little cars were made. When the big day came, all the Cub Scouts, with Boy Scout helpers from many groups, came together in the school gym where the race tracks were set up. There were many exciting races, and it was one of the best days of their Cub Scout years.

It was October 26, 1962 when we got a telegram from Amsterdam telling us that my father had died. Even though I knew that Father would not live long after he had visited us, it still came as a shock. Later we learned that Father had gone that day to his chess club even though he had not been feeling too well. That afternoon while playing his favorite game he slumped over his chessboard. Immediately he was taken to the hospital where he died of a heart attack a hour later. Father was 67 years old. I will always be thankful that my father had come to America and that we had been together, and that he had seen his grandchildren again. I know that he had missed them in the six years we had been gone. Even though the language had sometimes been in the way when they were at our home, the children and their grandparents learned to love and appreciate each other again. He saw America and how we lived. Even though we were not rich in money, we were healthy and happy, and Father went back to Holland at peace.

# 42

## *THE NEW BABY*

The year 1963 and the years that followed were filled with social unrest. After the tension of a Cuban missile crisis the year before when the world was almost pushed to the brink of a nuclear war, the anti-war protesters, social demonstration groups and civil liberty organization groups led to massive disorders in America. The emerging generation demanded sexual and moral liberation, and all over the country blacks faced harassment as they fought for their civil rights. Also emerging were the "Hippies." They were young people who wanted a more "natural" existence and more personal pleasures and fulfillment and freedom of expression. They were wearing long hair and many times torn clothing and beads and often indulged in sex, drugs and rock and roll.

In those turbulent years a young rock and roll star rose to fame and soon became a superstar. His name was Elvis Presley. With his greased hair, surly expression and suggestively gyrating hips he played on his guitar a mixture of the blue music and rock and roll. Elvis became a symbol of rebellious youth, and parents became concerned about their children's future in this sexual revolution. Also in that time drugs became more and more a problem in the US culture and abroad and later became our gravest domestic threat.

It was not long until loud rock and roll music was playing throughout our home and our sixteen-year-old son had a haircut like Elvis. "Everyone has an Elvis haircut, Mom," he would say. Our oldest son had grown taller than I was and now had become excited about getting his driver's license and having his own car. It seemed like yesterday that he and his friend Billy Mc Laughlin had adventures beside the railroad track near the Papio Creek. Or they slept in our porch so they could go fishing at Hitchcock Park early in the morning when the sun came up. He was still always the happy-go-lucky child. With his sense of humor and jokes there was never a dull moment in our home when he was around. He now wanted a car but knew that we did not have the money to buy one for him. He also knew that his parents did not believe that a sixteen-year-old should drive a car—let alone own one.

When summer vacation came around the corner, Jozef said to his son, "Joe, why don't you find a summer job and start making some money for yourself. Maybe in a few years you can buy yourself a little second-hand car." So after looking here and there for summer work, he found his first job. His job was selling hot tamales from a cart on street corners in downtown and in evenings in the bars. He was taken there with his cart by a tamale business. As his mother, I did not like to have my sixteen-year-old son working in the evenings in the streets of downtown and going into bars. Jozef thought that there was nothing wrong with it, and he and I had some arguments about it. I was glad when vacation was over and his summer job ended.

Joe loved the great outdoors and loved to go camping with the Boy Scouts. For some years now he belonged to the Scouts and was working on his Eagle Scout badge. To become an Eagle Scout is not easy. It include many things a boy has to do and go through. One of them included a few winter camps. One winter he went camping with the scouts in deep blowing snow and below freezing temperatures. At night they slept in small tents while the wind was howling around them. They cooked their food on little stoves and explored the woods for wildlife. He enjoyed it tremendously and was ready to do it again, he told us when he came home after the long weekend.

Our oldest also loved sports, especially track, wrestling, shot-put and discus, and his favorite sport at home was weightlifting. Every fall for the last few years Joe went hunting for the weekend with his best friend Chuck Showalter and his father or alone with his uncle Toni. Loving the great outdoors Joe always looked forward to those great weekends. Usually they came home with a few pheasants. Joe had entered Ryan High School two years before in 1961. Ryan High School was then a Catholic all-boys school which was located at 60 and L Street. The first year he had to adjust himself to a more disciplined environment than that he was used to in his public grade school. Later after he was settled, he was happy in his high school and was involved in sports. A few times he received the special 'Sportsmanship of the Year' award. It was about in that time when Jozef was teaching his oldest son how to drive a car.

◆     ◆     ◆

It was about a month before Christmas when one day I decided to get an early start on Christmas shopping. When the children had left for school that morning, Jozef took me in his car to South Omaha and from there I took a bus to downtown and did my shopping. It must have been about 3:00 in the afternoon when I came home from my shopping spree. As I entered the living room with my packages, I saw my son Joe staring at the TV without eating his usual snack. Instantly I knew something was wrong. He turned to me with a worried look on his face and said, "Mom, they shot President Kennedy." We all knew we lived in a very turbulent time, but to shoot our popular President Kennedy was hard to understand. In the meantime Lia and Eddy had come home from school, and we all sat glued around the TV. About a hour later the news announcer, with tears in his eyes and shaken voice said, "Our President John F. Kennedy is dead." A stunned world watched on television as incredible events unfolded; the assassination of the president in a open car with his wife beside him, the arrest of the suspected killer, Lee Harvey Oswald, and the murder of Oswald. The following days were very sad and America mourned. His funeral, which was watched all around the world, was the only program on TV that day. Most people in America and abroad loved the young energetic president and his beautiful young wife and their two small children. Many tears were shed that day. The Kennedy years were a brief shining moment of promise, a lost era of "Camelot." John F. Kennedy is buried in Arlington Cemetery. An eternal flame is burning at the head of his grave.

In February of 1964 our friends Henk and Coby became the proud parents of a precious baby girl who they named Mary. Since their other two young daughters, Joanne and Connie were already attending school, this new baby had been a happy surprise for all of them. A few weeks later when Mary was baptized in Mary Our Queen Church, she became our little godchild.

That early spring kept us busy with the usual things as planting our garden and flowers and taking care of the house. Besides the baby chickens, there were doves, Ed's dog and Lia's turtle and now there was also a litter of guinea pigs. The little babies were so very cute, and we loved just to watch and hold them. Later, when the babies were about eight weeks old, Lia sold them to a pet store. Even though our daughter got very little money for them, she was happy with the few dollars she made.

For a while now my children loved to listen to the new rock group from England. Whenever the kids came into the house, they turned the radio on and there it was: Beatles music. The name of the popular group was The Beatles and consisted of four clean-cut young men. The group produced a wave of unheard of hysteria among the teen population when they brought their lively and upbeat music to America in 1964. It was not long until Lia had pictures of the Beatles hanging on the wall of her bedroom which she had cut out of magazines, and their music filled our home. Not only in our house, but also wherever I went shopping in stores I heard their uplifting songs and music and enjoyed it.

One night we told the kids that their parents were going out to celebrate. When they asked curiously what the celebration was about, we told them that we were going to celebrate the last payment on our house. The children were happy for us and when our youngest son enthusiastically said, "Now are we rich, huh, Dad?" we all agreed with him. After only eight years we had paid off our home and were very proud of it. It was just great! Who would have thought that some-day we would own a home! Jozef had been right—America is the land of oppor-tunity! Now Jozef wanted to save money for a business of his own. "If God willing," he said hopefully, "I will have my own bakery someday."

It was one day in that spring when Frank Kawa, Jozef's boss, died. For the last few years he had been sick and had suffered greatly with intestinal cancer. He died at his beloved restaurant Johnny's Café, at the age of 64. A few days later Jozef and I attended his funeral. Because he had been well known in and far out-side our city of Omaha, the church and cemetery was crowded with people. He left behind his wife, two sons and two daughters. For some time I would miss the slabs of bacon and the hams which Frank many times gave to Jozef to take home. His death also marked the end of the wonderful Johnny's Café Christmas parties and the summer picnics for the people who worked at his restaurant.

Almost all men and women of my generation were raised without a car. Even though many people in America and Canada already owned a car in the forties, the people of Europe did not. Because of WWII, the explosion of cars did not come there until the late-fifties. When living in Holland, I always had gone places by walking, bicycling or taking the bus. Because of this, I didn't miss driving a car myself now that we lived here in America. If I wanted to go to the South Omaha shopping street or to go downtown, I took the bus which was going or coming every hour on Q Street. But as the years went by I sometimes wished I could drive, especially when one of the kids wanted or needed to go someplace and there was no one who could drive them.

Jozef had told me a few times that he wanted to teach me how to drive. Also my friend Coby, who had received her driver's license earlier, had said to me a few times, "Eef, why don't you take a driver's education course and get your driver license. There is nothing to it. Later you will be glad you did." Then one day after the kids were in school, I felt brave and said to Jozef that I was ready for my first driving lesson. For the following few months once or twice a week, my husband gathered together his patience and took me to Harrison Street, which in that time was a very quiet mostly unpaved road out in the country. Even though I soon felt comfortable enough to drive in the streets, I still was not confident enough to take my driver's test.

That same spring to our great surprise we learned that I was pregnant. Coby and I must have been drinking something somewhere that we both had become pregnant again after such a long time! Eddy, our youngest, was now eleven years old, and we really didn't believe that this would happen again. I remembered changing diapers, enduring the screams of teething and the traumas of illnesses, and I was not especially looking forward to this. But after the doctor confirmed my suspicion, Jozef and I were very happy about it. I was excited that after so many years I would have another baby in my arms again. It was strange to buy baby things—but wonderful. Since I didn't have baby clothes or furniture any-more, I had to start all over again, which was something I loved to do.

June of 1964 brought us terrible flash floods in and around Omaha. One night vicious storms rolled down the Papio valleys and lingered over West Omaha. As the torrential rains came down, Papio Creek spilled over its banks and flooded large areas of land in and around West Omaha, Papillion and Mill-ard. Basements flooded and walls collapsed, cars stalled and many people had to be rescued from homes and cars. The following morning the death toll count was seven people. The receding water left deep mud and misery everywhere. The day after the flood our oldest son, who had received his driver's license, and I drove around in Jozef's car and saw the terrible floods from some streets on which we were still able to drive on. Many of the stores in Westgate Shopping Plaza which were under water, and the Brandeis Budget Store and the Baker's Supermarket, were closed. Later some of the stores had big sales and then moved out. Soon the Corps of Engineers began cleaning and widening Papio Creek and building dams which were long overdue.

Since I felt fine we decided to go on vacation that summer. First we were going to the Lewis and Clark Lake before going further to Ponca State Park, which was only about a two-hour drive north from Omaha. We wanted to rent one of the cabins in the park but had taken our chances to go without making a reservation. We were lucky. There was a empty cabin which had been canceled that morning. The Ponca State Park is a very pretty place to spend a week camping or a few days fishing, horseback riding or hiking. In the mornings after breakfast our children went horseback riding while Jozef and I went hiking in the woods. Later the kids went fishing in the Missouri River which is very wide there, or they went to the swimming pool. After supper, we played ball in the large open area in front of our cabin or took a long walk to the overlook which was a beautiful sight over the Missouri River and the Niobrara River Valleys.

After a few days of enjoyment at the State Park, we drove to South Dakota just over the Missouri River were we looked for a place with cabins, but did not find one. While driving on an old two-lane road the kids asked their father, who seemed to be lost, "Where are we, Dad?" He stopped the car abruptly in a small village and rented a cabin for the night beside the wide Missouri river. I think my husband had no energy left to look for a better place. We soon found out the cabin was so small that the five of us could hardly move around in it.

That evening Joe and Lia rented a boat and paddled on a large bay of the river which was wide and calm while Jozef, Eddy and I took a walk next to the river. In the evening after it got dark, we played cards sitting like sardines in a can around the table. Luckily our oldest with his sense of humor made the evening fun. I was happy when the time came to say goodnight, but the small beds which we were to sleep on we hardly could fit. I wonder after all those years if any of us got any sleep that night. The following morning it started to rain, and it did not became any better as the day went on. In the small village store we heard on the radio that they expected it to rain for the next two days. We had to cut our vacation short which was, of course, a disappointment for the kids who had hoped to go fishing and boating again that day. In a steady cold rain, with Jozef and his son taking turns driving, we drove the road home.

In September Lia started high school. She had graduated from junior high which was located in the same grade school where she had attended. On that special graduation night our daughter received many honors, and she and Mark Cizek, a brother of one of Joe's friends, received the most awards. Even though Lia first wanted to go to Ryan High School, which had its doors opened also for girls now, she went with her girlfriends to Bryan High School in South Omaha. This high school was a new school which had just been finished. Lia's class members were the first students in that school and would later became the first students who graduated from there. Besides being a good student Lia was also a cheerleader during her high school years. Most of the time she practiced her jumps in our backyard while the pigeons, sitting on the roof, would look at her with their little heads moving from one side to the other.

When the summer vacations were over and our children were in school, I went again with Jozef driving around in his car. That was until I was six months pregnant. I was beginning to get scared. I was worried that if I would be driving the car and was involved in an accident, I could hurt the baby. I said to Jozef that I was going to wait with driving until after the baby was born.

The holidays came and that year I was finished early with my shopping, which I usually always was; but now that I was expecting I was finished even earlier. The last thing I bought was a pair of snow skis for Eddy. He had wanted them for some time for skiing down the hill in our yard and down the side road close to our house. That year we had a big New Year's Eve party with all the Dutch people we knew in Omaha. Because the living room at Henry and Maria's house was quite large, the party was held at their home. It turned out to be a great night. There were about a 15 Dutch people from Omaha and Bellevue. We had a great time dancing and singing and eating the homemade Dutch pastries which everyone had made in their own kitchens for the party.

*January, 1965.* Very unexpectedly and to my great surprise I was given a baby shower. It happened one day in the beginning of that month. Because I was a Cub Scout leader, I came to know people from our neighborhood—mainly they were the parents from the boys of my Cub Scout group. Once a month the Scout organization held a meeting in Bellevue which I attended with two Scout leaders—fathers of two of my Cubs. One of the fathers lived two houses from us, and his wife Barbara and I had become friends. A few months earlier he and his wife had become the happy parents of a baby girl named Cathy. One day Barbara came to our house with her baby. After we talked for a while she asked me if I could come to her home the following Friday night. She told me her husband had something to show me which had to do with the Scouts. I didn't ask her more about it, and went that following Friday evening to her house. As I entered her living room, I saw to my great surprise the room full of women who I knew. On a table nearby were packages which were wrapped in blue and pink paper. In an instant I knew. It was a baby shower! Since weddings and baby showers were not known in Holland, I never had one before and Barbara knew about this. It was great, and I enjoyed myself very much. Later when I went home with all my new baby things, I thought how blessed I was. The world was still full of wonderful people.

◆　　　◆　　　◆

After more than twenty four hours in Bergan Mercy hospital, my baby finally decided it wanted to be born. It was a girl! A healthy baby girl. How thankful I was. Even though the men in our family didn't mind another boy, Lia and I had hoped it would be a girl. Even if there was fourteen years between them, finally Lia had the sister she always wanted. We named our new daughter Sandra Christina. Because two names were not always given in Holland, Sandra was the first of our children who had two names. After only four days in the hospital I was home again with our baby. This was strange to me since in Holland I was used to being in the hospital for ten days. Of course, I did breastfeed my baby as I always had done with our other babies, even though the younger women in the sixties looked at this strangely. When our baby was a few weeks old Jozef and I gave a small get together with our friends to show her to everyone. Later Maria and Henry became Sandy's godparents during a Baptismal ceremony at Holy Ghost Church.

I was not accustomed to having a baby in the house after so many years—but it was wonderful. When our three children left for school and later Jozef went to work, I was alone with the baby for the rest of the day and concentrated only on her. But when school was out, I had to switch myself to be the mother of two teenagers and a preteen and listen to their stories and worries about school and the things they planned, or not planned, to do.

It was a busy but happy time. I think that since I was now older and had more patience and appreciation of life and the pure innocence of a baby, I enjoyed this child more fully. That summer I always took her outside and walked through the garden while looking at the many flowers that bloomed there. She loved the long weeping willow tree branches which moved softly in the breeze and which she tried to grab with her little hands. We bought a baby stroller and, when weather was right and I was busy tending the garden, she was lying outside in the porch or yard. Some days I took her in the buggy for a walk around the neighborhood. Even though I didn't walk between lush meadows, it always reminded me of Holland when I walked with my babies on the small country roads behind our home in Breda.

From out of Africa came a package and a letter from Mother. After Father had passed away, Mother had become lonesome. Her sister, Tante Ann, asked her to come to South Africa to stay with her for half a year—which she did. Since she was alone, she had gone by airplane. More and more people were flying now to far away places instead of going by ship. Mother had left for South Africa in December and it seemed she was enjoying herself. Tante Ann, Mother and some friends had gone to Kruger Wildlife Park at the end of January, the place where Oom Gerard had always dreamed of going.

Mother wrote that every day for a whole week they went further through the park. At night they slept in camps which were protected from wild animals. She enjoyed this trip and the wild animals that she saw in their natural habitat. She wrote that on the way back to Bloemfontein, they went to the city of Durban, which is a resort city on the coast of the Indian Ocean in the southwest of South Africa. Mother thought it a very nice modern city and loved the large colorful markets with the smell of tropical spices and the different kinds of people who came there. After reading Mother's letter I opened the package which she had sent us. For Jozef it held a billfold in fine leather, for me a bracelet, for Lia a small purse made from the skin of zebra and for each of the boys a wooden handcrafted souvenir. Mother had bought it all in the overnight camps at Kruger National Park. Occasionally I still wear the pretty silver bracelet with African designs.

◆          ◆          ◆

"Mom, I need money for rental fees for a cap and gown to graduate," our eighteen-year-old son said while coming into the kitchen and throwing his books on the table. "I needed to have the money in by last week, but I still have time this week." "That makes sense," his sister said while holding one of her guinea pigs. I looked at my son who, even though he worked a few hours each week at the Omaha Word-Herald, always needed money for one or another something, especially now for his graduation.

It all had started with graduation pictures almost a year before. I couldn't figure out why we had to buy so many pictures. All that we needed and wanted was just two nice pictures and some small friendship pictures. Not a bundle of pictures in all sizes. When I told his father about it, he mumbled and said, "Everything is business here. "After the pictures were taken and we paid for them, next came a request for a yearbook. When our son talked about a class ring, his father said he didn't think so— it was just a waste of money. And that was the end.

None of our kids would own a class ring, and I think they never cared to have one. Now it was the graduation gown. Why they needed to wear those gowns, I said to myself, I don't know. I had heard people saying no one liked them—especially not the caps. Since we had no family here and didn't know many people beside our friends, we didn't need invitations which cost an arm and a leg.

Our oldest son's graduation ceremony was held at the Civic Auditorium. It was the first time we attended a graduation ceremony and it was very impressive. After the graduation was over and we met with our son in the hallway of the Auditorium to congratulate him, he asked his father for money to celebrate—he was going out with his friends. The day after graduation our son said, "Mom, Dad, I need a car of my own. I just cannot live a normal life anymore without one." It was a few weeks later that our oldest child got his own car—a 1959 Ford Falcon.

After working at the Omaha World-Herald for awhile Joe started to work that spring at Skagway. Skagway was a Jewish-owned store which they had built just outside the city limits on 72nd and L Street. It was a large one story structure and built like a barn with no decorations and only a cement floor. It was not only that the prices of their merchandise were below other stores, but it also opened its doors on Sundays which was something that had never happened before in Omaha. Sunday was Sunday and stores were closed—this was the law. It was not long until people from everywhere began to pour into the new store, especially on Sundays. Because of this it brought a lot of commotion in our city from other stores who felt cheated that they couldn't open their doors on Sundays also. This fight between the Omaha businesses continued for sometime until finally the Sunday closing law was lifted. Even though Joe had to work many times on a Sunday, he enjoyed working there. It was not far from where we lived and the pay was not bad. That fall Joe enrolled at Omaha University for further studies. His dream was to go into forestry.

Something new had come to our town which was great fun for teenagers and peace of mind for their parents. Someone got the bright idea to open a discotheque for teenagers on Friday and Saturday nights until 11:00. It was a place where, for an admission, teens from 14 to 19 years old could dance and have a great time. There was strict supervision and only soft drinks were served. Parents could stop by anytime they wanted but could not stay. A policeman stood outside in case of an undesirable who would try to make trouble. The dance music they played was popular and had a strong Latin American beat and was accompanied by pulsating lights. This discotheque became so successful that in a year's time discos flourished like mushrooms all over our city.

They were great places for the teenager to spend an evening dancing. It was not long until a teen discotheque opened up in our neighborhood also. Joe and Lia had talked about those popular dance places before and, even though Lia was only fifteen years old, Jozef and I didn't mind if the two went there together. I always had told my daughter that she could not date before her sixteenth birthday, the same as my mother always had told me when I was young. Lia had never thought anything about it because that was the way it was. Now that she went to the disco, we told her to have fun but to come home after closing and not to make any dates. Usually she answered me with "Oh, Mom!" We were happy that Lia always was busy being a cheerleader, which she loved.

In the last year our oldest son had dated some girls but it never had lasted long. Sometimes our kids went to the disco in our neighborhood, but their favorite place was in Benson by the name of, "Sandy's Escape ." It was too bad that those places had to close their doors when the Liability Act was passed in the mid-sixties. Since the discotheques sold only soft drinks and the admission fee was not high, they were not able to pay the high cost of liability insurance. Some discos began to sell sandwiches and raised the price of the admission, but it was not enough. Just a few short years later they had to close their doors.

While our two oldest began to enjoy a different kind of entertainment, our son Eddy loved to shoot baskets in the backyard. His dog Star was always lying close by ready to jump up when the ball rolled too far. Eddy was still always busy making, painting or repairing one or another something such as the sled I remember which was painted in an array of colors and designs. One day in their summer vacation he and his friend Ricky Karasek made a treehouse in the large maple tree which stood in a corner of our backyard. It had taken them more than a week and when they were finished with their treehouse, I had to come and see it on the inside. I took some cookies with me for them and said that it was just a great place, and that they had done a good job.

For the following few weeks they played in or around their treehouse, until the day that our son's dad was home and needed nails. Jozef wanted to work on the fence by his vegetable garden that day and needed his large nails which he had bought a while back especially for this work. After looking everywhere for the sack of large nails, I suddenly remembered that a few weeks before the boys had been talking and searching for nails. I turned to my husband and said, "I know where they probably are. In the treehouse!"Immediately Jozef went to the tree where he found out that the whole sack of large nails was hammered into the tree trunk. The boys had made steps for going up into their treehouse with pieces of wood which they had pounded to the trunk. Jozef took a nail remover and a day later the steps to their treehouse were gone. For some time the treehouse without steps was still there and, as I recall, since it was close to the end of the summer vacation the boys never replaced the treehouse steps again.

*January 1966.* A year had passed and it was our baby's first birthday. How fast the time had flown. When I took her out of her baby bed and gave her an extra morning kiss she giggled as if she knew it was her birthday. A few weeks before she had loved all the excitement of Christmas. Even though she didn't know what it was all about, she loved the glitter and shimmer of the Christmas tree. She was such a happy child. She loved her sister and brothers who spoiled her sometimes too much, especially when it came to feeding her things she loved but shouldn't eat. When Christmas night came and we opened presents our youngest daughter sat in the middle of all the papers, ribbons and boxes. I think she enjoyed this more than all the presents she got. But now today was her birthday. I had invited Coby with Mary and Barbara with Cathy to our home in the morning for coffee with cake. Mary and Cathy, who were almost a year older than Sandy, soon took charge of the birthday girl—something which did not always go well. Later in the afternoon after her nap and when her sister and brothers were home, she had another party.

In the summer of 1966 Henk and Annie with their children came by car from Canada for a week. Jozef had taken his one week vacation and every day we went places—going swimming, picnicking and shopping. Only our son Joe, who had to work, could not join us. The week had gone by too fast, but it had been great to see each other and the children again.

One day that summer, when we were swimming with Henry and Maria and their boys at a lake behind Merritts Beach, we learned to our regrets that they had plans to move away from Omaha. We knew that Henry had family living in California and that someday they would settle there. Also Ken, who was transferred to the air force base in Colorado, was going to leave. We all would miss them and the Dutch parties we had together, and we wished them well. For some years we wrote to each other, and Ken and Liz visited us a few times in Omaha. But when time went by, we lost contact.

Our children were growing up and Joe now had his own car. Even though he and Lia would rather hang around with their own friends on summer Sundays, occasionally we all went together to Merritt's Beach as a family. By now they had built a dance floor on the beach, and every Sunday afternoon and evening a band played. The beach was crowded with young people. Many were dancing, and others were showing off their skills on the trampoline. There always was a group of young men, our oldest son included, who had to show off their weightlifting skills, but I think it was intended to impress the girls. Lia and her girlfriend ogled the young men on the beach and giggled whenever they saw a cute guy. We saw her only when she got hungry and it was time for our picnic. Eddy loved to play Tarzan diving in the water from a high swing, and we would not see him much either except for our picnic.

Only Sandy stayed close to us away from the crowd while playing in the sand and water. Yes, it was a great place for some years but, as with so many things, it started to change. Because of the high cost of liability insurance the once so very popular trampoline was removed. After that they began to ask a much higher entry fee and in a few years time the once so popular Merritts Beach was in financial trouble and closed the dance floor and other amusements which had made it such a great place. A few years later they closed the gates.

One Sunday morning Jozef was looking outside the kitchen window and said puzzled to me, "Eef, did you see any of my pigeons this morning? I didn't see them yet. It is so quiet." When I answered him that no, I had not seen them, he went outside to the chicken house from where they flew in and out and where all his pigeons had their own nests. By now Jozef had about fourteen pairs of King Pigeons. They were tame and very pretty, and we all enjoyed watching them. Most of the time they sat on the roof of their chicken house or on the electrical wires or pecked in the soil in the backyard. Not much later Jozef walked back into the house. He looked very upset and told me that someone had stolen all his pigeons that night—not one was left. In the meantime our kids had come from their bed and soon we all stood looking in the empty chicken house. Only feathers where left.

I felt very bad for my husband—he had so enjoyed his pigeons. Why had someone stolen all of them, we asked ourselves. We had no idea who could have done this. The first week after the theft Jozef hoped some of his pigeons would return home. Maybe some of the older ones could free themselves from their prison, he said, and find their way back home. It was few weeks later when we saw a few White King Pigeons sitting on the roof of the house for the whole afternoon. But by evening they were gone again instead of going inside our chicken house. Joe Latek offered Jozef a couple of pigeons to start over, but somehow he didn't want to start again and take the risk of losing them once more

# 43

## *WESTGATE BAKERY*

(Jozef) After the death of Frank Kawa in 1964, things at Johnny's Café began to change. I didn't like what happened and could not agree with their new management; but before I decided to make any changes, I wanted first to look the situation over for awhile. When nothing had changed within a few weeks, I told myself that I was going to quit my bakery work at Johnny's Café and go to work someplace else until the opportunity came along to start my own bakery. I had now money enough to finally make this dream come true.

One day I learned from a man who worked at Johnny's Café that the owner of a hotel in downtown Omaha was looking for a baker. The hotel was named the Castle Hotel. The following morning I drove downtown to find out more about the baking, the working hours and how much they paid. The pay was less than I received now, but because I would work less hours, I figured I probably could bake a few hours somewhere else and make up the difference. It was about two weeks later when I baked for the last time the pies and dinner rolls for Johnny's Café and said goodbye to the people I had worked with. I had been at Johnny's Café for almost nine years.

And so I began to bake for the large Castle Hotel. It has since been torn down and made into a parking place. I started to work there at 6:00 every morning, except Sundays, baking dinner rolls, pies and other pastries until the baking was done late in the morning. The working conditions were pleasant at the Castle Hotel, but I needed more hours to make more money. After working there a few weeks I heard that the North Omaha Country Club needed a baker for a few hours each day. Immediately I went to their clubhouse and talked to the manager. That following week, after I was done baking for the Castle Hotel, I began baking small fancy pastries and tiny dinner rolls for the North Omaha Country Club. The delicate pastries and rolls which were mainly baked for their ladies' lunches or parties, took me only a few hours to make.

It was about at that same time when someone told me that the Lamplighter Hotel at 72 and Center Street was looking for a baker. They needed someone who could bake some good dinner rolls everyday for their restaurant. Since this Lamplighter Hotel was located not too far from where we lived, I decided that a few more hours of baking every day would not hurt me and would bring in some extra money. And so, after my work for the North Omaha Country Club, I baked now also for the Lamplighter Hotel. It was already late in the afternoon when I finally was done with my baking and went home.

I baked for those three places for one and a half years until one day in August of 1966, opportunity knocked on my door. I learned from the Omaha Bakery Supply Company about the closing of the Cinderella Market. This well-known grocery store with a bakery had been on Dodge Street in downtown Omaha for many years. As soon as I heard that all their bakery equipment was for sale, I went to the Cinderella Market as soon as I was done with my baking at the Lamplighter. When I got there, I looked at their ovens, machinery, the showcases and their many baking pans and everything that is needed for a bakery.

Even though much of their equipment was well used, the ovens and most of the machinery were in good condition. The many showcases were of an older model but in good shape and, with some buffing up, it would do just fine. I looked everything over once more and came in contact with the owner of the Cinderella Market that same late afternoon. We talked for the longest time and finally the price of the entire bakery inventory—from ovens to machinery, bakery table, showcases, shelves, cash registers and pots and pans—was decided on. But first I had to go home and tell Eef about it. It was already late when I walked into the house where Eef had been waiting for me. I told her about the closing of the Cinderella Market and the equipment which was for sale and the price they asked for it. For many years Eef had known that I wanted a bakery business of my own, but I needed to be sure that she would agree on all of this before I could make the deal.

A few weeks later after the signing of papers, we looked around for the best place that we could rent and open our own bakery. It did not take long until we decided on Westgate Plaza where a place to rent became available. It was a place which formerly had been used by Rogers, the owner of the plaza. Since the empty place was not made for a bakery, we first had to install a partition to divide the bakery area from the front store. Then came the installing of the oven which Omaha Bakery Supply took care of. A plumbing company installed the sinks but had great trouble finding the drainage pipes. After they tore up half of the floor, went four feet deep and finally, after consulting a pipe finder, the drainage pipes were found. What a mess!

A few weeks later and after everything was cleaned up, we installed the showcases which we gave a good cleaning and waxing job. It was not long until things began to take shape. The hundreds of baking and sheet pans had to be scrubbed which Eef took care of. It was an enormous job and Eef and I worked hard for weeks to get everything ready for our opening day.

Finally in October we were ready to open our bakery. When I had bought all the bakery equipment in August, I also had hired the women baker and a sales lady from the former Cinderella Market. The day before the opening, the baker lady and I baked many pans of cookies in great variety. I don't think I slept very much that night. It was very early in the morning when I started to make the coffee cakes and sweet rolls, so everything would be ready before the store opened its door. After those were baked I began frying the different kinds of donuts.

Later, just before opening, I stood in my store looking at the pecan and cinnamon rolls which were laying invitingly on their plates in the showcase. For a moment my thoughts went back to a place of long ago. I thought about a bakery in far away East Poland and about Jan and his bakery where we worked together side by side. We had made big plans, and we had been so sure our bakery would grow into the largest in the whole area. While Jan's life had been cut short in that terrible war, my life had gone on and finally after many years, I now had opened my own bakery. Jan would have been proud and happy for me, I said to myself while looking at the showcase where the poppy seed rolls looked as if they were smiling. They were baked the same way as Jan always had done.

That morning before Joe went to his college classes, he drove his mother and his sister Sandy to the bakery because, as Eef had said, she didn't wanted to miss out on anything. For the opening of our bakery we received a beautiful vase of red roses from an optometrist who had his office next door. Even though I was very tired that morning, I was excited and ready for our first customers. Seven o'clock that morning after we opened the door of our bakery, the first customers walked in. It was the beginning of Westgate Bakery. The date was October 1966.

(Eef) Ever since Jozef purchased the entire baking inventory of the Cinderella Market, his goal of owning his own bakery was becoming closer to a realization. I was very happy for my husband that finally after so many years his dream had become real. It was something he always had wanted and had talked about. Even though he knew that it would not always be easy, he was determined to make a go of it no matter what obstacles would be in his way. Since I didn't know anything about a bakery business, I had to learn everything about the items we were selling in our store. I had no idea what the names were of the many kinds of cookies, the donuts with their different fillings, or the sweet rolls and the other pastries which we sold. I also had to learn the prices of each item by the piece or by the dozen and to take cake orders. The cakes came in different sizes and flavors and decorations. It was not very complicated, and I soon learned everything from the dough to selling and folding boxes. Our sales lady worked every day in the store except on Sunday and on Monday. Because Saturday was always our busiest time, Lia helped out in the store. Since we were open from 9 a.m. until 1 p.m. on Sundays, I did the selling of the pastries usually by myself and left Sandy home with Lia. On Sunday mornings our customers liked the cinnamon and pecan rolls and—best of all—the eclairs.

Besides working in the bakery with his father on Saturdays, our son Joe helped during those times when he had no school. Eddy cleaned pots and pans and washed the floor after school and on Saturdays. Our closing time was at 6:00. Jozef and I decided that because Sandy was so young and still needed my full attention, I would work in the bakery only when necessary and would take our young daughter with me. She had been sick with a cold and an ear infection and it had taken her awhile to get over it.

It was the month of December when I was busy not only with helping out in the bakery, but also writing long Christmas letters to Holland, Canada and to my Tante Ann in South Africa. Of course, I had to write everyone about the opening of our bakery. Jozef was going to write to Poland to tell the family there about the opening of his own bakery. In that time it still took at least two weeks for letters to arrive in Poland

Snow fell during the last weeks in December and it looked as if we would have a white Christmas, something that did not happen often. The days before Christmas had been busy, and our help, Jozef and the kids worked hard in the bakery until closing. It had been a good Christmas business in our store and my husband was satisfied. Christmas Eve we closed our store early and when everyone came home, I had a nice Christmas Eve dinner waiting for them. After singing our Christmas songs and the gifts were unwrapped, we spent the rest of the evening playing games, something we always had done ever since I remember. Later our son Joe and Lia walked in the brisk air the two blocks to church for midnight mass while the snow crunched under their feet. On Christmas morning we had Christmas stolen for breakfast as we did every year, only this time they were baked in our bakery instead of in my kitchen. When we came home from Christmas morning service, Eddy went outside with his dog Star beside him to see if he could do some skiing in our back yard. As I did every year, I fried oliebollen and apple flappen for Old and New Year's Day, not only as tradition but because everyone loved to eat them.

**(Jozef)** Before Christmas the bakery business had been reasonably good, but during January of 1967 with the holidays gone, our business slowed down. To bring more money in I started to bake not only for my own store, but also for places such as the Blackstone Hotel on Dodge Street and a few restaurants. Many a day, while frying the donuts and baking the sweet rolls in my oven for the restaurants which needed the rolls for their breakfast customers, I told myself that as soon as my store business picked up again, I would quit doing this. It was just too much work.

Since we had no back door in the bakery, I always had the front door of our store open at night while I was baking. It was not long until early in the morning before I opened the store, that people walked through the store and into the part of the bakery where I was working, and asked if they could buy some of my fresh baked sweet rolls. Some of them came as early as 5:30 going or coming from their work. They just loved the hot fresh baked rolls right out of the oven.

Many of those customers came almost every morning and soon we began to know each other. We talked about politics and the weather while I put their just-baked rolls in a sack. As I recall, some of those early customers came for many years, and later after my retirement I would miss the conversations we had.

**(Eef)** At the end of the winter we received a letter from Mother in which she wrote that she had plans to come by airplane to America in June of 1967. She not only wanted to meet her new granddaughter, Sandy, but also to see our bakery. After reading her letter I thought about the last time she had been here with us in Omaha. She and Father had made the trip by ship and train in that time. It seemed as though people now traveled mostly by airplane when flying long distance, and that our planet earth had become a smaller world.

A small house was located on the other side of our street. It had been built many years ago in the middle of a large property. It always had been a place of beauty during spring and summer when flowers of all colors and varieties grew in abundance. The old couple who had lived in the tiny house had moved into a retirement home a few years earlier. Since then no one had taken care of the property where the flowers had been growing wildly that following spring and summer. I always had loved to look at the many large irises which were growing close to the street. They were in colors of deep purple to lilac, yellow and white.

A year later when the irises bloomed again and no one attended the large garden, the temptation to leave the irises where they were had been too much. And so I committed my second crime in life. My first crime had been stealing apples at boer Backx orchard during the war. One day while sitting outside I told Lia about my plan. I said to her that I wanted to dig some of the iris bulbs out and plant them in a row by the street in our front yard. She looked at me and said, "Why not, Mom? One of these days they probably will come with a bulldozer and plow the whole field for new houses!" One evening a few days later, Lia and I took our shovel and a large sack and went across the road and dug up many of the old large iris bulbs. The next day I planted them all in our yard on our side of the street. The following spring they were in full bloom, and it was the most beautiful sight to see. As Lia had foreseen, it was not two years later the property with the many lovely flowers was plowed and now three houses with small yards have been built in its place.

◆     ◆     ◆

It was in June and some of the irises were still flowering when Mother arrived from Holland to stay with us for six weeks. It was great to have her again in our home, and we had to tell each other many things which had happened but are not always easy to write about in a letter. When Mother held her new granddaughter for the first time, Sandy began to cry about all the fuss that was being made over her by her grandmother who she had never seen. When Mother gave her a doll dressed in Dutch costume, she came around but still didn't trust the situation. Mother, who was impressed with our bakery, had difficulty understanding that we owned it, even though we told her that the place where our bakery was located was rented. "Things like that just don't happen much in Holland," she said. "Everything is strictly regulated and to get a license to open a bakery is very difficult. The examinations for bakers, or for any other occupation, are very rigid and the cost to open a store is very high."

The weeks that followed were great—only I missed Father. I missed talking to him and seeing him sitting in our backyard in the warm sunshine. It was something he had enjoyed so much when he had been here with us some years before.

It was a busy time. Besides taking care of my family I helped out many times in the bakery which left Mother alone too many times. Since Sandy and her grandmother couldn't speak the same language, I took my little girl with me to the bakery. Sometimes when I came home from our store, Mother was sitting by herself at the table playing solitaire or was knitting a sweater. Besides our shopping it was only on Sundays that we went to the places Mother loved to go. Usually it was the Fremont Lakes where we had picnics and the kids went swimming and fishing. Joe and his girlfriend Sandra Kane went with us occasionally, especially to Merritt's Beach.

The weeks had gone by fast and before we knew it, the time had come for Mother to go back to her home in Amsterdam. We all took her to the airport and said goodbye at the airplane. Sandy, who had come to love her grandmother, started to cry and didn't want her grandmother to leave. In that time the propeller airplanes were not yet connected to the terminal to let passengers in or out. The people who said goodbye to family and friends walked together to the airplane which were parked not far from the airport terminal. There people waited and talked together until it was time for the airplane to leave. How simple and uncomplicated flying was in that time.

After the plane took off and made a half circle in the sky, Sandy waved with both hands and said as loud as she could, "Bye Grandma! Bye Grandma!" For the longest time afterwards whenever she saw a airplane in the sky, she would point her little finger and while waving she said over and over, "Bye Grandma!" A week later I received a letter from Mother telling us that she had arrived home safely.

The Ottos' youngest child, Sandy, fishing with big brother Eddy during
the summer of 1967.

(Jozef) *1968.* Even before the opening of our bakery we knew we had to move
closer to our store. Since I started baking very early each morning, it was not only
better for me but also for Eef and our children. All three kids had to help out in
the bakery when they were not in school. It would be much better to live within
walking distance from our store, we said. To find a house in the Westgate neighborhood close to the store was not as easy as we had hoped. Not only were there
few houses for sale, but the ones which were for sale were not always what we
wanted. Finally one day when driving through the neighborhood again, I saw a
sign "House for Sale"on Grover Street. The house looked very nice on the outside and the yard was well taken care of. It also was in walking distance to our

bakery. Eef and I went back a few times to the house to look it over before we decided to buy it. Even though Eef was disappointed there was only one bathroom in the house and that it was located on a busy street in the Westgate neighborhood, it was a nicely built and good-looking house. On April of 1968 we bought the house at 7917 Grover Street. The price was $18,500.

(Eef) The house on the Grover Street was larger and nicer than any house I had ever lived in. I really had hoped for a two-bathroom house so there would not be a bathroom congestion every morning as had been the case in our other house. Jozef told me that we always could build a shower in the basement since there was a drain in the basement floor, but we never did. Although I never got my second bathroom, I was thrilled when we bought a new washing machine and a dryer. It was my first dryer! What a great way to do the laundry I thought when for the first time I took my fluffy towels out of the dryer. It brought memories back to me of a time when I did the weekly laundry by hand on the washboard in a tub, and hung my laundry on the washline outside to dry.

Something else I was looking forward to was that our home was cooled on hot summer days by central air-conditioning. It would cool our entire house! Even though our new home was larger and nicer than the one on 52 Street, I missed our yard with the weeping willows and the open spaces. I missed the many flowers and my daydreaming on the porch stairs outside while listening to the twittering of birds and the wind rustling through the trees. We always had complained about the mud in late winter, but we knew when spring was finally here when Jozef came home with a box full of little fuzzy chickies. For eleven years we had lived on the quiet 52 Street where our children had grown up free to play and roam.

Joe and Lia had friends away from the neighborhood, but Eddy missed our yard and his old neighborhood friends. Leaving all your friends at the age of fifteen is not easy. He also missed Star, his dog, who had died just before we moved away to the Grover Street. Instead of shooting ball in his basketball hoop or making things or just bumming around with his friends, our youngest son had now to work in the bakery on Saturdays. His job was washing pans and cleaning floors.

A few weeks after we moved to Grover Street, Lia graduated from Bryan High School. It was her special day which we celebrated with a party in the evening. Lia had invited her friends from school, but as it turned out more kids came than were invited. Some of them she never had seen before. I was glad that her boyfriend Chuck was at the party and kept an eye on the young people who came to celebrate. Jozef and I had retired to our bedroom thinking the party would soon end. It was 1:00 before we heard the last car leave.

After our daughter's graduation from high school, she enrolled in a business college for a two-year course in business administration. She finally drove her own car now which was a red convertible Mustang. I never will forget seeing her driving the bright red car with the top folded down and her long light blonde hair waving in the wind. After two years of schooling, Lia worked at the City Bank at Leavenworth Street.

Now that we lived on Grover Street, I went to the bakery a few times a week not only to help out, but also to learn about how to decorate cakes. I never before had decorated a cake in my life. A few times after watching how our woman baker used the decorating tubes, I began to practice on cardboard circles. As with every beginning I made many mistakes and then started all over again. I remember one time when our woman baker was not there and I had to decorate my first birthday cake. A lady had come in the store and wanted a birthday cake with pink flowers. Jozef who was at that moment busy with taking cookies out of the oven said for me to decorate the cake. Here I was. "Now or never," I told myself and, with determination to make it a pretty cake, I began first by making a border carefully around the cake. I then wrote "Happy Birthday" and the name in pink icing which turned out just great. Since I didn't know yet how to make nice-looking roses, I decided to make the simpler rose buds instead. After decorating the whole cake with pink and red rosebuds I made light green leaves. They didn't turn out too great, but I didn't think they were bad looking either. When the cake was all finished, I proudly showed it to Jozef. He was still busy with his cookies and said with a grin that it was a masterpiece. Later when the customer picked up her cake, she said that it was just fine.

Even though we didn't have too many cake orders that first year, I slowly became better at decorating them. It was not long thereafter that our woman baker left. Her husband was transferred to another state and now they had to move. Luckily our oldest son worked with his father in the bakery when not in school and could help his father out.

On those days when I went to the bakery, I always had to take Sandy along with me. She usually played with some empty pots and pans we didn't use or stood behind a rack full of rolls and looked at the customers who came into the store. She was a good child and not much in the way, but sometimes she was bored and wanted to go home. When September came, I enrolled Sandy for two mornings a week in a preschool which was located close to the other side of our bakery. Sandy loved to go there especially because Cathy Lane, her little playmate from the 52 Street, was also in her playroom. On Saturday morning I brought Sandy with her 'blanky' to Coby's house where she played with Mary until I picked her up later after the bakery closed.

In spring of 1969 I became pregnant again. This time, after my visit to the obstetrician who confirmed my suspicion, I was very unhappy with the idea of having another child. It was not only that I had my hands full with my family, the bakery and the bookkeeping of the bakery, but I felt I was too old to have another child. I was 44 years old! Also our oldest children came into a marrying age. Our son Joe, who was very much in love with Sandra, was already talking about getting married. Also Lia had become serious about an Air Force man by the name of Charles (Chuck) Langston. He came from Kentucky and was stationed at SAC Air Force base in Bellevue. Even though Jozef and the children were very supportive of me and said that I would be happy later with another baby in the house, it was not exactly what I wanted and needed.

To get more perspective, I said one day to Jozef that I needed to go away for a few days. I was going to visit my brother Henk and his family in Canada and was planning to go on my very first airplane flight. Since Sandy loved to go places, I said to Jozef that I was taking our four-year-old daughter with me. We would be gone only for five days. I never had been in an airplane, but I always had wanted to. I wondered how it would feel to be so high in the skies.

One morning in the spring of 1969 Jozef took Sandy and me in his car to the airport. Earlier when we got out of bed, we saw it was raining and we were disappointed for we had hoped for a nice clear day. Later when we reached Eppley Airport the sun came through the dark clouds. Our airplane was waiting for us when we stepped outside the terminal. Sandy was excited and hugged her daddy goodbye as we boarded the plane and settled in our seats. The airplanes in that time had only two rows of seats on each side of the aisle. Sandy wanted to sit by the window so she could see the houses and the cars and people from high up, as she happily told me. From Omaha we would be flying to Chicago, and from there we would board another airplane to Toronto.

As soon as we were airborne, we ran into bad weather. As this was my first flight, I did not know what to expect. Even though it was a big airplane for those days, by modern standards it was small. The turbulence was severe, and it was not long until the plane was thrown around like a toy. I was hoping that the pilot would take his airplane above the clouds and that maybe then the shaking and going up and down would stop. Sandy was not happy that she had to wear her seat belt all the time and disappointed that she saw nothing when looking out through the window of the plane. All that she saw was a dark gray mass. After she spilled her drink on the floor, I said to myself that if someone ever tells me again that flying is fun—I would scream. Soon the airplane began circling and circling above the Chicago O' Hara Airport, and I wondered why our airplane was not landing. Later I heard that this circling was normal for the airplanes which were going to land there.

Finally our plane flew below the dark clouds, and we saw Chicago below us. Because the plane was flying low now, my daughter could see all the houses and cars in miniature as much as she wanted and with her little nose glued to the window, she happily told me all that she saw. Was I ever relieved when the plane landed and taxied to the terminal. When Sandy and I walked down the stairs out of the airplane, the rain came pouring down. We started to run but still got wet before entering the Chicago's airport terminal. In that time not only were the airports smaller but also there were not so many people around in the terminals as is now the case.

After finding our flight connection to Toronto, we didn't have long to wait until going further with another airplane which, I hoped, would be an easier flight. As soon as we were airborne, the plane flew higher and higher until we were far above the heavy clouds in brilliant sunshine and deep blue sky. The airplane was flying smoothly by now, and everyone could take off their seat belts. Sandy got a coloring book with crayons from the flight attendant and colored happily away while sometimes looking out the window and wondering why the clouds were so far below and not above her. When they came around with a great lunch and drinks, I knew then that this was the way flying was supposed to be as I had heard people talking about. After a hour when we landed at Toronto's airport, my brother Henk was waiting for us. It had been my and Sandy's first airplane adventure

It was in late August when our oldest son told us that he was going to Texas with Sandra. He had gone there before on vacation and had fallen in love with the lifestyle and the wonderful beaches of the Gulf of Mexico, and wanted to live there. To say the least, it was a disappointment for Jozef and me. As all parents, we had hoped that our children would stay near us and live their lives close to our home—which is, of course, not very reasonable. Jozef and I ourselves had moved far from our parent's home when we were young. Now our first-born would leave the nest, and I knew we were going to miss him. Even though Joe returned many times to his home in Omaha, we missed his happy-go-lucky and loving ways. Joe and Sandra settled in the city of Corpus Christi on the Gulf of Mexico. There he worked in construction together with Sandra's brother in-law who lived in the same city. A few months later in October, Joe and Sandra were married in a small church ceremony.

For the last few years America and Russia were working hard to put a man on the moon. It had been an exciting time in the last years. First they sent rockets around the earth and the moon. This was televised and discussed at length in newspapers and in living rooms. Then on July 20, 1969 the world watched on television the fantastic event as the first man ever walked on the moon's dead surface. The first two men were Commander Neil Armstrong and Air Force Colonel Edwin Aldrin. All mankind who had ever lived had looked to the moon but never ever could they have dreamed that one day man would walk on the moon, and that day was now.

People in homes everywhere were glued to their television sets. In schools, stores and offices, TVs were set up especially so that everyone could watch this great event. It was exciting as we watched Armstrong and Aldrin explore the ice-cold lunar surface for almost two hours and heard Aldrin say, "That's one small step for man, one giant leap for mankind." As I watched this fantastic achievement, I wondered what would happen in the next generation and what affect it would have on their lives. The fulfillment of this goal, declared by the late President John Kennedy, cost 24 billion dollars.

Jozef had been working extremely hard, and I felt he needed a break. It didn't take much to talk him into going on a week vacation. First we talked about the different places we could go to before we decided on Colorado. At first Jozef had been a little skeptical about going there. Even though it had been many years since his terrible flight through the Carpathian Mountains during the war, he still did not feel good about mountains, he said. But knowing a vacation in Colorado was going to be a completely different experience as in Poland, he said that it would probably be a nice vacation for me since I never had seen the mountains.

It was August of that same year when I packed our suitcases. Jozef got his car ready, Eddy his fishing gear, Sandy got her favorite stuffed animal—a monkey. At that time Lia was going to school and also was working in a discount store in the Westroads Shopping Center and was not going with us. First we drove to Lake McConaughy where we planned to stay for the night in one of the cabins close to the dam. Very early the next morning while I was still in bed and Jozef and Sandy were sleeping, Eddy got his fishing gear and went fishing.

It was a few hours later when he came back proudly carrying with him seven white bass. After some discussion as what to do with all the fish, we decided to wrap them in paper and take them with us to Sterling, Colorado, look for a park and fry them for our lunch. Which we did. Eddy and his father cleaned the fish in a park which I then fried in the frying pan which we had taken with us from home. The fresh fried fish tasted delicious, and we had a great lunch. Before we left, we cleaned up and threw the leftover fish meat to the birds who were happy with the unexpected treat.

After driving a few hours and passing Greeley, I saw for the first time the mountains in the far distance. At first I thought I saw dark clouds on the horizon until Jozef said, "Do you see there those far away high dark areas? Those are the mountains." The kids and I got all excited, but it was still more than a hour's drive through what looked like a very wide open valley, before we came to the beautiful Colorado mountain range. What a spectacular sight! How mighty they looked. To see this for the first time is an unforgettable experience, and I think we all were in awe. Even Jozef, who had bad memories about mountains, thought this was a beautiful sight. Since it was getting late in the day, we began to look for a motel or cabin. Cabins always had been popular but were on the way out when the modern motels came. We saw a nice motel outside Estes Park close to the entrance of the Colorado Rocky Mountains and rented a room for the night. Even though the bed was great, the wild tumbling stream on the side of our cabin kept me awake most of the night.

The following day we began our trip through the mountains. Even it was the beginning of August and still vacation time, it was quiet everywhere. The weather was great with bright warm sunshine, and soon we entered the beautiful Rocky Mountains National Park. It is difficult to describe the incredible beauty I saw that day— my very first day in the mountains. We stopped at overlooks, fast running streams and took short nature walks over boulders and through tall pine tree woods. Sandy loved to feed the little ground squirrels which were everywhere and ate the small pieces of bread out of her hand. When we came to the higher elevation, Eddy and his little sister walked in the snow and threw snowballs at each other.

Later we stood at the highest point of the Rocky Mountain National Park. There we looked around us at the high snow capped mountains glistening in the sunlight. While I stood there I said to Jozef, "So, these are the Rocky Mountains we have heard so much about. What fantastic scenery. I could stay here the whole day!" But it was cold on the high mountains and even though we had put on our warm sweaters, we couldn't stay for a long period of time in that area. Soon we went further, while stopping here and there for something to see or for something to eat or to fish besides a stream. It was almost evening when we came out of the park and looked for a motel or a cabin. It had been a great day, and we all had enjoyed every moment of it.

After a good night sleep we drove to Sulphur Springs and visited Marble City where the beginnings of a village, built of marble, are to be seen. It was interesting, and we marveled at the beautiful large marble stones with which the bridges, half-finished houses and water wells were made. From there we went further to a ghost town close to Ashcroft and walked the path of a time past. Before looking for a place to spend the night we went to a Siberian husky dog range and visited the many wonderful dogs which were bred there and which Sandy loved to pet.

As soon as we finally left there, it got dusk suddenly. Instead of going to a town for a motel Jozef stopped at a small group of cabins out in nowhere. "It is getting too dark to be driving any further on those small roads in the mountains," he said. Luckily there was a cabin for rent which we took. In the meantime it got cold outside and my husband tried to light the stove for warmth. In no time our cabin filled with smoke, and we had to open the cabin door wide. I was glad that my husband knew what was wrong with the pipe and could fix it. By now it had started to rain and since the cabin door had to be open to get rid of the smoke, it got wet inside. What a mess! Later we finally could close the door and leave the cold and rain outside even though it smelled of smoke inside the cabin. When it was time for bed, Sandy jumped on Eddy's bed which came down with a loud bang on the floor. That night our son slept on his mattress on the floor. What a cabin this was!

The following day the sun was shining in a cloudless sky. When we opened the door of our cabin that morning and went outside, we looked at a most beautiful peaceful scenery around us and forgot the uncomfortable night. Eddy, who had seen that there were horses for rent at the place where we were, wanted to ride a horse. Of course Sandy wanted to ride a horsey too. After renting the horses Sandy rode her pony on the cabin grounds with her daddy beside her while her brother went riding by himself—a little further up in the hills.

When Eddy's two hours of rental were up, he still was nowhere to be seen. I got worried but after I asked his father to look for his son, we saw him coming down a path out of the forest. When we asked him what happened, he told us that he was stuck for two hours on the narrow path of the forest close to where we were. As soon as he was in the forest going up the hill, his horse had decided that he wanted to go back to his stable. Whatever Eddy tried, the stubborn animal did not want to go a step further. After a hour of trying our son decided to go back down the path and back to the stables. As soon as he got the horse turned half way around—it got stuck. The path was too narrow. Whatever Eddy tried to do, it was of no use. A hour later the horse probably got tired of the whole thing, or maybe our son finally talked some sense into the horse, because it turned further around and went with Eddy on his back down the narrow path out of the forest. We told our son that he never should ride a horse by himself if he wanted to go further away.

We had an early lunch and drove to Maroon Peak and from there farther close to Aspen where we visited a Christmas Village. It is a very pretty place to visit and browse in the many cute little Christmas stores which are located there. Of course we had to buy some souvenirs and Christmas ornaments for our Christmas tree in December. After our shopping Jozef took Sandy to feed the baby animals, Eddy and I enjoyed a large ice cream concoction at the village's ice cream terrace.

From the Christmas Village we went for a short while to the Garden of the Gods where we walked and climbed the tall red-stone formations. Later we drove close to Colorado Springs where we rented a very nice log cabin overlooking the mountains. The following day we visited the Colorado Springs Zoo which is build against a mountain. We enjoyed the many animals there especially the giraffes which they had many of. In the afternoon we went to the Air Force Academy which Jozef and I wanted to visit. The academy is a very nice building and is well worth seeing the inside. We thought it very interesting and beautiful. It was almost dark when we parked our car in front of the door of our last overnight stay on this trip before going home

It had been a great vacation. Eddy, who was sixteen years old and had received his driver's license, drove many times on this trip. It was good practice for him. It had been our first Colorado visit, but not our last one. In the future many more vacations in Colorado would follow. Jozef and I always enjoyed Colorado, and still do.

A few weeks later Eddy went back to Westside High School while Sandy went back to her preschool—this time for three mornings a week. After her school was out I took Sandy back to the bakery. There she played not only with some toys which I had there for her, but she also wanted to learn how to make a border and flowers from icing on a cardboard circle. As young as she was, she did a good job and by the time she was about five years old, she know how to make roses from icing. We proudly called her, "The youngest cake decorator in the world!" When we were home Sandy loved to dance around the house to any kind of music, and I enrolled her in the well-known Pat Carlson's Dance Studio which was located close to our bakery. It was the first time that Pat Carlson had begun a dance class that fall for four-year-old children.

Every spring for the next fourteen years, most of our family would attend the yearly Pat Carlson Dance Recital at the Orpheum Theater. Even though her dad got tired of seeing the dance show every year, he always attended. Chuck would tease me saying that this was our yearly social event. I always have enjoyed seeing my daughter dance in those recitals and never missed them. The girl's costumes were beautiful, but as they got older and they needed at least three different costumes for their performances, it became quite expensive. Though the location of the dance studio has been changed a few times, Sandy danced there until she was eighteen years old and graduated from Pat Carlson's Dance Studio.

◆     ◆     ◆

After two days of lying in the labor room of Bergen Mercy Hospital I gave birth to another son on December 16. We named him James. When I held our beautiful baby son for the first time in my arms, I was so thankful he was a healthy baby and prayed that he would grow up as fine a boy as his two brothers. How could I have been so unhappy with the thought of another child, I said to myself while gently kissing his tender little face. A few days later I came home, but our baby Jimmy had to stay another few days in the hospital because of jaundice.

That Christmas was a very busy time for our family. Even though we had more help now in our bakery, Jozef and Eddy worked very hard. It was almost Christmas and, as every year, there were many things to bake such as cakes and especially cookies and pastries. At home I was busy, especially now with our newborn baby. It seemed by itself to be a twenty-four-hour job. Even so, I made a nice Christmas Eve dinner for our son Joe and Sandra his wife who had come from Texas for a few days to visit us. Early in the evening when Chuck came to our house, we all celebrated Christmas Eve together. Later, after the opening of the presents, I took our baby out his crib and went to the living room. As I was sitting there with our little boy in my arms, I looked at my husband and children who were laughing and joking with each other, and I thought how lucky and blessed I was. How little I knew that things would soon change.

It was on the fifth of February 1970 when, after feeding my baby, we sat down for supper. Since Jimmy had been crying, I went upstairs to see if he was lying comfortably in his crib. It was very quiet and I thought that he was sleeping, but I felt that something was not right when I saw him lying in an awkward position. He had scooted himself up to the headboard and was lying with his head bent backward. When I tried to lay him straight and looked closer, my heart stopped. My little boy was dead. We called the rescue squad who took me and our baby to the hospital. A few days later after an autopsy we learned how Jimmy had died. Because he had been lying with his head backward against the headboard and had vomited, the milk he had drunk earlier had gone into his lungs. Our little son Jimmy had been only seven weeks old. A few days earlier he had been baptized in our church with our son Joe and our daughter Lia as his godparents. The months that followed were difficult. Even though I had at first not wanted this child in my early pregnancy, I had loved this little boy so very much after he was born.

# 44

## *OUR TRIP HOME*

*1970.* Since there was a period of relaxed tensions in the Cold War between the Soviet Union and America, Jozef thought about going back to Poland and seeing his mother, brothers and sisters. It had been many years since he saw his family for the last time—which was in 1938. Many times in the last years we had wanted to go back to our countries, but somehow it never had been the right time.

It was earlier that summer when Jozef decided to close the bakery for two weeks and visit our families in Poland and Holland sometime that August. Lia and Sandy were going with us and Eddy wanted to stay home. We planned that we all would fly together to Holland. From there Jozef would fly to Poland by himself for the first week. After that first week he then would fly back to Holland and stay with us for another week before flying home by himself to America.

Lia, Sandy and I planned to stay in Holland for another week before we would return home. We thought also it would be better if Jozef on this very first visit to his family went by himself. There was so much they had to tell each other after all those years in only a week's time. This way he would not be distracted by his two daughters and me who could not speak the Polish language. We also reasoned that now that the situations were better for us, that within two years we would go back to Poland, and this way we all could enjoy each other much more.

It was August of that year when we packed our suitcases. Lia, who wanted to take too many summer clothes with her, had to repack her suitcase after I explained to her that most of the time Holland is a little cool. Our daughter Sandy insisted on taking her stuffed animals with her. "All of them," she said. The end decision was that only her favorite monkey was going.

It was early in the morning when we boarded an airplane to Chicago. From there we were going to fly by KLM to Amsterdam. In Chicago we had a long time to wait in a small closed-in area (since then long gone) from where the international airplanes departed before boarding the KLM plane to Holland. The flight from Chicago to Amsterdam is 5.600 mile and would take nine hours. The new jet engine airplane was huge. It was the first time we had seen such an airplane and couldn't believe its immense size. It was also large on the inside where we saw three seats on each side of the plane and a row with three seats in the middle. From Chicago we flew over the northeastern side of Canada and further over the Labrador Sea. Hours later we flew over the most southern tip of Greenland before going further over the Atlantic Ocean toward Northern Europe.

It was a very comfortable flight, and we were spoiled with great tasting food and drinks. From the flight attendant Sandy got a KLM pin and other surprises which she happily showed to everyone who sat around her. Because the plane was flying very high and with great speed, the time quickly changed from light to dark. After a short period of darkness during which my family and most of the people in the plane were sleeping, except me, it changed to light again. I looked through the small window of the plane and saw in the eastern sky the sun coming up in a large hazy orange ball. As the early morning clouds where lifting over the Atlantic Ocean, I thought about the time when I had left my country. Now I came back almost sixteen years later, and I wondered how much my country had changed.

The flight attendant came around and after each passenger received a warm wash cloth to refresh our faces and hands, we got a hearty breakfast. Not much later the plane flew over the North Sea and slowly it began to fly lower. Our oldest daughter was looking out of her window and suddenly said excitedly that there was a fleet of fishing boats in the dark water below us. We all looked and Sandy said that they looked like small toys floating in the wind. It was such a peaceful sight, this scene on the endless water. The plane began to slow down and there it was, a golden strip glistening in the sunlight. It was the coastline of Holland with its wide beaches and beautiful dunes—the sand dunes where as child I loved to play and dream during our vacations in Haarlem. I told Lia that this was the land where she was born and played the very first years of her life. She answered me that she still could remember a few things, such as the ducks in the Wilhelmina Park and the street where she played with her little friends.

By now the plane flew low over Holland's landscape with its crisp cleanliness of soil and air which I remember so well when growing up in Holland. It was the flat land with here and there a typical Dutch village and a windmill with its sails turning in the wind. My Holland, how lovely it looked. My heart went open wide for my country. I had missed it and it was good to come home. Come home to the country where I was born and where I grew up and to see my family again.

It was 7:00 in the morning when our plane landed with a slight bounce at the International Airport of 'Schiphol' by Amsterdam. My brother Jan and his wife Gerda were waiting for us. It had been a long time since I had seen them—not since our immigration to America. Following a very happy reunion at the large terminal, Jan quickly took us to his car and out of the crowded area. Soon we were on the way to Mother's house in Amsterdam where there again was another wonderful reunion, this time with Mother and our daughters' grandmother.

As Jan and Gerda left for their home, they told us that they were going to pick us up for a walk on the beach in the afternoon. Because of the seven hour time difference from Omaha we were tired, but Jan and Gerda insisted that the walk would be good for us and we would have a good night sleep. It was that same afternoon when we met their son Rob and their daughter Irene—Jan and Gerda's two children. We had seen them only in photographs which they had sent us throughout the years. Lia, who was now nineteen, had been four years old when Jan and Gerda had last seen her, and she had grown into a young women. And there was Sandy—the baby in the family. We all had to get acquainted with each other which did not take long. The only problem for the children was the language, but since Jan knew English well, he was of great help. Early in the morning of the following day, Jan came with his car to bring Jozef back again to Schiphol. He was going to fly with a Polish airplane to Warsaw, Poland.

(Jozef) The airplane flight from Amsterdam to Warsaw took about two hours. This is a short flight by America standards, but for the Europeans the distance between Amsterdam to Warsaw is considered far. After I was settled in my seat, it did not take long before the airplane was flying over the border of Holland into Germany. Since I had a window seat, I was able to look out of the plane's window where I saw the German landscape below me. So many years have past, I thought, so many years since I was there in my tank and listened on my radio while grenades exploded around me. And I thought about my Army buddies who were buried in the German soil far away from their homes and loved ones. I never could forget them, or the war which we had fought together.

When the flight attendant came around with coffee, I thought about my family who would be waiting for me at the airport, and I wondered if I would recognize them. Even though I had seen my family in pictures which they had sent to us over the years, it probably would be different when I saw them again in real life. Later, as the plane was flying over Poland, I suddenly felt elated and sad at the same time. I was happy that finally I would not only see my family again, but also walk on the soil of my country Poland. During the war years I had said many times to myself that I was going home. And even though I had ultimately found my own home with Efka, this Poland was my country and the home of my family and childhood. It was only sad that my country after all those years was still not free from the Communist grip. As the airplane descended and I looked out of the window, I saw Warsaw below me. A few minutes later the plane landed. Finally I had returned home.

As I came from the airplane and walked to the airport terminal, I noticed many soldiers with guns around the plane. This was something I had not seen in a long time, not since the war years. It gave me an uneasy feeling, and I thought that this Poland was sure not the land of the free. When I came into the hall where security inspected everyone's papers and suitcases, I noticed the many people who were standing around a balcony above the hall. They were looking at the incoming passengers below them. When they saw a loved one coming, they waved their arms and screamed their names. Looking at the people who stood there, I hoped that I would recognize some of them as my family. Then suddenly I saw my brother Kazek and my sister Victoria. They were waving their arms excitedly and calling my name. About that same time, as I waved back to them, I saw my other sister Irene and Victoria's husband Cheslow. There they were, my two sisters and my youngest brother. They weren't children anymore, but adults with families of their own.

Later when I was done with my papers and had my suitcase, we came together. It was a very happy and emotional reunion at the airport in Warsaw. I don't recall how long we stood there hugging each other before we drove in a taxi to Victoria and Cheslow's apartment. There we talked until early in the morning the following two days before I was going to leave for Miedzychud to visit my mother and my other two brothers.

My sisters, Kazek and Cheslow asked many questions about my family and our life in America. After all those years we had so much to talk about, and I heard many stories—serious and funny ones. We talked especially about the war years which had been a difficult time for all of us. Kazek told me about what happened to our father and about his death, but I didn't get all the answers I wanted to know. Kazek, who had received his forest management degree from the University in Warsaw, was living close to Miedzychud with his wife and three children. It was not far from where my mother lived. While my sister's husband Cheslow was an engineer at airfields, Victoria was busy raising their son and being a dentist. My older sister Irene was not married and was an accountant for the city of Warsaw.

Even though we all talked together most of the time, Kazek took me away for a few hours to show me the inner city of Warsaw which had been completely destroyed in the Warsaw-Uprising in 1945. He showed me how they had rebuilt the inner city, stone by stone, so that it looked the same as it always had looked before those dreadful months. How much I wanted to see more of that great city and learn more about what had happened there.

On the third day of my stay in Poland I went by train with Kazek to Miedzy-chud to see my mother and my other brothers, Stanly and Marian who lived not far from there. While the train sped to the city of Poznan, we spent most of the time sleeping. In the last two days we both had only slept a few hours. From Poznan we took another train to the town of Miedzychud which was about a hour train ride.

As I looked out of the window over the warm rich yellow summer fields with their bleu cornflowers and bright golden buttercups, I thought about my father and our mushroom trips in the woods. How good it would have been if he had been here. Since I came to Poland, he had been on my mind many times.

It was not far to walk from the train station to the apartment of our mother. Even before we knocked on the door, she opened it, and I fell into my mother's arms. I think she had been looking out of her window since early morning to see me coming. It had been thirty two years ago that we had said goodbye. That was the day when I left for Eastern Poland, and now finally I had come back to her. At first I did not recognize my mother. The young slender mother who I had remembered through the years was no more. After such a long time and years of suffering during the war, she was now a much older and more serious woman. Her hair had grown gray, and her beautiful face was now laced with wrinkles. As she held me in her arms, I suddenly felt as if all the years disappeared and I was young again. I don't remember how long we stood there, holding each other. We wanted to say so many things to each other, but somehow we could not find the words. Finally she asked me if I was hungry; she had some nice chicken soup made for me. She had remembered that I always had enjoyed her chicken soup. She was still the same mother as I remembered.

That same evening my two brothers, Marian and Stanly came with their families to see me. It was because of the pictures they had sent me in the last years that I could recognize them; otherwise, I would not have known that they were my brothers. Marian had grown over six feet tall and Stanly, who always had been a little husky as a boy, was now a big man. We had much to talk about. Especially Stanly who had been in serious trouble with the Communists and had been in prison for political reasons. (The story is too long to write in this book.) He now had a farm and lived with his wife and two sons in a village twenty minutes from my mother. Marian, who was married and had a daughter, was an electrician.

Miedsychud, Poland, 1970: Stanley, Jozef, Mother, Marian, and Kazek.

The following few days I spend mostly at my mother's house but, because of the many people who wanted to see and talk to me, we had very little privacy. One morning Mother and I visited Father's grave where she told me about my father and what happened to him and, even though I got many of the answers I was looking for, I had the feeling that she did not tell me everything. From the cemetery Mother and I walked to the market square. As a boy I always had enjoyed seeing the farm animals which had been bought and sold there by the farmers. The square was still the same, but no markets were held anymore, as Mother told me. Instead there now was a fountain in a large flower bed. Our former house where I grew up had been made into an apartment, and I didn't recognize it anymore. The wide open grass area which had been behind our house where I had kept my animals, and where sometimes one of my chickens was killed by a slow moving train on the railroad track, was also gone. The property also had shrunk to half its size because of another building. It was not the place anymore as I had it remembered. The rest of Miedzychud was the same as when I had left thirty-two years ago. Not much was built since then.

The few days with my mother and brothers had gone too fast and the moment came that I had to say goodbye again. They all brought me to the train station—the same as they had done so many years before. Only Father was missing. I still could hear him say, "Go with God, my son," before I had entered the train going to East Poland. As then, Mother was holding back her tears and tried to be brave. As the train was leaving I looked at my mother and two brothers one more time and I wished I could have stayed longer. There had been not enough time to talk about everything I wanted too hear and wanted too say.

Only Kazek went with me back to Warsaw where I had to catch a airplane to Holland the next day. The last night of my stay in Poland I slept at Victoria and Cheslow's house before going back the following day to Holland.

As I was sitting in the Dutch KLM plane going to Amsterdam, I thought how the week had flown by like a whirlwind. It had been way too short, I thought. I was very tired and was glad that Eef and I had made the decision before planning this trip, that I should go alone to Poland. It would have been no good with all the traveling, sleeping arrangements, language barrier and with all those people around me, many who I didn't know.

As I was thinking about the lives of my family and the other people which I had met in Warsaw and in Miedzychud, I came to the conclusion that life was not very good in Poland. Yes, everyone had work—this is the Communist system—but no one made any money. Doctors or other more educated men or women made the same money as the blue collar workers, which was not much. Only for the man or woman who belonged to the Communist party it was a different story—they got adequate wages. Even though there was enough of food and merchandise in the stores, no one had the money to buy it. I also had noticed that everything looked old, run-down and not kept up. Not much was changed or improved or built since the war had ended in 1945. In the meantime, as I was thinking about my family, our plane had reached Holland. As the plane was ready to land at the airport Schiphol, I thought about all those people who, for so many years already, were still living behind the iron curtain.

As soon as the airplane landed in Holland, I could feel the difference. There were no soldiers in the airport walking with guns, and as I walked inside the terminal the atmosphere was much more pleasant. Jan was waiting for me and soon we drove in his car to Amsterdam where Eef, her mother and Lia and Sandy were waiting for me. While I drank a cup of tea and ate Dutch pastry, I had to tell everything about my family and my stay in Poland. Even though I still had to sort out many things in my mind, I could tell them that everything was well with my family.

The week that followed in Holland was great. Eef, the girls and I went by train for a few days to Breda. We wanted to go back there and show our daughters the town and the house we had lived in. As soon as we came out of Breda's train station we walked through the beautiful old Valkenburg Park to the Grote Mart (city square), where twice a week open market-day always were held. It was the place where Eef had gone on Fridays to buy fish, flowers and such. She always had enjoyed the market when we lived in Breda. It turned out disappointing for her and Lia when they heard that there was no market that day. The market had been the day before. Since it was lunch time, we decided to eat lunch at one of the restaurants which were located at the Grote Mart. We looked around until the girls saw an old and typical Dutch restaurant. That was the place where they wanted to eat.

As soon as we walked in, a waitress helped us to sit at a table by a window. It overlooked the Grote Mart and the magnificent Grote Kerk (church) which was build around the year 1300. While looking the menu over, we spoke English to each other as we always did. What we didn't know was that the waitress, who could hear our conversation, became very nervous. Since Breda is not a tourist town, they probably never had seen an American family in their restaurant. When I asked the girl if we could order only sandwiches and a drink, she blushed and stammered and went to her boss. I had not realized at that moment that I had spoken English to her. A few seconds later her boss came to our table followed by the nervous girl, and introduced himself as the owner of the restaurant. In broken English he asked us where we came from and if he could be of any service. I told him in English that we came from America and were visiting his city. I then said to him that we wanted to order sandwiches and drinks. The boss and the waitress then went behind the counter to prepare our order.

From the conversation between them we understood that they thought we were a rich American family. Eef and Lia didn't want to spoil the fun and said that we should keep up the image. I think they both liked to act as if we were people of influence. Sandy had no idea what we were talking about and just blabbered on—telling her monkey that he had to behave himself because we were in a restaurant. It was not much later when the waitress came in with a large tray of the most fantastic sandwiches, her boss whispered to her not to be so nervous because, as he said, "They are people, the same as anyone else." Eef and Lia tried hard not to laugh. They got a real kick out of this and, as they both said, "It feels great to get all that attention and to be treated like a movie star." Since we didn't want to spoil this special treatment, we said nothing and enjoyed the great lunch. Once in awhile the owner came over to our table and wanted to know about living in America. The bill for our lunch was high but, since the American dollar stood high in those years, the price for our lunch was very low.

As we walked out of the restaurant, Lia asked her mother if people were allowed to see the inside of the Grote Kerk. When Eef told her that it always had been open, Lia said that she was interested to see this beautiful church on the inside. Luckily it was open, but only for certain hours of the day. The high and large church was very impressive to our two daughters, especially the many marble tombstones with angels and the large statues of saints. After having seen everything in the church which was from a time of long ago, we went further. From the Grote Mart we walked through the cobbled shopping streets which the city had closed for traffic. Most of the old narrow inner city streets of Europe have been closed to traffic ever since the large number of cars began to jam the small roads. We walked further and looked at all the merchandise in the windows of the stores and trendy boutiques. Eef and I noticed the many new businesses which had come to Breda since we lived there. Lia, who held her sister by the hand, looked at a small chapel in the shopping street. It always had been there ever since people could remember. It must have been as old as when they first began building the city. We went inside, looked around the well-preserved small chapel and said a little prayer in one of the few pews.

From there we walked further to the Wilhelmina Park where we planned to rest for a while. As soon as we came to the park, where the rhododendrons stood in full bloom and where ducks and geese were swimming or sitting in the grass, Sandy became suddenly upset and said that she had lost her monkey. We figured she must have lost it in the chapel. As fast as we could we walked back to the little chapel, but when we came there and looked around, her monkey was gone. Sandy was sad about it, and I think she never forgot her favorite stuffed animal. After we comforted her, she fed the ducks and swans in the Wilhelmina Park and felt better. Soon we walked further to the street where we had lived—the Zeisstraat. Compared with American houses, these brick houses which are built side by side against each other, looked small and compact. We were not used to seeing that anymore in Omaha.

It was quiet in the street as it always had been when we lived there. The bakery on the corner was still in business. We walked in and after we bought some cookies, we asked if the owner of the bakery, who had served us fifteen years ago, was still working there. The salesgirl answered us that her father was not well and had retired. From the bakery we went further and stopped for a moment at the front yard entrance of our former house. From the outside it looked still the same—nice and clean and well taken care of as all houses were in our street. Lia said that she remembered it well. She then looked at the other side of the street where her little playmate Anja used to live.

As we walked to the backside of our house where once the cows grazed in the fields, we saw only houses. In the years we were gone whole new neighborhoods were built behind the Zeisstraat. Eef and I looked at each other and while staring at the jungle of houses, Eef said, "How well I remember the earth smell after the winter was gone. You knew springtime was on its way when the farmers fertilized their land. Look now, what happened! There is no soil and the wonderful fresh smell of earth is gone forever from here." Yes, I answered her sadly, it is not the same anymore as that it was so many years ago.

We also noticed that we didn't recognize some of the name plates on the houses where once our neighbors lived. Our former neighbors in the Zeisstraat had probably moved somewhere else, except for a neighbor who Eef had known well. She lived above the house where our close neighbors, Jan and Geertje van Dort, had lived before they moved away to one of the new neighborhoods.

After we rang the doorbell, our old neighbor opened the door. At first she did not recognize us but, after she looked closer she began to scream and told us to come inside. She made coffee and said she was going to call Geertje to come over. It was not much later that Geertje, Eef's old friend and neighbor, walked in and after an emotional greeting she later took us to her new house. Even though it was great for Eef and Geertje to see each other again and to talk about the children, and for me to talk to her husband Jan about the new expanding Breda, there was not much left to say anymore. They didn't seem too interested in America and our life there. Probably too many years had passed. We all had gone our way and had found new interests. It was also too bad that our daughters couldn't speak and understand the Dutch language enough to have a conversation. Later we said goodbye and we waved until we went around the corner of their new street, a street which was not long ago a waving wheat field.

Before going to our hotel for the night Eef wanted to walk by boer Backx farm. She was hoping it would still be there. As we came close to what used to be the end of the Poolse weg (former Molengracht straat) the first thing Eef and I noticed was that all the tall old cottonwood trees were gone. The fields and the lovely stream, the Lyke, with the salamanders and many frogs was also no more.

Now they were busy building an interstate going from Amsterdam to Antwerp and further to Brussels, Belgium. Instead of the sound from twittering birds and the wind in the trees, there was now the noise of heavy machines. Soon the sound of traffic would spoil the solitude we remembered so well when Eef and I walked there on the small paths between the summer fields.

In such a short time things had changed dramatically from the way it used to be. Except boer Backx. The farm, which is now under the protection of historical buildings, is still there. On the land and the orchard around the farmhouse is now a new neighborhood, but the house itself and some flower gardens are there and always will be. We noticed people living in the house because of some laundry which was blowing in the wind on a wash line and also a child's tricycle in front of the door. Even though Eef felt sad that everything she remembered about the land, farms, trees and even the smell of fresh cow manure was gone, I think she was glad that the boer Backx farm house will for always be saved. I think also that Eef had wanted to show Lia the way it used to be when she lived in the Zeisstraat.

Many places were the same though, as the Wilhelmina Park and the Mastbos where we went the following day. After a good night sleep and an excellent breakfast in a nice hotel in the middle of Breda, we walked to the Mastbos. The Mastbos, which seems to go on forever, is still the same as it always had been since I came to Breda. We walked not too far into the forest for it would become too tiresome for our young daughter Sandy. We all four loved the forest with its stillness, its tall pine trees and its sandy winding paths. Eef told the girls about when she and her brother went to the forest to pick blueberries during their summer vacations from school. "More berries went in our mouth than into the container we carried," she said. She also told them about the kikker place in the forest but, as she said, it was too far to walk there. We rested under the trees on the side of a lonely small road before we continued on with our tour to the Castle Bouvigne.

The small lovely castle with all its memories for Eef was still the same as it always had been. An office is now located inside the castle. Tourists are welcome to walk through the flower gardens behind the castle which we did and enjoyed very much. Before we realized it was late in the afternoon. We walked further and soon came to the very old village of Ginneken. There we ate some croquettes from an automate which was located on the other side of a dark 300-year-old church. The tomb of the Prince of Oranje is located beside the entrance. Since everything was enclosed by iron fencing and it was "dark and spooky there," as Lia said, we walked further on while looking for a bus to take us to the train station. It had been a few great days in Breda which we remember well. Late in the evening we arrived tired at Mother's house in Amsterdam.

It was the next day that we went with Mother and Gerda by train to the town of Hoek van Holland. It was the town where Tante Ann and her new husband lived. A few years after the death of Oom Gerard, Tante Ann met a Dutchman in Africa by the name of Jan van Schalke. He owned a bakery in Holland. It was a year later when, after their wedding, she had gone with him to Holland. It was already a few years now that they lived there. After her husband's retirement from the bakery, they moved to the town of Hoek van Holland where they have since lived in a retirement housing. Tante Ann, who always had been a happy-go-lucky woman, and her husband Jan were happy to see us all. The table was full of pastries, drinks and more.

After a pleasant few hours we all went to the corner of Hoek van Holland where the river Waal spills out into the North Sea. It was the place our ship had passed as we were going to America, and the last we had seen of Holland. The beach is wide there and, even though there was a cold wind blowing, we enjoyed walking on the white sand beside the churning sea. After Sandy rode a pony on the beach, we all went for lunch to a poffertjes pavilion. The pavilion was like a large closed-in beach tent with a terrace. Sitting inside we ate the famous Dutch poffertjes, little pancakey things covered with butter and powdered sugar. It is a Dutch specialty we all loved, especially Lia and Sandy, who couldn't eat enough of them. From the pavilion we walked to the river Waal where we saw a few large cargos and a passenger ship coming from over the North Sea. It was a great sight. It was there, Eef said, where she had said goodbye to her country for the last time when our ship passed this point before going over the sea. I understood the emotions which she felt. We lingered some more at the beach. The day had gone by too fast.

The following day the weather was cool and gloomy. Since it was my last day in Holland Eef and I decided to stay home that day, but later go out and take Lia to one of Amsterdam's great nightclubs. As we drank our coffee with a Dutch pastry, Sandy announced that she was going outside too play. Almost every day when we came home from one or another outing, children were playing in front of her grandmother's house. A few times Sandy had looked through the widow to see them playing a game. Eef went outside with her and asked if Sandy could play with them but—that she couldn't speak Dutch. Curious, they looked at her. After she had introduced our daughter to the children, she left and went inside the house. About a half an hour later, after the kids played ball together, Sandy came into the house announcing that she didn't want to play anymore. "Mom,"she said. "Why are those children talking so funny. I can't understand what they are saying to me!" Even though we tried our best to make her understand why this was, she did not want to play outside anymore.

That same night when we were ready to leave for an evening out, our youngest child was running through her grandmother's hallway to have a last hug from her mom. While holding the Dutch doll which she got from her uncle Jan, she slipped over the threshold which was located between the hallway and front door. She hit her face on the wooden shoes of her doll and cut the area between her upper lip and her nose. Our poor girl! She was crying in pain and it took awhile before we finally left for the nightclub. And, as Eef told me later, for the following few days she walked around with a swollen upper lip. The scar is still there today as a souvenir from Holland.

My two weeks in Europe were over, and I had to go home. It had been two great weeks. I was pleased and happy that I had seen all of my family in Poland and Eef's family in Holland. Besides Jan and Gerda and their children Rob and Irene, I also met Tante Dien again. One evening we had a great get-together with Coby and her husband Jaap in their home. It all had gone by too fast and I wished I could stay longer.

After a goodbye to Eef's mother and our daughters, I left with Jan and Eef in his car. In a cool mist under a heavy cloudy sky we drove to the International Airport of Shiphol from where I planned to take an airplane to Chicago. Schiphol is a very large and crowded airport, but it is modern and it is not difficult to find your way around. It was about 3:00 in the afternoon when the airplane left Holland and, because of time change, arrived at 4:00 that same afternoon in Chicago. When the airplane reached the terminal and I walked through the plane's open door, a wave of hot air greeted me. It was 104 degrees! After a few hours of waiting at the O'Hare Airport and another hour of flying, I finally arrived in Omaha. As the airplane landed and I stepped down, I suddenly felt that I had come home. Even though I had been very happy and glad to have been in Holland again and finally have seen my family in Poland, this Omaha, this America had become a part of me.

(Eef) Two days later it was beautiful and warm. It was early in the morning when my cousin Coby called and said that she and her husband Jaap were going cruising. She asked if I and my two girls wanted to go with them. Jaap and Coby always had loved boating and had owned a sailboat in the first years after they were married. A few years ago they had bought a very nice cabin cruiser. Since Coby and Jaap had no children and enjoyed cruising, they spent most of their vacations and their free time on the water. Many a time they went for a week or more cruising, going through Holland from one place to the other. It was a life-style they both enjoyed. Holland with its many waterways and lakes is a perfect place for sailing and cruising.

It did not take us long until we were ready to be picked up for our day on the water. It was great. The weather could not have been better and, while sitting or lying on the cruiser in our bathing suits, we took in the sun. We cruised through the Dutch canals with their windmills and through the rivers until we came to a large lake. I forgot the name of the lake. It was not long until Jaap anchored his boat on the side of a wooded area where we ate the lunch which Coby had taken with her. Most of the time Lia and Sandy had been lying on top of the cruiser, and I think if it had not been for the suntan lotion they would have been burned to a crisp. Coby and I were reminiscing about the time when we were not yet married and I came to Amsterdam during my vacations. Sometimes Jaap shook his head just hearing about it. It was late in the afternoon when Jaap anchored his cabin cruiser in a private harbor close to Amsterdam. It had been a great day. Sandy was sleeping in Jaap's car when he brought us home. Mother had been waiting for us.

On the last day of my stay in Holland we went with Jan, Gerda and Mother to the well-known fishing village of Volendam. It always was, and always will be, a typical Dutch fishing village on the former Zuider Zee. Since the making of an enclosing dike between the North Sea and the Zuider Zee, it is now called Ysselmeer. Because of the many tourists who come to Volendam, it became with time a village of souvenir shops and eating places. Sitting on small terraces on the dike, eating their herring, eel or other fish on soft buns, the tourists are looking at the many fishing boats which are anchored close to the shore. As we walked in the bright warm sun on the dike with the village on one side and the Yselmeer on the other side, we looked at the fishing boats at sea and the many seagulls which were trying to catch a fish. From there we went into the small souvenir stores which, of course, we had to see, especially Lia.

After seeing, and walking in and out of the souvenir stores, we each had to eat a salty herring. While Sandy giggled, Jan, Gerda, Lia and I stood there on the dike holding on to the fish's tail. With our heads bent backwards, we ate our her-ring as only Dutch people do. We didn't see many natives in their colorful cos-tumes anymore as there used to be. Now young people and children of

Volendam are wearing blue jeans. After a little discussion about if we had enough time, we took a boat ride to the small Island of Marken. A few years before the island had been connected to the mainland by a dike so people could reach it also by car. The small fishing village on the island is now preserved and kept the same as it had been for hundreds of years. Fishermen and their families still live in the tidy small houses. Only now many families make their living from tourism.

It was there in a tiny store that I bought a special vase which I still have displayed in my home. As we walked around the village, I told Lia about the life in those small villages of long ago. Later we stopped in a typical restaurant where we ate smoked eel. Both girls didn't trust eating those 'water snakes' as they called them and ordered something else. We took pictures and looked one more time at the picturesque village where I missed the colorful costumes of the people from a time which I remembered. We went back to our touring ship and reached the mainland a hour later.

The week before when Jozef had left for his family in Poland, one day Jan had brought Mother and us to the largest open market in Amsterdam. Lia and I had really enjoyed the crowded and colorful marketplace. Only Sandy didn't know what to make out of all this until we came to a stand where they sold parakeets in all colors and sizes. She was fascinated by seeing all those pretty birds and didn't want to leave. That lasted until Mother said to her granddaughter that there was an oliebollen stand close by and that she could buy some.

Another day Jan and Gerda with their daughter Irene took us for a long walk in the beautiful high dunes where many seabirds were nesting. Sometimes when Sandy got tired from walking in the sea sand Jan carried her on his schoulders. Finally, after we walked more than a halve hour, we reached the beach. When I stood on the top of the golden dunes with my hair blowing in the wind and looked out over the wide beach with the dark restless sea behind, I felt such a peace and was thankful that I was blessed to see this wonderful sight of my country once again. I think that our oldest daughter enjoyed this sight of Holland as much as I did.

In the weeks that we had been in Holland, Jan and Gerda went with us to many places. Nothing was ever too much for them. In the years that followed Jozef and I have been back to Holland many times and always have greatly enjoyed their company. Jan, who has an appetite for adventure, took us not only everywhere in Holland in their BMW car, but also to many other places in Europe as Rome, Switzerland, North Italy, Germany, Luxembourg and Brussels in Belgium. We always had a great time seeing the many very interesting places which we will never forget. A great trip was to Switzerland and northern Italy where we took a boat ride over the Lago Maggiore where we visited the three most picturesque tiny islands in the world. On another trip in Germany we saw old castles on the high hills of the river Rhine, where we visited a most beautiful castle named Schlok Dradjenburg. Here we drove through the wine fields and later drank wine at a wine festival. We saw many great churches—hundreds of years old—built in Gothic style. We also saw the great art treasures in the beautiful museums. We enjoyed seeing many flower baskets hanging on the windowsills of the houses in the mountains of Switzerland and Italy. But we also saw the war monuments of our time, especially the memorial in Bastogne, Belgium, of the Battle of the Bulge. We saw cities with great architecture from a time of long ago. It was a different culture then.

The time had gone by too fast. Soon the day arrived when we said goodbye to my family. When I hugged Mother, she said that she was coming next year again to see us in America—which she did.

After Jan brought us to the airport of Schiphol we said goodbye, promising to see each other soon again. First we went through the ticket and passport counter before going to the large tax-free shopping area. There we bought the big size Dutch chocolates and other Dutch items at a very reasonable price and took them back to Omaha with us. We left Holland at 3:00 in the afternoon and arrived at 4:00 in Chicago. The same as Jozef's flight had been. When we landed in Omaha and walked out of the plane, Jozef and Eddy were waiting for us. We had arrived back home in Omaha.

# 45

## *THE TORNADO*

*Summer of 1975.* Five years had passed since our first trip back to our countries. Since then it had become quiet in our home. First it had been our son Joe and his wife Sandra who had moved away. After they lived in Texas for about two years they moved to Florida. In October of 1970, when they still lived in Texas, they were blessed with a little girl who they named Tracy. She became our first grandchild. A few years later, when they lived in Florida, they were blessed with a baby boy. They named him Jozef. Hopefully he would carry the name of Jozef Otto further to the next generation. In the beginning our oldest son had worked for a construction company in Florida, but later began his own company and did well.

Four years before in June of 1971, our daughter Lia was married to Charles Langston. It was a small but lovely church wedding. Afterwards when family and friends went to a restaurant for reception and dinner, the thermometer read 102 degrees outside. Chuck's family had come from Paduca, Kentucky for their son's special day. After their honeymoon the newlyweds moved into an apartment close to Lia's work. Lia worked at the Leavenworth City Bank before working for an insurance company. After Chuck retired from active duty in the Air Force, he began working for OPPD while staying active in the Air Force reserve. About two years later they moved into a house two doors down from where we live on Grover Street. In February of 1974 they held their first-born child in their arms. His name was Matthew. A few years later, in 1976, Chuck and Lia were blessed with a daughter. They named her Julie. Then in 1979 their last child and daughter was born. Her name was Jill.

Also in that same year of 1971 our son Ed had graduated from Westside High School. He went three months later to Oklahoma to study bakery management and baking. He wanted to work with his father in our bakery and hoped later to take over his father's business. Ed had fallen in love with a girl by the name of Marlene Zack. She lived with her parents in our neighborhood. When Ed left for Oklahoma, I was sure we would not see much of him in the following two years.

Maybe once in awhile for a vacation break, I thought. He was our fourth child to leave home in two years time. First it had been our baby Jimmy who left us, then Joe and his wife Sandra went to Texas, then Lia our oldest daughter married and moved away, and now our youngest son left home. I missed all of them and felt very lonesome for the time they all were home. In that time Jozef and I were thankful that our home was filled with the happy sound of a ten-year-old girl. Even though Sandy was sometimes lonesome for her sister and brothers, with her laughter and her friends' chipper voices, she took the blues away. But I was mistaken about our youngest son who I thought I would not see much for two years. He had not been gone for a few weeks when I heard his car coming into our driveway. He missed Omaha and his family and came home for the weekend, he said while opening the refrigerator door. But I think it was more that he missed his girlfriend Marlene.

During the following two years when he was in Oklahoma, he drove home many times on weekends. If the weather was good, we didn't mind so much, even we thought it too far a drive for a weekend. However when wintertime came and snowstorms were possible, I worried. I remember well one time when Ed was ready to leave to go back to Oklahoma. Our son Joe, who had been in Omaha for a few days, was also ready to leave to go back to his home in Corpus Christi, Texas. Since early morning the weather forecaster had warned our region about a snowstorm in the afternoon. After some talk our two sons decided to take a chance and go anyway. They planned to drive to Kansas City together each in their own car. From there they had to split up, each taking another Interstate to their cities. Joe was all right and drove without difficulties to his home in Corpus Christi. Ed, however, ran into a snowstorm. Later he told us how difficult it had been to drive in the dark with no other cars to follow on the snow-covered Interstate. It was scary to be alone on a desolate road in the blowing snow. He would not have made it further, he told us later, if it had not been for a large snowplower on the Interstate. As soon as Ed saw the plow, he pulled behind him and safely drove out of the deep snow a few hours later. How lucky he had been. It was late at night when he reached Oklahoma.

It must have been a year later when one day our youngest son called us and said that he was coming home by airplane and would stay for awhile. He had broken his collarbone from playing football. After staying home for a few weeks he went back to his school promising he would not play football again without the proper football gear on. A year later Ed graduated from Oklahoma State and came home. Since then he has worked with his father in the bakery.

Even though the outside of our store remained unchanged over the years, the inside changed a great deal. The first change came when Jozef rented the space west of our bakery after it became available when the optometrist next door retired. When 84th Street was widened to a four-lane street in 1969, and a new bridge was built over the Papio Creek, our business had been growing steadily. It was not long until we could use some more space. After Jozef had rented the space next door, he enlarged his bakery by opening up some walls. We made the front of the new section into a room where people could sit at a table and order their wedding or other cakes from books. On the wall we made shelves for our display of wedding cake tops.

During the two years that Ed had been at school in Oklahoma, I had worked every day in the bakery. I decorated all the birthday cakes and wedding cakes during that time. First I studied them from decorating books, and then I copied them as accurately as I could. Together with a young man who occasionally worked in our bakery, I delivered the wedding cakes to the reception places. Usually I decorated the wedding cakes on Friday evenings so that I could have the whole bakery table to myself and stay out of the way of my husband. In time I became good at decorating and as the saying goes, "Practice makes perfect." Of course, I never became as good at it as our son. When Ed graduated and began working in our bakery, he became a big help to his father. Understandably he had different ideas than his father as how to do things, but it mostly worked out well between them. Since the day he began working in the bakery, our son took over most of the decorating of cakes and wedding cakes. Even though I still did some of the decorating, I was now mainly in the store selling.

It must have been in the year 1972 when we bought property at the new Beaver Lake recreational lake development community which is located north of Plattsmouth. A year later we also bought property at the new development of Lake Land, which is located between Omaha and Blair. We have enjoyed both places very much—entertaining friends and family or just having a picnic and walking with Sandy and her dog Tootsy. We also tried to grow a vegetable garden at Lake Land but, because of the hot sun and grasshoppers, it never turned out too well. When Sandy was older, we bought a sailboat for her which was especially fun at Beaver Lake when she took her girlfriends with her, or when Jozef and I went there with friends such as Henk and Coby.

The years had gone fast and now April of 1975 was here—it was our youngest son's wedding. Even though his father and I thought that they were too young to get married, he and Marlene didn't think so and went on with making their plans. The wedding was held in Omaha's St.Cecillia's Cathedral. Our son Joe and his wife Sandra came with their children from Florida to attend the wedding. It was a very lovely wedding with a reception and a dinner dance for the many invited guests afterwards at the German American Club. It was not only the bride and groom who went on a honeymoon the day after their wedding, but Jozef and I also went on a trip.

We had planned to go to Mexico for two weeks together. Our daughter Sandy was going to stay at Lia and Chuck's home. The first week of our vacation we went to Acapulco and stayed at the Holiday Inn which was on the beach. Even though Jozef and I enjoyed the beautiful surroundings, the cliff divers and the colorful markets, the beach was disappointing. The water of the Pacific Ocean was very high and wild that week we were there, and it was impossible to swim or even walk with our bare feet in the strong surge. Also the many natives on the beach, who begged the tourists to buy something from them, soon became annoying. Seeing poor women with small children sleeping on the sidewalks or in cardboard tents beside the beach, was a depressing sight to see.

After we spent a week at Acapulco, we went by airplane to Mexico City where we had a room in an older but first-class hotel beside a large park in the middle of the city. From there we could walk to interesting places such as the great Opera Theater where one night we saw the National Mexico Folk Dancers perform which we very much enjoyed. We also were able to walk from our hotel to the centrum of the city. There we visited a great Cathedral and other places of interest which were built around a large square where national parades were held, especially military parades. One day as we came back to our hotel from a whole day of walking through a beautiful park with monuments of another time, we signed up for a tour to the pyramids of the Sun and Moon for the following day.

It was 8:00 the next morning when our guide, a Mexican university student with his own car, was waiting for us. He spoke the English language well. With us came also a young American couple, she was a teacher and he a correspondent. It was a day which turned out to be one of those great days you will never forget. Our guide drove us not only to the most interesting places in Mexico City, but he also knew about their history which he explained to us. Later in the morning we drove to the great pyramids of the Sun and Moon and also saw the temples. Since the weather is hot there, we stopped half way to the pyramids for a drink and, of course, I had to take a picture of Jozef there and buy a souvenir at a large stand. A half an hour later we walked through the Avenue of the Dead and climbed the stairs of the imposing ancient pyramid of the Sun. From there we went to the Temple of Quetzalcoat and saw the great carvings in stone. It was most interesting to see the ancient city and learn about a time long ago in history. After a late Mexican lunch in an colorful restaurant, our guide took us to see other places of interest before returning to our hotel. It had been a great day with not only the guide who was interesting, but also with a pleasant couple in the car. It was our last day in Mexico.

The following morning we returned from breakfast in our hotel and opened the door of our room. We found a note on the floor saying that we had to call Omaha, U S A . The phone number was Lia's. Of course it scared me since we told them to call only in case of emergency. First I thought that maybe something had happened to Sandy, who was staying at her house, or maybe it was their little boy Matthew. As I called back, we soon found out that a tornado had hit Omaha. We should not be worried, Lia said, because everything was all right with the family. Our house was damaged—but not badly. Lia said she called in case we should hear something about it on the way home. Even though Lia told us that everyone was okay, I was upset and hoped that she was telling the situation as it was in Omaha and not better than it really was. Jozef and I were glad that we already had packed our suitcases and were about to go to the airport and home.

A few hours later, when we arrived at the Dallas airport, I saw at a newsstand headlines describing the terrible tornado that had hit Omaha. On the front pages were pictures of destroyed houses in our neighborhood. We did not buy a newspaper but said a prayer that our house would be all right as Lia had said. The waiting at the Dallas airport for our plane home seemed to take forever. It was already dark when we arrived in Omaha where Lia's husband Chuck was waiting for us. When we were settled in the car and were on the way home, he told us everything about the tornado—probably so we would be prepared as we came to our neighborhood. As soon as we drove off the Interstate and into our Westgate neighborhood, we noticed all the lights were out. It was dark. The only sound we heard was from a helicopter which was hovering above the houses and streets of our neighborhood with its searchlight on. It was eerie.

Our car was stopped by guards who wanted to know what we were doing here. After Chuck told them who we were and that we lived on Grover Street, they said we could pass. As we reached our house, I stepped out of the car and looked around me. The first thing I saw was that our home was still there in one piece. We went inside and with Chuck's flashlight on, he showed us around our house. All the windows were blown out, and the tornado had smashed large pieces of wood with great power through the wall and had done damage in the living room. He told us that there was a hole in the roof of our house which Ed had covered with a sheet of plastic. Also the siding of our house was damaged, and the whole wooden fencing of our yard was gone and had totally disappeared. Our beautiful large apple tree had been ripped out of the ground by the roots and our evergreen in the front yard was gone.

Chuck told us that early that morning Ed had cleaned our house as good as he could from glass and debris. He also had cleaned the yard from all the debris which had flown around and sometimes had come from far away. The broken limbs or fallen trees he had cut up and laid on the side of the street. "As soon as the tornado had left," Ed told us later, "the city had closed those neighborhoods who were hardest hit by the tornado. The National Guard and Red Cross came and began immediately with helping and cleaning. Large city trucks took all the mess that was laying in the streets which came from houses and trees and had been thrown around the neighborhood by the tornado."

Luckily Chuck and Lia's house was not damaged. We were thankful that everyone had been saved. Sandy and Lia were still shaken. Sandy told us that her whole school was gone, and she and all the children had been very fortunate that the school was dismissed just one and a half hours before the tornado struck. She then told us how she had gone to our house after school to get another dress for herself for the next day, when suddenly it became very dark and the sirens went off again, as it had been doing throughout most of the afternoon. She had closed the front door and went as fast as she could to her sister's home which was only a few houses from us. As soon as she arrived, Lia took Matthew out of his crib and together with Sandy they ran into the basement. It was not a second too early. Suddenly they heard a loud sound like a train coming and saw through the small basement window debris flying around. "It was a terrible sound, Mom," she said. Before Lia and Sandy knew what happened, it was over and only heavy rain was pouring down. Chuck, who was driving home from his work that afternoon, was not allowed to go into our neighborhood. He and more people were held back by police after the tornado struck. These were very scary moments for him when he knew what had happen and could not go to his house and family. Ed and Marlene lived in another part of Omaha and this vicious tornado luckily did not hit them.

The following day I woke up to a drab and torn neighborhood. As I walked into our backyard, I saw that the houses behind us were gone and also all the houses behind them. The sun was shining on piles and piles of debris and toppled trees. The house on the east side was heavily damaged and was not livable as were all house further up the hill. To the west not much was damaged. The tornado had made a long path through Omaha. As I later walked with Sandy through a street to her school, I saw that on both sides of the street all the houses were gone.

Not a stone was left. Many of those houses were wrenched from their foundations and thrown far away. Most people found nothing of their belongings. The people, who lived in houses which were gone or were heavily damaged, had saved their lives by going into their basements when the sirens went off. When Sandy and I came to the place where her school once was, I could hardly believe that this rubble had been a school. How thankful I was that all the children had been sent home before disaster struck. Since the school had no basement it could have been very tragic. After the tornado our city immediately began with the rebuilding of a new school, which they mostly finished that following October.

This tornado which happened in 1975 was the second disaster that had struck Omaha. The first one had been a heavy ferocious blizzard in January. People are still talking about "The Snowstorm of the Century." Because the storm struck in the afternoon with fast dropping temperatures, many people could not make it home in time and monumental traffic jams developed on the main streets. By then twelve inches of snow had accumulated and the forty-mile-an-hour winds took the wind chill index to 27 below zero. People, who were stuck in their cars on highways and main streets with nowhere to go, left their cars and walked to nearby businesses and houses. Luckily the schools were dismissed early and the children made it home safely. Even though the travelers on Interstate 80 and other highways couldn't get to their stranded cars for days and people were snowed in, the children had the best of times. Their schools were closed, and they made large igloos and snow forts. This blizzard, which was not only in Nebraska but also in Iowa and South Dakota, cost many people their lives. The year of 1975 was a year of major disasters for Omaha and surrounding areas.

"Mom, what about a game of badminton?" Sandy asked many times while walking to the back yard were our badminton game was set up. She always enjoyed playing a game with her mother, especially after the evening meal. Our daughter was now ten years old and had grown tall. She felt she was too tall and was not very happy with that situation. Gina Fallen, who had been her best friend since kindergarten, and Sandy played many a day in our room downstairs with their Barbies—especially during the winter months. The first Barbies, which had come out in 1959, had grown over the years to a sale of one billion dollars. The two girls would set up a whole household for their Barbies together and play for hours, dressing and undressing them. Sometimes they sewed Barbie clothes by hand and were very proud of them when they fit the doll.

On summer Sundays when the weather was sunny and warm, we went for the day with Sandy and Gina to Lake Land or Beaver Lake to swim or just to lay on the beach and have a picnic. Together they had gone to religion classes and later they had received their First Holy Communion at the St. Joan of Arc Church when they were eight years old. Our youngest daughter's communion day was a very special day. In her lovely white dress which I had made myself and the lace veil, she looked so precious kneeling there before the altar and receiving her first Holy Communion. She had a big smile on her face when the ceremonies were over and walked with the other children back to the entrance of the church. Later the family all went home for coffee and cake.

Sandy had not been very happy when her brothers and sister moved out of our home. She not only missed her sister, but had been especial unhappy when her brother Ed moved out. When Chuck and Lia moved back to the street where we lived, she was very happy—especially since Lia didn't work anymore and was home with little Matthew. It was about in that time that Sandy got a bunny rabbit which she gave the name of Fluffy. Her dad told her that she could keep it outside in a cage, but in winter when it was very cold, it had to go into the garage. In time Fluffy became a very tame bunny hopping occasionally around the living room and kitchen. When she was hungry or wanted some water, she went in the kitchen and stood by the sink on her two hind legs and made a sound almost like a cat, until she got something to eat or drink. During the cold winter months Fluffy was in her cage in the garage and sometimes hopped around between wooden poles which were laying there. Because of Jozef 's large station wagon which did not fit into our garage and always stood outside in the driveway, the garage door was always closed.

One day our bunny was not in her cage in the garage and was nowhere to be found. We called her and looked everywhere, but no Fluffy. For days we looked everywhere until we gave up thinking that she somehow got away and had decided not to come home again. A few months later when Jozef was cleaning up the garage, he found our bunny between some wood under the wooden poles in the garage. Fluffy probably had died of old age in her sleep. It looked as if our bunny had been frozen and dried out after it died, because it never smelled in the garage. Our bunny Fluffy was one of the pets which was buried besides our house. Now beautiful peonies are growing there every spring—and doing well. A succession of pets as fish, guinea pig, cat and dogs followed in the years to come. Some of them we had for many years, and they died of old age. Others died of a car accident or of sickness. Our last pet, a dog by the name of Corky, we had for many years until she died of old age.

After WW II the oil and gasoline were plentiful and cheap. We took it for granted that we could drive far and pay little for our gasoline. This all would change when a renewed violence in the Middle East broke out. Because of this resulting situation an oil embargo produced a global shortage and a sharp rise in the cost of oil. The gasoline price for our cars not only became sky high, but we were also warned that we had to conserve the oil we had by not driving if not needed. It was not long thereafter that our government took several measures to conserve our resources. One was that the national speed limit was set at 55 miles per hour. This was no problem when driving in the city, but it was a different story for the people driving on the Interstates and highways.

It was that winter of 1976 when Jozef and I planned to go to Florida for two weeks. At first we were not too sure if we would go with driving the slow speed and the problem of not getting gasoline. The 'No Gasoline' signs on many gas pumps everywhere was something which had become a serious problem. "Maybe on the Interstate it will be not so bad," my husband said. "Cars there have to drive!" It was a few weeks later when we began driving to St. Petersburg for a visit with our son Joe and his family. We left Omaha early in the morning and drove, as posted, 55 miles a hour. Soon Jozef said angrily, "This is crazy. It will take us a week before we are in Florida!"Even though in that time there were many state troopers patrolling the Interstates and we risked a speed ticket, Jozef soon drove 60-65 miles a hour. This is, of course, still slow on an Interstate.

Our real problem soon came when we needed gasoline for the car. At first we passed a few gasoline stations with a sign saying "Out Of Gas." At the third station they could help us on gasoline. At first we were happy and relieved, but soon found out that we could have only five gallons of gasoline. "Five gallons of gasoline!" we said. This, of course, doesn't go far on the road, but we were glad to have something anyway. Since then we stopped at almost every gasoline station we saw. It became a nerve-wracking sport. At some places we got some gas and others had nothing, but we never completely ran out of gasoline and made it safely to Joe's home in St. Petersburg. The trip back home must have been much better because I don't remember too much about it.

Besides the well-known Mangelsens Store in Westgate Plaza, there also was a home decorating store. There they sold paint, wallpaper, paintings, mirrors and other items. One day when I walked into the store I saw a sign saying, "Painting Lessons. Every Thursday Night." When I asked the owner of the store for some more details about the lessons and I got the answer I was looking for, I signed up.

I then went to the Mangelsens store and bought canvas as well as brushes and different colors of acrylic paint. I still had an easel at home. I had not painted since our immigration to America, but many times I thought about returning to my painting again, especially when I saw a lovely scene. Usually six women and two men were there in our class. Our teacher's name was Rachel Delord. She was a painter of landscapes and animals. The room where we painted was a back room of the home decorating store. It was great to paint again and for the following six years I went to my painting classes every Thursday night. One day the owner of the store told us that he was going to retire and was closing up. Even though I was disappointed, I had learned many new technics in painting and had enjoyed the lessons very much. Due to my writing I have greatly neglected my painting in the last years, but I have promised myself to resume it again when my book is finished.

◆        ◆        ◆

In the summer of 1977 Jozef, Sandy, and I went on a trip to Wisconsin to visit Cesia and Frank and their son Conrad. Some years before they had moved to the village of Almond which is located toward the northern part of Wisconsin and had taken up farming. Also there would be Cesia's brother Henry, Palasia and her daughters, and Tadeus with his wife Mary. They all were planning to come for a few day's visit from Chicago. They had written us that we also had to come so we could spend some time together. Chelca, Cesias's mother, had past away a few years before, and Jozef had gone to her funeral in Chicago. Since then he had not seen his family.

The weather was great that day when we drove on Interstate 80 toward Wisconsin and reached the Mississippi River by early afternoon. From there we drove north on a road which is on the east side of the beautiful Mississippi. As we drove north, we found the river was very wide in most places and had islands and spectacular scenery. When we arrived late that day at Frank and Cesia's large farm home, we were surprised to find all the family from Chicago had already arrived there. It was a very nice farm with many barns and acres of ground around it. Trees and flowers were everywhere, and it looked more like a large park than a farm.

It was so good to see everyone again after such a long time, and the days that followed were just great. Besides discussing the events of the last few years there was lots of joking and laughing and mountains of food to eat. We all had fun playing croquet on their lawn and watching the calves playing in the field. Sandy had a great time with a girl who lived not far from the farm. Cesia knew her well and had asked her mother if her daughter could stay at her house. It was not long before the two girls jumped from the stacks of hay which were in the large barn and had a great time. When evening came, they wanted to sleep there also.

One night, while having a late party, someone called from the yard, "Come outside! The Northern Lights are fantastic!" Soon we all stood outside where it was pitch dark and stared at the spectacular sight of the Northern Lights. Jozef and I had never seen anything like it. The streaks of lights in hues of yellow, green, blue and orange moved and twisted above our heads. They turned and moved over each other as far as the eye could see. It was eerie and strange and beautiful and frightening all at the same time. This spectacular show in the sky lasted for hours. Even though I had sometimes seen Northern Lights in Holland, I never had seen them this brilliant. Because the farm was far away from any traffic or light, it was very quiet and pitch dark at night which made it especially impressive.

It was a day later when the family members who lived in Chicago had to go back home and back to their place of work. Before they left we promised each other that, if possible, the following year we would come together again—which we did. It was too bad that we didn't see Halina in those years. She had divorced her husband and now lived in North Carolina with her children.

After that first year we have been back at Frank and Cesia's farmhouse in Wisconsin many times, and we have the fondest memories of our vacations there. As the years passed, everything changed when Frank and Cesia's only child and son, Conrad, was in a motorcycle accident in Kansas City. Ever since his accident he has been paralyzed from the neck down. A few years later Palasia passed away followed by Frank and a year later by Ann in North Carolina. Some years later Toni and Tadeus died and last to die was Henry. Even as things have changed, we stay in contact with Cesia and still go there occasionally to see her and her son who she is taking care of.

One decision I am very glad I made was to finally get my driver's license. I still didn't have my license to drive yet after all those years. Finally I had enough of always having to rely on someone else to drive me to the malls and other places. As long as the children were home, there had been no problem—there always had been someone who was willing to drive me around in their car. However, this changed when our three older children left home, and I found myself stranded. Jozef did not always have the time to take me to the places I wanted to go. One day I decided to put an end to this dependency on someone else and was determined to do something about it. I called a driver's school and told them that I wanted to get my driver's license. Since I wanted to keep this a surprise to my family, I said that they had to pick me up from my house and only in the mornings. I knew that was the time when no one was at home. I drove three mornings a week for two weeks with Jerod Sendol, the instructor, and learned all that I had to know about traffic signs and traffic situations.

One day Mr. Sendal said that I was ready for my driver's examination. I looked at him and said that I really didn't feel comfortable enough yet for this, and maybe I should drive another week with him. The good man didn't answer me but told me to drive to the nearest Douglas County Office. There I was. Now or never, I told myself and slid behind the steering wheel of the car after first having passed my written test. The instructor let me drive around Rockbrook first and then I had to drive on the interstate before driving back to the Douglas County Office. When I stopped the car in front of the office he said that I had passed with flying colors. About ten minutes later I walked out of the Douglas County Office with my driver's license and felt as though I was in seventh heaven. I was very proud of myself. I then asked Mr. Sendal if I could drive to the bakery because I wanted to surprise my husband and son who were there. As I walked into the bakery, I happily waved my driver's license in the air. I think that at first they didn't believe me. They looked from my driver's license in my hand to Mr. Sendal and back again, before they finally understood what I had done. Of course, everyone was happy for me not only that I could now drive myself but, I think, also for themselves that from now on they didn't have to drive me around anymore. A little later when Sandy walked into the bakery and I proudly showed her my driver's license she said, "Mom, I knew you were up to something, but I couldn't figure out what it was."When I drove Jozef's car home, I told myself that I would drive every day in and around our neighborhood until I felt comfortable enough to drive further away. Since that very first day I have been driving not only in Omaha but also later on trips to Florida and other vacations.

That same year of 1977 we received a notice in the mail saying that a meeting was scheduled for people of Dutch origin, and anyone who was interested was asked to attend. The meeting was going to be held in the basement of the Commercial Federal Bank on Center Street. Of course, Jozef and I went there to find out what this was about. Besides Henk and Coby Hendrix and Chris and Janneke Vredefeld and their daughter Dina with her husband Bill, we didn't know of any other families in Omaha who had come from Holland. Ever since we opened the bakery, I never had looked further into it. It seemed as though we had been too busy with our children and building a business.

As we walked into the Commercial Federal Bank basement, we were surprised by how many people we saw there. We soon noticed that most of the people there were of second and third generation Dutch. People whose parents or grandparents who had come from Holland wanted to know more about the country of their forefathers. The meeting was called to see if there was an interest in forming a Dutch Club—were there enough people in and around our city who were interested in this. The meeting was not long, and Jozef and I started to talk to Henk and Coby who we had not seen for quite some time. They also were surprised by the many people who had come. I think this idea of bringing people of Dutch origin together had been successful because, after the initial meeting, most of the people who had been there came together again at a later meeting.

It was only a few months later when our organization was officially formed and received the name of the Holland America Society. We had about thirty members. A few were Dutch families who had emigrated from Holland after the war. Others were Dutch and had married an American man or woman. Others were born in America from Dutch parents or grandparents. Once a month we had a board meeting at one or another board member's home to talk about the business of the month. Also once a month all the members of our organization came together in a clubhouse in north Omaha. Besides talking about Holland, we always had great fun singing the old familiar Dutch songs we all knew. Chris Vredefelt, who had a good voice, especially loved to sing the many old sentimental songs from Holland. Among the many new people we met, there was a Dutch family by the name of Jan and Henny Oldenhuis. They had emigrated from The Hague to America after the war. They had three sons. There was also a couple who lived in our neighborhood. He was a Dutchman by the name of Rockie Vander Mark and was married to Sue, a pretty young woman from Norway. While we ate Dutch treats which we had made ourselves, Jan Oldenhuis enjoyed to play on his harmonica. We have many happy memories of those evenings.

When the warm days of spring came, our organization went by bus to Orange City or to the tulip festival in Pella. There we saw not only the hundreds of tulips in bloom but also the Dutch windmill and the parade. In summer time our organization always held a family picnic in a park and had fun playing games. In the fall we had our yearly breakfast outdoors in a park, frying pancakes and sausages on the grills. On those special days everyone came, and together we had a good time. In the beginning of December St.Nicolas (Jan Oldenhuis) and his two helpers (Henk Hendrix and Rockie vander Mark) came to the clubhouse dressed in original costumes which came from Holland. Since this was a family night Sandy and Coby and Henk's youngest daughter Mary were there also. In turn the girls had to sit on St. Nicolas' lap, and they had to tell him what they wanted from Santa. Being fifteen years old Sandy probably said something clever because zwarte Piet wanted to put her in the jute sack. We all had a good laugh.

Once a year a large ethnic festival was held at the Civic Auditorium in Omaha. Many organizations, who represented their countries from around the world, came together once a year. Each country had their own booth from where they sold their native foods and handcrafted ware. The people who worked in the booths were dressed in original costumes of their countries. When we had become an official Dutch organization, the invitation came to participate in this yearly event and set up a Dutch booth in the auditorium. We thought this was a great idea. Beside making money for our organization perhaps we could also get some more members to sign up. Since it was our first year of participating in this festival, we didn't know what to expect and what to make to sell. We also had to start sewing Dutch costumes and order wooden shoes from Holland.

Even so by the time the Ethnic Festival came along, we were pretty well ready for our very first festival. Even though our booth looked simple that first year, it looked Dutch with its tulips and posters from Holland. Too soon we were sold out of the Dutch apple and chocolate sheet cakes which Jozef had baked and of the many knypertje (a small Dutch waffle) which Chris and Janneke had baked. It was the first time for us and we had to learn. That following year we had our Dutch booth very beautifully decorated not only with tulips and posters from Holland again but also with a windmill and other Dutch decorations and small flags. It was two years later when I painted scenes from the tulip fields in bright colors on two large boards for the background of our, by then, two booths. Since we now had more space, people could try on and buy wooden shoes. Also we had more place for the 'Dutch Blue' souvenirs and Dutch Cheese from Holland.

For a few years our club baked pigs in a blanket in our bakery which was very successful as were the oliebollen we fried at the festival. Besides the crowd of people who came to the yearly festival to eat the ethnic foods and buy the crafts of their countries, they also enjoyed watching the folk dancers each country performed in their original costumes. In the second year of our Ethnic Festival we had formed a group of klompen dansers. (wooden shoe dancers). Since we needed Dutch boy trousers for the boy dancers, we began to sew them ourselves. We needed the trousers not only for our dances but also for the men who helped in the booth. We also had ordered from Holland the original women's lace head covers. Sometimes when one of the women of our organization went to Holland on a visit, they bought the lace Dutch women's hats usually in Volendam.

One year when I went to Holland to see my family, I bought many yards of the original striped flannel material for the women's long skirts. Since Sandy and Mary helped at the festival selling things at our booths, they also were willing to dance with our small group of dancers. Sandy decided to be a boy dancer instead of a girl. This was great since we needed boys more than girls who are always ready to dance. Of course, I had to make her a boy's costume which was no problem, only we had a problem finding a boy or man's hat which would fit her. They were too large or too small. Finally I sewed one myself which fit. At that year's opening ceremony Sandy in her boy costume and Mary in a girl costume carried the Dutch flag onto the podium.

For some years we worked hard for our booth and enjoyed the Ethnic Festival. Our large double booth became one of the best and nicest booths at the festival. One year our organization received an award for the best decorated booths at the Civic Auditorium. A few years later less and less people came to the festival. Probably people got tired of it or too many other events were happening at the same time in Omaha. Whatever it was, a few years later the Omaha Ethnic Festival had its last show. Sometimes I still miss wearing my Dutch costume and wooden shoes.

◆     ◆     ◆

(Jozef) *September 3, 1982.* It was not only my 65th birthday but also the day of my retirement which I was looking forward to. Finally I could say goodbye to the years of hard working and to a life of abnormal sleeping hours. Hopefully I could now enjoy my life for a few years with Eef. Now I could get up every morning at a normal time and eat breakfast with her which was something I never had done except on Sundays and vacations. Eef told me that since Sunday was only a few days away, we were going to celebrate my birthday at Lia's house.

A few years earlier Chuck and Lia had moved away with their children from Grover Street to an acreage between Omaha and Blair. Our oldest daughter loved the great outdoors and wanted to live with her family away from the big city, which was all right with her husband who thought it would be better for their children. It was Sunday early afternoon when Eef and I drove to their house for what I thought was going to be a birthday party with only our children and grandchildren.

When we reached their property which was on a dead-end road, I saw not only many cars parked there but also balloons and small flags waving in the wind. I looked at my wife who said nothing but had a smile on her face. I knew then that this was not only a birthday party but also a retirement party for me. Later I discovered that our youngest daughter Sandy and two of her girlfriends from Highschool had decorated the place, while our other kids did the rest. All our family, friends and the sales ladies who worked in our bakery were invited to the party. I never had expected it, and I think this was very thoughtful and nice of them. The afternoon was filled with games, dancing and eating and drinking. Even though the weather was not the greatest, we all had a good time.

Later that day when Eef and I drove home after the party, we started to talk about when I first began to work in Breda at the rayon factory after the war. How monotonous the work had been—watching the rayon strings winding on large cones. And later in Chicago it had been like hell working in the iron factory. Even though it had been for only a short time, I shall never forget the terrible heat and dust in that place. When we came to Omaha and I worked at Johnny's Café, it was much better, but I didn't make much money the first few years. Then finally, when I was 49 years old, I started my own business. It had not been easy in the beginning and I had worked very hard to make a go of it, but everything had come out all right in the end and we had made it. Now our son Ed goes on from where I left off. I knew he had different ideas about the bakery than I had. He was young and was raised here and went to school in the States. Our son wanted a cake business and to stop making donuts and sweet rolls which we had sold. I was a little skeptical about that idea of his, thinking that it was difficult to earn a living by making only cakes. We just had to see.

Ed's cake business had grown tremendously in the years following my retirement. He had stop making the donuts and sweetrolls, as he had told me he would, but continued our line of cookies and brownies. He now was concentrated on making party and wedding cakes. Many are truly a work of art. Because of his success, he now didn't have enough room to work and to display the many cakes which people in and around Omaha order. So, when Ed heard that the store east of our bakery came for rent, he immediately rented the place. He then completely remodeled the bakery by making the three rental places into one. It became a very attractive and busy place with seventeen people working there. After the remodeling he gave his business the new name, "The Cake Gallery".

(**Eef**) May of 1983 was a special time for our daughter Sandy, who graduated from Westside High School. As the school's band played the recessional, our daughter walked down the large hall with a smile on her face—waving her graduation certificate in her hand. Our little girl. There she was—a young woman now. In the fall she was going to enter the University of Nebraska at Lincoln for further studies. Even though Lincoln is only a hour drive from our house, she would be living there in a dorm at the university. We would miss her.

The only thing which I would not miss were the weekend nights. Many times we told her not to be late coming home. While my husband was in dreamland, I was waiting in bed unable to sleep until I heard her or her boyfriend's car coming in the driveway and her quick footsteps coming up the stairs to the house. Then I knew she was home safe. With her graduation from high school she also ended her cheerleader years which she had always very much enjoyed. It had been great for her to belong to that group of girls. Now after all those years they are still close friends. She also said goodbye to her years of dancing at Pat Carlson Dance Studio. Two weeks before, she had performed at the dance recital at the Orpheum Theater for the last time. It was a great night. Later I would miss the yearly dance performance of my youngest daughter.

In 1986 Sue Vander Mark and I flew to Holland. I had met Sue for the first time in 1977 during the meeting at the Commercial Federal Bank about forming a Dutch organization. Sue, who comes from Norway, and her Dutch husband Rockie live just a few blocks from us and we had become friends. I had told her one day that I wanted to go to my mother's 90th birthday in January, but since Jozef didn't feel like making the trip I was going by myself. It was a week later when Sue came to my house and said that, if I was going to Holland, she was going with me. She then said, "Eve, I am flying with you to Amsterdam, and from there I am taking the plane further to Norway and surprise my mother and sister in Oslo."

It was the fourth of January when we left Omaha for Amsterdam which we reached the following morning. While Sue went on to her mother in Oslo, I went to my mother in the town of Purmerend where she had lived in a retirement home for some years. Tante Ann, Mother's sister, had died a few years before and, after the death of her girlfriend, Mother became very lonesome. I knew that by coming to her 90th birthday, it would be special for her. Before I left Omaha, I had bought some birthday decorations—something I thought she would like. Jan met me at the airport, and together we drove to Mother's very nice apartment. She had been looking out her window since early morning, she said, while happily embracing me. She was so very happy that I had come for her birthday.

The evening before her party when Mother was sleeping, I decorated her large living room before I went to bed. How surprised she was when she got up in the morning! Mother's birthday turned out great with many people from the home coming to her 90th birthday. One by one they came wishing Mother health and happiness. After drinking coffee and eating a pastry and some more talking, each went back to their own apartment again. Although Mother truly enjoyed all that attention, it had made her tired, and when afternoon came she was ready for a nap. In the evening Jan, Gerda and their children came and took Mother and me for a nice dinner. It had been a tiring but happy day for Mother, and I was happy I had come for her special day.

Before I went on this trip, I had written to Mother and Jan that, when I was in Holland, I planned to spend a few days in Norway with Sue. After the first week with Mother, I told her that I was leaving for Norway for four days and then would come back to her to stay for another week. Even so, I think Mother was not happy with the idea of me going away again from her, even if it was only for a few days.

The morning flight to Oslo was great. Since it was a short airplane flight from Amsterdam, the plane did not fly high but remained low over the Ysel Meer. The many fishing boats on the gray water were a very pretty sight. Especially lovely was when we flew over Holland's most northern islands in the Wadden Sea. Those small islands are rich with wildlife such as seal and many birds. From there the plane flew further over the North Sea until it reached Norway and the city of Oslo where Sue was waiting for me. First we had coffee and talked a mile a minute at a restaurant. From there she showed me the palace of Norway's King Olaf, which is located in the same area.

It was about 3:00 in the afternoon when, while walking in a shopping street, I turned to Sue and said, "It looks like we are getting some bad weather. It is getting dark." Sue said nothing and only smiled. Not much later I looked up in the sky wondering about the darkness but, as far as I could see, there were no clouds. Sue laughed and said, "Eef, don't you know where you are?" Suddenly I realized that I was in a northern country in the middle of the winter. Three o'clock in the afternoon and already dark on a clear day! I soon found out that the people of the north go on with their lives normally even if it is dark. There are not only light poles everywhere, but the people are used to the long dark days in winter.

As we came into a park, I saw families with small children going for a 'stroll' on skis. The babies were all bundled up in fur wraps and were sitting in some sort of baby buggy connected to skis. I especially enjoyed watching the rosy cheeked young children on their small skis. I think the children of the north can ski before they can walk. I also enjoyed the spectacular tall northern pine trees with their sweeping branches all covered with snow. They look prettier than a postcard. My four days in Norway were great. We slept at Sue's sister's house and ate dinner at her mother's. One day we went to a famous ski resort Frognerseteren with Sue and her sister and saw in awe the very high ski jumping ramps which they had used during the Olympic games. I could not believe how high they actually were. We watched the many skiers and besides walking and falling in the deep snow, we ate lunch at the large Olympic restaurant.

We spent one day and night at Sue's married girlfriend's house. Their beautiful home, encircled with many pine trees, is built outside Oslo close to the water. The bay was frozen and that night we three walked over the ice to an small island. It was very still and our only light was the moon. I would have been frightened if it wouldn't have been for Sue and her friend who knew the way over the ice. Even though it had been exciting, I was glad when we went back and reached the shore again. The house was very beautiful and different. The large wooden living room floor was heated which was wonderfully warm to our cold feet when we came back in the house. Because of the long lingering dusk in morning and afternoon I saw many candles burning everywhere. I also tried my luck on skies, but I think I was too old for this because I gave up after I fell down a few times.

The next day before Sue and I went to the famous Vigelandsparken, I asked her why it was that most women were wearing fur coats. It was something we did not see anymore in America and Holland. Sue answered me that the women in the Scandinavian countries do not see why all the fuss is about wearing fur coats as that they do in many other countries. They feel that since those animals are specially raised for this purpose there is nothing wrong with. When we came later into the large snow covered park, I saw hundreds or more stone statues of men, women and children. They were all naked and each in a different and natural pose, such as running, playing, sleeping or eating. It is a truly beautiful park. In the middle of it all stand a high column of carved bodies all twined around each other.

Too soon my four days in Norway came to an end. After I bought a change purse made from seal skin for each of my girls back home, I said goodbye to all the wonderful people I had met in Norway. When the airplane was in the air, I looked out of the window and saw the sun as a huge gray-orange ball behind the thick morning mist which hung over the Oslofjorden. It was the first time I ever had seen the sun this way. It was most beautiful.

After a few more days in Holland with Mother, I had to say goodbye. As always, it had been good to come back again to my country and see Mother and Jan and Gerda and their two children, Irene and Rob, who were married now. It had also been great to see my cousin Coby and her husband Jaap. We talked not only about our lives but also about a time when we were young and free and about our adventures in Amsterdam. As the plane flew high over the Atlantic Ocean, my thoughts went to Mother. She had become old, and she could not always grasp what I or other people were saying to her. Even after the motor accident from some years back and, because of this, a kidney operation, she was physically a very strong woman. The last time Mother had come to Omaha was when she was 83 years old. A year later she visited Henk and Annie in Canada. When we told Mother, after her last visit to Canada, that she was too old to travel alone by herself, she answered that this was nonsense.

As the plane flew further and further from Holland, I knew that it was the last time Mother and I would talk as mother and daughter. Our conversations had not been the same as before. Too many times she did not understand what I was saying and then stared out of her window.

Two years later Mother's memory left her completely, and she was taken to a nursing home. Since then I have held mother in my arms a few more times when we were in Holland, but she did not recognize me or her sons anymore. On July 8, 1992, Mother passed away peacefully at the age of 96.

◆        ◆        ◆

*November of 1987.* To Jozef's happy surprise he received a letter from Poland from his brother Kazek in which he wrote that he was coming to America for a visit. He would spent Christmas and New Years Day with us before returning home the second week in January. Jozef had not seen his brother since his visit to his family in Poland in 1970. Since that time his mother, his two sisters Irene and Victoria, his brother Stanley, and Kazek's wife had died. Jozef's mother passed away after she broke her hip in 1979 at the age of 84. Victoria had died of a heart attack when she was only 58 years old, and Irene had died when she was 72. Their brother Stanley had died of kidney failure when he was in his early 60s. Kazek's wife passed away because of diabetes when she also was in her late 50s.

It was on a cold but sunny day in December of 1988 when Kazek arrived by plane from Poland. Before he arrived, Jozef had told Sandy and me that his brother looked like him and he would be easy to recognize amongst the passengers. Sandy and her boyfriend James, or Jamo as everyone called him, went with us to the airport. Sandy, who had graduated from college the year before, was now working for Younker's Bridal Registry. She and Jamo were high school sweethearts and were serious about each other. They had plans to be married sometime that following year in 1989. As soon as Kazek came from the airplane, we recognized him—he looked like Jozef. After the two brothers hugged each other for the longest time, the rest of us were introduced.

Christmas, 1988: Jozef and Eve
with Jozef's brother Kazek.

The weeks that followed must have been like a dream to Kazek. When the Second World War had started in 1939, he was a child. Later after the war, Poland was under communist rule and since then nothing had been built or replaced except in Warsaw. The food and clothing had never been plentiful and most the time it was to expensive. Even though everyone worked, no one made much money except the ones who belonged to the Communist party. The first few days Jozef and his brother talked and talked as if there was no tomorrow. Everything was unbelievable great to Kazek, not only the food I served but everything in the house was a new experience for him—as the dishwasher and refrigerator.

One day I said to Jozef that I was going to the grocery store, and I was going to take his brother with me. I never forget his face when we walked into the supermarket. He couldn't believe the huge amount of food and the different sorts of everything that people could buy. He looked around and shook his head at the many different kinds of fruit which were displayed. He seldom had eaten a banana or an orange in his life, he had told us before. He couldn't understand why there were so many different flavors of ice cream in the freezers—why not just vanilla and cherry? Or the many flavors of jams or kinds of noodles. I walked with him through all the aisles and although we could not speak and understand the same language, I did understand that he was overwhelmed by what he saw. It must have hurt him to see the abundance of food we have in America compared to the shortage of food that had existed for the last few years in his own country. (In the mid-1980s the situation with food had become bad in the Eastern European countries.)

Later when we came home, I told Jozef about it. He said that his brother told him he never had seen so much food in his whole life. He couldn't understand why we needed so many different varieties of the same kind of food. From that day on I took Kazek with me whenever I went shopping. We also took him to the mall a few times. He could not believe the many stores that were located in the mall—each one crowded with merchandise. While he looked around, he asked Jozef, "Who is going to buy all that merchandise?" Even though Jozef tried to explain the way of living in America to his brother I think that, though he loved it, he had difficulty understanding why people needed so much clothing.

Besides all the new shopping experiences, he also was confused by the many parties we had. It just happened that in the time Kazek was here in Omaha, we had many different parties to attend. Beside the parties with friends, there were also parties from the German-American Society of which we had become members. This more than 105-year old society is great for dinner dances. The many members of this organization are about our age and are a mixture of different nationalities. They come not only from Germany and other countries in Europe, but also from Asia. Some of the members are immigrants, as we are. Others are descended from German parents or grandparents and are interested in the culture of their forefathers. Our friends Henk and Coby, and Rockie and Sue, and Jan and Henny also had become members. Twice a month a life band plays and we dance to the big band music of a time when we all were young. At first Kazek liked the many parties, but I think at the end of his stay he got tired of them.

He not only loved Sandy, but I think especially our little granddaughter Ashley. Ashley, the daughter of our youngest son Ed and his wife Marlene, was born in 1984. We always enjoyed having her come to our home and many times we went for walks in the park. We also loved to take her to the zoo, which over the years had grown into a very attractive and large place with many animals.

It was Christmas. After Jozef and I went to Church with Kazek and our daughter Sandy and Jamo came to our house, we had a Christmas party for Jozef's brother. Not only all our children and grandchildren came but also our friends and our granddaughter Tracy who had come from Florida and stayed at her other grandmother's house. Kazek received many gifts from everyone, especially shirts and sweaters. We told him he needed a new suitcase before going home. Everyone had spoiled Kazek, and he sometimes became shy under all that attention. The Old and New Year's Party at the German American Society was as always a great celebration with not only all our friends coming, but also Chuck and Lia who loved dancing. With great music we danced and sang the evening away. Kazek, who could speak German and had learned some English words in that short time he was with us, enjoyed himself greatly with the crowd.

During the last two weeks of Kazek's stay we went to different places and also took walks if the weather was not too cold. One day I remember we took Kazek, Tracy and Sandy to Boys Town and to the Mormon Cemetery. It was unbelievably cold, but we went anyway—all bundled up. We had a lot of fun that day. Too soon the day came for Kazek to go back to his home in Poland. Before he left we bought other things besides gifts. There was peanut butter, bananas and oranges for his grandchildren. We packed everything in one of the large suitcases we had in our basement. Both men had a hard time to closing it, and I wondered how Kazek would get the very heavy suitcase home. Before he left, I gave him an album with pictures which I had taken during his stay in Omaha. There were pictures of him with the family and friends which I thought he would like to have and show his family back home. We all took Kazek to the airport. It had been good to have Jozef's brother at our home, and we missed him in the weeks that followed.

The year 1989 was another busy year. It was May when our youngest daughter was married to her long time sweetheart, James Bolamperti. The same as her brother Ed, this wedding was also going to be a big celebration. After months of preparations—such as invitations, flowers and fittings for wedding dress, bridesmaid's dresses and mother of the bride dress, the wedding day was here. How beautiful our daughter looked in her wedding gown made from an off-white material adorned with pearls and sequins. A few days before the great day Jan and Gerda had come from Holland for the occasion. The wedding ceremony was held in the Lady Our Queen Church and afterwards there was a dinner-dance at the German American Society. Our youngest child was now married and moved out of the house. How fast the years had gone by. Even though Sandy and her husband Jamo had bought a house not far from us, and we saw each other many times, we missed having her around. Jamo is an arbortist and works in the tree and lawn maintenance business for himself.

Now that there were no children living at home anymore and Jozef was retired, we wanted to travel from home for longer periods. Not that we had not traveled before, but now it was different. Two days after the wedding, while Sandy and Jamo left for their honeymoon to Paradise Island, we left with my brother and his wife for Utah. First we drove in our car to Colorado. Since it was early in the season, snow was everywhere at the higher elevations, which made it a most beautiful scenery. From Colorado we drove to Utah where we saw in wonderment the enormous red stone formations at Arches National Park. The bright red colored stone of the very high and strange formations against the bright blue sky was a fantastic sight to see. Because it was not yet vacation time, we saw almost no people. It gave us the feeling as if we had landed on another planet.

For two days we walked with our four in this strange world and loved every minute of it before we went on. The next day we admired the great beauty of the Dead Horse Cliff. The following day we climbed the stairs of the ancient Indian cliff dwellers at Mesa Verda National Park. Before going home we went for a river raft ride, but since the water was low the river ride was not very wild which was a disappointment for the guys. It had been a great trip and too soon we had to bring Jan and Gerda back to the airport. They have been back in America a few more times. In 1993 my two brothers Jan and Henk with their wives Gerda and Annie and Jozef and I came together for two weeks in Florida. It was the first time in many years that we all were together. It was great!

Family gathering in Florida, 1993:
Eve, Annie, Gerda, Henk (standing),
Jozef and Jan (seated).

# 46

# *POLAND*

*1989.* **(Eef)** When Russia had lost more than 20 million people in WWII, Soviet leader Joseph Stalin wanted to control Poland. His idea had been to establish a buffer zone in Eastern Europe and dominate the Balkans. This resulted in hostility between Moscow and Washington that lasted for 45 years. It was in 1989 when, in an attempt to save the Soviet economy from collapse, they began to ease tensions with the United States. Gorbachev pulled Soviet troops out of Afghanistan and announced that the "Postwar period was over."In 1989-1990, the end came for most communist regimes in the Eastern Block. The Berlin Wall was torn down, and Germany was united. Finally the Soviet Union ceased to exist and became Russia once again as it always had been for hundreds of years. After 45 years not only the cold war had come to an end, but also communism in Eastern Europe.

This very moment of collapse came when Jozef and I were in Poland. We had gone to Poland for three weeks first, and then were planning to spent two weeks in Holland. After a long tiresome flight by the Dutch airliner KLM we landed in Warsaw, Poland. Before landing we had been warned by the captain of the plane not to take pictures of the airfield and airport terminal, but to put our camera away. As soon as the airplane landed, we saw armed soldiers around our airplane which didn't look like a welcome to me. Finally I was in Poland, the land of so much struggling and difficulties—the land my husband had told me so much about. When we walked into the hall where we had to show our papers and suitcases, we saw Jozef's brothers, Kazek and Marian, standing on the balcony of the hall. We waved at them and I thought how much taller Marian was than his two brothers. After a spontaneous welcome we went to Jozef's brother-in-law Cheslow's apartment where we would stay for about five days before going to the west part of Poland. Cheslow was retired from the air force and lived alone since the death of his wife Victoria, Jozef's sister.

The first impression I got of Warsaw was that it is one of those great and old European cities with a mighty background of art and history. It is a wonderful city to visit and, although it was not kept up in many years because of communist ruling, I could feel and see its greatness. The beautiful museums, the castles, churches and cathedral, the many carved stone statues of men from a time long past, and the many flowers in the parks and wide streets make this a very interesting city. Jozef had told me about how beautiful the Polish people had rebuilt the inner city which had been completely destroyed during the Polish uprising against the German power. One day we went there with Jozef's brothers and Lech, the son of Cheslow. He is a civil engineer and I was glad that he could speak English. He is interested in art and, after learning that I painted, he took us first to a bridge of a very old castle where many painters were painting and were selling their work. It was very interesting to see this. From there we walked to the large old historic square where the destroyed buildings were rebuilt in the same way as before. I was amazed at how they could have done this exact rebuilding with the same stones—stone by stone.

The first Sunday morning after arriving, we went to a beautiful park where they play the music of Chopin every Sunday. The music is played on a piano which is on a high stone platform beside a statue of the Polish composer Chopin. Even though it was crowded, we found a seat on a bank which stood between the hundreds of roses bushes which grew there. After the piano concert we took a walk through the very large and lovely park where also a castle was located.

Our visit in Warsaw would have been great if the stores would not have been empty of food and merchandise. In the time we arrived in Poland the situation of politics and money and everything else was bad, and it was hard for the people to get a meal on the table. Early in the morning people went to stores and market places hoping they could buy food. At 7:00 in the morning Cheslow went to places he knew, hoping to get food for the day. Many a time Jozef and I felt bad when we knew that our host served us food but had barely enough for himself.

It was not only extremely bad with the food and merchandise, but also with telephone and other equipment that didn't worked. Since for a long time there had been no new parts available to replace the old ones, eventually everything began to break down. Not much worked anymore, not even water faucets. It looked as if time had stood still in Poland after the war. In everything they were fifty years behind Western Europe and America. I knew that in the last years many people in America gave clothing to their churches to be sent to Poland, and that the Red Cross was sending food and medicine. Soon we also found out that the American dollar was sky high. When Jozef and I were walking on the street,

604 Our Times, Our Lives

soon some men would approach us and asked Jozef if he wanted to change dollars for Polish sloty. At that time one dollar of American money could be exchanged on the black market for 10,000 Polish slotys, which was a lot of money. I still wonder after all those years how they knew we were Americans since we dressed in casual clothing. Even though there was not much to buy in stores, the black market flourished.

One night anyone who had a radio in Poland sat before their crackling radio to listen. It was the night that, for the first time after Poland's domination by the Soviet Union, Poland prepared for a free election once again. After an uprising against communism, Lech Walesa had not only become a popular leader of the men in the shipbuilding company where he worked, but also throughout the whole of Poland. Since the uprising, communism in Poland was on the way to a total collapse. That night when Jozef and I were there, Walesa announced the candidates for a President and a free parliament after 45 years of oppression by communism. The living room of Cheslow was full of men listening to the old radio. Looking at the men I remembered a night long ago when Mother and Father and my brother and I were sitting around our crackling radio listening to the war situation. Only this time it was a happy occasion; this time it was freedom for the Polish people. Freedom to speak and freedom to write and live life once again. It had taken many years and many lives, but finally here it was. How happy I was for this country and its people. They had suffered so much for too long.

Besides seeing Warsaw we also went to the town Miedzychud where not only Jozef's two brothers Marian and Kazek lived close by, but also where Jozef had lived when he was a boy. We went by express train which came from Moscow and went to Berlin in Germany. Even though it was crowded in the train, we could find room to sit. It was interesting to hear the Russian language, but I could not understand the strange words they spoke. After three hours on the express we reached the city of Poznan where we had to change trains. One hour later we reached the small town of Miedzychud. As we came from the train we were greeted by Waldek. He is married to Kazek's daughter Krasina. Later we would meet her and their two young daughters. From the train we went with Waldek's car to Kazek's apartment where we stayed for a few days.

The days that followed were filled with old memories for Jozef and his brothers. I saw the house where they had lived and had so much heard about. And saw the school they had attended and all the places they had played and had been fishing as children. So many times Jozef had told me about his childhood memories and what life was like when growing up in Miedzychud. I was happy and felt fortunate to see all those places which were so dear to my husband.

Waldek, who is a forester, asked us one day if we wanted to go with him. He and another man by the name of Jurek had to inspect the forest around a lake for illegal campers. It was against the law to camp there. They were going with their patrol boat. It sounded interesting to us and not much later we sped away over a low-lying water area in the forest. As soon as we reached the very large lake and we slowed down, I noticed that there were no other boats to be seen on the water. It was very still. We saw only many water birds on the side of the clear water searching for fish. When I asked Waldek (with Jozef's help) if no one used the lake, he explained that only people with rowboats came to fish, and also younger people with their canoe were sometimes on the lake. "People cannot afford a motor boat here," he said.

As the boat slowly slid through the water close to the water's edge, Waldek looked into the forest while sometimes using his binoculars. As he told us about the great forests in Poland and the many different kinds of wildlife that live there, Jurek steered their patrol boat. Since the lake was very large, it took a while before we were on the other side of the water going back. So far Waldek had seen no campers. That was until we were about three-fourths of the way around the lake. There between the trees of the forest stood a small tent with some things needed for camping lying around it. Waldek gave Jurek a signal and slowly we went to the side where we anchored. Waldek told us to stay in the boat while he and Jurek were going to inspect the tent. Jozef and I saw no one around except the two men. We were sitting for some time there in the patrol boat. The only the sounds we heard were of birds and the rustling of the wind in the forest. "What a beautiful place to camp," I said to Jozef. "I wouldn't mind staying here in a tent for a few weeks or so." When the two men came back from their investigation, they told us that there was no one to be seen. "They probably heard us coming and now are hiding. We will be back when evening comes," Waldek said.

Not much later they drove their patrol boat back through the low area in the forest to where we had started from. It had been an interesting morning which was followed later that day by a ride in the forest together with Waldek's two young daughters. Waldek had rented a horse-and-buggy. The buggy was one of those of olden times with two large wheels and a folded down rooftop. As soon as we were in the forest, Waldek let the large black horse gallop on a path between the very high lush trees. Jozef and I enjoyed the ride very much. It was fun and the girls giggled with pleasure all the way home again.

It was a few days later when Waldek drove us to Marian's apartment where we would stay for a few days. Marian and his wife lived in small town not far from Miedzychud. It was there that Jozef and I went with Marian to a cemetery where their father and mother and a young child of Kazek, lay buried in one large grave. Marian had borrowed two bicycles for Jozef and me to use that day. The cemetery, which is not large, is very pretty with tall trees and many flowering bushes. Since it is full, it is closed for further burial. I was amazed at the large beautiful carved marble grave stones at each grave. Soon we came to the burial site of Jozef and his brother's parents. It was the first time that Jozef saw the place where his father and mother were buried. The grave which has a large beautiful marble stone of different colors is engraved with the names of their father, mother and the name of a four-year old granddaughter. It took awhile before we were ready to leave.

From the cemetery we drove on our bicycles about a half hour further to another burial ground. This time it was something Jozef and I never had seen. It was in the forest—alone by itself. There were about twelve large square dirt graves. Each of the graves had a dark gray stone on which the names were engraved of four or five Russian soldiers. It was strange to see this dark and sober place. All over Russia and Eastern Europe are the graves of the million and more Russian soldiers who are buried there.

When we looked at the burial site, I said that there must have been someone who had brought flowers because of a few wilted rose petals on one of the graves. While we stood beside our bicycles in the stillness of the forest, Marian told us about the old Russian woman who had come the week before from her country and stood before a grave. For 45 years she had searched for the grave of her son. She never had given up hope. Every summer she went to a different place, hoping that before she died she would find her son's grave. She had come to the village, which is not far from the burial ground, and learned about the burial ground of Russian soldiers in the forest. When she came there and stood before one of the gray stones, she saw the name of her son engraved. When the people in the village heard about the woman, they helped her with a room to sleep and flowers to bring to her son's grave.

When we drove home on a small sandy road beside the forest, we saw the place where Russian soldiers had been during the war in 1945. It was all so long ago but yet, when I saw this area, it placed me right back in the time when the war was fought all over the world.

Another day Waldek drove Jozef, Kazek, and me to the farm of their brother Stanley's widow. She lived in a village with her only son. Another son, who had been a frogman in the Navy, had drowned during an accident while repairing the bottom of a war ship. Jozef and I saw the village which was not only small but where the time had stood still. I loved to see the cows walking through the main street going to their stables, and enjoyed seeing the many small and pretty road-side chapels.

After a few interesting days with Marian and his wife and with Kazek and his family we had to say goodbye and went back to Warsaw together with Kazek and Marian. We took the early morning train to Poznan and further by express to Warsaw where we arrived in the late afternoon.

On the last Sunday of our stay in Warsaw we went together with Kazek, Marian and Lech by taxi to the cemetery where Victoria and Irene are buried. As the taxi stopped on a large paved parking area, I saw many people as well as cars, busses and taxis coming and going. It looked as if it was a very busy cemetery. At the front of the entrance there were many stalls where people could buy flowers—which Jozef and I did. Because of the high dollar value we paid very little for the two beautiful bouquets. As soon as we entered the cemetery, we noticed that this was a very large place. It was so large that it had lanes with numbers and names to help with finding a grave. On the crossroads were signs with names of the next lanes. Jozef and I couldn't believe our eyes. It was overwhelming. It was like a city! Between the trees and flowers we saw everywhere benches and drinking fountains. The graves were tomb-like.

Nowhere did we see graves such as those we were used to seeing in Holland and America. Not only was one grave more elaborate then the other, but also all of them were made from marble. It was most beautiful and suddenly I understood what Kazek had told us when he was in Omaha. He had walked one day to the cemetery on Center Street, and when he came home he had said that in Poland, dogs have a nicer grave. I didn't know what he had meant then, but now I understood. I still have a (peaceful) argument about it with Kazek. I told him that people in Poland give their life savings for a grave or are in debt their whole life just to have the same or nicer grave as another. In America we are all, rich or poor, the same in death.

After we walked further, we came to the beautiful grave of Victoria where we placed our bouquet of flowers and stood for awhile. God had taken her too soon from her family. Not much further in another lane was the grave of Irene where we placed the other bouquet of flowers and stood also for a while. It was evening when we came home to Cheslow and told him about our trip to the cemetery and that we had visited his wife's grave.

The day before we left for Holland, we went to a large castle which is known for its flower gardens. We all went there by bus. The lovely gardens with many fountains were a delight, and I took many pictures there. After spending a few hours between the many flowers, statues and waterfalls, we went for something to eat at a small but very pretty eating place at the castle grounds. We had not much choice but were happy we could order something. It was there I ate the Polish borscht for the first time. The red-beet soup together with a slice of bread tasted very good. There was also an apple dessert we all enjoyed. Jozef paid for the five of us, which was altogether three American dollars.

The following morning we said goodbye to family, Warsaw and Poland. As Jozef and I were sitting in the KLM airplane going to Holland, we talked about the last three weeks. I said to Jozef that I was happy that I had gone to visit his country and, even though most of his family had passed away in the last years, I had met some of them. I also had learned about the people's struggles and the different way of life and traditions. Sometimes it had been a little difficult when I was hungry, and we could not buy anything to eat. "You know Jozef," I said to him, "the people in America don't realize what a good life most of us have."

The following day, accompanied by Gerda and Jan, the first thing we did in Holland was to buy two nice dolls for the young granddaughters of Kazek. When we were in Miedzychud and I looked at the girls' toys one day, I noticed that there were not many. Each had only one small raggedy doll. One day Jozef and I looked for a toy store but we found it empty. In that time when we were in Poland, there were no playthings to buy for children. Jozef and I were thankful that now after the fall of communism and the coming of democracy in Poland, life there would finally change for the better in the coming years.

We were in Holland a few days when together with Jan and Gerda, we went to Italy to see Rome and the Vatican. Since it was too far to drive, we went by airplane and took a taxi to our hotel which was located in the center of Rome. From our hotel we were able to walk to all the interesting places which Rome has to offer. I think back on this trip as having been one of the most interesting and great places of Europe. Especially the huge historic Saint Peter's Church at the Vatican. Words cannot describe the inside of this magnificent church where people come from all around the globe. The church, which is the largest in the world, has enormous dimensions. It is very impressive with huge statues on the Pope's graves. It has three aisles with many side chapels. Besides the church there are buildings which are home to museums, galleries, archives and libraries. We also visited the large Coliseum and the fantastic Pantheon. Besides the great interesting monuments and the temples of ancient Rome, we also saw the beautiful fountains which are in nearly every square. I wish for my children and grand-children that sometime in their life they will see Rome and visit this great city and the magnificent Vatican.

After a whole week of walking and visiting the great places of Rome, we went back to Holland where we stayed for another week. It had not only been a very interesting trip but also a trip we never would forget. As always my brother Jan and his wife Gerda were our perfect host and guide.

◆     ◆     ◆

As most winters after Jozef's retirement, we went to Florida in February of 1991. Not only did we spend time with our son Joe and our daughter-in-law Sandra, but also especially with our grandchildren. The first few years we stayed at their home, but as their family grew we decided to rent a monthly rental place on St. Petersburg Beach not far from our kid's home and close to the beach. They have six children. The oldest is Tracy, their only daughter. Then come five more children, all boys. Their names are Joey, Eric, Casey, Rick and the youngest Chad. They are all fine young people now with great ambitions. We always have enjoyed staying in Florida and taking our grandchildren to different places. Beside our son's family we love the great white sandy Florida beaches and the warm sunshine. In the beginning we were there three months but that was a little too long and I started to miss my life in Omaha. Since then we are gone from the cold Nebraska winters for two months.

That winter of 1991 we planned with our friends Henk and Coby and our new friends John and Marlene Sanders to go on a five-day cruise. We went with the Royal Caribbean to Nassau, Freeport and Little Stirrup Cay. It was great and we all had a wonderful time sailing the blue waters of the Caribbean and seeing the three islands. When we came from our ship which anchored early in the morning in Miami, we drove in our cars to Alligator Alley in the Everglades. Jozef and I had been there before, and we knew that they had bicycles for rent there. It was not long until we were riding on our bicycles on a path through the Everglades and saw the alligators on the side of the road. Half-way around we took a rest. After walking beside a small lake and seeing many alligators in the water, we saw from a high tower the great expanse of the Everglades. Since some of us had not been on a bicycle for a long time, it became harder and harder to reach the place from where we had started. When we returned after more than three hours, everyone had muscle pain and stiff legs. It was late that night when we returned to our motel in St. Petersburg Beach. While John and Marlene drove home a few days later by car, Henk and Coby stayed with us for another week. Together we had a great time going places.

After spending two months in Florida we had to say goodbye to our family and hoped to return soon. It always took us two and half days of driving to get home just in time for Jozef to start his spring garden.

Jozef and I always enjoyed taking our granddaughter Ashley for walks, especially during the summer vacations. It was that August when we went to Two Rivers State Park to spend the afternoon. After a picnic we planned a walk on the side of the river and then though another part of the park and back to our car. We soon came to an area where trees had been cut down and were laying one behind the other in a long row. When Ashley saw the trees she said, "Come, grandma, let us walk on those trees!"So far as I remember, I never in my life had limited myself of any activity when it come to doing things. I always have been in good shape and I still am. I never have smoked or drank more than one or two drinks at an occasional party or had serious health problems.

As Ashley began to run over the cut down trees, I soon followed her. While our seven year old granddaughter and I had fun trying to keep our balance, Jozef walked a little further to look at something in the river. As we were close to the end of the row of tree trunks, Ashley shouted to me that the last tree had no more bark and that it was slippery. I should have stopped and stepped off of the tree trunk but I didn't and, before I was only a few steps from the very end, I slipped and fell down. I fell on my knee first and, because my feet slid under the trunk, I fell sideways on my side. I did not feel any pain, and I wondered why I could not get up when I wanted to. Ashley, who had come to where I was lying, tried to help me but it was of no use. I said to her to go to grandpa and tell him that I fell and was unable to get up. A few minutes later Jozef arrived and, while putting his hands under my arms, he wanted to lift me up. Suddenly everything spun around in front of my eyes and I knew that something was wrong. Jozef lay me down again and, while Ashley was sitting beside me, he went to the Park office to get help. I kept on talking to my little granddaughter so she would not be frightened. It was not long until the ambulance came and took me to the hospital. Since Ashley's mom was working, Jozef took her to her other grandmother's home.

Here I was lying in the hospital with a broken hip. I never had pain until after the operation when the doctor put four pins in my hip. I was in terrible pain. I asked the doctor when I could walk again and he said, "Four months." Four months, I said to myself, maybe it will take this long to heal but I do not plan to sit in the house for that long! Three weeks later I went shopping with my husband on crutches for a housecoat at the Brandeis store at the corner of our street. I remember that I was not feeling too well. The months that followed were not easy. Because of the pain I spent a lot of time in bed or on the sofa in the living room. When the weather was nice, Jozef took me in the car to Chalco Hills Park where I sat on a bench looking over the water. It always made me feel much better.

When I was lying in bed, I sometimes thought about the fact that one's life could end suddenly without any warning, and it made me think. Jozef and I had always talked about going someday to the West Coast but never had gone further than planning. One day I said to Jozef, "When I am able to walk again, let us go to see the rain forest in California and the rugged coast of Oregon and Mt. Rainier in Washington. I sure had big plans, which my husband thought great but not before I felt much better and could walk without crutches again. I always answered him that I would be the same as before in about a half year. Not only did I want to go on this trip, but I wanted to be all right again when our new grandchild was born. Our daughter Sandy and her husband expected their first baby in the beginning of March, and I wanted to help her the first few weeks.

It was the beginning of December when the doctor said that I could put my crutches in the closet. Even though I had pain, I was more than ready to walk again. The Holiday season came and went too fast that year. It was not only a great time having everyone coming to our home, but it was especially great when Joe and his whole family from Florida came to Omaha for Christmas. They came from St. Petersburg driving their large van, but halfway to Omaha they ran into a snowstorm. The grandchildren had been excited to see the blowing snow and to roll in it when they had to stop and spend the night at a hotel outside St Louis. Living in Florida they never had seen much snow!

On the morning of my birthday of March 6, 1992, Sandy went to the hospital to have her baby. My daughter had told me before she left home that she was going to give me a birthday present. All along I had been hoping that the baby would be born on my birthday but, as babies do, it had its own mind and decided to wait until one hour after midnight. It was a girl! Our new precious granddaughter was named Laura.

◆　　　◆　　　◆

It was in May of 1992 that we drove our car going west. Since we like to escape the rush of the summer vacations, we always like to go on trips in May or

September. After our first night in Cheyenne, Wyoming, we drove beside large oil refineries to Laramie. Not much further the terrain changed and become hilly with buttes. We saw only sagebrush as far as the eye could see and many prong-horn antelopes. After a lunch at the Flaming Gorge Reservoir we decided to go off I-80 and drive to Salt Lake City, Utah. After a good night's sleep in a motel before Salt Lake City, we went to the Temple Square and visited the famous Mormon buildings. We listened also to the famed tabernacle organ with its 2000 pipes which was being played there. We truly enjoyed visiting all the places which are so dear to the Mormons. After leaving this beautiful and interesting city, we stopped at the Great Salt Lake but did not go into the water. Because of a few year drought the Salt Lake was very low and smelled terrible.

When driving further on I 80 we came to the Salt Flats where we stopped our car. It was very strange to see this enormous white salt lake desert where nothing lives or grows. Of course Jozef had to taste the 'soil' which, as he said, tasted salty. We stood there in awe for awhile before driving further. We ended that day in a casino on the Utah-Nevada border.

The following day we entered a mountain area and crossed several passes in beautiful sunshine. After leaving this area the terrain became flat, and we entered the area of enormous cattle ranges in northeast Nevada. Some hours later we reached the hot and dry Nevada desert where for the first time we saw the strange sand-surfs (sand devils) which look like small tornadoes. As we drove further we came to a desolate forty mile stretch of white alkali desert and stopped at a resting place. Since there is no water in the desert, the state of Nevada sees to it that there is always water in large tanks available for travelers to drink at resting places. Just before reaching Reno we ran into a heavy thunderstorm. Luckily we were close to a large hotel with a casino where we spent that night.

The next day we drove under a blue sky to Lake Tahoe and stayed in a nice hotel on the beach for two days to rest. Because it was May and off-season time, it was everywhere very quiet. After some relaxing we planned to drive further first on Highway 20 and then on Highway 299 until we reached the Pacific Ocean. This took us the whole day. It was a most beautiful drive through mountain and ponderosa country which was especially pretty after the hot dry desert of Nevada. It was turning dusk when we reached Highway 101 on the Pacific Ocean in California. This Highway 101 is said to be the most beautiful highway in the world. We stopped on the side of the road on a parking place and together we saw the last rays of the sun fading over the rugged beauty of the Pacific coast. It was just breathtaking. After we stood there for awhile we drove further and found in a picturesque village a small but very pretty quaint motel where we spent the night.

We paid only $43 including a great breakfast. The following morning we enjoyed looking at the many woodcarving shops which were located in the small village.

From there we drove further to the famous ancient Redwood Forest of California which was on our agenda. First we went to a visitor's center for directions. This is something which we always do to find the most interesting places to see. As we came to the Redwood Forest, we parked the car and walked on a path through a part of the 300,000 acre rain forest. This forest had become a National Park in 1968. It was very quiet and we saw no one. The soundless moving of the fog through the enormous 2000-year-old redwood trees was eerie to say the least. Those giant trees are 367.8 feet high and the base is 22 feet in diameter. They are the largest living things on earth. It was incredible, beautiful and mighty all at the same time to see those huge trees in a setting of lush vegetation of all kinds of ferns and plants. As we were walking there alone in the soundless forest, I said to Jozef, "It gives me a feeling as if time is set back millions of years. Maybe we will see dinosaurs walking out from behind the trees." We were in the forest for hours and saw only two other couples enjoying this strange wondrous world of the redwood rain forest.

When we came out of the forest, we walked through to a fern canyon which was close to the rugged coast. After spending some time there we drove a few miles further and came to a very wide beach and were surprised to find not one person there. The weather was fantastic, warm and not a cloud in the sky. The only sound which we heard was the waves of the sea. We walked for a while on the beach and looked at the fog in the distance which drifted from the ocean into the rain forest. That evening we had dinner at a fish restaurant on an island overlooking the Pacific. We saw many sea lions sitting on boulders.

Even though the next day was again a beautiful sunny day, a cold wind was blowing from the north. For the first time we needed our jackets. That day we visited again more of the redwood forest before driving north on the coast on Highway 101. We stopped at the great overlooks and watched more sea lions lying in the sun on large boulders. We marveled at the tiny islands covered with fir trees, and the rugged North California and Oregon coastlines. We stayed that night in Reedsport and the next morning visited one of the largest sawmills in Oregon. This state is largely a lumber and fish industry. In the afternoon we went to Oregon Dunes National Recreation Area, and after enjoying a long walk through high sand dunes, we spent leisurely hours on the lonely beach.

The next morning, when we got up from bed, it was raining. It was the first rainy day since we had left Omaha. We decided that day to drive further North and reach the Columbia River. The mouth of this river is very wide, and it is here where every year millions of salmon come in from the ocean. As soon as we reached this mighty and beautiful river, the sky cleared. As we drove further we came into the State of Washington. There Highway 101 turns for a short time away from the ocean and becomes fir lined and narrow. While driving we saw mostly trucks full of lumber. By evening we reached Olympic National Park which is on the Pacific Ocean

The following day we spent hiking in Olympic National Park and slept for two nights in a large new motel in Port Angles. This small town lies next to the Strait of Juan de Fuco and has many motels. From Port Angles tourists went by ferry over to Victoria City which is on Vancouver Island, British Columbia. It was a gorgeous but chilly day when we boarded the large ferry early in that morning. After we parked our car on the deck of the ferry, we had breakfast on board ship. A hour later the ferry anchored at the English town of Victoria, B.C. Canada. When we left the ferry, we first visited a square which was close by and listened to the many musicians and saw artists who were painting there. The atmosphere was very pleasant with outside terraces and many tourists. Following an early lunch of the best clam chowder we ever ate and drinking wine, we drove to the Butchart Gardens. Those gardens are well known worldwide. They are large fabulous gardens with tens of thousands of flowers in all colors and sorts and many flowering trees.

After spending the afternoon at the gardens we went back to the harbor. While we were waiting for the ferry to leave, Jozef saw two bald eagles flying low over the water and told me to watch this. "We are going to have a show," he said. It was not long until one of the eagles swooped down and scooped a seagull out of the water. At that same moment about a fifty seagulls and blackbirds started to attack the two bald eagles. It became a war in the sky. Finally the seagulls gave up and the two eagles disappeared with their prey. As our ferry was halfway to Port Angles the captain, who had shut down his engines, announced that we had whales in front of the ferry. Immediately Jozef and I went on deck and while the sun was setting on the horizon, we watched the four whales passing our ferry. It was an incredible sight to see those enormous creatures of the sea from so close up. It was late when we arrived back in our hotel. It had been a great day.

As we drove Highway101 further east and later south, we reached the wide river Hood. The edge of the river, which is rich in clams, shrimp and other shellfish, is privately owned by large fish companies. The whole area there is a quiet wilderness which we both enjoyed. It was the following day when we drove to Mount Rainier National Park in Washington. As soon as we entered the park, the road started to wind and climb higher and higher. We drove to the highest located lodge in the park and asked if they still had a room for two nights. We were lucky. Lodge Paradise is a large and beautiful building with large fireplaces and a great dining room with wonderful food. For two days we hiked the mountain paths and rested at streams or watched the spectacular Mount Rainier glaciers. Sometimes my hip hurt me a lot, but I always tried to put it out of my mind. On the morning of our descent to the world below we saw many mountain climbers arriving at the lodge—ready to take on Mount Rainier.

From this breathtaking high world we drove down in the direction Mount St. Helen which had erupted in 1980. First we went to St. Helen Monument and the Visitor Center which is like a museum. There we learned about the explosive eruption which devastated 200 square miles. Since it had been twelve years and vegetation had come back, we did not drive the narrow unpaved road to the north side of the mountain where the eruption had been, but we drove further south. Later after a lunch beside a lake, we decided to take the road which is on the south side of the mighty Columbia River. From there we hoped to reach Hells Canyon which is located at the border of Washington, Oregon and Idaho.

It was early the next morning when we got up from bed in a motel not far from the canyon. The weather was hot. As soon as we drove into Hell's Canyon, we both understood the name they had given to this hot, dry, dead and forsaken place. The only road there is narrow, winding and unpaved and runs beside the Snake River. The road went higher and we did not see any cars, people or any other form of life except the many fish which we saw in the clear fast-running water. One time we stopped for a drink of water which we had in our car and to stretch our legs, but it was too hot. The temperature there must have been well over the hundred-degree mark. After reaching and watching the dam which is on the end of the 41-mile-long canyon, we turned around and drove the long road back. Even though it was a hot forsaken wilderness, it had its own beauty and we enjoyed seeing this. The first thing we did when we came to a motel was take a shower.

We went Interstate 84 East and stopped at different places in Idaho but we saw not the potato fields we had hoped for too see. Soon we followed the Snake River and came to a wilderness area. In the Snake River, which is wide in that region, we saw many white pelicans, eagles, large water birds and many beavers. We also saw hundreds of large fish close to the shore, and we almost could grab them with our hands. Beside the largest trout farm in Idaho, we also visited a large lava area with enormous lava boulders.

It was already evening as we drove further on I-84 East. There were very few cars on this highway which went through an inhospitable region of broad expanses and some mountains. Some of the mountains were a pinkish-red in the setting sun and it was a fantastic sight. It was a very beautiful drive to Ogden where we stayed for the night.

It was the following day that we again reached I-80 in Wyoming. From there we took the loop at Highway 130 at Walcott which is a scenic drive to Laramie. It brought us to a high mountain range with snow and ice covered lakes. It was very pretty there but too cold, something we were not used to in the last weeks. From there we drove on home arriving two days later. We had driven 5.800 miles in 24 days and spent $191.50 on gasoline.

Since our retirement we have gone on many trips in America, but this trip and the one to New Mexico, Arizona and the Grand Canyon in 1994, have been the most fabulous and interesting to us.

At Beaver Lake near Omaha, 1994: Jozef, Ashley, daughter Sandy with Laura, and daughter-in-law Sandra with Rick, Eric, Casey, and Chad.

# 47

## *FIFTIETH WEDDING ANNIVERSARY*

I will end this book with our golden wedding anniversary. How fast the years have gone by. It seems such a short time ago that I was a young bride—excited to begin a life together with Jozef. Who could have dreamed then that we would celebrate this day, fifty years later, in the heart of America with our children and grandchildren.

As I did fifty years ago, on the morning of my wedding day, I woke up early again this morning. Quietly so as not to wake my husband and son Joe, who came from Florida for this special celebration, I went downstairs. I made myself a cup of tea and walked outside into our backyard and sat down in one of the patio chairs. The weather was sunny, just as it was fifty years ago and a beautiful day was forecast. As I sipped my tea, I watched two young squirrels playfully jumping from branch to branch through our ash tree. Blue jays were twittering in the lilac bushes at the back of our yard; they were probably unhappy with me because I interfered with their morning bath. We have a birdbath in our backyard which we always try to keep full of water. The whole year through we enjoy seeing many different kinds of birds coming to drink or taking a bath there. We still like to grow flowers, and every year we have our yard full of different kinds of flowering plants. While I take care of the flowers, Jozef likes to grow tomatoes and vegetables—sometimes too many. Even now at the end of August after the long hot summer, many of the flowers and vegetables we seeded or planted are still doing very nicely.

While I looked at the tea rose bush, my thoughts drifted back fifty years, and I smiled about the memories of that day. How romantic it had been riding in a carriage pulled by two white horses with plumes on their heads—me in my white rented wedding gown carrying a bouquet of white carnations and Jozef in a tuxedo instead of his soldiers uniform. How young and in love we were. After all those years I still wonder how Mother was able to make such a nice dinner for so many people with the few ingredients she had to work with. Even with the large amount of veal, which we had thankfully received from Jozef's army buddy, it must have been a great effort for her. I also smiled thinking about the impossibly heavy suitcase full of bottles of drinks that Jozef carried with them to our home—just to have a toast on our wedding day.

The squirrels left our yard and, as I heard the 7:30 morning train coming by in the distance, my mind wandered to the difficult train trip to Limburg when we were going on our honeymoon. We accepted conditions the way they were in that time and never complained about the problems which were all around us. I thought about the more than full train and the many hours of traveling in an air-raid damaged train without windows. The bridges across the rivers were out and, after the train came to a halt, we walked over a pontoon bridge to board another train. How different life was in that time. Also I thought how two generations have grown up since then without the memory of WW II, but how clearly it still is in my and Jozef's minds. Today I said to myself, today three generations will come together, and we celebrate our golden wedding anniversary. This time there will be plenty of food and drinks. No one expects anything less and are taking the good life for granted.

I was still dreaming when Jozef came into the yard with our son and said, "Oh, here you are!" I made coffee and, while we ate our breakfast on the patio, we talked with our oldest child about the day that we got married and the time in which we lived. Soon our conversation was about the enormous changes that had taken place in the world since then. When Joe asked his father which changes he thought were the most impressive to him, he answered his son that it was probably in the communication and health field. "Since the coming of the satellites and powerful computer systems, we are able to reach each other in an instant anywhere in the world. And when it comes to health, it is unbelievable what they can do in these days. Do you realize how many new parts in the human body they can replace now." Jozef then turned to me and said, "Do you remember, Eef, when people died from pneumonia or other sicknesses which are now simple to treat or the inoculation of babies for those diseases. Yes, we live in a remarkable time." He then continued, "People have more of everything than ever before. Look at the larger and larger houses they build, the luxury cars, home gym equipment, home entertainment centers and, don't forget, modern jet travel which has made it possible for many people to travel to places which before were only for the very rich." Thinking about it for a few moments, I answered Jozef, "Yes, it is fantastic with all that prosperity we now have in the nineties in America, Western

Europe and other countries. I don't want to sound pessimistic, but with all the good things which came along also came along very sad situations as drugs, the many divorces and the breaking up of the extended families. Another thing which I think is sad is that people have become more isolated in everyday living. For example, when central air conditioning came along, something got lost. Now on summer nights people are inside their homes instead of sitting outside and talking to the neighbors or telling the kids stories while drinking lemonade." While pouring another cup of coffee for Jozef, I continued, "This is the same as with the television. Sure, it is a great invention and I am glad we have one, but I am thinking about another time before TV when, instead of staring at the tube the whole evening, the family talked with one another or played games. I know the new inventions are all great, but people are not much happier than before—rather they are more lonesome. Perhaps many suicides come from this." While eating another sandwich Joe said, "Mom, you may be right in some ways but, beside seeing great movies on TV, do you know one of the greatest days in the fall is when on a Saturday afternoon all our kids are over at the house, and together we watch the Nebraska football game on television. I would not like to miss this for anything!" How well I understood. I remembered the great soccer games of Holland vs. Belgium when I was a child, and everyone in Holland was glued around the radio listening. How great it would have been seeing this on a television.

We then talked some about our immigration to the States and the tearful good-byes, the difficult times in Chicago and the adjustments we had to make in our new lives. We discussed also how we coped with life's ups and downs. How good it was to come to Omaha and live on 52nd Street, and we remembered the hilarious and also the sad moments of our time there. We were interrupted by a ring of our doorbell. It was a delivery of two bouquets of flowers from friends for our anniversary.

Our Golden Wedding Anniversary was held that Saturday evening at the German American Society Hall. The children had told us to come early because they wanted to take some nice pictures of only our family before everyone else arrived—which we did. Our granddaughter Tracy and her fiancé had come from Florida for our anniversary and were staying for a few days at the home of Sandy and Jamo. As Jozef and I walked all dressed up that late afternoon into the hall, we were greeted not only by our children and grandchildren but also by a beautifully decorated place. White carnations in golden vases stood on round dinner tables which were covered with white linen. A beautiful centerpiece of pink and white carnations was on our family table. On a separate table was a gorgeous four-tiered wedding cake. Close to the entryway was a table set up with our wedding picture and also pictures from the last fifty years of our family. Here and there stood clusters of soft pink, white, and silver balloons. Everything looked just great.

Jozef and Eve Otto on their 50th wedding anniversary, August 1995.

August 1995: Chuck (Lia's husband), Lia, Eve, Jozef, Sandy with husband
Jamo, Joe, Marlene (Ed's wife), Ed.

After Lia and Joe pinned a corsage on each of us—which looked the same as the ones we wore on our wedding day—our youngest son Ed took pictures of the "golden couple" and of the whole family with his professional camera. This anniversary was the right occasion to take many pictures of the family since this does not happen much anymore that the whole family comes together all dressed up. As I looked at my children and their children, I felt rich and joyful. We were proud of them—all of them were successful. There was our firstborn son Joe with his oldest child Tracy—Sandra, our daughter-in law, was home in Florida with their five sons. Then our oldest daughter Lia with her husband Chuck and son Matt and daughters Julie and Jill. Then came our son Ed with his wife Marlene and daughter Ashley. And last our youngest child Sandy with husband Jamo and their three-year-old daughter Laura. A few years later they would be blessed with two more children, a daughter Grace and a son James (Jimmy).

About a hour later friends and neighbors began walking through the door, and the festivities began. A few weeks before, I had asked our granddaughter Ashley's piano teacher to play music during our dinner hour, and afterward for some sing-along. Our son-in-law Jamo had told us that he would take care of the music for dancing and set up his own stereo set. When everyone was seated and the wine glasses were filled, our oldest son began the evening with a short speech and a toast which was followed by a prayer by our son-in-law Chuck. While the pianist played soft music, we had our well-prepared stuffed pork chop dinner. After more wine and toasts our daughter Lia and granddaughters, Tracy and Julie, took care of the dessert which was a large piece of the fruit-filled wedding cake.

When the piano music stopped, Sandy, who stood beside a big screen television, asked for everyone's attention. When the music began to play "Memories," she said she was going to show on the TV pictures of her parents' life together called, "This is Your Life." The show began with a picture from our wedding day fifty years ago and some pictures of our honeymoon. It soon was followed by a picture of our first child—then came pictures of the other children and so on all through our lives. We then saw our children's wedding days and the pictures of our precious grandchildren. Everything was set to music, and it was moving and wonderful at the same time. The second half consisted of pictures with our friends throughout the years. Many of them were hilarious and everyone who had been there on those outings had a good laugh remembering those happy times. Jozef and I thought what our children had done for us was wonderful and very nice. Especially Sandy must have put a great deal of time into this. After the show we had a sing-along. I don't know if everyone liked this, but I sure did—standing there between our sons and Chuck who added humor throughout the whole show. I think especially Chuck pulled us through the whole set of popular songs. The piano player sometimes could not keep up with us as we sang faster than she could play. As soon as the last song was over, Jan Oldenhuis began to play some of the old Dutch melodies on his harmonica. This was followed by dance music from Jamo's stereo which sounded great. After Jozef and I danced the first dance together, our three-year-old granddaughter Laura stepped in and wanted to dance with her grandpa. She would have danced with him for the rest of the night if we would have let her.

It was a night to remember. It was midnight when we had to end our party, and one by one our guests said goodbye. Even though we didn't have to clean up, there were things we took home with us such as the leftover wedding cake, the flowers, and some decorations. As our children left for their homes and Joe was getting the car, Jozef and I stood outside looking at the stars which were bright that night. While pulling my arm through his I said, "Jozef, do you remember the times we walked outside on nights like this in Holland and dreamed big plans?" While he looked at the moon, he said softly, "Yes, I remember well, Efka. I also know that most of the dreams we had then we have accomplished in our lives." Moments later our son arrived with our car. As I stepped into the waiting vehicle my thoughts went back for a moment to many years ago in Holland. It was on the night just before we left for our new world when I had mailed a letter to my girlfriend Mies in the mailbox close to the Teolin factory at the Poolse Weg. That night as I walked home, I had looked up at the moon as I did now, and I knew wherever we would be in our uncertain future, God would always be looking out for us, and the moon would always be there.

The End

0-595-33563-2

Printed in the United States
131686LV00001B/24/A